MW00774272

Langenscheidt Universal Dictionary

Swedish

Swedish – English
English – Swedish

edited by the
Langenscheidt editorial staff

Langenscheidt
Munich · Vienna

Neither the presence nor the absence of a designation
indicating that any entered word constitutes a trademark
should be regarded as affecting the legal status thereof.

© 2018 Langenscheidt GmbH & Co. KG, Munich
Printed in Germany

18010

Contents
Innehållsförteckning

Preface

In selecting the vocabulary and phrases for this dictionary, the editors have had the traveller's needs foremost in mind. This book will prove a useful companion to casual tourists and business travellers alike who appreciate the reassurance a small and practical dictionary can provide. It offers them – as well as beginners and students – all the basic vocabulary they will encounter and have to use, providing them with the key words and expressions to allow them to cope in everyday situations.

This dictionary is designed to slip into a pocket or bag so that it's always at hand.

It contains just about everything you would normally find in dictionaries, including these extras:

- simplified pronunciation after each foreign entry, making it easy to read and enunciate words with tricky spelling
- useful information on how to tell the time and how to count, on conjugating irregular verbs, common abbreviations and converting to the metric system, in addition to basic phrases.

While no dictionary of this size can claim to be complete, we are confident this dictionary will help you get the most out of your trip abroad.

Förord

När vi valt ut ord och uttryck för varje språk har vi framför allt tänkt på resenärens behov. Denna ordbok blir säkert ovärderlig för alla resenärer, turister och affärsfolk som uppskattar en liten, tillförlitlig och praktisk bok. Men inte bara resenärer utan även studerande och nybörjare kan ha nytta av det basordförråd som ordboken erbjuder.

Utöver det som man vanligen hittar i ordböcker kan den här boken erbjuda:

- en ljudskrift som följer det internationella fonetiska alfabetet (IPA)

- praktiska upplysningar om hur man anger klockslag, räkneord, oregelbundna verb, vanliga förkortningar och några användbara uttryck.

Ingen ordbok i detta format kan anses vara fullständig, men vi hoppas ändå att du känner dig väl rustad att göra en resa utomlands.

Introduction

This dictionary has been designed to take account of your practical needs. Unnecessary linguistic information has been avoided. The entries are listed in alphabetical order, regardless of whether the entry is printed as a single word or as two or more separate words. The only exception to this rule is that a few idiomatic expressions are listed alphabetically as main entries, according to the most significant word of the expression. When an entry is followed by sub-entries, such as expressions and locutions, these are also listed in alphabetical order*.

Each headword is followed by a phonetic transcription (see guide to pronunciation). Following the transcription the part of speech of the headword is provided whenever applicable. If a headword is used as more than one part of speech, the translations are grouped together after the respective part of speech.

Irregular plurals are given in brackets after the part of speech.

Whenever a headword is repeated in irregular forms or sub-entries, a tilde (~) is used to represent the full word. With plurals of long words, only the part that changes is written out fully, whereas the unchanged part is represented by a hyphen (-).

Entry word: behållare (pl ~)   Plural: behållare
            anställd (pl ~a)   anställda
            antibiotikum (pl -ka)   antibiotika

An asterisk (*) in front of a verb indicates that it is irregular. For more details, refer to the list of irregular verbs.

---

* Note that Swedish alphabetical order differs from our own for three letters: å, ä and ö. These are considered independent characters and come after z, in that order.

Inledning

Vid utarbetandet av denna ordbok har vi framför allt strävat efter att göra den så praktisk och användbar som möjligt. Mindre viktiga språkliga upplysningar har utelämnats. Uppslagsorden står i alfabetisk ordning oavsett om uppslagsordet skrivs i ett, två eller flera ord eller med bindestreck. Det enda undantaget från denna regel är några få idiomatiska uttryck som i stället står under huvudordet i uttrycket. När ett uppslagsord följs av flera sammansättningar och uttryck har dessa också satts i alfabetisk ordning.

Varje huvuduppslagsord följs av ljudskrift (se Uttal) och i de flesta fall av ordklass. Då uppslagsordet kan tillhöra mer än en ordklass står de olika betydelserna efter respektive ordklass. Oregelbundna pluralformer av substantiv har angivits och vi har också satt ut pluralformen i en del fall där tvekan kan uppstå. I stället för att upprepa uppslagsordet vid oregelbundna pluralformer eller i sammansättningar och uttryck används en symbol (∿) som står för hela uppslagsordet i fråga.

Vid oregelbundna pluralformer av sammansatta ord skrivs endast den del ut som förändras, medan den oförändrade delen ersätts med ett streck (–).

En asterisk (*) före ett verb anger att detta är oregelbundet och att dess böjningsmönster återfinns i listan över oregelbundna verb. Ordboken är baserad på brittisk engelska. Amerikanska ord och uttryck har markerats med *Am*.

Guide to Pronunciation

Each main entry in this part of the dictionary is followed by a phonetic transcription which shows you how to pronounce the words. This transcription should be read as if it were English. It is based on Standard British pronunciation, though we have also tried to take account of General American pronunciation. Below is a list of those letters and symbols which we consider likely to be ambiguous or not immediately understood.

Syllables are separated by hyphens, and stressed syllables are printed in *italics*.

Of course, the sounds of any two languages are never exactly the same, but if you follow our instructions carefully, you should be able to pronounce the foreign words in such a way that will make you understood. To make your task easier, our transcriptions occasionally simplify the sound system of the language slightly while still reflecting the essential sound differences.

Consonants

g	always hard, as in **g**o
s	always hard, as in **s**o
t^y	more or less as in hi**t y**ou: sometimes rather like **h** in **h**uge

The consonants **d, l, n, s, t**, if preceded by **r**, are generally pronounced with the tip of the tongue turned up well behind the front teeth. The **r** then ceases to be pronounced.

Vowels and diphthongs

aa	long **a**, as in c**a**r, but without any r-sound
ah	a short version of **aa**; between **a** in c**a**t and **u** in c**u**t
æ	like **a** in c**a**t
ææ	a long **æ**-sound
ai	as in **ai**r, without any r-sound
eh	like **e** in g**e**t
er	as in oth**er**, without any r-sound
ew	a "rounded **ee**-sound". Say the vowel sound **ee** (as in s**ee**), and while saying it, round your lips as for **oo** (as in s**oo**n), without moving your tongue; when your lips are in the **oo** position, but your tongue in the **ee** position, you should be pronouncing the correct sound
igh	as in s**igh**
o	as in h**o**t (British pronunciation)
ou	as in l**ou**d
ur	as in f**ur**, but with rounded lips and no r-sound

1) A bar over a vowel symbol (e.g. $\overline{ew}$) shows that this sound is long.
2) Raised letters (e.g. ᵞ**aa**) should be pronounced only fleetingly.

Tones

In Swedish there are two tones: one is falling, the other consists of two falling pitches, with the second starting higher than the first. As these tones are complex and very hard to copy, they have not been indicated, but their position has been marked as stressed.

Uttal

I denna del av ordboken anges uttalet av huvuduppslagsorden med internationell ljudskrift (IPA). Varje tecken i ljudskriften står för ett bestämt ljud. De tecken som inte närmare förklaras här uttalas ungefär som motsvarande svenska ljud.

Konsonanter

ð	tonande läspljud, dvs. med tungspetsen mot övre framtändernas baksida
g	alltid som i gå
k	alltid som i kall
ŋ	som ng i lång
r	som slappt r i rar (ung. som r uttalas i Stockholmstrakten)
ʃ	tonlöst sje-ljud (ung. som i mellansvenskt uttal av rs i fors)
θ	tonlöst läspljud, dvs. med tungspetsen mot övre framtändernas baksida
w	mycket kort o-ljud (ung. som oä i oändlig)
z	tonande s-ljud
ʒ	som g i gelé, men tonande
Obs!	[sj] skall läsas som [s] följt av ett [j]-ljud och *inte* som sj i sjö.

Vokaler

ɑː	som a i dag
æ	som ä i smärre
ʌ	ung. som a i katt
e	som i bett
ɛ	som ä i källa
ə	som e i gosse (med dragning åt ö)
i	som i sitt
ɔ	som å i fått
u	som o i bott

1) Kolon [ː] efter vokalljudstecknet anger lång vokal.
2) Ett fåtal franska lånord innehåller nasala vokaler, vilket anges med en til [˜] över vokalen (t. ex. [ɑ̃]). Nasala vokaler uttalas samtidigt genom munnen och näsan.

Diftonger

En diftong är en förening av två vokaler, varav en är starkare (betonad) och en svagare (obetonad). De uttalas tillsammans glidande, ung. som **au** i mj**au**. I engelska språket är alltid andra vokalen svagare.

Betoning

Tecknet ['] står framför betonad stavelse och [ˌ] framför stavelse med biaccent.

Amerikanskt uttal

Vår ljudskrift återger brittiskt-engelskt riksspråk. Det amerikanska uttalet skiljer sig från engelska på några punkter (det finns även en mängd lokala variationer, som vi inte tar upp här).

1) I motsats till brittiskt-engelskt uttal uttalas **r** även före en konsonant och i slutet av ett ord.
2) I många ord som t. ex. *ask*, *castle*, *laugh* osv. blir [ɑː] till [æː].
3) En amerikan uttalar [ɔ]-ljudet som [ɑ] eller också ofta som [ɔː].
4) I ord som *duty*, *tune*, *new* osv. bortfaller ofta [j]-ljudet framför [uː].
5) Många ord betonas annorlunda.

Abbreviations
Förkortningar

adjective	*adj*	adjektiv
adverb	*adv*	adverb
American	*Am*	amerikanska
article	*art*	artikel
common gender	*c*	realgenus
conjunction	*conj*	konjunktion
noun	*n*	substantiv
noun (American)	*nAm*	substantiv (amerikanska)
neuter	*nt*	neutrum
numeral	*num*	räkneord
past tense	*p*	preteritum
plural	*pl*	pluralis
plural (American)	*plAm*	pluralis (amerikanska)
past participle	*pp*	perfekt particip
present tense	*pr*	presens
prefix	*pref*	prefix (förstavelse)
preposition	*prep*	preposition
pronoun	*pron*	pronomen
suffix	*suf*	suffix (ändelse)
verb	*v*	verb
verb (American)	*vAm*	verb (amerikanska)

Swedish – English
Svensk – Engelsk

A

abborre (*ah*-bo-rer) *c* bass, perch

abonnemang (ah-bo-ner-*mahng*) *nt* subscription

abonnemangskort (ah-bo-ner-*mahngs*-koort) *nt* season ticket

abort (ah-*bort*) *c* abortion

absolut (ahp-so-*lēwt*) *adv* absolutely; *adj* very

abstrakt (ahp-*strahkt*) *adj* abstract

absurd (ahp-*sewrd*) *adj* absurd

accent (ahk-*sehnt*) *c* accent

acceptera (ahks-ehp-*tāy*-rah) *v* accept

ackompanjera (ah-*kom*-pahn-*ʸāy*-rah) *v* accompany

adapter (ah-*dahp*-terr) *c* adaptor

addera (ah-*dāy*-rah) *v* add

addition (ah-di-*shōōn*) *c* addition

adekvat (ah-der-*kvaat*) *adj* adequate

adel (*aa*-derl) *c* nobility

adjektiv (*ahd*-ʸayk-teev) *nt* adjective

adjö! (ah-*dʸur*) goodbye!

administration (ahd-mi-ni-strah-*shōōn*) *c* administration

administrativ (ahd-mi-ni-strah-*teev*) *adj* administrative

adoptera (ah-doap-*tāy*-rah) *v* adopt

adress (ahd-*rayss*) *c* address

adressat (ahd-ray-*saat*) *c* addressee

adressera (ahd-ray-*sāy*-rah) *v* address

adress-förteckning (ahd-*rayss*-furr-*tayk*-ning) *c* directory of adresses

adverb (ahd-*værb*) *nt* adverb

advokat (ahd-voo-*kaat*) *c* lawyer; attorney, barrister, solicitor

affisch (ah-*fish*) *c* poster

affär (ah-*fæær*) *c* store; business

affärer (ah-*fææ*-rerr) *pl* business; **göra ~ med* *deal with; *i ~* on business

affärsbiträde (ah-*fæærs*-bi-trai-der) *nt* shop assistant

affärscentrum (ah-*fæærs*-sehnt-rewm) *nt* (pl -ra, -rer) shopping centre

affärsinnehavare (ah-*fæærs*-

i-ner-*haa*-vah-rer) c (pl ~) shopkeeper

affärskvinna (ah-*fæærs*-kvi-nah) c (pl -kvinnor) businesswoman

affärsman (ah-*fæærs*-mahn) c (pl -män) businessman

affärsmässig (ah-*fæærs*-meh-si) adj business-like

affärsresa (ah-*fæærs*-rāy-sah) c business trip

affärstid (ah-*fæærs*-teed) c business hours

affärstransaktion (ah-*fæærs*-trahn-sahk-*shōōn*) c deal

affärsuppgörelse (ah-*fæærs*-ewp-*ȳur*-rayl-ser) c deal

affärsverksamhet (ah-*fæærs*-værk-sahm-hāyt) c business

Afrika (*aaf*-ri-kah) Africa

afrikan (ahf-ri-*kaan*) c African

afrikansk (ahf-ri-*kaansk*) adj African

aftonklädsel (*ahf*-ton-klaid-serl) c evening dress

agent (ah-*gaynt*) c agent; distributor

agentur (ah-gayn-*tēwr*) c agency

aggressiv (*ahg*-rer-seev) adj aggressive

aids (eids) c AIDS

akademi (ah-kah-day-*mee*) c academy

akt (ahkt) c act; nude

akta (*ahk*-tah) v mind; ~ **sig** beware; ~ **sig för** mind

aktie (*ahkt*-si-ay) c share

aktiv (*ahk*-teev) adj active

aktivitet (ahk-ti-vi-*tāyt*) c activity

aktning (*ahkt*-ning) c esteem, respect

aktningsvärd (*ahkt*-nings-væærd) adj respectable

aktris (ahk-*treess*) c actress

aktuell (ahk-tew-*ehl*) adj topical

aktör (ahk-*tūrr*) c actor

akut (ah-*kēwt*) adj acute

akvarell (ahk-vah-*rayl*) c watercolo(u)r

alarm (ah-*lahrm*) nt alarm

album (*ahl*-bewm) nt album

aldrig (*ahl*-dri) adv never

alfabet (*ahl*-fah-*bāyt*) c alphabet

algebra (*ahl*-ˠer-brah) c algebra

algerier (ahl-*shāy*-ri-err) c (pl ~) Algerian

Algeriet (ahl-shāy-*ree*-ert) Algeria

algerisk (ahl-*shāy*-risk) adj Algerian

alkohol (*ahl*-ko-*hōāl*) c alcohol

alkoholhaltig (ahl-ko-*hōāl*-hahl-ti) adj alcoholic

all (ahl) adj (nt ~t, pl ~a) all; *pron* all

alldaglig (*ahl*-daag-li) adj ordinary

alldeles (*ahl*-day-lerss) adv quite

allergi (ah-lær-*gee*) c allergy

allians (ah-li-*ahns*) c alliance

(de) allierade (ah-li-*āy*-rah-der) Allies *pl*

allmän (*ahl*-mehn) *adj*
universal, general, public,
common; broad

i allmänhet (i *ahl*-mehn-hāyt)
in general

allsmäktig (ahls-mehk-ti) *adj*
omnipotent

alltför (*ahlt*-fürr) *adv* too

alltid (*ahl*-teed) *adv* ever,
always

allting (*ahl*-ting) *pron*
everything

allvar (*ahl*-vaar) *nt*
seriousness; gravity

allvarlig (*ahl*-vaar-li) *adj*
serious; bad, grave

alm (ahlm) *c* elm

alpstuga (*ahlp*-stew-gah) *c*
chalet

alstra (*ahlst*-rah) *v* generate

alt (ahlt) *c* alto

altare (*ahl*-tah-rer) *nt* altar

alternativ (ahl-tayr-nah-*teev*)
nt alternative

alternerande (ahl-tayr-*nāy*-
rahn-der) *adj* alternate

ambassad (ahm-bah-*saad*) *c*
embassy

ambassadör (ahm-bah-sah-
dūrr) *c* ambassador

ambition (ahm-bee-*shōōn*) *c*
ambition

ambulans (ahm-bew-*lahns*) *c*
ambulance

Amerika (ah-*māy*-ri-kah) *c*
America

amerikan (ah-may-ri-*kaan*) *c*
American

amerikansk (ah-*māy*-ri-

kaansk) *adj* American

ametist (ah-mer-*tist*) *c*
amethyst

amma (*ahm*-ah) *v* nurse

ammoniak (ah-*mōō*-ni-ahk)
c ammonia

amnesti (ahm-ner-*stee*) *c*
amnesty

amulett (ah-mew-*layt*) *c*
charm, lucky charm

analfabet (ahn-ahl-fah-*bāyt*)
c illiterate

analys (ah-nah-*lēwss*) *c*
analysis

analysera (ah-nah-lew-*sāy*-
rah) *v* analyse

analytiker (ah-nah-*lēw*-ti-
kerr) *c* (pl ~) analyst

ananas (*ah*-nah-nahss) *c* (pl
~, ~er) pineapple

anarki (ah-nahr-*kee*) *c*
anarchy

anatomi (ah-nah-to-*mee*) *c*
anatomy

anbefalla (ahn-ber-*fah*-lah) *v*
enjoin, recommend

anda (*ahn*-dah) *c* breath

andas (*ahn*-dahss) *v* breathe

ande (*ahn*-der) *c* spirit, ghost

andedräkt (*ahn*-der-drehkt) *c*
breath

andlig (*ahnd*-li) *adj* spiritual

andning (*ahnd*-ning) *c*
respiration, breathing

andra (*ahnd*-rah) *num* second

anfall (*ahn*-fahl) *nt* attack; fit

***anfalla** (*ahn*-fah-lah) *v* attack

anförande (ahn-*fūr*-rahn-
der) *nt* speech

anförtro (*ahn*-furr-*trōō*) *v*

entrust; commit

*ange (*ahn-ᵞay*) v ***give**;
report

angelägen (*ahn-ᵞay-lai-gern*)
adj urgent; anxious

angelägenhet (*ahn-ᵞay-leh-gayn-hāyt*) c matter, affair,
concern

angenäm (*ahn-ᵞay-naim*) adj
agreeable, pleasant,
pleasing

*angripa (*ahn-gree-pah*) v
assault

angränsande (*ahn-grehn-sahn-der*) adj neighbouring

*angå (*ahn-goā*) v concern

angående (*ahn-goā-ern-der*)
prep concerning; as regards,
about, regarding

anhängare (*ahn-heh-ngah-rer*) c (pl ~) supporter

aning (*aa-ning*) c notion

anka (*ahng-kah*) c duck

ankare (*ahng-kah-rer*) nt
anchor

ankel (*ahng-kayl*) c (pl
anklar) ankle

anklaga (*ahn-klaa-gah*) v
accuse; charge; **anklagad
person** accused

anklagelse (*ahn-klaa-gayl-ser*) c charge

*anknyta (*ahn-knēw-tah*) v
connect

anknytning (*ahn-knēwt-ning*) c connection

anknytningslinje (*ahn-knēwt-nings-lin-ᵞer*) c
extension

ankomst (*ahn-komst*) c

arrival; coming

ankomsttid (*ahn-komst-teed*) c time of arrival

anledning (*ahn-lāyd-ning*) c
occasion; cause; **med ~ av**
owing to

anlända (*ahn-lehn-dah*) v
arrive

anmäla (*ahn-mæ-lah*) v
announce; report; **~ sig**
report

anmärka (*ahn-mær-kah*) v
remark

anmärkning (*ahn-mærk-ning*) c remark

anmärkningsvärd (*ahn-mærk-nings-væærd*) adj
remarkable; noticeable

annan (*ahn-nahn*) pron other;
different; **en ~** another

annars (*ah-nahrs*) adv else,
otherwise

annektera (ah-nehk-*tāy*-rah)
v annex

annex (ah-*nayks*) nt annex

annons (ah-*nongs*) c
advertisement

annorlunda (*ahn-or-lewn-dah*) adv otherwise

annullera (ah-new-*lāy*-rah) v
cancel

annullering (ah-new-*lāy-ring*) c cancellation

anonym (*ah-no-nēwm*) adj
anonymous

anordning (*ahn-ord-ning*) c
apparatus, appliance

anpassa (*ahn-pah-sah*) v
adapt, adjust

*anse (*ahn-sāy*) v regard,

consider, reckon

anseende (*ahn-sāy-ern-der*) *nt* reputation

ansenlig (*ahn-sāyn-li*) *adj* substantial

ansikte (*ahn-sik-ter*) *nt* face

ansiktsdrag (*ahn-sikts-draag*) *nt* feature

ansiktskräm (*ahn-sikts-kraim*) *c* face cream

ansiktsmask (*ahn-sikts-mahsk*) *c* face pack

ansiktsmassage (*ahn-sikts-mah-saash*) *c* face massage

ansiktspuder (*ahn-sikts-pēw-derr*) *nt* face-powder

ansjovis (ahn-*shōō*-viss) *c* anchovy

anskaffa (*ahn-skahf-ah*) *v* *buy

anslag (*ahn-slaag*) *nt* bulletin; ~ **stavla** *c* bulletin board

*ansluta (*ahn-slēw-tah*) *v* connect; plug in; ~ **sig till** join; **ansluten** affiliated, connected

anspråk (*ahn-sprōak*) *nt* claim

anspråksfull (*ahn-sprōaks-fewl*) *adj* presumptuous

anspråkslös (*ahn-sprōaks-lūrss*) *adj* modest

anstalt (*ahn-stahlt*) *c* institute

anstränga sig (*ahn-strehng-ah*) labour

ansträngning (*ahn-strehng-ning*) *c* effort; strain

anställa (*ahn-stehl-ah*) *v* engage; appoint, employ

anställd (*ahn-stehld*) *c* (pl ~a)

employee

anställning (*ahn-stehl-ning*) *c* employment; situation

anständig (*ahn-stehn-di*) *adj* decent; proper

anständighet (*ahn-stehn-di-hāyt*) *c* decency

anstöt (*ahn-stūrt*) *c* offence

anstötlig (*ahn-stūrt-li*) *adj* offensive

ansvar (*ahn-svaar*) *nt* responsibility

ansvarig (ahn-*svaa*-ri) *adj* responsible; ~ **för** in charge of

ansvarighet (*ahn-svaa-ri-hāyt*) *c* responsibility

ansöka (*ahn-sūr-kah*) *v* apply

ansökan (*ahn-sūr-kahn*) *c* (pl -kningar) application

*anta (*ahn-taa*) *v* assume, suppose; suspect; ~ **att** supposing that

antal (*ahn-taal*) *nt* number, quantity

anteckna (*ahn-tayk-nah*) *v* note; record

anteckning (*ahn-tehk-ning*) *c* note; entry

anteckningsblock (*ahn-tehk-nings-blok*) *nt* writing pad

anteckningsbok (*ahn-tehk-nings-bōōk*) *c* (pl -böcker) notebook

antenn (*ahn-tayn*) *c* aerial

antibiotikum (ahn-ti-bi-*ōā*-ti-kewm) *nt* (pl -ka) antibiotic

antik (ahn-*teek*) *adj* antique

antikvitet (ahn-ti-kvi-*tāyt*) *c*

antikvitetshandlare 18

antique; **antikviteter**
antiquities *pl*
antikvitetshandlare (ahn-ti-
kvi-*tāyts*-hahnd-lah-rer) *c*
(pl ∼) antique dealer
antingen ... eller (*ahn*-ting-
en ... *eh*-lerr) either ... or
antipati (ahn-ti-pah-*tee*) *c*
dislike
antyda (*ahn*-tēw-dah) *v*
imply, indicate
antydan (*ahn*-tēw-dahn) *c* (pl
-dningar) indication
anvisning (*ahn*-veess-ning) *c*
directions *pl*, instructions *pl*
använda (*ahn*-vehn-der) *v*
use; employ; apply
användbar (*ahn*-vehnd-baar)
adj usable, useful
användning (*ahn*-vehnd-
ning) *c* use; application
apa (*aa*-pah) *c* monkey
apelsin (ah-payl-*seen*) *c*
orange
aperitif (ah-pay-ri-*tif*) *c*
aperitif
apotek (ah-poo-*tāyk*) *nt*
pharmacy; chemist's;
drugstore *nAm*
apotekare (ah-poo-*tāy*-kah-
rer) *c* (pl ∼) chemist,
pharmacist *nAm*
app (ahp) *c* app
apparat (ah-pah-*raat*) *c*
apparatus; machine,
appliance
applåd (ahp-*lōad*) *c* applause
applådera (ahp-lo-*dāy*-rah) *v*
applaud
aprikos (ah-pri-*kōōss*) *c*

apricot
april (ahp-*ril*) April
aptit (ahp-*teet*) *c* appetite
aptitlig (ahp-*teet*-li) *adj*
appetizing
aptitretare (ahp-*teet*-rāy-tah-
rer) *c* (pl ∼) appetizer
arab (ah-*raab*) *c* Arab
arabisk (ah-*raa*-bisk) *adj*
Arab
arbeta (*ahr*-bāy-tah) *v* work
arbetare (*ahr*-bāy-tah-rer) *c*
(pl ∼) worker; workman;
labourer
arbete (*ahr*-bāy-ter) *nt* work;
employment, labour, job
arbetsbesparande (*ahr*-
bāyts-bay-spaa-rahn-der)
adj labour-saving
arbetsdag (*ahr*-bāyts-daag) *c*
working day
arbetsförmedling (*ahr*-
bayts-furr-*māyd*-ling) *c*
employment exchange
arbetsgivare (*ahr*-bāyts-ᵞee-
vah-rer) *c* (pl ∼) employer
arbetskraft (*ahr*-bāyts-
krahft) *c* man-power
arbetslös (*ahr*-bayts-*lürss*)
adj jobless
arbetslöshet (*ahr*-bayts-
lürss-*hāyt*) *c* unemployment
arbetsnarkoman (*ahr*-bayts-
nahr-ko-*maan*) *c* workaholic
arbetsrum (*ahr*-bayts-rewm)
nt study
arbetstillstånd (*ahr*-bayts-til-
stond) *nt* work permit; labor
permit *Am*
arg (ahrᵞ) *adj* angry, cross

Argentina (ahr-gehn-*tee*-nah) Argentina

argentinare (ahr-gehn-*tee*-nah-rer) *c* (pl ~) Argentinian

argentinsk (ahr-gehn-*teensk*) *adj* Argentinian

argument (ahr-gew-*mehnt*) *nt* argument

argumentera (ahr-gew-mehn-*tāy*-rah) *v* argue

ark (ahrk) *nt* sheet

arkad (ahr-*kaad*) *c* arcade

arkeolog (ahr-kay-o-*lōāg*) *c* archaeologist

arkeologi (ahr-kay-o-loa-*gee*) *c* archaeology

arkitekt (ahr-ki-*taykt*) *c* architect

arkitektur (ahr-ki-tehk-*tēwr*) *c* architecture

arkiv (ahr-*keev*) *nt* archives *pl*

arm (ahrm) *c* arm; **arm i arm** arm-in-arm

armband (*ahrm*-bahnd) *nt* bracelet

armbandsur (*ahrm*-bahnds-ewr) *nt* wristwatch

armbåge (*ahrm*-bōā-gay) *c* elbow

armé (ahr-*māy*) *c* army

armstöd (*ahrm*-stürd) *nt* arm

arom (ah-*rōam*) *c* aroma

arrangera (ah-rahn-*shāy*-rah) *v* arrange

arrende (ah-*rayn*-der) *nt* lease

arrendera (ah-rern-*dāyr*-ah) *c* lease; ~ **ut** lease

arrestera (ah-rayss-*tāy*-rah) *v* arrest

arrestering (ah-rayss-*tāy*-ring) *c* arrest

art (aart) *c* species; breed

artig (*aar*-ti) *adj* polite; courteous

artikel (ahr-*ti*-kerl) *c* (pl -klar) article

artistisk (ahr-*tiss*-tisk) *adj* artistic

arton (*aar*-ton) *num* eighteen

artonde (*aar*-ton-der) *num* eighteenth

arv (ahrv) *nt* inheritance

arvinge (*ahrv*-ing-er) *c* (pl arvingar) heir

arvode (*ahr*-vōō-der) *nt* fee

arvtagerska (*ahrv*-taag-er-skah) *c* (pl -gerskor) heiress

asbest (*ahss*-behst) *c* asbestos

asfalt (*ahss*-fahlt) *c* asphalt

asiat (ah-si-*aat*) *c* Asian

asiatisk (ah-si-*aa*-tisk) *adj* Asian

Asien (*aa*-si-ern) Asia

ask (ahsk) *c* box

aska (*ahss*-kah) *c* ash

askkopp (*ahsk*-kop) *c* ashtray

aspekt (ah-*spehkt*) *c* aspect

assistent (ah-si-*staynt*) *c* assistant

associera (ah-so-si-*āy*-rah) *v* associate

astma (*ahst*-mah) *c* asthma

astronaut (*ahss*-tro-nout) *c* astronaut

astronomi (ahss-tro-no-*mee*) *c* astronomy

asyl (ah-*sēwl*) *c* asylum

ateist (ah-ter-*ist*) *c* atheist

Atlanten (aht-*lahn*-tern)

Atlantic

atlet (aht-*lāyt*) c athlete

atmosfär (aht-moss-*fæær*) c atmosphere

atom (ah-*tōam*) c atom; **atom-** atomic

att (aht) conj that; **för ~ in** order to

attest (ah-*tayst*) c certificate

attraktion (ah-trahk-*shōōn*) c attraction

augusti (ah-*gewss*-ti) August

auktion (ouk-*shōōn*) c auction

auktoritet (ouk-too-ri-*tāyt*) c authority

auktoritär (ouk-too-ri-*tæær*) adj authoritarian

Australien (ou-*straa*-li-ayn) Australia

australier (ou-*straa*-li-err) c (pl ~) Australian

australisk (ou-*straa*-lisk) adj Australian

autentisk (ou-*tayn*-tisk) adj authentic

automat (ou-to-*maat*) c vending machine, automat

automatisering (ou-to-mah-ti-*sāy*-ring) c automation

automatisk (ou-to-*maa*-tisk) adj automatic

automobilklubb (ou-to-mo-*beel*-klewb) c automobile club

autonom (ou-to-*nōam*) adj autonomous

av (aav) prep off, for, with, by, from; adv off

avancerad (ah-vahng-*sāy*-rahd) adj advanced

avbeställa (*aav*-ber-stehl-ah) v cancel

avbetala (*aav*-ber-taa-lah) v *pay on account

avbetalning (*aav*-ber-taal-ning) c instalment

avbetalningsköp (*aav*-ber-taal-nings-t*ȳurp*) nt hire purchase, installment plan Am

avbrott (*aav*-brot) nt interruption

***avbryta** (*aav*-br*ēw*t-ah) v interrupt; discontinue

avdelning (*aav*-dāyl-ning) c division; department, section

avdrag (*aav*-draag) nt discount

avdunsta (*aav*-dewns-tah) v evaporate

aveny (ah-vay-*nēw*) c avenue

avfall (*aav*-fahl) nt garbage, litter

avfatta (*aav*-fah-tah) v *draw up

avföringsmedel (*aav*-f*ūr*-rings-māy-dayl) nt laxative

avgaser (*aav*-gaa-serr) pl exhaust gases

avgasrör (*aav*-gaass-r*ūr*) nt exhaust pipe

avgift (*aav*-ȳift) c charge; **avgifter dues** pl

avgud (*aav*-gēwd) c idol

***avgå** (*aav*-gōa) v pull out; resign

avgång (*aav*-gong) c departure

avgångstid (*aav*-gongs-teed) *c* time of departure

*avgöra (*aav*-y͞ur-rah) *v* decide

avgörande (*aav*-y͞ur-rahn-der) *nt* decision

avhandling (*aav*-hahn-dling) *c* treatise; thesis

*avhålla sig från (*aav*-hol-ah) abstain from

avigsida (*aa*-vig-see-dah) *c* reverse

avkalkningsmedel (*aav*-kahlk-nings-mā͞y-dayl) *nt* water softener

avkoppling (*aav*-kop-ling) *c* relaxation

avlagring (*aav*-laag-ring) *c* deposit

*avlida (*aav*-lee-dah) *v* pass away

avlopp (*aav*-lop) *nt* drain

avlång (*aav*-long) *adj* oblong

avlägsen (*aav*-laig-sern) *adj* remote; distant, far-off

avlägset (*aav*-laig-sayt) *adj* far

avlägsna (*aav*-laigs-nah) *v* remove; ~ sig depart

avlämna (*aav*-lehm-nah) *v* deliver

avlöna (*aav*-l͞urn-ah) *v* remunerate

avlöning (*aav*-lur-ning) *c* pay, salary

avlösa (*aav*-lur-sah) *v* relieve

avog (*aa*-v͞oog) *adj* averse

avpassa (*aav*-pah-sah) *v* suit

avresa (*aav*-rā͞y-sah) *v* depart; *c* departure

avråda (*aav*-r͞oā-dah) *v* dissuade from

avrättning (*aav*-reht-ning) *c* execution

*avse (*aav*-sā͞y) *v* destine

avsevärd (*aav*-say-væærd) *adj* considerable

avsides (*aav*-see-derss) *adj* remote; out of the way

avsikt (*aav*-sikt) *c* purpose, intention

avsiktlig (*aav*-sikt-li) *adj* intentional

avskaffa (*aav*-skah-fah) *v* abolish

avsked (*aav*-shā͞yd) *nt* parting; resignation

avskeda (*aav*-shā͞y-dah) *v* dismiss; fire

avskedsansökan (*aav*-shā͞yds-ahn-s͞ur-kahn) *c* (pl -kningar) resignation

avskilja (*aav*-shil-ʸah) *v* detach

*avskjuta (*aav*-shē͞w-tah) *v* launch

avskrift (*aav*-skrift) *c* copy

avsky (*aav*-shew) *v* detest, loathe; *c* disgust, loathing

avskyvärd (*aav*-shew-væærd) *adj* horrible; hideous

avsluta (*aav*-slē͞w-tah) *v* finish

avslutning (*aav*-slēwt-ning) *c* conclusion, end

*avslå (*aav*-sl͞oā) *v* reject

avslöja (*aav*-slur-ʸah) *v* reveal

avslöjande (*aav*-slur-ʸahn-der) *nt* revelation

avsnitt (*aav*-snit) *nt* passage

avspark (*aav*-spahrk) *c*
kickoff

avspänd (*aav*-spehnd) *adj*
easy-going, relaxed

*****avstå från** (*aav*-stōa) abstain
from

avstånd (*aav*-stond) *nt*
distance; space, way

avståndsmätare (*aav*-
stonds-mai-tah-rer) *c* (pl ∼)
range finder

avsända (*aav*-sehn-dah) *v*
dispatch

avsändare (*aav*-sehn-dah-
rer) *c* (pl ∼) sender

avsändning (*aav*-sehnd-
ning) *c* dispatch

avsky (*aav*-shew) *v* detest; *c*
disgust

*****avta** (*aav*-taa) *v* decrease

avtal (*aav*-taal) *nt* agreement,
treaty

avtryck (*aav*-trewk) *nt* print

avtryckare (*aav*-trew-kah-
rer) *c* (pl ∼) trigger

avtäcka (*aav*-teh-kah) *v*
uncover

avundas (*aav*-ewn-dahss) *v*
envy

avundsam (*aav*-ewnd-sahm)
adj envious

avundsjuk (*aav*-ewnd-
shewk) *adj* envious

avundsjuka (*aa*-vewnd-
shēw-kah) *c* envy

*****avvika** (*aav*-vee-kah) *v*
deviate

avvisa (*aav*-vee-sah) *v* reject

axel (*ahks*-ayl) *c* (pl axlar)
shoulder; axis, axle

B

baby (*bai*-bi) *c* baby

babykorg (*bai*-bi-kor³) *c*
carrycot

bacill (bah-*sil*) *c* germ

backa (*bah*-kah) *v* reverse

backe (*bah*-ker) *c* hill; slope

backhoppning (*bahk*-hop-
ning) *c* ski jump

backkrön (*bahk*-krūrn) *nt*
hilltop

backväxel (*bahk*-vehks-ayl) *c*
(pl -växlar) reverse

bad (baad) *nt* bath

bada (*baa*-dah) *v* bathe

badbyxor (*baad*-bewk-serr)
pl bathing suit,

swimmingtrunks *pl*

badda (*bah*-dah) *v* dab

baddräkt (*baad*-drehkt) *c*
bathing suit; swimsuit,
swimming suit *Am*

badhandduk (*baad*-hahnd-
dēwk) *c* bath towel

badmössa (*baad*-murss-sah)
c bathing cap

badort (*baad*-oort) *c* seaside
resort

badrock (*baad*-roak) *c*
bathrobe

badrum (*baad*-rewm) *nt*
bathroom

badsalt (*baad*-sahlt) *nt* bath

salts

badvakt (*baad*-vahkt) *c* pool attendant

bagage (bah-*gaash*) *nt* baggage, luggage

bagagehylla (bah-*gaash*-hew-lah) *c* luggage rack

bagageinlämning (bah-*gaash*-in-lehm-ning) *c* left luggage office; baggage deposit office *nAm*

bagageutrymme (bah-*gaash*-ēwt-rew-mer) *nt* boot; trunk *nAm*

bagare (*baa*-gah-rer) *c* (pl ~) baker

bageri (baa-ger-*ree*) *nt* bakery

baka (*baa*-kah) *v* bake

bakdel (*baak*-dāyl) *c* bottom

bakelser (*baa*-kerl-serr) *pl* pastry

bakgrund (*baak*-grewnd) *c* background

baklykta (*baak*-lewk-tah) *c* rear light; taillight

bakom (*baak*-om) *prep* behind; *adv* behind

baksida (*baak*-seedah) *c* rear

baksmälla (*baak*-smeh-lah) *c* hangover

bakterie (bahk-*tai*-ri-er) *c* bacterium

bakverk (*baak*-vehrk) *nt* pastry, cake

bakåt (*baa*-kot) *adv* backwards

bal (baal) *c* ball

balansräkning (bah-*lahngs*-raik-ning) *c* balance sheet

balett (bah-*layt*) *c* ballet

balja (*bahl*-ᵞah) *c* basin

balkong (bahl-*kong*) *c* balcony; circle

ballong (bah-*long*) *c* balloon

balsal (*baal*-saal) *c* ballroom

bana (*baa*-nah) *c* track

banan (bah-*naan*) *c* banana

band (bahnd) *nt* band; ribbon

bandspelare (*bahnd*-spāy-lah-rer) *c* (pl ~) tape recorder

baner (bah-*nāyr*) *nt* banner

bank (bahngk) *c* bank

bankett (bahng-*keht*) *c* banquet

bankkonto (*bahngk*-kon-too) *nt* bank account

bankomat (bahng-ko-*maat*) *c* ATM; automatic teller machine; cash dispenser; cash machine

bankrutt (bahng-*krewt*) *adj* bankrupt

bar (baar) *c* bar, saloon; *adj* bare

bara (*baarah*) *adv* only

bark (bahrk) *c* bark

barm (bahrm) *c* bosom

barmhärtighet (bahrm-*hær*-ti-hāyt) *c* mercy

barn (baarn) *nt* child; kid; **föräldralöst ~** orphan

barnbarn (*baarn*-baarn) *nt* (pl ~) grandchild

barnförlamning (*baarn*-furr-*laam*-ning) *c* polio

barnkammare (*baarn*-kah-mah-rer) *c* (pl ~) nursery

barnmorska (*baarn*-moors-kah) *c* midwife

barnsjukdom (*baarn*-shewk-doom) *c* children's disease

barnsköterska (*baarn*-shür-terr-skah) *c* nurse

barnsäng (*baarn*-sehng) *c* cot

barnvagn (*baarn*-vahngn) *c* pram; baby carriage *Am*

barnvakt (*baarn*-vahkt) *c* babysitter

barock (bah-*rok*) *adj* baroque

barometer (bah-ro-*may*-terr) *c* (pl -trar) barometer

barriär (bah-ri-*²ǣr*) *c* barrier

barrträd (*bahr*-traid) *nt* conifer, fir tree

barsk (bahrsk) *adj* grim

baryton (*bah*-ri-ton) *c* baritone

bas (baass) *c* base; bass

baseboll (*bayss*-bol) *c* baseball

basera (bah-*say*-rah) *v* base

basilika (bah-*see*-li-kah) *c* basilica

basis (*baa*-siss) *c* basis

bassäng (*bah*-sehng) *c* pool

bastard (bah-*staard*) *c* bastard

bastu (*bahss*-tew) *c* sauna

batteri (bah-tay-*ree*) *nt* (pl ~er) battery

***be** (*bay*) *v* ask; beg

beakta (bay-*ahk*-tah) *v* pay attention to

bebo (bay-*boo*) *v* inhabit

beboelig (ber-*boo*-ay-li) *adj* habitable; inhabitable

***bedja** (*bayd*-²ah) *v* pray

***bedra** (ber-*draa*) *v* deceive; cheat

bedrägeri (ber-drai-ger-*ri*) *nt* (pl ~er) deceit; fraud

bedrövad (ber-*drür*-vahd) *adj* distressed; sad

bedrövelse (ber-*drür*-verl-ser) *c* sorrow; grief

bedrövlig (ber-*drürv*-li) *adj* lamentable

bedårande (ber-*dóā*-rahn-der) *adj* adorable; enchanting

bedöma (ber-*dur*-mah) *v* judge

bedövning (ber-*dürv*-ning) *c* anaesthesia

bedövningsmedel (ber-*durv*-nings-*may*-dayl) *nt* anaesthetic

befalla (ber-*fah*-lah) *v* command

befallning (ber-*fahl*-ning) *c* order, command

befatta sig med (ber-*fah*-tah) *deal with, concern oneself with

befolkning (ber-*folk*-ning) *c* population

befordra (ber-*fōō*-drah) *v* promote

befordran (ber-*fōōd*-rahn) *c* (pl -ringar) promotion

befria (*ber*-free-ah) *v* rid

befriad (ber-*free*-ahd) *adj* exempt; liberated

befrielse (ber-*free*-erl-ser) *c* liberation; exemption

befruktning (ber-*frewkt*-

ning) c conception

befälhavare (ber-*fail*-haa-vah-rer) c (pl ~) commander

begagnad (ber-*gahng*-nahd) adj second-hand

begeistrad (bay-*gighst*-rahd) adj enthusiastic

begrava (ber-*graa*-vah) v bury

begravning (ber-*graav*-ning) c funeral; burial

begravningsplats (bay-*graav*-nings-plahts) c cemetery; graveyard

begrepp (ber-*grayp*) nt idea, notion

***begripa** (bay-*gree*-pah) v grasp, *understand

begränsa (ber-*grehn*-sah) v limit

begränsad (ber-*grehn*-sahd) adj limited

begränsning (ber-*grehns*-ning) c limitation

begynna (ber-*yew*-nah) v *begin

begynnelse (ber-*yew*-nerl-ser) c beginning

***begå** (ber-*goa*) v commit

begåvad (ber-*goa*-vahd) adj brilliant, talented, gifted

begåvning (ber-*goav*-ning) c talent; mind

begär (ber-*Yӕer*) nt desire

begära (ber-*Yӕӕ*-rah) v ask, demand, request

begäran (ber-*gӕӕ*-rahn) c request; demand

behaglig (ber-*haag*-li) adj pleasant, delightful

behandla (ber-*hahnd*-lah) v treat; handle

behandling (ber-*hahnd*-ling) c treatment

behov (ber-*hōōv*) nt need, want; **starkt ~** urge

behå (*bay*-hoa) c bra

***behålla** (ber-*ho*-lah) v *keep

behållare (ber-*ho*-lah-rer) c (pl ~) container

behändig (ber-*hehn*-di) adj handy; sweet

behärska (ber-*hӕӕrs*-kah) v master; **~ sig** control oneself

behöva (ber-*hūū*-vah) v need

beige (baish) adj beige

bekant (ber-*kahnt*) c (pl ~a) acquaintance

beklaga (ber-*klaa*-gah) v regret; pity

beklagande (ber-*klaa*-gahn-der) nt regret

beklaglig (ber-*klaag*-li) adj regrettable

bekräfta (ber-*krehf*-tah) v confirm; acknowledge

bekräftelse (ber-*krehf*-tayl-ser) c confirmation

bekväm (ber-*kvaim*) adj comfortable; convenient; easy

bekvämlighet (ber-*kvaim*-li-hāyt) c comfort

bekymmer (ber-*tˢew*-merr) nt worry; anxiety; care; trouble

bekymrad (ber-*tˢewm*-rahd) adj concerned

bekämpa (ber-*tˢehm*-pah) v combat

bekänna (ber-*t*ᵉeh-nah) *v* confess

bekännelse (ber-*t*ᵉeh-naylser) *c* confession

belastning (ber-*lahst*-ning) *c* charge

belgare (*bayl*-gah-rer) *c* (pl ~) Belgian

Belgien (*bayl*-g*ᵉ*ayn) Belgium

belgisk (*bayl*-gisk) *adj* Belgian

belopp (ber-*lop*) *nt* amount

belysning (ber-*lewss*-ning) *c* illumination; lighting

belåten (ber-*lōa*-tern) *adj* satisfied, happy

belåtenhet (ber-*lōa*-ternhāyt) *c* satisfaction

belägen (ber-*lai*-gern) *adj* situated

belöna (ber-*lūr*-nah) *v* reward

belöning (ber-*lūr*-ning) *c* prize, reward; remuneration

bemästra (ber-*mehst*-rah) *v* master

bemöda sig (ber-*mūr*-dah) try, endeavour

bemötande (beh-*mur*-tahnder) *nt* treatment; reply

ben (bāyn) *nt* leg; bone

bena (*bāy*-nah) *c* parting

bensin (bayn-*seen*) *c* fuel, petrol; gasoline *nAm*, gas *nAm*; **blyfri ~** unleaded petrol

bensindunk (bayn-*seen*-dewngk) *c* jerrycan

bensinmack (bayn-*seen*-mahk) *c* petrol station

bensinpump (bayn-*seen*-pewmp) *c* petrol pump; fuel pump *Am*; gas pump *Am*

bensinstation (bayn-*seen*-stah-*shōōn*) *c* service station, filling station; gas station *Am*

bensintank (bayn-*seen*-tahngk) *c* petrol tank; gas tank *Am*

benådning (ber-*nōad*-ning) *c* pardon

benägen (ber-*nai*-gern) *adj* inclined; ***vara ~** *be inclined to

benägenhet (ber-*nai*-gernhāyt) *c* tendency; inclination

benämning (ber-*nehm*-ning) *c* denomination

beredd (ber-*rayd*) *adj* prepared

berg (bær*ᵉ*) *nt* mountain; mount

bergig (*bær*-*ᵉ*i) *adj* mountainous

bergsbestigning (*bær*ᵉs-ber-*steeg*-ning) *c* mountaineering

bergskam (*bær*ᵉs-kahm) *c* mountain ridge

bergskedja (*bær*ᵉs-t*ᵉ*āyd-*ᵉ*ah) *c* mountain range

bergsklyfta (*bær*ᵉs-klewf-tah) *c* gorge

bergspass (*bær*ᵉs-pahss) *nt* mountain pass

bero på (ber-*rōō*) depend on

beroende (ber-*rōō*-ern-der) *adj* dependant

berusad (ber-*rew*-sahd) *adj*

intoxicated; drunk
beryktad (ber-*rewk*-tahd) *adj*
notorious
beräkna (ber-*raik*-nah) *v*
calculate
beräkning (ber-*raik*-ning) *c*
calculation; estimate
berätta (ber-*reh*-tah) *v* *tell;
relate
berättelse (ber-*reh*-tayl-ser) *c*
tale
berättiga (ber-*reh*-ti-gah) *v*
entitle, justify
berättigad (ber-*reh*-ti-gahd)
adj entitled, justified
beröm (ber-*rurm*) *nt* praise
berömd (ber-*rurmd*) *adj*
famous
berömdhet (ber-*rurmd*-hāyt)
c celebrity
berömma (ber-*rur*-mah) *v*
praise
berömmelse (ber-*rur*-mayl-
ser) *c* fame; glory
beröra (ber-*rūr*-rah) *v* touch;
affect
beröring (ber-*rūr*-ring) *c*
touch, contact
beröva (ber-*rūr*-vah) *v*
deprive of
besatt (ber-*saht*) *adj*
possessed
besatthet (ber-*saht*-hāyt) *c*
obsession
besegra (ber-*sāyg*-rah) *v*
defeat; beat, conquer
beskatta (ber-*skah*-tah) *v* tax
beskattning (ber-*skaht*-ning)
c taxation
besked (ber-*shāyd*) *nt*

message
***beskriva** (ber-*skree*-vah) *v*
describe
beskrivning (ber-*skreev*-
ning) *c* description
beskylla (ber-*shew*-lah) *v*
accuse
beslut (ber-*slēwt*) *nt* decision
***besluta** (ber-*slēw*-tah) *v*
decide
beslutsam (ber-*slēwt*-sahm)
adj determined, resolute
besläktad (ber-*slehk*-tahd)
adj related
besmitta (ber-*smi*-tah) *v*
infect
besparingar (ber-*spaa*-ring-
ahr) *pl* savings *pl*
bestick (ber-*stik*) *nt* cutlery
***bestiga** (ber-*stee*-gah) *v*
ascend; mount
***bestrida** (ber-*stree*-dah) *v*
dispute; deny
***bestå av** (ber-*stoa*) consist of
beståndsdel (ber-*stonds*-
dāyl) *c* element
beställa (ber-*steh*-lah) *v*
order; reserve
beställning (ber-*stehl*-ning) *c*
order; booking; **gjord på ~**
made to order
bestämd (ber-*stehmd*) *adj*
definite
bestämma (ber-*steh*-mah) *v*
decide; determine, define;
designate
bestämmelse (ber-*stehm*-
erl-ser) *c* stipulation
bestämmelseort (ber-*steh*-
merl-ser-oort) *c* destination

beständig (ber-*stehn*-di) *adj*
permanent

besvara (ber-*svaa*-rah) *v*
answer

besvikelse (ber-*svee*-kerl-ser) *c* disappointment; ***vara en ~ *be disappointing

besviken (ber-*svee*-kern) *adj*
disappointed; ***göra ~**
disappoint

besvär (ber-*svæær*) *nt*
trouble; inconvenience;
nuisance; ***göra sig ~** bother

besvära (ber-*svææ*-rah) *v*
trouble; bother

besvärlig (ber-*svæær*-li) *adj*
inconvenient, troublesome

besynnerlig (ber-*sewn*-err-li)
adj strange; queer

***besätta** (ber-*seht*-ah) *v*
occupy

besättning (ber-*seht*-ning) *c*
crew

besök (ber-*surk*) *nt* visit; call

besöka (ber-*sur*-kah) *v* visit;
call on

besökare (ber-*sur*-kah-rer) *c*
(pl ~) visitor

besökstid (ber-*surks*-teed) *c*
visiting hours

beta (*bay*-tah) *c* beet; *v* graze

betala (ber-*taa*-lah) *v* *pay

betalbar (ber-*taal*-baar) *adj*
due

betalning (ber-*taal*-ning) *c*
payment

bete (*bay*-ter) *nt* bait

beteckna (ber-*tehk*-nahn-der) *adj* characteristic

beteckning (ber-*tehk*-ning) *c*

denomination, designation

betesmark (*bay*-terss-mahrk) *c* pasture

betjäning (ber-*t*ᵞ*ai*-ning) *c*
service

betjäningsavgift (ber-*t*ᵞ*ai*-nings-aav-ᵞ*ift*) *c* service
charge

betjänt (ber-*t*ᵞ*ehnt*) *c* valet,
servant

betona (ber-*too*-nah) *v* stress;
emphasize

betong (ber-*tong*) *c* concrete

betoning (ber-*too*-ning) *c*
stress

betrakta (ber-*trahk*-tah) *v*
consider, regard; watch,
view

beträda (ber-*trai*-dah) *v*
*tread, *set foot on

beträffa (ber-*trehf*-ah) *v*
concern

beträffande (ber-*trehf*-ahn-der) *prep* concerning; about,
regarding; with reference to

bett (bayt) *nt* bite

betvivla (ber-*tveev*-lah) *v*
doubt; query

betyda (ber-*tew*-dah) *v*
*mean

betydande (ber-*tew*-dahn-der) *adj* considerable

betydelse (ber-*tew*-derl-ser)
c importance; sense

betydelsefull (ber-*tew*-derl-ser-*fewl*) *adj* important;
significant

betydlig (ber-*tewd*-li) *adj*
considerable

betydligt (ber-*tÿwd*-lit) *adj* by

far

betyg (ber-*tewg*) nt mark

betänklig (ber-*tængk*-li) adj dubious; serious, critical

beundra (ber-*ewnd*-rah) v admire

beundran (ber-*ewnd*-rahn) c admiration

beundrare (ber-*ewnd*-rahrer) c (pl ∼) admirer; fan

bevaka (ber-*vaa*-kah) v guard

bevara (ber-*vaa*-rah) v *keep; preserve

bevilja (ber-*vil*-ʸah) v grant; allow

beviljande (ber-*vil*-ʸahn-der) nt concession

bevis (ber-*veess*) nt proof, evidence; token

bevisa (ber-*vee*-sah) v prove; demonstrate; *show

beväpna (ber-*vaip*-nah) v arm

beväpnad (ber-*vaip*-nahd) adj armed

bi (bee) nt bee

*bibehålla (*bee*-ber-ho-lah) v *hold, *keep, preserve

bibel (*bee*-berl) c (pl biblar) bible

bibetydelse (*bee*-ber-*tew*-derl-ser) c connotation, subordinate sense

bibliotek (bi-bli-oo-*tayk*) nt library

*bidra (*bee*-draa) v contribute

bidrag (*bee*-draag) nt contribution; grant

bifall (*bee*-fahl) nt approval; consent

biff (bif) c steak

biffburgare (*bif*-bewr-ʸahrer) c (pl ∼) beefburger

biflod (*bee*-flood) c tributary

bifoga (bee-*foo*-gah) v attach; enclose

bijouterier (bee-shoo-ter-ree-err) pl costume jewellery

bikt (bikt) c confession; **bikta sig** confess

bikupa (*bee*-kew-pah) c beehive

bil (beel) c car; automobile, motorcar

bila (*bee*-lah) v motor

bilaga (*bee*-laa-gah) c enclosure; annex

bild (bild) c picture; image

bilda (*bil*-dah) v form

bildad (*bil*-dahd) adj cultivated

bildskärm (*bild*-shærm) c screen

bilist (bi-*list*) c motorist

biljard (bil-ʸaard) c billiards pl

biljett (bil-ʸayt) c ticket; coupon

biljettautomat (bil-ʸayt-ou-too-*maat*) c ticket machine

biljettkassa (bil-ʸayt-kahsah) c box office

biljettlucka (bil-ʸayt-lewkah) c booking-office

biljettpris (bil-ʸayt-preess) nt (pl ∼, ∼er) fare

bilkapning (*beel*-kaap-ning) c carjacking

billig (*bil*-i) adj inexpensive; cheap

biltur (*beel-tewr*) c drive

biluthyrning (*beel-ewt-hewr-ning*) c car hire; car rental *Am*

***binda** (*bin-dah*) v *bind, tie

bindestreck (*bin-der-strehk*) nt hyphen

bio (*bee-oo*) c pictures; movies *Am*, movie theater *Am*

biograf (*bee⁰⁰-graaf*) c cinema

biologi (*bee-o-lo-gee*) c biology

biologiskt nedbrytbar (*bee-o-lo-giskt nayd-brewt-baar*) adj biodegradable

bipolär (*bee-poo-lœœr*) adj bipolar

biskop (*biss-kop*) c bishop

***bistå** (*bee-stoa*) v *assist; aid

bistånd (*bee-stond*) nt assistance

bit (*beet*) c bit; piece; morsel, lump, scrap

***bita** (*bee-tah*) v *bite

bitter (*bi-terr*) adj bitter

***bjuda** (*bʸew-dah*) v offer

bjälke (*bʸehl-ker*) c beam

björk (*bʸurrk*) c birch

björn (*bʸurrn*) c bear

björnbär (*bʸurrn-bæær*) c blackberry

Blackberry® (*blehk-ber-ri*) c Blackberry®

blad (*blaad*) nt leaf; sheet

bladguld (*blaad-gewld*) nt gold leaf

bland (*blahnd*) prep among; amid; ~ **annat** among other things

blanda (*blahn-dah*) v mix; shuffle; ~ **sig i** interfere with

blandad (*blahn-dahd*) adj mixed; miscellaneous

blandning (*blahnd-ning*) c mixture

blank (*blahngk*) adj blank; glossy

blazer (*blai-serr*) c (pl -zrar) blazer

bleckburk (*blehk-bewrk*) c canister

blek (*blayk*) adj pale

bleka (*blay-kah*) v bleach

blekna (*blayk-nah*) v turn pale; fade

***bli** (*blee*) v *become; *get; *grow, *go

blick (*blik*) c look; glance; **kasta en** ~ glance

blid (*bleed*) adj gentle

blind (*blind*) adj blind

blindtarm (*blin-tahrm*) c appendix

blindtarmsinflammation (*blin-tahrms-in-flah-mah-shoon*) c appendicitis

blinker (*bling-kerr*) c (pl -krar) indicator

blixt (*blikst*) c lightning

blixtlampa (*blikst-lahm-pah*) c flashgun; flashbulb

blixtlås (*blikst-loass*) nt zip, zipper

block (*blok*) nt pad; pulley

blockera (*blo-kay-rah*) v block

blod (*blood*) nt blood

blodbrist (*blood-brist*) c

anaemia
blodcirkulation (blōōd-seer-kew-lah-shōōn) c circulation
blodförgiftning (blōōd-fŭrr-ᵞift-ning) c blood poisoning
blodig (blōō-day) adj bloody
blodkärl (blōōd-t¹ᵞæærl) nt blood vessel
blodtryck (blōōd-trewk) nt blood pressure
blogg (blohg) c Blog
blomkål (bloom-kōal) c cauliflower
blomlök (bloom-lūrk) c bulb
blomma (bloo-mah) c (pl blommor) blossom
blomsterhandel (bloms-terr-hahn-dayl) c flower shop
blomstrande (blomst-rahn-der) adj prosperous
blond (blond) adj fair
blondin (blon-deen) c (pl blondiner) blond
blott (blot) adv only
blus (blewss) c blouse
bly (blew) nt lead
blyertspenna (blew-errts-peh-nah) c pencil
blyg (blewg) adj timid, shy
blyghet (blewg-hāyt) c timidity
blygsam (blewg-sahm) adj modest
blygsamhet (blewg-sahm-hāyt) c modesty
blå (blōa) adj blue
blåmussla (blōa-mewss-lah) c mussel
blåmärke (blōa-mær-ker) nt bruise

blåsa (blōa-sah) v *blow; ~ upp blow up
blåsig (blōa-si) adj windy
blåsinstrument (blōass-in-strēw-mehnt) nt horn
bläck (blehk) nt ink
bläckfisk (blehk-fisk) c octopus
blända (blehn-dah) v blind
bländande (blehn-dahn-der) adj glaring
blänka (blehng-kah) v *shine
blöda (blūr-dah) v *bleed
blödning (blūrd-ning) c haemorrhage
blöja (blur-ᵞah) c nappy; diaper nAm
blöta (blūr-tah) v soak
bo (bōō) v live; reside; nt nest
bock (bok) c bow; tick; buck colloquial
bocka (bo-kah) v bow, *bend; tick
bod (bōōd) c booth
bofast (bōō-fahst) adj resident
bofink (bōō-fingk) c finch
bogsera (boog-sāy-rah) v tow, tug
bogserbåt (boog-sāyr-bōat) c tug
boj (boi) c buoy
bok¹ (bōōk) c (pl böcker) book
bok² (bōōk) c beech
boka (bōō-kah) v book
bokband (bōōk-bahnd) nt volume
bokföra (bōōk-fūr-rah) v book

bokhandel (*bōōk*-hahn-dayl)
c (pl -dlar) bookstore

boklåda (*bōōk*-lōa-dah) *c*
bookstore

bokomslag (*bōōk*-om-slaag)
nt jacket; wrapper

bokstav (*book*-staav) *c* (pl
-stäver) letter; **stor ~** capital
letter

bokstånd (*bōōk*-stond) *nt*
bookstand

bolag (*bōō*-laag) *nt* company

Bolivia (boo-*lee*-v^{y}ah)
Bolivia

bolivian (boo-li-v^{y}aan) *c*
Bolivian

boliviansk (boo-liv-^{y}aansk)
adj Bolivian

boll (bol) *c* ball

bollplan (*bol*-plaan) *c*
recreation ground

bom (boom) *c* (pl ~mar)
barrier

bomb (bomb) *c* bomb

bombardera (bom-bahr-*dā*-
rah) *v* bomb

bomull (*boo*-mewl) *c* cotton
wool; cotton; **bomulls-
cotton**

bomullssammet (*boo*-
mewls-sah-mayt) *c*
velveteen

bonde (*boon*-der) *c* (pl
bönder) peasant

bondgård (*boond*-gōard) *c*
farmhouse

bong (bong) *c* voucher

bord (bōōrd) *nt* table;
gående ~ buffet

bordduk (*bōōrd*-dewk) *c*
tablecloth

bordell (bor-*dehl*) *c* brothel

bordtennis (*bōōrd*-tehn-iss) *c*
ping-pong; table tennis

borg (bor^y) *c* castle

borgen (*bor*-^{y}ern) *c* (pl ~)
bail; security

borgerlig (*bor*-^{y}ehr-li) *adj*
middle-class

borgmästare (*bor*^{y}-mehss-
tah-rer) *c* (pl ~) mayor

borr (bor) *c* drill

borra (*bor*-ah) *v* drill; bore

borsta (*bors*-tah) *v* brush

borste (*bors*-ter) *c* brush

bort (bort) *adv* away

borta (*bor*-tah) *adv* gone

bortkommen (*bort*-ko-mern)
adj lost

bortom (*bort*-om) *adv*
beyond; *prep* beyond

bortre (*bort*-rer) *adj* farther

bortsett från (*bort*-sayt)
apart from

boskap (*bōō*-skaap) *c* cattle
pl

bostad (*bōō*-staad) *c* (pl
-städer) house; residence

*bosätta sig (*bōō*-seh-tah)
settle down

bota (*bōō*-tah) *v* cure

botanik (boo-tah-*neek*) *c*
botany

botemedel (*bōō*-ter-māy-
dayl) *nt* remedy

botten (*bo*-tern) *c* bottom

bottenvåning (*bo*-tern-vōa-
ning) *c* ground floor

boutique (boo-*tik*) *c*
boutique

33 **brodera**

bowlingbana (*bov*-ling-baa-nah) *c* bowling alley
boxas (*books*-ahss) *v* box
boxningsmatch (*books*-nings-mahch) *c* boxing match
boyscout (*boi*-skahewt) *c* scout
bra (brah) *adv* well; *adj* good; **bra!** all right!
brak (braak) *nt* boom
brandalarm (*brahnd*-ah-lahrm) *c* fire alarm
brandgul (brahnd-gewl) *adj* orange
brandkår (brahnd-koar) *c* fire brigade
brandman (*brahnd*-mahn) *c* (pl -män) firefighter
brandsläckare (*brahnd*-sleh-kah-rer) *c* (pl ~) fire extinguisher
brandstege (*brahnd*-stāy-ger) *c* fire escape
brandsäker (brahnd-sai-kerr) *adj* fireproof
brandvägg (brahnd vehg) *c* firewall
brant (brahnt) *adj* steep
brasilianare (brah-si-li-*aa*-nah-rer) *c* (pl ~) Brazilian
brasiliansk (brah-si-li-*aansk*) *adj* Brazilian
Brasilien (brah-*see*-li-ern) Brazil
bred (brāyd) *adj* wide, broad
bredband (brāyd-bahnd) *c* broadband
bredd (brayd) *c* breadth; width

breddgrad (brayd-graad) *c* latitude
bredvid (brāy-veed) *prep* beside; next to
brev (brāyv) *nt* letter; **rekommenderat** ~ registered letter
brevbärare (brāyv-bææ-rah-rer) *c* (pl ~) postman
brevkort (brāyv-koort) *nt* postcard; card
brevlåda (brāyv-loā-dah) *c* pillarbox, letterbox; mailbox *nAm*
brevlådstömning (brāyv-lods-turm-ning) *c* collection
brevpapper (brāyv-pah-pahr) *nt* notepaper, writing paper
brevväxling (brāyv-vehks-ling) *c* correspondence
bricka (bri-kah) *c* tray
bridge (bridsh) *c* bridge
briljant (bril-*yahnt*) *adj* brilliant
*brinna (bri-nah) *v* *burn
bris (breess) *c* breeze
brist (brist) *c* shortage, lack, want; deficiency
*brista (briss-tah) *v* *burst
bristfällig (brist-feh-li) *adj* defective; faulty
britt (brit) *c* Briton
brittisk (bri-tisk) *adj* British
bro (broō) *c* bridge
brock (brok) *nt* hernia
broder (broō-derr) *c* (pl bröder) brother
brodera (broo-*dāy*-rah) *v* embroider

broderi (broo-der-*ree*) nt (pl ~er) embroidery

broderlighet (*broo*-derr-li-hāyt) c fraternity

brokig (*broo*-ki) adj gay

broms (broms) c brake

bromsa (*brom*-sah) v brake

bromsljus (*broms*-ˠēwss) nt brake lights

bromstrumma (*broms*-trewmah) c brake drum

brons (brons) c bronze; **brons-** bronze

bror (brōōr) c (pl bröder) brother

brorsdotter (*brōōrs*-do-tay) c (pl -döttrar) niece

brorson (*brōōr*-sōān) c (pl -söner) nephew

brosch (brōāsh) c brooch

broschyr (bro-*shēwr*) c brochure

brosk (brosk) nt cartilage

brott (brot) nt crime; fracture

brottslig (*brots*-li) adj criminal

brottslighet (*brots*-li-hāyt) c criminality

brottsling (*brots*-ling) c criminal; convict

brottstycke (*brot*-stew-ker) nt fragment

brud (brēwd) c bride

brudgum (*brēwd*-gewm) c (pl -gummar) groom

bruk (brēwk) nt custom

bruka (*brēw*-kah) v use, employ; cultivate

bruklig (*brēwk*-li) adj customary

bruksanvisning (*brēwks*-ahn-*veess*-ning) c directions for use

brun (brēwn) adj brown

brunett (brew-*nayt*) c brunette

brunn (brewn) c well

brus (brēwss) nt fizz

brutal (brew-*taal*) adj brutal

brutto- (brew-too) gross

bry sig om (brēw) care for; mind; care about

brydsam (*brēwd*-sahm) adj awkward

brygga (*brew*-gah) v brew; c landingstage

bryggeri (brew-ger-*ree*) nt (pl ~er) brewery

brysselkål (*brew*-serl-kōal) c Brussels sprouts

***bryta** (*brēw*-tah) v *break; fracture; ~ samman collapse

brytning (*brēwt*-ning) c breaking, refraction; accent

brådska (*bross*-kah) c hurry, haste

brådskande (*bross*-kahn-der) adj urgent; pressing

bråk (brōāk) nt row; fuss

bråkdel (*brōāk*-dāyl) c fraction

***ha bråttom** (*bro*-tom) *be in a hurry

bräckjärn (*brehk*-ˠæærn) nt crowbar

bräcklig (*brehk*-li) adj fragile

bräda (*brai*-dah) c board

brädd (brehd) c brim

bränna (*breh*-nah) v *burn

brännmärke (*brehn*-mær-

35

byte

ker) *nt* brand

brännolja (brehn-ol-*y*ah) *c* fuel oil

brännpunkt (brehn-pewngkt) *c* focus

brännsår (brehn-soar) *nt* burn

bränsle (brehns-lay) *nt* fuel

bröd (brūrd) *nt* bread; **rostat ~ toast**

brödrost (brūrd-rost) *c* toaster

bröllop (brur-lop) *nt* wedding

bröllopsresa (brur-lops-*rāy*-sah) *c* honeymoon

bröst (brurst) *nt* breast; bosom, chest

bröstkorg (brurst-kor*y*) *c* chest

bröstsim (brurst-sim) *nt* breaststroke

bubbla (bewb-lah) *c* bubble

buckla (bewk-lah) *c* dent

bud (bēwd) *nt* messenger; bid

budget (bewd-*y*ert) *c* budget

buga sig (bew-gah) bow

buk (bēwk) *c* belly; abdomen

bukett (bew-*kayt*) *c* bunch, bouquet

bukt (bewkt) *c* gulf

bula (bew-lah) *c* lump

bulgar (bewl-*gaar*) *c* Bulgarian

Bulgarien (bewl-*gaa*-ri-ern) Bulgaria

bulgarisk (bewl-*gaa*-risk) *adj* Bulgarian

bulle (bewl-er) *c* bun

buller (bew-lerr) *nt* noise

bullrig (bewl-ri) *adj* noisy

bult (bewlt) *c* bolt

bundsförvant (bewnds-furr-vahnt) *c* associate; ally, confederate

bunt (bewnt) *c* bundle; batch

bunta ihop (bewn-tah i-*hōōp*) bundle

bur (bēwr) *c* cage

burk (bewrk) *c* tin

busig (bēw-si) *adj* rowdy

buske (bewss-ker) *c* bush; shrub

buss (bewss) *c* bus; coach

butik (bew-*teek*) *c* shop

by (bēw) *c* village

bygga (bew-gah) *v* *build; construct

bygge (bew-ger) *nt* construction

byggnad (bewg-nahd) *c* building, construction

byggnadskonst (bewg-nahds-konst) *c* architecture

byggnadsställning (bewg-nahds-stehl-ning) *c* scaffolding

byrå¹ (bēw-ro) *c* (pl ~ar) chest of drawers; bureau *nAm*

byrå² (bēw-ro) *c* (pl ~er) agency

byråkrati (bēw-ro-krah-*tee*) *c* bureaucracy

byrålåda (bēw-ro-*lōa*-dah) *c* drawer

byst (bewst) *c* bust

bysthållare (bewst-ho-lah-rer) *c* (pl ~) brassiere

byta (bēw-tah) *v* change; swap; ~ **ut** exchange

byte (bēw-ter) *nt* exchange;

byxdräkt 36

prey

byxdräkt (*bewks*-drehkt) *c* pant suit

byxor (*bewk*-serr) *pl* trousers *pl*, pants *plAm*

båda (*bōa*-dah) *pron* both, either

både ... och (*bōa*-der ... ok) both ... and

båge (*bōa*-ger) *c* bow

bågformig (*bōag*-for-mi) *adj* arched

bår (bōar) *c* stretcher

båt (bōat) *c* boat

bäck (behk) *c* stream, brook

bäcken (behk-ern) *nt* pelvis

bädda (*beh*-dah) *v* *make the bed

bälte (*behl*-ter) *nt* belt

bänk (behngk) *c* bench

bär (bæær) *nt* berry

*bära (*bææ*-rah) *v* carry; *wear; *bear

bärbar (*bæær*-baar) *adj* portable

bärbar dator (*bæær*-baar *dah*-torr) *c* laptop

bärare (*bææ*-rah-rer) *c* (pl ~) porter

bärgningsbil (*bærʸ*-nings-beel) *c* breakdown truck

bärnsten (*bæærn*-stāyn) *c* amber

bäst (behst) *adj* best

bättre (*beht*-rer) *adj* superior; better

bäver (*bai*-verr) *c* (pl bävrar) beaver

bödel (*būr*-derl) *c* (pl bödlar) executioner

böja (*bur*-ʸah) *v* *bend; ~ sig *bend down

böjd (burʸd) *adj* bent; curved

böjlig (*burʸ*-li) *adj* flexible, supple

böjning (*burʸ*-ning) *c* bending; flexion

böld (burld) *c* abscess

bön (būrn) *c* prayer

böna (*būr*-nah) *c* bean

*bönfalla (*būrn*-fahl-ah) *v* beg

bör (būr) *v* ought

*böra (*būr*-rah) *v* *ought to

börda (*būr*-dah) *c* burden, load; charge

börja (burr-ʸah) *v* *begin; commence, start; ~ om recommence

början (*burr*-ʸahn) *c* beginning; start; **i ~** at first

börs (burrs) *c* purse; exchange; **svarta börsen** black market

böter (*būr*-terr) *pl* ticket, fine; penalty

C

cancer (*kahn*-serr) *c* cancer

cape (käyp) *c* cape; cloak

CD-(ROM) (säy-day-rohm) *c* (pl ~) CD(-ROM)

CD-skiva (*säy*-day-*sheev*-ah) *c* compact disc

CD-spelare (*säy*-day-*späy*-lah-rer) *c* compact disc player

cell (sayl) *c* cell

cement (say-*maynt*) *nt* cement

censur (sayn-*sewr*) *c* censorship

center (*sayn*-ter) *nt* center

centimeter (sayn-ti-*mäy*-terr) *c* (pl ~) centimetre

central (sayn-*traal*) *adj* central

centralisera (sayn-trah-li-*säy*-rah) *v* centralize

centralvärme (sayn-*traal*-vær-mer) *c* central heating

centrum (*sehnt*-rewm) *nt* centre

ceremoni (say-ray-mo-*nee*) *c* ceremony

certifikat (sehr-ti-fi-*kaat*) *nt* certificate

champagne (shahm-*pahn*^{y}) *c* champagne

champinjon (shahm-pin-^{y}*oon*) *c* button mushroom

chans (shahngs) *c* chance

charlatan (shahr-lah-*taan*) *c* quack

charm (shahrm) *c* charm

charmerande (shahr-*mäy*-rahn-der) *adj* charming

charterflyg (t^y*aar*-terr-flëwg) *nt* charter flight

chassi (*shah*-si) *nt* chassis

chaufför (sho-*furr*) *c* chauffeur

check (t^{y}ayk) *c* cheque, check *nAm*

checka in (t^y*eh*-kah) check in

checkhäfte (t^y*ayk*-hehf-ter) *nt* chequebook; checkbook *nAm*

chef (shäyf) *c* boss; manager, chief

chefssekreterare (*shäyfs*-sayk-ray-*täy*-rah-rer) *c* executive assistant

chic (shik) *adj* smart

Chile (t^y*ee*-ler) Chile

chilenare (t^{y}i-*lee*-nah-rer) *c* (pl ~) Chilean

chilensk (t^{y}i-*läynsk*) *adj* Chilean

chock (shok) *c* shock

chockera (sho-*käy*-rah) *v* shock

chockerande (sho-*käy*-rahn-der) *adj* shocking

choke (shoak) *c* choke

choklad (shook-*laad*) *c* chocolate

chokladpralin (shook-*laad*-prah-leen) *c* chocolate

cigarr (si-*gahr*) *c* cigar

cigarraffär (si-*gahr*-ah-*fæær*)
c cigar shop
cigarrett (si-gah-*rayt*) *c*
cigarette
cigarrettetui (si-gah-*rayt*-ay-
tew-*ee*) *nt* cigarette case
cigarrettmunstycke (si-gah-
rayt-mewn-stew-ker) *nt*
cigarette holder
cigarrettobak (si-gah-*reht*-
too-bahk) *c* cigarette
tobacco
cigarrettändare (si-gah-*rayt*-
tehn-dah-rer) *c* (pl ~)
cigarette lighter
cirka (*seer*-kah) *adv*
approximately
cirkel (*seer*-kerl) *c* (pl -klar)
circle
cirkulation (seer-kew-lah-
shoon) *c* circulation
cirkus (*seer*-kewss) *c* circus
cirkusarena (*seer*-kewss-ah-
ray-nah) *c* ring
citat (si-*taat*) *nt* quotation
citationstecken (si-tah-
shoons-tay-kern) *pl*
quotation marks
citera (si-*tay*-rah) *v* quote

citron (si-*troon*) *c* lemon
civil (si-*veel*) *adj* civilian
civilisation (si-vi-li-sah-
shoon) *c* civilization
civiliserad (si-vi-li-*say*-rahd)
adj civilized
civilist (si-vi-*list*) *c* civilian
civilrätt (si-*veel*-reht) *c* civil
law
clown (kloun) *c* clown
cocktail (*kok*-tayl) *c* cocktail
Colombia (ko-*lom*-bi-ah)
Colombia
colombian (ko-lom-bi-*aan*) *c*
Colombian
colombiansk (ko-lom-bi-
aansk) *adj* Colombian
container *c* (pl ~, -nrar)
container
crawlsim (*krōal*-sim) *nt* crawl
curry (*kew*-ri) *c* curry
cykel (*sew*-kerl) *c* (pl cyklar)
bicycle; cycle
cykla (*sewk*-lah) *v* *ride a
bicycle
cyklist (sewk-*list*) *c* cyclist
cylinder (sew-*lin*-derr) *c* (pl
-drar) cylinder

D

dag (daag) *c* day; **om dagen**
by day; **per ~** per day
dagbok (*daag*-book) *c* (pl
-böcker) diary
dagbräckning (*daag*-brehk-
ning) *c* daybreak
dagg (dahg) *c* dew

daghem (*daag*-hehm) *nt* day
nursery
daglig (*daag*-li) *adj* everyday,
daily
dagning (*daag*-ning) *c* dawn
dagordning (*daag*-ord-ning)
c agenda

delning

dagsljus (*dahgs-*ˈ*ewss*) *nt*
daylight
dagsnyheter (*daags-new-*
hāy-terr) *pl* news
dagstidning (*dahgs-teed-*
ning) *c* daily; newspaper
dagsutflykt (*dahgs-ewt-*
flewkt) *c* day trip
dal (*daal*) *c* valley
dalsänka (*daal-sehng-kah*) *c*
depression, valley
dam (*daam*) *c* lady
dambinda (*daam-bin-dah*) *c*
sanitary towel
damfrisör (*daam-fri-sürr*) *c*
hairdresser
damm (*dahm*) *nt* dust; *c* dam
dammig (*dah-mi*) *adj* dusty
*****dammsuga** (*dahm-sēw-gah*)
v hoover; vacuum *vAm*
dammsugare (*dahm-sēw-*
gah-ray) *c* (pl ~) vacuum
cleaner
damspel (*daam-spāyl*) *nt*
draughts; checkers *plAm*
damtoalett (*daam-tooah-*
layt) *c* ladies' room
damunderkläder (*daam-*
ewn-derr-klai-derr) *pl*
lingerie
Danmark (*dahn-mahrk*) *c*
Denmark
dans (*dahns*) *c* dance
dansa (*dahn-sah*) *v* dance
dansk (*dahnsk*) *c* Dane; *adj*
Danish
darra (*dah-rah*) *v* tremble
data (*daa-tah*) *pl* data *pl*
dator (*daa-tor*) *c* computer
datum (*daa-tewm*) *nt* (pl *data*,

~) date
de (*dāy*) *pron* they; ~ **där**
those; ~ **här** these
debatt (*der-baht*) *c* debate;
discussion
debattera (*der-bah-tāy-rah*) *v*
discuss; argue
debet (*dāy-bayt*) *c* debit
december (*der-saym-berr*)
December
decimalsystem (*day-si-*
maal-sew-stāym) *nt* decimal
system
defekt (*der-fehkt*) *c* fault
definiera (*der-fi-ni-āy-rah*) *v*
define
definition (*der-fi-ni-shōōn*) *c*
definition
deg (*dāyg*) *c* dough
deklaration (*day-klah-rah-*
shōōn) *c* declaration;
statement
dekoration (*day-ko-rah-*
shōōn) *c* decoration
dekorera (*day-ko-rāy-rah*) *v*
decorate
del (*dāyl*) *c* part; share
dela (*dāy-lah*) *v* divide; share;
~ **sig** fork; ~ **ut** *****deal;
administer
delegat (*day-ler-gaat*) *c*
delegate
delegation (*day-ler-gah-*
shōōn) *c* delegation
delfin (*dayl-feen*) *c* dolphin
delikatess (*day-li-kah-tayss*)
c delicacy
delikatessaffär (*day-li-kah-*
tayss-ah-fær) *c* delicatessen
delning (*dāyl-ning*) *c* division

delta 40

*delta (dāyl-taa) *v* participate
deltagande (dāyl-taa-gahn-der) *adj* sympathetic; *nt* attendance
deltagare (dāyl-taa-gah-rer) *c* (pl ~) participant
delvis (dāyl-veess) *adv* partly; *adj* partial
delågare (dāyl-ai-gah-rer) *c* (pl ~) associate
dem (dom) *pron* them
demokrati (day-mo-krah-tee) *c* democracy
demokratisk (day-moa-kraa-tisk) *adj* democratic
demonstration (day-mons-trah-shōōn) *c* demonstration
demonstrera (day-mons-trāy-rah) *v* demonstrate
den (dayn) *pron* (nt det, pl de) that; ~ **där** that; ~ **här** this
denna (deh-nah) *pron* (nt detta, pl dessa) this
dental (dayn-taal) *adj* dental
deodorant (dāy-o-do-rahnt) *c* deodorant
departement (der-pahr-ter-mehnt) *nt* department; ministry
deponera (der-po-nāy-rah) *v* deposit; bank
depression (der-pray-shōōn) *c* depression
deprimera (der-pri-māy-rah) *v* depress
deprimerad (der-pri-māy-rahd) *adj* depressed
deputation (der-pew-tah-shōōn) *c* deputation, delegation

deputerad (der-pew-tāy-rahd) *c* (pl ~e) deputy
depå (der-pōa) *c* depot
deras (dāy-rahss) *pron* their
desertera (der-sehr-tāy-rah) *v* desert
desinfektera (diss-in-fayk-tāy-rah) *v* disinfect
desinfektionsmedel (diss-in-fayk-shōōns-māy-dayl) *nt* disinfectant
desperat (derss-pay-raat) *adj* desperate
dess (dehss) *pron* its
dessert (der-sǣær) *c* dessert; sweet
dessförinnan (dehss-fur-ri-nahn) *adv* before then
dessutom (dehss-ēw-tom) *adv* besides; moreover, also, furthermore
dessvärre (dehss-vǣ-rer) *adv* unfortunately
ju ... desto (Yēw ... dehss-too) the ... the
det (dāy) *pron* it; **det beror på** that depends
detalj (der-tahlY) *c* detail
detaljerad (der-tahl-YāY-rahd) *adj* detailed
detaljhandel (der-tahlY-hahn-dayl) *c* retail trade
detaljhandlare (der-tahlY-hahnd-lah-rer) *c* (pl ~) retailer
detaljist (der-tahl-Yist) *c* retailer
detektiv (day-tehk-teev) *c* detective
detektivroman (day-tehk-

teev-roo-*maan*) *c* detective story
devalvera (der-vahl-*vay*-rah) *v* devalue
devalvering (der-vahl-*vay*-ring) *c* devaluation
diabetes (diah-*bay*-terss) *c* diabetes
diabetiker (dee-ah-*bay*-ti-kerr) *c* (pl ~) diabetic
diagnos (dee-ahg-*nōass*) *c* diagnosis; **ställa en ~** diagnose
diagonal (dee-ah-go-*naal*) *c* diagonal; *adj* diagonal
diagram (dee-ah-*grahm*) *nt* graph; chart, diagram
dialekt (dee-ah-*laykt*) *c* dialect
diamant (dee-ah-*mahnt*) *c* diamond
diapositiv (*dee*-ah-poo-si-*teev*) *nt* slide
diarré (dee-ah-*ray*) *c* diarrhoea
diesel (*dee*-serl) *c* diesel
diet (di-*ayt*) *c* diet
difteri (dif-ter-*ree*) *c* diphtheria
dig (day) *pron* you, yourself
digital (di-gi-*taal*) *adj* digital
digital projektor (di-gi-*taal* pro-*shayk*-torr) *nt* digital projector
digitalfoto (di-gi-*taal* -*fōo*-too) *nt* digital photo
digitalkamera (di-gi-*taal*-*kaa*-meh-rah) *c* digital camera
dike (*dee*-ker) *nt* ditch

dikt (dikt) *c* poem
diktamen (dik-*taa*-mern) *c* (pl ~, -mina) dictation
diktare (*dik*-tah-rer) *c* (pl ~) poet
diktator (dik-*taa*-tor) *c* dictator
diktera (dik-*tay*-rah) *v* dictate
dimension (di-mehn-*shōon*) *c* dimension, size
dimma (*di*-mah) *c* mist, fog
dimmig (*di*-mi) *adj* foggy
din (din) *pron* yours
diplom (di-*plōam*) *nt* diploma; certificate
diplomat (di-plo-*maat*) *c* diplomat
diplomatisk (dip-lo-*maa*-tisk) *adj* diplomatic
direkt (di-*raykt*) *adj* direct
direktion (di-rehk-*shōon*) *c* direction, management
direktiv (di-rehk-*teev*) *nt* directive
direktmeddelande (di-*raykt*-*mayd*-day-lahn-der) *nt* instant message
direktör (di-rayk-*tūrr*) *c* director; executive, manager
dirigent (di-ri-*shaynt*) *c* conductor
dirigera (di-ri-*shay*-rah) *v* conduct
dis (deess) *nt* haze
disciplin (di-si-*pleen*) *c* discipline
disig (*dee*-si) *adj* misty, hazy
disk (disk) *c* counter, bar; washingup
diska (*diss*-kah) *v* wash up

diskbråck (*disk-*brok) *nt*
slipped disc

diskonto (diss-*kon-*too) *c*
bank rate

diskussion (diss-kew-*shoon*)
c discussion; argument

diskutera (diss-kew-*tāy-*rah)
v argue, discuss

disponibel (diss-poo-*nee-*
berl) *adj* available

dispyt (diss-*pēwt*) *c* dispute

distrikt (dist-*rikt*) *nt* district

dit (deet) *adv* there

djungel (*ᵞewng-*ayl) *c* (pl
djungler) jungle

djup (*ᵞewp*) *nt* depth; *adj*
deep, low

djupsinnig (*ᵞewp-*si-ni) *adj*
profound

djur (*ᵞewr*) *nt* beast, animal

djurkretsen (*ᵞewr-*kreht-
sern) zodiac

djurpark (*ᵞewr-*pahrk) *c*
zoological gardens

djurreservat (*ᵞewr-*ray-sær-
vaat) *nt* game reserve

djurskinn (*ᵞewr-*shin) *nt* skin

djärv (*ᵞærv*) *adj* bold

djävul (*ᵞai-*vewl) *c* (pl -vlar)
devil

dock (dok) *conj* yet,
nevertheless; but; yet

docka[1] (*doa-*kah) *c* doll

docka[2] (*doa-*kah) *c* dock; *v*
dock

dockteater (*dok-*tay-aa-terr)
c (pl -trar) puppet-show

doft (doft) *c* scent

doktor (*doak-*toar) *c* doctor

dokumentportfölj (do-kew-

maynt-port-*furlᵞ*) *c* attaché
case

dollar (*dol-*laar) *c* (pl ∼)
dollar

dom (doom) *c* judgment;
verdict, sentence; **fällande** ∼
conviction

domare (*doo-*mah-rer) (pl ∼)
judge; *c* umpire, referee

domkraft (*doom-*krahft) *c*
jack

domkyrka (*doom-*tᵞewr-kah)
c cathedral

domnad (*dom-*nahd) *adj*
numb

domslut (*doom-*slēwt) *nt*
verdict

domstol (*doom-*stool) *c*
court; law court

donation (do-nah-*shoon*) *c*
donation

donator (do-*naa-*tor) *c* donor

donera (do-*nāy-*rah) *v* donate

dop (dōōp) *nt* baptism;
christening

doppvärmare (*dop-*vær-mah-
rer) *c* (pl ∼) immersion
heater

dos (dōōss) *c* dose

dotter (*do-*terr) *c* (pl döttrar)
daughter

dotterdotter (*do-*terr-do-
terr) *c* (pl -döttrar)
granddaughter

dotterson (*do-*terr-*sōan*) *c* (pl
-söner) grandson

dov (dōav) *adj* dull

***dra** (draa) *v* *draw; pull; ∼ av
deduct; ∼ ifrån subtract; ∼
sig tillbaka *v* retire; ∼ till

43 **durkslag**

tighten; ~ **tillbaka**
*withdraw; ~ **upp** *wind; ~
ur disconnect; ~ **åt** tighten
drag (draag) nt move; trait;
draught
dragning (draag-ning) c
draw; tendency; tinge
drake (draa-ker) c dragon
drama (draa-mah) nt (pl
-mer) drama
dramatisk (drah-maa-tisk)
adj dramatic
dressera (drer-say-rah) v
train
*dricka** (dri-kah) v *drink
drickbar (drik-baar) adj for
drinking
dricks (driks) c tip
dricksvatten (driks-vah-tern)
nt drinking water
drink (drink) c drink
*driva** (dree-vah) v drift; ~
framåt propel; ~ **med** kid
drive-in (driye-in) c drive-
-thru
drivhus (dreev-hewss) nt
greenhouse
drivkraft (dreev-krahft) c
driving force
drog (droag) c drug
droppe (dro-per) c drop
drottning (drot-ning) c queen
drunkna (drewngk-nah) v *be
drowned
dryck (drewk) c drink;
beverage; **alkoholfri** ~ soft
drink
dränera (dreh-nay-rah) v
drain
dränka (drehng-kah) v drown

dröm (drurm) c (pl ~mar)
dream
drömma (drur-mah) v
*dream
du (dew) pron you
dubbdäck (dewb-dehk) nt
spiked tyre
dubbel (dew-behl) adj double
dubbelsäng (dew-berl-
sehng) c double bed
duggregn (dewg-rehngn) c
drizzle
duglig (dewg-li) adj capable,
able
duk (dewk) c tablecloth
duka (dew-kah) v *set the
table
duka under (dew-kah)
succumb
duktig (dewk-ti) adj capable;
skilful, smart
dum (dewm) adj silly; foolish,
stupid, dumb
dumbom (dewm-boom) c (pl
~mar) fool
dumdristig (dewm-driss-ti)
adj daring, foolhardy
dumheter (dewm-hay-terr) pl
nonsense
dun (dewn) nt down
dunka (dewng-kah) v thump;
bump
dunkel (dewng-kerl) adj
obscure; dim
dunkelhet (dewng-kerl-hayt)
c gloom
duntäcke (dewn-teh-ker) nt
eiderdown
durkslag (dewrk-slaag) nt
strainer

dusch 44

dusch (dewsh) c shower
duschgelé (dewsh-shay-lay) c or nt shower gel
dussin (dew-sin) nt dozen
duva (dew-vah) c pigeon
DVD (day-vay-day) c DVD
DVD-ROM (day-vay-day-raam) c DVD-ROM
dvärg (dvær^y) c dwarf
dygd (dewgd) c virtue
dygn (dewngn) nt twenty-four hours
*dyka (dew-kah) v dive
dykarglasögon (dew-kahr-glaa-sur-gon) pl diving goggles
dylik (dew-leek) adj such, similar
dyn (dewn) c dune
dyna (dew-nah) c pad
dynamo (dew-nah-moo) c dynamo
dynga (dewng-ah) c dung
dyr (dewr) adj expensive; dear
dyrbar (dewr-baar) adj precious; dear, valuable, expensive
dyrka (dewr-kah) v worship
dyster (dewss-terr) adj gloomy; sombre
då (doa) adv then; conj when; då och då occasionally; now and then
dålig (doa-li) adj bad; ill
dån (doan) nt roar
dåraktig (doar-ahk-ti) adj foolish

dåre (doa-rer) c fool
däck (dehk) nt tire, tyre; deck
däckshytt (dehks-hewt) c deck cabin
däggdjur (dehg-^yewr) nt mammal
där (dæær) adv there; ~ borta over there; ~ nere downstairs; down there; ~ uppe upstairs; up there
därefter (dæær-ayf-terr) adv afterwards; then
däremot (dæær-ay-moot) adv on the other hand
därför (dæær-fürr) adv therefore; ~ att because, as
därifrån (dæær-i-froan) adv from there
*dö (dur) v die
död (durd) c death; adj dead
döda (dur-dah) v kill
dödlig (durd-li) adj mortal, fatal
dödsstraff (durds-strahf) nt death penalty
*dölja (durl-^yah) v conceal; *hide
döma (dur-mah) v judge; sentence
döpa (dur-pah) v baptize; christen
dörr (durr) c door
dörrklocka (durr-klo-kah) c doorbell
dörrvaktmästare (durr-vahkt-mehss-tah-rer) c (pl ~) doorman
döv (dürv) adj deaf

E

ebb (ayb) *c* low tide

ebenholts ($\overline{ay}$-bayn-holts) *c* ebony

e-biljett ($\overline{ay}$-bil-*yayt*) *c* e-ticket

e-brev ($\overline{ay}$-br$\overline{ay}$v) *nt* e-mail

Ecuador (ayk-vah-*d$\overline{oa}$r*) Ecuador

ecuadorian (ayk-vah-*d$\overline{oa}$*-ri-aan) *c* Ecuadorian

ed ($\overline{ay}$d) *c* oath, vow

effektförvaring (ay-fehkt-furr-vaa-ring) *c* left-luggage office

effektiv (ay-fayk-*teev*) *adj* effective; efficient

efter (*ayf*-terr) *prep* after

efterforska (*ayf*-terr-fors-kah) *v* investigate

efterfrågan (*ayf*-terr-fr$\overline{oa}$-gahn) *c* demand

efterlikna (*ayf*-terr-leek-nah) *v* imitate

efterlämna (*ayf*-terr-lehm-nah) *v* *leave behind

eftermiddag (*ayf*-terr-mi-daag) *c* afternoon; **i ~** this afternoon

efternamn (*ayf*-terr-nahmn) *nt* surname; family name

eftersom (*ayf*-terr-som) *conj* because, as, since

eftersträva (*ayf*-terr-strai-vah) *v* pursue; aim at

eftersända (*ayf*-terr-sehn-dah) *v* forward

efterträda (*ayf*-terr-trai-dah) *v* succeed

efteråt (*ayf*-terr-$\overline{oa}$t) *adv* afterwards

egen ($\overline{ay}$-gayn) *adj* own

egendom ($\overline{ay}$-gayn-doom) *c* property

egendomlig ($\overline{ay}$-gern-doom-li) *adj* peculiar

egendomlighet ($\overline{ay}$-gern-doom-li-*h$\overline{ay}$t*) *c* peculiarity

egenskap ($\overline{ay}$-gern-skaap) *c* quality; property

egentligen (ay-^{y}*aynt*-li-ern) *adv* really

egoism (ay-goo-*ism*) *c* selfishness

Egypten (ay-^{y}*ewp*-tern) Egypt

egypter (ay-^{y}*ewp*-terr) *c* (pl **~**) Egyptian

egyptisk (ay-^{y}*ewp*-tisk) *adj* Egyptian

ehuru ($\overline{ay}$-*h$\overline{ew}$*-rew) *conj* though

ek ($\overline{ay}$k) *c* oak

eker ($\overline{ay}$-kerr) *c* (pl ekrar) spoke

ekipage (ay-ki-*paash*) *nt* carriage

eko ($\overline{ay}$-koo) *nt* echo

ekollon ($\overline{ay}$k-o-lon) *nt* acorn

ekonom (ay-ko-*n$\overline{oa}$m*) *c* economist

ekonomi (ay-ko-no-*mee*) *c* economy

ekonomisk

ekonomisk (ay-ko-*nōā*-misk) *adj* economical, economic; thrifty

ekorre (*āy*k-orer) *c* squirrel

ekoturist (*āy*-ko-*tēw*-rist) *c* eco-tourist

eksem (ehk-*sāym*) *nt* eczema

ekvatorn (ayk-*vaa*-torn) equator

elak (ay-lahk) *adj* evil; ill

elakartad (*āy*-lahk-aar-tahd) *adj* malignant

elasticitet (ay-lahss-ti-si-*tāyt*) *c* elasticity

elastisk (ay-*lahss*-tisk) *adj* elastic

eld (ayld) *c* fire; ~ **upphör** ceasefire

eldfarlig (*ayld*-faar-li) *adj* inflammable

eldfast (*ayld*-fahst) *adj* fireproof

eldstad (*ayld*-staad) *c* (pl -städer) hearth

eldsvåda (*aylds*-vōā-dah) *c* fire

elefant (ay-lay-*fahnt*) *c* elephant

elegans (ay-lay-*gahns*) *c* elegance

elegant (ay-lay-*gahnt*) *adj* elegant

elektricitet (ay-layk-tri-si-*tāyt*) *c* electricity

elektriker (ay-*layk*-tri-kerr) *c* (pl ~) electrician

elektrisk (ay-*layk*-trisk) *adj* electric

elektronisk (ay-layk-*trōā*-nisk) *adj* electronic

element (ay-lay-*mehnt*) *nt* element

elementär (ay-lay-mehn-*tæær*) *adj* primary

elev (ay-*lāyv*) *c* pupil

elfenben (*ayl*-fayn-bāyn) *nt* ivory

elfte (*aylf*-tay) *num* eleventh

eliminera (ay-li-mi-*nāy*-rah) *v* eliminate

eller (*ayl*-err) *conj* or

elva (*ayl*-vah) *num* eleven

elände (ay-*lehn*-der) *nt* misery

eländig (ay-*lehn*-di) *adj* miserable

emalj (ay-*mahlʸ*) *c* enamel

emaljerad (ay-mahl-*ʸāy*-rahd) *adj* enamelled

embargo (aym-*bahr*-goo) *nt* embargo

embarkering (aym-bahr-*kāy*-ring) *c* embarkation

emblem (aym-*blāym*) *nt* emblem

emellertid (ay-*meh*-lerr-teed) *adv* though, however

emot (ay-*mōōt*) *prep* against; towards; ***ha något ~** mind

en¹ (ayn) *art* (nt ett) a art

en² (ayn) *num* one

-en³ (ayn) *suf* (nt -et) the *art*

enaktare (*āy*n-ahk-tah-rer) *c* (pl ~) one-act play

enastående (*āy*-nah-stōā-ayn-der) *adj* exceptional

enbart (*āy*n-baart) *adv* exclusively

enda (*ayn*-dah) *pron* only; **en ~** single

endast (*ayn*-dahst) *adv* alone, only; merely

endera (*ayn*-dā̄y-rah) *pron* either

endossera (ayn-do-sā̄y-rah) *v* endorse

energi (ay-nær-*shee*) *c* power, energy

energisk (ay-*nær*-gisk) *adj* energetic

engelsk (*ehng*-erlsk) *adj* English

Engelska kanalen (*eh*-ngerls-kah kah-*naa*-lern) English Channel

engelsman (*ehng*-erls-mahn) *c* (pl -män) Englishman

England (*ehng*-lahnd) England; Britain

engångs- (*ā̄y*n-gongs) disposable

engångsflaska (*ā̄y*n-gongs-flahss-kah) *c* no return bottle

enhet (*ā̄y*n-hāyt) *c* unit, unity

*vara enig (vaa-rah *ā̄y*-ni) agree

enighet (*ā̄y*-ni-hāyt) *c* agreement

enkel (*ayng*-kayl) *adj* simple; plain

enkelrum (*ayng*-kayl-rewm) *nt* single room

enkelt (*ayng*-kerlt) *adv* simply; **helt ~** simply

enligt (*ā̄y*n-lit) *prep* according to

enorm (ay-*norm*) *adj* enormous; immense

ensam (*ayn*-sahm) *adj* lonely;

sole

ensidig (*ā̄y*n-see-di) *adj* one-sided

enskild (*ā̄y*n-shild) *adj* individual

enstämmig (*ā̄y*n-stehm-i) *adj* unanimous

entreprenör (ehnt-rer-pray-*nūrr*) *c* contractor

entusiasm (ayn-tew-si-*ahsm*) *c* enthusiasm

entusiastisk (ayn-tew-si-*ahss*-tisk) *adj* enthusiastic

envar (ayn-*vaar*) *pron* everyone

envis (*ā̄y*n-veess) *adj* stubborn; obstinate

epidemi (ay-pi-der-*mee*) *c* epidemic

epilepsi (ay-pi-lehp-*see*) *c* epilepsy

epilog (eh-pi-*lōāg*) *c* epilogue

episk (*ā̄y*-pisk) *adj* epic

episod (eh-pi-*sōōd*) *c* episode

epos (*ā̄y*-poss) *nt* epic

e-post (*ā̄y*-post) *c* (pl ~) e-mail

e-postadress (*ā̄y*-post-ahd-rayss) *c* e-mail address

e-postmeddelande (*ā̄y*-post-*mā̄y*-day-lahn-der) *nt* e-mail

er (āyr) *pron* you; your; yourselves

era (*ā̄y*-rah) *pron* your

*erbjuda (*ā̄y*r-bʸ*ēw*-dah) *v* offer; **~ sig** offer one's services

erbjudande (*ā̄y*r-bʸ*ēw*-dahn-der) *nt* offer

*erfara (*ā̄y*r-faa-rah) *v*

experience

erfaren (*ayr*-faa-rern) *adj*
experienced

erfarenhet (*ayr*-faa-rern-hayt) *c* experience

erforderlig (*ayr*-foor-derr-li) *adj* requisite

*****erhålla** (*ayr*-ho-lah) *v* obtain

erinra sig (*ayr*-in-rah) recall

erkänna (*ayr*-t'eh-nah) *v* admit; confess, acknowledge, recognize

erkännande (*ayr*-t'eh-nahn-der) *nt* recognition

*****ersätta** (*ayr*-seh-tah) *v* substitute; replace

ersättning (*ayr*-seht-ning) *c* indemnity; compensation

erövra (*ayr*-*ūrv*-rah) *v* conquer

erövrare (*ayr*-*ūrv*-rah-rer) *c* (pl ~) conqueror

erövring (*ayr*-*ūrv*-ring) *c* conquest; capture

eskort (ayss-*kort*) *c* escort

eskortera (ayss-kor-*tay*-rah) *v* escort

esplanad (ayss-plah-*naad*) *c* esplanade

essens (ay-*sehns*) *c* essence

essä (ay-*sai*) *c* essay

etablera (ay-tah-*blay*-rah) *v* establish

etapp (ay-*tahp*) *c* stage, lap

eter (*ay*-terr) *c* ether

etikett (ay-ti-*kayt*) *c* label; tag

etikettera (ayti-keh-*tay*-rah) *v* label

Etiopien (ay-ti-*ōō*-pi-ern) Ethiopia

etiopier (ay-ti-*ōō*-pi-err) *c* (pl ~) Ethiopian

etiopisk (ay-ti-*ōō*-pisk) *adj* Ethiopian

etsning (*ehts*-ning) *c* etching

etui (ay-tew-*ee*) *nt* case

EU (*ay*-*ew*) EU

euro (*ēw*-rōō) *c* (pl ~) Euro

Europa (*ay*-*rōō*-pah) Europe

europé (*ay*-roo-*pay*) *c* European

europeisk (*ay*-roo-*pay*-isk) *adj* European

Europeiska Unionen (ay-roo-*pay*-is-kah *ēw*-ni-*ōōn*-en) *c* European Union

evakuera (ay-vah-kew-*ay*-rah) *v* evacuate

evangelium (ay-vahn-*ʸay*-li-ʸewm) *nt* (pl -lier) gospel

eventuell (ay-vehn-tew-*ayl*) *adj* possible

evolution (ay-vo-lew-*shōōn*) *c* evolution

exakt (ayks-*ahkt*) *adv* exactly; *adj* exact

examen (ayk-*saa*-mern) *c* examination; *****ta ~** graduate

excentrisk (ayk-*sehnt*-risk) *adj* eccentric

exempel (ayk-*sehm*-perl) *nt* example; instance; **till ~** for example; for instance

exemplar (ayks-aym-*plaar*) *nt* copy; specimen

existens (ayk-si-*stehns*) *c* existence

existera (ayk-si-*stay*-rah) *v* exist

exklusiv (*ehks*-kloo-*seev*) *adj*

exclusive
exotisk (ehk-*sōa*-tisk) *adj*
exotic
expansion (ehks-*pahng*-shōn) *c* expansion
expedit (ehks-pay-*deet*) *c*
shop assistant
expedition (ayks-pay-di-*shōōn*) *c* expedition
experiment (ayks-peh-ri-*mehnt*) *nt* experiment
experimentera (ayks-peh-ri-mayn-*tāy*-rah) *v* experiment
expert (ayks-*pært*) *c* expert
explodera (ayks-plo-*dāy*-rah) *v* explode
explosion (ayks-plo-*shōōn*) *c* blast, explosion
explosiv (ayks-plo-*seev*) *adj* explosive
exponering (ayks-po-*nāy*-ring) *c* exposure
exponeringsmätare (ayks-po-*nāy*-rings-*mai*-tah-rer) *c* (pl ~) exposure meter
exportera (ayks-por-*tāy*-rah) *v* export
expresståg (ayks-*prayss*-tōāg) *nt* express train
expressutdelning (ayks-*prayss*-ewt-*dāyl*-ning) *c* special delivery
extas (ayks-*taass*) *c* ecstasy
extra (*aykst*-rah) *adj* extra, additional; spare
extrastorlek (*aykst*-rah-stōōr-layk) *c* outsize
extravagant (ayks-trah-vah-*gahnt*) *adj* extravagant
extrem (ehk-*strāym*) *adj* extreme

F

fabrik (fahb-*reek*) *c* factory; works *pl*; plant, mill
fabrikant (fahb-ri-*kahnt*) *c* manufacturer
fack (fahk) *nt* compartment; trade
fackförening (*fahk*-furr-*āy*-ning) *c* trade union
fackla (*fahk*-lah) *c* torch
fackman (*fahk*-mahn) *c* (pl -män) expert
fager (*faa*-gerr) *adj* fair
faktisk (*fahk*-tisk) *adj* actual, factual
faktiskt (*fahk*-tist) *adv* in
effect, actually, as a matter of fact, really
faktor (*fahk*-tor) *c* factor
faktum (*fahk*-tewm) *nt* (pl fakta) fact
faktura (fahk-*tew*-rah) *c* invoice
fakturera (fahk-tew-*rāyrah*) *v* bill
fakultet (fah-kewl-*tāyt*) *c* faculty
falk (fahlk) *c* hawk
fall (fahl) *nt* fall; case, instance; **i varje ~** at any rate; anyway

*falla (*fahl-*ah) *v* *fall

fallenhet (*fahl-*ern-hayt) *c* faculty

fallfärdig (*fahl-*fæær-di) *adj* ramshackle

falsk (fahlsk) *adj* false

familj (fah-*mil^y*) *c* family

familjär (fah-mil-*^{y}æær*) *adj* familiar

famn (fahmng) *c* (pl famnar) arms

fanatisk (fah-*naa-*tisk) *adj* fanatical

fantasi (fahn-tah-*see*) *c* imagination, fantasy

fantasilös (fahn-tah-*see-*lürss) *adj* unimaginative

fantastisk (fahn-*tahss-*tisk) *adj* fantastic

fantom (fahn-*tōam*) *c* phantom

far (faar) *c* (pl fäder) father

fara (*faa-*rah) *c* peril, risk, danger

*fara (*faa-*rah) *v* *go away; ~ **runt om** by-pass

farbror (*fahr-*brōōr) *c* (pl -bröder) uncle

farfar (*fahr-*faar) *c* (pl -fäder) grandfather

farföräldrar (*faar-*furr-ehld-rahr) *pl* grandparents *pl*

farlig (*faar-*li) *adj* dangerous

farmakologi (fahr-mah-ko-loo-*gee*) *c* pharmacology

farmor (*fahr-*mōōr) *c* (pl -mödrar) grandmother

fart (faart) *c* speed; rate

fartbegränsning (*faart-*bay-grehns-ning) *c* speed limit

fartyg (*faar-*tewg) *nt* ship; vessel

fas (faass) *c* stage, phase

fasa (*faa-*sah) *c* horror

fasad (fah-*saad*) *c* façade

fasan (fah-*saan*) *c* pheasant

fascinera (fah-shi-*nay-*rah) *v* fascinate

fascism (fah-*shism*) *c* fascism

fascist (fah-*shist*) *c* fascist

fascistisk (fah-*shiss-*tisk) *adj* fascist

fast (fahst) *adj* fixed; firm; permanent; *adv* tight

faster (*fahss-*terr) *c* (pl -trar) aunt

fastighet (fahss-ti-*hayt*) *c* house, property; premises *pl*

fastighetsmäklare (*fahss-*ti-hayts-*maik*-lah-rer) *c* (pl ~) house agent

fastland (*fahst-*lahnd) *nt* mainland

fastställa (*fahst-*steh-lah) *v* establish; determine, ascertain, state

fastän (*fahst-*ehn) *conj* though, although

fat (faat) *nt* dish; barrel

fatal (fah-*taal*) *adj* fatal

fatta (*fah-*tah) *v* conceive; *take

fattas (*fah-*tahss) *v* fail

fattig (*fah-*ti) *adj* poor

fattigdom (*fah-*ti-*doom*) *c* poverty

fatöl (*faat-*ürl) *nt* draught beer

favorit (fah-vōō-*reet*) *c* favourite

51 **finansiera**

fax (fahgs) *nt* fax; **skicka ett ~** send a fax
fe (fāy) *c* fairy
feber (fāy-berr) *c* fever
febrig (fāyb-ri) *adj* feverish
februari (fayb-rew-*aa*-ri) February
federation (fay-day-rah-*shōōn*) *c* federation
feg (fāyg) *adj* cowardly
fel (fāyl) *nt* mistake, error, fault; *adj* false, wrong; ***ha ~** *be wrong; ***ta ~** err
felaktig (*fāyl*-ahk-ti) *adj* incorrect; mistaken
felfri (*fāyl*-free) *adj* faultless
felsteg (*fāyl*-stāyg) *nt* slip
fem (fehm) *num* five
feminin (*fāy*-mi-neen) *adj* feminine
femte (fehm-ter) *num* fifth
femtio (fehm-ti) *num* fifty
femton (fehm-ton) *num* fifteen
femtonde (fehm-ton-der) *num* fifteenth
feodal (fay-o-daal) *adj* feudal
ferieläger (*fāy*-ri-er-lai-gerr) *nt* holiday camp
fernissa (fær-*nee*-sah) *c* varnish; *v* varnish
fest (fehst) *c* party; feast
festival (fayss-ti-*vaal*) *c* festival
festlig (fayst-li) *adj* festive
fet (fāyt) *adj* fatty; fat; corpulent
fett (fayt) *nt* fat, grease
fettfri (fayt-free) *adj* fat free
fettsugning (*fayt-sēwg*-ning) *c* liposuction

fiber (*fee*-berr) *c* fibre
ficka (*fi*-kah) *c* pocket
fickalmanacka (*fik*-ahl-mah-nah-kah) *c* diary
fickkniv (*fik*-kneev) *c* pocketknife
ficklampa (*fik*-lahm-pah) *c* torch; flashlight
fiende (*fee*-ayn-der) *c* enemy
fientlig (fi-*ehnt*-li) *adj* hostile
figur (*fi*-gēwr) *c* figure
fikon (*fee*-kon) *nt* fig
fiktion (fik-*shōōn*) *c* fiction
fil (feel) *c* file; row; lane
filial (fil-i-*aal*) *c* branch
Filippinerna (fi-li-*pee*-nerr-nah) Philippines *pl*
filippinsk (fi-li-*peensk*) *adj* Philippine
film (film) *c* film; movie; **tecknad ~** cartoon
filma (*fil*-mah) *v* film
filmduk (*film*-dēwk) *c* screen
filmkamera (*film*-kaa-mer-rah) *c* film camera
filosof (fi-lo-*sōaf*) *c* philosopher
filosofi (fi-lo-so-*fee*) *c* philosophy
filt (filt) *c* blanket; felt
fint! all right!; okay!
finanser (fi-*nahng*-serr) *pl* finances *c*
finansiell (fi-nahng-si-*ayl*) *adj* financial
finansiera (fi-nahng-si-*āy*-rah) *v* finance
fin (feen) *adj* fine; delicate;

finger (*fing*-err) *nt* (pl fingrar) finger

fingeravtryck (*fing*-err-aav-trewk) *nt* fingerprint

fingerborg (*fing*-er-borʸ) *c* thimble

finhacka (*feen*-hah-kah) *v* mince

Finland (*fin*-lahnd) Finland

finländare (*fin*-lehn-der-rer) *c* (pl ∼) Finn

finmala (*feen*-maa-lah) *v* *grind

*finna (*fi*-nah) *v* *find

finne (*fi*-ner) *c* pimple; finnar acne

finsk (finsk) *adj* Finnish

fiol (fi-*ōōl*) *c* violin

fira (*fee*-rah) *v* celebrate

firande (fee-rahn-der) *nt* celebration

firma (*feer*-mah) *c* firm; company

fisk (fisk) *c* fish

fiska (*fiss*-kah) *v* fish

fiskaffär (*fisk*-ah-*fæær*) *c* fish shop

fiskare (*fiss*-kah-rer) *c* (pl ∼) fisherman

fiskben (*fisk*-bᾱyn) *nt* fishbone; bone

fiskedon (*fiss*-ker-dōōn) *nt* fishing tackle

fiskekort (*fiss*-ker-kōōrt) *nt* fishing licence

fiskerinäring (fiss-ker-*ree*-næ-ring) *c* fishing industry

fiskmås (*fisk*-mōᾱss) *c* seagull

fisknät (*fisk*-nait) *nt* fishing net

fiskredskap (*fisk*-rᾱyd-skaap) *nt* fishing gear

fiskrom (*fisk*-rom) *c* roe

fjorton (*fʸōōr*-ton) *num* fourteen

fjortonde (*fʸōōr*-ton-der) *num* fourteenth

fjäder (*fʸai*-derr) *c* (pl -drar) feather; spring

fjäderfä (*fʸai*-derr-fai) *nt* poultry; fowl

fjädring (*fʸaid*-ring) *c* suspension

fjäll (fʸehl) *nt* scale; mountain

fjälla (*fʸeh*-lah) *v* peel

fjärde (*fʸæær*-der) *num* fourth

fjäril (*fʸææ*-ril) *c* butterfly

fjärilsim (*fʸææ*-ril-sim) *nt* butterfly stroke

fjärrkontroll (*fʸairr*-kon-troll) *c* remote control

flagga (*flah*-gah) *c* flag

flamingo (flah-*ming*-goo) *c* flamingo

flanell (flah-*nayl*) *c* flannel

flanera (flah-*nᾱy*-rah) *v* stroll

flanör (flah-*nüürr*) *c* stroller

flaska (*flahss*-kah) *c* bottle

flaskhals (*flahsk*-hahls) *c* bottleneck

flasköppnare (*flahsk*-urp-nah-rer) *c* (pl ∼) bottle opener

flat (flaat) *adj* flat

fler (flᾱyr) *adj* more; (de) flesta most; flera several

flicka (*fli*-kah) *c* girl

flicknamn (*flik*-nahmn) *nt*

maiden name; girl's name

flickvän (flik-vehn) *c*
girlfriend

flin (fleen) *nt* grin

flina (flee-nah) *v* grin

flintskallig (flint-skah-li) *adj*
bald

flintsten (flint-stayn) *c* flint

flisa (flee-sah) *c* chip

flit (fleet) *c* diligence

flitig (flee-ti) *adj* industrious,
diligent

flod (flōōd) *c* river; flood

flodbank (flōōd-bahngk) *c*
bank

flodmynning (flōōd-mew-
ning) *c* river mouth, estuary

flodstrand (flōōd-strahnd) *c*
(pl -stränder) riverside; river
bank

flott (flott) *adj* posh *colloquial*

flotta (flo-tah) *c* navy; fleet;
flott- naval

flotte (flo-ter) *c* raft

flottig (flo-ti) *adj* greasy

flottör (flo-t**urr**) *c* float

fluga (flew-gah) *c* fly; bow tie

fly (flew) *v* flee

flyg (flewg) *nt* flight

*flyga (flew-gah) v *fly

flygbolag (flewg-bōō-laag) *nt*
airline

flygel (flew-gerl) *c* (pl -glar)
grand piano

flygfält (flewg-fehlt) *nt*
airfield

flygkapten (flewg-kahp-tayn)
c captain

flygolycka (flewg-oo-lew-
kah) *c* plane crash

flygplan (flewg-plaan) *nt*
aeroplane, aircraft, plane;
airplane *nAm*

flygplats (flewg-plahts) *c*
airport

flygpost (flewg-post) *c*
airmail

flygresa (flewg-rāy-sah) *c*
flight

flygsjuka (flewg-shew-kah) *c*
airsickness

flygvärdinna (flewg-vær-di-
nah) *c* stewardess

flykt (flewkt) *c* escape

flyktig (flewk-ti) *adj* passing;
volatile

flykting (flewk-ting) *c* refugee

*flyta (flew-tah) v flow; float

flytande (flew-tahn-der) *adj*
fluent; liquid, fluid

flytta (flewt-ah) *v* move

flyttbar (flewt-baar) *adj*
movable

flyttning (flewt-ning) *c* move

flytväst (flewt-vehst) *c* life
jacket

fläck (flehk) *c* stain, spot;
speck, blot; **fläcka ned** stain

fläckborttagningsmedel
(flehk-boart-taag-nings-
māy-dayl) *nt* stain remover

fläckfri (flehk-free) *adj*
spotless, stainless

fläckig (fleh-ki) *adj* spotted

fläkt (flehkt) *c* breath of air,
breeze; fan

fläktrem (flehkt-rehm) *c* (pl
~mar) fan belt

flämta (flehm-tah) *v* pant

flöjt (flur^yt) *c* flute

fnittra (*fnit*-rah) v giggle

foajé (foo-ah-ʸ*ay*) c lobby, foyer

foder (*foo*-derr) nt lining; forage

foderbehållare (*foo*-derr-bay-*ho*-lah-rer) c (pl ∼) manger

fodral (foo-*draal*) nt case; cover

fogde (*foog*-der) c bailiff

folk (folk) nt folk, nation, people; pl people pl; **folk-**national, popular

folkdans (*folk*-dahns) c folk dance

folklore (*folk*-lo̅a̅r) c folklore

folkmassa (*folk*-mah-sah) c crowd

folkrik (*folk*-reek) adj populous

folkvisa (*folk*-vee-sah) c folk song

fond (fond) c fund

fondbörs (*fond*-burrs) c stock exchange

fondmarknad (*fond*-mahrk-nahd) c stock market

fonetisk (fo-*na̅y*-tisk) adj phonetic

fontän (fon-*tain*) c fountain

forcera (for-*sa̅y*-rah) v force

fordon (*foo*-doon) nt vehicle

fordra (*foo̅d*-rah) v demand; claim

fordran (*foo̅d*-rahn) c (pl -ringar) claim

fordringsägare (*foo̅d*-rings-ai-gah-rer) c (pl ∼) creditor

forell (fo-*rayl*) c trout

form (form) c form; shape

forma (*for*-mah) v form; model, shape

formalitet (for-mah-li-*ta̅yt*) c formality

format (for-*maat*) nt format; size

formel (*for*-merl) c (pl -mler) formula

formell (for-*mehl*) adj formal

formulär (for-mew-*læær*) nt form

forntida (*foorn*-tee-dah) adj ancient

forskning (*forsk*-ning) c research

fort (foort) adv in a hurry

*fortgå (*foort*-go̅a̅) v continue

fortkörning (*foort*-tʸ*urr*-ning) c speeding

*fortsätta (*foort*-seh-tah) v *keep on; continue; *go on, *go ahead, carry on; proceed

fortsättning (*foort*-seht-ning) c continuation

fosterföräldrar (*fooss*-terr-furr-*ehld*-rahr) pl foster parents pl

fosterland (*fooss*-terr-lahnd) nt (pl -länder) native country

fot (foot) c (pl fötter) foot; **till fots** on foot; walking

fotboll (*foot*-bol) c football; soccer

fotbollslag (*foot*-bols-laag) nt soccer team

fotbollsmatch (*foot*-bols-mahch) c football match

fotbroms (*fōōt*-broms) *c* foot brake

fotgängare (*fōōt*-Yehng-ah-rer) *c* (pl ~) pedestrian

fotnot (*fōōt*-nōōt) *c* note

foto (*fōō*-too) *nt* photo

fotoaffär (*fōō*-too-ah-*fæær*) *c* camera shop

fotogen (fo-to-*shāyn*) *c* paraffin; kerosene

fotograf (foo-too-*graaf*) *c* photographer

fotografera (foo-too-grah-*fāy*-rah) *v* photograph

fotografering (foo-too-grah-*fāy*-ring) *c* photography

fotografi (foo-too-grah-*fee*) *nt* photograph

fotomeddelande (*fōō*-too-may-*dāy*-lahn-der) *nt* photo message

fotostatkopia (*foo*-too-staat-koo-*pee*-ah) *c* photostat

fotpuder (*fōōt*-pēw-derr) *nt* foot powder

frakt (frahkt) *c* freight

fram (frahm) *adv* forward

framför (frahm-*fūrr*) *prep* before; in front of; *adv* ahead

framföra (frahm-*fūr*-rah) *v* present, state

***framgå** (frahm-*goa*) *v* appear

framgång (frahm-gong) *c* prosperity

framgångsrik (frahm-gongs-reek) *adj* successful

framkalla (frahm-kah-lah) *v* develop

***framlägga** (frahm-lehg-ah) *v* present

framsida (frahm-see-dah) *c* front; face

framsteg (frahm-stāyg) *nt* progress; advance; ***göra ~** advance, *make progress; *get on

framstegsvänlig (frahm-stāygs-vehn-li) *adj* progressive

framstående (frahm-stōā-ayn-der) *adj* prominent; distinguished

framställa (frahm-steh-lah) *v* produce, represent

framtid (frahm-teed) *c* future

framtida (frahm-tee-dah) *adj* future

framträda (frahm-trai-dah) *v* appear

framträdande (frahm-treh-dahn-der) *nt* appearance

framvisa (frahm-vee-sah) *v* *show

framåt (frahm-*ōāt*) *adv* onwards, forward, ahead

framåtsträvande (frahm-ōāt-strai-vahn-der) *adj* progressive

frankera (frahng-*kāy*-rah) *v* stamp

franko (frahng-koo) *adj* post-paid

Frankrike (frahngk-ri-ker) France

frans (frahns) *c* fringe

fransa sig (frahn-sah) fray

fransk (frahnsk) *adj* French

fransman (frahns-mahn) *m*

(pl -män) Frenchman
fras (fraass) c phrase
frasig (fraa-si) adj crisp
fred (frayd) c peace
fredag (fray-daag) c Friday
frekvens (frer-kvehns) c
frequency
fresta (frayss-tah) v tempt
frestelse (frayss-tayl-ser) c
temptation
fri (free) adj free
fribiljett (free-bil-Yayt) c free
ticket
frid (freed) c peace
fridfull (freed-fewl) adj
peaceful; serene
***frige** (fri-Yay) v release
frigivande (free-Yee-vahn-
der) nt liberation
frigörelse (free-Yur-rerl-ser) c
emancipation, liberation
frihet (free-hayt) c liberty,
freedom
friidrott (free-ee-drot) c
athletics pl
frikalla (free-kah-lah) v
exempt
frikostig (free-koss-ti) adj
liberal
friktion (frik-shoon) c friction
frikännande (free-tYeh-nahn-
der) nt acquittal
frimärke (free-mær-ker) nt
postage stamp
frisk (frisk) adj well, healthy
friskintyg (frisk-in-tewg) nt
health certificate
frisyr (fri-sewr) c hairdo
***frita** (free-taa) v exempt; ~
från discharge of

fritid (free-teed) c spare time
fritidscenter (free-teeds-
sehn-terr) nt recreation
centre
frivillig[1] (free-vi-li) c (pl ~a)
volunteer
frivillig[2] (free-vi-li) adj
voluntary
frivol (fri-vol) adj frivolous
from (froom) adj pious
frost (frost) c frost
frostskyddsvätska (frost-
shewds-vehts-kah) c
antifreeze
frotté (fro-tay) c terry cloth
fru (frew) c madam
frukost (frew-kost) c
breakfast
frukt (frewkt) c fruit
frukta (frewk-tah) v dread,
fear
fruktan (frewk-tahn) c dread,
fright
fruktansvärd (frewk-tahns-
væærd) adj awful
fruktbar (frewkt-baar) adj
fertile
fruktos (frewk-toos) c
fructose; **fruktosfri** (frewk-
toos-free) adj fructose-free
fruktsaft (frewkt-sahft) c
squash, juice
fruktträdgård (frewkt-trai-
goard) c orchard
frusen (frew-sern) adj frozen,
cold
frys (frewss) c (pl frysar)
freezer
***frysa** (frew-sah) v *be cold;
*freeze

fryspunkt (*frewss*-pewngkt) *c* freezing point

fråga (*frōa*-gah) *c* question; matter, issue; *v* ask

frågesport (*frōa*-ger-sport) *c* quiz

frågetecken (*frōa*-ger-tay-kern) *nt* question mark

frågvis (*frōag*-veess) *adj* inquisitive

från (*frōan*) *prep* from; off, as from, out of; ~ **och med** from; as from

frånstötande (*frōan*-stūr-tahn-der) *adj* repellent; repulsive

frånvarande (*frōan*-vaa-rahn-der) *adj* absent

frånvaro (*frōan*-vaa-roo) *c* absence

fräck (frehk) *adj* impertinent, insolent; bold; cheeky *colloquial*

fräckhet (*frehk*-hāyt) *c* nerve

frälsa (*frehl*-sah) *v* redeem; deliver

frälsning (*frehls*-ning) *c* delivery

främling (*frehm*-ling) *c* stranger; alien

främmande (*frehm*-ahn-der) *adj* strange; foreign

frö (frūr) *nt* seed

fröjd (frūr³d) *c* joy

fröken (*frūr*-kayn) *c* miss; spinster

fukt (fewkt) *c* damp

fukta (*fewk*-tah) *v* moisten; damp

fuktig (*fewk*-ti) *adj* damp;

humid, moist

fuktighet (*fewk*-ti-hāyt) *c* humidity, moisture

ful (fēwl) *adj* ugly

full (fewl) *adj* full; drunk

fullborda (*fewl*-boor-dah) *v* accomplish; finish

***fullgöra** (*fewl*-³ur-rah) *v* fulfill; perform

fullkomlig (*fewl*-kom-li) *adj* complete; perfect

fullkomligt completely; entirely

fullkomlighet (*fewl*-kom-li-hāyt) *c* perfection

fullkornsbröd (*fewl*-kōorns-brūrd) *nt* wholemeal bread

fullpackad (*fewl*-pahk-ahd) *adj* chockfull; crowded

fullsatt (*fewl*-saht) *adj* full up

fullständig (*fewl*-stehn-di) *adj* complete, total, utter;

fullständigt completely

fullända (*fewl*-ehn-dah) *v* complete

fundera på (fewn-*dāy*-rah) *think over, ponder upon

fungera (fewng-*gāy*-rah) *v* work; operate

funktion (fewngk-*shōōn*) *c* function; working, operation

funktionsoduglig (fewngk-shōōns-ōō-dewg-li) *adj* out of order

fuska (*fewss*-kah) *v* cheat

fy! (fēw) shame!

fylla (*few*-lah) *v* fill; ~ **i** fill in; fill out *Am*

fylld (fewld) *adj* stuffed

fyllning (*fewl*-ning) *c* filling;

fynd 58

stuffing
fynd (fewnd) *nt* discovery, find; bargain
fyr (fewr) *c* lighthouse
fyra (few-rah) *num* four
fyrtio (furr-ti) *num* forty
fysik (few-seek) *c* physics
fysiker (few-si-ker) *c* (pl ~) physicist
fysiologi (few-si-o-lo-gee) *c* physiology
fysisk (few-sisk) *adj* physical
få (foa) *adj* few
*få (foa) *v* *get; *may, *have, *be allowed to
fåfänglig (foa-fehng-li) *adj* vain
fågel (foa-gerl) *c* (pl fåglar) bird
fåll (fol) *c* hem
fånga (fong-ah) *v* *catch
fånge (fong-er) *c* prisoner
fångenskap (fong-ayn-skaap) *c* imprisonment
får (foar) *nt* sheep
fåra (foa-rah) *c* furrow, groove
fårkött (foar-t∫urt) *nt* mutton
*få tag i (faw taag ee) *come across
fåtölj (foa-turly) *c* armchair; easy chair
fäkta (fehk-tah) *v* fence
fälg (fehly) *c* rim
fälla (fehl-ah) *c* trap
fält (fehlt) *nt* field
fältkikare (fehlt-t∫ee-kah-rer) *c* (pl ~) field glasses
fältsäng (fehlt-sehng) *c* camp bed
fängelse (fehng-ayl-ser) *nt*

prison; jail
fångsla (fehngs-lah) *v* imprison, captivate
färdig (fær-di) *adj* finished; ready
färg (færy) *c* colour; dye
färga (fær-yah) *v* dye
färgad (fær-yahd) *adj* coloured, dyed
färgblind (færy-blind) *adj* colour-blind
färgfilm (færy-film) *c* colour film
färglåda (færy-loa-dah) *c* paintbox
färgrik (færy-reek) *adj* richly coloured, vivid
färgstark (færy-stahrk) *adj* colourful
färja (fær-yah) *c* ferry-boat
färsk (færsk) *adj* fresh
fästa (fehss-tah) *v* attach, fasten; *stick; ~ **med nål** pin; **fäst vid** attached to
fästman (fehst-mahn) *c* (pl -män) fiancé
fästmö (fehst-mür) *c* fiancée
fästning (fehst-ning) *c* fortress; stronghold
föda (für-dah) *c* food
född (furd) *adj* born
födelse (für-dayl-ser) *c* birth
födelsedag (für-dayl-ser-daag) *c* birthday
födelseort (für-dayl-ser-oort) *c* place of birth
födsel (furd-serl) *c* (pl -slar) birth
föga (für-gah) *adj* little
följa (furl-yah) *v* accompany;

follow; ~ **efter** follow

följaktligen (*furl*ᵞ-ahkt-li-gayn) *adv* consequently

följande (furl-ᵞahn-der) *adj* following; next, subsequent

följd (furl³d) *c* consequence; result; succession

följeslagare (furl-ᵞer-slaa-gah-rer) *c* (pl ~) companion

följetong (*furl*-ᵞer-tong) *c* serial

fönster (furns-terr) *nt* window

fönsterbräde (furn-sterr-braider) *nt* windowsill

fönstergaller (furns-terr-gahl-err) *nt* bar

fönsterlucka (furns-terr-lew-kah) *c* shutter

för (fürr) *prep* for, conj for; ~ **alltid** forever, for ever; ~ **att** to; ~ **en gångs skull** for once

föra (fü̃-rah) *v* convey, carry

förakt (furr-ahkt) *nt* scorn, contempt

förakta (furr-ahk-tah) *v* despise; scorn

förare (fü̃-rah-rer) *c* (pl ~) driver

förarga (furr-ahr-ᵞah) *v* annoy; displease

förargelse (furr-ahr-ᵞerl-ser) *c* annoyance

förarglig (furr-ahrᵞ-li) *adj* annoying

förband (furr-bahnd) *nt* bandage

förbandslåda (furr-bahnds-lōā-dah) *c* first aid kit

förbanna (furr-bahn-ah) *v*

damn; **förbannat** Damn!

förbehåll (fürr-ber-hol) *nt* reservation; qualification; **utan** ~ unconditionally

förbereda (fürr-ber-rãy-dah) *v* prepare

förberedelse (fürr-ber-rãy-dayl-ser) *c* preparation

förbi (furr-bee) *prep* past; *gå ~ pass by

***förbinda** (furr-bin-dah) *v* connect; join; dress

förbindelse (furr-bin-dehl-ser) *c* connection

förbipasserande (furr-bee-pah-sãy-rahn-der) *c* (pl ~) passer-by

***förbise** (fürr-bi-sãy) *v* overlook

förbiseende (fürr-bi-sãy-ayn-der) *nt* oversight

***förbjuda** (furr-bᵞēw-dah) *v* *forbid; prohibit

förbjuden (furr-bᵞēw-dayn) *adj* prohibited

***förbli** (furr-blee) *v* remain; stay

förbluffa (furr-blew-fah) *v* amaze

förbruka (furr-brēw-kah) *v* consume; *spend; use up

förbrukning (furr-brēwk-ning) *c* consumption

förbryllande (furr-brew-lahn-der) *adj* puzzling

förbrytare (furr-brēw-tah-rer) *c* (pl ~) criminal

förbud (furr-bēwd) *nt* prohibition

förbund (furr-bewnd) *nt*

league; **förbunds-** federal

förbundsstat (furr-*bewnd-staat*) c federation

förbättra (furr-*beht*-rah) v improve

förbättring (furr-*beht*-ring) c improvement

fördel (fūr-dāyl) c advantage; profit

fördelaktig (fūr-dāyl-ahk-ti) adj advantageous; attractive

fördom (fūr-doom) c prejudice

*****fördriva** (furr-*dree*-vah) v expel, chase

fördröja (furr-*drur-ʸah*) v delay; slow down

fördämning (furr-*dehm*-ning) c dike

fördärva (furr-*dær*-vah) v *spoil

före (fūr-rer) prep before; ahead of; ~ **detta** former

förebrå (fūr-rer-brōa) v reproach; blame

förebråelse (fūr-rer-brōa-ayl-ser) c reproach

förebygga (fūr-rer-bewg-ah) v prevent

förebyggande (fūr-rer-bewg-gahn-der) adj preventive

*****föredra** (fūr-rer-draa) v prefer

föredrag (fūr-rer-draag) nt lecture, talk

*****föregripa** (fūr-rer-gree-pah) v anticipate

*****föregå** (fur-rer-gōa) v precede

föregående (fūr-rer-gōa-ern-

der) adj previous; preceding; prior

föregångare (fūr-rer-gong-ah-rer) c (pl ~) predecessor

*****förekomma** (fūr-rer-ko-mah) v occur; anticipate

förekomst (fūr-rer-komst) c frequency

föreläsning (fūr-rer-laiss-ning) c lecture

föremål (fūr-rer-mōal) nt object

förena (furr-āy-nah) v join, unite

förenad (furr-āy-nahd) adj united, combined, joint

förening (furr-āy-ning) c association; society, club; union

Förenta Staterna (fur-rayn-tah-*staa*-terr-nah) United States; the States

*****föreslå** (fūr-rer-slōa) v propose; suggest

förespråkare (fūr-rer-sprōa-kah-ray) c (pl ~) spokesman, advocate

förestående (fūr-rer-stōa-ayn-der) adj oncoming

föreståndarinna (fūr-rer-ston-dah-*ri*-nah) c matron; manageress

föreställa (fūr-rer-stehl-ah) v introduce; represent; ~ **sig** imagine; fancy

föreställning (fūr-rer-stehl-ning) c idea; performance, show

*****företa** (fūr-rer-tah) v *undertake

förhöra

företag (*fūr*-rer-taag) *nt*
enterprise; undertaking;
concern, company

företräde (*fūr*-rer-trai-der) *nt*
priority

förevisa (*fūr*-rer-vee-sah) *v*
exhibit

förevändning (*fūr*-rer-
vehnd-ning) *c* pretence

förfader (furr-faa-derr) *c* (pl
-fäder) ancestor

förfall (furr-*fahl*) *nt* decay

*förfalla (furr-*fah*-lah) *v*
deteriorate; expire

förfallen (furr-*fahl*-ern) *adj*
dilapidated; ~ **till betalning**
overdue

förfallodag (furr-*fah*-lo-
daag) *c* due date, day of
maturity

förfalska (furr-*fahls*-kah) *v*
forge; counterfeit

förfalskning (furr-*fahlsk*-
ning) *c* fake, falsification

förfaringssätt (furr-*faa*-
rings-seht) *nt* method

författare (furr-*fah*-tah-rer) *c*
(pl ~) author; writer

förfluten (furr-*flew*-tayn) *adj*
past; **det förflutna** the past

*förflyta (furr-*flew*-tah) *v* pass

förflyttning (furr-*flewt*-ning)
c transfer

förfogande (furr-*fōōg*-ahn-
der) *nt* disposal

förfriskning (furr-*frisk*-ning)
c refreshment

förfråga sig (furr-*frōāg*-ah)
inquire

förfrågan (furr-*frōā*-gahn) *c*

(pl -gningar) request,
inquiry; query

förfärlig (furr-*fæær*-li) *adj*
terrible; dreadful, frightful

förfölja (furr-*furl*-^yah) *v*
pursue; chase

förföra (furr-*fūr*-rah) *v* seduce

förförisk (furr-*fūr*-risk) *adj*
seductive

förgasare (furr-*gaa*-sah-rer)
c (pl ~) carburettor

förgifta (furr-*y*if-tah) *v* poison

förgrena (furr-*grāy*-nahss) *v*
fork, ramify

förgrund (*fūrr*-grewnd) *c*
foreground

förgylld (furr-*y*ewld) *adj* gilt

*förgå sig (furr-*gōā*) offend

förgäves (furr-*y*aiv-erss) *adv*
in vain

på förhand (pōā *fūrr*-hahnd)
in advance

förhandla (furr-*hahnd*-lah) *v*
negotiate

förhandling (furr-*hahnd*-
ling) *c* negotiation

förhandsvisning (furr-
hahnds-veess-ning) *c*
preview

förhastad (furr-*hahss*-tahd)
adj rash; premature

förhindra (furr-*hin*-drah) *v*
prevent

förhoppning (furr-*hop*-ning)
c hope

förhållande (furr-*hol*-ahn-
der) *nt* relation; affair

förhör (furr-*hūrr*) *nt*
interrogation; examination

förhöra (furr-*hūr*-rah) *v*

interrogate; ~ **sig** inquire;
enquire

förkasta (furr-*kahss*-tah) *v*
reject; turn down

förklara (furr-*klaa*-rah) *v*
explain; declare; ~ **skyldig**
convict

förklaring (furr-*klaa*-ring) *c*
explanation; declaration

förklä sig (furr-*klai*) disguise

förkläde (furr-*klai*-der) *nt*
apron

förklädnad (furr-*klaid*-nahd)
c disguise

förkorta (furr-*kor*-tah) *v*
shorten

förkortning (furr-*kort*-ning) *c*
abbreviation

förkylning (furr-t^y*ewl*-ning) *c*
cold; *bli **förkyld** *catch a
cold

förkämpe (*fürr*-t^yehm-per) *c*
advocate, champion

förkärlek (*fürr*-t^yæær-layk) *c*
preference

förkörsrätt (*fürr*-t^yürrs-reht)
c right of way

förlag (furr-*laag*) *nt*
publishing house

förlamad (furr-*laa*-mahd) *adj*
paralyzed; lame

förlikning (furr-*leek*-ning) *c*
settlement

förlopp (furr-*lop*) *nt* process

förlora (furr-*loo*-rah) *v* *lose

förlorare (furr-*loh*-rah-rer) *c*
(pl ~) loser

förlossning (furr-*loss*-ning) *c*
delivery; redemption

förlovad (furr-*loa*-vahd) *adj*
engaged

förlovning (furr-*loav*-ning) *c*
engagement

förlovningsring (furr-*loav*-
nings-ring) *c* engagement
ring

förlust (furr-*lewst*) *c* loss

*förlåta** (furr-*loa*-tah) *v*
*forgive; **förlåt**! sorry!

förlåtelse (furr-*loa*-tayl-ser) *c*
pardon

förlägen (furr-*lai*-gern) *adj*
embarrassed; *göra ~
embarrass

förlägenhet (furr-*lai*-gen-
hä<u>y</u>t) *c* embarrassment

*förlägga** (furr-*leh*-gah) *v*
place; *mislay

förläggare (furr-*leh*-gah-rer)
c (pl ~) publisher

förlänga (furr-*lehng*-ah) *v*
lengthen; extend; renew

förlängning (furr-*lehng*-
ning) *c* extension

förlängningssladd (furr-
lehng-nings-slahd) *c*
extension cord

förlöjliga (furr-*lur*^y-li-gah) *v*
ridicule

förman (*fürr*-mahn) *c* (pl
-män) foreman

förmedlare (furr-*mayd*-lah-
rer) *c* (pl ~) intermediary

förmiddag (*fürr*-mi-daag) *c*
morning

förminska (furr-*mins*-kah) *v*
lessen, reduce

förmoda (furr-*mood*-ah) *v*
suppose; guess, reckon,
assume

förmodan (furr-*mōōd*-ahn) c
(pl ~den) supposition

förmyndare (furr-mewn-dah-
rer) c (pl ~) tutor; guardian

förmynderskap (furr-mewn-
derr-*skaap*) nt custody,
guardianship

förmå att (furr-*mōa*) *be able
to; cause to

förmåga (furr-*mōa*-gah) c
ability; faculty, capacity

förmån (*fūrr*-mōan) c benefit;
till ~ för in favour of …

förmånlig (furr-*mōan*-li) adj
advantageous

förmögen (furr-*mūr*-gern)
adj wealthy

förmögenhet (furr-*mūr*-
gern-hāyt) c fortune

förmörkelse (furr-*murr*-kehl-
ser) c eclipse

förnamn (*fūrr*-nahmn) nt first
name; Christian name

förneka (furr-*nāy*-kah) v deny

*förnimma (furr-*nim*-ah) v
sense, perceive; apprehend

förnimmelse (furr-*nim*-erl-
ser) c sensation; perception

förnuft (furr-*newft*) nt reason;
sense

förnuftig (furr-*newf*-ti) adj
reasonable, sensible

förnya (furr-*nēw*-ah) v renew

förnybar (*fūrr*-nēw-baar) adj
renewable

förnämst (furr-*naimst*) adj
leading, foremost, greatest

förolämpa (furr-ōō-lehm-
pah) v insult

förolämpning (furr-ōō-

lehmp-ning) c insult

förorda (furr-ōōr-dah) v
recommend

förorena (*fūrr*-oo-rāy-nah) v
pollute

förorening (*fūrr*-oo-*rāy*-
ning) c pollution

förorsaka (*fūrr*-oor-saa-kah)
v cause

förort (*fūrr*-oort) c suburb

förpackning (furr-*pahk*-
ning) c packing; package

förpliktelse (furr-*plik*-terl-
ser) c obligation;
engagement

förr (furr) adv formerly

förra (*furr*-ah) adj last; past

förresten (furr-*rehss*-tayn)
adv by the way; besides

i förrgår (ee *furr*-gōar) the
day before yesterday

förråd (furr-*rōad*) nt supply

förråda (furr-*rōad*-ah) v
betray; *give away

förrådsbyggnad (fur-*rōads*-
bewg-nahd) c warehouse

förrädare (furr-*rai*-dah-rer) c
traitor

förräderi (furr-aid-er-*ree*) nt
treason

förrätt (*furr*-reht) c hors
d'œuvre; first course

församling (furr-*sahm*-ling)
c assembly; parish,
congregation

*förse (furr-*sāy*) v supply,
furnish

förseelse (furr-*sāy*-ayl-ser) c
offence

försena (furr-*sāy*-nah) v

delay; **försenad** late;
delayed; overdue

försening (furr-*sāy*-ning) *c*
delay

försiktig (furr-*sik*-ti) *adj*
cautious, careful

försiktighet (furr-*sik*-ti-hāyt)
c caution; precaution

försiktighetsåtgärd (furr-*sik*-ti-hayts-ōāt-˅æærd) *c*
precaution

förskott (*fūrr*-skot) *nt*
advance; **betald i ~** prepaid

förskottera (*fūrr*-sko-*tāy*-rah)
v advance

förskräcka (furr-*skreh*-kah) *v*
terrify; ***bli förskräckt** *be
frightened

förskräcklig (furr-*skrehk*-li)
adj frightful; dreadful,
terrible, horrible

förslag (furr-*slaag*) *nt*
proposal; suggestion,
proposition

försoning (furr-*sōōn*-ing) *c*
reconciliation

*försova sig (furr-*sōā*-vah)
*oversleep

försprång (*fūrr*-sprong) *nt*
lead, start

först (furrst) *adv* at first

första (furrs-tah) *num* first;
adj foremost, initial, earliest,
original

förstad (*fūrr*-staad) *c* (pl
-städer) suburb; **förstads-**
suburban

förstavelse (*fūrr*-staa-vayl-ser) *c* prefix

förstklassig (*furrst*-klahss-i)

adj first-class; first-rate

förstoppning (furr-*stop*-ning) *c* constipation

förstora (furr-*stōō*-rah) *v*
magnify

förstoring (furr-*stōō*-ring) *c*
enlargement

förstoringsglas (furr-*stōō*-rings-glaass) *nt* magnifying
glass

förströelse (furr-*strūr*-ayl-ser) *c* amusement; diversion

*förstå (furr-*stōā*) *v*
*understand; *see;
comprehend

förståelse (furr-*stōā*-ayl-ser)
c understanding

förstående (furr-*stōā*-ern-der) *adj* understanding

förstånd (furr-*stond*) *nt*
intellect; reason, brain

förstöra (furr-*stūr*-rah) *v*
damage, destroy

förstörelse (furr-*stūr*-rayl-ser) *c* destruction

försumlig (furr-*sewm*-li) *adj*
neglectful

försumma (furr-*sewm*-ah) *v*
neglect; fail

försvar (furr-*svaar*) *nt*
defence

försvara (furr-*svaa*-rah) *v*
defend, justify

*försvinna (furr-*svi*-nah) *v*
disappear; vanish

försvunnen (furr-*svew*-nayn)
adj lost; missing

försäkra (furr-*saik*-rah) *v*
assure; insure; affirm

försäkring (furr-*saik*-ring) *c*

insurance

försäkringsbrev (furr-*saik*-rings-bray̆v) *nt* insurance policy; policy

försäkringspremie (furr-*saik*-rings-pray̆-mi-ay) *c* premium

försäljare (furr-*sehl*-Ꭹah-rer) *c* (pl ~) salesman

försäljerska (furr-*sehl*-Ꭹerrs-kah) *c* salesgirl

försäljning (furr-*sehl*Ꭹ-ning) *c* sale

försändelse (furr-*sehn*-dayl-ser) *c* consignment; item of mail

försök (furr-*sūrk*) *nt* attempt; experiment, try

försöka (furr-*sūr*-kah) *v* try; attempt

förtal (furr-*taal*) *nt* slander, calumny

förteckning (furr-*tayk*-ning) *c* index, list

förtjusande (furr-t Ꭹ*ewss*-ahn-der) *adj* delightful; lovely

förtjusning (furr-t Ꭹ*ewss*-ning) *c* delight

förtjust (furr-t Ꭹ*ewst*) *adj* delighted; joyful

förtjäna (furr-t Ꭹ*ai*-nah) *v* merit, deserve; earn

förtjänst (furr-t Ꭹ*ehnst*) *c* gain; merit

förtret (furr-*trāy̆t*) *c* annoyance

förtroende (furr-*trōō*-ern-der) *nt* confidence; trust

förtrolig (furr-*trōō*-li) *adj* intimate

förtrollande (furr-*trol*-ahn-der) *adj* enchanting; glamorous

förtrycka (furr-*trew*-kah) *v* oppress

förträfflig (furr-*trehf*-li) *adj* excellent

förtulla (furr-*tew*-ler) *v* declare

förtunna (furr-*tewn*-ah) *v* dilute

förtvivla (furr-*tveev*-lah) *v* despair

förtvivlan (furr-*tveev*-lahn) *c* despair

förundran (furr-*ewnd*-rahn) *c* wonder

förundra sig (furr-*ewnd*-rah) wonder

förut (*fūrr*-ēwt) *adv* before; formerly

förutsatt att (furr-*ēwt*-saht aht) provided that

*****förutse** (*fūrr*-ēwt-say̆) *v* anticipate

förutspå (*fūrr*-ēwt-spōā) *v* predict

*****förutsäga** (*fūrr*-ēwt-seh-Ꭹah) *v* forecast

förutsägelse (*fūrr*-ēwt-sayal-ser) *c* forecast

förutvarande (*fūr*-rēwt-vaa-rahn-der) *adj* former

förvaltande (*fūrr*-vahl-tahn-der) *adj* administrative

förvaltare (furr-*vahl*-tah-rer) *c* (pl ~) administrator; trustee

förvaltning (furr-*vahlt*-ning)

förvaltningsrätt   66

c administration
förvaltningsrätt (furr-*vahlt*-nings-reht) c administrative law
förvandla (furr-*vahnd*-lah) v transform; **förvandlas till** turn into
förvaring (furr-*vaa*-ring) c custody
förvaringsbox (furr-*vaa*-rings-boks) c locker
förverkliga (furr-*værk*-li-gah) v realize
förvirra (furr-*vi*-rah) v confuse; muddle
förvirrad (furr-*vi*-rahd) adj confused
förvirring (furr-*vi*-ring) c confusion
förvissa sig om (furr-*viss*-ah) ascertain
förvåna (furr-*vōān*-ah) v astonish; surprise; amaze
förvånansvärd (furr-*vōā*-nahns-væærd) adj astonishing

förvåning (furr-*vōā*ning) c astonishment; amazement
i förväg (ee *furr*-vaig) in advance
förväntan (furr-*vehn*-tahn) c (pl -tningar) expectation
förvänta sig (furr-*vehn*-tah) expect
förvärv (furr-*værv*) nt acquisition
förväxla (furr-*vehks*-lah) v *mistake, confuse, mix up
föråldrad (furr-*old*-rahd) adj antiquated, out-of-date
förälder (fūrr-*ehl*-der) c (pl föräldrar) parent
föräldrar (furr-*ehld*-rahr) pl parents pl
förälskad (furr-*ehls*-kahd) adj in love
förändra (furr-*ehnd*-rah) v change; alter
förändring (furr-*ehnd*-ring) c change, variation, alteration
föröva (furr-*ūrv*-ah) v commit

G

gagnlös (*gahngn*-lūrss) adj futile, useless, fruitless
galen (*gaa*-lern) adj crazy
galge (*gahl*-ʸer) c coat hanger; gallows pl
galla (*gahl*-ah) c bile; gall
gallblåsa (*gahl*-blōäss-ah) c gall bladder
galleri (gah-ler-*ree*) nt gallery
gallsten (*gahl*-stäyn) c

gallstone
galopp (gah-*lop*) c gallop
gam (gaam) c vulture
gammal (*gahm*-ahl) adj old; ancient, aged; stale
gammaldags (*gahm*-ahl-dahks) adj old-fashioned; quaint
gammalmodig (*gahm*-ahl-mōō-di) adj old-fashioned,

outmoded

ganska (*gahns*-kah) *adv* fairly; pretty, rather, quite

gap (gaap) *nt* jaws *pl*; mouth

gapa (*gaapah*) *v* open one's mouth

garage (gah-*raash*) *nt* garage

garantera (gah-rahn-*tay*-rah) *v* guarantee

garanti (gah-rahn-*tee*) *c* guarantee

garderob (gahr-der-*rōab*) *c* wardrobe; closet *nAm*; checkroom *nAm*

gardin (gahr-*deen*) *c* curtain

garn (gaarn) *nt* (pl ⁓er) yarn

gas (gaass) *c* gas

gaskök (*gaass*-tᵞūrk) *nt* gas cooker

gaspedal (*gaass*-pay-*daal*) *c* accelerator

gasspis (*gaass*-speess) *c* gas cooker

gastronom (gahst-ro-*nōām*) *c* gourmet

gasverk (*gaass*-værk) *nt* gasworks

gata (gaa-tah) *c* street; road

gatubeläggning (*gaa*-tew-bay-*lehg*-ning) *c* pavement

gatukorsning (*gaatew*-*kors*-ning) *c* crossroads

gavel (*gaa*-vayl) *c* (pl gavlar) gable

*****ge** (ᵞay) *v* *give; pass; ⁓ **efter** *give in; indulge; ⁓ **sig** surrender; ⁓ **sig av** *set out, *leave; ⁓ **upp** *give up; quit; ⁓ **ut** publish

gedigen (ᵞay-*dee*-gern) *adj*

solid

gelé (shay-*lāy*) *c* jelly

gemen (ᵞay-*māyn*) *adj* mean, foul

gemensam (ᵞay-*māyn*-sahm) *adj* common; joint, mutual; **gemensamt** jointly; in common

gemenskap (ᵞay-*māyn*-skaap) *c* community, fellowship

genast (ᵞay-nahst) *adv* immediately, at once, straight away

genera (shay-*nāy*-rah) *v* embarrass

general (ᵞay-nay-*raal*) *c* general

generation (ᵞay-nay-nay-rah-*shōōn*) *c* generation

generator (ᵞay-nay-*raa*-tor) *c* generator

generös (shay-nay-*rūrss*) *adj* generous

geni (ᵞay-nee) *nt* (pl ⁓er) genius

genljud (ᵞayn-ᵞēwd) *nt* echo

genom (ᵞay-nom) *prep* through

genomborra (ᵞay-nom-bo-rah) *v* pierce

genomföra (ᵞay-nom-*fūr*-rah) *v* carry out

*****genomgå** (ᵞay-nom-*gōa*) *v* *go through

genomresa (ᵞay-nom-*rāy*-sah) *c* passage, transit

genomskinlig (ᵞay-nom-*sheen*-li) *adj* transparent; sheer

genomsnitt (*ˈäy*-nom-snit)
nt average; mean; **i ~** on the
average

genomsnittlig (*ˈäy*-nom-
snit-li) *adj* average; medium

genomsöka (*ˈäy*-nom-sür-
kah) *v* search, ransack

genomtränga (*ˈäy*-nom-
trehng-ah) *v* penetrate

gentemot (*ˈäynt*-ay-mōōt)
prep towards

genus (*ˈäy*-newss) *nt* gender

geografi (*ˈäy*-o-grah-*fee*) *c*
geography

geologi (*ˈäy*-o-lo-*gee*) *c*
geology

geometri (*ˈäy*-o-mayt-*ree*) *c*
geometry

gest (shehst) *c* gesture

gestikulera (shehss-ti-kew-
*läy*r-ah) *v* gesticulate

get (*ˈäyt*) *c* (pl ~ter) goat;
getabock billy goat

geting (*ˈäy*-ting) *c* wasp

getskinn (*ˈäy*t-shin) *nt* kid

gevär (*ˈer-væær*) *nt* rifle; gun

gift (*ˈift*) *nt* poison

gifta sig (*ˈif*-tah) marry

giftig (*ˈif*-ti) *adj* poisonous;
toxic

gikt (*ˈikt*) *c* gout

gilla (*ˈi*-lah) *v* like; approve

gillande (*ˈi*-lahn-der) *nt*
approval

giltig (*ˈil*-ti) *adj* valid

gips (*ˈips*) *c* plaster

gissa (*ˈi*-sah) *v* guess

gisslan (*ˈiss*-lahn) *c* hostage

gitarr (*ˈi-tahr*) *c* guitar

givetvis (*ˈee*-vert-veess) *adv*

of course

givmild (*ˈeev*-mild) *adj*
generous; liberal

givmildhet (*ˈeev*-mild-hāyt) *c*
generosity

*gjuta (*ˈ*ew-tah) *v* *cast

glaciär (glah-si-*ˈæer*) *c*
glacier

glad (glaad) *adj* glad;
cheerful, joyful

gladlynt (*glaad*-lewnt) *adj*
good-humoured

glans (glahns) *c* gloss

glas (glaass) *nt* glass; **färgat ~**
stained glass; **glas-** glass

glasera (glah-*säy*-rah) *v* glaze

glass (glahss) *c* ice cream

glasögon (*glaass*-ūr-gon) *pl*
glasses; spectacles

*glida (*glee*-dah) *v* *slide;
glide

glidning (*gleed*-ning) *c* slide

glimt (glimt) *c* glimpse; flash

glob (glōōb) *c* globe

globalisera (glōō-baal-i-*säy*-
rah) *v* globalize

globalisering (glōō-baali-
säy-ring) *c* globalization

global uppvärmning (glōō-
baal ewp-værm-ning) *c*
global warming

glupsk (glewpsk) *adj* greedy

gluten (*glew*-tern) *nt* gluten;
glutenfri (*glew*-tern-free)
adj gluten-free

*glädja (*glaid*-*ˈ*ah) *v* please,
delight

glädje (*glaid*-*ˈ*er) *c* joy,
pleasure; gladness; **med ~**
gladly

granne

glänsa (*glehn*-sah) v *shine
glänsande (*glehn*-sahn-der)
adj shining, lustrous
glänta (*glehn*-tah) c glade
glöd (glürd) c embers pl; glow
glöda (*glūr*-dah) v glow
glödlampa (*glürd*-lahm-pah)
c light bulb
glödlampshållare (*glürd*-
lahmps-*ho*-lah-rer) c (pl ~)
socket
glömma (*glur*-mah) v *forget
glömsk (glurmsk) adj
forgetful
***gnida** (*gneed*-ah) v rub
gnissla (*gniss*-lah) v creak
gnista (*gniss*-tah) c spark
gnistra (*gnist*-rah) v sparkle
gnistrande (*gnist*-rahn-der)
adj sparkling
god (gōōd) adj nice; good;
kind; **var ~** please; **var så ~**
here you are
goddag! (gōō-daa) hello!
godis (*gōōd*-iss) nt candy
nAm
godkänna (*gōōd*-t⁵ehn-ah) v
approve of
godlynt (*gōōd*-lewnt) adj
good-tempered
godmodig (*gōōd*-mōō-di)
adj good-natured
gods (goods) nt estate
godståg (*goods*-tōåg) nt
goods train; freight train
nAm
godsvagn (*goods*-vahngn) c
waggon
godtrogen (*gōōd*-trōō-gern)
adj credulous

godtycklig (*gōōd*-tewk-li) adj
arbitrary, fortuitous
golf (golf) c golf
golfbana (*golf*-baa-ner) c
golf course; golf links
golv (golv) nt floor
gondol (gon-*dōål*) c gondola
gosse (*goss*-er) c lad
gottaffär (*got*-ah-fæær) c
sweetshop; candy store Am
gotter (*got*-err) pl sweets
***gottgöra** (*got*-⁵ūrr-ah) v
*make good, indemnify
gottgörelse (*got*-⁵ūr-rerl-ser)
c indemnity
GPS (ge-peh-s) c GPS ; global
positioning system
grabb (grahb) c chap
grace (graass) c grace
graciös (grah-si-*ürss*) adj
graceful
grad (graad) c degree; grade;
till den ~ so
gradvis (*graad*-veess) adj
gradual
grafisk (*graa*-fisk) adj
graphic; ~ **framställning**
diagram
gram (grahm) nt gram
grammatik (grah-mah-*teek*) c
grammar
grammatisk (grah-*mah*-tisk)
adj grammatical
grammofon (grah-mo-*fōån*) c
record player; gramophone
grammofonskiva (grah-mo-
fōån-shee-vah) c record; disc
gran (graan) c fir tree
granit (grah-*neet*) c granite
granne (*grah*-ner) c

neighbour
grannskap (*grahn*-skaap) *nt* neighbourhood
grapefrukt (*graip*-frewkt) *c* grapefruit
gratis (*graa*-tiss) *adj* free; gratis
gratulation (grah-tew-lah-*shōōn*) *c* congratulation
gratulera (grah-tew-*lāy*-rah) *v* compliment, congratulate
grav (graav) *c* grave; tomb
gravera (grah-*vāy*-rah) *v* engrave
gravid (grah-*veed*) *adj* pregnant
gravsten (*graav*-stāyn) *c* gravestone; tombstone
gravsättning (*graav*-seht-ning) *c* burial
gravyr (grah-*vewr*) *c* engraving
gravör (grah-*vürr*) *c* engraver
grej (gray) *c* gadget
grek (grāyk) *c* Greek
grekisk (*grāy*-kisk) *adj* Greek
Grekland (*grāyk*-lahnd) Greece
gren (grāyn) *c* branch
grepp (grayp) *nt* grasp; clutch, grip
greve (*grāy*-ver) *c* count; earl
grevinna (gray-*vi*-nah) *c* countess
grevskap (*grāyv*-skaap) *nt* county
griffeltavla (*gri*-ferl-taav-lah) *c* slate
grill (grill) *c*; (pl griller) barbecue

grilla (*gri*-lah) *v* grill; roast
grillrestaurang (*gril*-rayss-tew-*rahng*) *c* grillroom
grind (grind) *c* gate
***gripa** (*greep*-ah) *v* grasp; *take, grip, seize, *catch
gripbar (*greep*-baar) *adj* tangible
gris (greess) *c* pig
griskött (*greess*-t'urt) *nt* pork
groda (*grōō*-dah) *c* frog
grodd (grood) *c* germ
grop (grōōp) *c* pit
gropig (*grōō*-pi) *adj* bumpy, rough
gross (gross) *nt* gross
grossist (gro-*sist*) *c* wholesale dealer
grotta (*gro*-tah) *c* grotto; cave
grov (grōōv) *adj* coarse; gross
grund (grewnd) *c* cause; ground; *adj* shallow; **på ~ av** because of; on account of, for
grunda (*grewn*-dah) *v* found; base, ground
grundlag (*grewnd*-laag) *c* constitutional law
grundlig (*grewnd*-li) *adj* thorough
grundläggande (*grewnd*-leh-gahn-der) *adj* fundamental; basic
grundprincip (*grewnd*-prin-seep) *c* basis
grundsats (*grewnd*-sahts) *c* fundamental principle
grundval (*grewnd*-vaal) *c* base, foundation
grupp (grewp) *c* group; set

grus (grewss) nt gravel; grit

grusväg (grewss-vaig) c gravelled road

gruva (grew-vah) c mine; pit

gruvarbetare (grewv-ahr-bay-tah-rer) c (pl ~) miner

gruvdrift (grewv-drift) c mining

grym (grewm) adj cruel; harsh

gryning (grew-ning) c dawn

gryta (grew-tah) c pot, casserole

grå (groa) adj grey

*gråta (groa-tah) v cry; *weep

grädde (greh-der) c cream

gräddfärgad (grehd-fær-yahd) adj cream

gräl (grail) nt quarrel; dispute

gräla (grai-lah) v argue, quarrel; ~ på scold

gränd (grehnd) c alley; lane

gräns (grehns) c frontier, border; limit, bound

gränslinje (grehns-lin-yer) c boundary

gräs (graiss) nt grass

gräshoppa (graiss-ho-pah) c grasshopper

gräslig (graiss-li) adj horrible

gräslök (graiss-lürk) c chives pl

gräsmatta (graiss-mah-tah) c lawn

grässtrå (graiss-stroa) nt blade of grass

gräva (grai-vah) v *dig; ~ ut excavate

grön (grürn) adj green

grönsak (grürn-saak) c vegetable

grönsakshandlare (grürn-saaks-hahnd-lah-rer) c (pl ~) greengrocer; vegetable merchant

grönsallad (grürn-sahl-ahd) c lettuce

gud (gewd) c god

gudfar (gewd-faar) c (pl -fäder) godfather

gudinna (gew-din-ah) c goddess

gudmor (gewd-moor) c (pl -mödrar) godmother

gudomlig (gew-doom-li) adj divine

gudstjänst (gewds-tyehnst) c worship, divine service

guide (gighd) c guide

gul (gewl) adj yellow

guld (gewld) nt gold

guldsmed (gewld-smayd) c goldsmith

gulsot (gewl-soot) c jaundice

gummi (gew-mi) nt rubber; gum

gummiband (gew-mi-bahnd) nt rubber band

gunga (gewng-ah) c swing; v rock, *swing

gungbräda (gewng-brai-dah) c seesaw

gunstling (gewnst-ling) c favourite

gurgla (gewrg-lah) v gargle

gurka (gewr-kah) c cucumber

guvernant (gew-verr-nahnt) c governess

guvernör (gew-verr-nürr) c governor

gylf (ˀewlf) c fly

gyllene (ˀewl-ler-ner) adj golden

gymnast (ˀewm-*nahst*) c gymnast

gymnastik (ˀewm-nah-*steek*) c gymnastics pl

gymnastikbyxor (ˀewm-nah-*steek*-bewk-serr) pl trunks pl

gymnastiksal (ˀewm-nah-*steek*-saal) c gymnasium

gymnastikskor (ˀewm-nah-*steek*-skoor) pl gym shoes; plimsolls pl; sneakers plAm

gynekolog (ˀew-nay-ko-*loag*) c gynaecologist

gynna (ˀewn-ah) v favour

gynnsam (ˀewn-sahm) adj favourable

gyttja (ˀewt-ˀah) c mud

***gå** (goa) v *go; walk; ~ **förbi** pass by; ~ **igenom** pass through; ~ **i land** land; ~ **in** enter; ~ **med på** consent to; ~ **ombord** embark; ~ **till val** go to the polls; ~ **upp** *rise; ~ **ut** *go out

gång (gong) c time; passage, corridor, aisle; **en** ~ once; some time; **en** ~ **till** once more; **gång på gång** again and again; **någon** ~ some day; **två gånger** twice

gångart (gong-aart) c gait

gångbana (gong-baan-ah) c sidewalk nAm

gångjärn (gong-ˀæærn) nt hinge

gångstig (gong-steeg) c footpath

gård (goard) c farm; yard

gås (goass) c (pl gäss) goose

gåshud (goass-hewd) c goose flesh

gåta (goa-tah) c riddle; enigma

gåtfull (goat-fewl) adj mysterious

gåva (goa-vah) c gift; present

gädda (ˀeh-dah) c pike

gäl (ˀail) c gill

gäll (ˀehl) adj loud

gälla (ˀehl-ah) v apply

gällande (ˀehl-ahn-der) adj current, valid

gäng (ˀehng) nt gang

gärna (ˀæær-nah) adv gladly, willingly

gärning (ˀæær-ning) c deed, act

gäspa (ˀehss-pah) v yawn

gäst (ˀehst) c guest

gästfri (ˀehst-free) adj hospitable

gästfrihet (ˀehst-free-hāyt) c hospitality

gästrum (ˀehst-rewm) nt guest room; spare room

gödsel (ˀur-serl) c manure

gök (ˀürk) c cuckoo

gömma (ˀur-mah) v *hide

***göra** (ˀūr-rah) v *do; *make; ~ **illa** harm; ~ **ljusare** brighten; ~ **modfälld** discourage; ~ **sig av med** get rid of; ~ **upp** settle; *make up

gördel (ˀūrr-dayl) c (pl -dlar) girdle

H

*ha (haa) v *have
habegär (haa-bay-ᵞæær) nt greed
hacka (hahk-ah) c hoe; v hoe, chop
hagalen (haa-gaa-lern) adj greedy
hagel (haa-gerl) nt hail
haj (high) c shark
haka (haa-kah) c chin
hal (haal) adj slippery
halka (hahl-kah) v slip
hall (hahl) c hall
hallon (hah-lon) nt raspberry
halm (hahlm) c straw
halmtak (hahlm-taak) nt thatched roof
hals (hahls) c throat; neck
halsband (hahls-bahnd) nt necklace; collar
halsbränna (hahls-breh-nah) c heartburn
halsduk (hahls-dēwk) c scarf
halsfluss (hahls-flewss) c tonsilitis
halsmandlar (hahls-mahnd-lahr) pl tonsils pl
halsont (hahls-oont) nt sore throat
halstra (hahl-strah) v roast
halt (hahlt) adj lame
halta (hahl-tah) v limp
halv (hahlv) adj half
halvcirkel (hahlv-seer-kerl) c (pl -klar) semicircle
halvera (hahl-vāȳ-rah) v halve

halvlek (hahlv-lāyk) c half time
halvpension (hahlv-pahng-shōōn) c half board
halvvägs (hahl-vaigs) adv halfway
halvö (hahlv-ūr) c peninsula
hammare (hah-mah-rer) c (pl ~) hammer
hamn (hahmn) c port, harbour
hamnarbetare (hahmn-ahr-bāȳ-tah-rer) c (pl ~) docker
hamnpir (hahmn-peer) c jetty
hamnstad (hahmn-staad) c (pl -städer) seaport
hampa (hahm-pah) c hemp
han (hahn) pron he
han- (haan) pref male
hand (hahnd) c (pl händer) hand; hand- handheld; *ta ~ om look after; *take care of
handarbete (hahnd-ahr-bāȳt-er) nt needlework
handbagage (hahnd-bah-gaash) nt hand luggage; hand baggage Am
handbojor (hahnd-bo-ᵞor) pl handcuffs pl
handbok (hahnd-bōōk) c (pl -böcker) handbook
handbroms (hahnd-broms) c handbrake
handduk (hahnd-dēwk) c

towel

handel (*hahn*-derl) *c* trade; business, commerce; *driva ~ trade; **handels-** commercial

handelsidkare (*hahn*-derls-eed-kaar-er) *c* (pl ~) tradeswoman

handelsman (*hahn*-derls-mahn) *c* (pl -män) tradesman

handelsrätt (*hahn*-derls-reht) *c* commercial law

handelsvara (*hahn*-derls-vaa-rah) *c* merchandise

handfat (*hahnd*-faat) *nt* washbasin

handflata (*hahnd*-flaa-tah) *c* palm

handfull (*hahnd*-fewl) *c* handful

handgjord (*hahnd*-ˈyoord) *adj* hand-made

handikapp (*hahn*-di-kahp) *nt* (pl ~) handicap

handikappad (*hahn*-di-kahp-ahd) *adj* handicapped, disabled

handkräm (*hahnd*-kraim) *c* hand cream

handla (*hahnd*-lah) *v* shop; act

-handlare (*hahnd*-lah-rer) dealer

handled (*hahnd*-layd) *c* wrist

handling (*hahnd*-ling) *c* action; act, plot, deed; certificate; **handlingar** documents *pl*

handpenning (*hahnd*-pay-ning) *c* down payment, deposit

handske (*hahnd*-sker) *c* glove

handslag (*hahnd*-slaag) *nt* handshake

handstil (*hahnd*-steel) *c* handwriting

handtag (*hahnd*-taag) *nt* knob, handle

handväska (*hahnd*-vehss-kah) *c* handbag; bag

hans (hahns) *pron* his

hantera (hahn-ˈtay-rah) *v* handle

hanterlig (hahn-ˈtayr-li) *adj* manageable

hantverk (*hahnt*-værk) *nt* handicraft

hare (*haa*-rer) *c* hare

harmoni (hahr-mo-*nee*) *c* harmony

harpa (*hahr*-pah) *c* harp

hasselnöt (*hahss*-erl-*nurt*) *c* (pl -ter) hazelnut

hast (hahst) *c* haste

hastig (*hahss*-ti) *adj* fast, rapid; hasty

hastighet (*hahss*-ti-hāyt) *c* speed

hastighetsbegränsning (*hahss*-ti-hāyts-ber-grehns-ning) *c* speed limit

hastighetsmätare (*hahss*-ti-hāyts-*mai*-tah-rer) *c* (pl ~) speedometer

hat (haat) *nt* hatred, hate

hata (*haa*-tah) *v* hate

hatt (haht) *c* hat

hatthylla (*haht*-hew-lah) *c* hat

rack

hav (haav) *nt* sea

havande (*haa*-vahn-der) *adj* pregnant

havre (*haav*-rer) *c* oats *pl*

havsstrand (*hahvs*-strahnd) *c* (pl -stränder) seashore

havsvatten (*hahvs*-vah-tern) *nt* sea water

hebreiska (hay-*brāy*-iss-kah) *c* Hebrew

hed (hāyd) *c* heath

heder (*hāy*-derr) *c* honour

hederlig (*hāy*-derr-li) *adj* honest, straight

hederskänsla (*hāy*-derrs-t^y ehns-lah) *c* sense of honour

hedning (*hāyd*-ning) *c* pagan, heathen

hednisk (*hāyd*-nisk) *adj* heathen; pagan

hedra (*hāyd*-rah) *v* honour

hej! (hay) hello!; **hej då!** Bye-bye! *colloquial*

hel (hāyl) *adj* entire; whole

helgdag (*hehl^y*-daag) *c* holiday

helgedom (*hehl*-ger-doom) *c* shrine, sanctuary

helgeflundra (*hehl*-^y er-flewnd-rah) *c* halibut

helgerån (*hehl*-^y eh-rōan) *nt* sacrilege

helgon (*hehl*-gon) *nt* saint

helhet (*hāyl*-hayt) *c* whole

helig (*hāy*-li) *adj* holy; sacred

helikopter (heh-li-*kóp*-ter) *c* (pl -koptrar) helicopter

hellre (*hehl*-rer) *adv* rather;

sooner

helpension (*hāyl*-pahng-shōōn) *c* full board; bed and board; board and lodging

helt (hāylt) *adv* entirely; quite; ~ **och hållet** wholly; altogether

helvete (*hehl*-vāy-ter) *nt* hell

hem (hehm) *nt* home; *adv* home; **~gå** ~ ***go** home; **hem-** domestic

hembiträde (*hehm*-bee-*trai*-der) *nt* housemaid

hemgjord (*hehm*-^y ōōrd) *adj* home-made

hemland (*hehm*-lahnd) *nt* (pl -länder) native country

hemlig (*hehm*-li) *adj* secret

hemlighet (*hehm*-li-hāyt) *c* secret

hemlängtan (*hehm*-lehng-tahn) *c* homesickness

hemma (*hehm*-ah) *adv* at home; home

hemmafru (heh-mah-frew) *c* house-wife

hemorrojder (heh-mo-*roi*-derr) *pl* haemorrhoids *pl*; piles *pl*

hemort (*hehm*-oort) *c* domicile

hemsk (hehmsk) *adj* terrible

hemtrevlig (*hehm*-trāyv-li) *adj* cosy

henne (*hehn*-er) *pron* her

hennes (*hehn*-erss) *pron* her

herde (*hāyr*-der) *c* shepherd

herr (*hær*) *mister*

herravälde (*hær*-ah-vehl-der) *nt* domination;

dominion
herre (*hær*-er) *c* gentleman; min ~ sir
herrfrisör (*hær*-fri-*surr*) *c* barber
herrgård (*hær*-gōard) *c* manor house
herrtoalett (*hær*-tōo-ah-*layt*) *c* men's room
hertig (*hær*-tig) *c* duke
hertiginna (*hær*-ti-*gin*-ah) *c* duchess
hes (hāyss) *adj* hoarse
het (hāyt) *adj* hot
heta (*hāy*-tah) *v* *be called
heterosexuell (heh-ter-ro-sehk-sew-*ayl*) *adj* heterosexual
hetlevrad (*hāyt*-lāyv-rahd) *adj* hot-tempered
hetta (*hay*-tah) *c* heat
hicka (*hi*-kah) *c* hiccup
hierarki (hi-err-ahr-*kee*) *c* hierarchy
himmel (*him*-erl) *c* (pl -mlar) sky; heaven
hinder (*hin*-derr) *nt* obstacle; impediment
hindra (*hind*-rah) *v* hinder; impede; embarrass
hink (hingk) *c* bucket
hinna (*hin*-ah) *c* membrane
***hinna** (*hin*-ah) *v* *catch; *find time
hip-hop (hip-hop) *c* hip-hop
hiss (hiss) *c* lift; elevator *nAm*
hissa (*hiss*-ah) *v* hoist
historia (hiss-*tōo*-ri-ah) *c* history; story

historiker (hiss-*tōo*-ri-kerr) *c* (pl ~) historian
historisk (hiss-*tōo*-risk) *adj* historic; historical
hitta (*hit*-ah) *v* *find
hittegods (*hi*-ter-goods) *nt* lost and found
hittegodsmagasin (*hi*-ter-goods-mah-gah-*seen*) *nt* lost property office
hittills (*heet*-tils) *adv* so far
hjord (*yōord*) *c* herd; flock
hjort (*yoort*) *c* deer
hjortkalv (*yoort*-kahlv) *c* fawn
hjul (*yewl*) *nt* wheel
hjulaxel (*yewl*-ahk-serl) *c* (pl -axlar) axle
hjälm (*yehlm*) *c* helmet
hjälp (*yehlp*) *c* help; aid, assistance; relief; helper; första hjälpen first aid
hjälpa (*yehl*-pah) *v* help; aid, assist
hjälpsam (*yehlp*-sahm) *adj* helpful
hjälpstation (*yehlp*-stah-*shōon*) *c* first aid post
hjälte (*yehl*-ter) *c* hero
hjärna (*yæær*-nah) *c* brain
hjärnskakning (*yæærn*-skaak-ning) *c* concussion
hjärta (*yær*-tah) *nt* heart
hjärtattack (*yært*-ah-*tahk*) *c* heart attack
hjärtklappning (*yært*-klahp-ning) *c* palpitation
hjärtlig (*yært*-li) *adj* cordial; hearty
hjärtlös (*yært*-lūrss) *adj*

heartless
hobby (*ho*-bi) *c* (pl -bies, ~er)
hobby
hockey (*ho*-ki) *c* hockey
hoj (hōōy) *c* (pl hojar) bike
colloquial
Holland (*ho*-lahnd) Holland
holländare (*ho*-lehn-dah-rer)
c (pl ~) Dutchman
holländsk (*ho*-lehndsk) *adj*
Dutch
homosexuell (*ho*-moo-sehk-
sew-*ayl*) *adj* homosexual
hon (hoon) *pron* she
hon- (hōōn) *pref* female
honom (*ho*-nom) *pron* him
honung (*hōa*-newng) *c* honey
hop (hōōp) *c* crowd; bunch
hopp (hop) *nt* hope; jump,
leap, hop
hoppa (*ho*-pah) *v* jump;
*leap, hop; ~ **över** skip, jump
over
hoppas (*ho*-pahss) *v* hope
hoppfull (*hop*-fewl) *adj*
hopeful, confident
hopplös (*hop*-lūrss) *adj*
hopeless
hora (*hōō*-rah) *c* whore
horisont (ho-ri-*sont*) *c*
horizon
horisontal (ho-ri-son-*taal*)
adj horizontal
horn (hoorn) *nt* horn
hos (hooss) *prep* at
hosta (*hooss*-tah) *v* cough; *c*
cough
hot (hōōt) *nt* threat
hota (*hōō*-tah) *v* threaten
hotande (*hōō*-tahn-der) *adj*

threatening
hotell (ho-*tayl*) *nt* hotel
hov¹ (hōav) *nt* court
hov² (hōōv) *c* hoof
hovmästare (*hōav*-mehss-
tah-rer) *c* (pl ~) head waiter
hud (hēwd) *c* skin
hudkräm (*hēwd*-krehm) *c*
skin cream
hudutslag (*hēwd*-ēwt-slaag)
nt rash
***hugga** (hew-gah) *v* *hew
humle (*hewm*-lay) *nt* hop
hummer (*hew*-merr) *c* (pl
-mrar) lobster
humor (*hēw*-mor) *c* humour
humoristisk (hēw-mo-*riss*-
tisk) *adj* humorous
humör (hēw-*mūrr*) *nt* mood;
temper, temperament
hund (hewnd) *c* dog
hundkoja (*hewnd*-ko-ʸah) *c*
kennel
hundra (*hewnd*-rah) *num*
hundred
hunger (*hewng*-err) *c* hunger
hungrig (*hewng*-ri) *adj*
hungry
hur (hūūr) *adv* how; ~ **mycket**
how much; ~ **många** how
many; ~ **som helst** anyhow;
any way
hus (hēwss) *nt* house; home
husblock (*hēwss*-blok) *nt*
house block *Am*
husbåt (*hēwss*-bōat) *c*
houseboat
hushåll (*hēwss*-hol) *nt*
household
hushållerska (*hēwss*-ho-

hushållning

lerrs-kah) c housekeeper

hushållning (hewss-hol-ning) c housekeeping; economy

hushållsarbete (hewss-hols-ahr-bay-ter) nt housework

hushållssysslor (hewss-hols-sewss-lor) pl housekeeping

husmor (hewss-moor) c (pl -mödrar) mistress

husrum (hewss-rewm) nt accommodation; lodging

hustru (hewst-rew) c wife

husvagn (hewss-vahngn) c caravan; trailer nAm

huttra (hewt-rah) v shiver

huvud (hew-er) nt (pl ~, ~en) head; **huvud-** main; chief, cardinal, principal, capital, primary

huvudbry (hew-verd-brew) nt puzzle

huvudgata (hew-verd-gaa-tah) c main street; thoroughfare

huvudkudde (hew-verd-kew-der) c pillow

huvudledning (hew-verd-layd-ning) c mains pl

huvudlinje (hew-verd-lin-Yer) c main line

huvudrätt (hew-verd-reht) c main course

huvudsaklig (hew-verd-saak-li) adj cardinal, capital; **huvudsakligen** mainly

huvudstad (hew-verd-staad) c (pl -städer) capital

huvudväg (hew-verd-vaig) c

main road; thoroughfare

huvudvärk (hew-verd-værk) c headache

hy (hew) c complexion, skin

hycklande (hewk-lahn-der) adj hypocritical

hycklare (hewk-lah-rer) c (pl ~) hypocrite

hyckleri (hewk-ler-ree) nt (pl ~er) hypocrisy

hydda (hew-dah) c hut; cabin

hygien (hew-gi-ayn) c hygiene

hygienisk (hew-gi-ay-nisk) adj hygienic

hylla (hew-lah) v congratulate, honour; c shelf, rack

hyllning (hewl-ning) c tribute; homage; congratulations pl

hymn (hewmn) c hymn, anthem

hypotek (hew-po-tayk) nt mortgage

hyra (hew-rah) v rent, hire; lease; c rent; ~ **ut** *let

hyresgäst (hew-rerss-Yehst) c tenant

hyreshus (hew-rerss-hewss) nt block of flats; apartment house Am

hyreskontrakt (hew-rerss-kon-trahkt) nt lease

hyresvärd (hew-rerss-væærd) c landlord

hyresvärdinna (hew-rerss-vær-di-nah) c landlady

hysterisk (hewss-tay-risk) adj hysterical

hytt (hewt) c cabin; booth
hyttventil (hewt-vehn-teel) c
porthole
hågkomst (hōag-komst) c
remembrance
hål (hōal) nt hole; *göra ~
pierce
håla (hōal-ah) c cavern
hålighet (hōal-i-hāyt) c
cavity, hollow
håll (hol) nt way; stitch
*hålla (ho-lah) v *hold;
*keep; ~ av love; ~ fast
*hold; ~ tillbaka restrain;
uppe support; *hold up; ~
upp med stop; ~ ut *keep up
hållning (hol-ning) c gait,
carriage; attitude
hållplats (hol-plahts) c stop,
halt
hån (hōan) nt scorn; mockery,
derision
håna (hōa-nah) v mock,
deride
hår (hōar) nt hair; ~ gelé ~
hair gel
hårborste (hōar-bors-ter) c
hairbrush
hård (hōard) adj hard
hårdnackad (hōard-nahk-
ahd) adj obstinate, stubborn
hårig (hōar-i) adj hairy
hårklippning (hōar-klip-
ning) c haircut
hårklämma (hōar-kleh-mah)
c bobby pin Am
hårkräm (hōar-kraim) c hair
cream
hårnål (hōar-nōal) c hairpin
hårnät (hōar-nait) nt hair net

hårolja (hōar-ol-ʸah) c hair
oil
hårrullar (hōar-rew-lahr) pl
hair rollers
hårspray (hōar-spray) nt hair
spray
hårspänne (hōar-speh-nay)
nt hairgrip
hårtork (hōar-tork) c
hairdrier, hairdryer
hårvatten (hōar-vah-tern) nt
hair tonic
häck (hehk) c hedge
häftig (hehf-ti) adj violent,
severe; intense, fierce
häftklammer (hehft-klah-
merr) c (pl ~, -mrar) staple
häftplåster (hehft-ploss-terr)
nt sticking-plaster
häftstift (hehft-stift) nt
drawing pin; thumbtack
nAm
häger (hai-gerr) c heron
häkte (hehk-ter) nt custody
häl (hail) c heel
hälft (hehlft) c half; till ~
hälften half
hälla (heh-lah) v pour
hälsa (hehl-sah) v greet;
salute; c health
hälsning (hehls-ning) c
greeting
hälsosam (hehl-soo-sahm)
adj wholesome, salubrious
hälsovårdscentral (hehl-
soo-vōards-sehn-traal) c
health centre
hämma (hehm-mah) v inhibit
hämnd (hehmnd) c revenge
hämta (hehm-tah) v fetch;

*get, collect, pick up
hända (*hehn*-dah) *v* happen;
occur
händelse (*hehn*-dayl-ser) *c*
event, happening; incident; **i**
~ av in case of
händig (*hehn*-di) *adj* skilful
hänga (*hehng*-ah) *v* *hang; ~
med *keep up with
hängare (*hehng*-ah-rer) *c* (pl
~) peg, hook, hanger
hängbro (*hehng*-broo) *c*
suspension bridge
hänglås (*hehng*-loäss) *nt*
padlock
hängmatta (*hehng*-mah-tah)
c hammock
hängslen (*hehngs*-lern) *pl*
braces *pl*; suspenders *plAm*
hängsmycke (*hehng*-smew-
ker) *nt* pendant
hänsyn (*hain*-sēwn) *c* regard;
med ~ till considering; as
regards; ***ta ~ till** consider
hänsynsfull (*hain*-sēwns-
fewl) *adj* considerate
hänsynsfullhet (*hain*-sewns-
fewl-hāyt) *c* consideration
hänvisa till (*hain*-vee-sah)
refer to
hänvisning (*hain*-veess-
ning) *c* reference
häpnads-väckande (*hep*-
nahds-*vayk*-ahn-der) *adj*
amazing
här (hæær) *adv* here
härbärge (*hæær*-bær-Yah)
hostel
härbärgera (*hær*-bær-Yāy-
rah) *v* accommodate

härkomst (*hæær*-komst) *c*
origin
härleda (*hæær*-lāyd-ah) *v*
deduce
härlig (*hæær*-li) *adj*
wonderful; delightful; fine
häromdagen (*hæær*-om-daa-
gern) *adv* recently
härskare (*hærs*-kah-rer) *c* (pl
~) ruler; sovereign
härsken (*hærs*-kayn) *adj*
rancid
härstamning (*hæær*-stahm-
ning) *c* origin
häst (hehst) *c* horse
hästkapplöpning (*hehst*-
kahp-lūrp-ning) *c* horserace
hästkapplöpningsbana
(*hehst*-kahp-lūrp-nings-baa-
nah) *c* racecourse
hästkraft (*hehst*-krahft) *c*
horsepower
hästsko (*hehst*-skoo) *c*
horseshoe
hävarm (*haiv*-ahrm) *c* lever
hävstång (*haiv*-stong) *c* (pl
-stänger) lever
häxa (*hehk*-sah) *c* witch
hö (hūr) *nt* hay
höft (hurft) *c* hip
höfthållare (*hurft*-ho-lah-rer)
c (pl ~) girdle
hög (hūrg) *c* lot, heap, pile;
adj high; tall
högdragen (*hūrg*-draa-gern)
adj haughty
höger (*hūr*-gerr) *adj* right,
right-hand; **på ~ hand** on the
right-hand side; **till ~** to the
right

högkvarter (*hūrg*-kvahr-*tair*) *nt* headquarters *pl*

högland (*hūrg*-lahnd) *nt* (pl -länder) uplands *pl*

högljudd (*hūrg*-ʸewd) *adj* loud

högmodig (*hūrg*-mōō-di) *adj* haughty

högskola (*hūrg*-skōō-lah) *c* college

högsäsong (*hūrg*-seh-song) *c* peak season; high season

högt (hurkt) *adv* aloud

högtalare (*hūrg*-taa-lah-rer) *c* loudspeaker

högtalartelefon (*hūrg*-taa-lahr-tay-lay-*fōan*) *c* speaker phone

högtidlig (*hūrg*-teed-li) *adj* solemn, ceremonious

högvatten (*hūrg*-vah-tern) *nt* high tide

höja (*hur*ʸ-ah) *v* raise; lift

höjd (hurʸd) *c* height; altitude; **på sin ~** at most

höjdpunkt (*hur*ʸd-pewngt) *c* height; peak, climax

hök (hūrk) *c* hawk

höna (*hū*-nah) *c* hen

höra (*hū*-rah) *v* *hear

hörbar (*hūrr*-baar) *adj* audible

hörn (hūrrn) *nt* corner

hörsal (*hūrr*-saal) *c* auditorium

hörsel (*hurr*-sayl) *c* hearing

hösnuva (*hū*-snēw-vah) *c* hay fever

höst (hurst) *c* autumn; fall *nAm*

hövding (*hurv*-ding) *c* chieftain

hövlig (*hūrv*-li) *adj* polite, civil

***iaktta** (ee-ahkt-taa) *v* observe; watch

I

iakttagelse (*eeahkt*-taa-gerl-ser) *c* observation

ibland (i-*blahnd*) *adv* sometimes; *prep* among

icke-rökare (*i*-keh-*rūr*-kah-rer) *c* (pl ~) non-smoker

idag (i-*daag*) *adv* today

idé (i-*dāy*) *c* idea

ideal (i-day-*aal*) *nt* ideal

idealisk (i-day-*aal*-isk) *adj* ideal

identifiera (i-dayn-ti-fi-*āyr*-ah) *v* identify

identifiering (i-dayn-ti-fi-*āy*-ring) *c* identification

identisk (i-*dayn*-tisk) *adj* identical

identitet (i-dayn-ti-*tāyt*) *c* identity

identitetskort (i-dayn-ti-*tāyts*-koort) *nt* identity card

idiom (i-di-*ōam*) *nt* idiom

idiomatisk (i-di-o-*maa*-tisk) *adj* idiomatic

idiot (i-di-*ōōt*) *c* idiot

idiotisk (i-di-*ōōt*-isk) *adj*

idol 82

idiotic
idol (i-dōal) *c* idol
idrottskvinna (*eed*-rots-*kvi*-nah) *c* (pl -kvinnor)
sportswoman
idrottsman (*eed*-rots-mahn) *c* (pl -män) sportsman
ifall (i-*fahl*) *conj* if; in case
igelkott (*ee*-gerl-kot) *c* hedgehog
igen (i-*Yehn*) *adv* again
igenvuxen (i-*Y*n-vewk-sern) *adj* overgrown
ignorera (ing-noa-*ray*-rah) *v* ignore
igår (i-*gōar*) *adv* yesterday
ihålig (*ee*-hōa-li) *adj* hollow
ihärdig (*ee*-hæær-di) *adj* persevering, tenacious
ikon (i-*kōan*) *c* icon
illaluktande (i-lah-lewk-tahn-der) *adj* smelly
illamående (i-lah-*mōa*-ayn-der) *nt* nausea, sickness; *adj* sick
illegal (il-er-*gaal*) *adj* illegal
illtjut (*il-t*Yēwt) *nt* shriek
illusion (il-ew-*shōōn*) *c* illusion
illustration (i-lew-strah-*shōōn*) *c* illustration; picture
illustrera (i-lew-*stray*-rah) *v* illustrate
illvillig (*il*-vi-li) *adj* spiteful, malicious
ilska (*ils*-kah) *c* anger
imitation (i-mi-tah-*shōōn*) *c* imitation
imitera (i-mi-*tay*-rah) *v* imitate

immigrera (i-mi-*gray*-rah) *v* immigrate
immunisera (i-mew-ni-*say*-rah) *v* immunize
immunitet (i-mew-ni-*tayt*) *c* immunity
imperium (im-*pay*-ri-ewm) *nt* empire; **imperial-** imperial
imponera (im-po-*nay*-rah) *v* impress
imponerande (im-po-*nay*-rahn-der) *adj* impressive; imposing
impopulär (*im*-po-pew-*læær*) *adj* unpopular
import (im-*port*) *c* import
importera (im-por-*tay*-rah) *v* import
importtull (im-*port*-tewl) *c* import duty
importvara (im-*port*-vaa-rah) *c* import
importör (im-por-*tūrr*) *c* importer
impotens (im-po-*tayns*) *c* impotence
impotent (im-po-*taynt*) *adj* impotent
impregnerad (im-prayng-*nay*-rahd) *adj* rainproof, impregnated
improvisera (im-pro-vi-*say*-rah) *v* improvise
impuls (im-*pewls*) *c* impulse
impulsiv (im-pewl-*seev*) *adj* impulsive
in (in) *adv* in; ***gå ~** *go in; **~ i** into; inside
inackordering (*in*-ahk-or-*day*-ring) *c* boarder; lodger

inandas (*in*-ahn-dahss) *v*
inhale

*inbegripa (*in*-ber-*gree*-pah)
v comprise

inberäknad (*in*-ber-*raik*-
nahd) *adj* included

inbetalning (*in*-ber-*taal*-
ning) *c* payment, deposit

inbillad (*in*-bi-lahd) *adj*
imaginary

inbilla sig (*in*-bi-lah) imagine

inbillning (*in*-bil-ning) *c*
imagination

*inbjuda (*in*-b^yēw-dah) *v*
invite; ask

inbjudan (*in*-b^yēw-dahn) *c*
invitation

inblanda (*in*-blahn-dah) *v*
involve

inblandad (*in*-blahn-dahd)
adj involved; concerned

inblandning (*in*-blahnd-
ning) *c* interference

inbrott (*in*-brot) *nt* burglary;
*göra ~ burgle

inbrottstjuv (*in*-brots-t^yēwv)
c burglar

inbördes (*in*-bŭrr-derss) *adj*
mutual

indela (*in*-dāyl-ah) *v* divide;
classify

indian (*in*-di-aan) *c* Indian

indiansk (*in*-di-aansk) *adj*
Indian

Indien (*in*-di-ayn) India

indier (*in*-di-^yerr) *c* (pl ~)
Indian

indignation (*in*-ding-nah-
shōōn) *c* indignation

indirekt (*in*-di-raykt) *adj*

indirect

indisk (*in*-disk) *adj* Indian

individ (*in*-di-*veed*) *c*
individual

individuell (*in*-di-vee-dew-
ayl) *adj* individual

indones (*in*-doo-*nāyss*) *c*
Indonesian

Indonesien (*in*-doo-*nāy*-si-
^yern) Indonesia

indonesisk (*in*-doo-*nāyss*-
isk) *adj* Indonesian

industri (*in*-dewss-*tree*) *c*
industry

industriell (*in*-dewss-tri-*ayl*)
adj industrial

industriområde (*in*-dew-
stree-om-*rōā*-der) *nt*
industrial area

ineffektiv (*in*-ay-fehk-*teev*)
adj ineffective; inefficient

infall (*in*-fahl) *nt* whim; idea

infanteri (*in*-fahn-ter-*ree*) *nt*
infantry

infektion (*in*-fehk-*shōōn*) *c*
infection

infinitiv (*in*-fi-ni-teev) *c*
infinitive

inflammation (*in*-flah-mah-
shōōn) *c* inflammation; *bli
inflammerad *become
septic

inflation (*in*-flah-*shōōn*) *c*
inflation

influensa (*in*-flēw-*ayn*-sah) *c*
flu; influenza

inflytelserik (*in*-flēw-*tayl*-
say-reek) *adj* influential

infoga (*in*-fōō-gah) *v* insert

informator (*in*-for-*maa*-tor) *c*

tutor
informell (in-for-*mayl*) *adj*
informal; casual
informera (in-for-*māȳr*-ah) *v*
inform
infraröd (in-frah-*rūrd*) *adj*
infra-red
infödd (*in*-furd) *adj* native
inföding (*in*-fūr-ding) *c*
native
införa (*in*-fūrr-ah) *v* import;
introduce
införsel (*in*-fūrr-serl) *c* (pl
-slar) import
ingefära (*i*-nger-fææ-rah) *c*
ginger
ingen (*ing*-ayn) *pron* nobody;
none, no one; no
ingendera (*i*-ngayn-dāȳ-rah)
pron neither
ingenjör (in-shayn-*ȳūrr*) *c*
engineer
ingenstans (*ing*-ayn-stahns)
adv nowhere
ingenting (*ing*-ayn-ting) *pron*
nothing; nil
ingrediens (ing-gray-di-*ayns*)
c ingredient
***ingripa** (*in*-gree-pah) *v*
interfere; intervene
ingång (*in*-gong) *c* entrance;
way in, entry
inhemsk (*in*-haymsk) *adj*
domestic
initial (i-ni-tsi-*aal*) *c* initial
initiativ (i-nit-si-ah-*teev*) *nt*
initiative
injektion (in-*ȳ*ayk-*shōōn*) *c*
injection
injektionsspruta (in-*ȳ*ehk-

shōōns-sprēw-tah) *c* syringe
inkassera (*in*-kah-sāȳ-rah) *v*
cash
inklusive (ing-klew-*see*-ver)
adj inclusive; **allt inkluderat**
all included, all in
inkompetent (in-kom-per-
tehnt) *adj* incompetent
inkomst (*in*-komst) *c* income;
revenue; **inkomster**
earnings *pl*
inkomstskatt (*in*-komst-
skaht) *c* income tax
inkräkta (*in*-krehk-tah) *v*
trespass
inkräktare (*in*-krehk-tah-rer)
c (pl ~) trespasser
inkvartera (*in*-kvahr-*tāȳ*-rah)
v lodge
inkvartering (*in*-kvahr-*tāȳ*-
ring) *c* lodgings *pl*
inköpspris (*in*-t*ȳ*ūrps-preess)
nt cost price
inledande (in-*lāȳd*-ahn-der)
adj preliminary
inledning (in-*lāȳd*-ning) *c*
introduction
innan (*i*-nahn) *conj* before;
adv before
innanför (in-ahn-*fūrr*) *prep*
inside
innanmäte (*in*-ahn-mait-er)
nt entrails, pulp
inne (*i*-ner) *adv* inside,
indoors
***innebära** (*i*-ner-bææ-rah) *v*
imply
innefatta (*i*-ner-fah-tah) *v*
include
innehavare (*i*-ner-haa-vah-

rer) *c* (pl ~) owner; occupant
innehåll (*i*-ner-hol) *nt*
contents *pl*
***innehålla** (*i*-ner-ho-lah) *v*
contain
innehållsförteckning (*i*-ner-
hols-furr-*tayk*-ning) *c* table
of contents
innerslang (*in*-err-slahng) *c*
inner tube
innersta (*in*-ayrs-tah) *nt* heart
innertak (*i*-nerr-taak) *nt*
ceiling
***innesluta** (*i*-ner-*slewt*-ah) *v*
encircle; enclose
inneställe (*i*-ner-*steh*-ler) *c*
hotspot
inofficiell (*in*-o-fi-si-*ayl*) *adj*
unofficial
inom (*in*-om) *prep* within; ~
kort soon; shortly
inomhus (*in*-om-*hewss*) *adj*
indoor; *adv* indoors
inre (*in*-rer) *adj* inner;
internal, inside
inrikes (*in*-reeh-kez) *adj*
domestic
inringa (*in*-ring-ah) *v* encircle
inrätta (*in*-reh-tah) *v* institute,
establish
insats (*in*-sahts) *c* bet, inset;
contribution
***inse** (*in*-*say*) *v* realize; *see
insekt (*in*-sehkt) *c* insect; bug
nAm
insektsgift (*in*-sehkts-ʸift) *nt*
insecticide
insektsmedel (*in*-sehkts-
may-dayl) *nt* insect repellent
insida (*in*-seed-ah) *c* inside;

interior
insikt (*in*-sikt) *c* insight
insistera (in-si-*stayr*-ah) *v*
insist
inskription (in-skrip-*shoon*) *c*
inscription
***inskriva** (*in*-skree-vah) *v* list,
enter, inscribe; ~ **sig** register
inskrivningsblankett (*in*-
skreev-nings-blahng-*kayt*) *c*
registration form
inskränkning (*in*-skrehngk-
ning) *c* restriction, limitation
inskränkt (*in*-skrehngkt) *adj*
restricted; limited; narrow-
-minded
inspektera (in-spayk-*tay*-rah)
v inspect
inspektion (in-spayk-*shoon*)
c inspection
inspektör (in-spayk-*turr*) *c*
inspector
inspelning (*in*-spāyl-ning) *c*
recording
inspirera (in-spi-*rayr*-ah) *v*
inspire
inspruta (*in*-sprew-tah) *v*
inject
instabil (in-stah-*beel*) *adj*
unstable
installation (in-stah-lah-
shoon) *c* installation
installera (in-stah-*lay*-rah) *v*
install; induct
instinkt (in-stingt) *c* instinct
institut (in-sti-*tewt*) *nt*
institute
institution (in-sti-tew-*shoon*)
c institution
instruera (in-strew-*āy*-rah) *v*

instruct
instruktion (in-strewk-*shoōn*) *c* direction
instruktör (in-strewk-*tūrr*) *c* instructor
instrument (in-strew-*maynt*) *nt* instrument
instrumentbräda (in-strew-*maynt*-brai-dah) *c* dashboard
inställning (*in*-stehl-ning) *c* attitude; position
instämma (*in*-stehm-ah) *v* agree
***inta** (*in*-taa) *v* capture, take
intagning (*in*-taag-ning) *c* admission
intakt (in-*tahkt*) *adj* unbroken; intact
inte (*in*-ter) *adv* not; ~ **alls** by no means; ~ **desto mindre** nevertheless; ~ **ens** not even; ~ **heller** nor; ~ **längre** no longer
inteckning (*in*-tayk-ning) *c* mortgage
integrera (in-ter-*grāy*-rah) *v* integrate
intellekt (in-ter-*laykt*) *nt* intellect
intellektuell (in-ter-layk-tew-*ayl*) *adj* intellectual
intelligens (in-ter-li-*gayns*) *c* intelligence
intelligent (in-ter-li-*gaynt*) *adj* intelligent; clever
intendent (in-tern-*daynt*) *c* superintendent, curator, controller
intensiv (in-tayn-*seev*) *adj*

intense
intern (in-*tæærn*) *c* prisoner
internationell (in-terr-naht-shoo-*nayl*) *adj* international
internatskola (in-terr-*naat*-skoō-lah) *c* boarding school
Internet (in-terr-nayht) *nt* (pl ~) Internet
interrogativ (in-ter-ro-gahteev) *adj* interrogative
intervall (in-terr-*vahl*) *c* interval
intervju (in-terr-*v*ᵞ*ew*) *c* interview
intet (*in*-tert) *nt* nothing
intetsägande (*in*-tert-sai-gahn-der) *adj* insignificant
intressant (in-tray-*sahnt*) *adj* interesting
intresse (in-*treh*-ser) *nt* interest
intressera (in-trer-*sāy*-rah) *v* interest
intresserad (in-trer-*sāy*-rahd) *adj* interested
introducera (in-tro-dew-*sāy*-rah) *v* introduce
intryck (*in*-trewk) *nt* impression; ***göra ~ på** impress
inträde (*in*-trai-der) *nt* entrance; admission
inträdesavgift (*in*-traiderss-aav-ᵞift) *c* entrance fee
intyg (in-*tēwg*) *nt* certificate; document; testimonial
intyga (*in*-tēwg-ah) *v* attest
intäkter (*in*-tehk-terr) *pl* earnings *pl*
inuti (in-*ēw*-ti) *adv* within,

inside
invadera (in-vah-*dāy*-rah) v
  invade
invalid (in-vah-*leed*) c invalid
invalidiserad (*in*-vah-li-di-
  sāy-rahd) adj crippled;
  invalid, disabled
invand (*in*-vaand) adj
  habitual
invandrare (*in*-vahnd-rah-
  rer) c (pl ~) immigrant
invandring (*in*-vahnd-ring) c
  immigration
invasion (in-vah-*shōōn*) c
  invasion
invecklad (*in*-vayk-lahd) adj
  complicated; complex,
  involved
inventering (in-vayn-*tāy*-
  ring) c inventory
investera (in-vayss-*tāy*-rah) v
  invest
investering (in-vayss-*tāy*-
  ring) c investment
invånare (*in*-voā-nah-rer) c
  (pl ~) inhabitant; resident
invända (*in*-vehn-dah) v
  object
invändig (*in*-vehn-di) adj
  internal, inside
invändning (*in*-vehnd-ning)
  c objection
inåt (*in*-ōāt) adv inwards
inälvor (*in*-ehl-vor) pl bowels
  pl; intestines pl
Irak (i-*raak*) Iraq
irakier (i-*raa*-ki-err) c (pl ~)
  Iraqi
irakisk (i-*raak*-isk) adj Iraqi
Iran (i-*raan*) Iran

iranier (i-*raan*-i-err) c (pl ~)
  Iranian
iransk (i-*raansk*) adj Iranian
Irland (*eer*-lahnd) Ireland
irländsk (*eer*-lehnsk) adj Irish
ironi (i-roo-*nee*) c irony
ironisk (i-*rōōn*-isk) adj
  ironical
irra (eer-ah) v err
irritera (eer-i-*tāyr*-ah) v
  irritate; annoy
is (eess) c ice
isblåsa (*eess*-blōā-sah) c ice
  bag
iskall (*eess*-kahl) adj freezing
Island (*eess*-lahnd) Iceland
isländsk (*eess*-lehnsk) adj
  Icelandic
islänning (*eess*-lehn-ing) c
  Icelander
isolator (i-soo-laa-*tor*) c
  insulator, insulant
isolera (i-soo-*lāy*-rah) v
  isolate; insulate
isolerad (i-soo-*lāy*-rahd) adj
  isolated
isolering (i-soo-*lāy*-ring) c
  isolation; insulation
Israel (*eess*-rah-ayl) Israel
israelier (iss-rah-*āy*-li-err) c
  (pl ~) Israeli
israelisk (iss-rah-*āy*-lisk) adj
  Israeli
isvatten (*eess*-vah-tern) nt
  iced water
isär (i-*sær*) adv apart
Italien (i-*taal*-^yayn) Italy
italienare (i-tahl-^y*āy*-nah-rer)
  c (pl ~) Italian
italiensk (i-tahl-^y*aynsk*) adj

Italian
iver (*ee*-verr) *c* zeal; eagerness
ivrig (*eev*-ri) *adj* eager;

anxious
iväg (i-*vaig*) *adv* off

J

ja (ᶥaa) yes; **ja ja!** well!
jacka (ᶥ*ah*-kah) *c* jacket
jade (ᶥ*aa*-der) *c* jade
jag (ᶥaa) *pron* I; *nt* self
jaga (ᶥ*aa*-gah) *v* hunt; ~ **bort** chase; ~ **efter** hunt for
jakande (ᶥ*aa*-kahn-der) *adj* affirmative
jakt (ᶥahkt) *c* hunt; chase
jaktstuga (ᶥ*ahkt*-stewg-ah) *c* lodge
januari (ᶥah-new-*aa*-ri) January
Japan (ᶥ*aa*-pahn) Japan
japan (ᶥah-*paan*) *c* Japanese
japansk (ᶥah-*paansk*) *adj* Japanese
jeans (djiins) *pl* jeans
jerseytyg (ᶥ*urr*-si-tewg) *nt* jersey
jet lag (ᶥeyt lehg) *c* jet lag
jetplan (ᶥeht-plaan) *nt* jet
jobb (ᶥob) *nt* job
jockey (*djo*-ki) *c* jockey
jod (ᶥod) *c* iodine
jolle (ᶥo-ler) *c* dinghy
jord (ᶥord) *c* earth; soil
Jordanien (ᶥoor-*daa*-ni-ern) Jordan
jordanier (ᶥoor-*daa*-ni-err) *c* (pl ~) Jordanian
jordansk (ᶥoor-*daansk*) *adj* Jordanian

jordbruk (ᶥoord-brewk) *nt* agriculture
jordbävning (ᶥoord-behv-ning) *c* earthquake
jordgubbe (ᶥoord-gew-ber) *c* strawberry
jordisk (ᶥoor-disk) *adj* earthly
jordklot (ᶥoord-kloot) *nt* globe
jordlott (ᶥoord-lot) *c* allotment, plot
jordmån (ᶥoord-moan) *c* soil
jordnöt (ᶥoord-nurt) *c* (pl ~ter) peanut
jordvall (ᶥoord-vahl) *c* dam
journalfilm (shoor-*naal*-film) *c* newsreel
journalism (shoor-nah-*lism*) *c* journalism
journalist (shoor-nah-*list*) *c* journalist
jubileum (ᶥew-bi-*lay*-ewm) *nt* (pl -leer) jubilee
judisk (ᶥ*ew*-disk) *adj* Jewish
juice (ᶥ*ooss*) *c* juice
jul (ᶥewl) *c* Christmas; Xmas; **god ~!** Merry Christmas!; ~ **gåva** *c* Christmas present
juli (ᶥ*ew*-li) July
jumper (ᶥewm-perr) *c* (pl -prar) jumper
jude (ᶥ*ew*-der) *c* Jew

kaki

jungfru (⁹*ewng*-frēw) *c* virgin

juni (⁹*ēw*-ni) June

junior (⁹*ēw*-ni-or) *adj* junior

juridik (⁹ew-ri-*deek*) *c* law

juridisk (⁹ew-*ree*-disk) *adj* juridical, legal

jurist (⁹ew-*rist*) *c* lawyer

jury (⁹*ewr*-i) *c* jury

just¹ (⁹*ewst*) *adv* just

just² (shewst) *adj* fair

justera (shew-*stayr*-ah) *v* adjust

juvel (⁹ew-*vāyl*) *c* gem; **juveler** jewellery

juvelerare (⁹*ew*-ver-*lāy*-rah-rer) *c* (pl ∼) jeweller

jägare (⁹*ai*-gah-rer) *c* (pl ∼) hunter

jämföra (⁹*ehm*-fūr-rah) *v* compare

jämförelse (⁹*ehm*-fūr-rayl-say) *c* comparison

jämlikhet (⁹*ehm*-leek-hāyt) *c* equality

jämlöpande (⁹*ehm*-lūr-pahn-der) *adj* parallel

jämn (⁹*ehmn*) *adj* even; smooth, level

jämna (⁹*ehm*-nah) *v* level

jämra sig (⁹*ehm*-rah) moan

jämvikt (⁹*ehm*-vikt) *c* balance

järn (⁹*æærn*) *nt* iron; **järn-** iron

järnhandel (⁹*æærn*-hahn-dayl) *c* hardware store

järnvaror (⁹*æærn*-vaa-ror) *pl* hardware

järnväg (⁹*æærn*-vaig) *c* railway; railroad *nAm*

järnvägsspår (⁹*æærn*-vaig-spōar) *nt* track

järnvägsstation (⁹*æærn*-vaig-stah-*shōōn*) *c* station

järnvägsvagn (⁹*æærn*-vaigs-vahngn) *c* carriage; passenger car *Am*

järnvägsövergång (⁹*æærn*-vaigs-ūr-verr-gong) *c* railway crossing, level crossing

jäsa (⁹*aiss*-ah) *v* ferment

jäst (⁹*ehst*) *c* yeast

jätte (⁹*eht*-er) *c* giant

jättestor (⁹*eh*-ter-stōōr) *adj* huge

K

kabel (*kaab*-erl) *c* (pl kablar) cable

kabin (kah-*been*) *c* cabin

kabinett (kah-bi-*nayt*) *nt* cabinet

kafé (kah-*fay*) *nt* (pl ∼er) café

kafeteria (kah-fer-*tāy*-ri-ah) *c* cafeteria

kaffe (*kah*-fay) *nt* coffee

kaffebryggare (*kah*-fay-brew-gah-rer) *c* (pl ∼) percolator

kagge (*kah*-ger) *c* cask

kaj (kigh) *c* quay; dock

kajuta (kah-⁹*ēw*-tah) *c* cabin

kaka (*kaa*-kah) *c* cake

kakel (*kaa*-kerl) *nt* tile

kaki (*kaa*-ki) *c* khaki

kal

kal (kaal) *adj* bare, naked

kalas (kah-*laass*) *nt* party

kalcium (*kahl*-si-ewm) *nt* calcium

kalender (kah-*layn*-derr) *c* (pl -drar) calendar

kalk (kahlk) *c* lime

kalkon (kahl-*kōōn*) *c* turkey

kall (kahl) *adj* cold

kalla (*kahl*-ah) *v* call; **så kallad** so-called

kalori (kah-loo-*ree*) *c* calorie

kalsonger (kahl-*song*-err) *pl* drawers; briefs *pl*; shorts *plAm*; underpants *plAm*

kalv (kahlv) *c* calf

kalvinism (kahl-vi-*nism*) *c* Calvinism

kalvkött (*kahlv*-tᵞurt) *nt* veal

kalvskinn (*kahlv*-shin) *nt* calf skin

kam (kahm) *c* (pl ⁓mar) comb

kamé (kah-*māy*) *c* cameo

kamel (kah-*mayl*) *c* camel

kamera (*kaa*-mer-rah) *c* camera

kamin (kah-*meen*) *c* heater, stove

kamma (*kah*-mah) *v* comb

kammare (*kah*-mah-rer) *c* (pl ⁓, kamrar) chamber

kammartjänare (*kahm*-ahr-tᵞai-nah-her) *c* (pl ⁓) valet

kamp (kahmp) *c* fight; struggle, combat, battle

kampa (*kahm*-pah) *v* camp

kampanj (kahm-*pahn*ᵞ) *c* campaign

kampare (*kahm*-pah-rer) *c* (pl ⁓) camper

kampingplats (*kahm*-ping-plahts) *c* camping site

kamrat (kahm-*raat*) *c* comrade

Kanada (*kah*-nah-dah) Canada

kanadensare (kah-nah-*dayn*-sah-rer) *c* (pl ⁓) Canadian

kanadensisk (kah-nah-*dayn*-sisk) *adj* Canadian

kanal (kah-*naal*) *c* canal; channel

kanariefågel (kah-*naa*-ri-er-fōā-gerl) *c* (pl -glar) canary

kandidat (kahn-di-*daat*) *c* candidate

kanel (kah-*nāyl*) *c* cinnamon

kanhända (kahn-*hehn*-dah) *adv* perhaps

kanin (kah-*neen*) *c* rabbit

kanon (kah-*nōōn*) *c* gun

kanot (kah-*nōōt*) *c* canoe

kanske (*kahn*-sher) *adv* perhaps; maybe

kant (kahnt) *c* edge; border; verge, rim

kantin (kahn-*teen*) *c* canteen

kaos (*kaa*-oss) *nt* chaos

kaotisk (kah-*ōā*-tisk) *adj* chaotic

kapa (*kaa*-pah) *v* hijack

kapabel (kah-*paa*-berl) *adj* capable

kapacitet (kah-pah-si-*tāyt*) *c* capacity

kapare (*kaa*-pah-rer) *c* (pl ⁓) hijacker

kapell (kah-*payl*) *nt* chapel

kapital (kah-pi-*taal*) *nt* capital

kapitalism (kah-pi-tah-*lism*)
c capitalism

kapitalplacering (kah-pi-
taal-plah-*sāy*-ring) *c*
investment

kapitulation (kah-pi-tew-lah-
shōōn) *c* capitulation,
surrender

kaplan (kah-*plaan*) *c* chaplain

kappa (*kah*-pah) *c* coat

kapplöpning (*kahp*-lūrp-
ning) *c* race

kapplöpningshäst (*kahp*-
lūrp-nings-hehst) *c*
racehorse

kapprum (*kahp*-rewm) *nt*
cloakroom

kappsegling (*kahp*-sāyg-
ling) *c* regatta

kappsäck (*kahp*-sehk) *c*
suitcase, grip

kapsyl (kahp-*sewl*) *c* capsule

kapten (kahp-*tāyn*) *c* captain

kapuschong (kah-pew-
shong) *c* hood

karakterisera (kah-rahk-terri-*sāy*-rah) *v* characterize

karakteristisk (kah-rahk-terriss-tisk) *adj* characteristic;
typical

karaktär (kah-rahk-*tæær*) *c*
character

karaktärsdrag (kah-rahk-
tæærs-draag) *nt*
characteristic

karamell (kah-rah-*mayl*) *c*
caramel, sweet; candy *nAm*

karantän (kah-rahn-*tain*) *c*
quarantine

karat (kah-*raat*) *c* (pl ~) carat

karbonkopia (kahr-*bōōn*-
koo-*pee*-ah) *c* carbon copy

karbonpapper (kahr-*bōōn*-
pah-perr) *nt* carbon paper

kardinal (kahr-di-*naal*) *c*
cardinal

karg (kahrʸ) *adj* bare

karl (kaar) *c* guy; chap, fellow

karmosinröd (kahr-mo-*seen*-
rūrd) *adj* crimson

karneval (kahr-nay-*vaal*) *c*
carnival

kaross (kah-*ross*) *c* coach

karosseri (kah-ro-ser-*ree*) *nt*
(pl ~er) motor body *Am*

karp (kahrp) *c* carp

karriär (kah-ri-*ær*) *c* career

karta (*kaar*-tah) *c* map

kartong (kahr-*tong*) *c* carton

karusell (kah-rew-*sayl*) *c*
merry-go-round

kaschmir (kahsh-*meer*) *c*
cashmere

kasern (kah-*sæærn*) *c*
barracks *pl*

kasino (kah-*see*-no) *nt* casino

kassa (*kah*-sah) *c* cash, fund;
pay desk

kassaskåp (*kah*-sah-skōap)
nt safe

kassavalv (*kah*-sah-vahlv) *nt*
vault

kasse (*kah*-ser) *c* shopping
bag

kassera (kah-*sāy*-rah) *v*
discard

kassett (kah-*seht*) *c* cassette

kassör (kah-*sūrr*) *c* cashier

kassörska (*kah*-sūrrs-kah) *c*
cashier

kast (kahst) *nt* throw; cast

kasta (*kahss*-tah) *v* *throw; toss, *cast; *overcast

kastanj (kahss-*tahnʸ*) *c* chestnut

kastby (*kahst*-bew) *c* gust

kastrull (kahst-*rewl*) *c* saucepan

katakomb (kah-tah-*komb*) *c* catacomb

katalog (kah-tah-*lōāg*) *c* catalogue

katarr (kah-*tahr*) *c* catarrh

katastrof (kah-tah-*strōāf*) *c* catastrophe; disaster; calamity

katastrofal (kah-tah-stro-*faal*) *adj* disastrous

katedral (kah-ter-*draal*) *c* cathedral

kategori (kah-ter-gōā-*ree*) *c* category

katolsk (kah-*tōōlsk*) *adj* catholic; **romersk ~** Roman Catholic

katrinplommon (kaht-*reen*-ploo-mon) *nt* prune

katt (kaht) *c* cat

kavaj (kah-*vigh*) *c* jacket

kaviar (*kah*-vi-ʸahr) *c* caviar

kedja (*tʸayd*-ʸah) *c* chain

kejsardöme (*tʸay*-sahr-dūr-mer) *nt* empire

kejsare (*tʸay*-sah-rer) *c* (pl ∼) emperor

kejsarinna (tʸay-sah-*ri*-nah) *c* empress

kejserlig (*tʸay*-serr-li) *adj* imperial

kelgris (*tʸayl*-greess) *c* pet

kemi (tʸay-*mee*) *c* chemistry

kemikalieaffär (tʸay-mi-*kaa*-li-ay-ah-*fær*) *c* chemist's; drugstore *nAm*

kemisk (*tʸay*-misk) *adj* chemical

kemtvätt (*tʸaym*-tveht) *c* dry cleaner's

kemtvätta (*tʸaym*-tveh-tah) *v* dry-clean

kennel (*keh*-nerl) *c* (pl -nlar) kennel

Kenya (*kāyn*-i-ah) Kenya

keramik (tʸay-rah-*meek*) *c* ceramics *pl*; pottery

kex (kayks) *nt* biscuit; cookie *nAm*; cracker *nAm*

kika (*tʸee*-kah) *v* peep

kikare (*tʸee*-kah-rer) *c* (pl ∼) binoculars *pl*

kikhosta (*tʸeek*-hooss-tah) *c* whooping-cough

kil (tʸeel) *c* wedge, gusset

kilo (*tʸee*-loo) *nt* kilogram

kilometer (tʸee-loo-*māy*-terr) *c* (pl ∼) kilometre

Kina (*tʸee*-nah) China

kind (tʸind) *c* cheek

kindben (*tʸind*-bāyn) *nt* cheekbone

kindtand (*tʸind*-tahnd) *c* (pl -tänder) molar

kines (tʸi-*nāyss*) *c* Chinese

kinesisk (tʸi-*nāy*-sisk) *adj* Chinese

kinkig (*tʸing*-ki) *adj* difficult

kiosk (tʸi-*osk*) *c* kiosk

kirurg (tʸi-*rewrg*) *c* surgeon

kissekatt (ki-ser-*kaht*) *c* pussy-cat

kista (t⁹iss-tah) c chest; coffin

kittel (t⁹i-terl) c (pl -tlar) kettle

kittla (t⁹it-lah) v tickle

kiv (t⁹eev) nt strife, quarrelling

kivas (t⁹eev-ahss) v quarrel

kjol (t⁹ool) c skirt

klack (klahk) c heel

klaga (klaa-gah) v complain

klagomål (klaa-goo-mōal) nt complaint

klander (klahn-derr) nt blame

klandra (klahn-drah) v blame

klang (klahng) c tone

klar (klaar) adj ready; clear, serene

klara (klaa-rah) v cope with; **klara sig** manage; get along; pass; **klara sig med** *make do with

***klargöra** (klaar-ᵞ̶ūr-rah) v clarify

***klarlägga** (klaar-lehg-ah) v elucidate

klass (klahss) c class; form

klassificera (klah-si-fi-sāy-rah) v classify, grade

klassisk (klah-sisk) adj classical

klasskamrat (klahss-kahm-raat) c classmate

klassrum (klahss-rewm) nt classroom

klatsch (klahch) c smack

klausul (klahew-sēwl) c clause

klenod (klay-nōōd) c gem

klia (klee-ah) v itch

klibbig (kli-bi) adj sticky

klicka (klik-ah) v click; ~ **fast** click into place

klient (kli-aynt) c client; customer

klimat (kli-maat) nt climate

klimpig (klim-pi) adj lumpy

klinik (kli-neek) c clinic

klippa¹ (kli-pah) v *cut; ~ **av** *cut off

klippa² (kli-pah) c rock; cliff

klippbok (klip-bōōk) c (pl -böcker) scrapbook

klippig (kli-pi) adj rocky

klipsk (klipsk) adj smart, shrewd

klister (kliss-terr) nt gum

klistermärke (kliss-terr-mær-ker) nt sticker

klisterremsa (kliss-terr-raym-sah) c adhesive tape

klistra (kliss-trah) v paste; *stick

klo (klōō) c claw

kloak (kloo-aak) c sewer

klocka (klo-kah) c watch; bell; **klockan ... at ...** o'clock; **klockan tolv** noon

klockarmband (klok-ahrm-bahnd) nt watchstrap

klockspel (klok-spāyl) nt chimes pl

klok (klōōk) adj clever

klon (klōān) c clone

klona (klōā-nah) v clone

klor (klōar) c chlorine

kloss (kloss) c block

kloster (kloss-terr) nt cloister; convent, monastery

klot (klōōt) nt sphere

klubb   94

klubb (klewb) *c* club
klubba (*klew*-bah) *c* club;
mallet; lollipop
klump (klewmp) *c* lump
klumpig (*klewm*-pi) *adj*
clumsy; awkward
klumpsumma (*klewmp*-
sewm-ah) *c* lump sum
klyfta (*klewf*-tah) *c* cleft;
cleavage; segment
***klyva** (*klēw*-vah) *v* *split
klåda (*klōa*-dah) *c* itch
klä (klai) *v* *become; clothe;
cover; ~ **av sig** undress; ~
om sig change; ~ **på** dress; ~
på sig *put on; ~ **sig** dress;
***vara klädd i** *wear
kläder (*klai*-derr) *pl* clothes
pl
klädhängare (*klehd*-hehng-
ah-rer) *c* (pl ~) hanger
klädskåp (*klaid*-skōap) *nt*
wardrobe
klämma (*klehm*-ah) *c* clamp;
v squeeze
klänga sig (*klenhg*-ah say) *v*
cling; ~ **fast** cling to
klänning (*klehn*-ing) *c* dress;
frock, gown
klättra (*kleht*-rah) *v* climb
klättring (*kleht*-ring) *c* climb
klösa (*klūr*-sah) *v* scratch
klöver (*klūr*-verr) *c* clover
knacka (*knah*-kah) *v* knock;
tap
knackning (*knahk*-ning) *c*
knock
knapp[1] (knahp) *c* button
knapp[2] (knahp) *adj* scarce;
knappast scarcely; **knappt**

adv hardly
knappast (*knahp*-ahst)
hardly
knapphet (*knahp*-hāyt) *c*
scarcity
knapphål (*knahp*-hōal) *nt*
buttonhole
knappnål (*knahp*-nōal) *c* pin
knaprig (*knaap*-ri) *adj* crisp
knekt (knehkt) *c* knave
***knipa** (*knee*-pah) *v* pinch
kniptång (*kneep*-tong) *c* (pl
-tänger) pincers *pl*
kniv (kneev) *c* knife
knivblad (*kneev*-blaad) *nt*
blade
knoge (*knōō*-ger) *c* knuckle
knopp (knop) *c* bud
knorra (*kno*-rah) *v* grumble
knubbig (*knewb*-i) *adj* plump
knuff (knewf) *c* push
knulla (*knewl*-ah) *v* fuck V
knut (knēwt) *c* knot
knutpunkt (*knēwt*-pewngkt)
c junction
***knyta** (*knēw*-tah) *v* tie; knot;
~ **upp** untie
knytnäve (*knēwt*-nai-ver) *c*
fist
knytnävsslag (*knēwt*-naivss-
slaag) *nt* punch
knä (knai) *nt* knee
knäböja (*knai*-bur-ʸah) *v*
*kneel
knäppa (*knehp*-ah) *v* button;
zap; ~ **upp** unbutton
knäskål (*knai*-skōal) *c*
kneecap
ko (kōō) *c* cow
kock (kok) *c* cook

kod (kōad) c code

koffein (ko-fer-*een*) nt caffeine

koffeinfri (ko-fer-*een*-free) adj decaf(feinated)

koffert (*ko*-ferrt) c trunk

kofta (*kof*-tah) c cardigan

kofångare (*kōō*-fong-ah-rer) c (pl ~) bumper

koj (koi) c bunk

koka (*kōō*-kah) v boil

kokain (koo-kah-*een*) nt cocaine

kokbok (*kōōk*-bōōk) c (pl -böcker) cookery book; cookbook nAm

kokmöjligheter (*kōōk*-murᵞ-li-hāy-ter) pl cooking facilities pl

kokosnöt (*koo*-kooss-nūrt) c (pl ~ter) coconut

kol (kōal) nt coal

kola (*kōa*-lah) c toffee

kolja (*kol*-ᵞah) c haddock

kolla (*kol*-ah) v check

kollapsa (ko-*lahp*-sah) v collapse

kollega (ko-*lāy*-gah) c colleague

kollektiv (*ko*-lehk-teev) adj collective

kollidera (ko-li-*dāy*-rah) v collide; crash

kollision (ko-li-*shōōn*) c collision; crash

koloni (ko-lo-*nee*) c colony

kolonn (ko-*lon*) c column

kolossal (ko-lo-*saal*) adj huge

koltrast (*kōal*-trahst) c blackbird

kolumn (ko-*lewmn*) c column

kolv (kolv) c piston

kolvring (*kolv*-ring) c piston ring

koma (*kōa*-mah) c coma

kombination (kom-bi-nah-*shōōn*) c combination

kombinera (koam-bi-*nāy*-rah) v combine

komedi (ko-may-*dee*) c comedy; **musikalisk ~** musical comedy

komfort (kom-*fort*) c comfort

komfortabel (kom-for-*taa*-berl) adj comfortable

komiker (*kōō*-mi-kerr) c (pl ~) comedian

komisk (*kōō*-misk) adj comic

***komma** (*ko*-mah) v *come; ~ ihåg** remember; **~ tillbaka** return; ***get back

kommatecken (*ko*-mah-tay-kern) nt comma

kommentar (ko-mayn-*taar*) c comment

kommentera (ko-mayn-*tāy*-rah) v comment

kommersiell (ko-mær-si-*ayl*) adj commercial

kommission (ko-mi-*shōōn*) c commission

kommitté (ko-mi-*tāy*) c committee

kommun (ko-*mēwn*) c municipality; commune; **kommunal-** municipal

kommunfullmäktige (ko-*mēwn*-fewl-mehk-ti-ger) pl municipality council

kommunikation (ko-mew-ni-kah-_shōōn_) c
communication

kommuniké (ko-mew-ni-_kāy_) c communiqué

kommunism (ko-mew-_nism_) c communism

kommunist (ko-mew-_nist_) c communist

kompakt (kom-_pahkt_) adj compact

kompanjon (koam-pahn-_yōōn_) c partner; associate

kompass (kom-_pahss_) c compass

kompensation (kom-payn-sah-_shōōn_) c compensation

kompensera (kom-pern-_sāy_-rah) v compensate

kompetent (koam-pay-_taynt_) adj qualified

kompis (_kom_-piss) c buddy _colloquial_

komplett (kom-_playt_) adj complete

komplex (kom-_plehks_) nt complex

komplicerad (kom-pli-_sāy_-rahd) adj complicated

komplimang (kom-pli-_mahng_) c compliment

komplimentera (kom-pli-mern-_tāy_-rah) v compliment

komplott (kom-_plot_) c plot; conspiracy

komponera (kom-poo-_nāy_-rah) v compose

komposition (kom-po-si-_shōōn_) c composition

kompositör (kon-ī-po-si-_tūrr_)

c composer

kompromiss (kom-pro-_miss_) c compromise

koncentration (kon-sayn-trah-_shōōn_) c concentration

koncentrera (kon-sayn-_trāy_-rah) v concentrate

koncern (kon-_surrn_) c concern

koncession (kon-ser-_shōōn_) c concession

koncis (kon-_seess_) adj concise

kondition (kon-di-_shōōn_) c condition

konditor (kon-_dee_-toar) c confectioner

konditori (kon-di-too-_ree_) nt (pl ∼er) pastry shop

kondom (kon-_dōam_) c condom

konduktör (kon-dewk-_tūrr_) c ticket collector

konfektionssydd (kon-fayk-_shōōn_-sewd) adj ready-made

konferens (kon-fer-_rayns_) c conference

konfidentiell (kon-fi-daynt-si-_ayl_) adj confidential

konfiskera (kon-fi-_skāyr_-ah) v confiscate

konflikt (kon-_flikt_) c conflict

konfrontera (kon-fron-_tāy_-rah) v confront, face

kongregation (kon-gray-gah-_shōōn_) c congregation

kongress (kong-_rayss_) c congress

konjak (_kon_-yahk) c cognac

konkret (kon-*krayt*) *adj*
concrete

konkurrens (kon-kew-*rayns*)
c competition

konkurrent (kon-kew-*raynt*)
c competitor

konkurrera (kon-kew-*rayr*-ah) *v* compete

konkursmässig (kon-*kewrs*-meh-si) *adj* bankrupt

konsekvens (kon-ser-*kvayns*) *c* consequence;
issue

konsert (kon-*sær*) *c* concert

konsertsal (kon-*sær*-saal) *c*
concert hall

konservativ (kon-sær-vah-*teev*) *adj* conservative

konservatorium (kon-*sær*-vah-*too*-ri-ewm) *nt* (pl -rier)
music academy

konservburk (kon-*særv*-bewrk) *c* can, tin

konserver (kon-*særv*-err) *pl*
tinned food

konservera (kon-sær-*vayr*-ah) *v* preserve

konservering (kon-sær-*vay*-ring) *c* preservation

konservöppnare (kon-*særv*-urp-nah-rer) *c* (pl ~) can
opener, tin opener

konst (konst) *c* art; **de sköna
konsterna** fine arts

konstakademi (*konst*-ah-kah-dah-*mee*) *c* art school

konstatera (kons-tah-*tayr*-ah) *v* ascertain, establish;
diagnose

konstgalleri (*konst*-gah-ler-

ri) *nt* (pl ~er) art gallery;
gallery

konstgjord (konst-*yoord*) *adj*
artificial

konsthantverk (*konst*-hahnt-værk) *nt* handicraft

konsthistoria (*konst*-hiss-*too*-ri-ah) *c* art history

konstig (*kons*-ti) *adj* funny,
odd; queer

konstindustri (*konst*-in-dew-stree) *c* arts and crafts

konstnär (*konst*-næær) *c*
artist

konstnärinna (*konst*-næ-ri-nah) *c* artist

konstnärlig (konst-*næær*-li)
adj artistic

konstruera (kon-strew-*ayr*-ah) *v* construct

konstruktion (kon-strewk-*shoon*) *c* construction

konstsamling (*konst*-sahm-ling) *c* art collection

konstsiden (*konst*-see-dern)
c rayon

konststycke (*konst*-stew-ker) *nt* trick

konstutställning (*konst*-*ewt*-stehl-ning) *c* art exhibition

konstverk (*konst*-værk) *nt*
work of art

konsul (*kon*-sewl) *c* consul

konsulat (kon-sew-*laat*) *nt*
consulate

konsultation (kon-sewl-tah-*shoon*) *c* consultation

konsument (kon-sew-*maynt*)
c consumer

konsumera (kon-sew-*may*-

rah) *v* consume

kontakt (kon-*tahkt*) *c* contact

kontakta (kon-*tahk*-tah) *v* contact

kontaktlinser (kon-*tahkt*-lin-serr) *pl* contact lenses

kontanter (kon-*tahn*-terr) *pl* cash

kontinent (kon-ti-*naynt*) *c* continent

kontinental (kon-ti-nayn-*taal*) *adj* continental

kontinuerlig (kon-ti-new-*āyr*-li) *adj* continuous

konto (*kon*-too) *nt* account

kontokort (*kon*-toh-koort) *nt* debit card

kontor (kon-*tōōr*) *nt* office

kontorist (kon-too-*rist*) *c* clerk

kontorsartiklar (kon-*tōōrs*-ahr-tik-lahr) *pl* stationery

kontorstid (kon-*tōōrs*-teed) *c* office hours; business hours

kontra (*kont*-rah) *prep* versus

kontrakt (kon-*trahkt*) *nt* contract; agreement

kontrast (kon-*trahst*) *c* contrast

kontroll (kon-*trol*) *c* control; inspection; supervision

kontrollera (kon-tro-*lāy*-rah) *v* control; check, inspect, supervise

kontur (kon-*tēwr*) *c* contour

konversation (kon-vær-sah-*shōōn*) *c* conversation

kooperation (koo-o-per-rah-*shōōn*) *c* co-operative

kooperativ (koo-o-per-rah-teev) *adj* co-operative

kopia (ko-*pee*-ah) *c* copy

kopiera (koo-pi-*āyr*-ah) *v* copy

kopp (kop) *c* cup

koppar (*ko*-pahr) *c* copper

koppel (*ko*-payl) *nt* leash; lead

koppla (*kop*-lah) *v* connect; ~ av relax; ~ på switch on; ~ till connect; ~ ur disconnect; declutch

koppling (*kop*-ling) *c* clutch

kopplingsbord (*kop*-lings-bōōrd) *nt* switchboard

korall (ko-*rahl*) *c* coral

korg (korᵛ) *c* basket; hamper

korint (ko-*rint*) *c* currant

kork (kork) *c* cork

korka upp (*kor*-kah) uncork

korkskruv (*kork*-skrēwv) *c* corkscrew

korn (kōōrn) *nt* grain; corn, barley

korp (korp) *c* raven

korpulent (kor-pew-*laynt*) *adj* corpulent; stout

korrekt (ko-*raykt*) *adj* correct

korrespondens (ko-ray-spon-*dahngs*) *c* correspondence

korrespondent (ko-rayss-pon-*daynt*) *c* correspondent

korrespondera (ko-rayss-pon-*dāy*-rah) *v* correspond

korridor (ko-ri-*dōar*) *c* corridor

korrumpera (ko-rewm-*pāy*-rah) *v* corrupt

korrumperad (ko-rewm-*pāy*-

rahd) *adj* corrupt

korruption (ko-rewp-*shōōn*) *c* corruption

kors (kors) *nt* cross

korsett (kor-*sayt*) *c* corset

korsfästa (*kors*-fehss-tah) *v* crucify

korsfästelse (*kors*-fehss-tayl-ser) *c* crucifixion

korsning (*kors*-ning) *c* crossing

korståg (*kors*-tōāg) *nt* crusade

kort[1] (kort) *adj* short; brief

kort[2] (koort) *nt* card; snapshot; **grönt ~** green card

kortfattad (*kort*-faht-ahd) *adj* brief; concise

kortslutning (*kort*-slēwt-ning) *c* short circuit

korv (korv) *c* sausage

kosmetika (koss-*māy*-ti-kah) *pl* cosmetics *pl*

kost (kost) *c* fare

kosta (*koss*-tah) *v* *cost

kostnad (*kost*-nahd) *c* cost

kostnadsfri (*kost*-nahds-free) *adj* free of charge

kostsam (*kost*-sahm) *adj* expensive

kostym (koss-*tēwm*) *c* suit

kotlett (kot-*leht*) *c* chop; cutlet

krabba (*krah*-bah) *c* crab

kraft (krahft) *c* force; energy, strength, power

kraftig (*krahf*-ti) *adj* strong, powerful; robust

kraftverk (*krahft*-værk) *nt* power station

krage (*kraa*-gay) *c* collar

kragknapp (*kraag*-knahp) *c* collar stud

kram (kraam) *c* hug

krama (*kraam*-ah) *v* cuddle, embrace

kramp (krahmp) *c* cramp; convulsion

krampa (*krahm*-pah) *c* clamp

kran (kraan) *c* tap

kranvatten (*kraan*-vah-tern) *nt* tap water

krasslig (*krahss*-li) *adj* unwell

krater (*kraa*-terr) *c* (pl -trar) crater

kratta (*krah*-tah) *c* rake

krav (kraav) *nt* requirement

kreativ (*kray*-ah-teev) *adj* creative

kredit (kray-*deet*) *c* credit

kreditera (kray-di-*tāy*-rah) *v* credit

kreditiv (kray-*di*-teev) *nt* letter of credit

kreditkort (kray-*deet*-koort) *nt* credit card; charge card *nAm*

kremera (kray-*māyr*-ah) *v* cremate

krets (krayts) *c* circuit; circle

kretslopp (*krayts*-lop) *nt* circulation, orbit, cycle

kricket (*kri*-kayt) *nt* cricket

krig (kreeg) *nt* war

krigsfånge (*kriks*-fong-er) *c* prisoner of war

kriminell (kri-mi-*nayl*) *adj* criminal

kringliggande (*kring*-li-

gahn-der) *adj* surrounding
kris (kreess) *c* crisis
kristall (kriss-*tahl*) *c* crystal;
 kristall- crystal
kristen[1] (*kriss*-tern) *c* (pl
 -tna) Christian
kristen[2] (*kriss*-tern) *adj*
 Christian
Kristus (*kriss*-tewss) Christ
krita (*kreet*-ah) *c* chalk
kritik (kri-*teek*) *c* criticism
kritiker (*kree*-ti-kerr) *c* (pl ~)
 critic
kritisera (kri-ti-*saÿ*-rah) *v*
 criticize
kritisk (*kree*-tisk) *adj* critical
krockkudde (*crock-kew*-day)
 c airbag
krog (krōōg) *c* restaurant
krok (krōōk) *c* hook
krokig (*krōōk*-i) *adj* crooked,
 curved, bent
krokodil (kroo-koo-*deel*) *c*
 crocodile
krona (*krōō*-nah) *c* crown
kronblad (*krōōn*-blaad) *nt*
 petal
kronisk (*krōō*-nisk) *adj*
 chronic
kronologisk (kroo-noo-*lōāg*-
 isk) *adj* chronological
kronärtskocka (*krōōn*-ærts-
 ko-kah) *c* artichoke
kropp (krop) *c* body; **fast ~**
 solid
krossa (*krōss*-sah) *v* crush
krucifix (krew-si-*fiks*) *nt*
 crucifix
kruka (*krew*-kah) *c* jar
krus (krēwss) *nt* pitcher

krusa (*krew*-sah) *v* curl
krusbär (*krēwss*-bæær) *nt*
 gooseberry
krut (krēwt) *nt* gunpowder
krycka (*krew*-kah) *c* crutch
krydda (*krew*-dah) *c* spice; *v*
 flavour
kryddad (*krew*-dahd) *adj*
 spiced; spicy
krympa (*krewm*-pah) *v*
 *shrink
krympfri (*krewmp*-free) *adj*
 shrinkproof
*****krypa** (*krēwp*-ah) *v* *creep;
 crawl
kryssning (*krewss*-ning) *c*
 cruise
kråka (*krōāk*-ah) *c* crow
kräfta (*krehf*-tah) *c* crayfish
kräkas (*krai*-kahss) *v* vomit
kräldjur (*krail*-ýēwr) *nt*
 reptile
kräm (kraim) *c* cream
krämpa (*krehm*-pah) *c*
 ailment
kränka (*krehng*-kah) *v* offend
kränkande (*krehng*-kahn-
 der) *adj* offensive
kränkning (*krehngk*-ning) *c*
 offence; violation
kräsen (*krai*-sern) *adj* choosy,
 fastidious, particular
kräva (*krai*-vah) *v* demand;
 require, claim
krök (krūrk) *c* bend
kröna (*krūr*-nah) *v* crown
kub (kēwb) *c* cube
Kuba (*kēw*-bah) Cuba
kuban (kew-*baan*) *c* Cuban
kubansk (kew-*baansk*) *adj*

Cuban

kudde (*kew*-day) *c* cushion; pillow

kuggas (*kewg*-ahss) *v* fail

kula (*kew*-lah) *c* bullet

kull (kewl) *c* litter

kulle (*kew*-lay) *c* hill; mound

kullkasta (*kewl*-kahss-tah) *v* *upset

kulspetspenna (*kewl*-spayts-pay-nah) *c* ballpoint pen

kultiverad (kewl-ti-*vāy*-rahd) *adj* cultured, refined

kultur (kewl-*fēwr*) *c* culture

kund (kewnd) *c* customer; client

kung (kewng) *c* king

kungarike (*kewng*-ah-ree-ker) *nt* kingdom

kunglig (*kewng*-li) *adj* royal

***kungöra** (*kewn*-ʸ*urr*-ah) *v* proclaim

kungörelse (*kewn*-ʸ*ur*-rayl-ser) *c* announcement; proclamation; notice

***kunna** (*kewn*-ah) *v* *can; *may, *be able to

kunskap (*kewn*-skaap) *c* knowledge

kupé (kēw-*pāy*) *c* compartment

kuperad (kēw-*pāy*-rahd) *adj* hilly

kupol (kēw-*pōal*) *c* dome

kupong (kēw-*pong*) *c* coupon; voucher

kur (kēwr) *c* cure

kurort (*kēwr*-oort) *c* spa

kurs (kewrs) *c* course

kurva (*kewr*-vah) *c* curve,

turning, bend

kusin (kew-*seen*) *c* cousin

kuslig (*kewss*-li) *adj* creepy

kust (kewst) *c* coast; seashore, seaside

kuvert (kew-*væær*) *nt* envelope

kuvertavgift (kēw-væær-aav-ʸift) *c* cover charge

kvacksalvare (*kvahk*-sahl-vah-rer) *c* (pl ~) quack

kvadrat (kvah-*draat*) *c* square

kvadratisk (kvah-*draa*-tisk) *adj* square

kvalificera sig (kvah-li-fi-*sāyr*-ah) qualify

kvalificerad (kvah-li-fi-*sāyr*-ahd) *adj* qualified

kvalifikation (kvah-li-fi-kah-*shōōn*) *c* qualification

kvalitet (kvah-li-*tāyt*) *c* quality

kvantitet (kvahn-ti-*tāyt*) *c* quantity

kvar (kvaar) *adv* left

kvarleva (*kvaar*-lāy-vah) *c* remnant

kvarn (kvaarn) *c* mill

kvart (kvahrt) *c* quarter of an hour; quarter

kvartal (kvahr-*taal*) *nt* quarter; **kvartals-** quarterly

kvarter (kvahr-*tāyr*) *nt* block

kvast (kvahst) *c* broom

kvav (kvaav) *adj* stuffy

kvick (kvik) *adj* quick

kvicksilver (*kvik*-sil-vehr) *nt* mercury

kvicktänkt (*kvik*-tehngkt) *adj* bright

kvinna (*kvi*-nah) *c* woman

kvinnlig (*kvin*-li) *adj* feminine

kvist (kvist) *c* twig

kvitto (*kvi*-too) *nt* receipt

kvot (kvōōt) *c* quota

kväll (kvehl) *c* evening; night; **i ~** tonight

kvällsmat (*kvehls*-maat) *c* supper

kväva (*kvai*-vah) *v* choke

kvävas (*kvai*-vahss) *v* choke

kväve (*kvai*-ver) *nt* nitrogen

kyckling (*tᵞewk*-ling) *c* chicken

kyla (*tᵞēw*-lah) *c* cold

kylig (*tᵞēw*-li) *adj* cool; chilly

kylskåp (*tᵞēwl*-skoap) *nt* fridge, refrigerator

kypare (*tᵞēw*-pah-rer) *c* (pl ~) waiter

kyrka (*tᵞewr*-kah) *c* church

kyrkogård (*tᵞewr*-koo-goard) *c* churchyard; cemetery

kyrktorn (*tᵞewrk*-toorn) *nt* church tower

kyrkvaktmästare (*tᵞewrk*-vahkt-mehss-tah-rer) *c* (pl ~) sexton

kysk (tᵞewsk) *adj* chaste

kyss (tᵞewss) *c* kiss

kyssa (*tᵞew*-sah) *v* kiss

kål (koal) *c* cabbage

käck (tᵞehk) *adj* plucky

käft (tᵞehft) *c* mouth

kägelspel (*tᵞai*-gerl-spāyl) *nt* bowling

käke (*tᵞai*-ker) *c* jaw

kälkborgerlig (*tᵞehlk*-bor-ᵞerr-li) *adj* bourgeois

kälke (*tᵞehl*-ker) *c* sleigh, sledge

källa (*tᵞehl*-ah) *c* spring; source, fountain

källare (*tᵞeh*-lah-rer) *c* (pl ~) cellar

källarvåning (*tᵞeh*-lahr-vōā-ning) *c* basement

kämpa (*tᵞehm*-pah) *v* *fight; struggle, combat, battle

känd (tᵞehnd) *adj* famous, known, noted

känguru (*tᵞehng*-gew-rew) *c* kangaroo

känna (*tᵞehn*-ah) *v* *feel; *know; ~ **igen** recognize

kännare (*tᵞeh*-nah-rer) *c* (pl ~) connoisseur

kännbar (*tᵞehn*-baar) *adj* perceptible, noticeable

kännedom (*tᵞehn*-er-doom) *c* knowledge

kännemärke (*tᵞehn*-er-mær-ker) *nt* feature

kännetecken (*tᵞeh*-ner-tay-kern) *nt* characteristic

känsel (*tᵞehn*-serl) *c* touch; feeling; **utan ~** numb

känsla (*tᵞehns*-lah) *c* emotion, sensation

känslig (*tᵞehns*-li) *adj* sensitive; delicate

känslolös (*tᵞayns*-loo-*lūrss*) *adj* insensitive

käpp (tᵞehp) *c* cane; stick

käpphäst (*tᵞehp*-hehst) *c* hobbyhorse

kär (tᵞær) *adj* dear

kärl (tᵞærl) *nt* vessel

kärlek (*tᵞær*-lāyk) *c* love

103

kött

kärleksaffär (t³æær-lāyks-ah-fæær) c affair

kärleksfull (t³æær-lāyks-fewl) adj affectionate

kärlekshistoria (t³æær-lāyks-hiss-tōō-ri-ah) c love story

kärn- (t³æærn) nuclear; atomic

kärna (t³ær-nah) c stone, pip; core, essence; nucleus

kärnhus (t³æærn-hēwss) nt core

kärnkraft (t³æærn-krahft) c nuclear energy

kärra (t³æ-rah) c cart; barrow

kö (kūr) c queue

köa (kūr-ah) v queue; stand in line Am

kök (t³urk) nt kitchen

kökschef (t³urks-shāyf) c chef

kökshandduk (t³urks-hahn-dēwk) c kitchen towel

köksredskap (t³urks-rāyd-skaap) nt utensil

köksspis (t³urk-speess) c stove, cooker

köksträdgård (t³urks-trai-gōārd) c kitchen garden

köl (t³ūrl) c keel

kön (t³ūrn) nt sex; **köns-genital**

könssjukdom (t³ūrns-shēwk-doom) c venereal disease

köp (t³ūrp) nt purchase

köpa (t³ūr-pah) v *buy; purchase

köpare (t³ūr-pah-rer) c (pl ~) buyer; purchaser

köpcenter (t³ūr-sayn-ter) nt (pl -centra) mall

köpesumma (t³ūr-per-sew-mah) c purchase price

köpman (t³ūrp-mahn) c (pl -män) merchant; trader

***köpslå** (t³ūrp-sloa) v bargain

kör (kūrr) c choir

köra (t³ūr-rah) v *drive; ~ för fort *speed; ~ om *overtake; pass vAm

körbana (t³ūrr-baan-ah) c carriageway; roadway nAm

körfil (t³ūrr-feel) c lane

körkort (t³ūrr-koort) nt (pl ~) driver's licence, driving licence

körriktningsvisare (t³ūrr-rikt-nings-vee-sah-rer) c (pl ~) trafficator; directional signal Am

körsbär (t³ūrrs-bæær) nt cherry

körsnär (t³ūrrs-næær) c furrier

körtel (t³ūrr-terl) c (pl -tlar) gland

kött (t³urt) nt flesh; meat

L

labyrint (lah-bew-*rint*) c
labyrinth; maze

lack (lahk) *nt* lacquer; varnish

lada (*laa*-dah) c barn

laddare (*laa*-dah-rer) c
charger

ladda upp (lah-dah *ewp*) v
upload

laddning (*lahd*-ning) c
charge; cargo

lag (laag) c law; *nt* team

laga (*laa*-gah) v fix; mend

lager (*laa*-gerr) *nt* store,
stock; layer

laglig (*laag*-li) *adj* legal;
lawful

lagra (*laag*-rah) v store; stock

lagring (*laag*-ring) c storage

lagun (lah-*gewn*) c lagoon

lakan (*laa*-kahn) *nt* sheet

lakrits (*laa*-krits) c liquorice

laktos (lahk-*toos*) c lactose

laktosfri (lahk-*toos*-free) *adj*
lactose-free

laktosintolerant (lahk-*toos*-
in-tool-e-*rahnt*) *adj* lactose
intolerant

lamm (lahm) *nt* lamb

lammkött (*lahm*-t^{y}urt) *nt*
lamb

lampa (*lahm*-pah) c lamp

lampskärm (*lahmp*-shærm) c
lampshade

land (lahnd) *nt* (pl länder)
land; country; *gå i ~ land,
disembark; **i ~** ashore

landa (*lahn*-dah) v land

landgräns (*lahnd*-grehns) c
boundary

landgång (*lahnd*-gong) c
gangway

landmärke (*lahnd*-mær-ker)
nt landmark

landsbygd (*lahnds*-bewgd) c
countryside; country

landsflykt (*lahnds*-flewkt) c
exile

landsflykting (*lahnds*-flewk-
ting) c exile

landskap (*lahnd*-skaap) *nt*
province, landscape;
scenery

landsman (*lahnds*-mahn) c
(pl -män) countryman

***landstiga** (*lahnd*-steeg-ah) v
disembark

landsväg (*lahnds*-vaig) c
highway

lantbruk (*lahnt*-br$\overline{\text{ew}}$k) *nt*
farm

lantbrukare (*lahnt*-br$\overline{\text{ew}}$-kah-
rer) c (pl ~) farmer

lantlig (*lahnt*-li) *adj* rural

lantställe (*lahnt*-steh-ler) *nt*
country house

larma (*lahr*-mah) v alarm;
clamour

lasarett (lah-sah-*reht*) *nt*
hospital

last (lahst) c cargo; load,
freight; vice

lasta (*lahss*-tah) v load;

charge; ~ **av** unload

lastbil (*lahst*-beel) c lorry; truck *nAm*

lastkaj (*lahst*-kigh) c wharf

lastrum (*lahst*-rewm) nt hold

lat (laat) adj lazy; idle

Latinamerika (lah-*teen*-ah-*māy*-ri-kah) Latin America

latinamerikansk (lah-*teen*-ah-*may*-ri-*kaansk*) adj Latin-American

lavin (lah-*veen*) c avalanche

lax (lahks) c salmon

***le** (lāy) v smile

led (lāyd) c joint; **ur ~** dislocated

leda (*lāy*-dah) v *lead; head, direct

ledande (*lāy*-dahn-der) adj leading

ledare (*lāy*-dah-rer) c (pl ~) leader

ledarhund (*lāyd*-ahr-hewnd) c guide dog

ledarskap (*lāyd*-ahr-skaap) nt leadership

ledig (*lāy*-di) adj vacant; unoccupied

ledighet (*lāy*-di-hāyt) c leave; leisure

ledning (*lāyd*-ning) c lead, guidance; management

ledsaga (*lāyd*-saag-ah) v accompany; conduct

ledsen (*lay*-sayn) adj sad, sorry

ledstång (*lāyd*-stong) c (pl -stänger) rail, banister

leende (*lāy*-ern-der) nt smile

legal (lay-*gaal*) adj legal

legalisering (lay-gah-li-*sāyr*-ing) c legalization

legat (lay-*gaat*) nt legacy

legation (lay-gah-*shōōn*) c legation

legitimation (lay-gi-ti-mah-*shōōn*) c identification

legitimera (lay-gi-ti-*māy*-rah) v *lead; head, direct

lejon (*lay*-on) nt lion

lek (lāyk) c play

leka (*lāyk*-ah) v play

lekman (*lāyk*-mahn) c (pl -män) layman

lekplats (*lāyk*-plahts) c playground

leksak (*lāyk*-saak) c toy

leksaksaffär (*lāyk*-sahks-ah-*fæær*) c toyshop

lekskola (*lāyk*-skōōl-ah) c kindergarten

lektion (lehk-*shōōn*) c lesson

lektor (*lehk*-tor) c lecturer, senior master

lem (laym) c (pl ~mar) limb

len (lāyn) adj soft, smooth

lera (*lāy*-rah) c clay

lergods (*lair*-goods) nt pottery, ceramics pl; crockery

lerig (*lāy*-ri) adj muddy

leta efter (*lāy*-tah) look for

leva (*lāy*-vah) v live

levande (*lāy*-vahn-der) adj alive; live

lever (*lāy*-verr) c (pl levrar) liver

leverans (lay-vay-*rahns*) c delivery; supply

leverera (lay-vay-*rāy*-rah) v deliver; furnish

levnadsstandard (*lāyv*-nahds-stahn-dahrd) c

standard of living
levnadssätt (*läyv*-nahds-seht) nt (pl ~) living
libanes (li-bah-*näyss*) c Lebanese
libanesisk (li-bah-*näyss*-isk) adj Lebanese
Libanon (*lee*-bah-non) Lebanon
liberal (li-bay-*raal*) adj liberal
Liberia (li-*bäyri*-ah) Liberia
liberian (li-bay-ri-*aan*) c Liberian
liberiansk (li-bay-ri-*aansk*) adj Liberian
licens (li-*sayns*) c licence
***lida** (*lee*-dah) v suffer
lidande (*leed*-ahn-der) nt suffering
lidelse (*leed*-erl-ser) c passion
lidelsefull (*leed*-erl-ser-*fewl*) adj passionate
lifta (*lif*-tah) v hitchhike
liftare (*lif*-tah-rer) c (pl ~) hitchhiker
***ligga** (*li*-gah) v *lie; *be situated
lik (leek) nt corpse; adj alike, like
lika (*lee*-kah) adj equal; even; adv equally, as; ~ mycket as much
likadan (*lee*-kah-*daan*) adj alike
likaledes (*lee*-kah-*läyd*-erss) adv likewise
likasinnad (*lee*-kah-*sin*-ahd) adj like-minded
likaså (*lee*-kah-*soa*) adv

likewise; as well, as much
likformig (*leek*-for-mi) adj uniform, homogeneous
likgiltig (*leek*-*y*il-ti) adj indifferent
likhet (*leek*-häyt) c resemblance; similarity
likna (*leek*-nah) v resemble
liknande (*leek*-nahn-der) adj similar, such
liksom (*lik*-som) conj as
likström (*leek*-strurm) c direct current
liktorn (*leek*-toarn) c corn
likväl (leek-*vail*) adv yet; however, still
likvärdig (*leek*-vær-di) adj equivalent; *vara ~ equal
likör (li-*kürr*) c liqueur
lilja (*lil*-ya) c lily
lillfinger (*lil*-fing-ayr) nt (pl -fingrar) little finger
lim (lim) nt glue
limpa (*lim*-pah) c loaf; carton of cigarettes
lina (*leen*-ah) c cord, line
lind (lind) c lime; limetree
linda (*lin*-dah) v *wind
lindra (*lind*-rah) v relieve, mitigate, soothe
linjal (lin-*y*aal) c ruler
linje (*lin*-*y*er) c line
linjefartyg (*leen*-*y*er-faar-tewg) nt line
linjerederi (*lin*-*y*er-ray-day-ree) nt (pl ~er) shipping line
linne (*li*-ner) nt linen
lins (lins) c lens; lentil
list (list) c ruse; artifice; border

lista (*liss*-tah) *c* list
listig (*liss*-ti) *adj* cunning
lita på (*lee*-tah) trust; rely on
liten (*lee*-tern) *adj* (pl små)
minor, small; little; petty,
short; **ytterst ~** minute
liter (*lee*-terr) *c* litre
litteratur (li-ter-rah-*tewr*) *c*
literature; **litteratur-** literary
litterär (li-ter-*ræær*) *adj*
literary
liv (*leev*) *nt* life
livbälte (*leev*-behl-ter) *nt*
lifebelt
livfull (*leev*-fewl) *adj* lively
livförsäkring (*liv*-furr-*saik*-
ring) *c* life insurance
livlig (*leev*-li) *adj* vivid; busy
livmoder (*leev*-mood-err) *c*
(pl -drar) womb
livräddare (*leev*-reh-dah-rer)
c (pl ~) life-saver
livsfarlig (*lifs*-faar-li) *adj*
perilous
livsmedel (*lifs*-may-derl) *nt*
food
livsmedelsbutik (*lifs*-may-
derls-bew-teek) *c* grocer's
livstid (*lifs*-teed) *c* lifetime
livsviktig (*lifs*-vik-ti) *adj* vital
livvakt (*leev*-vahkt) *c*
bodyguard
ljud (*Yewd*) *nt* sound
*ljuda (*Yew*-dah) *v* sound
ljudband (*Yewd*-bahnd) *nt*
tape
ljuddämpare (*Yewd*-dehm-
pah-rer) *c* (pl ~) silencer;
muffler *nAm*
ljudisolerad (*Yewd*-i-soo-*lay*-

rahd) *adj* soundproof
*ljuga (*Yewg*-ah) *v* lie
ljum (*Yewm*) *adj* lukewarm,
tepid
ljumske (*Yewms*-ker) *c* groin
ljung (*Yewng*) *c* heather
ljunghed (*Yewng*-hāyd) *c*
moor
ljus (*Yewss*) *adj* light; *nt* light
ljushårig (*Yewss*-hoā-ri) *adj*
fair
ljuvlig (*Yewv*-li) *adj* lovely
lock (lok) *nt* cover, lid, top; *c*
curl
locka (*lok*-ah) *v* curl; entice,
tempt
lockelse (*lo*-kayl-ser) *c*
attraction
lockig (*lo*-ki) *adj* curly
lodrät (*lood*-rait) *adj* vertical;
perpendicular
logera (lo-*shāy*-rah) *v*
accommodate
logga in (log-gah-*in*) *v* log in;
~ ut log off
logi (lo-*shee*) *nt* (pl ~er, ~n)
accommodation
logik (loo-*geek*) *c* logic
logisk (*lawg*-isk) *adj* logical
lojal (lo-*Yaal*) *adj* loyal
lok (lōōk) *nt* locomotive
lokal (loo-*kaal*) *adj* local;
lokal- local
lokalisera (loo-kah-li-*sāy*-
rah) *v* locate
lokalsamtal (loo-*kaal*-sahm-
taal) *nt* local call
lokaltåg (loo-*kaal*-tōāg) *nt*
local train
lokomotiv (loo-koo-moo-

teev) *nt* engine

longitud (*long*-gi-te̅w̅d) *c* longitude

lopp (lop) *nt* race; course

lort (loort) *c* dirt, filth

lortig (*loort*-i) *adj* filthy, dirty

lossa (*loss*-ah) *v* loosen; unfasten; discharge

lots (loots) *c* pilot

lott (lot) *c* lot; lottery ticket

lotteri (lo-ter-*ree*) *nt* lottery

lov (lo̅a̅v) *nt* vacation; permission

lova (*lo̅a̅*-vah) *v* promise

LP-skiva (ayl-pay-*shee*-vah) *c* long-playing record

lucka (*lew*-kah) *c* hatch

luffare (*lewf*-ah-rer) *c* (pl ~) tramp

luft (lewft) *c* air; sky; **luft-** air-; pneumatic

lufta (*lewf*-tah) *v* air, ventilate

luftfilter (*lewft*-fil-terr) *nt* (pl ~, -terr) air-filter

luftig (*lewf*-ti) *adj* airy

luftkonditionerad (*lewft*-kon-di-shoo-*na̅y*-rahd) *adj* air-conditioned

luftkonditionering (*lewft*-kon-di-shoo-*na̅y*-ring) *c* air conditioning

luftrörskatarr (*lewft*-ru̅rrs-kah-*tahr*) *c* bronchitis

lufttryck (*lewft*-trewk) *c* atmospheric pressure

lufttät (*lewft*-tait) *adj* airtight

lugn (lewngn) *adj* calm; quiet, tranquil; restful

lugna (*lewng*-nah) *v* calm down; reassure; ~ **sig** calm

down

lukt (lewkt) *c* smell; odour

lukta (*lewk*-tah) *v* *smell

lunch (lewnsh) *c* lunch; luncheon

lunga (*lewng*-ah) *c* lung

lunginflammation (*lewng*-in-flah-mah-*shoo̅n*) *c* pneumonia

lura (*le̅w̅r*-ah) *v* cheat

lus (le̅w̅ss) *c* (pl löss) louse

lust (lewst) *c* desire; zest; ***ha ~ att** *feel like; fancy

lustig (*lewss*-ti) *adj* funny; amusing, jolly, humorous

lustjakt (*lewst*-*y*ahkt) *c* yacht

lustspel (*lewst*-spayl) *nt* comedy

luta (*le̅w̅*-tah) *v* *lean; ~ **sig** *lean

lutande (*le̅w̅*-tahn-der) *adj* slanting

lutning (*le̅w̅t*-ning) *c* inclination

luxuös (lewk-sew-*u̅rss*) *adj* luxurious

lya (*le̅w̅*-ah) *c* den

lycka (*lewk*-ah) *c* happiness; fortune, luck; ~ **till!** Good luck!

lyckas (*lewk*-ahss) *v* manage, succeed

lycklig (*lewk*-li) *adj* happy; fortunate; **lyckligtvis** *adv* fortunately

lyckosam (*lew*-ko-sahm) *adj* lucky

lyckönska (*lewk*-urns-kah) *v* congratulate

lyckönskning (*lewk*-urnskning) c congratulation

lyda (*lewd*-dah) v obey

lydig (*lew*-di) adj obedient

lydnad (*lewd*-nahd) c
obedience

lyfta (*lewf*-tah) v lift; *take off

lyftkran (*lewft*-kraan) c crane

lykta (*lewk*-tah) c lantern

lymmel (*lew*-merl) c (pl
-mlar) rascal

lysande (*lew*-sahn-der) adj
luminous

lysa upp (*lew*-sah) illuminate,
light up; brighten

lyssna (*lewss*-nah) v listen

lyssnare (*lewss*-nah-rer) c (pl
~) listener

lyx (lewks) c luxury

låda (*lōa*-dah) c drawer

låg (lōag) adj low

låga (*lōa*-gah) c flame

lågland (*lōag*-lahnd) nt (pl
-länder) lowlands pl

lågsäsong (*lōag*-seh-*song*) c
low season; off season

lågtryck (*lōag*-trewk) nt
depression

lågvatten (*lōag*-vaht-ern) nt
low tide

lån (lōan) nt loan

låna (*lōa*-nah) v borrow; ~ **ut**
*lend

lång (long) adj long; tall

långbyxor (*long*-bewks-err)
pl trousers pl; slacks pl

långsam (*long*-sahm) adj
slow

långt (longt) adv far; **längre
bort** further away; **längst
bort** furthest; **långt bort** far

away; **på ~ när** by far

långtråkig (*long*-trōa-ki) adj
boring; dull

långvarig (*long*-vaar-i) adj
long, lengthy

lår (lōar) nt thigh

lås (lōass) nt lock

låsa (*lōa*-sah) v lock; ~ **in** lock
up; ~ **upp** unlock

***låta** (*lōa*-tah) v sound; allow
to, *let; *leave

låtsa (*lot*-sah) v simulate,
pretend

läcka (*leh*-kah) v leak; v leak

läcker (*lehk*-err) adj delicious

läder (*leh*-derr) nt leather;
läder- leather

läge (*lai*-ger) nt location;
position; situation, site

lägenhet (*lai*-gern-hāyt) c
flat; apartment *nAm*

läger (*lai*-gerr) nt camp

***lägga** (*lehg*-ah) v *put; *lay;
~ **på** *put on; apply; add; ~
sig *lie down; ~ **till** add; ~ **ut**
på entreprenad outsource

läggningsvätska (*lehg*-
nings-vehts-kah) c setting
lotion

läka (*lai*-kah) v heal

läkare (*lai*-kah-rer) c (pl ~)
doctor; physician;
allmänpraktiserande ~
general practitioner

läkarmottagning (*lai*-kahr-
moot taag-ning) c surgery

läkarvetenskap (*lai*-kahr-
vāy-tern-skaap) c medicine

läkemedel (*lai*-ker-*māy*-dayl)
nt remedy

läktare (*lehk*-tah-rer) *c* (pl ~)
stand

lämna (*lehm*-nah) *v* *leave;
check out; ~ **i sticket** *let
down

lämplig (*lehmp*-li) *adj*
appropriate; proper, fit,
convenient

län (lain) *nt* province

längd (lehngd) *c* length; **på
längden** lengthways

längs (lehngs) *prep* along;
past

längta (*lehng*-tah) *v* desire; ~
efter long for

längtan (*lehng*-tahn) *c*
longing; wish

länk (lehngk) *c* link

läpp (lehp) *c* lip

läppstift (*lehp*-stift) *nt*
lipstick

lära (*lær*-ah) *c* teachings *pl*;
v *teach; ~ **sig** *learn; ~ **sig
utantill** memorize

lärare (*lær*-ah-rer) *c* (pl ~)
teacher; master,
schoolmaster, schoolteacher

lärarinna (*lær*-ah-*rin*-ah) *c*
teacher

lärd (læærd) *c* scholar

lärka (*lær*-kah) *c* lark

lärling (*læær*-ling) *c*
apprentice

lärobok (*lææ*-roo-bō̄k) *c* (pl
-böcker) textbook

lärorik (*lææ*-roo-reek) *adj*
instructive

läroverk (*lææ*-roo-værk) *nt*
secondary school

läsa (*lai*-sah) *v* *read

läsesal (*lai*-ser-saal) *c*
reading room

läsk (lehsk) *c* soda

läskedryck (*lehss*-ker-drewk)
c lemonade

läskpapper (*lehsk*-pahp-err)
nt blotting paper

läslampa (*laiss*-lahm-pah) *c*
reading lamp

läslig (*laiss*-li) *adj* legible

läsning (*laiss*-ning) *c* reading

lätt (leht) *adj* easy; light,
slight

lätta (*leht*-ah) *v* relieve;
lighten, ease

lätthanterlig (*leht*-hahn-tayr-
li) *adj* easy to handle

lätthet (*leht*-hāyt) *c* ease

lättnad (*leht*-nahd) *c* relief

lättretad (*leht*-rāy-tahd) *adj*
irritable

lättretlig (*leht*-rāyt-li) *adj*
touchy; quick-tempered

lättsmält (*leht*-smehlt) *adj*
digestible

läxa (*lehks*-ah) *c* (pl läxor)
homework, lesson

lödder (*lur*-derr) *nt* lather

löfte (*lurf*-ter) *nt* promise;
vow

lögn (lurngn) *c* lie

lögnare (*lurng*-nah-rer) *c* (pl
~) liar

löjeväckande (*lur*-Yer-veh-
kahn-der) *adj* ludicrous

löjlig (*lur*Y-li) *adj* ridiculous;
ludicrous, foolish

lök (lūrk) *c* onion

lön (lūrn) *c* salary; wages *pl*,
pay

löna sig (*lūrn*-ah) *pay

lönande (*lūrn*-ahn-der) *adj* paying

löneförhöjning (*lūrn*-er-furr-hur*ʸ*-ning) *c* rise; raise *nAm*

lönlös (*lūrn*-lūrss) *adj* useless, futile

lönn (lurn) *c* maple

lönsam (*lūrn*-sahm) *adj* profitable

löntagare (*lūrn*-taa-gah-rer) *c* (pl ~) employee

löpare (*lūr*-pah-rer) *c* (pl ~) runner

lördag (*lūrr*-daag) *c* Saturday

lös (lūrss) *adj* loose

lösa (*lūr*-sah) *v* solve; ~ **in** cash; ~ **upp** *undo

lösen (*lūr*-sern) *c* ransom

lösenord (*lūrss*-ern-ōōrd) *nt* password

löshår (*lūrss*-hoar) *nt* hair piece

löslig (*lūrss*-li) *adj* soluble

lösning (*lūrss*-ning) *c* solution

löständer (*lūrss*-tehn-derr) *pl* false teeth

löv (lūrv) *nt* leaf

M

madrass (mah-*drahss*) *c* mattress

magasin (mah-gah-*seen*) *nt* store house; warehouse

mage (*maa*-ger) *c* stomach; **mag-** gastric

mager (*maa*-gerr) *adj* thin; lean

magisk (*maag*-isk) *adj* magic

magnetapparat (mahng-*nāyt*-ah-pah-raat) *c* magneto

magnetisk (mahng-*nāy*-tisk) *adj* magnetic

magnifik (mahng-ni-*feek*) *adj* magnificent

magont (*maag*-oont) *nt* stomach ache

magplågor (*maag*-plōag-or) *pl* stomach ache

magra (*maag*-rah) *v* slim

magsår (*maag*-soar) *nt*

gastric ulcer

maj (migh) May

major (mah-*ʸōōr*) *c* major

majoritet (mah-*ʸ*oo-ri-*tāyt*) *c* majority

majs (mighss) *c* maize

majskolv (*mighss*-kolv) *c* corn on the cob

maka (*maak*-ah) *c* wife

make (*maak*-er) *c* husband

makrill (*mahk*-ril) *c* mackerel

makt (mahkt) *c* power; might, force; rule

maktbefogenhet (*mahkt*-bay-fōō-gern-hāyt) *c* authority

maktlös (*mahkt*-lūrss) *adj* powerless

mal (maal) *c* moth

mala (*maa*-lah) *v* *grind

malaria (mah-*laa*-ri-*ʸ*ah) *c*

malaria

Malaysia (mah-*ligh*-si-ah) Malaysia

malaysier (mah-*ligh*-si-err) *c* (pl ~) Malay

malaysisk (mah-*ligh*-sisk) *adj* Malaysian

mallig (*mahl*-i) *adj* cocky

malm (mahlm) *c* ore

malplacerad (mahl-plah-*sayr*-ahd) *adj* misplaced

man[1] (mahn) *pron* one

man[2] (mahn) *c* (pl män) man

manchester (mahn-*shayss*-terr) *c* corduroy

mandarin (mahn-dah-*reen*) *c* mandarin; tangerine

mandat (mahn-*daat*) *nt* mandate

mandel (*mahn*-dayl) *c* (pl -dlar) almond

manet (mah-*nayt*) *c* jellyfish

mani (mah-*nee*) *c* craze

manikyr (mah-ni-*kewr*) *c* manicure

manikyrera (mah-ni-kew-*ray*-rah) *v* manicure

manlig (*mahn*-li) *adj* masculine

mannekäng (mah-ner-*kehng*) *c* model

manschett (mahn-*shayt*) *c* cuff

manschettknappar (mahn-*shayt*-knah-pahr) *pl* cuff links *pl*

manuskript (mah-new-*skript*) *nt* manuscript

mardröm (*maar*-drurm) *c* (pl ~mar) nightmare

margarin (mahr-gah-*reen*) *nt* margarine

marginal (mahr-[y]i-*naal*) *c* margin

marinmålning (mah-*reen*-mōal-ning) *c* seascape

maritim (mah-ri-*teem*) *adj* maritime

mark (mahrk) *c* ground, earth; grounds

markant (mahr-*kahnt*) *adj* striking

markera (mahr-*kay*-rah) *v* mark

markis (mahr-*keess*) *c* awning; marquis

marknad (*mahrk*-nahd) *c* fair

marmelad (mahr-may-*laad*) *c* marmalade

marmor (*mahr*-moor) *c* marble

marockan (mah-ro-*kaan*) *c* Moroccan

marockansk (mah-ro-*kaansk*) *adj* Moroccan

Marocko (mah-*rok*-o) Morocco

mars (mahrs) March

marsch (mahrsh) *c* march

marschera (mahr-*shāy*-rah) *v* march

marschfart (*mahrsh*-faart) *c* cruising speed

marsvin (*maar*-sveen) *nt* guinea pig

martyr (mahr-*tēwr*) *c* martyr

mask (mahsk) *c* worm; mask

maska (*mahss*-kah) *c* mesh; ladder

maskara (mahss-*kaa*-rah) *c*

medan

mascara

maskin (mah-*sheen*) c
engine; machine;
livsuppehållande ~ life
support; ***skriva** ~ type

maskineri (mah-shi-ner-*ree*)
nt (pl ~er) machinery

maskinskriverska (mah-
sheen-skree-vayrs-kah) c
typist

maskros (*mahsk*-rōōss) c
dandelion

massa (*mahss*-ah) c mass;
bulk

massage (mah-*saash*) c
massage

massera (mah-*sāy*-rah) v
massage

massförstörelsevapen
(*mahss*-furr-stūr-ayl-se-
vaap-ern) nt (pl ~) weapons
of mass destruction; WMD

massiv (mah-*seev*) adj solid;
massive

massmöte (*mahss*-mūr-ter)
nt rally

massproduktion (*mahss*-
pro-dewk-shōōn) c mass
production

massör (mah-*sūrr*) c masseur

mast (mahst) c mast

mat (maat) c food; fare;
djupfryst ~ frozen food;
laga ~ cook; ~ och logi bed
and board; room and board,
board and lodging; smälta
maten digest

mata (*maa*-tah) v *feed

match (mahch) c match

matematik (mah-tay-mah-

teek) c mathematics

matematisk (mah-tay-*maat*-
isk) adj mathematical

materia (mah-*tāy*-ri-ah) c
matter

material (mah-teh-ri-*aal*) nt
material

materiell (mah-teh-ri-*ayl*) adj
material

matförgiftning (maat-furr-
ᵞ*ift*-ning) c food poisoning

matlust (*maat*-lewst) c
appetite

matros (mah-*trōōss*) c
seaman

maträtt (*maat*-reht) c dish

matsal (*maat*-saal) c dining
room

matsedel (*maat*-sāy-derl) c
menu

matservis (*maat*-sehr-veess)
c dinner service

matsked (*maat*-shāyd) c
tablespoon

matsmältning (maat-smehlt-
ning) c digestion

matsmältningsbesvär
(*maat*-smehlt-nings-bay-
svæær) nt indigestion

matt (maht) adj dim, mat; dull

matta (*mah*-tah) c carpet; mat

matvaror (*maat*-vaa-roor) pl
foodstuffs pl

mausoleum (mou-so-*lāy*-
ewm) nt (pl -leer)
mausoleum

med (māyd) prep with; by;
*ha ~ **sig** *bring

medalj (may-*dahl*ᵞ) c medal

medan (*māy*-dahn) conj

while; whilst

medarbetare (*mayd*-ahr-*bay*-tah-rer) *c* (pl ~) colleague

medborgare (*mayd*-bor-*y*ah-rer) *c* (pl ~) citizen; **medborgar-** civic

medborgarskap (*mayd*-bor-*y*ahr-skaap) *nt* citizenship

medborgerlig (*mayd*-bor-*y*ayr-li) *adj* civil

meddela (*mayd*-*day*-lah) *v* inform; report, communicate, notify

meddelande (*mayd*-*day*-lahn-day) *nt* message; information, communication

meddelandeforum (*may*-*day*-lahn-day-*foar*-ewm) *c* message board

medel (*may*-derl) *nt* means; **antiseptiskt ~** antiseptic; **lugnande ~** sedative; tranquillizer; **smärtstillande ~** analgesic; **stärkande ~** tonic

medel- (*may*-derl) medium

Medelhavet (*may*-derl-haa-vert) Mediterranean

medelklass (*may*-derl-klahss) *c* middle class

medelmåttig (*mayd*-erl-mot-i) *adj* moderate; medium

medelpunkt (*mayd*-erl-pewngt) *c* centre

medeltida (*may*-derl-tee-dah) *adj* mediaeval

Medeltiden (*may*-derl-tee-dern) Middle Ages

medfödd (*mayd*-furd) *adj*

inborn

medföra (*mayd*-*fur*-rah) *v* *bring

*medge (*mayd*-*yay*) *v* admit; grant

medhjälpare (*mayd*-*y*ehl-pah-rer) *c* (pl ~) assistant

media (*may*-di-ah) *pl* media

medicin (may-di-*seen*) *c* medicine; drug

medicinsk (may-di-*seensk*) *adj* medical

meditera (may-di-*tayr*-ah) *v* meditate

medkänsla (*mayd*-t*y*ehns-lah) *c* sympathy

medla (*mayd*-lah) *v* mediate

medlare (*mayd*-lah-rer) *c* (pl ~) mediator

medlem (*mayd*-laym) *c* (pl ~mar) member; associate

medlemskap (*mayd*-laym-skaap) *nt* membership

medlidande (*mayd*-lee-dahn-der) *nt* pity; ***ha ~ med** pity

medräkna (*mayd*-raik-nah) *v* count, include

medströms (*mayd*-strurms) *adv* downstream

medtävlare (*mayd*-taiv-lah-rer) *c* (pl ~) competitor

medvetande (*mayd*-*vay*-tahn-der) *nt* consciousness

medveten (*mayd*-*vay*-tern) *adj* conscious; aware

medvetslös (*mayd*-*vay*ts-lurss) *adj* unconscious

mejeri (may-*y*ay-ree) *nt* (pl ~er) dairy

mejsel (*may*-sayl) *c* (pl -slar)
chisel
mekaniker (may-*kaa*-ni-kerr)
c (pl ~) mechanic
mekanisk (may-*kaa*-nisk) *adj*
mechanical
mekanism (may-kah-*nism*) *c*
mechanism
mellan (*may*-lahn) *prep*
between; among
mellanmål (*may*-lahn-*mo͞al*)
nt snack
mellanrum (*may*-lahn-rewm)
nt space
mellanspel (*may*-lahn-spāyl)
nt interlude
mellantid (*may*-lahn-teed) *c*
interim
mellersta (*may*-lerrs-tah) *adj*
middle
melodi (may-lo-*dee*) *c*
melody; tune
melodisk (mer-*lo͞od*-isk) *adj*
melodious
melodrama (may-loo-*draam*-
ah) *nt* (pl -mer) melodrama
melon (may-*lo͞on*) *c* melon
memorandum (may-moo-
rahn-dewm) *nt* (pl -da)
memo
men (mayn) *conj* but; only
mena (*mayn*-ah) *v* *mean
mened (*mayn*-āyd) *c* perjury
mening (*māy*-ning) *c*
sentence; sense; meaning
meningslös (*māy*-nings-
lūrss) *adj* meaningless
menstruation (mayn-strew-
ah-*sho͞on*) *c* menstruation
mental (mayn-*taal*) *adj*

mental
mentalsjukhus (mehn-*taal*-
shĕwk-hĕwss) *nt* asylum
meny (mer-*new*) *c* menu; **fast
~** set menu
mer (māyr) *adv* more; **lite ~**
some more
mest av allt (mayst aav ahlt)
most of all
för det mesta (furr day
mayss-tah) mostly
meta (*māyt*-ah) *v* fish; **angle**
metall (may-*tahl*) *c* metal;
metall- metal
meter (*māy*-terr) *c* (pl ~)
metre
metkrok (*māyt*-kro͞ok) *c*
fishing hook
metod (may-*to͞od*) *c* method
metodisk (may-*to͞o*-disk) *adj*
methodical
metrev (*māyt*-rāyv) *c* fishing
line
metrisk (*māyt*-risk) *adj*
metric
metspö (*māyt*-spur) *nt*
fishing rod
mexikanare (mayks-i-*kaa*-
nah-rer) *c* (pl ~) Mexican
mexikansk (mayks-i-*kaansk*)
adj Mexican
Mexiko (*mayks*-i-koo)
Mexico
middag (*mi*-dah) *c* dinner;
*äta ~ dine
midja (*meed*-ʸah) *c* waist
midnatt (*meed*-naht) *c*
midnight
midsommar (*mid*-so-mahr) *c*
midsummer

mig (may) *pron* me; myself

migrän (mi-*grain*) *c* migraine

mikrofon (mik-ro-*foan*) *c* microphone

mil (meel) *c* ten kilometres

mild (mild) *adj* mild; gentle

miljard (mil-*Yaard*) *c* billion

miljon (mil-*Yoon*) *c* million

miljonär (mil-*Yoo-nœœr*) *c* millionaire

miljö (mil-*Yur*) *c* environment; milieu

milstolpe (*meel-*stol-per) *c* milestone

min (min) *pron* (nt mitt, pl mina) my

mindervärdig (*min-*derr-vœœr-di) *adj* inferior

minderårig (*min-*derr-oa-ri) *adj* under age; *c* minor

mindre (*mind-*rer) *adv* less; *adj* minor

mineral (mi-ner-*raal*) *nt* mineral

mineralvatten (mi-ner-*raal-*vah-tern) *nt* mineral water; soda water

mingla (*ming-*lah) *v* mingle

miniatyr (mi-ni-ah-*tewr*) *c* miniature

minimum (*mee-*ni-mewm) *nt* (pl ∿, -ma) minimum

minister (mi-*niss-*terr) *c* (pl -trar) minister

mink (mingk) *c* mink

minnas (*min-*ahss) *v* remember, recollect

minne (*minah*) *nt* memory; remembrance

minnesfest (*mi-*nayss-fehst)

c commemoration

minnesmärke (*mi-*nayss-mœr-ker) *nt* memorial; monument

minnesvärd (*mi-*nayss-vœœrd) *adj* memorable

minoritet (mi-noo-ri-*tāyt*) *c* minority

minska (*mins-*kah) *v* decrease; subtract; lower

minskning (*minsk-*ning) *c* decrease, reduction

minst (minst) *adj* least

minus (*mee-*newss) *prep* minus

minut (mi-*newt*) *c* minute

mirakel (mi-*raa-*kayl) *nt* (pl -kler) miracle

missa (*miss-*ah) *v* miss

missbelåten (*miss-*ber-*loa-*tern) *adj* discontented

missbruk (*miss-*brewk) *nt* abuse; misuse

missbruka (*miss-*brewkah) *v* abuse

missfall (*miss-*fahl) *nt* miscarriage

missfärgad (*miss-*fœr-*Yahd*) *adj* discoloured

*****missförstå** (*miss-*furr-*stoa*) *v* *misunderstand

missförstånd (*miss-*furr-stond) *nt* misunderstanding

misshaga (*miss-*haa-gah) *v* displease

misslyckad (*miss-*lew-kahd) *adj* unsuccessful

misslyckande (*miss-*lew-kahn-der) *nt* failure

misslyckas (*miss-*lew-kahss)

monark

v fail

missnöjd (miss-nur-ᵞd) *adj* dissatisfied

*missta (miss-taa) **be mistaken; err*

misstag (miss-taag) *nt* mistake; error

misstanke (miss-tahng-ker) *c* suspicion

misstro (miss-troo) *v* mistrust; *c* distrust

misstrogen (miss-troo-gern) *adj* distrustful

misstänka (miss-tehng-kah) *v* suspect

misstänksam (miss-tehngk-sahm) *adj* suspicious

misstänksamhet (miss-tayngk-sahm-hāyt) *c* suspicion

misstänkt¹ (miss-tehngt) *c* (pl ∼a) suspect

misstänkt² (miss-tehngt) *adj* suspicious, suspected

missunna (miss-ewn-ah) *v* grudge

missöde (miss-ūr-day) *nt* mishap

mista (miss-tah) *v* *lose

mitt (mit) *c* middle; midst; ∼ i amid; ∼ **ibland** amid

mittemellan (mit-ay-may-lahn) *adv* in between

mittemot (mit-ay-mōōt) *prep* opposite; facing

mixer (miks-err) *c* (pl ∼) mixer

mjuk (mᵞewk) *adj* soft; smooth; supple

mjuka upp (mᵞew-kah)

soften

mjäll (mᵞehl) *nt* dandruff; *adj* tender

mjöl (mᵞūrl) *nt* flour

mjölk (mᵞurlk) *c* milk

mjölkig (mᵞurl-ki) *adj* milky

mjölnare (mᵞurl-nah-rer) *c* (pl ∼) miller

mobil (moo-bēēl) *adj* mobile; *c* mobile (phone), cell(phone)

mobiltelefon (moo-bēēl-tay-lay-fōån) *c* mobile (phone), cell(phone)

mockaskinn (mo-kah-shin) *nt* suede

mod (mōōd) *nt* courage; guts

mode (mōō-der) *nt* fashion

modell (moo-dayl) *c* model

modellera (moo-day-lāyr-ah) *v* model

modem (mōō-daym) *nt* (pl ∼) modem

moderat (moo-der-raat) *adj* moderate

modern (moo-dæærn) *adj* modern; fashionable

modersmål (mōō-derrs-mōāl) *nt* mother tongue; native language

modig (mōō-di) *adj* brave, courageous

mogen (mōō-gayn) *adj* mature; ripe

mognad (mōōg-nahd) *c* maturity

moln (mōāln) *nt* cloud

molnig (mōāl-ni) *adj* cloudy

monark (moo-nahrk) *c* monarch

monarki (moo-nahr-_kee_) c
monarchy

monetär (mo-ner-_tæær_) adj
monetary

monolog (mo-noo-_lōāg_) c
monologue

monopol (mo-no-_pōāl_) nt
monopoly

monoton (mo-no-_tōān_) adj
monotonous

monter (mon-terr) c (pl -trar)
showcase

montera (mon-_tāy_-rah) v
assemble

montering (mon-_tāy_-ring) c
assembly

montör (mon-_tūrr_) c fitter,
assembler

monument (mo-new-_mehnt_)
nt monument

moped (moo-_pāyd_) c moped;
motorbike nAm

mor (mōōr) c (pl mödrar)
mother

moral (moo-_raal_) c moral

moralisk (moo-_raa_-lisk) adj
moral

morallära (moo-_raal_-lææ-
rah) c morality

morbror (_moor_-broor) c (pl
-bröder) uncle

mord (mōōrd) nt murder;
assassination

morfar (_moor_-fahr) c (pl
-fäder) grandfather

morfin (mor-_feen_) nt
morphine

morgon (_mor_-on) c (pl -gnar)
morning; **i ~** tomorrow

morgonrock (_mo_-ron-rok) c

dressing gown

morgontidning (_mo_-ron-
teed-ning) c morning paper

morgonupplaga (_mor_-on-
ewp-laag-ah) c morning
edition

mormor (_moor_-moor) c (pl
-mödrar) grandmother

morot (_mōō_-rōōt) c (pl
mörötter) carrot

morra (_mor_-ah) v growl

i morse (ee _mor_-ser) this
morning

mosa (_mōōs_-ah) v mash

mosaik (moo-sah-_eek_) c
mosaic

moské (moss-_kay_) c mosque

moskit (mo-_skeet_) c mosquito

mossa (_moss_-ah) c moss

moster (_mooss_-terr) c (pl
-trar) aunt

mot (mōōt) prep against;
towards

motbjudande (_mōōt_-b^yēw-
dahn-day) adj revolting

motell (moo-_tayl_) nt motel

motgång (_mōōt_-gong) c
adversity

motion (mot-_shōōn_) c
exercise; motion

motiv (moo-_teev_) nt motive

motivera (moo-tee-_vāy_-rah)
v motivate

motor (_mōō_-tor) c engine,
motor

motorbåt (_mōō_-tor-bōāt) c
motorboat

motorcykel (_mōō_-tor-sew-
kerl) c (pl -klar) motorcycle

motorfartyg (_mōō_-tor-faar-

murgröna

tēwg) *nt* motor vessel
motorhuv (mōō-tor-hēwv) *c*
  bonnet; hood *nAm*
motorskada (mōō-tor-skaa-
  dah) *c* engine failure
motorstopp (mōō-tor-stop)
  nt breakdown
motorväg (mōō-tor-vaig) *c*
  motorway; highway *nAm*
motsats (mōōt-sahts) *c*
  contrary; reverse
motsatt (mōōt-saht) *adj*
  opposite; contrary
motstående (mōōt-stoa-ayn-
  der) *adj* opposite
motstånd (mōōt-stond) *nt*
  resistance; resistor
motståndare (mōōt-ston-
  dah-rer) *c* (pl ~) opponent
motsvara (mōōt-svaar-ah) *v*
  correspond to
motsvarande (mōōt-svaar-
  ahn-der) *adj* equivalent
motsvarighet (mōōt-svaa-ri-
  hāyt) *c* equivalence
***motsäga** (mōōt-say-ah) *v*
  contradict
motsägande (mōōt-say-ahn-
  der) *adj* contradictory
***motta** (mōōt-taa) *v* receive;
  accept
mottagande (mōōt-taag-
  ahn-der) *nt* reception;
  receipt
mottagning (mōōt-taag-
  ning) *c* reception;
  mottagningstid
    consultation hours
mottagningsbevis (mōōt-
  taag-nings-ber-veess) *nt*

receipt
motto (mot-oo) *nt* motto
motvilja (mōōt-vil-ʸah) *c*
  antipathy; dislike; aversion
mousserande (moo-sāy-
  rahn-der) *adj* sparkling
mugg (mewg) *c* mug
mulen (mēwl-ern) *adj*
  overcast, cloudy
multikulturell (mewl-ti-kewl-
  tew-*rell*) *adj* multicultural
multiplex (mewl-ti-*plex*) *c*
  multiplex
multiplicera (mewl-ti-pli-
  sāy-rah) *v* multiply
multiplikation (mewl-ti-pli-
  kah-*shōōn*) *c* multiplication
mulåsna (mēwl-ōass-nah) *c*
  mule
mun (mewn) *c* (pl ~nar)
  mouth
munk (mewngk) *c* monk
munsbit (mewns-beet) *c* bite
munstycke (mewn-stew-ker)
  nt nozzle
munter (mewn-terr) *adj*
  merry; gay, cheerful
munterhet (mewn-terr-hāyt)
  c gaiety
muntlig (mewnt-li) *adj* oral;
  verbal
muntra upp (mewnt-rah)
  cheer up
munvatten (mewn-vah-tern)
  nt mouthwash
mur (mēwr) *c* wall
mura (mēwr-ah) *v* *lay bricks
murare (mēw-rah-rer) *c* (pl ~)
  bricklayer
murgröna (mēwr-grūr-nah) *c*

ivy

mus (mewss) c (pl möss)
mouse

museum (mew-sáy-ewm) nt
(pl museer) museum

musik (mēw-seek) c music

musikal (mēw-si-kaal) c
musical

musikalisk (mēw-si-kaa-lisk)
adj musical

musiker (mēw-si-kerr) c (pl
~) musician

musikinstrument (mew-
seek-in-strēw-mehnt) nt
musical instrument

muskel (mewss-kerl) c
muscle

muskotnöt (mewss-kot-núrt)
c (pl ~ter) nutmeg

muskulös (mewss-kew-lúrss)
adj muscular

muslin (mewss-leen) nt
muslin

mustasch (mewss-taash) c
moustache

muta (mēwt-ah) v bribe

mutning (mēwt-ning) c
bribery

mutter (mew-terr) c (pl -trar)
nut

mycket (mew-ker) adv very;
much, far

mygga (mewg-ah) c mosquito

myggnät (mewg-nait) nt
mosquito net

myndig (mewn-di) adj of age

myndigheter (mewn-di-háy-
terr) pl authorities pl

mynning (mewn-ing) c
mouth

mynt (mewnt) nt coin

mynta (mewn-tah) c mint

myntenhet (mewnt-áyn-háyt)
c monetary unit

myntöppning (mewnt-urp-
ning) c slot

myra (mēw-rah) c ant

mysig (mēw-si) adj cosy

mysterium (mewss-táy-ri-
ewm) nt (pl -rier) mystery

mystisk (mewss-tisk) adj
mysterious

myt (mēwt) c myth

myteri (mew-ter-ree) nt (pl
~er) mutiny

må (moa) v *feel

mål (moal) nt goal; meal

måla (moál-ah) v paint

målare (moá-lah-rer) c (pl ~)
painter

målarfärg (moá-lahr-færⁿ) c
paint

mållinje (moál-lin-ⁿer) c
finish, finishing line

mållös (moál-lürss) adj
speechless

målning (moál-ning) c
painting

målsättning (moál-seht-
ning) c objective, aim

måltavla (moál-taav-lah) c
target

måltid (moál-teed) c meal

målvakt (moál-vahkt) c
goalkeeper

månad (moá-nahd) c month

månadstidning (moá-nahds-
teed-ning) c monthly
magazine

månatlig (moá-naht-li) adj

monthly
måndag (*mon-daag*) *c*
Monday
måne (*mōa-ner*) *c* moon
många (*mong-ah*) *adj* many;
much
månsken (*mōan-shäyn*) *nt*
moonlight
mås (*mōass*) *c* gull
*måste (*moss-ter*) *v* *must;
*be obliged to, *have to,
need to; *be bound to
mått (*mot*) *nt* measure
måttband (*mot-bahnd*) *nt*
tape measure
måttlig (*mot-li*) *adj* moderate
mäklare (*maik-lah-rer*) *c* (pl
~) broker
mäktig (*mehk-ti*) *adj*
powerful; mighty
mängd (*mehngd*) *c* amount;
lot
människa (*meh-ni-shah*) *c*
human being; man
mänsklig (*mehnsk-li*) *adj*
human
mänsklighet (*mehn-skli-
häyt*) *c* humanity; mankind
märg (*mæær^y*) *c* marrow
märka (*mæær-kah*) *v* notice,
sense; mark
märkbar (*mærk-baar*) *adj*
noticeable; perceptible
märke (*mær-ker*) *nt* mark;
brand; ***lägga ~ till** notice
märkvärdig (*mærk-væær-di*)
adj curious
mässa (*meh-sah*) *c* Mass
mässing (*meh-sing*) *c* brass
mässling (*mehss-ling*) *c*

measles
mästare (*mayss-tah-rer*) *c* (pl
~) master; champion
mästerverk (*mehss-terr-
værk*) *nt* masterpiece
mäta (*mai-tah*) *v* measure
mätare (*mait-ah-rer*) *c* (pl ~)
meter; gauge
möbelben (*mūr-berl-bäyn*) *nt*
leg
möbler (*mūrb-lerr*) *pl*
furniture
möblera (*mūr-blāy-rah*) *v*
furnish
möda (*mūrdah*) *c* pains,
trouble
mögel (*mūr-gerl*) *c* mildew
möglig (*mūrg-li*) *adj* mouldy
möjlig (*mur^y-li*) *adj* possible
*möjliggöra (*mur^y-li-yūr-
rah*) *v* *make possible;
enable
möjlighet (*mur^y-li-hāyt*) *c*
possibility
mönster (*murns-terr*) *nt*
pattern
mör (*mūrr*) *adj* tender
mörda (*mūrr-dah*) *v* murder
mördare (*mūrr-dah-rer*) *c* (pl
~) murderer
mörk (*murrk*) *adj* dark;
obscure
mörker (*murr-kerr*) *nt* dark;
darkness
mört (*murrt*) *c* roach
mössa (*mur-sah*) *c* cap
möta (*mūr-tah*) *v* *meet;
encounter
mötande (*mūr-tahn-der*) *adj*
oncoming

möte (*mūrt*-er) *nt* meeting;
avtalat ~ appointment;
engagement

mötesplats (*mūr*-tayss-plahts) *c* meeting place

N

nacke (*nahk*-er) *c* nape of the neck

nagel (*naa*-gayl) *c* (pl naglar) nail

nagelfil (*naa*-gayl-feel) *c* nail file

nagellack (*naa*-gayl-lahk) *nt* nail polish

nagelsax (*naa*-gayl-sahks) *c* nail scissors *pl*

naiv (nah-*eev*) *adj* naïve

nakenstudie (*naa*-kern-*stēw*-di-er) *c* nude

namn (nahmn) *nt* name; i ... **namn** in the name of

narkos (nahr-*kōass*) *c* narcosis

narkotika (nahr-*kōa*-ti-kah) *c* narcotic

nation (naht-*shōon*) *c* nation

nationaldräkt (naht-shoo-*naal*-drehkt) *c* national dress

nationalisera (naht-shoo-nah-li-*sayr*-ah) *v* nationalize

nationalitet (naht-shoo-nah-li-*tāyt*) *c* nationality

nationalpark (naht-shoo-*naal*-pahrk) *c* national park

nationalsång (naht-shoo-*naal*-song) *c* national anthem

nationell (naht-shoo-*nayl*) *adj* national

natt (naht) *c* (pl nätter) night; i ~ tonight; **om natten** by night; **över natten** overnight

nattaxa (*naht*-tahk-sah) *c* night rate

nattflyg (*naht*-flēwg) *nt* night flight

nattklubb (*naht*-klewb) *c* nightclub; cabaret

nattkräm (*naht*-kraim) *c* night cream

nattlig (*naht*-li) *adj* nightly

nattåg (*naht*-tōag) *nt* night train

natur (nah-*tēwr*) *c* nature

naturlig (nah-*tēwr*-li) *adj* natural

naturligtvis (nah-*tēwr*-lit-veess) *adv* of course; naturally

naturskön (nah-*tēwr*-shürn) *adj* scenic

naturvetenskap (nah-*tēwr*-vāyt-ern-*skaap*) *c* physics

navel (*naav*-erl) *c* (pl navlar) navel

navigation (nah-vi-gah-*shōon*) *c* navigation

navigationssystem (nah-vi-gah-*shōons*-sewss-*tāym*) *nt* navigation system, sat nav, GPS

navigera (nah-vi-*gāy*-rah) *v*

navigate
necessär (nay-ser-*sær*) c
toilet case
ned (nayd) adv down
nedan (*nay*-dahn) adv
beneath, below
nedanför (*nay*-dahn-*für*)
prep below; under
nederbörd (nayd-err-*bürrd*)
c precipitation
nederlag (*nayd*-err-laag) nt
defeat
nederländare (*nay*-derr-
lehn-dah-rer) c (pl ~)
Dutchman
Nederländerna (*nay*-derr-
lehn-derr-nah) the
Netherlands
nederländsk (*nay*-dayr-
lehnsk) adj Dutch
nedersta (*nay*-derr-stah) adj
bottom, lowest
nedladdning (*nayd*-lahd-
ning) c download
nedre (*nayd*-rer) adj inferior,
lower
nedslående (*nayd*-sloa-ayn-
der) adj depressing
nedsmutsad (*nayd*-smewt-
sahd) adj soiled
nedstigning (*nayd*-steeg-
ning) c descent
nedstämd (*nayd*-stehmd) adj
low; down, down-hearted
nedåt (*nayd*-ot) adv down;
downwards
negativ (*nay*-gah-teev) adj
negative; nt negative
negligé (nay-gli-*shay*) c
negligee

nej (nay) no
neka (*nayk*-ah) v deny
nekande (*nayk*-ahn-der) adj
negative
ner (nayr) adv down,
downstairs
nerladdning (*nayr*-lahd-
ning) c download
nerv (nærv) c nerve
nervös (nær-*vürss*) adj
nervous
netto- (*nayt*-oo) net
neuralgi (nayv-rahl-*gee*) c
neuralgia
neuros (nayv-*rōass*) c
neurosis
neutral (nay^ew-traal) adj
neutral
neutrum (*nay*-ewt-rewm) c
neuter
ni (nee) pron you
nick (nik) c nod
nicka (*nik*-ah) v nod
nickel (*nik*-erl) c nickel
***niga** (*nee*-gah) v curtsy
Nigeria (ni-*gayr*-i-ah) Nigeria
nigerian (ni-gay-ri-*aan*) c
Nigerian
nigeriansk (ni-gay-ri-*aansk*)
adj Nigerian
nikotin (ni-koo-*teen*) nt
nicotine
nio (*neeoo*) num nine
nionde (*nee*-on-der) num
ninth
nit (neet) nt zeal, ardour
nittio (*nit*-i) num ninety
nitton (*nit*-on) num nineteen
nittonde (*nit*-on-der) num
nineteenth

nivå (ni-*voa*) c level

njure (n*Yew*-rer) c kidney

*njuta (n*Yew*-tah) v enjoy

njutning (n*Yewt*-ning) c delight

nog (noog) adv enough; probably

noga (*noo*-gah) adj precise

noggrann (*noog*-rahn) adj accurate, precise

nolla (*no*-lah) c zero; nought

nominell (noo-mi-*nayl*) adj nominal

nominera (noo-mi-*nay*r-ah) v nominate

nominering (noo-mi-*nay*r-ing) c nomination

nord (noord) c north

nordlig (*noord*-li) adj northern;north

nordost (noord-*oost*) c north-east

Nordpolen (*noord*-poo-lern) North Pole

nordväst (noord-*vehst*) c north-west

Norge (nor-*Yer*) Norway

norm (norm) c norm, standard

normal (nor-*maal*) adj normal; regular

norrman (*nor*-mahn) c (pl -män) Norwegian

norsk (norsk) adj Norwegian

nos (nooss) c snout

noshörning (*nooss*-hürr-ning) c rhinoceros

nota (*noot*-ah) c bill; check nAm

notera (noo-*tayr*-ah) v note

novell (noo-*vehl*) c short story

november (noo-*vehm*-berr) November

nu (new) adv now

nudistbadstrand (new-*dist*-baad-strahnd) c (pl -stränder) nudist beach

nuförtiden (*new*-furr-*tee*-dayn) adv nowadays

nummer (newm-err) nt number; act

nummerplåt (new-*merr*-plōat) c registration plate; licence plate nAm

nummerpresentatör (newm-err-pray-sayn-tah-*türr*) c caller ID

nunna (*newn*-ah) c nun

nutid (*new*-teed) c present

nutida (*new*-tee-dah) adj contemporary

nuvarande (*new*-vaa-rahn-der) adj present; current

ny (new) adj new; recent; splitter ~ brand-new

nyans (n*ahngs*) c nuance; shade

Nya Zeeland (*newah* *say*-lahnd) New Zealand

nybörjare (*new*-burr-*Y*ah-rer) c (pl ~) beginner; learner

nyck (newk) c whim; fancy

nyckel (new-kerl) c (pl -klar) key

nyckelben (new-kerl-*bayn*) nt collarbone

nyckelhål (new-kerl-*hōal*) nt keyhole

nyfiken (*new*-fee-kern) adj

curious; nosy *colloquial*
nyfikenhet (*new̄*-fee-kern-
hāyt) *c* curiosity
nyhet (*new̄*-hāyt) *c* news
nyheter (*new̄*-hāy-terr) *pl*
news
nykter (*newk*-terr) *adj* sober
nyligen (*new̄*-li-gayn) *adv*
recently; lately
nylon (*new̄*-lōan) *nt* nylon
nynna (*newn*-ah) *v* hum
***nypa** (*new̄*-pah) *v* pinch
***nysa** (*new̄*-sah) *v* sneeze
nyss (newss) *adv* a moment
ago
nytta (*new̄*-tah) *c* use; benefit,
profit; ***ha ~ av** benefit by,
profit by
nyttig (*new̄*-ti) *adj* useful
nyttighet (*new̄*-ti-hāyt) *c*
utility
nyttja (*newt̄*-ᵛah) *v* use,
employ
nyår (*new̄*-ōar) *nt* New Year
nå (nōa) *v* reach
nåd (nōad) *c* grace; mercy
någon (*nōa*-gon) *pron*
somebody; any, someone
någonsin (*nōa*-gon-sin) *adv*
ever
någonstans (*nōa*-gon-
stahns) *adv* somewhere
någorlunda (*nōa*-goor-lewn-
dah) *adv* quite; rather
något (*nōa*-got) *pron*
something, some
några (*nōag*-rah) *pron* some;
adj some
nål (nōal) *c* needle
näbb (nehb) *c* beak

näktergal (*nehk*-terr-gaal) *c*
nightingale
nämligen (*nehm*-li-gern) *adv*
namely
nämna (*nehm*-nah) *v*
mention
när (næær) *adv* when; *conj*
when
nära (*næær*-ah) *adj* near;
close
närande (*næær*-ahn-der) *adj*
nourishing; nutritious
närapå (*nææ*-rah-poa) *adv*
nearly
närbelägen (*næær*-bay-laig-
ern) *adj* near
närgången (*næær*-gong-ern)
adj inquisitive
närhelst (næær-*hehlst*) *conj*
whenever
närhet (*næær*-hāyt) *c* vicinity
närliggande (*næær*-li-gahn-
der) *adj* nearby
närma sig (*næær*-mah)
approach
närmast (*næær*-mahst) *adv*
closest; nearest
närsynt (næær-*sēwnt*) *adj*
short-sighted
närvarande (*næær*-vaa-rahn-
der) *adj* present; ***vara ~ vid**
attend, assist at
närvaro (*næær*-vaa-roo) *c*
presence
näsa (*nai*-sah) *c* nose
näsblod (naiss-blōōd) *nt*
nosebleed
näsborre (naiss-bo-rer) *c*
nostril
näsduk (naiss-dēwk) *c*

handkerchief
nästa (*nehss*-tah) *adj*
following, next
nästan (*nehss*-tahn) *adv*
practically; almost; nearly
näsvis (*naiss*-veess) *adj*
impertinent
näsvishet (*naiss*-veess-hāyt)
c impertinence
nät (nait) *nt* net
näthinna (*nait*-hin-ah) *c*
retina
nätverk (*nait*-værk) *nt*
network
nätverksarbete (*nait*-verks-
ahr-*bāy*-ter) *c* networking
nöd (nūrd) *c* misery; distress
nödläge (*nūrd*-lai-ger) *nt*
emergency
nödsignal (*nūrd*-sing-naal) *c*
distress signal
nödsituation (*nūrd*-si-tew-

ah-*shōon*) *c* emergency
nödtvång (*nūrd*-tvong) *nt*
urgency
nödutgång (*nūrd*-ēwt-gong)
c emergency exit
nödvändig (*nūrd*-vehn-di)
adj necessary
nödvändighet (*nūrd*-vehn-
di-hāyt) *c* necessity; need
nöja sig (*nur*-ʸah) content
oneself
nöjd (nurʸd) *adj* content;
pleased
nöje (*nur*ʸ-er) *nt* pleasure;
enjoyment, fun, amusement
nöt (nūrt) *c* (pl ⁓ter) nut
nötknäppare (*nūrt*-knehp-
ah-rer) *c* (pl ⁓) nutcrackers
pl
nötskal (*nūrt*-skaal) *nt*
nutshell

O

oaktat (*ōo*-ahk-taht) *prep* in
spite of
oanad (*ōo*-aan-ahd) *adj*
unexpected
oangenäm (*ōo*-ahn-ʸer-
naim) *adj* unpleasant
oansenlig (*ōo*-ahn-sāyn-li)
adj insignificant;
inconspicuous
oanständig (*ōo*-ahn-stehn-
di) *adj* obscene
oantagbar (*ōo*-ahn-taag-
baar) *adj* unacceptable
oas (oo-*aass*) *c* oasis

oavbruten (*ōo*-aav-brēw-
tern) *adj* continuous;
uninterrupted
oavsiktlig (*ōo*-aav-sikt-li) *adj*
unintentional
obduktion (ob-dewk-*shōon*)
c autopsy
obebodd (*ōo*-ber-bood) *adj*
uninhabited
obeboelig (*ōo*-ber-*boo*-ay-li)
adj uninhabitable
obegriplig (*ōo*-ber-greep-li)
adj incomprehensible
obegränsad (*ōo*-ber-*grehn*-

sahd) *adj* unlimited

obehaglig (ōō-ber-*haag*-li) *adj* unpleasant; disagreeable

obekant (ōō-ber-*kahnt*) *adj* unfamiliar

obekväm (ōō-ber-*kvaim*) *adj* uncomfortable, inconvenient

oberoende (ōō-ber-rōō-ayn-der) *adj* independent

oberättigad (ōō-ber-*reh*-ti-gahd) *adj* unauthorized

obestämd (ōō-ber-*stehmd*) *adj* indefinite

obesvarad (ōō-ber-*svaa*-rahd) *adj* unanswered

obetydlig (ōō-ber-*tewd*-li) *adj* insignificant; petty

obetänksam (ōō-ber-*tehngk*-sahm) *adj* thoughtless, rash

obildad (ōō-*bil*-dahd) *adj* uneducated

objekt (ob-ᵞaykt) *nt* object

objektiv (ob-ᵞerk-teev) *adj* objective

obligation (ob-li-gah-*shōōn*) *c* bond

obligatorisk (ob-li-gah-*tōō*-risk) *adj* compulsory; obligatory

oblyg (ōō-*blewg*) *adj* immodest

obotlig (ōō-*bōōt*-li) *adj* incurable

observation (ob-serr-vah-*shōōn*) *c* observation

observatorium (ob-serr-vah-*tōō*-ri-ewm) *nt* (pl -rier) observatory

observera (ob-serr-*vāyr*-ah) *v*
observe; note

och (o) *conj* and

också (*ok*-soa) *adv* also; too

ockupation (o-kew-pah-*shōōn*) *c* occupation

ockupera (o-kew-*pāy*-rah) *v* occupy

odla (*ōōd*-lah) *v* cultivate; *grow, raise

oduglig (ōō-*dewg*-li) *adj* incapable, incompetent

odygdig (ōō-*dewg*-di) *adj* mischievous, naughty

***vara oenig** (vaa-rah ōō-*āy*-ni) disagree

***vara oense** (vaa-rah ōō-*ayn*-say) disagree

oerfaren (ōō-āyr-*faa*-rern) *adj* inexperienced

oerhörd (ōō-ayr-*hūrrd*) *adj* immense; tremendous

ofantlig (oo-*fahnt*-li) *adj* vast

ofarlig (ōō-*faar*-li) *adj* harmless

ofattbar (ōō-*faht*-baar) *adj* incomprehensible, inconceivable

offensiv (of-ern-*seev*) *adj* offensive; *c* offensive

offentlig (o-*faynt*-li) *adj* public

***offentliggöra** (o-*faynt*-li-ᵞūr-rah) *v* announce; publish

offentliggörande (o-*faynt*-li-ᵞūr-rahn-der) *nt* publication

offer (o-ferr) *nt* sacrifice; victim; casualty

officer (o-fi-*sāyr*) *c* officer

officiell (o-fi-si-*ayl*) *adj* official

offra (*of*-rah) *v* sacrifice
ofog (*oo*-foog) *nt* mischief
oframkomlig (*oo*-frahm-kom-li) *adj* impassable
ofta (*of*-tah) *adv* often; frequently
ofullkomlig (*oo*-fewl-kom-li) *adj* imperfect
ofullständig (*oo*-fewl-stehn-di) *adj* incomplete
ofärdig (*oo*-fæær-di) *adj* crippled, disabled
oförarglig (*oo*-furr-ahr^y-li) *adj* harmless
oförklarlig (*oo*-furr-*klaar*-li) *adj* inexplicable, unaccountable
oförmodad (*oo*-furr-*moo*-dahd) *adj* unexpected, casual
oförmögen (*oo*-furr-*mur*-gern) *adj* incapable, unable
oförskämd (*oo*-furr-*shehmd*) *adj* impertinent; insolent, impudent
oförskämdhet (*oo*-furr-*shehmd*-hāyt) *c* insolence
oförståndig (*oo*-furr-*ston*-di) *adj* unwise
oförtjänt (*oo*-furr-*t^y aint*) *adj* unearned
ogift (*oo*-^yift) *adj* single
ogilla (*oo*-^yi-lah) *v* disapprove of, dislike
ogiltig (*oo*-^yil-ti) *adj* invalid; expired, void
ogräs (*oo*-graiss) *nt* weed
ogynnsam (*oo*-^yewn-sahm) *adj* unfavourable
ohälsosam (*oo*-hehl-soo-sahm) *adj* unhealthy

ohövlig (*oo*-hürv-li) *adj* impolite; rude
ojust (*oo*-shewst) *adj* unfair
ojämn (*oo*-^yehmn) *adj* uneven; rough
ok (*ook*) *nt* yoke
oklanderlig (oo-*klahn*-derr-li) *adj* faultless
oklar (*oo*-klaar) *adj* dim; obscure
okonstlad (*oo*-konst-lahd) *adj* simple, ingenious
okrossbar (*oo*-kross-baar) *adj* unbreakable
oktober (ok-*too*-berr) October
okunnig (*oo*-kew-ni) *adj* ignorant
okvalificerad (*oo*-kvah-li-fi-*sāy*-rahd) *adj* unqualified
okänd (oo-t^yehnd) *adj* unknown
olaglig (*oo*-laag-li) *adj* unlawful; illegal
olik (*oo*-leek) *adj* different; distinct, unlike; *vara ~ differ; vary
olika (*oo*-lee-kah) *adj* different; unequal; various
oliv (o-*leev*) *c* olive
olivolja (o-*leev*-ol-^yah) *c* olive oil
olja (*ol*-^yah) *c* oil; *v* lubricate
oljebyte (*ol*-^yer-*bēw*-ter) *nt* oil-change
oljefilter (*ol*-^yer-*fil*-terr) *nt* (pl -trer, ~) oil filter
oljefyndighet (*ol*-^yer-fewn-di-hāyt) *c* oil well

oljekälla (*ol-*^{y}*er-t*^{y}*eh-lah*) *c* oil well

oljemålning (*ol-*^{y}*er-mōal-ning*) *c* oil painting

oljeraffinaderi (*ol-*^{y}*er-rah-fi-nah-der-ree*) *nt* (pl ~*er*) oil refinery

oljetryck (*ol-*^{y}*er-trewk*) *nt* oil pressure

oljig (*ol-*^{y}*i*) *adj* oily; greasy

oljud (*ōō-*^{y}*ewd*) *nt* noise

olustig (*ōō-lewss-ti*) *adj* uneasy; out of spirits

olycka (*ōō-lew-kah*) *c* accident; misfortune, calamity, disaster

olycklig (*ōō-lewk-li*) *adj* unhappy; miserable, unfortunate

olycksbådande (*ōō-lewks-bōad-ahn-der*) *adj* ominous; sinister

olycksfall (*ōō-lewks-fahl*) *nt* accident

olägenhet (*ōō-leh-gern-hāyt*) *c* inconvenience

olämplig (*ōō-lehmp-li*) *adj* inconvenient; inappropriate

oläslig (*ōō-laiss-li*) *adj* illegible

om (om) *conj* if; whether; *prep* about, in; **runt** ~ round

ombord (om-*bōōrd*) *adv* aboard; ***gå** ~ embark

ombordläggning (om-*bōōrd-lehg-ning*) *c* collision

omdirigering (om-di-ri-*shāy-*ring) *c* diversion, detour

omdöme (om-*dur-mer*) *nt* judgement

omdömesgill (om-*dur-merss-*^{y}il) *adj* judicious

omedelbar (*ōō-*māy-dayl-baar) *adj* immediate; spontaneous; **omedelbart** instantly, immediately, straight away

omedveten (*ōō-*māyd-vāy-tern) *adj* unaware

omelett (o-mer-*layt*) *c* omelette

omfamna (om-*fahm-*nah) *v* embrace; hug

omfamning (om-*fahm-*ning) *c* embrace

omfartsled (om-*faarts-*lāyd) *c* by-pass

omfatta (om-*fah-*tah) *v* comprise; include

omfattande (om-*faht-*ahn-der) *adj* extensive; comprehensive

omfång (om-*fong*) *nt* extent

omfångsrik (om-*fongs-reek*) *adj* bulky, big; extensive

*omge (om-*gāy*) *v* surround; circle

omgivning (om-*^{y}*eev-ning) *c* setting; environment

omgående (om-*gōa-*ayn-der) *adj* prompt

*omkomma (om-*kom-*ah) *v* perish

omkostnader (om-*kost-*nah-derr) *pl* expenses *pl*

omkring (om-*kring*) *prep* round; around; *adv* about

omkull (om-*kewl*) *adv* down, over; ***slå** ~ knock down

omkörning förbjuden (om-

t^yurr-ning furr-*b^yew*-dayn)
no overtaking; no passing
Am

omlopp (*om*-lop) *nt* (pl ~)
circulation; orbit

omnämna (*om*-nehm-nah) *v*
mention

omnämnande (*om*-nehm-nahn-der) *nt* mention

omodern (ōō-moo-*dæærn*)
adj out of date

omringa (*om*-ring-ah) *v*
surround; encircle

område (*om*-rōad-er) *nt*
district; region, area, zone

omräkna (*om*-raik-nah) *v*
convert

omräkningstabell (*om*-raik-nings-tah-*bayl*) *c* conversion
chart

omslagspapper (*om*-slaags-pah-perr) *nt* wrapping paper

*omsluta** (*om*-slew-tah) *v*
surround; encircle

omsorgsfull (*om*-sor^ys-fewl)
adj thorough, careful

omstridd (*om*-strid) *adj*
controversial

omständighet (*om*-stehn-di-hāyt) *c* circumstance

omsvängning (*om*-svehng-ning) *c* sudden change

omsättning (*om*-seht-ning) *c*
turnover

omtvistad (*om*-tviss-tahd)
adj controversial

omtänksam (*om*-tehngk-sahm) *adj* considerate,
thoughtful

omtänksamhet (*om*-tehngk-

sahm-*hāyt*) *c* thoughtfulness

omvandla (*om*-vahnd-lah) *v*
transform

omväg (*om*-vaig) *c* detour

omvänd (*om*-vehnd) *adj*
inverted; converted

omvända (*om*-vehn-dah) *v*
convert

omväxlande (*om*-vehks-lahn-der) *adj* varied

omväxling (*om*-vehks-ling) *c*
change; variety; **som** ~ for a
change

omåttlighet (ōō-mot-li-hāyt)
c immoderation

omöjlig (ōō-mur^y-li) *adj*
impossible

ond (oond) *adj* evil; wicked

ondska (*oond*s-kah) *c* (pl
ondskor) evil; spite

ondskefull (*oond*-skay-fewl)
adj vicious; spiteful

onsdag (*ons*-daag) *c*
Wednesday

ont (oont) *nt* harm

onyx (ōa-newks) *c* onyx

onödig (ōō-nūr-di) *adj*
unnecessary

oordentlig (ōō-or-*daynt*-li)
adj untidy; sloppy

oordning (ōō-oard-ning) *c*
mess

opal (oo-*paal*) *c* opal

opartisk (ōō-paart-isk) *adj*
impartial

opassande (ōō-pah-sahn-der) *adj* improper; indecent;
unsuitable

opera (ōō-per-rah) *c* opera

operahus (ōō-per-rah-hēwss)

nt opera house

operation (o-per-rah-*shōōn*) *c* operation

operera (o-per-*rāyr*-ah) *v* operate

opersonlig (ōō-pehr-*sōōn*-li) *adj* impersonal

opponera sig (o-po-*nāy*-rah) oppose

opposition (o-po-si-*shōōn*) *c* opposition

optiker (*op*-ti-kerr) *c* (pl ~) optician

optimism (op-ti-*mism*) *c* optimism

optimist (op-ti-*mist*) *c* optimist

optimistisk (op-ti-*miss*-tisk) *adj* optimistic

opålitlig (ōō-pōā-leet-li) *adj* unreliable; untrustworthy

ord (ōōrd) *nt* word

ordbok (*ōōrd*-bōōk) *c* (pl -böcker) dictionary

ordentlig (or-*dehnt*-li) *adj* thorough

order (*ōar*-derr) *c* (pl ~) order

orderblankett (*ōar*-derr-blahng-*keht*) *c* order form

ordförande (*ōōrd*-fūr-rahn-der) *c* (pl ~) chairperson; president

ordförråd (*ōōrd*-furr-*rōad*) *nt* vocabulary

ordinera (ōar-di-*nāy*-rah) *v* prescribe

ordinär (ōar-di-*nær*) *adj* ordinary, common

ordlek (*ōōrd*-layk) *c* pun

ordlista (*ōōrd*-liss-tah) *c*

vocabulary, wordbook

ordna (*ōard*-nah) *v* arrange; settle; sort

ordning (*ōard*-ning) *c* order; method; tidiness; *göra i ~ prepare; i ~ in order

ordningsföljd (*awrd*-nings-furl*y*d) *c* order; sequence

ordspråk (*ōōrd*-sprōak) *nt* proverb

ordväxling (*ōōrd*-vehks-ling) *c* argument

oreda (ōō-*rāyd*-ah) *c* disorder; mess, muddle

oregelbunden (ōō-*rāy*-gayl-bewn-dayn) *adj* irregular

oren (ōō-*rāyn*) *adj* unclean

organ (or-*gaan*) *nt* organ

organisation (or-gah-ni-sah-*shōōn*) *c* organization

organisera (or-gah-ni-*sāy*-rah) *v* organize

organisk (or-*gaa*-nisk) *adj* organic

orgel (*or-*ᵉerl) *c* (pl orglar) organ

orientalisk (o-ri-ayn-*taa*-lisk) *adj* oriental

Orienten (o-ri-*ayn*-tayn) the Orient

orientera sig (o-ri-ayn-*tāy*-rah) orientate oneself

originell (or-gi-*nayl*) *adj* original

oriktig (ōō-*rik*-ti) *adj* incorrect; inaccurate

orimlig (ōō-*rim*-li) *adj* unreasonable; absurd

orkan (or-*kaan*) *c* hurricane

orkester (or-*kayss*-terr) *c* (pl

-trar) orchestra

orm (oorm) *c* snake

oro (ōō-rōō) *c* concern; disturbance, fear, worry; unrest

oroa (ōō-rōō-ah) *v* alarm; ~ **sig** worry

orolig (ōō-roo-li) *adj* anxious

oroväckande (ōō-rōō-veh-kahn-der) *adj* alarming

orsak (ōōr-saak) *c* cause; reason

orsaka (ōōr-saa-kah) *v* cause

ort (oort) *c* place

ortodox (or-to-*doks*) *adj* orthodox

orubblig (ōō-rewb-li) *adj* steadfast

orätt (ōō-reht) *c* wrong; *adj* wrong; ***göra ~** wrong

orättvis (ōō-reht-veess) *adj* unfair, unjust

orättvisa (ōō-reht-veesah) *c* injustice

osann (ōō-sahn) *adj* untrue

osannolik (ōō-sah-noo-leek) *adj* unlikely

osjälvisk (ōō-shehl-visk) *adj* unselfish

oskadad (ōō-skaa-dahd) *adj* unhurt; whole

oskuld (ōō-skewld) *c* innocence; virgin; virginity

oskyddad (ōō-shew-dahd) *adj* unprotected

oskyldig (ōō-shewl-di) *adj* innocent, harmless

osnygg (ōō-snewg) *adj* slovenly, foul

oss (oss) *pron* us; ourselves

ost (oost) *c* cheese

ostadig (ōō-staa-di) *adj* unsteady

ostlig (*oost*-li) *adj* eastern

ostron (*oost*-ron) *nt* oyster

osund (ōō-sewnd) *adj* unsound

osympatisk (ōō-sewm-*paat*-isk) *adj* disagreeable

osynlig (ōō-*sewn*-li) *adj* invisible

osäker (ōō-sai-kerr) *adj* uncertain

osäkerhet (ōō-sai-kerr-hāyt) *c* insecurity; incertainty

otacksam (ōō-tahk-sahm) *adj* ungrateful

otillfredsställande (ōō-til-frāyds-*steh*-lahn-der) *adj* unsatisfactory

otillgänglig (ōō-til-*y*ehng-li) *adj* inaccessible

otillräcklig (ōō-til-rehk-li) *adj* insufficient; inadequate

otrevlig (ōō-trāyv-li) *adj* unpleasant

otrogen (ōō-trōō-gayn) *adj* unfaithful

otrolig (ōō-trōō-li) *adj* incredible; improbable

otur (ōō-tēwr) *c* bad luck; misfortune

oturlig (ōō-tēwr-li) *adj* unlucky

otvivelaktigt (ōō-tveev-erl-ahk-tit) *adv* undoubtedly

otålig (ōō-tōal-i) *adj* impatient; eager

otäck (ōō-tehk) *adj* nasty

otät (ōō-tait) *adj* leaky

oöverträffad

oumbärlig ($\overline{oo}$-ewm-bæær-li)
  adj indispensable

oundviklig ($\overline{oo}$-ewnd-veek-li)
  adj unavoidable, inevitable

oupphörligen ($\overline{oo}$-ewp-hüürl-li-ern) *adv* continually

ouppodlad ($\overline{oo}$-ewp-$\overline{oo}$d-lahd) *adj* uncultivated

outhärdlig ($\overline{oo}$-ewt-hæærd-li)
  adj unbearable, intolerable

ouvertyr (oo-vær-*tewr*) *c*
  overture

oval (oo-*vaal*) *adj* oval

ovan[1] ($\overline{oa}$-vahn) *adv* above;
  overhead

ovan[2] ($\overline{oo}$-vaan) *adj*
  unaccustomed

ovanför ($\overline{oa}$-vahn-füür) *prep*
  over; above

ovanlig ($\overline{oo}$-vaan-li) *adj*
  unusual; uncommon;
  exceptional

ovanpå ($\overline{oa}$-vahn-p$\overline{oa}$) *prep*
  on top of

overall ($\overline{oa}$-ver-*r$\overline{oa}$l*) *c*
  overalls *pl*

overklig ($\overline{oo}$-værk-li) *adj*
  unreal

overksam ($\overline{oo}$-værk-sahm)
  adj idle

oviktig ($\overline{oo}$-vik-ti) *adj*
  unimportant; insignificant

ovillig ($\overline{oo}$-vi-li) *adj* unwilling

ovillkorlig ($\overline{oo}$-vil-*k$\overline{oa}$r*-li) *adj*
  unconditional

oviss ($\overline{oo}$-viss) *adj* uncertain;
  vague

oväder ($\overline{oo}$-vai-derr) *nt*
  tempest

ovälkommen ($\overline{oo}$-verl-ko-mern) *adj* unwelcome,
  undesirable

ovänlig ($\overline{oo}$-vehn-li) *adj*
  unkind; unfriendly

oväntad ($\overline{oo}$-vehn-tahd) *adj*
  unexpected

ovärderlig ($\overline{oo}$-vær-*d$\overline{a}$yr*-li)
  adj priceless

oväsen ($\overline{oo}$-vai-sayn) *nt*
  noise; racket

oväsentlig ($\overline{oo}$-vai-*sehnt*-li)
  adj petty

oxe (*ooks*-er) *c* ox

oxkött (*ooks*-t^{j}urt) *nt* beef

ozon ($\overline{oo}$-s$\overline{oo}$n) *nt* (pl ~)
  ozone

oåterkallelig ($\overline{oo}$-$\overline{oa}$t-err-*kahl*-er-li) *adj* irrevocable

oäkta ($\overline{oo}$-ehk-tah) *adj* false

oändlig ($\overline{oo}$-*ehnd*-li) *adj*
  infinite, endless; immense

oärlig ($\overline{oo}$-æær-li) *adj*
  dishonest; crooked

oätbar ($\overline{oo}$-ait-baar) *adj*
  inedible

oöverkomlig ($\overline{oo}$-$\overline{oo}$r-verr-kom-li) *adj* insurmountable;
  prohibitive

oöverträffad ($\overline{oo}$-$\overline{oo}$rv-err-trehf-ahd) *adj* unsurpassed

P

pacifist (pah-si-*fist*) c pacifist

pacifistisk (pah-si-*fiss*-tisk) adj pacifist

packa (*pah*-kah) v pack; ~ **in** pack; ~ **upp** unpack

packning (*pahk*-ning) c pack; packing

padda (*pahd*-ah) c toad

paddel (*pah*-dayl) c (pl -dlar) paddle

paket (pah-*kāyt*) nt packet; parcel, package

Pakistan (pah-ki-*staan*) Pakistan

pakistanier (pah-ki-*staa*-ni-err) c (pl ~) Pakistani

pakistansk (pah-ki-*staansk*) adj Pakistani

pakt (pahkt) c pact

palats (pah-*lahts*) nt palace

palm (pahlm) c palm

panel (pah-*nāyl*) c panel; panelling

panik (pah-*neek*) c panic

pank (pahngk) adj broke

panna (*pahn*-ah) c forehead; pan

pant (pahnt) c pledge; security

pantlånare (*pahnt*-lōa-nah-ray) c (pl ~) pawnbroker

*pantsätta (*pahnt*-seh-tah) v pawn

papegoja (pah-per-*goi*-ah) c parakeet, parrot

papiljott (pah-pil-*ʸot*) c curler

papp (pahp) c cardboard; **papp-** cardboard

pappa (*pah*-pah) c daddy

papper (*pah*-perr) nt paper; **pappers-** paper

pappershandel (*pah*-perrs-hahn-dayl) c (pl -dlar) stationer's

papperskniv (*pah*-perrs-kneev) c paper knife

papperskorg (*pah*-perrs-korʸ) c wastepaper basket

pappersnäsduk (*pah*-perrs-naiss-dēwk) c paper hanky, tissue

papperspåse (*pah*-perrs-pōa-ser) c paper bag

pappersservett (*pah*-perrs-sær-*vayt*) c paper napkin

par (paar) nt pair; couple; **äkta ~** married couple

parabol (pah-rah-*bōal*) c satellite dish

parad (pah-*raad*) c parade

paradis (pah-rah-dees) nt (pl ~) paradise

parafera (pah-rah-*fāy*-rah) v initial

paragraf (pah-rah-*graaf*) c paragraph

parallell (pah-rah-*layl*) c parallel, adj parallel

paralysera (pah-rah-lew-*sāy*-rah) v paralyse

paraply (pah-rah-*plēw*) nt umbrella

parfym (pahr-*fewm*) *c*
perfume

park (pahrk) *c* park; **offentlig**
~ public garden

parkera (pahr-*kāy*-rah) *v*
park

parkering (pahr-*kāy*-ring) *c*
parking; ~ **förbjuden** no
parking

parkeringsavgift (pahr-*kāy*-
rings-*aav*-ᵞift) *c* parking fee

parkeringsljus (pahr-*kāy*-
rings-ᵞ*ēwss*) *nt* parking light

parkeringsmätare (pahr-
kāy-rings-mai-tah-rer) *c* (*pl*
~) parking meter

parkeringsplats (pahr-*kāy*-
rings-plahts) *c* car park;
parking lot *Am*

parkeringszon (pahr-*kāy*-
rings-sōōn) *c* parking zone

parkett (pahr-*kayt*) *c* parquet;
stall; orchestra seat *Am*

parlament (pahr-lah-*maynt*)
nt parliament

parlamentarisk (pahr-lah-
mayn-*taar*-isk) *adj*
parliamentary

parlör (pahr-*lurr*) *c* phrase
book

parti (pahr-*tee*) *nt* (*pl* ~er)
party; side

partisk (*paar*-tisk) *adj* partial

partner (*paart*-nerr) *c* (*pl* ~)
partner

pass (pahss) *nt* passport; pass

passa (*pahss*-ah) *v* fit; suit;
look after, match

passage (pah-*saash*) *c*
passage

passagerare (pah-sah-*shāy*-
rah-rer) *c* (*pl* ~) passenger

passande (*pahss*-ahn-der)
adj proper, suitable;
convenient, adequate

passera (pah-*sāy*-rah) *v* pass

passfoto (*pahss*-foo-too) *nt*
passport photograph

passion (pah-*shōōn*) *c*
passion

passiv (*pah*-seev) *adj* passive

passkontroll (*pahss*-kon-
trol) *c* passport control

patent (pah-*taynt*) *nt* patent

patentbrev (pah-*taynt*-brāyv)
nt patent

patient (pah-si-*ehnt*) *c* patient

patricierhus (paht-*ree*-si-err-
hēwss) *nt* mansion

patriot (paht-ri-*ōōt*) *c* patriot

patron (paht-*rōōn*) *c*
cartridge

patrull (paht-*rewl*) *c* patrol

patrullera (pah-trew-*lāyr*-ah)
v patrol

paus (pouss) *c* pause;
intermission, interval; ***göra**
~ pause

paviljong (pah-vil-ᵞ*ong*) *c*
pavilion

pedal (pay-*daal*) *c* pedal

peka (*pāyk*-ah) *v* point

pekdator (*pāyk*-daa-tor) *c*
tablet

pekfinger (*pāyk*-fing-err) *nt*
(*pl* -grar) index finger

pelare (*pāyl*-ah-rer) *c* (*pl* ~)
column; pillar

pelargång (*pāy*-lahr-gong) *c*
arcade

pelikan (pay-li-*kaan*) *c*
pelican
pendlare (*pehnd*-lah-rer) *c*
(pl ~) commuter
pengar (*payng*-ahr) *pl*
money; **placera ~** invest
penicillin (pay-ni-si-*leen*) *nt*
penicillin
penna (*peh*-nah) *c* pen
penningförsändelse (*payn*-
ing-furr-*sehn*-dayl-ser) *c*
remittance
pennkniv (*pehn*-kneev) *c*
penknife
pennvässare (*pehn*-veh-sah-
rer) *c* (pl ~) pencil sharpener
penny (*peh*-nee) *c* penny
pensel (*pehn*-serl) *c* (pl -slar)
paintbrush
pension (pahng-*shōōn*) *c*
pension; board
pensionat (pahng-shoo-*naat*)
nt boardinghouse; pension;
guesthouse
pensionerad (pahng-shoo-
nāy-rahd) *adj* retired
pensionering (pahng-shoo-
nehr-ing) *c* retirement
peppar (*pay*-pahr) *c* pepper
pepparmint (*pay*-pahr-mint)
nt peppermint
pepparrot (*pay*-pahr-rōōt) *c*
horseradish
per (payr) *prep* per
perfekt (pær-*faykt*) *adj*
perfect
period (pay-ri-*ōōd*) *c* period;
term
periodisk (pay-ri-*ōō*-disk)
adj periodical

permanent (pær-mah-*naynt*)
c permanent wave
permanentveck (pær-mah-
naynt-vayk) permanent
press
perrong (pæ-*rong*) *c* platform
perrongbiljett (pæ-*rong*-bil-
ᵞayt) *c* platform ticket
perser (*pær*-serr) *c* (pl ~)
Persian
Persien (*pær*-si-ern) Persia
persienn (pær-si-*æn*) *c* blind;
shutter
persika (*pær*-si-kah) *c* peach
persilja (pær-*sil*-ᵞah) *c*
parsley
persisk (*pær*-sisk) *adj* Persian
person (pær-*sōōn*) *c* person;
enskild ~ individual; **per ~**
per person
personal (pær-soo-*naal*) *c*
staff; personnel
personbil (pær-*sōōn*-beel) *c*
car
personlig (pær-*sōōn*-li) *adj*
personal; private
personlighet (pær-*sōōn*-li-
hāyt) *c* personality
persontåg (pær-*sōōn*-tōag)
nt slow train
perspektiv (pær-spayk-*teev*)
nt perspective
peruk (per-*rēwk*) *c* wig
pessimism (pay-si-*mism*) *c*
pessimism
pessimist (pay-si-*mist*) *c*
pessimist
pessimistisk (pay-si-*miss*-
tisk) *adj* pessimistic
petition (pay-ti-*shōōn*) *c*

petition

pianist (pi-ah-*nist*) c pianist

piano (pi-*aa*-noo) nt piano

pickels (*pik*-erls) pl pickles pl

picknick (*pik*-nik) c picnic

picknicka (*pik*-ni-kah) v picnic

pigg (pig) adj brisk; alert

piggsvin (*pig*-sveen) nt porcupine

pikant (pi-*kahnt*) adj spicy

pil (peel) c arrow; willow

pilgrim (*peel*-grim) c pilgrim

pilgrimsfärd (*peel*-grims-fæærd) c pilgrimage

piller (*pi*-lerr) nt pill

pilot (pi-*lōōt*) c pilot

pimpsten (*pimp*-stäyn) c pumice stone

PIN (peen) c PIN; personal identification number

pina (*pee*-nah) v torment

pincett (pin-*sayt*) c tweezers pl

pingst (pingst) c (pl pingster) Whitsun, Pentecost

pingvin (ping-*veen*) c penguin

pinsam (*peen*-sahm) adj embarrassing

pionjär (pi-on-ʸæær) c pioneer

pipa (*pee*-pah) c pipe

***pipa** (*pee*-pah) v chirp

piprensare (*peep*-rayn-sah-rer) c (pl ∼) pipe cleaner

piptobak (*peep*-too-bahk) c pipe tobacco

pir (peer) c pier

pirog (pee-*roog*) c pasty

piska (*piss*-kah) c whip

pistol (piss-*fōōl*) c pistol

pittoresk (pi-to-*raysk*) adj picturesque

pjäs (pʸaiss) c play

pjäxor (pʸehks-or) pl ski boots

placera (plah-*sāyr*-ah) v place; *lay, *put

plakat (plah-*kaat*) nt placard

plan (plaan) c plan; project, scheme, map; nt level; adj even, level, plane

planera (plah-*nāy*-rah) v plan

planet (plah-*nāyt*) c planet

planetarium (plah-nay-*taa*-ri-ewm) nt (pl -rier) planetarium

planka (*plahng*-kah) c plank

***planlägga** (*plaan*-leh-gah) v plan, design

planta (*plahn*-tah) c plant

plantage (plahn-*taash*) c plantation

plantera (plahn-*tāy*-rah) v plant

plantskola (*plahnt*-skōōl-ah) c nursery

plast (plahst) c plastic; **plast-** plastic

platina (plah-*tee*-nah) c platinum

plats (plahts) c place; spot; seat; room; job; **ställa på** ∼ *put away; **öppen** ∼ square

platsbiljett (*plahts*-bil-ʸeht) c seat reservation

platt (plaht) adj flat

platta (*plaht*-ah) c plate

plattform (*plaht*-form) c

platå 138

platform
platå (plah-*tōā*) c plateau
plikt (plikt) c duty
plocka (*plok*-ah) v pick; ~ **upp**
pick up
plog (plōōg) c plough
plomb (plomb) c filling
plommon (*ploom*-on) nt
plum
plural (*plēw*-raal) c plural
plus (plewss) prep plus
plåga (*plōāg*-ah) c plague; v
torment
plånbok (*plōan-bōōk*) c (pl
-böcker) wallet; pocketbook
plåster (*ploss*-terr) nt plaster
plåt (plōat) c sheet metal;
plate
plåtburk (*plōat*-bewrk) c tin,
can
plädera (pleh-*dāyr*-ah) v
plead
plöja (*plur*ʸ-ah) v plough
plötslig (*plurts*-li) adj
sudden; **plötsligt** suddenly
pocketbok (*po*-kert-bōōk) c
(pl -böcker) paperback
poesi (poo-ay-*see*) c poetry
pojke (*poi*-ker) c boy
pojkvän (poik-vehn) c (pl
-vänner) boyfriend
pokal (poo-*kaal*) c cup
Polen (*pōā*-lern) Poland
polera (poo-*lāy*-rah) v polish
polio (*pōō*-li-oo) c polio
polis (poo-*leess*) c police pl;
policeman
poliskonstapel (poo-*leess*-
kon-*staa*-perl) c (pl -plar)
policeman

polisonger (po-li-*song*-err)
pl whiskers pl; sideburns pl
polisstation (poo-*leess*-stah-
shōōn) c police station
politik (poo-li-*teek*) c politics;
policy
politiker (poo-*lee*-ti-kerr) c
(pl ~) politician
politisk (poo-*lee*-tisk) adj
political
pollett (po-*layt*) c token
polsk (pōalsk) adj Polish
pommes frites (pom-*frit*)
chips; nAm french fries
ponny (*po*-new) c (pl -nies,
~er) pony
popmusik (*pop-mēw-seek*) c
pop music
populär (po-pēw-*læær*) adj
popular
porslin (pors-*leen*) nt china;
crockery, porcelain
port (pōōrt) c front door, gate
portfölj (port-*furl*ʸ) c
briefcase
portier (port-ʸ*āy*) c hall
porter, receptionist
portion (port-*shōōn*) c
portion; helping
portmonnä (port-mo-*nai*) c
purse
portnyckel (*poort*-new-kerl)
c (pl -klar) latchkey
porto (*por*-too) nt postage
portofri (*por*-too-free) adj
postage paid
porträtt (poort-*reht*) nt
portrait
Portugal (*por*-tew-gahl)
Portugal

portugis (por-tew-*geess*) c
Portuguese

portugisisk (por-tew-*gee*-
sisk) *adj* Portuguese

portvakt (*poort*-vahkt) c
janitor, concierge

position (po-si-*shōōn*) c
position; station

positiv (poo-si-*teev*) *adj*
positive

post (post) c item; mail; post

posta (*poss*-tah) *v* mail; post

postanvisning (*post*-ahn-
veess-ning) c postal order;
money order; mail order
nAm

poste restante (post rer-
stahnt) poste restante

postkontor (*post*-kon-*tōōr*)
nt post-office

postnummer (*post*-new-
merr) *nt* zip code *Am*

postväsen (*post*-vai-sern) *nt*
postal service

potatis (poo-*taa*-tiss) c potato

potatismos (poo-*taa*-tiss-
moos) *nt* mashed potatoes

poäng (po-*ehng*) c point; *få
~ score

poängsumma (po-*ehng*-sew-
mah) c score

prakt (prahkt) c splendour

praktfull (*prahkt*-fewl) *adj*
splendid; magnificent,
glorious, gorgeous

praktik (prahk-*teek*) c
practice

praktikant (prahk-tee-*kahnt*)
c trainee

praktisera (prahk-ti-*sāy*-rah)
v practise

praktisk (*prahk*-tisk) *adj*
practical

prat (praat) *nt* chat

prata (*praat*-ah) *v* chat; talk; ~
strunt talk rubbish

pratmakare (*praat*-maa-kah-
rer) c (pl ~) chatterbox

pratsam (*praat*-sahm) *adj*
talkative

pratstund (*praat*-stewnd) c
chat

precis (pray-*seess*) *adj* exact,
precise; *adv* exactly, just

predika (pray-*deek*-ah) *v*
preach

predikan (pray-*deek*-ahn) c
sermon

predikstol (*pray*-dik-stōōl) c
pulpit

preliminär (pray-li-mi-*næær*)
adj preliminary

premiärminister (pray-mi-
ær-mi-niss-terr) c (pl -trar)
premier

prenumerant (pray-new-
mer-*rahnt*) c subscriber

preposition (pray-po-si-
shōōn) c preposition

present (pray-*saynt*) c
present

presentation (pray-sayn-tah-
shōōn) c introduction

presentera (pray-sayn-*tāy*-
rah) *v* introduce; present

presentkort (pray-*saynt*-
koort) *nt* (pl ~) gift card

president (pray-si-*daynt*) c
president

pressa (*prayss*-ah) *v* press

presskonferens (*prayss-kon-fer-rayns*) *c* press conference

prestation (*prayss-tah-shōōn*) *c* achievement; feat

prestera (*pray-stáy-*rah) *v* achieve

prestige (*pray-steesh*) *c* prestige

preventivmedel (*pray-vayn-teev-máy-*dayl) *nt* contraceptive

pricka av (*prik-*ah) tick off

prickskytt (*prik-*shewt) *c* sniper

primär (*pri-mǽær*) *adj* primary

princip (*prin-seep*) *c* principle

prins (*prins*) *c* prince

prinsessa (*prin-say-*sah) *c* princess

prioritet (*pri-o-ri-táyt*) *c* priority

pris (*preess*) *nt* (*pl* ~, ~er) price; cost, rate; award, prize

prisfall (*preess-*fahl) *nt* fall in prices; break; slump

prislista (*preess-*liss-tah) *c* price list

prisnedsättning (*preess-náyd-*seht-ning) *c* reduction

*prissätta (*preess-*seh-tah) *v* price

privat (*pri-vaat*) *adj* private

privatliv (*pri-vaat-*leev) *nt* privacy

privilegiera (*pri-vi-lay-gi-áyr-*ah) *v* privilege, favour

privilegium (*pri-vi-láy-*gi-ewm) *nt* (*pl* -gier) privilege

problem (*proo-bláym*) *nt* problem; question

procedur (*proo-ser-dēwr*) *c* procedure

procent (*proo-saynt*) *c* (*pl* ~) per cent

procentsats (*proo-saynt-*sahts) *c* percentage

process (*proo-sayss*) *c* process; lawsuit

procession (*proo-seh-shōōn*) *c* procession

pro-choice (*pro-t'ōōys*) *adj* pro-choice

producent (*proo-dēw-sehnt*) *c* producer

produkt (*proo-dewkt*) *c* produce; product

produktion (*proo-dewk-shōōn*) *c* production; output

professor (*pro-fay-*sor) *c* professor

profet (*pro-fáyt*) *c* prophet

program (*proo-grahm*) *nt* programme

programvara (*proo-grahm-*vaar-ah) *c* (*pl* -varor) software

projekt (*pro-shaykt*) *nt* project

proklamera (*prok-lah-máy-*rah) *v* proclaim

pro-life (*pro-layf*) *adj* pro-life

promenad (*pro-mer-naad*) *c* walk; promenade, stroll

promenadkäpp (*pro-mer-naad-*t'ehp) *c* walking stick

promenera (*pro-mer-náy-*rah) *v* walk

pumpa

pronomen (pro-*nōa*-mayn) nt
pronoun
propaganda (pro-pah-*gahn*-
dah) c propaganda
propeller (pro-*pay*-lerr) c (pl
-lrar) propeller
proportion (pro-por-*shōōn*) c
proportion
proportionell (pro-por-shōō-
nayl) adj proportional
propp (prop) c stopper; fuse
proppfull (*prop*-fewl) adj
chock-full
prospekt (proo-*spaykt*) nt
prospectus
prostituerad (pross-ti-tew-
ay-rahd) c (pl ~e) prostitute
protein (proo-tay-*een*) nt
protein
protest (proo-*tayst*) c protest
protestantisk (proo-tay-
stahn-tisk) adj Protestant
protestera (proo-tay-*stay*-
rah) v protest; object; ~ **mot**
object to
protokoll (pro-to-*kol*) nt
record; minutes
prov (prōōv) nt test; trial;
proof; sample; **skriftligt** ~
written test; exercise
prova (*prōō*-vah) v try on
proviant (proo-vi-*ahnt*) c
provisions pl
provinsiell (proo-vin-si-*ayl*)
adj provincial
provisorisk (proo-vi-*sōōr*-
isk) adj temporary;
provisional
provrum (*prōōv*-rewm) nt
fitting room

pruta (*prēw*-tah) v bargain
prydlig (*prēwd*-li) adj neat
präst (prehst) c clergyman;
parson, minister, rector;
katolsk ~ priest
prästgård (prehst-*gōard*) c
vicarage; parsonage
pröva (*prēw*-vah) v attempt;
test
prövning (*prēwv*-ning) c test
psalm (sahlm) c hymn
psykiater (psew-ki-*a*-terr) c
(pl ~) psychiatrist
psykisk (*psēw*-kisk) adj
mental, psychic
psykoanalytiker (psew-ko-
ah-nah-*lēw*-ti-kerr) c (pl ~)
analyst; psychoanalyst
psykolog (psew-ko-*lōag*) c
psychologist
psykologi (psew-ko-lo-*gee*) c
psychology
psykologisk (psew-ko-*lōa*-
gisk) adj psychological
publicera (pewb-li-*sāy*-rah) v
publish
publicitet (pewb-li-si-*tāyt*) c
publicity
publik (pew-*bleek*) c
audience; public
puder (*pēw*-derr) nt powder
puderdosa (*pēw*-derr-dōō-
sah) c powder compact
pullover (pew-*lōav*-err) c
pullover
puls (pewls) c pulse
pulsåder (*pewls*-ōa-derr) c
(pl -dror) artery
pump (pewmp) c pump
pumpa (*pewm*-pah) v pump

pund (pewnd) *nt* pound

pung (pewng) *c* pouch

punkt (pewngkt) *c* point; item; full stop, period

punkterad (pewngk-*tāy*-rahd) *adj* punctured

punktering (pewngk-*tāy*-ring) *c* puncture; flat tyre, blowout

punktlig (pewngkt-li) *adj* punctual

pur (pewr) *adj* sheer

purpur (pewr-pewr) *adj* purple

puss (pewss) *c* kiss

pussel (pewss-erl) *nt* jigsaw puzzle; puzzle

pyjamas (pew-*ʸ*aa-mahss) *c* (pl ~, ~ar) pyjamas *pl*

pytteliten (pew-ter-lee-tern) *adj* tiny

på (pōa) *prep* on; upon; at; in; ~ en gång at once; ~ TV on TV

påbörja (pōa-burr-*ʸ*ah) *v* initiate

påfallande (pōa-fahl-ahn-der) *adj* striking

påfrestning (pōa-frayst-ning) *c* strain

påfyllningsförpackning (pōa-fewl-nings-furr-*pahk*-ning) *c* refill

påfågel (pōa-fōag-erl) *c* (pl -glar) peacock

*pågå (pōa-gōa) *v* *be in progress

påhitt (pōa-hit) *nt* idea, invention

påklädningsrum (pōa-klaid-nings-rewm) *nt* dressing room

påle (pōa-ler) *c* pole

pålitlig (pōa-leet-li) *adj* reliable; sound, trustworthy

*pålägga (pōa-leh-gah) *v* impose, inflict

påminna (pōa-mi-nah) *v* remind

påpeka (pōa-pāy-kah) *v* remark; indicate

påringning (pōa-ring-ning) *c* call

påse (pōa-ser) *c* bag

påsk (posk) *c* Easter

påsklilja (posk-lil-*ʸ*ah) *c* daffodil

påssjuka (pōass-shew-kah) *c* mumps

*påstå (pōa-stōa) *v* claim

påstående (pōa-stōa-ayn-der) *nt* statement

påtryckning (pōa-trewk-ning) *c* pressure

påve (pōa-ver) *c* pope

påverka (pōa-vær-kah) *v* affect; influence

påverkan (pōa-vær-kahn) *c* (pl -kningar) influence

päls (pehls) *c* fur coat; fur

pärla (pæær-lah) *c* pearl; bead

pärlemor (pæær-ler-mōōr) *c* mother of pearl

pärlhalsband (pæærl-hahls-bahnd) *nt* pearl necklace, beads *pl*

pärm (pærm) *c* cover

päron (pææ-ron) *nt* pear

pöl (pūrl) *c* puddle

R

rabarber (rah-*bahr*-berr) c
rhubarb
rabatt (rah-*baht*) c discount;
rebate; flowerbed
rabies (*raa*-bi-erss) c rabies
racket (*rah*-kayt) c (*tennis*)
racket
rad (raad) c row; line, file,
rank
radband (*raad*-bahnd) nt
rosary; beads pl
radergummi (rah-*dayr*-gew-
mi) nt eraser
radie (*raa*-di-?er) c radius
radikal (rah-di-*kaal*) adj
radical
radio (*raa*-di-oo) c radio;
wireless
raffinaderi (rah-fi-nah-der-
ree) nt (pl ~er) refinery
rak (raak) adj straight
raka sig (*raa*-kah) shave
rakapparat (*raak*-ah-pah-
raat) c electric razor; shaver
rakblad (*raak*-blaad) nt razor
blade
rakborste (*raak*-bors-ter) c
shaving brush
raket (rah-*kayt*) c rocket
rakhyvel (*raak*-hew-verl) c
(pl ~vlar) safety razor
rakkniv (*raak*-kneev) c razor
rakkräm (*raak*-kraim) c
shaving cream
rakt (raakt) adv straight; ~
fram straight ahead; straight

on
raktvål (*raak*-tvoal) c shaving
soap
rakvatten (*raak*-vah-tern) nt
aftershave lotion
ram (raam) c frame
ramp (rahmp) c ramp
rand (rahnd) c (pl ränder)
stripe
randig (*rahn*-di) adj striped
rang (rahng) c rank
ranson (rahn-*soon*) c ration
rapp (rahp) c rap
rapphöna (*rahp*-hūrn-ah) c
partridge
rappning (*rahp*-ning) c
plaster
rapport (rah-*port*) c report
rapportera (rah-por-*tay*-rah)
v report
raring (*raa*-ring) c sweetheart
ras (raass) c breed, race; nt
landslide; **ras-** racial
rasa (*raass*-ah) v collapse;
rage
rasande (*raass*-ahn-der) adj
furious; mad; *vara ~ rage
raseri (raa-say-*ree*) nt fury,
rage
rask (rahsk) adj swift
rast (rahst) c break
rastlös (*rahst*-lūrss) adj
restless
rastlöshet (*rahst*-lūrss-hayt) c
unrest
ratt (raht) c steering wheel

rattstång (*raht*-stong) *c* (pl -stänger) steering column

reagera (ray-ah-*gay*-rah) *v* react

reaktion (ray-ahk-*shoon*) *c* reaction

realisation (ray-ah-li-sah-*shoon*) *c* sales; clearance sale

realisera (ray-ah-li-*sayr*-ah) *v* realize

recension (ray-sayn-*shoon*) *c* review

recept (ray-*saypt*) *nt* prescription; recipe

reception (ray-sayp-*shoon*) *c* reception office

receptionist (ray-sayp-shoo-*nist*) *c* receptionist

redaktör (ray-dahk-*turr*) *c* editor

redan (*ray*-dahn) *adv* already

redigera (ray-di-*shay*-rah) *v* edit; *write, *draw up

redogörelse (*ray*-doo-Yur-rayl-ser) *c* report; account

redovisa (*ray*-doo-vee-sah) *v* account for

redskap (*rayd*-skaap) *nt* tool; implement, utensil

reducera (ray-dew-*say*-rah) *v* reduce

reduktion (ray-dewk-*shoon*) *c* reduction

referens (ray-fer-*rayns*) *c* reference

reflektera (ray-flayk-*tay*-rah) *v* reflect

reflektor (ray-*flayk*-tor) *c* reflector

reflex (rayf-*lehks*) *c* reflection

Reformationen (ray-for-mah-*shoo*-nern) reformation

regel[1] (*ray*-gerl) *c* rule; regulation; **som ~** as a rule

regel[2] (*ray*-gerl) *c* bolt

regelbunden (*ray*-gerl-bewn-dayn) *adj* regular

regelmässig (*ray*-gerl-mehss-i) *adj* regular

regent (ray-*Yehnt*) *c* ruler

regera (ray-*Yay*-rah) *v* rule; govern, reign

regering (ray-*Yay*-ring) *c* government; rule

regeringstid (ray-*Yay*-rings-teed) *c* reign

regi (ray-*shee*) *c* direction

regim (ray-*sheem*) *c* régime

region (ray-gi-*oon*) *c* region

regional (ray-gi-oo-*naal*) *adj* regional

regissera (rer-shi-*sayr*-ah) *v* direct

regissör (ray-shi-*surr*) *c* director

register (ray-Yiss-terr) *nt* index

registrering (ray-Yi-*stray*-ring) *c* registration

registreringsnummer (ray-Yi-*stray*-rings-newm-err) *nt* registration number; licence number *Am*

registreringsskylt (rayg-Yi-*stray*-rings-shewlt) *c* license plate

reglemente (rayg-ler-*mayn*-ter) *nt* regulation

reparera

reglera (ray-*glay*-rah) *v*
regulate

reglering (ray-*glay*r-ing) *c*
regulation

regn (rehngn) *nt* rain

regna (*rehng*-nah) *v* rain

regnbåge (*rehngn*-bōa-ger) *c*
rainbow

regnig (*rehng*-ni) *adj* rainy

regnrock (*rehng*-rok) *c*
mackintosh; raincoat

regnskur (rehngn-skēwr) *c*
shower

reguljär (ray-gewl-ʸ*ææ*r) *adj*
regular

rehabilitering (ray-hah-bi-li-
tay-ring) *c* rehabilitation

reklam (rayk-*laam*) *c*
advertising

reklamationsbok (rayk-lah-
mah-*shōon*s-bōok) *c* (pl
-böcker) complaints book

reklamsändning (rayk-*laam*-
sehnd-ning) *c* commercial

rekommendation (ray-ko-
mayn-dah-*shōon*) *c*
recommendation

rekommendationsbrev
(ray-ko-mayn-dah-*shōon*s-
brāyv) *nt* letter of
recommendation

rekommendera (ray-ko-
mayn-*day*-rah) *v*
recommend; register

rekonstruktiv kirurgi (ray-
kon-strewk-*teev* ʸt-i-rewrg-
ee) *c* reconstructive surgery

rekord (rer-*kord*) *nt* record

rekreation (rayk-ray-ah-
shōon) *c* recreation

rekryt (ray-*krēwt*) *c* recruit

rektangel (rayk-*tahng*-erl) *c*
(pl -glar) rectangle; oblong

rektangulär (rayk-tahng-
gew-*læær*) *adj* rectangular

rektor (*rayk*-tor) *c*
headmaster; principal

relatera (ray-lah-*tay*-rah) *v*
relate

relation (ray-lah-*shōon*) *c*
relation

relativ (*ray*-lahteev) *adj*
relative; comparative

relief (ray-li-*ayf*) *c* relief

religion (ray-li-ʸ*ōon*) *c*
religion

religiös (ray-li-*shürss*) *adj*
religious

relik (ray-*leek*) *c* relic

relikskrin (ray-*leek*-skreen) *nt*
shrine

rem (raym) *c* strap

remsa (*raym*-sah) *c* strip

ren¹ (*rāyn*) *c* reindeer

ren² (*rāyn*) *adj* pure, neat,
clean; sheer

***rengöra** (*rāyn*-ʸ*ür*-rah) *v*
clean

rengöring (*rāyn*-ʸ*ür*-ring) *c*
cleaning

rengöringsmedel (*rāyn*-ʸ*ür*-
rings-māy-dayl) *nt* cleaning
fluid; detergent

renommé (rer-no-*māy*) *c*
reputation

rep (rāyp) *nt* rope; cord

repa (*rāyp*-ah) *c* scratch

reparation (rer-pah-rah-
shōon) *c* repair; reparation

reparera (rer-pah-*rāyr*-ah) *v*

repair; mend
repertoar (ray-pær-too-*aar*) c repertory
repetera (ray-pay-*tāy*-ah) v rehearse
repetition (ray-pay-ti-*shōōn*) c rehearsal; repetition; revision
reporter (ray-*pōar*-terr) c (pl -trar) reporter
representant (rer-pray-sayn-*tahnt*) c representative, agent
representation (rer-pray-sayn-tah-*shōōn*) c representation
representativ (rer-pray-sayn-tah-*teev*) adj representative
representera (rer-pray-sayn-*tāy*-rah) v represent
reproducera (rer-pro-dew-*sāy*-rah) v reproduce
reproduktion (rer-pro-dewk-*shōōn*) c reproduction
republik (rer-pew-*bleek*) c republic
republikansk (rer-pewb-li-*kaansk*) adj republican
resa (*rāy*-sah) c journey; voyage, trip; v travel; ~ **bort** *leave; ~ **sig** *get up
resebyrå (*rāy*-ser-bew-*rōa*) c travel agency
resecheck (*rāy*-ser-t^yayk) c traveller's cheque
reseförsäkring (*rāy*-ser-furr-saik-ring) c travel insurance
resehandbok (*rāy*-ser-hahnd-bōōk) c (pl -böcker) guidebook

resekostnader (*rāy*-ser-kost-nah-derr) pl travelling expenses
reseledare (*rāy*-ser-lāy-dah-rer) c (pl ~) guide, tour leader
resenär (rāy-ser-*næær*) c traveller
reserv (rer-*særv*) c reserve; reserv- spare
reservation (rer-sær-vah-*shōōn*) c reservation; booking
reservdel (rer-*særv*-dāyl) c spare part
reservdäck (rer-*særv*-dehk) nt spare tyre
reservera (rer-sær-*vāyr*-ah) v reserve; book
reserverad (rer-sær-*vāy*-rahd) adj reserved
reservhjul (rer-*særv*-^yēwl) nt spare wheel
reservoar (rer-sær-voo-*aar*) c reservoir
reservoarpenna (rer-sær-voo-*aar*-pay-nah) c fountain pen
resgodsfinka (*rāyss*-goots-fin-kah) c luggage van
resolut (rer-so-*lēwt*) adj resolute
resonera (rer-so-*nāyr*-ah) v reason
respekt (rer-*spaykt*) c respect; esteem
respektabel (rer-spayk-*taa*-berl) adj respectable
respektera (rer-spayk-*tāy*-rah) v respect

respektfull (rer-*spaykt*-fewl)
adj respectful

respektive (rayss-payk-teev-
er) *adj* respective

resplan (*rayss*-plaan) *c*
itinerary

resrutt (*rayss*-rewt) *c*
itinerary

rest (rayst) *c* rest; remnant,
remainder

restaurang (rayss-to-*rahng*) *c*
restaurant

restaurangvagn (rayss-to-
rahng-vahngn) *c* dining car

resterande (ray-*stayr*-ahn-
der) *adj* remaining

restriktion (rayst-rik-*shoon*) *c*
restriction

resultat (ray-sewl-*taat*) *nt*
result; outcome; issue

resultera (rer-sewl-*fāy*-rah) *v*
result

resväska (*rāyss*-vehss-kah) *c*
suitcase; case, bag

resårband (ray-*sōar*-bahnd) *
nt* elastic band

reta (*rāyt*-ah) *v* tease; annoy,
irritate

retsam (*rāyt*-sahm) *adj*
teasing, annoying

returflyg (ray-tewr-flēwg) *nt*
return flight

returnera (ray-tewr-*nāy*-rah)
v *send back

reumatism (ray-ew-mah-
tism) *c* rheumatism

rev (rāyv) *nt* reef

reva (*rāy*-vah) *c* tear

revben (*rāyv*-bāyn) *nt* rib

revidera (rer-vi-*dāy*-rah) *v*
revise

revision (rer-vi-*shōōn*) *c*
revision

revolt (rer-*volt*) *c* revolt

revolution (rer-vo-lew-
shōōn) *c* revolution

revolutionär (rer-vo-lew-
shoo-*næær*) *adj*
revolutionary

revolver (rer-*vol*-verr) *c*
revolver

revy (rer-*vēw*) *c* revue

revyteater (rer-*vēw*-tay-aa-
terr) *c* (pl -trar) music hall

***rida** (*reed*-ah) *v* *ride

riddare (*rid*-ah-rer) *c* (pl ~)
knight

ridning (*reed*-ning) *c* riding

ridskola (*reed*-skool-ah) *c*
riding school

ridå (ri-*doā*) *c* curtain

rik (reek) *adj* rich

rike (*reek*-er) *nt* country;
kingdom; empire

rikedom (*ree*-ker-doom) *c*
wealth; riches *pl*

riklig (*reek*-li) *adj* abundant;
plentiful

riklighet (*reek*-li-hāyt) *c*
plenty

riksdagsman (*riks*-dahks-
mahn) *c* (pl -män) Member
of Parliament

rikssamtal (*riks*-sahm-taal)
nt long-distance call

riksväg (*riks*-vaig) *c* trunk
road

rikta (*rik*-tah) *v* direct

riktig (*rik*-ti) *adj* right; just,
correct, proper

riktighet (*rik*-ti-hāyt) *c*
correctness

riktlinje (*rikt*-leen-⁻ʸer) *c*
guideline

riktning (*rikt*-ning) *c*
direction; way

riktnummer (*rikt*-new-merr)
nt area code

rim (rim) *nt* rhyme

rimlig (*rim*-li) *adj* reasonable

ring (ring) *c* ring

ringa (*ring*-ah) *v* call; *ring;* ~
upp phone, ring up; call up
Am

ringaktning (*ring*-ahkt-ning)
c contempt

ringklocka (*ring*-klo-kah) *c*
bell

*****rinna** (*ri*-nah) *v* *run

ris (reess) *nt* rice

risk (risk) *c* risk; hazard,
chance

riskabel (riss-*kaa*-berl) *adj*
unsafe

riskera (ri-*skāyr*-ah) *v* risk

riskfylld (*risk*-fewld) *adj* risky

rispa (*riss*-pah) *v* scratch

rita (*ree*-tah) *v* *draw

*****riva** (*ree*-vah) *v* *tear,
demolish; grate

rival (ri-*vaal*) *c* rival

rivalitet (ri-vah-li-*tāyt*) *c*
rivalry

rivjärn (*reev*-ʸærn) *nt* grater

rivning (*reev*-ning) *c*
demolition

ro (rōō) *v* quiet; *v* row

roa (*rōō*-ah) *v* amuse;
entertain

roande (*rōō*-ahn-der) *adj*

entertaining

robust (ro-*bewst*) *adj* robust

rock (rok) *c* coat

rockslag (*rok*-slaag) *nt* lapel

roddbåt (*rood*-bōāt) *c* rowing
boat

roder (*rōō*-derr) *nt* rudder

rodna (*rōād*-nah) *v* blush

rolig (*rōō*-li) *adj* funny;
enjoyable

Rollerblade® (roo-lerr-
blayd) *c* Rollerblade®

rom (rom) *c* roe

roman (roo-*maan*) *c* novel

romanförfattare (roo-maan-
furr-*fah*-tah-rer) *c* (pl ~)
novelist

romans (roo-*mahns*) *c*
romance

romantisk (roo-*mahn*-tisk)
adj romantic

rond (rond) *c* round

rondell (ron-*dayl*) *c*
roundabout

rop (rōōp) *nt* call; cry

ropa (*rōō*-pah) *v* call; cry

rorkult (*rōōr*-kewlt) *c* helm

rorsman (*rōōrs*-mahn) *c* (pl
-män) steersman; helmsman

ros (rōōss) *c* rose

rosa (*rōā*-sah) *adj* rose, pink

rost (rost) *c* rust

rostig (*ross*-ti) *adj* rusty

rot (rōōt) *c* (pl rötter) root

rotting (*rot*-ing) *c* rattan

rouge (rōōsh) *c* rouge

rovdjur (*rōōv*-ʸewr) *nt* beast
of prey

rubin (rew-*been*) *c* ruby

rubrik (rew-*breek*) *c* headline,

heading

ruin (rew-*een*) c ruins

ruinera (rew-ee-*nay*-rah) v ruin

rulett (rew-*layt*) c roulette

rulla (*rewl*-ah) v roll

rulle (*rewl*-er) c roll

rullgardin (rewl-gahr-*deen*) c blind

rullskridskoåkning (*rewl*-skri-skoo-*oak*-ning) c roller-skating

rullstol (*rewl*-stool) c wheelchair

rulltrappa (*rewl*-trah-pah) c escalator

rum (rewm) nt room; space; ~ **med frukost** bed and breakfast

rumsbetjäning (*rewms*-ber-t'ai-ning) c room service

rumstemperatur (*rewms*-taym-per-rah-*tewr*) c room temperature

rumän (rew-*main*) c Rumanian

Rumänien (rew-*mai*-ni-ern) Rumania

rumänsk (rew-*mainsk*) adj Rumanian

rund (rewnd) adj round

rundad (*rewn*-dahd) adj rounded

rundhänt (*rewnd*-hehnt) adj liberal

rundresa (*rewnd*-*ray*-sah) c tour

runt (rewnt) adv around

rusa (*rewss*-ah) v rush; dash

rusningstid (*rewss*-nings-

teed) c rush hour; peak hour

russin (*rewss*-in) nt raisin

rustik (rew-*steek*) adj rustic

rustning (*rewst*-ning) c armour

ruta (*rewt*-ah) c square; pane

rutin (rew-*teen*) c routine

rutschbana (rewch-*baan*-ah) c slide

rutt (rewt) c route

rutten (*rewt*-ern) adj rotten

ryck (rewk) nt tug; wrench

rygg (rewg) c back

ryggrad (*rewg*-raad) c backbone; spine

ryggskott (*rewg*-skot) nt lumbago

ryggsäck (*rewg*-sehk) c rucksack; knapsack

ryggvärk (*rewg*-værk) c backache

***ryka** (*rew*-kah) v smoke

ryktbarhet (*rewkt*-baar-*hayt*) c fame

rykte (*rewk*-ter) nt rumour; reputation; renown

rymd (rewmd) c space

rymdraket (*rewmd*-rah-*kay*) c space shuttle

rymlig (*rewm*-li) adj spacious; roomy, large

rymling (*rewm*-ling) c runaway

rymma (*rewm*-ah) v *run away; contain

rynka (*rewng*-kah) c wrinkle

rysk (rewsk) adj Russian

ryslig (*rewss*-li) adj horrible; awful

rysning (*rewss*-ning) c shiver;

shudder, *nt* chill
ryss (rewss) *c* Russian
Ryssland (*rewss*-lahnd)
Russia
***ryta** (*rēw*-tah) *v* roar
rytm (rewtm) *c* rhythm
ryttare (*rewt*-ah-rer) *c* (pl ~)
rider; horseman
rå (rōā) *adj* raw
råd (rōā) *nt* advice; ***ha ~
med** afford
råda (*rōā*-dah) *v* advise
rådfråga (*rōā*-frōā-gah) *v*
consult
***rådgiva** (*rōā*-ʸee-vah-her)
v advise
rådgivare (*rōā*-ʸee-vah-rer)
c (pl ~) counsellor
rådjurskalv (*rōā*-ʸewrs-
kahlv) *c* fawn
rådman (*rōā*-mahn) *c* (pl
-män) magistrate
rådsförsamling (*rōāds*-furr-
sahm-ling) *c* council
rådsmedlem (*rōāds*-mäyd-
lehm) *c* (pl ~mar) councillor
råmaterial (*rōā*-mah-tay-ri-
aal) *nt* raw material
rån¹ (rōān) *nt* robbery;
väpnat ~ hold-up
rån² (rōān) *nt* wafer
råna (*rōā*-nah) *v* rob
rånare (*rōā*-nah-reh) *c* (pl ~)
robber
råolja (*rōā*-ol-ʸah) *c*
petroleum
råtta (*ro*-tah) *c* rat
räcka (*rehk*-ah) *v* suffice
räcke (*rehk*-er) *nt* rail;
railing

räckhåll (*rehk*-hol) *nt* reach
räckvidd (*rehk*-vid) *c* range
räd (raid) *c* raid
rädda (*rehd*-ah) *v* save; rescue
räddning (rehd-ning) *c*
rescue
rädisa (*rai*-di-sah) *c* radish
rädsla (*raids*-lah) *c* fear
räka (*rai*-kah) *c* shrimp;
prawn
räkna (*raik*-nah) *v* reckon,
count; **~ ut** calculate
räknemaskin (*raik*-ner-mah-
sheen) *c* adding-machine
räkneord (*raik*-ner-ōōrd) *nt*
numeral
räkning (*raik*-ning) *c* bill;
arithmetic
rännsten (*rehn*-stäyn) *c*
gutter
ränta (*rehn*-tah) *c* interest
rätt¹ (reht) *c* course
rätt² (reht) *adj* appropriate,
right, correct; *adv* rather; *c*
justice; ***ha ~** be right; **med
rätta** rightly
rätta (*reht*-ah) *v* correct; **~ till**
correct, adjust
rättegång (*reh*-ter-gong) *c*
trial; lawsuit
rättelse (*reh*-terl-ser) *c*
correction
rättfärdig (reht-*fæær*-di) *adj*
righteous
rättighet (*reh*-ti-hāyt) *c* right
rättmätig (*reht*-mai-ti) *adj*
legitimate
rättskaffens (*reht*-skahf-
erns) *adj* honourable

salladsolja

rättvis (*reht-veess*) *adj* just; fair, right

rättvisa (*reht-vee-sah*) *c* justice

räv (raiv) *c* fox

röd (rūrd) *adj* red

rödbeta (*rūrd-bāy-tah*) *c* beetroot

rödhake (*rūrd-haa-ker*) *c* robin

rödlila (*rūrd-lee-lah*) *adj* mauve

rödspätta (*rūrd-speh-tah*) *c* plaice

rök (rūrk) *c* smoke

röka (*rū-kah*) *v* smoke

rökare (*rū-kah-rer*) *c* (pl ∼) smoker

rökelse (*rūrk-erl-ser*) *c* incense

rökfritt (*rūrk-freet*) *adj* smoke-free

rökkupé (*rūrk-kēw-pāy*) *c* smoker, smoking compartment

rökning förbjuden (*rūrk-

ning furr-b^{y}ēw-dern*) no smoking

röntga (*rurnt-kah*) *v* X-ray

röntgenbild (*rurnt-kern-bild*) *c* X-ray

rör (rūrr) *nt* pipe; tube; cane

röra[1] (*rūrr-ah*) *v* touch; move; ∼ **om** stir; ∼ **sig** move

röra[2] (*rūrr-ah*) *c* muddle

rörande (*rūrr-ahn-der*) *adj* touching; *prep* regarding

rörelse (*rūrr-erl-ser*) *c* motion, movement; emotion; *sätta i ∼* move

rörlig (*rūrr-li*) *adj* mobile

rörmokare (*rūrr-moo-kah-rer*) *c* (pl ∼) plumber

röst (rurst) *c* voice; vote

rösta (*rurss-tah*) *v* vote

röstbrevlåda (*rurst-brāyv-lōa-dah*) *c* (pl -lådor) voice mail

röstning (*rurst-ning*) *c* vote; poll

rösträtt (*rurst-reht*) *c* franchise; suffrage

S

safir (sah-*feer*) *c* sapphire

saft (sahft) *c* syrup

saftig (*sahf-*ti) *adj* juicy

saga (*saa-*gah) *c* fairytale; tale

sak (saak) *c* thing; matter, affair

sakkunnig (*saak-*kewn-i) *adj* expert

saklig (*saak-*li) *adj* matter-of-

-fact

sakna (*saak-*nah) *v* lack, miss

saknad (*saak-*nahd) *c* lack

sakta ned (*sahk-*tah) slow down

sal (saal) *c* hall

saldo (*sahl-*doo) *nt* balance

saliv (sah-*leev*) *c* saliva, spit

sallad (*sahl-*ahd) *c* salad

salladsolja (*sah-*lahds-ol-ᵞah) *c* salad-oil

salong (sah-*long*) *c* drawing room; salon

salt (sahlt) *nt* salt; *adj* salty

saltkar (*sahlt*-kaar) *nt* salt cellar, salt shaker *nAm*

salu: till ~ (til *saa*-lew) for sale

saluhall (saa-lew-hahl) *c* market

salva (*sahl*-vah) *c* ointment

samarbete (sahm-ahr-*bay*-tah) *nt* cooperation; *v* collaborate

samarbetsvillig (sahm-ahr-*bayts*-vi-li) *adj* co-operative

samband (sahm-bahnd) *nt* relation

samfund (sahm-fewnd) *nt* society

samhälle (sahm-heh-ler) *nt* community; locality; **samhälls-** social

samhällsbevarande (sahm-hehls-ber-*vaa*-rahn-der) *adj* conservative

samla (sahm-lah) *v* gather; assemble, collect; ~ **ihop** compile; ~ **in** collect

samlag (sahm-laag) *nt* sexual intercourse

samlare (*sahm*-lah-rer) *c* (pl ~) collector

samlas (sahm-lahss) *v* gather

samling (sahm-ling) *c* collection

samma (sahm-ah) *adj* same

*sammanbinda (sah-*mahn*-bin-dah) *v* link

sammandrag (sahm-mahn-

draag) *nt* summary

*sammanfalla (*sahm*-mahn-fahl-ah) *v* coincide

sammanfatta (*sahm*-ahn-fah-tah) *v* summarize

sammanfattning (*sah*-mahn-faht-ning) *c* summary, résumé

sammanfoga (sahm-ahn-*fōōg*-ah) *v* join, *put together

sammanhang (sahm-ahn-hahng) *nt* connection; coherence, reference

sammankomst (sahm-ahn-komst) *c* meeting; assembly

sammanlagd (sahm-ahn-lahgd) *adj* overall, total

sammanslagning (*sahm*-ahn-slaag-ning) *c* merger

sammanslutning (*sah*-mahn-slewt-ning) *c* society; association

sammanställa (*sahm*-ahn-stehl-ah) *v* compose; compile

sammanstöta (*sahm*-ahn-stūr-tah) *v* bump

sammanstötning (*sahm*-ahn-stūrt-ning) *c* collision

*sammansvärja sig (*sahm*-ahn-*svær*-ᵞah) conspire

sammansvärjning (sahm-ahn-*svær*ᵞ-ning) *c* conspiracy, plot

sammansättning (*sahm*-ahn-seht-ning) *c* composition

sammanträde (*sahm*-ahn-traid-er) *nt* meeting

sammanträffande (*sahm-ahn-trehf-ahn-der*) *nt*
concurrence; encounter

sammet (*sah-*mayt) *c* velvet

samordna (*sahm-*ord-nah) *v*
coordinate

samordning (*sahm-*ord-ning) *c* coordination

samtal (*sahm-*taal) *nt*
conversation; talk, discussion; ~ **väntar** *nt* call waiting

samtalsämne (*sahm-*taals-aim-ner) *nt* topic

samtida (*sahm-*tee-dah) *adj*
contemporary

samtidig (*sahm-*tee-di) *adj*
simultaneous

samtycka (*sahm-*tew-kah) *v*
consent

samtycke (*sahm-*tew-ker) *nt*
consent

samverkan (*sahm-*vær-kahn) *c* cooperation

samvete (*sahm-*vāy-ter) *nt*
conscience

samåka (*sahm-ōā-*kah) *v*
carpool

samåkning (*sahm-ōā*k-ning) *c* carpool

sanatorium (*sah-nah-tōō-*ri-ewm) *nt* (pl -rier)
sanatorium

sand (sahnd) *c* sand

sandal (sahn-*daal*) *c* sandal

sandig (*sahn-*di) *adj* sandy

sandpapper (*sahnd-*pahp-err) *nt* sandpaper

sanitär (*sah-ni-tæær*) *adj*
sanitary

sann (sahn) *adj* very, true

sannfärdig (*sahn-*fæær-di)
adj truthful

sanning (*sah-*ning) *c* truth

sannolik (*sahn-*oo-leek) *adj*
likely; probable

sansad (*sahns-*ahd) *adj* sober

sardin (sahr-*deen*) *c* sardine

satellit (sah-tay-*leet*) *c*
satellite

satellitradio (sah-tay-*leet-*raa-di-oo) *c* satellite radio

satäng (*sah-*tehng) *c* satin

Saudiarabien (*sou-di-ah-raa-*bi-ern) Saudi Arabia

saudiarabisk (*sou-di-ah-raab-*isk) *adj* Saudi Arabian

sax (sahks) *c* scissors *pl*

scen (sāyn) *c* scene, stage

schack (shahk) *nt* chess;
schack! check!

schackbräde (*shahk-*brai-der) *nt* checkerboard *nAm*

schal (shaal) *c* shawl

schampo (*shahm-*pōō) *nt*
shampoo

scharlakansfeber (shahr-*laa-*kahns-*fāy-*berr) *c* scarlet fever

scharlakansröd (shahr-*laa-*kahns-rūrd) *adj* scarlet

schema (*shāy-*mah) *nt*
scheme

schlager (*shlaa-*gerr) *c* (pl ~, -rar) hit

Schweiz (shvayts)
Switzerland

schweizare (*shvay-*tsah-rer) *c* (pl ~) Swiss

schweizisk (*shvay-*tsisk) *adj*

Swiss

scout (skout) *c* boy scout

*se (sāy) *v* *see; notice; ~ **på** look at; ~ **till** attend to; ~ **upp** look out; watch out; ~ **ut** look

sebra (sāyb-rah) *c* zebra

sedan (sāy-dahn) *adv* then; afterwards; *conj* since, after; *prep* since; **för** ... ~ ago; ~ **dess** since

sedel (sāy-dayl) *c* (pl sedlar) banknote

seder (sāy-derr) *pl* customs *pl*

sediment (say-di-maynt) *nt* deposit

sedvanlig (sāyd-vaan-li) *adj* customary

sedvänja (sāyd-vehn-yah) *c* usage

seg (sāyg) *adj* tough

segel (sāy-gerl) *nt* sail

segelbar (sāy-gerl-baar) *adj* navigable

segelbåt (sāy-gerl-bōat) *c* sailing boat

segelflygplan (sāy-gerl-flēwg-plaan) *nt* glider

segelsport (sāy-gerl-sport) *c* yachting

segelsällskap (sāy-gerl-sehl-skaap) *nt* yacht club

seger (sāy-gerr) *c* (pl segrar) victory

segerrik (sāy-gerr-reek) *adj* triumphant

segla (sāyg-lah) *v* sail; navigate

segra (sāyg-rah) *v* *win

segrare (sāyg-rah-ray) *c* (pl ~)

winner, victor

sekreterare (sayk-ray-tāy-rah-rer) *c* (pl ~) secretary; clerk

sektion (sehk-shōōn) *c* section

sekund (ser-kewnd) *c* second

sekundär (ser-kewn-dǣær) *adj* secondary

selleri (say-ler-ree) *nt* celery

selfie (seyl-fee) *c* selfie

semester (say-mayss-terr) *c* holiday

semesterort (say-mayss-terr-oort) *c* holiday resort

semikolon (say-mi-kōō-lon) *nt* semicolon

sen (sāyn) *adj* late; **för sent** too late

sena (sāyn-ah) *c* sinew; tendon

senap (sāy-nahp) *c* mustard

senat (ser-naat) *c* senate

senator (ser-naa-tor) *c* senator

senil (say-neel) *adj* senile

sensation (sayn-sah-shōōn) *c* sensation

sensationell (sayn-sah-shoo-nayl) *adj* sensational

sentimental (sayn-ti-mayn-taal) *adj* sentimental

separat (say-pah-raat) *adv* separately

september (sayp-taym-berr) September

septisk (sayp-tisk) *adj* septic

serie (sāy-ri-er) *c* series; **tecknad** ~ comics *pl*

seriös (say-ri-ūrss) *adj*

sinnessjuk

serious
servera (sær-*vāy*-rah) v serve
serveringsfat (sær-*vāy*-rings-faat) nt dish
servett (sær-*vayt*) c napkin; serviette
servitris (sær-vit-*reess*) c waitress
servitör (sær-vi-*tūrr*) c waiter
session (say-*shōōn*) c session
sevärdhet (*sāy*-væærd-hāyt) c sight
sex (sayks) num six
sextio (*sayks*-ti) num sixty
sextonde (*sayks*-ton-der) num sixteenth
sexualitet (sayk-sew-ah-li-*tāyt*) c sexuality
sexuell (sayk-sew-*ayl*) adj sexual
siames (see-ah-*māyss*) c Siamese
siamesisk (see-ah-*māyss*-isk) adj Siamese
sida (*see*-dah) c side; page; på andra sidan across; på andra sidan om beyond; åt sidan aside; sideways
siden (*see*-dayn) nt silk
sidogata (*see*-doo-gaat-ah) c side street
sidoljus (*see*-doo-*y*ewss) nt sidelight
sidoskepp (*see*-doo-shayp) nt aisle
siffra (*sif*-rah) c figure; digit
sig (say) pron himself, herself; themselves; itself
sigill (si-*y*ill) nt seal
signal (sing-*naal*) c signal

signalement (sing-nah-lay-*maynt*) nt description
signalera (sing-nah-*lāyr*-ah) v signal
signalhorn (sing-*naal*-hōōrn) nt hooter, horn
signatur (sing-nah-*tēwr*) c signature
sikt (sikt) c visibility
sikta¹ (*sik*-tah) v aim at; ~ på aim at
sikta² (*sik*-tah) v sift
sil (seel) c strainer
sila (*seel*-ah) v strain
sill (sil) c herring
silver (*sil*-verr) nt silver; silverware
silversmed (*sil*-verr-smāyd) c silversmith
simbassäng (*sim*-bah-sehng) c swimming pool
simma (*sim*-ah) v *swim
simmare (*si*-mah-rer) c (pl ~) swimmer
simning (*sim*-ning) c swimming
simpel (*sim*-perl) adj common
simulera (si-mew-*lāyr*-ah) v pretend
sin (sin) pron (nt sitt, pl sina) his, her, its, one's; their
singularis (*sing*-gēw-laa-riss) nt singular
sinne (*si*-ner) nt sense
sinnesförvirrad (*si*-nerss-furr-*vi*-rahd) adj mad
sinnesrörelse (*si*-nerss-*rūr*-rayl-ser) c emotion
sinnessjuk¹ (*si*-nerss-shēwk)

adj insane

sinnessjuk² (*si*-nerss-shewk) *c* (pl ~a) lunatic

sinnesstämning (*si*-nerss-stehm-ning) *c* state of mind

siren (si-*rayn*) *c* siren

sist (sist) *adj* last; **till ~** at last

sista (*siss*-tah) *adj* ultimate

*sitta (*sit*-ah) *v* *sit

sittplats (*sit*-plahts) *c* seat

situation (si-tew-ah-*shoon*) *c* situation

sju (shew) *num* seven

sjuk (shewk) *adj* ill; sick

sjukdom (*shewk*-doom) *c* illness; sickness, disease

sjukhus (*shewk*-hewss) *nt* hospital

sjukledighet (*shewk*-lay-di-hayt) *c* sick-leave

sjuksköterska (*shewk*-shürt-err-skah) *c* nurse

sjukvård (*shewk*-voård) *c* public health

sjunde (*shewn*-der) *num* seventh

*sjunga (*shewng*-ah) *v* *sing

*sjunka (*shewng*-kah) *v* *sink

sjuttio (*shewt*-ti) *num* seventy

sjutton (*shewt*-on) *num* seventeen

sjuttonde (*shewt*-on-der) *num* seventeenth

själ (shail) *c* soul

själv (shehlv) *pron* myself, yourself, himself, herself, itself, oneself

själva (*shehl*-vah) *pron* ourselves, yourselves, themselves

självbetjäning (*shehlv*-ber-t'ai-ning) *c* self-service

självgod (*shehlv*-good) *adj* self-righteous

självisk (*shehl*-visk) *adj* selfish

självklar (*shehlv*-klaar) *adj* self-evident

självmord (*shehlv*-moord) *nt* suicide

självmordsattack (*shehlv*-moords-ah-tahk) *c* suicide attack

självmordsbombare (*shehlv*-moords-bomb-arer) *c* (pl ~) suicide bomber

självservering (*shehlv*-sayr-vay-ring) *c* self-service restaurant

självstyre (*shehlv*-stew-rer) *nt* self-government

självständig (*shehlv*-stehn-di) *adj* independent

självständighet (*shehlv*-stehn-di-hayt) *c* independence

självupptagen (*shehlv*-ewp-taag-ern) *adj* self-centred

sjätte (*sheh*-ter) *num* sixth

sjö (shür) *c* lake

sjöborre (*shür*-bo-rer) *c* sea urchin

sjöfart (*shür*-faart) *c* navigation; shipping

sjöfågel (*shür*-foa-gayl) *c* (pl -glar) seabird

sjökort (*shür*-koort) *nt* nautical chart

sjöman (*shür*-mahn) *c* (pl -män) sailor

157   **skicklighet**

sjörövare (*shǖr-rǖr-vah-rer*) *c* (pl ~) pirate

sjösjuk (*shǖr-shewk*) *adj* seasick

sjösjuka (*shǖr-shew-kah*) *c* seasickness

sjösättning (*shǖr-seht-ning*) *c* launching

sjötunga (*shǖr-tewng-ah*) *c* sole

*ska (skaa) *v* *shall; *will

skada (*skaa-dah*) *c* injury; damage, mischief, harm; *v* *hurt, injure, harm

skadad (*skaa-dahd*) *adj* injured

skadeersättning (*skaa-der-āyr-seht-ning*) *c* compensation; indemnity

skadlig (*skaad-li*) *adj* harmful; hurtful

skaffa (*skahf-ah*) *v* get, procure, provide; ~ **sig** acquire; *v* acquire; obtain

skaft (skahft) *nt* handle

skaka (*skaa-kah*) *v* *shake

skal (skaal) *nt* skin, peel; shell

skala (*skaa-lah*) *c* scale; *v* peel

skalbagge (*skaal-bahg-er*) *c* beetle; bug

skald (skahld) *c* poet

skaldjur (*skaal-ȳewr*) *nt* shellfish

skalle (*skah-ler*) *c* skull

skam (skahm) *c* shame; disgrace

skamsen (*skahm-sayn*) *adj* ashamed

skandal (skahn-*daal*) *c* scandal

skandinav (skahn-di-*naav*) *c* Scandinavian

Skandinavien (skahn-di-*naav*-i-ern) Scandinavia

skandinavisk (skahn-di-*naav*-isk) *adj* Scandinavian

skanna (*skahn*-ah) *v* scan

skanner (*skahn*-ehr) *c* scanner

skanning (*skahn*-ing) *c* scan

skapa (*skaa*-pah) *v* create

skarp (skahrp) *adj* sharp; keen; strong

skatt (skaht) *c* tax; treasure

skattefri (*skah*-ter-free) *adj* tax-free

skattmästare (*skaht*-mehss-tah-rer) *c* (pl ~) treasurer

ske (shāy) *v* happen; occur

sked (shāyd) *c* spoon; spoonful

skelett (skay-*layt*) *nt* skeleton

skelögd (*shāyl*-ūrgd) *adj* cross-eyed

sken (shāyn) *nt* glare

skenhelig (*shāyn-hāy*-li) *adj* hypocritical

skepp (shayp) *nt* boat

skeppa (*shayp*-ah) *v* ship

skeppsredare (*shayps-rāy*-dah-rer) *c* (pl ~) shipowner

skeppsvarv (*shayps*-vahrv) *nt* shipyard

skicka (*shik*-ah) *v* *send; ~ **bort** dismiss; ~ **efter** *send for; ~ **iväg** *send off; ~ **tillbaka** *send back

skicklig (*shik*-li) *adj* skilled, skilful; clever

skicklighet (*shik*-li-hāyt) *c*

ability; skill
skida (*shee*-dah) *c* ski; **åka**
skidor ski
skidbyxor (*sheed*-bewks-err)
pl ski pants
skidlift (*sheed*-lift) *c* ski lift
skidstavar (*sheed*-staa-vahr)
pl ski sticks; ski poles *Am*
skidåkare (*sheed*-ōā-kah-rer)
c (pl ~) skier
skidåkning (*sheed*-ōāk-ning)
c skiing
skiffer (*shif*-err) *nt* slating
skift (shift) *nt* gang, shift
skiftnyckel (*shift*-new-kayl) *c*
(pl -klar) wrench
skilja (*shil*-ʸah) *v* separate;
part; **skiljas** divorce; ~ **sig**
divorce
skiljedomare (skil-ʸeh-doo-
mah-rer) *c* (pl ~) referee
skiljevägg (*shil*-ʸer-vehg) *c*
partition
skillnad (*shil*-nahd) *c*
difference; distinction;
*göra ~ distinguish
skilsmässa (*shils*-meh-sah) *c*
divorce
*skina (*shee*-nah) *v* *shine
skinka (*shing*-kah) *c* ham;
buttock
skinn (shin) *nt* hide; **skinn-**
leather
skinna (*shi*-nah) *v* skin,
fleece
skir (sheer) *adj* sheer
skiss (skiss) *c* sketch
skissera (ski-*sāy*-rah) *v*
sketch
skit (scheet) *c* crap V

skiva (*sheev*-ah) *c* slice; disc
skivenhet (*sheev*-en-*hāyt*) *c*
disk drive
skivspelare (*shiv*-spāy-lah-
rer) *c* (pl ~) record player
skjorta (*shoor*-tah) *c* shirt
skjul (shewl) *nt* shed
*skjuta (*shēwt*-ah) *v* fire,
*shoot; push
skjutdörr (*shēwt*-durr) *c*
sliding door
sko (skoo) *c* shoe
skoaffär (*skoo*-ah-fær) *c*
shoe shop
skog (skoog) *c* forest; wood
skogig (*skoog*-i) *adj* wooded
skogsdunge (skoogs-dew-
nger) *c* grove
skogstrakt (skoogs-trahkt) *c*
woodland
skogvaktare (*skoog*-vahk-
tah-rer) *c* (pl ~) forester
skoj (skoi) *nt* fun
skoja (*skoi*-ah) *v* joke, fool
skokräm (*skoo*-krehm) *c*
shoe polish
skola (*skool*-ah) *c* school
skolbänk (*skool*-behngk) *c*
desk
skolflicka (*skool*-fli-kah) *c*
schoolgirl
skolka (*skol*-kah) *v* play
truant
skollärare (*skool*-lær-ah-
rer) *c* (pl ~) schoolmaster,
schoolteacher
skolpojke (*skool*-poi-ker) *c*
schoolboy
skolväska (*skool*-vehss-kah)
c satchel

skomakare (*skōō*-maa-kah-rer) *c* (pl ~) shoemaker

skorpa (*skor*-pah) *c* crust; rusk

skorsten (*skors*-tāyn) *c* chimney

skosnöre (*skōō*-snūr-rer) *nt* shoelace

skotsk (skotsk) *adj* Scottish

skott (skot) *nt* shot

skottavla (*skot*-taav-lah) *c* target

skottkärra (*skot*-tᵞær-ah) *c* wheelbarrow

Skottland (*skot*-lahnd) Scotland

skottår (*skot*-ōår) *nt* leap year

skovel (*skōa*-verl) *c* (pl -vlar) shovel

skrapa (*skraap*-ah) *v* scrape; scratch

skratt (skraht) *nt* laugh; laughter

skratta (*skrah*-tah) *v* laugh

skreva (*skrāy*-vah) *c* cleft

skri (skree) *nt* scream

skridsko (*skri*-skoo) *c* skate; åka skridskor skate

skridskobana (*skri*-skoo-baa-nah) *c* skating rink

skridskoåkning (*skri*-skoo-ōåk-ning) *c* skating

skriftlig (*skrift*-li) *adj* written

skrik (skreek) *nt* cry; scream, shout

*skrika** (*skree*-kah) *v* shriek; scream, shout; cry

*skriva** (*skree*-vah) *v* *write; ~ in book; enter; ~ in sig check in; ~ om *rewrite; ~ på

endorse; ~ upp *write down

skrivblock (*skreev*-blok) *nt* writing pad

skrivbord (*skreev*-bōōrd) *nt* desk; bureau

skrivmaskin (*skreev*-mah-sheen) *c* typewriter

skrivmaskinspapper (*skreev*-mah-sheens-pah-perr) *nt* typing paper

skrivpapper (*skreev*-pah-perr) *nt* notepaper

skrovlig (*skrōav*-li) *adj* hoarse

skrubbsår (*skrewb*-sōår) *nt* graze

skruv (skrēwv) *c* screw

skruva (*skrēw*-vah) *v* screw; ~ av unscrew; ~ på screw on, turn on

skruvmejsel (*skrēwv*-may-sayl) *c* (pl -slar) screwdriver

skrymmande (*skrewm*-ahn-der) *adj* bulky

skrynkla (*skrewngk*-lah) *c* crease; *v* crease

*skryta** (*skrēwt*-ah) *v* boast

skråma (*skrōå*-mah) *c* scratch

skräck (skrehk) *c* scare; fright; horror, terror

skräddare (*skreh*-dah-rer) *c* (pl ~) tailor

skräddarsydd (*skreh*-dahr-sewd) *adj* tailor-made

skrämd (skrehmd) *adj* frightened

skrämma (*skrehm*-ah) *v* frighten; scare

skrämmande (*skrehm*-ahn-der) *adj* terrifying

skräp (skraip) *nt* rubbish; refuse, junk

skugga (*skewg*-ah) *c* shadow; shade

skuggig (*skewg*-i) *adj* shady

skuld (skewld) *c* guilt, fault; debt

skulptur (skewlp-*tewr*) *c* sculpture

skulptör (skewlp-*turr*) *c* sculptor

skum (skewm) *nt* foam; *adj* obscure

skumgummi (*skewm*-gewm-i) *nt* foam rubber

skumma (*skewm*-ah) *v* foam

skura (*skew*-rah) *v* scrub

skurk (skewrk) *c* villain

skutta (*skew*-tah) *v* skip; *leap

skvadron (skvah-*drōōn*) *c* squadron

skvaller (*skvah*-lerr) *nt* gossip

skvallra (*skvahl*-rah) *v* gossip

sky (shēw) *c* sky, cloud; gravy

skydd (shewd) *nt* protection; shelter, cover

skydda (*shewd*-ah) *v* protect; shelter

skygg (shewg) *adj* shy

skygghet (*shewg*-hāyt) *c* shyness

skyldig (*shewl*-di) *adj* guilty; *vara ~* owe

skyltdocka (*shewlt*-do-kah) *c* dummy, mannequin

skyltfönster (*shewlt*-furns-terr) *nt* shopwindow

skymfa (*shewm*-fah) *v* call names

skymning (*shewm*-ning) *c* twilight; dusk

skymt (shewmt) *c* glimpse

skymta (*shewm*-tah) *v* glimpse

skynda sig (*shewn*-dah) hurry; hasten

skyskrapa (*shēw*-skraa-pah) *c* skyscraper

skådespel (*skōā*-der-spāyl) *nt* spectacle; drama

skådespelare (*skōā*-der-spāy-lah-rer) *c* (pl ~) actor; comedian

skådespelerska (*skōā*-der-spāy-lerrs-kah) *c* actress

skådespelsförfattare (*skōā*-der-spāyls-furr-*fah*-tah-rer) *c* (pl ~) playwright

skål (skōal) *c* bowl; basin; toast

skåp (skōap) *nt* cupboard; closet

skåpvagn (*skōap*-vahngn) *c* pick-up van

skägg (shehg) *nt* beard

skäl (shail) *nt* reason

skälla (*shehl*-ah) *v* bark, bay; scold; *~ ut* scold

skälm (shehlm) *c* rascal

skälva (*shehl*-vah) *v* shiver; tremble

skämma bort (*sheh*-mah bort) *v* *spoil

skämmas (*shehm*-ahss) *v* *be ashamed

skämt (shehmt) *nt* joke

skämtsam (*shehmt*-sahm) *adj* humorous

skär (shæær) *adj* pink

*skära (*shææ-rah*) v *cut;
carve; ~ **av** *cut off; ~ **ned**
reduce, *cut down; decrease

skärgård (*shæær-*goård) c
archipelago

skärm (shærm) c screen

skärmmössa (*shærm-mur-*
sah) c cap

skärpt (shærpt) adj bright

skärsår (*shæær-*soar) nt cut

sköldpadda (*shurld-*pahd-
ah) c turtle

skölja (*shurl*ʸah) v rinse

sköljmedel (*shurl*ʸ-mäy-derl)
nt conditioner

sköljning (*shurl*ʸ-ning) c
rinse

skön (shūrn) adj beautiful;
fine; comfortable

skönhet (*shūrn-*häyt) c
beauty

skönhetsmedel (*shūrn-*
häyts-mäyd-ayl) pl
cosmetics pl

skönhetssalong (*shūrn-*
häyts-sah-*long*) c beauty
salon

skönhetsvård (*shūrn-*häyts-
voård) c beauty treatment

skör (shurr) adj fragile

skörd (shūrrd) c harvest; crop

skörda (*shūrr-*dah) v reap;
harvest; gather

sköta (*shūrr-*tah) v look after;
~ **om** *take care of

sladd (slahd) c flex, electric
cord; skid

slag¹ (slaag) nt a sort of, a
kind of; **all slags** all sorts of

slag² (slaag) nt battle; blow,

tap; bump; smash

slaganfall (*slaag-*ahn-fahl) nt
stroke

slagord (slaag-oōrd) nt (pl ~)
catchword

slagsmål (*slahgs-*moāl) nt
fight

slaktare (*slahk-*tah-rer) c (pl
~) butcher

slang (slahng) c slang

slangtryck (*slahng-*trewk) c
tyre pressure

slank (slahngk) adj slender;
slim

slant (slahnt) c coin

slapp (slahp) adj limp

slappna av (*slahp-*nah) relax

slarv (slahrv) nt neglect

slarvig (*slahr-*vi) adj careless;
slovenly

slav (slaav) c slave

slicka (*slik-*ah) v lick

slingra sig (*sling-*rah) *wind

slingrande (*sling-*rahn-der)
adj winding

slipa (*slee-*pah) v sharpen

*slippa (*slip-*ah) v not *have to

slipprig (*slip-*ri) adj slippery

slips (slips) c necktie

slira (*slee-*rah) v skid; slip

*slita (*slee-*tah) v *tear; ~ **ut**
wear out

sliten (*sleet-*ern) adj worn

slogan (*sloā-*gahn) c (pl ~)
slogan

slott (slot) nt castle

slug (slewg) adj sly

sluka (*slew-*kah) v swallow

slump (slewmp) c chance,
luck; **av en ~** by chance

slumpartad (*slewmp-ahr-tahd*) *adj* accidental

sluss (*slewss*) *c* lock

slut (*slewt*) *nt* end; finish

till slut at last

sluta (*slewt-ah*) *v* end; discontinue, finish

*****sluta** (*slewt-ah*) *v* close

slutbetala (*slewt-ber-taa-lah*) *v* *pay off

sluten (*slewt-ern*) *adj* closed; reserved

slutlig (*slewt-li*) *adj* final; eventual; **slutligen** *adv* finally

slutresultat (*slewt-ray-sewl-taat*) *nt* final result

slutsats (*slewt-sahts*) *c* conclusion

slutta (*slewt-ah*) *v* slope; slant

sluttning (*slewt-ning*) *c* hillside, slope; incline

*****slå** (*sloa*) *v* *beat; *strike, *hit; slap, punch; ~ **ifrån** switch off; ~ **igen** slam; ~ **ihop** merge; ~ **ihjäl** kill; ~ **in** wrap; ~ **till** *strike; ~ **upp** look up

slående (*sloa-ayn-der*) *adj* striking

*****slåss** (*sloss*) *v* struggle

släcka (*slehk-ah*) *v* *put out; extinguish

släde (*slai-der*) *c* sleigh, sledge

släkt (*slehkt*) *c* family

släkting (*slehk-ting*) *c* relative; relation

slänga (*slehng-ah*) *v* *throw

släpa (*slaip-ah*) *v* drag; haul

släppa in (*slehp-ah*) admit; *let in

släpvagn (*slaip-vahngn*) *c* trailer

slät (*slait*) *adj* smooth; level

slätt (*sleht*) *c* plain

slätvar (*slait-vaar*) *c* brill

slö (*slur*) *adj* blunt, dull

slöja (*slur-¹yah*) *c* veil

slösa bort (*slur-sah bort*) waste

slösaktig (*slurss-ahk-ti*) *adj* wasteful; lavish, extravagant

slöseri (*slur-ser-ree*) *nt* waste, wastefulness

smak (*smaak*) *c* taste; flavour

smaka (*smaa-kah*) *v* taste

smaklig (*smaak-li*) *adj* savoury

smaklös (*smaak-lürss*) *adj* tasteless

smaksätta (*smaak-say-tah*) *v* flavour

smal (*smaal*) *adj* narrow

smaragd (*smah-rahgd*) *c* emerald

smart (*smart*) *adj* smart

smartmobil (*smart-moo-beel*) *c* smartphone

smarttelefon (*smart-tay-lay-foan*) *c* smartphone

smed (*smayd*) *c* (black)smith

smekmånad (*smayk-mōa-nahd*) *v* honeymoon

smeknamn (*smayk-nahmn*) *nt* nickname

smet (*smayt*) *c* batter

smidig (*smeed-i*) *adj* supple; flexible

smink (*smingk*) *c* make-up

snarare

*smita (*smee-tah*) *v* slip away

smitta (*smit-ah*) *v* infect

smittande (*smi-tahn-der*) *adj* contagious

smittkoppor (*smit-ko-poor*) *pl* smallpox

smittosam (*smi-too-sahm*) *adj* infectious; contagious

smoking (*smōa-king*) *c* dinner jacket; tuxedo *nAm*

smuggla (*smewg-lah*) *v* smuggle

smula (*smēw-lah*) *c* crumb; bit

smultron (*smewlt-ron*) *nt* wild strawberry

smuts (smewts) *c* dirt

smutsig (*smewt-si*) *adj* dirty; filthy

smycke (*smew-ker*) *c* jewel; smycken jewellery

*smyga (*smēw-gah*) *v* sneak

småaktig (*smōa-ahk-ti*) *adj* stingy

småfranska (*smōa-frahns-kah*) *c* roll

småningom (*smōa-ning-om*) *adv* gradually; så ~ eventually

småpengar (*smōa-payng-ahr*) *pl* change

småprat (*smōa-praat*) *nt* chat

småprata (*smōa-praat-ah*) *v* chat

småskratta (*smōa-skraht-ah*) *v* chuckle

smäll (smehl) *c* spanking; crack

smälla (*smehl-ah*) *v* spank; crack

smälta (*smehl-tah*) *v* melt;

thaw; digest

smärta (*smær-tah*) *c* pain

smärtfri (*smært-free*) *adj* painless

smärting (*smær-ting*) *c* canvas

smärtsam (*smært-sahm*) *adj* painful

smärtstillande (*smært-sti-lahn-der*) *adj* pain-relieving, analgesic; ~ medel *nt* painkiller

smör (smūrr) *nt* butter

smörgås (*smūrr-gōass*) *c* sandwich

smörja (*smurr-ᵞah*) *c* trash

smörja (*smurr-ᵞah*) *v* grease, lubricate

smörjning (*smurrᵞ-ning*) *c* lubrication

smörjolja (*smurrᵞ-ol-ᵞah*) *c* lubrication oil

smörjsystem (*smurrᵞ-sew-stäym*) *nt* lubrication system

snabb (snahb) *adj* rapid; fast

snabbgående (*snahb-gōa-ayn-der*) *adj* express, high-speed

snabbhet (*snahb-hāyt*) *c* rapidity, swiftness

snabbkurs (*snahb-kewrs*) *c* intensive course

snabbköp (*snahb-tᵞūrp*) *nt* supermarket

snabbuppringning (*snabb-ewp-ring-ning*) *c* speed dial(ing)

snackbar (*snahk-baar*) *c* snack bar

snarare (*snaar-ah-rer*) *adv*

rather

snarka (*snahr*-kah) *v* snore

snart (snaart) *adv* soon; presently, shortly; **så ~ som** as soon as

snask (snahsk) *nt* candy *nAm*

sned (snäyd) *adj* slanting

snickare (*snik*-ah-rer) *c* (pl ~) carpenter

snida (*snee*-dah) *v* carve

snideri (snee-der-*ree*) *nt* carving

snideriarbete (snee-der-*ree*-ahr-*bāy*-ter) *nt* wood carving

snigel (*snee*-gayl) *c* (pl -glar) snail

snilleblixt (*sni*-ler-blikst) *c* brain wave

snitt (snit) *nt* cut

snodd (snood) *v* twine

snorkel (*snor*-kayl) *c* (pl -klar) snorkel

snubbla (*snewb*-lah) *v* stumble

snurra (*snew*-rah) *v* *spin

snygg (snewg) *adj* good-looking

***snyta sig** (*snēw*-tah) *blow one's nose

snäcka (*sneh*-kah) *c* seashell

snäckskal (*snehk*-skaal) *nt* shell

snäll (snehl) *adj* good; sweet, kind, nice

snälltåg (*snehl*-tōag) *nt* through train, express train

snäv (snaiv) *adj* narrow

snö (snūr) *c* snow

snöa (*snūr*-ah) *v* snow

snöig (*snūr*-i) *adj* snowy

snöre (*snūr*-rer) *nt* string; tape

snöslask (*snūr*-slahsk) *nt* slush

snöstorm (*snūr*-storm) *c* snowstorm; blizzard

social (soo-si-*aal*) *adj* social

socialism (soo-si-ah-*lism*) *c* socialism

socialist (soo-si-ah-*list*) *c* socialist

socialistisk (soo-siah-*liss*-tisk) *adj* socialist

socka (*sok*-ah) *c* sock

socker (*so*-kerr) *nt* sugar

sockerbit (*so*-kerr-beet) *c* lump of sugar

sockerlag (*so*-kerr-laag) *c* syrup

sockersjuk (*so*-kerr-shēwk) *c* (pl ~a) diabetic

sockersjuka (*so*-kerr-shēw-kah) *c* diabetes

sodavatten (*soo*-dah-vah-tern) *nt* soda water

soffa (*so*-fah) *c* sofa; couch

sol (sōōl) *c* sun

sol- (sōōl) *adj* solar

solbada (*sōōl*-baa-dah) *v* sunbathe

solbränd (*sōōl*-brehnd) *adj* tanned

solbränna (*sōōl*-breh-nah) *c* suntan

soldat (sol-*daat*) *c* soldier

solfjäder (*sōōl*-f³*eh*-derr) *c* fan

solglasögon (*sōōl*-glaass-*ūr*-goan) *pl* sunglasses *pl*

solid (so-*leed*) *adj* firm

solig (_sōō_-li) *adj* sunny

solistframträdande (_soo_-list-frahm-trai-dahn-der) *nt* recital

solljus (_sōōl_-^yewss) *nt* sunlight

solnedgång (_sōōl_-nāyd-gong) *c* sunset

sololja (_sōōl_-ol-^yah) *c* suntan oil

solparasoll (_sōōl_-pah-rah-sol) *nt* sunshade

solsken (_sōōl_-shāyn) *nt* sunshine

solsting (_sōōl_-sting) *nt* sunstroke

solsystem (_sōōl_-sewss-tāym) *nt* solar system

soluppgång (_sōōl_-ewp-gong) *c* sunrise

som (som) *conj* as; *pron* who, that, which; ~ **om** as if

somliga (_som_-li-gah) *pron* some

sommar (_so_-mahr) *c* summer

sommartid (_so_-mahr-teed) *c* summer time

son (sōān) *c* (pl söner) son

sondotter (_sōān_-do-terr) *c* (pl -döttrar) granddaughter

sonson (_sōān_-sōān) *c* (pl -söner) grandson

sopa (_sōō_-pah) *v* *sweep

sophink (_sōōp_-hingk) *c* rubbish bin

sopor (_soo_-por) *pl* garbage

soppa (_sop_-ah) *c* soup

soppsked (_sop_-shāyd) *c* soup spoon

sopptallrik (_sop_-tahl-rik) *c*

soup plate

soptunna (_sōōp_-tewn-ah) *c* dustbin; trash can *Am*

sorg (sor^y) *c* sorrow; mourning, grief

sorgespel (_sor_-^yer-spāyl) *nt* tragedy

sorglös (sor^y-lurss) *adj* carefree

sorgsen (sor^y-sayn) *adj* sad

sort (sort) *c* kind; sort

sortera (sor-_tāy_-rah) *v* sort; assort

sortiment (sor-ti-_maynt_) *nt* assortment

souvenir (soo-ver-_neer_) *c* souvenir

***sova** (_sōā_-vah) *v* *sleep

sovande (_sōāv_-ahn-der) *adj* asleep

sovbrits (_sōāv_-brits) *c* berth

sovjetisk (sov-^y_āy_-tisk) *adj* Soviet

sovkupé (sov-kew-_pāy_) *c* sleeping compartment

sovrum (_sōāv_-rewm) *nt* bedroom

sovsal (_sōāv_-saal) *c* dormitory

sovsäck (_sōāv_-sehk) *c* sleeping bag

sovvagn (_sōāv_-vahngn) *c* sleeping car; Pullman

spade (_spaa_-der) *c* spade

Spanien (_spah_-ni-ayn) Spain

spanjor (spahn-^y_ōōr_) *c* Spaniard

spannmål (_spahn_-mōal) *c* corn, cereals *pl*

spansk (spahnsk) *adj*

Spanish

spara (*spaa*-rah) *v* save; economize

sparbank (*spaar*-bahngk) *c* savings bank

spargris (spaar-greess) *c* piggy bank

spark (spahrk) *c* kick

sparka (*spahr*-kah) *v* kick

sparkcykel (*spahrk*-sew-kerl) *c* (pl ~-klar) scooter

sparris (*spahr*-iss) *c* asparagus

sparsam (*spaar*-sahm) *adj* economical

sparv (spahrv) *c* sparrow

speceriaffär (spay-say-*ree*-ah-*fæær*) *c* grocer's

specerier (spay-say-ree-*err*) *pl* groceries

specerihandlare (spay-say-*ree*-hahnd-lah-rer) *c* (pl ~) grocer

specialisera sig (spay-si-ah-li-*sāy*-rah) specialize

specialist (spay-si-ah-*list*) *c* specialist

specialitet (spay-si-ah-li-*tāyt*) *c* speciality

speciell (spay-si-*ayl*) *adj* special

specifik (spay-si-*feek*) *adj* specific

specimen (*spāy*-si-mern) *nt* specimen

spegel (*spāy*-gayl) *c* (pl -glar) mirror; looking-glass

spegelbild (*spay*-gerl-bild) *c* reflected image, reflection

spekulera (spay-kew-*lāyr*-ah)

v speculate

spel (spāyl) *nt* game

spela (*spāyl*-ah) *v* play; act

spelare (*spāy*-lah-rer) *c* (pl ~) player

spelkort (*spāyl*-koort) *nt* playing card

spelkula (*spāyl*-kēwl-ah) *c* marble

spelmark (*spāyl*-mahrk) *c* chip, counter

spenat (spay-*naat*) *c* spinach

spendera (spayn-*dāyr*-ah) *v* *spend

spets (spayts) *c* tip; point; lace

spetsig (*spayt*-si) *adj* pointed

spett (spayt) *nt* spit

spetälska (*spāyt*-ehls-kah) *c* leprosy

spik (speek) *c* nail

spikböld (*speek*-burld) *c* boil

spilla (*spil*-ah) *v* *spill

spindel (*spin*-dayl) *c* (pl -dlar) spider

spindelnät (*spin*-derl-nait) *nt* spider's web

***spinna** (*spin*-ah) *v* purr; *spin

spion (spi-*ōōn*) *c* spy

spira (*spee*-rah) *c* spire

spirituell (spi-ri-tēw-*ayl*) *adj* witty

spis (speess) *c* cooker; **öppen** ~ fireplace

spisgaller (*speess*-gah-lerr) *c* grate

spjut (sp³*ewt*) *nt* spear

spjäla (sp³*ai*-lah) *c* lath; bar; splint

spjällåda (sp^{y}ail-lōād-ah) c crate

splitter (spli-terr) nt splinter

splitterfri (spli-terr-free) adj shatterproof

spole (spōōl-er) c spool

spoliera (spoo-li-$\overline{ay}$-rah) v mess up

sporra (spo-rah) v incite

sport (sport) c sport

sportbil (sport-beel) c sports car

sportjacka (sport-^{y}ah-kah) c sports jacket

sportkläder (sport-klai-derr) pl sportswear

spott (spot) nt spit

spotta (spo-tah) v *spit

spratt (spraht) nt trick

spray (spray) c spray; atomizer

sprayflaska (spray-flahss-kah) c atomizer

spricka (sprik-ah) c crack

*spricka (sprik-ah) v crack; *burst

*sprida (spreed-ah) v *spread; *shed

*springa (spring-ah) v *run

sprit (spreet) c liquor; booze colloquial

spritdrycker (spreet-drewk-err) pl spirits

spritkök (spreet-t^{y}ürk) nt spirit stove

spritvaror (spreet-vaa-ror) pl spirits

spruta (sprēwt-ah) c shot

språk (sprōāk) nt language; speech

språklaboratorium (sprōāk-lah-bo-rah-tōō-ri-ewm) nt (pl -rier) language laboratory

språng (sprong) nt jump

spräcka (spreh-kah) v crack

sprängämne (sprehng-ehm-ner) nt explosive

spy (spēw) v vomit

spår (spōar) nt trace; trail

spåra (spōar-ah) v trace

spårvagn (spōar-vahngn) c tram; streetcar nAm

spädbarn (spaid-baarn) nt infant

spädgris (spaid-greess) c piglet

spänd (spehnd) adj tense

spänna fast (speh-nah) fasten

spännande (spehn-ahn-der) adj exciting

spänne (speh-ner) nt buckle; fastener

spänning (speh-ning) c excitement; voltage, tension

spärra (spæ-rah) v block

spöke (spūr-ker) nt ghost; spirit

spörsmål (spurrs-mōāl) nt question, problem

stabil (stah-beel) adj stable

stad (staad) c (pl städer) city, town; stads- urban

stadig (staa-di) adj steady

stadigvarande (staa-di-vaa-rahn-der) adj permanent

stadion (staad-^{y}on) nt stadium

stadium (staa-d^{y}ewm) nt (pl

-dier) stage
stadsbo (*stahds-bōō*) *c* citizen
stadscentrum (*stahds-sayntrewm*) *nt* town centre
stadsdel (*stahds-dāyl*) *c* district
stadshus (*stahds-hēwss*) *nt* town hall
staket (*stah-kāyt*) *nt* fence
stall (*stahl*) *nt* stable
stam (*stahm*) *c* trunk; tribe
stamanställd (*stahm-ahn-stehld*) *c* (pl ~a) cadre, regular
stamcell (*stahm-sayl*) *c* stem cell
stamma (*stahm-ah*) *v* falter
stampa (*stahm-pah*) *v* stamp
standard- (*stahn-dahrd*) standard
stanna (*stahn-ah*) *v* halt; pull up; ~ **kvar** stay
stapel (*staa-perl*) *c* (pl -plar) pile, stack
stapla (*staap-lah*) *v* pile, stack
stare (*staar-er*) *c* starling
stark (*stahrk*) *adj* strong; powerful
start (*staart*) *c* take-off
starta (*staar-tah*) *v* start
startbana (*stahrt-baa-nah*) *c* runway
stat (*staat*) *c* state; **stats-** national
station (*stah-shōōn*) *c* depot *nAm*
statistik (*stah-ti-steek*) *c* statistics *pl*
statskassa (*stahts-kah-sah*) *c* treasury

statsman (*stahts-mahn*) *c* (pl -män) statesman
statsminister (*stahts-mi-nisster*) *c* (pl -trar) Prime Minister
statstjänsteman (*stahtst'ehns-ter-mahn*) *c* (pl -män) civil servant
statsöverhuvud (*stahts-ūr-verr-hēw-vewd*) *nt* (pl ~, ~en) head of state
staty (*stah-tēw*) *c* statue
stava (*staa-vah*) *v* *spell
stavelse (*staa-vayl-ser*) *c* syllable
stavning (*staav-ning*) *c* spelling
stearinljus (*stāy-ah-reen-ⁱēwss*) *nt* candle
steg (*stāyg*) *nt* step, move; pace
stege (*stāy-ger*) *c* ladder
steka (*stāy-kah*) *v* fry
stekpanna (*stāyk-pahn-ah*) *c* frying pan
stel (*stāyl*) *adj* stiff
sten (*stāyn*) *c* stone; **sten-** stone
stenblock (*stāyn-blok*) *nt* boulder
stenbrott (*stāyn-brot*) *c* quarry
stengods (*stāyn-goods*) *nt* stoneware
*stenlägga (*stāyn-leh-gah*) *v* pave
stenografi (*stay-noo-grah-fee*) *c* shorthand
stereo (*stay-ree-oh*) *c* (pl ~)

stereo

steril (stay-*reel*) *adj* sterile

sterilisera (stay-ri-li-*say*-rah) *v* sterilize

steward (st'*oo*-ahrd) *c* steward

stick (stik) *nt* sting

sticka (*stik*-ah) *v* *knit; prick; ~ **in** plug in

***sticka** (*stik*-ah) *v* *sting; prick; ~ **in** plug in

stickkontakt (*stik*-kon-tahkt) *c* plug, socket

stifta (*stif*-tah) *v* found; institute

stiftelse (*stif*-tayl-ser) *c* foundation

stig (steeg) *c* trail, path

***stiga** (*steeg*-ah) *v* *rise; ascend; ~ **av** *get off; ~ **ned** descend; ~ **på** *get on; ~ **upp** *rise; *get up; ~ **uppåt** ascend

stigning (*steeg*-ning) *c* ascent

stil (steel) *c* style

stilla (*stil*-ah) *adj* quiet, calm, still

Stilla havet (*sti*-lah-*haa*-vert) Pacific Ocean

stillastående (*sti*-lah-stoa-ayn-der) *adj* stationary, still

stillhet (*stil*-hayt) *c* quiet

stillsam (*stil*-sahm) *adj* calm, quiet

stimulans (*sti*-mew-lahngs) *c* stimulant; impulse

stimulera (sti-mew-*lay*-rah) *v* stimulate

sting (sting) *nt* sting

***stinka** (*sting*-kah) *v* *stink

stipendium (sti-*payn*-di-

ewm) *nt* (pl -dier) grant, scholarship

stipulera (sti-pew-*lay*-rah) *v* stipulate

stirra (*sti*-rah) *v* gaze, stare

***stjäla** (*shail*-ah) *v* *steal

stjälk (shehlk) *c* stem

stjärna (*shæær*-nah) *c* star

stjärt (shært) *c* bottom

sto (st*oo*) *nt* mare

stock (stock) *c* log

stol (st*oo*l) *c* chair

stola (*stoa*l-ah) *c* stole

stolpe (*stol*-per) *c* post; pillar

stolpiller (*stool*-pi-lerr) *nt* suppository

stolt (stolt) *adj* proud

stolthet (*stolt*-hayt) *c* pride

stoppa (*stop*-ah) *v* stop; *put; darn; upholster; **stopp!** stop!

stoppgarn (*stop*-gaarn) *nt* (pl ~er) darning wool

stor (st*oo*r) *adj* large; great, big, major

storartad (*stoor*-aar-tahd) *adj* magnificent, superb, terrific

Storbritannien (*stoor*-bri-*tahn*-yayn) Great Britain

stork (stork) *c* stork

storlek (*stoor*-l*ay*k) *c* size

storm (storm) *c* gale, storm

stormig (*stor*-mi) *adj* stormy; gusty

stormlykta (*storm*-lewk-tah) *c* hurricane lamp

storslagen (*stoor*-slaa-gern) *adj* grand

straff (strahf) *nt* punishment; penalty

straffa 170

straffa (*strah-fah*) *v* punish
strafflag (*strahf-laag*) *c* criminal law
straffspark (*strahf-spahrk*) *c* penalty kick
stram (straam) *adj* tight
strama åt (*straa-mah*) tighten
strand (strahnd) *c* (pl stränder) beach; shore
strandsnäcka (*strahnd-sneh-kah*) *c* winkle
strandsten (*strahnd-stāyn*) *c* pebble
strax (strahks) *adv* presently
streberaktig (*strāy-berr-ahk-ti*) *adj* ambitious
streck (strayk) *nt* line
strejk (strayk) *c* strike
strejka (*stray-kah*) *v* *strike
stress (strayss) *c* stress
strid (streed) *c* fight; combat, struggle
*strida (*streed-ah*) *v* *fight
strikt (strikt) *adj* strict
strof (strōāf) *c* stanza
struktur (strewk-*tēwr*) *c* structure, fabric; texture
strumpa (*strewm-pah*) *c* stocking
strumpbyxor (*strewmp-bewks-err*) *pl* tights *pl*; panty hose
strumpebandshållare (*strewm-per-bahnds-ho-lah-rer*) *c* (pl ~) garter belt *Am*
strunt (strewnt) *nt* rubbish
strupe (strēw-per) *c* throat
strupkatarr (*strēwp-kah-tahr*) *c* laryngitis
struts (strewts) *c* ostrich

*stryka (*strēw-kah*) *v* iron; ~ **under** underline
strykfri (*strēwk-fri*) *adj* drip-dry; wash and wear
strykjärn (*strēwk-ᵞærn*) *nt* iron
*strypa (*strēw-pah*) *v* strangle; choke
strålande (*strōā-lahn-der*) *adj* splendid, bright
stråle (strōāl-er) *c* ray, beam; spout, jet, squirt
strålkastare (*strōāl-kahss-tah-rer*) *c* (pl ~) searchlight; spotlight, headlamp, headlight
sträcka (*streh-kah*) *c* stretch
sträng (strehng) *adj* severe; strict, harsh; *c* string
sträv (straiv) *adj* harsh
sträva (straiv-ah) *v* aspire; ~ **efter** aim at
strö (strūr) *v* scatter, strew; sprinkle
ström (strurm) *c* (pl ~mar) stream, current
strömbrytare (*strurm-brēw-tah-rer*) *c* (pl ~) switch
strömdrag (*strurm-draag*) *nt* rapids *pl*
strömfördelare (*strurm-furr-dāyl-ah-rer*) *c* (pl ~) distributor
strömma (*strurm-ah*) *v* stream; flow
ströva (strūrv-ah) *v* roam
stubintråd (*stew-been-trōād*) *c* fuse
student (stew-*daynt*) *c* student

studera (stew-*dayr*-ah) v
study

studerande (stew-*dayr*-rahn-der) c (pl ~) student

studier (*stew*-dee-er) pl
studies pl

studium (*stew*-di-ewm) nt (pl -dier) study

stuga (*stew*-gah) c cottage

stuka (*stew*-kah) v sprain

stukning (*stewk*-ning) c
sprain

stum (stewm) adj dumb; mute

stund (stewnd) c while

stup (stewp) nt precipice

stycke (*stewk*-er) nt piece;
part, chunk

stygg (stewg) adj naughty;
bad

stygn (stewngn) nt stitch

styra (*stew*-rah) v manage;
rule; steer

styrbord (*stewr*-boord)
starboard

styrelse (*stew*-rayl-ser) c
government; direction,
management; commitee

styrelseordförande (stew-rayl-ser-oord-fur-rahn-der) c
(pl ~) chairman of the board

styrelsesätt (stew-rayl-ser-seht) n rule

styrka (stewr-kah) c strength,
power; **beväpnade styrkor**
armed forces

styvbarn (*stewv*-baarn) nt
stepchild

styvfar (*stewv*-faar) c (pl
-fäder) stepfather

styvmor (*stewv*-moor) c (pl

-mödrar) stepmother

*****stå** (stoa) v *stand; ~ **ut med**
endure

stål (stoal) nt steel; **rostfritt ~**
stainless steel

ståltråd (*stoal*-troad) c wire

stånd (stond) nt stand; stall;
***vara i ~ till** *be able to

ståndpunkt (*stond*-poongkt) c
standpoint

stång (stong) c (pl stänger)
bar; rod

ståtlig (*stoat*-li) adj
magnificent

städa (staid-ah) v clean; tidy
up

städad (stai-dahd) adj tidy

städerska (stai-derr-skah) c
cleaning-woman

ställa (steh-lah) v *put; ~ **in**
tune in; ~ **ut** exhibit

ställe (steh-ler) nt place; spot
i stället för (ee steh-lert furr)
instead of

ställföreträdare (stehl-fūr-rer-trai-dah-rer) c (pl ~)
substitute; deputy

ställning (*stehl*-ning) c
position

stämma överens (steh-mah
ūrver-rayns) agree, tally

stämning (*stehm*-ning) c
atmosphere

stämpel (*stehm*-perl) c (pl
-plar) stamp

ständig (*stehn*-di) adj
constant; permanent,
continual

stänga (*stehng*-ah) v *shut,
close; fasten; ~ **av** turn off;

*cut off; ~ **in** *shut in
stängd (stehngd) *adj* closed; shut
stängsel (stehng-serl) *nt* fence
stänka (stehng-kah) *v* splash
stärkelse (stær-kayl-ser) *c* starch
stöd (stürd) *nt* support
stödja (stürd-ʸah) *v* support
stödstrumpor (stürd-strewm-por) *pl* support hose
stöld (sturld) *c* theft; robbery
stöna (stūūn-ah) *v* groan
störa (stūū-rah) *v* disturb; bother
störning (stūūr-ning) *c* disturbance
större (sturr-er) *adj* major, superior, bigger
störst (sturrst) *adj* major, main, biggest
störta (sturr-tah) *v* crash
störtregn (sturrt-rehngn) *nt* downpour
störtskur (sturrt-skēwr) *c* shower
stöt (stürt) *c* bump, thrust
stöta (stūūt-ah) *v* bump; ~ **emot** knock against; ~ **på** *come across
stötdämpare (stūūrt-dehm-pah-rer) *c* (pl ~) shock absorber
stötta (stur-tah) *v* *hold up, prop
stövel (stur-verl) *c* (pl -vlar) boot
subjekt (sewb-ʸehkt) *nt* subject

substans (sewb-stahns) *c* substance
substantiv (sewb-stahn-teev) *nt* noun
subtil (sewb-teel) *adj* subtle
succé (sewk-sāy) *c* success
suddgummi (sewd-gew-mi) *nt* eraser, rubber
suga (sēw-gah) *v* suck
sula (sēw-lah) *c* sole
summa (sewm-ah) *c* sum; total, amount
sumpmark (sewmp-mahrk) *c* marsh
supa (sēw-pah) *v* booze
super (sēw-perr) *adj* super *colloquial*
superlativ (sew-perr-lah-teev) *adj* superlative; *c* superlative
sur (sēwr) *adj* sour
surfa (sewr-fah) *v* surf
surfingbräda (sewr-fing-brai-dah) *c* surfboard
surfplatta (sewrf-plaht-ah) *c* tablet
surr (sewrr) *nt* buzz
surrogat (sew-roo-gaat) *nt* substitute
suspendera (sewss-payn-dāyr-ah) *v* suspend
SUV (s-ew-ve) *c* SUV; sport utility vehicle
svag (svaag) *adj* weak; faint, slight, feeble
svaghet (svaag-hāyt) *c* weakness
svala (svaal-ah) *c* swallow
svalka (svahl-kah) *v* refresh

svamp (svahmp) *c*
mushroom; toadstool
svan (svaan) *c* swan
svans (svahns) *c* tail
svar (svaar) *nt* answer; reply
svara (svaa-rah) *v* answer;
reply
svart (svahrt) *adj* black
svartsjuk (svahrt-shēwk) *adj*
jealous
svartsjuka (svahrt-shēw-kah)
c jealousy
svensk (svaynsk) *adj*
Swedish; *c* Swede
svepa (svāy-pah in) *v*
envelop
svepskäl (svāyp-shail) *nt*
pretext
Sverige (svær-Yer) Sweden
svetsa (svayt-sah) *v* weld
svetsfog (svayts-fōōg) *c*
welding seam
svett (svayt) *c* sweat;
perspiration
svettas (svay-tahss) *v* sweat,
perspire
svettning (svayt-ning) *c*
perspiration
***svika** (svee-kah) *v* fail; betray
svimma (svi-mah) *v* faint
svindel (svin-derl) *c* swindle
svindla (svind-lah) *v* swindle
svindlare (svind-lah-rer) *c* (pl
~) swindler
svinläder (sveen-lai-derr) *nt*
pigskin
svit (sveet) *c* suite
svordom (svōōr-doom) *c*
curse
svullnad (svewl-nahd) *c*
swelling
svulst (svewlst) *c* tumour,
growth
svåger (svōa-gerr) *c* (pl -grar)
brother-in-law
svår (svōar) *adj* difficult, hard
svårighet (svōa-ri-hāyt) *c*
difficulty
svägerska (svai-gayr-skah) *c*
sister-in-law
***svälja** (svehl-Yah) *v* swallow
svälla (sveh-lah) *v* *swell
svälta (svehl-tah) *v* starve
svänga (svehng-ah) *v* turn;
*swing
svängdörr (svehng-durr) *c*
revolving door
***svära** (svææ-rah) *v* *swear,
curse; vow
svärd (svæærd) *nt* sword
svärdotter (svæær-do-terr)
(pl -döttrar) daughter-in-law
svärfar (svæær-faar) *c* (pl
-fäder) father-in-law
svärföräldrar (svæær-furr-
ehld-rahr) *pl* parents-in-law
pl
svärmor (svæær-mōōr) *c* (pl
-mödrar) mother-in-law
svärson (svæær-sōān) *c* (pl
-söner) son-in-law
sväva (svai-vah) *v* float in the
air
swahili (svah-hee-li) Swahili
sy (sēw) *v* *sew; ~ ihop *sew
up
Sydafrika (sēwd-aaf-ri-kah)
South Africa
sydlig (sēwd-li) *adj* southern;
southerly

sydost (sewd-*oost*) c
southeast

Sydpolen (sewd-poo-lern)
South Pole

sydväst (sewd-*vehst*) c
southwest

syfte (sewf-ter) nt aim;
purpose, object

sylt (sewlt) c jam

symaskin (sew-mah-*sheen*) c
sewing machine

symbol (sewm-*boal*) c
symbol

symfoni (sewm-fo-*nee*) c
symphony

sympati (sewm-pah-*tee*) c
sympathy

sympatisk (sewm-*paat*-isk)
adj nice

symptom (sewmp-*toam*) nt
symptom

syn (sewn) c eyesight; sight;
outlook

synagoga (sew-nah-*goo*-gah)
c synagogue

synas (*sew*-nahss) v seem;
appear; **det syns att** it is
obvious that

synbar (*sewn*-baar) adj
visible

synbarligen (sewn-baar-li-
ern) adv apparently

synd (sewnd) c sin; **så synd!**
what a pity!

syndabock (sewn-dah-bok) c
scapegoat

synhåll (*sewn*-hol) nt sight

synlig (*sewn*-li) adj visible

synnerligen (sew-nerr-li-ern)
adj extremely

synonym (sew-noo-*newm*) c
synonym

synpunkt (*sewn*-pewngkt) c
point of view

syntetisk (sewn-*tay*-tisk) adj
synthetic

syre (*sew*-rer) nt oxygen

Syrien (*sewr*-i-ern) Syria

syrier (*sewr*-i-err) c Syrian

syrisk (*sewr*-isk) adj Syrian

syrsa (*sewr*-sah) c cricket

*sysselsätta (sew-serl-seht-
ah) v occupy, employ; ~ **sig**
occupy oneself

sysselsättning (sew-sayl-
seht-ning) c occupation;
employment

syssla (*sewss*-lah) c work,
task

system (sewss-*taym*) nt
system

systematisk (sewss-tay-*maa*-
tisk) adj systematic

systembolag (sewss-*staym*-
boo-laag) nt off-licence,
liquor store nAm

syster (*sewss*-terr) c (pl -trar)
sister

systerdotter (sewss-terr-do-
terr) c (pl -döttrar) niece

systerson (sewss-terr-soan) c
(pl -söner) nephew

så¹ (soa) adv how, so, such;
conj so that, so; ~ **att** so that

så² (soa) v *sow

sådan (*soa*-dahn) adj such; ~
som such as

såg (soag) c saw

sågspån (*soag*-spoan) nt
sawdust

sågverk (sōag-værk) nt sawmill

således (sōa-lāy-dayss) adv thus

sålla (sol-ah) v sift

sång (song) c song

sångare (song-ah-rer) c (pl ~) singer; **sångerska** (song-err-skah) c singer

sår (sōar) nt wound; ulcer, sore

såra (sōar-ah) v injure, wound; offend, *hurt

sårbar (sōar-baar) adj vulnerable

sås (sōass) c sauce

såsom (sōa-som) conj like

såväl som (sōa-vail som) as well as

säck (sehk) c sack

säd (said) c corn

sädesfält (sai-derss-fehlt) nt cornfield

sädeskorn (sai-derss-kōorn) nt grain

*säga (seh-ᵞah) v *say; ~ hej till say hello to

säker (sai-kerr) adj sure; certain; safe, secure; **helt säkert** without fail

säkerhet (sai-kerr-hāyt) c safety, security; guarantee

säkerhetsbälte (sai-kerr-hāyts-behl-ter) nt safety belt; seat belt

säkerhetsnål (sai-kerr-hāyts-nōal) c safety pin

säkerligen (sai-kerr-li-ern) adv surely

säkert (sai-kerrt) adv certainly

sål (sail) c seal

*sälja (sehl-ᵞah) v *sell

säljbar (sehlʸ-baar) adj saleable

sällan (sehl-ahn) adv seldom, rarely

sällsam (sehl-sahm) adj strange, singular

sällskap (sehl-skaap) nt society; company, party

sällskaplig (sehl-skaap-li) adj sociable

sällskapsdjur (sehl-skaaps-ᵞewr) nt pet

sällskapsrum (sehl-skaaps-rewm) nt lounge

sällsynt (sehl-sēwnt) adj rare; uncommon, infrequent

sämre (sehm-rer) adj worse; inferior

sända (sehn-dah) v *send; transmit

sändare (sehn-dah-rer) c (pl ~) transmitter

sändning (sehnd-ning) c transmission

säng (sehng) c bed

sängkläder (sehng-klai-derr) pl bedding

sängöverkast (sehng-ūr-verr-kahst) nt bedspread

sänka (sehng-kah) v lower

säregen (sæær-āy-gern) adj peculiar; singular

särskild (sæær-shild) adj special; particular, separate; **särskilt** especially; in particular

säsong (seh-song) c season

säte (*sai*-ter) nt seat

sätt (seht) nt way; fashion, manner; by samma ~ alike

*sätta (*seht*-ah) v place; *set; *lay; ~ ihop assemble; ~ in bank; ~ på turn on; ~ sig *sit down; ~ upp *make up

säv (saiv) c rush

söder (*sur*-derr) c south

söka (*sur*-kah) v *seek; search

sökare (*sur*-kah-rer) c (pl ~) viewfinder

söm (surm) c (pl ~mar) seam

sömmerska (*surm*-err-skah) c seamstress; dressmaker

sömn (surmn) c sleep

sömnig (*surm*-ni) adj sleepy

sömnlös (*surm*-lürss) adj

sleepless

sömnlöshet (*surmn*-lürss-hȳt) c insomnia

sömntablett (*surmn*-tahb-*layt*) c sleeping pill

söndag (*surn*-daag) c Sunday

sönder (*surn*-derr) adj broken; *gå ~ *break down; *riva ~ rip

sörja (*surr*-ʸah) v grieve; ~ för see to

söt (sürt) adj sweet; nice, pretty, lovely

söta (*sür*-tah) v sweeten

sötsaker (*sürt*-saa-kerr) pl sweets

sötvatten (*sürt*-vah-tern) nt fresh water

T

tabell (tah-*bayl*) c table; chart

tablett (tahb-*layt*) c tablet

tabu (tah-*bēw*) nt taboo

tack! (tahk) thank you!

tacka (*tahk*-ah) v thank; *ha att ~ för owe

tacksam (*tahk*-sahm) adj grateful; thankful

tacksamhet (*tahk*-sahm-hȳt) c gratitude

tagg (tahg) c thorn

taggtråd (tahg-trōad) c barbed wire

tak (tak) nt roof

takräcke (*taak*-reh-ker) nt roof-rack

takt (tahkt) c tact; beat

taktik (tahk-*teek*) c tactics pl

tal (taal) nt speech; number

tala (*taa*-lah) v *speak; talk; ~ om talk about; *tell

talang (tah-*lahng*) c gift, talent; faculty

talarstol (*taa*-lahr-stōol) c pulpit; desk

talförmåga (*taal*-furr-*mōa*-gah) c speech

talk (tahlk) c talc powder

tall (tahl) c pine

tallrik (*tahl*-rik) c plate; dish

talong (tah-*long*) c counterfoil; stub

talrik (*taal*-reek) adj numerous

tam (taam) adj tame

tampong (tahm-*pong*) c

tampon

tand (tahnd) *c* (pl tänder)
tooth

tandborste (*tahnd*-bors-ter)
c toothbrush

tandfyllning (*tahnd*-fewl-
ning) *c* filling, inlay

tandkräm (*tahnd*-kraim) *c*
toothpaste

tandkött (*tahnd*-t^yurt) *nt* gum

tandläkare (*tahnd*-lai-kah-
rer) *c* (pl ~) dentist

tandpetare (*tahnd*-pāy-tah-
rer) *c* (pl ~) toothpick

tandprotes (*tahnd*-proo-
tāyss) *c* denture

tandställning (*tahnd*-stehl-
ning) *c* brace, braces

tandtråd (*tahnd*-trōad) *c*
dental floss

tandvärk (*tahnd*-værk) *c*
toothache

tank (tahngk) *c* tank

tanka (*tahng*-kah) *v* fill up

tanke (*tahng*-ker) *c* idea,
thought

tankfartyg (*tahngk*-faar-
tēwg) *nt* tanker

tankfull (*tahngk*-fewl) *adj*
thoughtful

tanklös (*tahngk*-lūrss) *adj*
scatterbrained

tankstreck (*tahngk*-strayk) *nt*
dash

tant (tahnt) *c* aunt

tapet (tah-*pāyt*) *c* wallpaper

tappa (*tahp*-ah) *v* drop

tapper (*tahp*-err) *adj*
courageous; brave

tapperhet (*tahp*-err-hāyt) *c*
courage

tariff (tah-*rif*) *c* tariff

tarm (tahrm) *c* intestine; gut;
   tarmar bowels *pl*

tass (tahss) *c* paw

tavla (*taav*-lah) *c* picture;
board

taxa (*tahk*-sah) *c* rate

taxameter (tahks-ah-*māy*-
terr) *c* (pl -trar) taximeter

taxi (*tahk*-si) *c* (pl ~) taxi; cab

taxichaufför (*tahk*-si-sho-
fūrr) *c* cab driver; taxi driver

taxistation (*tahks*-i-stah-
shōōn) *c* taxi rank; taxi stand
nAm

te (tāy) *nt* tea

teater (tay-*aa*-terr) *c* (pl -trar)
theatre

tecken (*tay*-kayn) *nt* sign,
indication; token; signal

teckna (*tayk*-nah) *v* sketch

teckning (*tayk*-ning) *c*
drawing; sketch

tefat (*tāy*-faat) *nt* saucer

tegelpanna (*tāy*-gerl-pah-
nah) *c* tile

tegelsten (*tāy*-gerl-stāyn) *c*
brick

tejp (tayp) *c* adhesive tape

tekanna (*tāy*-kah-nah) *c*
teapot

teknik (tayk-*neek*) *c*
technique

tekniker (*tayk*-ni-kerr) *c* (pl
~) technician

teknisk (*tayk*-nisk) *adj*
technical

teknisk support (*tayk*-nisk
sew-*poort*) *c* technical

support
teknologi (tayk-no-lo-*gee*) *c*
  technology
teknologisk (tayk-no-*lo*-
  gisk) *adj* technological
tekopp (*tay*-kop) *c* teacup
telefon (tay-lay-*foān*) *c*
  telephone; phone
telefonera (tay-lay-foo-*nāyr*-
  ah) *v* phone
telefonhytt (tay-lay-*foān*-
  hewt) *c* telephone booth
telefonkatalog (tay-lay-*foān*-
  kah-tah-*loāg*) *c* telephone
  directory; telephone book
  Am
telefonkort (tay-lay-*foān*-
  koort) *nt* (pl ~) phone card
telefonsamtal (tay-lay-*foān*-
  sahm-taal) *nt* telephone call
telefonsvarare (tay-lay-foan-
  svää-rah-rer) *c* answering
  machine
telefonväxel (tay-lay-*foān*-
  vehks-ayl) *c* (pl -xlar)
  telephone exchange,
  switchboard
telegrafera (tay-ler-grah-*fāy*-
  rah) *v* telegraph; cable
telegram (tay-ler-*grahm*) *nt*
  telegram; cable
telekommunikation (*tay*-lay-
  ko-mew-ni-kah-*shoān*) *c*
  telecommunications
teleobjektiv (*tay*-ler-ob-ᵞayk-
  teev) *nt* telephoto lens
telepati (tay-ler-pah-*tee*) *c*
  telepathy
television (tay-ler-vi-*shoān*)
  c television; **kabel ~** *c* cable

TV; **satellit ~** *c* satellite TV
televisionsapparat (tay-ler-
  vi-*shoāns*-ah-pah-*raat*) *c*
  television set
telex (*tay*-layks) *nt* telex
tema (*tay*-mah) *nt* theme
tempel (*taym*-payl) *nt* temple
temperatur (taym-per-rah-
  tewr) *c* temperature
tempo (*taym*-poo) *nt* pace
tendens (tayn-*dayns*) *c*
  tendency
tendera (tayn-*dāyr*-ah) *v*
  tend; **~ åt** tend to
tenn (tayn) *nt* tin; pewter
tennis (*tayn*-iss) *c* tennis
tennisbana (*tayn*-iss-baa-
  nah) *c* tennis court
tennisskor (*tayn*-iss-skoōr)
  pl tennis shoes
teologi (tay-o-lo-*gee*) *c*
  theology
teoretisk (tay-o-*rāyt*-isk) *adj*
  theoretical
teori (tay-o-*ree*) *c* theory
terapi (tay-rah-*pee*) *c* therapy
term (tærm) *c* term
termin (tær-*meen*) *c* term
termometer (tær-moo-*māy*-
  terr) *c* (pl -trar)
  thermometer
termosflaska (tær-mooss-
  flahss-kah) *c* vacuum flask
termostat (tær-moo-*staat*) *c*
  thermostat
terpentin (tær-payn-*teen*) *nt*
  turpentine
terrass (tay-*rahss*) *c* terrace
territorium (tær-i-*toō*-ri-
  ewm) *nt* (pl -rier) territory

179   tilldela

terror (*teh*-ror) c terrorism
terrorism (teh-ro-*rism*) c
  terrorism
terrorist (teh-ro-*rist*) c
  terrorist
terräng (tær-*ehng*) c terrain
tes (tayss) c thesis
tesalong (*tay*-sah-*loang*) c
  tea-shop
teservis (*tay*-sær-*veess*) c tea
  set
tesked (*tay*-shayd) c
  teaspoon; teaspoonful
testa (*tayss*-tah) v test
testamente (tayss-tah-*mayn*-
  tay) nt will
text (*tehkst*) c text
textilier (tehk-*stee*-li-ayr) pl
  textiles pl
Thailand (*tigh*-lahnd)
  Thailand
thailändare (*tigh*-lehn-dah-
  rer) c (pl ~) Thai
thailändsk (*tigh*-lehndsk) adj
  Thai
tid (teed) c time; **hela tiden**
  all the time; **i ~** in time; **på
  sista tiden** lately
tidig (*tee*-di) adj early
tidigare (*tee*-di-gah-rer) adj
  previous
tidning (*teed*-ning) c paper
tidningsbilaga (*teed*-nings-
  bi-*laa*-gah) c supplement
tidningsförsäljare (*teed*-
  nings-furr-*sehl*-Yah-rer) c (pl
  ~) newsagent
tidningskiosk (*teed*-nings-
  t³osk) c newsstand
tidningspress (*teed*-nings-

  prayss) c press
tidsbesparande (*teeds*-ber-
  spaa-rahn-der) adj time-
  -saving
tidskrift (*teed*-skrift) c
  periodical; magazine,
  review, journal
tidsschema (*teeds*-shay-
  mah) nt schedule
tidtabell (*teed*-tah-*bayl*) c
  schedule, timetable
tidvatten (*teed*-vah-tern) nt
  tide
***tiga** (*teeg*-ah) v *be silent;
  *keep quiet
tiger (*teeg*-err) c (pl tigrar)
  tiger
tigga (*tig*-ah) v beg
tiggare (*ti*-gah-rer) c (pl ~)
  beggar
tik (teek) c bitch
till (til) prep to; for, until, till;
  en ~ another; **~ och med**
  even
tillaga (*til*-laag-ah) v cook
tillbaka (til-*baa*-kah) adv
  back; ***gå ~** *go back
tillbakagång (til-*baa*-kah-
  gong) c recession; decline
tillbakaväg (til-*baa*-kah-
  vaig) c way back
tillbehör (*til*-bay-*hūrr*) nt
  accessory
tillbringa (*til*-bring-ah) v
  *spend
tillbringare (*til*-bring-ah-rer)
  c (pl ~) jug
tillbörlig (*til*-būrr-li) adj
  proper
tilldela (*til*-dāyl-ah) v assign

to, award
tilldragande (*til*-draag-ahn-der) *adj* attractive
tilldragelse (*til*-draag-ayl-ser) *c* event, occurrence
*****tilldra sig** (til-*draa*) happen, occur; attract
tillfredsställa (*til*-fray-*stehl*-ah) *v* satisfy
tillfredsställd (*til*-fray-*stehld*) *adj* satisfied
tillfredsställande (*til*-frayds-*stehl*-ahn-der) *adj* satisfactory
tillfredsställelse (*til*-fray-*stehl*-ayl-ser) *c* satisfaction
tillfriskna (*til*-frisk-nah) *v* recover
tillfrisknande (*til*-frisk-nahn-der) *nt* recovery
*****tillfångata** (til-*fo*-ngah-taa) *v* capture
tillfångatagande (til-*fong*-ah-taag-ahn-der) *nt* capture
tillfälle (*til*-fehl-er) *nt* opportunity; occasion
tillfällig (*til*-feh-li) *adj* temporary; incidental, momentary
tillfällighet (*til*-feh-li-hāyt) *c* coincidence, chance
tillgiven (*til*-ᵞeev-ern) *adj* affectionate
tillgivenhet (*til*-ᵞeev-ern-hāyt) *c* affection
tillgjord (*til*-ᵞōōrd) *adj* affected
tillgång (*til*-gong) *c* asset; access
tillgänglig (*til*-ᵞehng-li) *adj*

accessible; available
tillhöra (*til*-hūr-rah) *v* belong to, belong
tillhörigheter (*til*-hūr-ri-hāy-terr) *pl* belongings *pl*
tillit (*til*-leet) *c* faith
tillitsfull (*til*-leets-fewl) *adj* confident
*****tillkännage** (*til*-tᵞeh-nah-ᵞay) *v* announce
tillkännagivande (*til*-tᵞehn-ah-ᵞeev-ahn-der) *nt* announcement
tillmötesgående (*til*-mūr-terss-gōa-ayn-der) *adj* obliging
tillråda (*til*-rōā-dah) *v* recommend
tillräcklig (*til*-rehk-li) *adj* sufficient; adequate, enough
tillrättavisa (til-*reht*-ah-veess-ah) *v* reprimand
tills (tils) *prep* till; until
tillsammans (til-*sah*-mahns) *adv* together
tillstånd (*til*-stond) *nt* permission, permit; condition, state
tillståndsbevis (*til*-stonds-ber-*veess*) *nt* licence, permit, permission
*****tillta** (*til*-taa) *v* increase
tilltagande (*til*-taa-gahn-der) *adj* increasing, progressive
tillträde (*til*-trai-der) *nt* entrance; access, admittance, entry; ~ **förbjudet** no entry, no admittance
tillvaro (*til*-vaa-roo) *c*

existence
tillverka (*til*-vær-kah) *v*
manufacture
*gå tillväga (gōā til-*vai*-gah)
proceed
tillvägagångssätt (til-*vai*-gah-gongs-seht) *nt*
procedure
*tillåta (*til*-lōā-tah) *v* allow;
permit; ***vara tillåten** *be
allowed
tillåtelse (*til*-lōāt-ayl-ser) *c*
authorization; permission
tillägg (*til*-lehg) *nt* addition;
surcharge
*tillägga (*til*-leh-gah) *v* add
tillämpa (*til*-lehm-pah) *v*
apply
timjan (*tim*-ᵞahn) *c* thyme
timme (*tim*-er) *c* hour; **varje ~**
hourly
timmer (*tim*-err) *nt* timber
tinning (*tin*-ing) *c* temple
tio (*tee*-oo) *num* ten
tionde (*tee*-on-der) *num*
tenth
tisdag (*teess*-daag) *c* Tuesday
tistel (*tiss*-terl) *c* (pl -tlar)
thistle
titel (*ti*-tayl) *c* (pl titlar) title
titt (tit) *c* look, glance
titta (*tit*-ah) *v* look; **~ på** look
at
tjata (*tᵞaa*-tah) *v* nag
Tjeckiska republiken (tᵞehk-kis-kah rer-pew-*blee*-kayn) *c*
Czech Republic
tjock (tᵞok) *adj* fat, big;
corpulent, thick, stout;
*göra ~ thicken

tjocklek (*tᵞok*-layk) *c*
thickness
tjockna (*tᵞok*-nah) *v* thicken;
swell; become wider
tjugo (*tᵞew*-goo) *num* twenty
tjugonde (*tᵞew*-gon-der)
num twentieth
tjur (tᵞewr) *c* bull
tjurfäktning (*tᵞewr*-fehkt-ning) *c* bullfight
tjurfäktningsarena (tᵞewr-fehkt-nings-ah-*rāy*-nah) *c*
bullring
tjurskallig (tᵞewr-skahl-i) *adj*
pig-headed
tjusa (*tᵞew*-sah) *v* charm,
captivate, delight
tjusig (tᵞew-si) *adj* charming
tjusning (tᵞewss-ning) *c*
charm
tjut (tᵞewt) *nt* yell
*tjuta (*tᵞewt*-ah) *v* yell;
scream; roar
tjuv (tᵞewv) *c* thief
tjuvlyssna (tᵞewv-lewss-nah)
v eavesdrop
*tjuvskjuta (tᵞewv-shewt-ah)
v poach
tjäder (*tᵞai*-derr) *c* (pl -drar)
capercailzie
tjäna (tᵞai-nah) *v* earn;
*make; **~ till** *be of use
tjänare (tᵞain-ah-rer) *c* (pl ~)
domestic; boy
tjänst (tᵞehnst) *c* service,
favour; post
tjära (tᵞær-ah) *c* tar
tjärn (tᵞæærn) *nt* tarn
toalett (too-ah-*layt*) *c* toilet,
bathroom, lavatory;

washroom *nAm*
toalettartiklar (too-ah-*layt*-ahr-tik-lahr) *pl* toiletry
toalettbord (too-ah-*layt*-boord) *nt* dressing table
toalettpapper (too-ah-*layt*-pahp-err) *nt* toilet paper
tobak (*too*-bahk) *c* tobacco
tobaksaffär (*too*-bahks-ah-*fæær*) *c* tobacconist's
tobakshandlare (*too*-bahks-hahnd-lah-rer) *c* (pl ~) tobacconist
tobakspung (*too*-bahks-pewng) *c* tobacco pouch
toffel (*to*-fayl) *c* (pl -flor) slipper
tofsvipa (*tofs*-veep-ah) *c* pewit
tokig (*tōō*-ki) *adj* mad; crazy
tolfte (*tolf*-ter) *num* twelfth
tolk (tolk) *c* interpreter
tolka (*tol*-kah) *v* interpret
tolv (tolv) *num* twelve
tom (toom) *adj* empty
tomat (too-*maat*) *c* tomato
tomt (tomt) *c* site
ton[1] (tōōn) *c* tone, note
ton[2] (ton) *nt* ton
tonfisk (*tōōn*-fisk) *c* tuna
tonskala (*tōōn*-skaa-lah) *c* scale
tonvikt (*tōōn*-vikt) *c* accent
tonåring (*ton*-ōā-ring) *c* teenager
topp (top) *c* top, peak; summit
topplock (*top*-lok) *nt* cylinder head
torg (tor[y]) *nt* marketplace;

square
torka (*tor*-kah) *v* dry; drought; ~ **av** wipe; ~ **bort** wipe
torktumlare (*tork*-tewm-lah-rer) *c* dryer
torn (tōōrn) *nt* tower
torr (tor) *adj* dry
***torrlägga** (*tor*-leh-gah) *v* drain
torsdag (*toors*-daag) *c* Thursday
torsk (torsk) *c* cod
tortera (tor-*tāÿr*-ah) *v* torture
tortyr (tor-*tēwr*) *c* torture
total (too-*taal*) *adj* total; utter; **totalt** completely
totalitär (to-tah-li-*tæær*) *adj* totalitarian
tradition (trah-di-*shōōn*) *c* tradition
traditionell (trah-di-shoo-*nayl*) *adj* traditional
trafik (trah-*feek*) *c* traffic; **enkelriktad** ~ one-way traffic
trafikljus (trah-*feek*-[y]ēwss) *nt* traffic light
trafikolycka (trah-*feek*-ōō-lew-kah) *c* traffic accident
trafikomläggning (trah-*feek*-om-lehg-ning) *c* diversion
trafikstockning (trah-*feek*-stok-ning) *c* traffic jam; jam
tragedi (trah-shay-*dee*) *c* tragedy
tragisk (*traa*-gisk) *adj* tragic
trakt (trahkt) *c* area
traktat (trahk-*taat*) *c* treaty
traktor (*trahk*-tor) *c* tractor

trampa (*trahm*-pah) *v* tread, tramp

trams (trahms) *nt* rubbish

transaktion (trahns-ahk-*shoon*) *c* transaction

transatlantisk (trahns-aht-*lahn*-tisk) *adj* transatlantic

transformator (trahns-for-*maa*-tor) *c* transformer

transpiration (trahn-spi-rah-*shoon*) *c* perspiration

transpirera (trahn-spi-*rāyr*-ah) *v* perspire

transport (trahns-*port*) *c* transportation; transport

transportbil (trahns-*port*-beel) *c* van

transportera (trahns-por-*tāy*-rah) *v* transport

trappa (*trah*-pah) *c* stairs *pl*; staircase

trasa (*traass*-ah) *c* rag; cloth

trasig (*traass*-i) *adj* broken

trast (trahst) *c* thrush

tratt (traht) *c* funnel

tre (trāy) *num* three

tredje (*trāyd*-ʸay) *num* third

trekantig (*trāy*-kahn-ti) *adj* triangular

trendig (*trayn*-day) *adj* trendy *colloquial*

trettio (*tray*-ti) *num* thirty

tretton (*tray*-ton) *num* thirteen

trettonde (*tray*-ton-der) *num* thirteenth

trevlig (*trāyv*-li) *adj* enjoyable, pleasant, nice

triangel (tri-*ahng*-erl) *c* (pl -glar) triangle

trick (trik) *nt* trick

trimma (*trim*-ah) *v* trim

tripp (trip) *c* trip

triumf (tri-*ewmf*) *c* triumph

triumfera (tri-ewm-*fāyr*-ah) *v* triumph

trivsam (*treev*-sahm) *adj* pleasant, comfortable, cosy

tro (trōō) *c* belief, faith; *v* believe

trofast (*trōō*-fahst) *adj* true

trogen (*trōō*-gern) *adj* faithful; true

trolig (*trōō*-li) *adj* presumable, probable

trolleri (tro-ler-*ree*) *nt* magic

trollkarl (*trol*-kaar) *c* magician

trollkonst (*trol*-konst) *c* magic

tron (trōōn) *c* throne

tropikerna (tro-*pee*-kerr-nah) *pl* tropics *pl*

tropisk (*trōa*-pisk) *adj* tropical

trosor (*trōō*-sor) *pl* panties *pl*; briefs *pl*

trots (trots) *prep* in spite of; despite

trottoar (troo-too-*aar*) *c* pavement; sidewalk *nAm*

trottoarkant (troo-too-*aar*-kahnt) *c* curb

trovärdig (*trōō*-væær-di) *adj* credible

trubbig (*trewb*-i) *adj* blunt

trumhinna (*trewm*-hin-ah) *c* eardrum

trumma (*trewm*-ah) *c* drum

trumpet (trewm-*pāyt*) *c*

trumpet

trupper (*trew*-perr) *pl* troops *pl*

tryck (trewk) *nt* pressure; print

trycka (*trewk*-ah) *v* press; print

tryckknapp (*trewk*-knahp) *c* pressstud; push button

tryckkokare (*trewk*-kōō-kah-rer) *c* (pl ~) pressure cooker

trycksak (*trewk*-saak) *c* printed matter

tråd (trōād) *c* thread

trådlös (trōād-*lürss*) *adj* wireless

trådsliten (trōād-slee-tern) *adj* threadbare

tråka ut (*trōā*-kah) bore

tråkig (*trōā*-ki) *adj* dull; boring

tråkmåns (*trōā*-mons) *c* bore

trång (trong) *adj* narrow; tight

trä (trai) *nt* wood; **trä-** wooden

trä upp (trai) thread

träd (traid) *nt* tree

trädgård (*treh*-gōārd) *c* garden

trädgårdsmästare (*treh*-gōārds-mehss-tah-rer) *c* (pl ~) gardener

trädgårdsodling (*treh*-gōārds-ōōd-ling) *c* horticulture

träff (trehf) *c* hit; date; get-together

träffa (*trehf*-ah) *v* encounter, *meet; *hit

träkol (*trai*-kōāl) *nt* charcoal

träna (*train*-ah) *v* train; drill

tränare (*trai*-nah-rer) *c* (pl ~) coach

tränga sig fram (*trehng*-ah) push one's way

trängande (*trehng*-ahn-der) *adj* pressing

träning (*trai*-ning) *c* training

träsk (trehsk) *nt* swamp; bog

träsko (treh-*skōō*) *c* clog, wooden shoe

trög (trürg) *adj* sluggish; inert

trögtänkt (*trürg*-tehngkt) *adj* slow

tröja (*trur*-ˢah) *c* sweater

tröskel (*trürss*-kayl) *c* (pl -klar) threshold

tröst (trurst) *c* comfort

trösta (*trurss*-tah) *v* comfort

tröstpris (*trurst*-preess) *nt* (pl ~, ~er) consolation prize

trött (trurt) *adj* tired; weary; ~ på tired of

trötta (*trurt*-ah) *v* tire

tröttsam (*trurt*-sahm) *adj* tiring

tub (tewb) *c* tube

tuberkulos (tew-behr-kew-*lōāss*) *c* tuberculosis

tugga (*tewg*-ah) *v* chew

tuggummi (*tewg*-gew-mi) *nt* chewinggum

tull (tewl) *c* Customs duty; Customs *pl*

tullavgift (*tewl*-aav-ˢift) *c* Customs duty; duty

tullfri (*tewl*-free) *adj* duty-free

tulltjänsteman (*tewl*-tˢehns-ter-mahn) *c* (pl -män)

Customs officer

tulpan (*tewl-paan*) *c* tulip

tum (tewn) *c* (pl ~) inch

tumme (*tewm*-er) *c* thumb

tumvantar (*tewm*-vahn-tahr) *pl* mittens *pl*

tumör (*tew-mūrr*) *c* tumour

tung (tewng) *adj* heavy

tunga (*tewng*-ah) *c* tongue

tunika (*tēw*-ni-kah) *c* tunic

Tunisien (tew-*nee*-si-ern) Tunisia

tunisier (tew-*nee*-si-err) *c* (pl ~) Tunisian

tunisisk (tew-*nee*-sisk) *adj* Tunisian

tunn (tewn) *adj* thin; weak, light

tunna (*tewn*-ah) *c* barrel; cask

tunnel (*tew*-nayl) *c* (pl -nlar) tunnel

tunnelbana (*tew*-nayl-baa-nah) *c* underground; subway *nAm*

tupp (tewp) *c* cock

tupplur (*tewp*-lēwr) *c* nap

tur (tēwr) *c* luck; turn; **~ och retur** round trip *Am*

turbin (tewr-*been*) *c* turbine

turbojet (*tewr*-bo-ʾeht) *c* turbojet

turism (tēw-*rism*) *c* tourism

turist (tēw-*rist*) *c* tourist

turistbyrå (tēw-*rist-bēw-rōa*) *c* tourist office

turistklass (tēw-*rist*-klahss) *c* tourist class

turistsäng (tēw-*rist*-sehng) *c* folding bed, cot *nAm*

Turkiet (tewr-*kee*-ayt) Turkey

turkisk (tewr-kisk) *adj* Turkish; **turkiskt bad** Turkish bath

turnering (tewr-*nāyr*-ing) *c* tournament

tusen (*tēw*-sern) *num* thousand

tuta (*tew*-tah) *v* hoot; honk *vAm*, toot *vAm*

tv (te-ve) *c* telly *colloquial*; television *nAm*

tveka (*tvāy*-kah) *v* hesitate

tvekan (*tvāy*-kahn) *c* hesitation

tvetydig (tvāy-tēwd-i) *adj* ambiguous

tvillingar (*tvi*-ling-ahr) *pl* twins *pl*

tvinga (*tving*-ah) *v* force; compel

tvist (tvist) *c* dispute

tvista (*tviss*-tah) *v* dispute

tvisteämne (*tviss*-ter-ehm-ner) *nt* controversial issue

tvivel (*tveev*-erl) *nt* doubt

tvivelaktig (*tvee*-verl-*ahk*-ti) *adj* doubtful

tvivla (*tveev*-lah) *v* doubt

två (tvōa) *num* two

tvådelad (*tvōa*-dāy-lahd) *adj* two-piece

tvål (tvōal) *c* soap

tvåltvättmedel (*tvōal*-tveht-māy-dayl) *nt* soap powder

tvång (tvong) *nt* compulsion; **med ~** by force; **ʾvara tvungen att** *be obliged to

tvåspråkig (*tvōa*-sprōak-i) *adj* bilingual

tvärtom (*tvært*-om) *adv* the

tvätt

contrary

tvätt (tveht) c laundry;
washing

tvätta (tveht-ah) v wash

tvättbar (tveht-baar) adj
washable

tvättinrättning (tveht-in-reht-
ning) c laundry

tvättmaskin (tveht-mah-
sheen) c washing machine

tvättmedel (tveht-māy-dayl)
nt washing powder

tvättomat (tveh-too-maat) c
launderette

tvättsvamp (tveht-svahmp) c
sponge

tvättäkta (tveht-ehk-tah) adj
washable, fast-dyed

tycka (tewk-ah) v think; **inte
~ om** dislike; **~ illa om**
dislike; **~ om** like; fancy, *be
fond of

tyckas (tewk-ahss) v look;
appear

tyda (tēw-dah) v decipher

tydlig (tēwd-li) adj clear;
obvious, evident, apparent,
distinct

tyfus (tēw-fewss) c typhoid

tyg (tēwg) nt cloth; fabric,
material

tygla (tēwg-lah) v curb;
restrain

tynga (tewng-ah) v oppress

tyngdkraft (tewngd-krahft) c
gravity

typ (tēwp) c type

typisk (tēw-pisk) adj typical

tyrann (tew-rahn) c tyrant

tysk (tewsk) adj German; c
German

Tyskland (tewsk-lahnd)
Germany

tyst (tewst) adj silent

tysta (tewss-tah) v silence

tystnad (tewst-nahd) c silence

tyvärr (tew-vær) adv
unfortunately

tå (tōa) c toe

tåg (tōag) nt train

tågfärja (tōag-fær-³ah) c train
ferry

tåla (tōal-ah) v *bear

tålamod (tōal-ah-mōōd) nt
patience

tålmodig (tōal-mōōd-i) adj
patient

tång (tong) c (pl tänger) tongs
pl; pliers pl

tår (tōar) c tear

tårta (tōar-tah) c cake

täcka (tehk-ah) v cover

täcke (tehk-er) nt quilt

tält (tehlt) nt tent

tältsäng (tehlt-sehng) c camp
bed

tämja (tehm-³ah) v tame

tämligen (tehm-li-ern) adv
fairly, rather, pretty

tända (tehn-dah) v *light;
turn on

tändare (tehn-dah-rer) c (pl
~) lighter

tändning (tehnd-ning) c
ignition; lighting

tändspole (tehnd-spōōl-er) c
ignition coil

tändsticka (tehnd-sti-kah) c
match

tändsticksask (*tehnd*-stiks-ahsk) *c* matchbox

tändstift (*tehnd*-stift) *nt* sparking plug

tänja (*tehn*-¹ah) *v* stretch

tänjbar (*tehn*ʸ-baar) *adj* elastic

tänka (*tehng*-kah) *v* *think; ~ **på** *think of; ~ **sig** imagine; fancy; ~ **ut** conceive

tärning (*tær*-ning) *c* dice *pl*; cube; **spela** ~ play dice

tät (tait) *adj* dense; thick

tätort (*tait*-oort) *c* built-up area

tävla (*taiv*-lah) *v* compete

tävlan (*taiv*-lahn) *c* (pl -lingar) competition

tävling (*taiv*-ling) *c* competition; contest

tävlingsbana (*taiv*-lings-baa-nah) *c* racetrack

töa (*tūr*-ah) *v* thaw

tölp (turlp) *c* lout, bastard

tömma (*tur*-mah) *v* empty

törst (turrst) *c* thirst

törstig (*turrs*-ti) *adj* thirsty

töväder (*tūr*-vai-derr) *nt* thaw

U

udda (*ewd*-ah) *adj* odd

udde (*ewd*-er) *c* cape

uggla (*ewg*-lah) *c* owl

ugn (ewngn) *c* stove; furnace, oven; **mikrovågs** ~ *c* microwave oven

ull (ewl) *c* wool

ultraviolett (*ewlt*-rah-vi-oo-*layt*) *adj* ultraviolet

*umgås med (*ewm*-gōāss) mix with;

undanröjning (*ewn*-dahn-rur ʸ-ning) *c* removal

undantag (*ewn*-dahn-taag) *nt* exception; **med** ~ **av** except

under¹ (*ewn*-derr) *prep* under; beneath, below; during; **av** underneath; ~ **tiden** meanwhile; in the meantime

under² (*ewn*-derr) *nt* wonder; marvel

underbar (*ewn*-derr-baar) *adj* wonderful; marvellous

underbyxor (*ewn*-derr-bewks-err) *pl* pants *pl*

underdrift (*ewn*-derr-*dreef*) *c* understatement

undergång (*ewn*-derr-*gong*) *c* ruin; destruction

underhåll (*ewn*-derr-*hol*) *nt* allowance; maintenance, upkeep

*underhålla (*ewn*-derr-*hol*-ah) *v* entertain; amuse

underhållande (*ewn*-derr-*hol*-ahn-der) *adj* entertaining

underhållning (*ewn*-derr-*hol*-ning) *c* entertainment

underjordisk (*ewn*-derr-ʸoor-disk) *adj* underground

underkasta sig (*ewn*-derr-*kahss*-tah) submit

underkläder (ewn-derr-klai-derr) pl underwear

underklänning (ewn-derr-kleh-ning) c slip

underkuva (ewn-derr-kēw-vah) v subdue, subjugate

underlagskräm (ewn-derr-laags-kraim) c foundation cream

underlig (ewn-derr-li) adj queer, odd

underlägsen (ewn-derr-laig-sern) adj inferior

undernäring (ewn-derr-næær-ing) c malnutrition

underordnad (ewn-derr-awrd-nahd) adj subordinate; minor

underrätta (ewn-derr-reht-ah) v inform; notify; ~ **sig** enquire

underrättelse (ewn-derr-reht-erl-ser) c notice, information, news

underskatta (ewn-derr-skah-tah) v underestimate

underskott (ewn-derr-skot) nt deficit

underström (ewn-derr-sturm) c (pl ~mar) undercurrent

understöd (ewn-derr-stürd) nt subsidy; assistance

understödja (ewn-derr-stürd-ʸah) v support

undersåte (ewn-derr-soã-ter) c subject

undersöka (ewn-derr-sür-kah) v examine; enquire

undersökning (ewn-derr-sūrk-ning) c inquiry; enquiry, examination; checkup

underteckna (ewn-derr-tayk-nah) v sign

undertitel (ewn-derr-ti-terl) c (pl -tlar) subtitle

undertrycka (ewn-derr-trewk-ah) v suppress

undertröja (ewn-derr-trur-ʸah) c vest; undershirt

undervattens- (ewn-derr-vah-tayns) underwater

undervisa (ewn-derr-vee-sah) v *teach

undervisning (ewn-derr-veess-ning) c instruction; tuition

***undgå** (ewnd-gōã) v avoid; escape

undra (ewnd-rah) v wonder

***undslippa** (ewnd-slip-ah) v escape

***undvika** (ewnd-veek-ah) v avoid

ung (ewng) adj young

ungdom (ewng-doom) c youth

ungdomlig (ewng-doom-li) adj juvenile

ungdomshärbärge (ewng-dooms-hæær-bær-ʸer) nt youth hostel

unge (ewng-er) c kid

ungefär (ewn-ʸay-fæær) adv about; approximately

ungefärlig (ewn-ʸay-fæær-li) adj approximate

Ungern (ewng-errn) Hungary

ungersk (ewng-ayrsk) adj

Hungarian
ungkarl (*ewng*-kaar) *c*
bachelor
ungrare (*ewng*-rah-rer) *c* (pl
~) Hungarian
uniform (ēw-ni-*form*) *c*
uniform
unik (ēw-*neek*) *adj* unique
union (ēw-ni-*ōōn*) *c* union
universell (ēw-ni-vær-*sayl*)
adj universal
universitet (ēw-ni-vær-si-
tāyt) *nt* university
universum (ēw-ni-*vær*-sewm)
nt universe
uns (ewns) *nt* ounce
upp (ewp) *adv* up; upwards;
upstairs; ~ **och ner** upside
down; up and down
uppassa (*ewp*-pah-sah) *v*
attend on, wait on
uppblomstring (*ewp*-blomst-
ring) *c* prosperity
uppblåsbar (*ewp*-blōass-
baar) *adj* inflatable
uppbygga (*ewp*-bewg-ah) *v*
erect; edify
uppdikta (*ewp*-dik-tah) *v*
invent
uppdrag (*ewp*-draag) *nt*
assignment
uppehåll (*ew*-pay-hol) *nt*
pause; **utan ~** without
stopping
uppehålla sig (*ew*-pay-hol-
ah) stay
uppehållstillstånd (*ew*-pay-
hols-til-stond) *nt* residence
permit
uppehälle (*ew*-per-hehl-er) *nt*

livelihood
uppenbar (*ewp*-ern-baar) *adj*
apparent
uppenbara (*ewp*-ern-baar-
ah) *v* reveal
uppfatta (*ewp*-faht-ah) *v*
apprehend, *catch
uppfattning (*ewp*-faht-ning)
c view, opinion; conception
*****uppfinna** (*ewp*-fin-ah) *v*
invent
uppfinnare (*ewp*-fi-nah-rer) *c*
(pl ~) inventor
uppfinning (*ewp*-fi-ning) *c*
invention
uppfinningsrik (*ewp*-fi-
nings-reek) *adj* inventive
uppfostra (*ewp*-foost-rah) *v*
*bring up; rear, educate;
raise
uppfostran (*ewp*-foost-rahn)
c education
uppfriskande (*ewp*-friss-
kahn-der) *adj* refreshing
uppföda (*ewp*-fūrd-ah) *v*
*breed; raise
uppför (*ewp*-fūrr) *adv* uphill
uppföra (*ewp*-fūrr-ah) *v*
construct; **~ sig** behave; act
uppförande (*ewp*-fūr-rahn-
day) *nt* behaviour; manners
pl, conduct; production;
construction
*****uppge** (*ewp*-ʸ*ay*) *v* state;
declare
uppgift (*ewp*-ʸ*ift*) *c* task;
information
*****uppgå till** (*ewp*-gōa) amount
to
uppgörelse (*ewp*-ʸ*ūr*-rayl-

ser) *c* settlement

upphetsa (*ewp*-hayt-sah) *v* excite

upphetsad (*ewp*-hayt-sahd) *adj* excited

upphängningsanordning (*ewp*-hehng-nings-ahn-*oard*-ning) *nt* suspension

upphäva (*ewp*-haiv-ah) *v* nullify; annul

upphöjning (*ewp*-hur^y-ning) *c* rise

upphöra (*ewp*-hūr-rah) *v* cease, stop; quit

uppkalla (*ewp*-kah-lah) *v* name

uppköp (*ewp*-t^{y}urp) *nt* purchase

upplaga (*ewp*-laa-gah) *c* edition; issue

uppleva (*ewp*-lāy-vah) *v* experience

upplevelse (*ewp*-lāy-vayl-say) *c* experience

upplopp (*ewp*-lop) *nt* riot

upplysa (*ewp*-lēwss-ah) *v* inform

upplysning (*ewp*-lēwss-ning) *c* information

upplysningsbyrå (*ewp*-lēwss-nings-*bēw*-roā) *c* information bureau; inquiry office

upplösa (*ewp*-lūrss-ah) *v* dissolve; ~ **sig** dissolve

uppmana (*ewp*-maan-ah) *v* exhort, urge

uppmuntra (*ewp*-mewn-trah) *v* encourage

uppmärksam (*ewp*-mærk-

sahm) *adj* attentive

uppmärksamhet (*ewp*-mærk-sahm-hāyt) *c* notice, attention

uppmärksamma (*ewp*-mærk-sahm-ah) *v* attend to, notice, *pay attention to

uppnå (*ewp*-noā) *v* achieve; attain

uppnåelig (*ewp*-noā-er-li) *adj* attainable

upprepa (*ewp*-rāy-pah) *v* repeat

upprepning (*ewp*-rāyp-ning) *c* repetition

uppriktig (*ewp*-rik-ti) *adj* sincere; honest

uppriktigt (*ewp*-rik-tit) *adv* sincerely

uppror (*ewp*-roōr) *nt* rebellion; rising; *göra ~ revolt

upprätt (*ewp*-reht) *adv* upright; *adj* erect, upright

upprätta (*ewp*-reh-tah) *v* found, establish

upprätthålla (*ewp*-reht-ho-lah) *v* maintain

upprättstående (*ewp*-reht-stoā-ayn-der) *adj* upright, erect

upprörande (*ewp*-rūr-rahn-der) *adj* shocking, revolting

upprörd (*ewp*-rūrrd) *adj* upset

uppsats (*ewp*-sahts) *c* essay, paper

uppseendeväckande (*ewp*-sāy-ern-der-*vehk*-ahn-der) *adj* sensational

uppsikt (*ewp*-sikt) *c*
supervision

uppskatta (*ewp*-skah-tah) *v*
appreciate; esteem

uppskattning (*ewp*-skaht-ning) *c* appreciation

***uppskjuta** (*ewp*-shew-tah) *v*
*put off; delay, postpone

uppskov (*ewp*-skōōv) *nt*
delay; respite

uppslagsbok (*ewp*-slaags-bōōk) *c* (pl -böcker)
encyclopaedia

uppstigning (*ewp*-steeg-ning) *c* rise, ascent

***uppstå** (*ewp*-stoā) *v* *arise

uppståndelse (*ewp*-stond-ayl-ser) *c* commotion,
excitement; resurrection

uppsving (*ewp*-sving) *nt* rise

uppsyningsman (*ewp*-sēw-nings-mahn) *c* (pl -män)
supervisor

uppsättning (*ewp*-seht-ning)
c set

***uppta** (*ewp*-taa) *v* *take up;
occupy

upptagen (*ewp*-taa-gern) *adj*
engaged; busy

uppträda (*ewp*-trææ-dah) *v*
act

upptäcka (*ewp*-teh-kah) *v*
discover; detect

upptäckt (*ewp*-tehkt) *c*
discovery

uppvisa (*ewp*-vee-sah) *v*
exhibit

uppvärma (*ewp*-vær-mah) *v*
heat

uppvärmning (*ewp*-værm-ning) *c* heating

uppåt (*ewp*-ot) *adv* up

ur (ēwr) *prep* out of; *nt* clock

urbena (ēwr-bāy-nah) *v* bone

urin (ew-reen) *nt* urine

urinblåsa (ew-reen-blōā-sah)
c bladder

urmakare (ēwr-maa-kah-rer)
c (pl ~) watchmaker

ursinne (ew-sin-er) *nt* rage;
fury

ursinnig (ew-si-ni) *adj*
furious

urskilja (ēwr-shil-ʸah) *v*
distinguish

urskog (ewr-skōōg) *c* jungle

ursprung (ēwr-sprewng) *nt*
origin

ursprunglig (ēwr-sprewng-li)
adj original; initial;
ursprungligen originally

ursäkt (ēwr-sehkt) *c* apology;
excuse; ***be om ~** apologize

ursäkta (ēwr-sehk-tah) *v*
excuse; **ursäkta!** sorry!

urtavla (ēwr-taav-lah) *c* (pl
urtavlor) dial

Uruguay (ew-rew-gew-*igh*)
Uruguay

uruguayare (ew-rew-gew-*igh*-ah-rer) *c* (pl ~)
Uruguayan

uruguaysk (ew-rew-gew-*ighsk*) *adj* Uruguayan

urval (ēwr-vaal) *nt* choice;
selection, assortment

usel (ēw-serl) *adj* poor

ut (ēwt) *adv* out; **~ och in**
inside out

utan (ēw-tahn) *prep* without;

*vara ~ *be without, spare

utandas ($\overline{ewt}$-ahn-dahss) v
expire; exhale

utanför ($\overline{ew}$-tahn-$f\overline{urr}$) prep
outside; out of

utantill ($\overline{ew}$-tahn-til) adv by
heart

utarbeta ($\overline{ewt}$-ahr-b$\overline{ay}$t-ah) v
compose, elaborate, prepare

utbetalning ($\overline{ewt}$-bay-taal-
ning) c payment

utbilda ($\overline{ewt}$-bil-dah) v
educate

utbildning ($\overline{ewt}$-bild-ning) c
education, background

utbreda ($\overline{ewt}$-br$\overline{ay}$d-ah) v
*spread; expand

utbrott ($\overline{ewt}$-brot) nt
outbreak; eruption

utbud ($\overline{ewt}$-bewd) nt supply

utbyta ($\overline{ewt}$-b$\overline{ew}$t-ah) v
exchange

utbyte ($\overline{ewt}$-b$\overline{ew}$-ter) nt
exchange; benefit

utdela ($\overline{ewt}$-d$\overline{ay}$l-ah) v
distribute

*utdra ($\overline{ewt}$-draa) v extract

utdrag ($\overline{ewt}$-draag) nt excerpt;
extract

ute ($\overline{ew}$-ter) adv out

utelämna ($\overline{ew}$-ter-lehm-nah)
v *leave out; omit

*utesluta ($\overline{ew}$-ter-sl$\overline{ew}$-tah) v
exclude

uteslutande ($\overline{ew}$-ter-sl$\overline{ew}$-
tahn-der) adv exclusively;
solely

utfart ($\overline{ewt}$-faart) c exit

utfattig ($\overline{ewt}$-fah-ti) adj
destitute

utflykt ($\overline{ewt}$-flewkt) c
excursion; trip

utforska ($\overline{ewt}$-fors-kah) v
explore

utföra ($\overline{ewt}$-f$\overline{ur}$-rah) v
perform; execute; carry out

utförbar ($\overline{ewt}$-f$\overline{urr}$-baar) adj
feasible; realizable

utförlig ($\overline{ewt}$-f$\overline{urr}$-li) adj
detailed

*utge ($\overline{ewt}$-g$\overline{ay}$) v issue;
publish

utgift ($\overline{ewt}$-^{y}ift) c expense;
utgifter expenditure

utgivning ($\overline{ewt}$-^{y}eev-ning) c
issue, publication

*utgjuta ($\overline{ewt}$-$^y\overline{ew}$-tah) v
*shed

utgrävning ($\overline{ewt}$-graiv-ning) c
excavation

utgång ($\overline{ewt}$-gong) c way out,
exit; expiration; result

utgångspunkt ($\overline{ewt}$-gongs-
pewngkt) c starting point

till uthyrning (til $\overline{ewt}$-hewr-
ning) for hire

uthållighet ($\overline{ewt}$-hol-i-h$\overline{ay}$t) c
perseverance

uthärda ($\overline{ewt}$-hæær-dah) v
*stand, endure

uthärdlig ($\overline{ewt}$-hæærd-li) adj
tolerable; endurable

utjämna ($\overline{ewt}$-^{y}ehm-nah) v
equalize; level

utkant ($\overline{ewt}$-kahnt) c outskirts
pl

utkast ($\overline{ewt}$-kahst) nt draft,
design

utled (ewt-l$\overline{ay}$d) adj fed up

utlämna ($\overline{ewt}$-lehm-nah) v

give out; extradite

utländsk ($\overline{ewt}$-lehnsk) *adj*
foreign; alien

utlänning ($\overline{ewt}$-lehn-ing) *c*
foreigner; alien

utlöpa ($\overline{ewt}$-lürp-ah) *v* expire

utmana ($\overline{ewt}$-maan-ah) *v*
challenge; dare

utmaning ($\overline{ewt}$-maan-ing) *c*
challenge

utmatta ($\overline{ewt}$-maht-ah) *v*
exhaust

utmattad ($\overline{ewt}$-maht-ahd) *adj*
exhausted

utmärka ($\overline{ewt}$-mær-kah) *v*
mark; ~ **sig** excel

utmärkt ($\overline{ewt}$-mærkt) *adj*
excellent

utnyttja ($\overline{ewt}$-newt-^{y}ah) *v*
exploit; utilize

utnämna ($\overline{ewt}$-nehm-nah) *v*
appoint

utnämning ($\overline{ewt}$-nehm-ning)
c appointment; nomination

utom ($\overline{ew}$-om) *prep* except;
but, besides

utomhus ($\overline{ew}$-tom-hēwss) *adv*
outdoors; outside

utomlands ($\overline{ewt}$-om-lahnds)
adv abroad

utomordentlig ($\overline{ewt}$-om-or-
daynt-li) *adj* extraordinary

utpeka ($\overline{ewt}$-pāy-kah) *v* point
out

utplocka ($\overline{ewt}$-plo-kah) *v*
select

utpressa ($\overline{ewt}$-prayss-ah) *v*
extort; ~ **pengar** blackmail

utpressning *c* blackmail,
extortion

utreda ($\overline{ewt}$-rāy-dah) *v*
investigate

utredning ($\overline{ewt}$-rāyd-ning) *c*
investigation

utrop ($\overline{ewt}$-rōop) *nt*
exclamation

utropa ($\overline{ewt}$-rōo-pah) *v*
exclaim

utrusta ($\overline{ewt}$-rewss-tah) *v*
equip

utrustning ($\overline{ewt}$-rewst-ning) *c*
outfit, equipment; kit, gear

utrymma ($\overline{ewt}$-rew-mah) *v*
vacate

utrymme ($\overline{ewt}$-rew-mer) *nt*
room

utsatt för ($\overline{ewt}$-saht) liable to,
subject to

utsätta ($\overline{ewt}$-seht-ah) *v*
expose

utseende ($\overline{ewt}$-sāy-ayn-der)
nt look; semblance,
appearance

utsida ($\overline{ewt}$-seed-ah) *c* outside

utsikt ($\overline{ewt}$-sikt) *c* view;
prospect, outlook

utskott ($\overline{ewt}$-skot) *nt*
committee

***utskära** ($\overline{ewt}$-shææ-rah) *v*
carve

utsliten ($\overline{ewt}$-slee-tern) *adj*
worn-out

utsmyckning ($\overline{ewt}$-smewk-
ning) *c* ornament

utspäda ($\overline{ewt}$-spai-dah) *v*
dilute

utsträckt ($\overline{ewt}$-strehkt) *adj*
extended

***utstå** ($\overline{ewt}$-stōa) *v* endure,
*bear

utställa (*ewt*-steh-lah) *v* issue;
show, exhibit; display
utställning (*ewt*-stehl-ning) *c*
exhibition; exposition,
display, show
*utsuga (*ewt*-sew-gah) *v*
exploit
utsåld (*ewt*-sold) *adj* sold out
utsända (*ewt*-sehn-dah) *v*
*broadcast
utsändning (*ewt*-sehnd-ning)
c broadcast
utsökt (*ewt*-sūrkt) *adj*
exquisite; delicious, superb
uttag (*ewt*-taag) *nt* socket,
outlet
uttagsautomat (*ewt*-taags-
ou-to-*maat*) *c* ATM, automatic teller machine, cash
dispenser, cash machine
uttal (*ewt*-taal) *nt*
pronunciation
uttala (*ewt*-taa-lah) *v*
pronounce; ~ fel
mispronounce
uttorkad (*ewt*-tor-kahd) *adj*
dried-up, parched
uttryck (*ewt*-trewk) *nt*
expression; *ge ~ åt express
uttrycka (*ewt*-trew-kah) *v*

uttrycklig (*ewt*-trewk-li) *adj*
explicit; express
uttröttad (*ewt*-trur-tahd) *adj*
overtired
utvald (*ewt*-vaald) *adj* select
utvandra (*ewt*-vahnd-rah) *v*
emigrate
utvandrare (*ewt*-vahnd-rah-
rer) *c* (pl ~) emigrant
utvandring (*ewt*-vahnd-ring)
c emigration
utveckla (*ewt*-vayk-lah) *v*
develop
utveckling (*ewt*-vayk-ling) *c*
development
utvidga (*ewt*-vid-gah) *v*
extend; enlarge, expand
utvidgande (*ewt*-vid-gahn-
der) *nt* extension
utvisa (*ewt*-vee-sah) *v* expel
utväg (*ewt*-vaig) *c* way out
*utvälja (*ewt*-vehl-ʸah) *v*
select
utvändig (*ewt*-vehn-di) *adj*
external
utåt (*ewt*-ot) *adv* outwards
utöva (*ewt*-ūrv-ah) *v* exercise
utöver (*ewt*-ūrv-err) *prep*
beyond, besides

V

vaccination (vahk-si-nah-
shōōn) *c* vaccination
vaccinera (vahks-i-*nāy*-rah) *v*
vaccinate
vacker (*vah*-kerr) *adj*
beautiful; pretty

vackla (*vahk*-lah) *v* stagger,
waver
vacklande (*vahk*-lahn-der)
adj tottering, failing
vad¹ (vaad) *pron* what; ~ som
helst anything; ~ som än

whatever
vad² (vaad) *nt* bet; ***slå ~ *bet**
vad³ (vaad) *c* calf
vada (*vaa*-dah) *v* wade
vadhållningsagent (*vaad*-hol-nings-ah-*gehnt*) *c* bookmaker
vag (vaag) *adj* faint, vague; dim
vagga (*vah*-gah) *c* cradle
vagn (vahngn) *c* carriage, coach
vakans (vah-*kahns*) *c* vacancy
vaken (*vaa*-kayn) *adj* awake
vakna (*vaak*-nah) *v* *wake up
vaksam (*vaak*-sahm) *adj* vigilant
vakt (vahkt) *c* guard; warden
vaktel (*vahk*-tayl) *c* (pl -tlar) quail
vaktmästare (*vahkt*-mehss-tah-rer) *c* (pl ~) waiter
vakuum (*vaa*-kewm) *nt* vacuum
val (vaal) *nt* election, pick, choice; *c* whale
valfri (*vaal*-free) *adj* optional
valkrets (*vaal*-krayts) *c* constituency
vallfartsort (*vahl*-faarts-oort) *c* place of pilgrimage
vallgrav (*vahl*-graav) *c* moat
vallmo (*vahl*-moo) *c* poppy
valnöt (*vaal*-nūrt) *c* (pl ~ter) walnut
vals (vahls) *c* waltz
valspråk (*vaal*-sprōak) *nt* motto

valuta (vah-*loo*-tah) *c* currency; **utländsk ~** foreign currency
valutakurs (vah-*lew*-tah-kewrs) *c* rate of exchange
valv (vahlv) *nt* vault; arch
valvbåge (*vahlv*-bōa-ger) *c* arch
van (vaan) *adj* accustomed; ***vara ~ vid** *be used to
vana (*vaa*-nah) *c* habit; custom
vandra (*vahnd*-rah) *v* wander; hike, tramp
vanilj (vah-*nilʸ*) *c* vanilla
vankelmodig (*vahng*-kerl-mōo-di) *adj* irresolute
vanlig (*vaan*-li) *adj* usual; normal, ordinary, common, plain; frequent; **vanligen** generally, as a rule
vanligtvis (*vaan*-lit-veess) *adv* usually
vansinne (*vaan*-sin-er) *nt* madness; lunacy
vansinnig (*vaan*-sin-i) *adj* crazy; lunatic
vanskapt (*vaan*-skaapt) *adj* deformed
vansklig (*vahnsk*-li) *adj* precarious
vanställd (*vaan*-stehld) *adj* deformed, disfigured
vanvettig (*vaan*-vay-ti) *adj* mad; absurd
vapen (*vaap*-ern) *nt* weapon; arm
var¹ (vaar) *conj* where; *adv* where; **~ som helst** anywhere

var² (vaar) *pron* each; ~ för
sig apart; ~ och en
everybody, everyone
var³ (vaar) *nt* pus
vara (*vaar*-ah) *v* last
*****vara** (*vaar*-ah) *v* *be
varaktig (vaar-*ahk*-ti) *adj*
lasting; permanent
varaktighet (vaar-ahk-ti-
hāyt) *c* duration
varandra (vaar-*ahnd*-rah)
pron each other
vardag (*vaar*-daag) *c*
weekday
vardagsrum (*vaar*-daags-
rewm) *nt* living room; sitting
room
vare sig ... eller (*vaa*-rer say
... eh-lerr) whether ... or
varelse (*vaa*-rayl-ser) *c*
being; creature
varför (*vahr*-furr) *adv* why;
what for
varg (vahr²) *c* wolf
varhelst (vaar-*hehlst*) *adv*
wherever
variation (vah-ri-ah-*shōōn*)
c variation, variety
variera (vah-ri-*āy*-rah) *v* vary
varierad (vah-ri-*āy*-rahd) *adj*
varied
varietéteater (vah-ri-ay-*tāy*-
tay-aa-terr) *c* (pl -trar)
variety theatre
varifrån (vaar-i-*frōan*) *adv*
from where
varje (*vahr*-³er) *pron* every;
anyone, each
varken ... eller (*vahr*-kern ...
eh-lerr) neither ... nor

varm (vahrm) *adj* warm; hot
varmvattensflaska (*vahrm*-
vah-terns-flahss-kah) *c* hot-
-water bottle
varna (*vaar*-nah) *v* warn;
caution
varning (*vaar*-ning) *c*
warning
varor (*vaar*-or) *pl* goods *pl*;
wares *pl*
varsam (*vaar*-sahm) *adj*
careful; wary
varubil (*vaa*-rēw-beel) *c*
delivery van
varuhus (*vaa*-rēw-hēwss) *nt*
department store
varumärke (*vaa*-rēw-mær-
ker) *c* trademark
varumässa (*vaa*-rēw-neh-
sah) *c* trade fair
varuprov (*vaarēw*-proov) *nt*
sample
varv (vahrv) *nt* revolution;
shipyard
vas (vaass) *c* vase
vask (vahsk) *c* sink
vass (vahss) *c* reed; *adj* sharp
vatten (*vah*-tern) *nt* water;
rinnande ~ running water
vattenblåsa (*vaht*-ern-blōa-
sah) *c* blister
vattenfall (*vaht*-ern-fahl) *nt*
waterfall
vattenfärg (*vaht*-ern-fær²)
c watercolour
vattenkran (*vaht*-ern-kraan)
c faucet, tap
vattenkrasse (*vaht*-ern-krah-
ser) *c* watercress
vattenmelon (*vah*-tern-may-

197 **verktyg**

lōon) c watermelon

vattenpass (*vaht-ern-pahss*)
nt level

vattenpump (*vaht-ern-pewmp*) c water pump

vattenskida (*vah-tern-shee-dah*) c water ski

vattentät (*vah-tern-tait*) *adj*
waterproof

vattkoppor (*vaht-ko-perr*) *pl*
chickenpox

vax (vahks) *nt* wax

vaxkabinett (*vahks-kah-bi-nayt*) *nt* waxworks *pl*

veck (vayk) *nt* fold; crease

vecka (*vay-kah*) c week;
vecko- weekly

veckla upp (*vayk-lah*)
unwrap

veckla ut (*vayk-lah*) unfold

veckopeng (*vay-koo-pehng*)
c weekly allowance

veckoslut (*vay-koo-slewt*) *nt*
weekend

veckotidning (*vay-koo-teed-ning*) c weekly magazine

vedervärdig (*vay-derr-væær-di*) *adj* repulsive

vedträ (*vāyd-trai*) *nt* log

vegan (vay-gaan) c vegan;
vegansk *adj* vegan

vegetarian (vay-ger-tahr-i-aan) c vegetarian;
vegetarisk *adj* vegetarian

vegetation (vay-ger-tah-shōōn) c vegetation

vem (vaym) *pron* who; **till ~** to
whom; **~ som helst**
anybody; **~ som än** whoever

vemod (*vāy-mōōd*) *nt*

melancholy; sadness

vemodig (*vāy-mōōd-i*) *adj*
melancholy, sad

Venezuela (vay-nay-tsew-*āy*-lah) Venezuela

venezuelan (vay-nay-tsew-ay-*laan*) c Venezuelan

venezuelansk (vay-nay-tsew-ay-*laansk*) *adj*
Venezuelan

ventil (vayn-*teel*) c valve

ventilation (vayn-ti-lah-shōōn) c ventilation

ventilator (vayn-ti-*laa*-tor) c
ventilator

ventilera (vayn-ti-*lāy*-rah) *v*
ventilate

veranda (vay-*rahn*-dah) c
veranda

verb (værb) *nt* verb

verifiera (vay-ri-fi-*āy*-rah) *v*
verify

verka (*vær*-kah) *v* appear,
seem

verkan (*vær*-kahn) c effect;
result; consequence

verklig (*vær*k-li) *adj* real;
actual, true; very; **verkligen**
really; indeed

verklighet (*vær*k-li-hāyt) c
reality

verksam (*vær*k-sahm) *adj*
active, effective

verkstad (*vær*k-staad) c
(pl -städer) workshop;
garage

verkställande (*vær*k-stehl-ahn-der) *adj* executive

verktyg (*vær*k-tewg) *nt* tool;
utensil

verktygslåda (*værk-tēwgs-lōa*-dah) *c* tool box
vers (værs) *c* verse
version (*vær-shōon*) *c* version
vespa (*vayss*-pah) *c* scooter
vestibul (vehss-ti-*bēwl*) *c* lobby
***veta** (*vāy*-tah) *v* *know
vete (*vāy*-tay) *nt* wheat
vetemjöl (*vāy*-tay-m^yürl) *nt* flour
vetenskap (*vāy*-tayn-skaap) *c* science
vetenskaplig (*vāy*-tayn-skaap-li) *adj* scientific
vetenskapsman (*vāy*-tayn-skaaps-mahn) *c* (pl -män) scientist
veterinär (vay-tay-ri-*næær*) *c* veterinary surgeon
vett (vaytt) *nt* wit
vevaxel (*vāy*-vahks-ayl) *c* (pl -xlar) crankshaft
vi (vee) *pron* we
via (*vee*-ah) *prep* via
viadukt (vee-ah-*dewkt*) *c* viaduct
vibration (vi-brah-*shōon*) *c* vibration
vibrera (vi-*brāy*-rah) *v* vibrate
vid (veed) *prep* on, by; *adj* wide
vidbränna (*veed*-breh-nah) *v* *burn
video (*vee*-day-oh) *c* video
video(bandspelare) (*vee*-day-o-bahnd-spāy-lay-rer) *c* video recorder
videoinspelning (*vee*-day-o-in-*spāyl*-ning) *c* video recording
videokamera (*vee*-day-o-*kāā*-mer-nah) *c* video camera
videokassett (*vee*-day-o-kah-*sēht*) *c* video cassette
videospel (*vee*-dee-o-*spāy*) *nt* video game
videospelare (*vee*-day-o-*spāy*-lah-rer) *c* (pl ~) video recorder
vidga (*vid*-gah) *v* widen
***vidhålla** (*veed*-hol-ah) *v* insist
vidrig (*veed*-ri) *adj* disgusting
vidröra (*veed*-rūr-rah) *v* touch
vidskepelse (*veed*-shāy-payl-ser) *c* superstition
vidsträckt (*vid*-strehkt) *adj* broad, vast; extensive
vigselring (*vig*-sehl-ring) *c* wedding ring
vik (veek) *c* bay; creek
***vika** (*vee*-kah) *v* fold
vikt (vikt) *c* weight
viktig (*vik*-ti) *adj* important, essential; self-important; *vara viktigt matter
vila (*veel*-ah) *v* rest; *c* rest
vild (vild) *adj* wild; fierce, savage
vilja (*vil*-^yah) *v* will; med ~ on purpose
***vilja** (*vil*-^yah) *v* want, *will
viljekraft (*vil*-^yer-krahft) *c* willpower
vilken (*vil*-kayn) *pron* which
villa (*vi*-lah) *c* villa
villebråd (*vi*-ler-*brōad*) *nt* game

villfarelse (vil-faa-rayl-ser) c illusion

villig (vi-li) adj willing

villkor (vil-koar) nt condition; term

villkorlig (vil-koar-li) adj conditional

villrådig (vil-roa-di) adj irresolute

vilohem (vee-loo-haym) nt rest home

vilsegången (vil-ser-gong-ern) adj lost

vilstol (veel-stool) c deck chair

vilthandlare (vilt-hahnd-lah-rer) c (pl ~) poulterer

vin (veen) nt wine

***vina** (vee-nah) v howl

vinbär (veen-bæær) nt currant; **svarta ~** blackcurrant

vind (vind) c wind; attic

vindbrygga (vind-brewg-ah) c drawbridge

vindpust (vind-pewst) c whiff of wind

vindruta (vind-rew-tah) c windscreen; windshield nAm

vindrutetorkare (vind-rew-ter-tor-kah-rer) c (pl ~) windscreen wiper; windshield wiper Am

vindruvor (veen-drew-voor) pl grapes pl

vindsrum (vinds-rewm) nt attic

vinge (ving-er) c wing

vingård (veen-goard) c vineyard

vinhandlare (veen-hahnd-lah-rer) c (pl ~) wine merchant

vink (vingk) c wave; hint

vinka (ving-kah) v wave

vinkel (ving-kerl) c (pl ~klar) angle

vinkällare (veen-tyeh-lah-rer) c (pl ~) wine cellar

vinlista (veen-liss-tah) c wine list

***vinna** (vi-nah) v *win; gain

vinnande (vi-nahn-der) adj winning

vinranka (veen-rahn-kah) c vine

vinskörd (veen-shūrrd) c grape harvest, vintage

vinst (vinst) c benefit; profit; **winnings** pl

vinstbringande (vinst-bring-ahn-der) adj profitable

vinter (vin-terr) c (pl ~trar) winter

vintersport (vin-terr-sport) c winter sports

vinthund (vint-hewnd) c greyhound

vinäger (vi-nai-gerr) c vinegar

viol (vi-ool) c violet

violett (vi-ew-layt) adj violet

VIP (vip) c VIP

virka (veer-kah) v crochet

virrvarr (veer-vahr) nt muddle

virus (vee-rews) c (pl ~) virus

vis (veess) nt way, manner; adj wise

visa¹ (veess-ah) v *show; indicate, point out, display

visa² (*veess*-ah) c tune

visdom (*veess*-doom) c wisdom

vision (vi-*shōōn*) c vision

visit (vi-*seet*) c visit

visitera (vi-si-*tāy*-rah) v search

visitering (vi-si-*tāy*-ring) nt search

visitkort (vi-*seet*-koort) nt visitingcard

viska (*viss*-kah) v whisper

viskning (*visk*-ning) c whisper

vispa (*viss*-pah) v whip

viss (viss) adj certain

visselpipa (*vi*-serl-pee-pah) c whistle

vissla (*viss*-lah) v whistle

vistas (*viss*-tahss) v stay

vistelse (*viss*-tayl-ser) c stay

visum (*vee*-sewm) nt (pl visa) visa

vit (veet) adj white

vitamin (vi-tah-*meen*) nt vitamin

vitling (*vit*-ling) c whiting

vitlök (*veet*-lūrk) c garlic

vits (vits) c joke

vittna (*vit*-nah) v testify

vittne (*vit*-ner) nt witness

vokal (voo-*kaal*) c vowel

vokalist (voo-kah-*list*) c vocalist

volt (volt) c (pl ∼) volt

volym (vo-*lewm*) c volume; bulk

vrak (vraak) nt wreck

vred (vrāyd) adj angry

vrede (*vrāy*-day) c anger

vresig (*vrāyss*-i) adj cross

*vrida (*vree*-dah) v twist, turn; wrench; ∼ om turn

vriden (*vreed*-ern) adj crooked

vridning (*vreed*-ning) c twist

vrål (vrōal) nt roar

vulgär (vewl-*gæær*) adj vulgar

vulkan (vewl-*kaan*) c volcano

vuxen¹ (*vewk*-sern) adj adult; grown-up

vuxen² (*vewk*-sern) c (pl vuxna) grown-up; adult

vykort (*vēw*-koort) nt picture postcard

våffla (*vof*-lah) c waffle

våg¹ (vōag) c (pl ∼or) wave

våg² (vōag) c (pl ∼ar) scales pl; weighing machine

våga (*vōa*-gah) v dare; venture

vågad (*vōag*-ahd) adj risky

vågig (*vōa*-gi) adj wavy

våglängd (*vōag*-lehngd) c wavelength

våld (vold) nt violence; force

våldsam (*vold*-sahm) adj violent

våldsdåd (*volds*-dōad) nt act of violence; outrage

*våldta (*vold*-taa) v rape; assault

vålla (*vol*-ah) v cause

våning (*vōan*-ing) c floor; storey; apartment nAm

vår (vōar) c spring; springtime; pron our

vård (vōard) c care

vårda (*vōar*-dah) v nurse; tend

vårdhem (*vōard*-haym) nt

välsignelse

nursing home

vårdslös (*vōards*-lūrss) *adj* careless

våt (vōat) *adj* wet

väcka (*veh*-kah) *v* *wake; *awake

väckarklocka (*veh*-kahr-klo-kah) *c* alarm-clock

väder (*vai*-derr) *nt* weather

väderkvarn (*vai*-derr-kvaarn) *c* windmill

väderleksrapport (*vai*-derr-lāyks-rah-*port*) *c* weather forecast

vädjan (*vaid*-^yahn) *v* appeal

vädra (*vaid*-rah) *v* ventilate

väg (vaig) *c* road; drive; way; **på ~ till** bound for

väga (*vai*-gah) *v* weigh

vägarbete (*vaig*-ahr-*bāy*-ter) *nt* road up, road work

vägavgift (*vaig*-aav-^yift) *c* toll

vägbank (*vaig*-bahngk) *c* embankment

vägg (vehg) *c* wall

vägglus (*vehg*-lēwss) *c* (pl -löss) bug

vägkant (*vaig*-kahnt) *c* roadside; wayside

vägkarta (*vaig*-kaar-tah) *c* road map

vägkorsning (*vaig*-kors-ning) *c* junction, intersection

vägleda (*vaig*-lāyd-ah) *v* direct; guide

vägmärke (*vaig*-mær-ker) *c* road sign

på ... vägnar (poā *vehng*-nahr) on behalf of

vägnät (*vaig*-nait) *nt* road system

vägra (*vaig*-rah) *v* refuse; deny

vägran (*vaig*-rahn) *c* refusal

vägräcke (*vaig*-rehk-er) *nt* crash barrier

vägskäl (*vaig*-shail) *nt* road fork

vägvisare (*vaig*-vee-sah-rer) *c* (pl ~) signpost

välbefinnande (*vail*-ber-*fin*-ahn-der) *nt* well-being; comfort

välbärgad (*vail*-bær-^yahd) *adj* well-to-do

väldig (*vehl*-di) *adj* enormous; huge, gigantic

välgrundad (*vail*-grewn-dahd) *adj* well-founded

välgång (*vail*-gong) *c* prosperity

välgörenhet (*vail*-^yur-rern-*hāyt*) *c* charity

***välja** (*vehl*-^yah) *v* *choose; elect, pick

väljare (*vehl*-^yah-rer) *c* (pl ~) voter

välkommen (*vail*-ko-mern) *adj* welcome

välkomna (*vail*-kom-nah) *v* welcome

välkomnande (*vail*-kom-nahn-der) *nt* welcome

välkänd (*vail*-t^yehnd) *adj* well-known; familiar

välsigna (vehl-*sing*-nah) *v* bless

välsignelse (vehl-*sing*-nayl-ser) *c* blessing

välsmakande (*vail*-smaak-ahn-der) *adj* tasty; savoury

välstånd (*vail*-stond) *nt* prosperity

välvilja (*vail*-vil-ʸah) *c* goodwill

välvårdad (*vail*-vōār-dahd) *adj* neat

vämjelig (*vehm*-ʸer-li) nauseous

vän (vehn) *c* (pl ~ner) friend

vända (*vehn* dah) *v* turn; ~ på turn round; ~ sig om turn round; ~ sig till address; ~ tillbaka turn back; ~ upp och ner turn over

vändning (*vehnd*-ning) *c* change, turn

vändpunkt (*vehnd*-pewngkt) *c* turning point

väninna (veh-*nin*-ah) *c* friend; girlfriend

*vänja (*vehn*-ʸah) *v* accustom

vänlig (*vehn*-li) *adj* friendly; kind

vänskap (*vehn*-skaap) *c* friendship

vänskaplig (*vehn*-skaap-li) *adj* friendly

vänster (*vehns*-terr) *adj* left; left-hand

vänsterhänt (*vehns*-terr-hehnt) *adj* left-handed

vänta (*vehn*-tah) *v* wait; ~ på await; ~ sig expect; await

väntad (*vehn*-tahd) *adj* due

väntan (*vehn*-tahn) *c* waiting

väntelista (*vehn*-ter-liss-tah) *c* waiting list

väntrum (*vehnt*-rewm) *nt* waiting room

värd (væærd) *c* host

värde (*væær*-der) *nt* worth, value; *vara värd *be worth

värdefull (*væær*-der-fewl) *adj* valuable

värdelös (*væær*-der-lūrss) *adj* worthless

värdepapper (*væær*-der-pah-perr) *pl* stocks and shares

värdera (vær-*dāyr*-ah) *v* value; estimate, evaluate

värdering (vær-*dāyr*-ing) *c* appraisal

värdesaker (*væær*-der-saa-kerr) *pl* valuables *pl*

*värdesätta (*væær*-der-seh-tah) *v* value, appreciate

värdig (*væær*-di) *adj* dignified; worthy of

värdighet (*væær*-di-heet) *c* dignity

värdinna (vær-*di*-nah) *c* hostess

värdshus (*væærds*-hēwss) *nt* inn; roadhouse; roadside restaurant

värk (værk) *c* ache; **värkar** labour pains

värka (*vær*-kah) *v* ache; *hurt

värld (væærd) *c* world

världsberömd (*væærds*-ber-rurmd) *adj* world-famous

världsdel (*væærds*-dāyl) *c* continent

världshav (*væærds*-haav) *nt* ocean

världskrig (*væærds*-kreeg) *nt* world war

världsomfattande (*væærds*-

WLAN

om-fah-tahn-der) *adj* global
världsomspännande
(*væærds-om-speh-nahn-*
der) *adj* world-wide
värma (*vær-mah*) *v* warm
värme (*vær-*mer) *c* heat;
warmth
värmedyna (*vær-mer-dēw-*
nah) *c* heating pad
värmeelement (*vær-mer-ay-*
ler-mehnt) *nt* radiator
värnpliktig (*væærn-*plik-tig) *c*
(pl ~a) conscript
värre (*væ-*rer) *adv* worse; *adj*
worse; värst worst
väsen (*vaiss-*ern) *nt* essence;
noise; fuss
väsentlig (veh-*saynt-*li) *adj*
essential; väsentligen
essentially
väska (*vehss-*kah) *c* bag
vässa (*veh-*sah) *v* sharpen
väst (vehst) *c* waistcoat, vest
nAm; west
väster (*vehss-*terr) *c* west
västlig (*vehst-*li) *adj* western;
westerly
väte (*vai-*ter) *nt* hydrogen
vätska (*veht-*skah) *c* fluid
väva (*vai-*vah) *v* *weave
vävare (*vai-*vah-rer) *c* (pl ~)

weaver
vävnad (*vaiv-*nahd) *c* tissue
växa (*vehks-*ah) *v* *grow
växel (*vehks-*ayl) *c* (pl växlar)
gear; draft
växelkontor (*vehks-*ayl-kon-
tōōr) *nt* exchange office;
money exchange
växelkurs (*vehks-*ayl-kewrs)
c exchange rate
växellåda (*vehks-*ayl-lōa-
dah) *c* gearbox
växelpengar (*vehks-*ayl-peh-
ngahr) *pl* small change
växelspak (*vehks-*ayl-spaak)
c gear lever
växelström (*vehks-*ayl-
strurm) *c* alternating current
växla (*vehks-*lah) *v* change;
switch, exchange; change
gear
växlande (*vehks-*lahn-der)
adj variable
växt (vehkst) *c* growth; plant
växthus (*vehkst-*hēwss) *nt*
greenhouse
vördnad (*vūrd-*nahd) *c*
veneration, respect
vördnadsvärd (*vūrd-*nahds-
væærd) *adj* venerable

W

watt (vaht) *c* (pl ~) watt
webbplats (*veb-*plahts) *c*
website
Wi-Fi (*oo-ay-*fi) (*nt*) wi-fi,
WiFi®; ~ **hotspot** *c* wi-fi

hotspot
WLAN (*vāy-*laan) *nt* wi-fi,
WiFi®

Y

ylle- (*ew*-ler) woollen

ylletröja (*ew*-ler-trur-ᵞah) *c* jersey

ympa (*ewm*-pah) *v* inoculate; graft

ympning (*ewmp*-ning) *c* grafting

ynkrygg (*ewngk*-rewg) *c* coward

yoghurt (*ᵞo*-gūrt) *c* yoghurt

yr (ēwr) *adj* dizzy; giddy

yrke (*ewr*-ker) *nt* profession; trade; **yrkes-** professional

yrkesutbildad (*ewr*-kerss-ēwt-bil-dahd) *adj* skilled, trained

yrsel (*ewr*-serl) *c* dizziness; giddiness

yta (*ēw*-tah) *c* surface; area

ytlig (*ēwt*-li) *adj* superficial

ytterlig (*ewt*-err-li) *adj* extreme

ytterligare (*ewt*-err-li-gah-rer) *adj* further; additional

ytterlighet (*ewt*-err-li-hāyt) *c* extreme

ytterlinje (*ewt*-err-lin-ᵞer) *c* outline

yttersta (*ew*-terrs-tah) *adj* utmost; extreme

yttra (*ewt*-rah) *v* utter

yttrande (*ewt*-rahn-der) *nt* expression

yttrandefrihet (*ewt*-rahn-der-fri-hāyt) *c* freedom of speech

yttre (*ewt*-rer) *nt* exterior; *adj* outer; exterior

yuppie (yew-pee) *c* yuppie

yxa (*ewks*-ah) *c* axe

Z

zenit (*sāy*-nit) zenith

zigenare (si-*ᵞāy*-nah-rer) *c* (pl ~) gipsy

zink (singk) *c* zinc

zon (sōōn) *c* zone

zoo (sōō) *nt* zoo

zoologi (so-o-lo-*gee*) *c* zoology

zoomlins (*sōōm*-lins) *c* zoom lens

Å

å (ōā) *c* river, stream

åder (*ōā*-derr) *c* (pl ådror) vein

åderbrock (*ōā*-derr-brok) *nt* varicose vein

*ådraga sig (*ōā*-draa-gah)

contract

åhörare (ōā-hǖrr-ah-rer) c (pl
~) listener, auditor

åka (ōā-kah) v *ride, *drive,
*go; ~ **bort** *go away; ~ **fort**
*speed; ~ **runt om** by-pass; ~
tillbaka *go back

åker (ōāk-err) c (pl åkrar)
field

ål (ōāl) c eel

ålder (ol-derr) c (pl åldrar)
age

ålderdom (ol-derr-doom) c
age; old age

åldrig (old-ri) adj aged

*ålägga (ōā-lehg-ah) v enjoin

ånga (ong-ah) c steam;
vapour

ångare (ong-ah-rer) c (pl ~)
steamer

ånger (ong-err) c repentance

ångest (ong-erst) c anguish;
fear

ångra (ong-rah) v regret,
repent

år (ōar) nt year; **per** ~ per
annum

åra (ōā-rah) c oar

årgång (ōā-gong) c vintage

århundrade (ōā-hewnd-rah-
der) nt century

årlig (ōā-li) adj annual;
yearly

årsbok (ōars-bōōk) c (pl
-böcker) annual

årsdag (ōars-daag) c
anniversary

årstid (ōars-teed) c season

åsikt (ōā-sikt) c opinion; view

åska (oss-kah) c thunder; v

thunder; **åsk-** thundery

åskväder (osk-vai-derr) nt
thunderstorm

åskådare (ōā-skōā-dah-rer) c
(pl ~) spectator

åsna (ōass-nah) c donkey

*åstadkomma (ōā-stah-kom-
ah) v effect

åsyn (ōā-sēwn) c sight

åt (ōāt) prep to; towards

åtala (ōā-taa-lah) v prosecute

*åta sig (ōā-taa) *take upon
oneself

åter (ōā-err) adv again

återbetala (ōāt-err-bay-taal-
ah) v *repay; reimburse,
refund

återbetalning (ōāt-err-bay-
taal-ning) c repayment;
refund

*återfå (ōā-terr-fōā) v *find
again, recover

återföra (ōāt-err-fǖrr-ah) v
*bring back

återförena (ōāt-err-fur-rāy-
nah) v reunite

återkalla (ōāt-err-kahl-ah) v
recall

återkomst (ōāt-err-komst) c
return

återresa (ōāt-err-rāy-sah) c
return journey

återstod (ōāt-err-stōōd) c
remainder

*återstå (ōāt-err-stōā) v
remain

*återuppta (ōāt-err-ewp-tah)
v resume

återvinna (oat-err-vi-nah) v
recycle

återvinningsbar (*oat-err-vin-nings-baar*) *adj* recyclable

återvända (*ōat-err-vehn-dah*) *v* return

återvändsgränd (*ōat-err-vehnds-grehnd*) *c* cul-de-sac

åtfölja (*ōat-furl-Yah*) *v* accompany

åtgärd (*ōat-Yærd*) *c* measure

åtkomlig (*ōat-kom-li*) *adj* attainable

åtminstone (*ōat-mins-toner*) *adv* at least

åtrå (*ōa-trōa*) *c* lust

åtråvärd (*ōa-trōa-væærd*) *adj* desirable

åtskild (*ōat-shild*) *adj* separate

åtskilja (*ōat-shil-Yah*) *v* divide; disconnect

åtskilliga (*ōat-shi-li-gah*) *adj* several; various

åtstrama (*ōat-straam-ah*) *v* tighten

åtta (*o-tah*) *num* eight

åttio (*o-ti*) *num* eighty

åttonde (*o-ton-der*) *num* eighth

åverkan (*ōa-vehr-kahn*) *c* damage, mischief

Ä

äcklig (*ehk-li*) *adj* disgusting; revolting

ädel (*ai-dayl*) *adj* noble

ädelsten (*ai-dayl-stäyn*) *c* stone; gem

äga (*ai-gah*) *v* own; possess; ~ **rum** *take place

ägare (*ai-gah-rer*) *c* (pl ~) owner; proprietor

ägg (*ehg*) *nt* egg

äggplanta (*ehg-plahn-tah*) *c* eggplant

äggula (*ehg-gēwl-ah*) *c* egg yolk; yolk

ägna (*ehng-nah*) *v* devote; dedicate

ägodelar (*ai-goo-dāyl-ahr*) *pl* property; possessions

äkta (*ehk-tah*) *adj* true; authentic, genuine; ~ **man** husband

äktenskap (*ehk-tayn-skaap*) *nt* marriage; matrimony

äldre (*ehld-rer*) *adj* elder; elderly; **äldst** eldest

älg (*ehlY*) *c* elk, moose

älska (*ehls-kah*) *v* love

älskad (*ehls-kahd*) *adj* beloved

älskare (*ehls-kah-rer*) *c* (pl ~) lover

älskarinna (*ehls-kah-rin-ah*) *c* mistress

älskling (*ehlsk-ling*) *c* darling; sweetheart; **älsklings-** favourite; pet

älv (*ehlv*) *c* river

ämbar (*ehm-baar*) *nt* pail

ämbete (*ehm-bāyt-er*) *nt* office

ämbetsdräkt (*ehm-bāyts-drehkt*) *c* official dress, robe

ämna (*ehm-nah*) *v* intend

ämne (*ehm-ner*) *nt* theme; matter

än (*ehn*) *conj* than

ända till (*ehn-dah til*) until; as far as

ändamål (*ehn-dah-mōal*) *nt* purpose; object

ändamålsenlig (*ehn-dah-mōals-āyn-li*) *adj* suitable, appropriate

ände (*ehn-der*) *c* end

ändra (*ehnd-rah*) *v* change

ändring (*ehnd-ring*) *c* alteration

ändstation (*ehnd-stah-shōōn*) *c* terminal

ändtarm (*ehnd-tahrm*) *c* rectum

äng (*ehng*) *c* meadow

ängel (*ehng-ayl*) *c* (pl änglar) angel

ängslig (*ehngs-li*) *adj* afraid; worried

änka (*ehng-kah*) *c* widow

änkling (*ehngk-ling*) *c* widower

ännu (*ehn-ew*) *adv* still; yet; ~ **en gång** once more

äpple (*ehp-lay*) *nt* apple

ära (*æær-ah*) *v* honour; *c* glory

ärelysten (*æær-er-lewss-tern*) *adj* ambitious

ärende (*ææ-rayn-der*) *nt* errand

ärftlig (*ærft-li*) *adj* hereditary

ärlig (*æær-li*) *adj* honest

ärlighet (*æær-li-hāyt*) *c* honesty

ärm (*ærm*) *c* sleeve

ärofull (*ææ-roo-fewl*) *adj* honourable

ärr (*ær*) *nt* scar

ärta (*ær-tah*) *c* pea

ärva (*ær-vah*) *v* inherit

*äta (*ai-tah*) *v* *eat

ätbar (*ait-baar*) *adj* edible

ättling (*eht-ling*) *c* descendant

även (*aiv-ern*) *adv* also; even; likewise; ~ **om** although; though

äventyr (*ai-vayn-tēwr*) *nt* adventure

Ö

ö (*ūr*) *c* island

öde (*ūrd-er*) *nt* fate; destiny, fortune; *adj* desert; waste

*ödelägga (*ūr-day-leh-gah*) *v* wreck; ruin

ödesdiger (*ūr-derss-dee-gerr*) *adj* fatal

ödla (*ūrd-lah*) *c* (pl ödlor)

lizard

ödmjuk (*ūrd-m'ōōk*) *adj* humble

öga (*ūr-gah*) *nt* (pl ögon) eye

ögla (*ūrg-lah*) *c* loop

ögonblick (*ūr-gon-blik*) *nt* moment; second, instant

ögonblickligen (*ūr-gon-blik-*

li-ern) *adv* instantly
ögonblicksbild (ūr-gon-bliks-*bild*) *c* snapshot
ögonbryn (ūr-gon-brēwn) *nt* eyebrow
ögonbrynspenna (ūr-gon-brēwns-peh-nah) *c* eyebrow pencil
ögonfrans (ūr-gon-frahns) *c* eyelash
ögonlock (ūr-gon-lok) *nt* eyelid
ögonläkare (ūr-gon-lai-kah-rer) *c* (pl ∼) eye specialist, oculist
ögonskugga (ūr-gon-skew-gah) *c* eye shadow
ögonvittne (ūr-gon-vit-ner) *nt* eyewitness
öka (ūr-kah) *v* increase; raise
öken (ūr-kern) *c* (pl öknar) desert
ökning (ūrk-ning) *c* increase
öl (ūrl) *nt* beer; ale
öm (urm) *adj* tender; sore
ömsesidig (urm-say-*seed*-i) *adj* mutual
ömtålig (urm-tōā-li) *adj* delicate; perishable
önska (urns-kah) *v* wish; desire, want
önskan (urns-kahn) *c* (pl -kningar) wish; desire
önskvärd (urnsk-væærd) *adj* desirable
öppen (ur-payn) *adj* open
öppenhjärtig (ur-pern-ᵞær-ti) *adj* open-hearted, frank
öppna (urp-nah) *v* open
öppnare (urp-nah-rer) *c* (pl

∼) opener
öppning (urp-ning) *c* breach, gap; opening
öra (ūr-rah) *nt* (pl öron) ear
örfil (ūrr-feel) *c* slap; blow; *ge en* ∼ smack
örhänge (urr-hehng-er) *c* earring
örlogsfartyg (ūrr-logs-faar-tēwg) *nt* man-of-war
örn (urrn) *c* eagle
örngott (ūrrn-got) *nt* pillowcase
örsprång (ūrr-sprong) *nt* earache
ört (urrt) *c* herb
öst (urst) east
öster (urss-terr) *c* east
österrikare (urss-terr-ree-kah-rer) *c* (pl ∼) Austrian
Österrike (urss-terr-ree-ker) Austria
österrikisk (urss-terr-ree-kisk) *adj* Austrian
östra (urst-rah) *adj* eastern
öva (ūrv-ah) *v* exercise; ∼ *sig* practise
över (ūrv-err) *prep* over; across, *adv* over; *gå* ∼ cross, pass; **över-** upper, chief
överallt (ūr-verr-*ahlt*) *adv* everywhere; throughout
överanstränga (ūr-verr-ahn-strehng-ah) *v* strain; ∼ *sig* overstrain, overwork
överdrift (ūr-verr-drift) *c* exaggeration
***överdriva** (ūr-verr-dree-vah) *v* exaggerate
överdriven (ūr-verr-dreev-

ern) *adj* excessive;
extravagant

överdäck (ūr-verr-dehk) *nt*
main deck

överenskommelse (ūr-verr-
ayns-ko-mayl-ser) *c*
settlement, agreement

överensstämma (ūr-verr-
ayns-steh-mah) *v*
correspond

överfart (ūr-verr-faart) *c*
crossing; passage

överflöd (ūr-verr-flūrd) *nt*
abundance; plenty; *finnas i
~ *be in plenty

överflödig (ūr-verr-flūrd-i)
adj superfluous; redundant

överfull (ūr-verr-fewl) *adj*
overfull, crowded

överföra (ūr-verr-fūr-rah) *v*
transfer

*överge (ūr-verr-ỹay) *v* desert

övergång (ūr-verr-gong) *c*
crossing, change over,
transition

övergångsställe (ur-verr-
gongs-steh-ler) *nt* zebra
crossing; crosswalk *nAm*

överlagd (ūr-verr-lahgd) *adj*
deliberate, premeditated

överleva (ūr-verr-lāy-vah) *v*
survive

överlevnad (ūr-verr-lāyv-
nahd) *c* survival

överlägga (ūr-verr-lehg-ah)
v deliberate

överläggning (ūr-verr-lehg-
ning) *c* discussion,
deliberation

överlägsen (ūr-verr-laig-

sern) *adj* superior

överlämna (ūr-verr-lehm-
nah) *v* deliver, hand ... over;
commit

överlärare (ūr-verr-læae-rah-
rer) *c* (pl ~) head teacher

övermodig (ūr-verr-mōōd-i)
adj presumptuous, reckless

överraska (ūr-verr-rahss-
kah) *v* surprise

överraskning (ūr-verr-rahsk-
ning) *c* surprise

överrock (ūr-verr-rok) *c*
overcoat

överrumpla (ūr-verr-rewmp-
lah) *v* surprise

översida (ūr-verr-see-dah) *c*
top side; top

översikt (ūr-verr-sikt) *c*
survey; summary

överskott (ūr-verr-skot) *nt*
surplus

*överskrida (ur-verr-skreed-
ah) *v* exceed

överskrift (ūr-verr-skrift) *c*
heading; headline

överspänd (ūr-verr-spehnd)
adj overstrung

överste (ūr-verrs-ter) *c*
colonel

översvallande (ūr-verr-
svahl-ahn-der) *adj*
exuberant

översvämning (ūr-verr-
svehm-ning) *c* flood

översända (ūr-verr-sehn-
dah) *v* *send, remit

*översätta (ūr-verr-seh-tah) *v*
translate

översättare (ūr-verr-seh-tah-

översättning 210

rer) *c* (pl ~) translator
översättning (*ūr*-verr-seht-
ning) *c* translation
***överta** (*ūr*-verr-taa) *v* *take
over
övertala (*ūr*-verr-taa-lah) *v*
persuade
övertrassera (*ūr*-verr-trah-
seh-rah) *v* overdraw
övertrassering (*ūr*-verr-trah-
seh-ring) *c* overdraft
överträffa (*ūr*-verr-trehf-ah)
v exceed; *outdo
övertyga (*ūr*-verr-tēw-gah) *v*
convince; persuade
övertygelse (*ūr*-verr-tew-
gayl-ser) *c* conviction;

persuasion
övervaka (*ūr*-verr-vaak-ah) *v*
supervise; watch
övervikt (*ūr*-verr-vikt) *c*
overweight
***övervinna** (*ūr*-verr-vin-ah) *v*
*overcome
överväga (*ūr*-verr-vaig-ah) *v*
consider; deliberate
övervägande (*ūr*-verr-vaig-
ahn-der) *nt* consideration
överväldiga (*ūr*-verr-vehl-di-
gah) *v* overwhelm
övning (*ūrv*-ning) *c* exercise
övre (*ūrv*-rer) *adj* upper; top
övrig (*ūrv*-ri) *adj* remaining;
för övrigt moreover

English – Swedish
Engelsk – Svensk

A

a [ei,ə] *art* (an) en *art*

abbey ['æbi] *n* kloster *nt*

abbreviation [ə,bri:vi'eiʃən] *n* förkortning *c*

ability [ə'biləti] *n* skicklighet *c*; förmåga *c*

able ['eibəl] *adj* i stånd att; duglig; ***be ~ to** *vara i stånd till; *kunna

aboard [ə'bɔ:d] *adv* ombord

abolish [ə'bɔliʃ] *v* avskaffa

abortion [ə'bɔ:ʃən] *n* abort *c*

about [ə'baut] *prep* om; beträffande, angående; *adv* ungefär, omkring

above [ə'bʌv] *prep* ovanför; *adv* ovan

abroad [ə'brɔ:d] *adv* utomlands

abscess ['æbses] *n* böld *c*

absence ['æbsəns] *n* frånvaro *c*

absent ['æbsənt] *adj* frånvarande

absolutely ['æbsəlu:tli] *adv* absolut

abstain from [əb'stein] *avstå från, *avhålla sig från

abstract ['æbstrækt] *adj* abstrakt

absurd [əb'sə:d] *adj* orimlig,

absurd

abundance [ə'bʌndəns] *n* överflöd *c*

abundant [ə'bʌndənt] *adj* riklig

abuse [ə'bju:s] *n* missbruk *nt*

academy [ə'kædəmi] *n* akademi *c*

accelerate [ək'seləreit] *v* öka farten

accelerator [ək'seləreitə] *n* gaspedal *c*

accent ['æksənt] *n* accent *c*; tonvikt *c*

accept [ək'sept] *v* acceptera, *motta

access ['ækses] *n* tillträde *nt*

accessible [ək'sesəbəl] *adj* tillgänglig

accessories [ək'sesəriz] *pl* tillbehör *pl*

accident ['æksidənt] *n* olycksfall *nt*, olycka *c*

accidental [,æksi'dentəl] *adj* slumpartad

accommodate [ə'kɔmədeit] *v* härbärgera, logera

accommodation [ə,kɔmə'deifən] *n* husrum *nt*, logi *nt*

accompany [ə'kʌmpəni] *v*

åtfölja; följa; ackompanjera

accomplish [əˈkʌmpliʃ] v
fullborda

in accordance with [in
əˈkɔːdəns wið] i enlighet
med

according to [əˈkɔːdiŋ tuː]
enligt

account [əˈkaunt] n konto nt;
redogörelse c; ~ **for**
redovisa; **on ~ of** på grund
av

accurate [ˈækjurət] adj
noggrann

accuse [əˈkjuːz] v beskylla;
anklaga

accused [əˈkjuːzd] n
anklagad person

accustom [əˈkʌstəm] v
*vänja; **accustomed** van

ache [eik] v värka; n värk c

achieve [əˈtʃiːv] v uppnå;
prestera

achievement [əˈtʃiːvmənt] n
prestation c

acknowledge [əkˈnɔlidʒ] v
erkänna; bekräfta

acne [ˈækni] n finnar

acorn [ˈeikɔːn] n ekollon nt

acquaintance [əˈkweintəns]
n bekant c

acquire [əˈkwaiə] v skaffa sig

acquisition [ˌækwiˈziʃən] n
förvärv nt

acquittal [əˈkwitəl] n
frikännande nt

across [əˈkrɔs] prep över;
adv på andra sidan

act [ækt] n handling c; akt c;
nummer nt; v handla;

uppträda; uppföra sig; spela

action [ˈækʃən] n handling c

active [ˈæktiv] adj aktiv

activity [ækˈtivəti] n aktivitet
c

actor [ˈæktə] n aktör c,
skådespelare c

actress [ˈæktris] n
skådespelerska c, aktris c

actual [ˈæktʃuəl] adj faktisk,
verklig

actually [ˈæktʃuəli] adv
faktiskt

acute [əˈkjuːt] adj akut

adapt [əˈdæpt] v anpassa

adaptor [əˈdæptə] n adapter c

add [æd] v addera; *lägga till

addition [əˈdiʃən] n addition
c; tillägg nt

additional [əˈdiʃənəl] adj
extra; ytterligare

address [əˈdres] n adress c; v
adressera; vända sig till

addressee [ˌædreˈsiː] n
adressat c

adequate [ˈædikwət] adj
tillräcklig; passande,
adekvat

adjective [ˈædʒiktiv] n
adjektiv c

adjust [əˈdʒʌst] v justera;
anpassa

administer [ədˈministə] v
dela ut

administration
[ədˌminiˈstreiʃən] n
administration c;
förvaltning c

administrative
[ədˈministrətiv] adj

administrativ; förvaltande;
~ **law** förvaltningsrätt c
admiration [,ædmə'reiʃən] n
beundran c
admire [əd'maiə] v beundra
admission [əd'miʃən] n
inträde nt; intagning c
admit [əd'mit] v *ta in, släppa
in; erkänna, *medge;
rymma
admittance [əd'mitəns] n
tillträde nt; **no** ~ tillträde
förbjudet
adopt [ə'dɔpt] v adoptera
adorable [ə'dɔ:rəbəl] adj
bedårande
adult ['ædʌlt] n vuxen c; adj
vuxen
advance [əd'vɑ:ns] n
framsteg nt; förskott nt; v
*göra framsteg; förskottera;
in ~ i förväg, på förhand
advanced [əd'vɑ:nst] adj
avancerad
advantage [əd'vɑ:ntidʒ] n
fördel c
advantageous
[,ædvən'teidʒəs] adj
fördelaktig
adventure [əd'ventʃə] n
äventyr c
adverb ['ædvə:b] n adverb nt
advertisement
[əd'və:tismənt] n annons c
advertising ['ædvətaiziŋ] n
reklam c
advice [əd'vais] n råd nt
advise [əd'vaiz] v råda
advocate ['ædvəkət] n
försvarare c, förespråkare c

aerial ['eəriəl] n antenn c
aeroplane ['eərəplein] n
flygplan nt
affair [ə'feə] n angelägenhet
c; förhållande nt,
kärleksaffär c
affect [ə'fekt] v påverka;
beröra
affected [ə'fektid] adj
tillgjord
affection [ə'fekʃən] n
tillgivenhet c
affectionate [ə'fekʃənit] adj
kärleksfull, tillgiven
affiliated [ə'filieitid] adj
ansluten
affirm [ə'fə:m] v försäkra
affirmative [ə'fə:mətiv] adj
jakande
afford [ə'fɔ:d] v *ha råd med
afraid [ə'freid] adj rädd,
ängslig; *be ~ *vara rädd
Africa ['æfrikə] Afrika
African ['æfrikən] adj
afrikansk; n afrikan c
after ['ɑ:ftə] prep efter; conj
sedan
afternoon [,ɑ:ftə'nu:n] n
eftermiddag c; **this** ~ i
eftermiddag
afterwards ['ɑ:ftəwədz] adv
sedan; efteråt
again [ə'gen] adv igen; åter; ~
and again gång på gång
against [ə'genst] prep mot
age [eidʒ] n ålder c; ålderdom
c; **of** ~ myndig; **under** ~
minderårig
aged ['eidʒid] adj åldrig;
gammal

agency ['eidʒənsi] n agentur c; byrå c

agenda [ə'dʒendə] n dagordning c

agent ['eidʒənt] n agent c, representant c

aggressive [ə'gresiv] adj aggressiv

ago [ə'gou] adv för … sedan

agree [ə'griː] v *vara enig; instämma; stämma överens

agreeable [ə'griːəbəl] adj angenäm

agreement [ə'griːmənt] n kontrakt nt; avtal nt, överenskommelse c

agriculture ['ægrikʌltʃə] n jordbruk nt

ahead [ə'hed] adv framför; ~ of före; *go ~ *fortsätta; straight ~ rakt fram

aid [eid] n hjälp c; v *bistå, hjälpa

AIDS [eidz] n aids c

airbag ['ɛəbæg] n krockkudde c

aim [eim] n syfte nt; ~ at sikta, sikta på; sträva efter

air [ɛə] n luft c; v lufta

air conditioning ['ɛəkən.diʃəniŋ] n luftkonditionering c; air-conditioned adj luftkonditionerad

airfield ['ɛəfiːld] n flygfält nt

air-filter ['ɛə.filtə] n luftfilter nt

airline ['ɛəlain] n flygbolag nt

airmail ['ɛəmeil] n flygpost c

airplane ['ɛəplein] nAm

flygplan nt

airport ['ɛəpɔːt] n flygplats c

airsickness ['ɛə.siknəs] n flygsjuka c

airtight ['ɛətait] adj lufttät

airy ['ɛəri] adj luftig

aisle [ail] n sidoskepp nt; gång c

alarm [ə'lɑːm] n alarm nt; v larma

alarm-clock [ə'lɑːmklɔk] n väckarklocka c

album ['ælbəm] n album nt

alcohol ['ælkəhɔl] n alkohol c

alcoholic [.ælkə'hɔlik] adj alkoholhaltig

ale [eil] n öl nt

algebra ['ældʒibrə] n algebra c

Algeria [æl'dʒiəriə] Algeriet

Algerian [æl'dʒiəriən] adj algerisk; n algerier c

alien ['eiliən] n utlänning c; främling c; adj utländsk

alike [ə'laik] adj likadan, lik; adv på samma sätt

alive [ə'laiv] adj levande

all [ɔːl] adj all; ~ in allt inkluderat; ~ right! fint!; at ~ överhuvudtaget

allergy ['ælədʒi] n allergi c

alley ['æli] n gränd c

alliance [ə'laiəns] n allians c

Allies ['ælaiz] pl (de) allierade

allow [ə'lau] v *tillåta, bevilja; ~ to *låta; *be allowed *vara tillåten; *be allowed to *få

allowance [ə'lauəns] n

215

analysis

fickpengar *pl*, underhåll *nt*
almond [ˈɑːmənd] *n* mandel *c*
almost [ˈɔːlmoust] *adv*
nästan
alone [əˈloun] *adv* endast; *adj*
ensam, för sig själv
along [əˈlɔŋ] *prep* längs
aloud [əˈlaud] *adv* högt
alphabet [ˈælfəbet] *n* alfabet
nt
already [ɔːlˈredi] *adv* redan
also [ˈɔːlsou] *adv* också;
dessutom, även
altar [ˈɔːltə] *n* altare *nt*
alter [ˈɔːltə] *v* förändra, ändra
alteration [ˌɔːltəˈreiʃən] *n*
ändring *c*, förändring *c*
alternate [ɔːlˈtəːnət] *adj*
alternerande
alternative [ɔːlˈtəːnətiv] *n*
alternativ *nt*
although [ɔːlˈðou] *conj*
fastän, även om
altitude [ˈæltitjuːd] *n* höjd *c*
alto [ˈæltou] *n* (*pl* ~s) alt *c*
altogether [ˌɔːltəˈgeðə] *adv*
helt och hållet
always [ˈɔːlweiz] *adv* alltid
am [æm] *v* (pr be)
amaze [əˈmeiz] *v* förbluffa,
förvåna
amazement [əˈmeizmənt] *n*
förvåning *c*
amazing [əˈmeiziŋ] *adj*
häpnadsväckande
ambassador [æmˈbæsədə] *n*
ambassadör *c*
amber [ˈæmbə] *n* bärnsten *c*
ambiguous [æmˈbigjuəs] *adj*
tvetydig

ambition [æmˈbiʃən] *n*
ambition *c*
ambitious [æmˈbiʃəs] *adj*
ambitiös; ärelysten
ambulance [ˈæmbjuləns] *n*
ambulans *c*
ambush [ˈæmbuʃ] *n* bakhåll
nt
America [əˈmerikə] Amerika
American [əˈmerikən] *adj*
amerikansk; *n* amerikan *c*
amethyst [ˈæmiθist] *n*
ametist *c*
amid [əˈmid] *prep* bland; mitt
ibland, mitt i
ammonia [əˈmouniə] *n*
ammoniak *c*
amnesty [ˈæmnisti] *n*
amnesti *c*
among [əˈmʌŋ] *prep* bland;
mellan, ibland; ~ **other**
things bland annat
amount [əˈmaunt] *n* mängd
c; summa *c*, belopp *nt*; ~ **to**
v uppgå till
amuse [əˈmjuːz] *v* roa,
*underhålla
amusement [əˈmjuːzmənt] *n*
nöje *nt*, förströelse *c*
amusing [əˈmjuːziŋ] *adj*
lustig
anaemia [əˈniːmiə] *n*
blodbrist *c*
anaesthesia [ˌænisˈθiːziə] *n*
bedövning *c*
anaesthetic [ˌænisˈθetik] *n*
bedövningsmedel *nt*
analyse [ˈænəlaiz] *v*
analysera
analysis [əˈnæləsis] *n* (pl

-ses) analys c

analyst ['ænəlist] n
analytiker c;
psykoanalytiker c

anarchy ['ænəki] n anarki c

anatomy [ə'nætəmi] n
anatomi c

ancestor ['ænsestə] n
förfader c

anchor ['æŋkə] n ankare nt

anchovy ['æntʃəvi] n sardell
c, ansjovis c

ancient ['einʃənt] adj
gammal; forntida

and [ænd, ənd] conj och

angel ['eindʒəl] n ängel c

anger ['æŋgə] n ilska c, vrede
c

angle ['æŋgəl] v meta; n
vinkel c

angry ['æŋgri] adj vred, arg

animal ['æniməl] n djur nt

ankle ['æŋkəl] n ankel c

annex¹ ['æneks] n annex nt;
bilaga c

annex² [ə'neks] v annektera

anniversary [,æni'və:səri] n
årsdag c

announce [ə'nauns] v
*tillkännage, *offentliggöra

announcement
[ə'naunsmənt] n
tillkännagivande nt,
kungörelse c

annoy [ə'nɔi] v förarga,
irritera; reta

annoyance [ə'nɔiəns] n
förargelse c

annoying [ə'nɔiiŋ] adj
förarglig, retsam

annual ['ænjuəl] adj årlig; n
årsbok c

per annum [pər 'ænəm] per
år

anonymous [ə'nɔniməs] adj
anonym

another [ə'nʌðə] adj en till;
en annan

answer ['ɑ:nsə] v svara;
besvara; n svar nt

answering machine
['ɑ:nsəriŋ mə'ʃi:n] n
telefonsvarare

ant [ænt] n myra c

antibiotic [,æntibai'ɔtik] n
antibiotikum c

anticipate [æn'tisipeit] v
*förutse, *föregripa;
*förekomma

antifreeze ['æntifri:z] n
frostskyddsvätska c

antipathy [æn'tipəθi] n
motvilja c

antique [æn'ti:k] adj antik; n
antikvitet c

antiquities pl antikviteter

antiseptic [,ænti'septik] n
antiseptiskt medel

anxiety [æŋ'zaiəti] n
bekymmer nt

anxious ['æŋkʃəs] adj ivrig;
orolig

any ['eni] adj någon

anybody ['enibɔdi] pron vem
som helst

anyhow ['enihau] adv hur
som helst

anyone ['eniwʌn] pron varje

anything ['eniθiŋ] pron vad
som helst

anyway ['eniwei] adv i varje
fall

anywhere ['eniwɛə] adv var
som helst

apart [ə'pɑ:t] adv isär, var för
sig; ~ from bortsett från

apartment [ə'pɑ:tmənt]
nAm våning c, lägenhet c; ~
house Am hyreshus nt

aperitif [ə'perətiv] n aperitif
c

apologize [ə'pɔlədʒaiz] v *be
om ursäkt

apology [ə'pɔlədʒi] n ursäkt c

app [æp] n app c

apparatus [,æpə'reitəs] n
anordning c, apparat c

apparent [ə'pærənt] adj
uppenbar; tydlig

apparently [ə'pærəntli] adv
tydligen

appeal [ə'pi:l] n vädjan c

appear [ə'piə] v verka,
tyckas; *framgå; synas;
framträda

appearance [ə'piərəns] n
utseende nt; framträdande
nt

appendicitis [ə,pendi'saitis]
n blindtarmsinflammation c

appendix [ə'pendiks] n (pl
-dices, -dixes) blindtarm c

appetite ['æpətait] n aptit c,
matlust c

appetizer ['æpətaizə] n
aptitretare c

appetizing ['æpətaiziŋ] adj
aptitlig

applaud [ə'plɔ:d] v
applådera

applause [ə'plɔ:z] n applåd c

apple ['æpəl] n äpple nt

appliance [ə'plaiəns] n
apparat c, anordning c

application [,æpli'keiʃən] n
användning c; ansökan c

apply [ə'plai] v tillämpa,
*lägga på; använda; ansöka;
gälla

appoint [ə'pɔint] v anställa,
utnämna

appointment [ə'pɔintmənt]
n avtalat möte, avtal nt;
utnämning c

appreciate [ə'pri:ʃieit] v
uppskatta, *värdesätta

appreciation [ə,pri:ʃi'eiʃən]
n värdestegring c;
uppskattning c

apprentice [ə'prentis] n
lärling c

approach [ə'proutʃ] v närma
sig; n tillvägagångssätt nt;
närmande c

appropriate [ə'proupriət] adj
rätt, lämplig, ändamålsenlig

approval [ə'pru:vəl] n
gillande nt; bifall nt

approve [ə'pru:v] v gilla; ~ of
godkänna

approximate [ə'prɔksimət]
adj ungefärlig

approximately
[ə'prɔksimətli] adv ungefär,
cirka

apricot ['eiprikɔt] n aprikos c

April ['eiprəl] april

apron ['eiprən] n förkläde nt

Arab ['ærəb] adj arabisk; n
arab c

arbitrary ['ɑ:bitrəri] *adj*
godtycklig

arcade [ɑ:'keid] *n* pelargång
c, arkad *c*

arch [ɑ:tʃ] *n* valvbåge *c*; valv
nt

archaeologist
[,ɑ:ki'ɔlədʒist] *n* arkeolog *c*

archaeology [,ɑ:ki'ɔlədʒi] *n*
arkeologi *c*

arched [ɑ:tʃt] *adj* bågformig

architect ['ɑ:kitekt] *n*
arkitekt *c*

architecture ['ɑ:kitektʃə] *n*
byggnadskonst *c*, arkitektur
c

archives ['ɑ:kaivz] *pl* arkiv
nt

are [ɑ:] *v* (pr be)

area ['ɛəriə] *n* område *nt*; yta
c; **~ code** riktnummer *nt*

Argentina [,ɑ:dʒən'ti:nə]
Argentina

Argentinian [,ɑ:dʒən'tiniən]
adj argentinsk; *n*
argentinare *c*

argue ['ɑ:gju:] *v*
argumentera, diskutera,
debattera; gräla

argument ['ɑ:gjumənt] *n*
argument *nt*; diskussion *c*;
ordväxling *c*

*****arise** [ə'raiz] *v* *uppstå

arithmetic [ə'riθmətik] *n*
räkning *c*

arm [ɑ:m] *n* arm *c*; vapen *nt*;
armstöd *nt*; *v* beväpna

armchair ['ɑ:mtʃɛə] *n* fåtölj *c*

armed [ɑ:md] *adj* beväpnad;
~ forces beväpnade styrkor

armour ['ɑ:mə] *n* rustning *c*

army ['ɑ:mi] *n* armé *c*

aroma [ə'roumə] *n* arom *c*

around [ə'raund] *prep*
omkring; *adv* runt

arrange [ə'reindʒ] *v* ordna;
arrangera

arrangement [ə'reindʒmənt]
n arrangemang *nt*; avtal *nt*;
åtgärd *c*

arrest [ə'rest] *v* arrestera; *n*
arrestering *c*

arrival [ə'raivəl] *n* ankomst *c*

arrive [ə'raiv] *v* anlända

arrow ['ærou] *n* pil *c*

art [ɑ:t] *n* konst *c*; skicklighet
c; list *c*; **~ collection**
konstsamling *c*; **~ exhibition**
konstutställning *c*; **~ gallery**
konstgalleri *nt*; **~ history**
konsthistoria *c*; **arts and
crafts** konstindustri *c*; **~
school** konstakademi *c*

artery ['ɑ:təri] *n* pulsåder *c*

artichoke ['ɑ:titʃouk] *n*
kronärtskocka *c*

article ['ɑ:tikəl] *n* artikel *c*

artificial [,ɑ:ti'fiʃəl] *adj*
konstgjord

artist ['ɑ:tist] *n* konstnär *c*;
konstnärinna *c*

artistic [ɑ:'tistik] *adj*
artistisk, konstnärlig

as [æz] *conj* liksom, som;
lika; därför att, eftersom; **~
from** från; från och med; **~** så
som om

asbestos [æz'bestɔs] *n*
asbest *c*

ascend [ə'send] *v* *stiga;

*stiga uppåt; *bestiga

ascent [ə'sent] n stigning c; bestigning c

ascertain [ˌæsə'tein] v konstatera; förvissa sig om, fastställa

ash [æʃ] n aska c

ashamed [ə'feimd] adj skamsen; *be ~ skämmas

ashore [ə'ʃɔ:] adv i land

ashtray [ˈæʃtrei] n askkopp c

Asia [ˈeiʃə] Asien

Asian [ˈeiʃən] adj asiatisk; n asiat c

aside [ə'said] adv åt sidan

ask [ɑ:sk] v fråga; *be; *inbjuda

asleep [ə'sli:p] adj sovande

asparagus [ə'spærəgəs] n sparris c

aspect [ˈæspekt] n aspekt c

asphalt [ˈæsfælt] n asfalt c

aspire [ə'spaiə] v sträva

aspirin [ˈæspərin] n aspirin nt

assassination [əˌsæsi'neiʃən] n mord nt

assault [ə'sɔ:lt] v *angripa; *våldta

assemble [ə'sembəl] v samla; *sätta ihop, montera

assembly [ə'sembli] n församling c, sammankomst c

assignment [ə'sainmənt] n uppdrag nt

assign to [ə'sain] tilldela; *överlåta

assist [ə'sist] v hjälpa, *bistå; ~ at *vara närvarande vid

assistance [ə'sistəns] n hjälp c; bistånd nt; understöd nt

assistant [ə'sistənt] n assistent c

associate[1] [ə'souʃiət] n kompanjon c, delägare c; kollega c; medlem c

associate[2] [ə'souʃieit] v associera; ~ with *umgås med

association [əˌsousi'eiʃən] n förening c, sammanslutning c

assort [ə'sɔ:t] v sortera

assortment [ə'sɔ:tmənt] n urval nt, sortiment c

assume [ə'sju:m] v *anta, förmoda

assure [ə'ʃuə] v försäkra

asthma [ˈæsmə] n astma c

astonish [ə'stɔniʃ] v förvåna

astonishing [ə'stɔniʃiŋ] adj förvånansvärd

astonishment [ə'stɔniʃmənt] n förvåning c

astronaut [ˈæstrənɔ:t] n astronaut c

astronomy [ə'strɔnəmi] n astronomi c

asylum [ə'sailəm] n asyl c; mentalsjukhus nt, vårdanstalt c

at [æt] prep på, hos, i

ate [et] v (p ate)

atheist [ˈeiθiist] n ateist c

athlete [ˈæθli:t] n atlet c

athletics [æθ'letiks] pl friidrott c

Atlantic [ət'læntik] Atlanten

ATM [ˈeiti:'em] n bankomat c

atmosphere ['ætməsfiə] *n* atmosfär *c*; stämning *c*

atom ['ætəm] *n* atom *c*

atomic [ə'tɔmik] *adj* atom-; kärn-

atomizer ['ætəmaizə] *n* sprayflaska *c*; spray *c*

attach [ə'tætʃ] *v* fästa; bifoga; attached to fäst vid

attack [ə'tæk] *v* *anfalla; *n* anfall *nt*

attain [ə'tein] *v* uppnå

attainable [ə'teinəbəl] *adj* uppnåelig; åtkomlig

attempt [ə'tempt] *v* försöka, pröva; *n* försök *nt*

attend [ə'tend] *v* *vara närvarande vid; ~ on uppassa; ~ to *ta hand om, *se till; beakta, uppmärksamma

attendance [ə'tendəns] *n* deltagande *nt*

attendant [ə'tendənt] *n* vaktmästare *c*

attention [ə'tenʃən] *n* uppmärksamhet *c*

attentive [ə'tentiv] *adj* uppmärksam

attest [ə'test] *v* intyga

attic ['ætik] *n* vindsrum *nt*

attitude ['ætitjuːd] *n* inställning *c*

attorney [ə'təːni] *n* advokat *c*

attract [ə'trækt] *v* *tilldra sig

attraction [ə'trækʃən] *n* attraktion *c*; lockelse *c*

attractive [ə'træktiv] *adj* tilldragande

auction ['ɔːkʃən] *n* auktion *c*

audible ['ɔːdibəl] *adj* hörbar

audience ['ɔːdiəns] *n* publik *c*

auditor ['ɔːditə] *n* åhörare *c*

auditorium [,ɔːdi'tɔːriəm] *n* hörsal *c*

August ['ɔːgəst] augusti

aunt [ɑːnt] *n* tant *c*, moster *c*, faster *c*

Australia [ɔ'streiliə] Australien

Australian [ɔ'streiliən] *adj* australisk; *n* australier *c*

Austria ['ɔstriə] Österrike

Austrian ['ɔstriən] *adj* österrikisk; *n* österrikare *c*

authentic [ɔː'θentik] *adj* autentisk; äkta

author ['ɔːθə] *n* författare *c*

authoritarian [ɔː,θɔri'teəriən] *adj* auktoritär

authority [ɔː'θɔrəti] *n* auktoritet *c*; maktbefogenhet *c*; authorities *pl* myndigheter *pl*

authorization [,ɔːθərai'zeiʃən] *n* tillåtelse *c*

automatic [,ɔːtə'mætik] *adj* automatisk; ~ teller machine *n* bankomat *c*

automation [,ɔːtə'meiʃən] *n* automatisering *c*

automobile ['ɔːtəməbiːl] *n* bil *c*; ~ club automobilklubb *c*

autonomous [ɔː'tɔnəməs] *adj* autonom

ball

autopsy ['ɔːtɔpsi] *n* obduktion *c*

autumn ['ɔːtəm] *n* höst *c*

available [ə'veiləbəl] *adj* disponibel, tillgänglig, i lager

avalanche ['ævəlɑːnʃ] *n* lavin *c*

avenue ['ævənjuː] *n* aveny *c*

average ['ævəridʒ] *adj* genomsnittlig; *n* genomsnitt *nt*; **on the ~** i genomsnitt

averse [ə'vəːs] *adj* obenägen, ovillig

aversion [ə'vəːʃən] *n* motvilja *c*

avoid [ə'vɔid] *v* *undgå;

*undvika

await [ə'weit] *v* vänta på, vänta upp

awake [ə'weik] *adj* vaken

*****awake** [ə'weik] *v* väcka

award [ə'wɔːd] *n* pris *nt*; *v* tilldela

aware [ə'wɛə] *adj* medveten

away [ə'wei] *adv* bort; *****go ~** åka bort

awful ['ɔːfəl] *adj* fruktansvärd, ryslig

awkward ['ɔːkwəd] *adj* brydsam; tafatt, klumpig

awning ['ɔːniŋ] *n* markis *c*

axe [æks] *n* yxa *c*

axle ['æksəl] *n* hjulaxel *c*

B

baby ['beibi] *n* baby *c*; **~ carriage** *Am* barnvagn *c*

babysitter ['beibi,sitə] *n* barnvakt *c*

bachelor ['bætʃələ] *n* ungkarl *c*

back [bæk] *n* rygg *c*; *adv* tillbaka; *****go ~** åka tillbaka

backache ['bækeik] *n* ryggvärk *c*

backbone ['bækboun] *n* ryggrad *c*

background ['bækgraund] *n* bakgrund *c*; utbildning *c*

backwards ['bækwədz] *adv* bakåt

bacon ['beikən] *n* bacon *nt*

bacterium [bæk'tiːriəm] *n* (pl -ria) bakterie *c*

bad [bæd] *adj* dålig, allvarlig; stygg

bag [bæg] *n* påse *c*; väska *c*, handväska *c*; resväska *c*

baggage ['bægidʒ] *n* bagage *nt*; **~ deposit office** *Am* bagageinlämning *c*; **hand ~** handbagage *nt*

bail [beil] *n* borgen *c*

bait [beit] *n* bete *nt*

bake [beik] *v* baka

baker ['beikə] *n* bagare *c*

bakery ['beikəri] *n* bageri *nt*

balance ['bæləns] *n* jämvikt *c*; våg *c*; saldo *nt*

balcony ['bælkəni] *n* balkong *c*

bald [bɔːld] *adj* flintskallig

ball [bɔːl] *n* boll *c*; bal *c*

ballet ['bæleɪ] n balett c

balloon [bə'luːn] n ballong c

ballpoint pen ['bɔːlpɔɪntpen] n kulspetspenna c

ballroom ['bɔːlruːm] n balsal c

banana [bə'nɑːnə] n banan c

band [bænd] n band c

bandage ['bændɪdʒ] n förband nt

bank [bæŋk] n flodbank c; bank c; v deponera, *sätta in; ~ account bankkonto nt

banknote ['bæŋknout] n sedel c

bank rate ['bæŋkreɪt] n diskonto nt

bankrupt ['bæŋkrʌpt] adj konkursmässig, bankrutt

banner ['bænə] n baner nt

banquet ['bæŋkwɪt] n bankett c

banqueting-hall ['bæŋkwɪtɪŋhɔːl] n bankettsal c

baptism ['bæptɪzəm] n dop nt

baptize [bæp'taɪz] v döpa

bar [bɑː] n bar c; stång c; fönstergaller nt

barbecue ['bɑːbɪkjuː] n grill; v grilla

barbed wire ['bɑːbd waɪə] n taggtråd

barber ['bɑːbə] n herrfrisör c

bare [beə] adj naken, bar; kal

barely ['beəlɪ] adv nätt och jämt

bargain ['bɑːgɪn] n fynd nt; v *köpslå, pruta

baritone ['bærɪtoun] n baryton c

bark [bɑːk] n bark c; v skälla

barley ['bɑːlɪ] n korn nt

barn [bɑːn] n lada c

barometer [bə'rɔmɪtə] n barometer c

baroque [bə'rɔk] adj barock

barracks ['bærəks] pl kasern c

barrel ['bærəl] n tunna c, fat nt

barrier ['bærɪə] n barriär c; bom c

barrister ['bærɪstə] n advokat c

bartender ['bɑː,tendə] n bartender c

base [beɪs] n bas c; grundval c; v basera

baseball ['beɪsbɔːl] n baseboll c

basement ['beɪsmənt] n källarvåning c

basic ['beɪsɪk] adj grundläggande

basilica [bə'zɪlɪkə] n basilika c

basin ['beɪsən] n balja c, skål c

basis ['beɪsɪs] n (pl bases) basis c, grundprincip c

basket ['bɑːskɪt] n korg c

bass[1] [beɪs] n bas c

bass[2] [bæs] n (pl ~) abborre c

batch [bætʃ] n parti nt; hop c

bath [bɑːθ] n bad nt; ~ salts badsalt nt; ~ towel

badhandduk c
bathe [beið] v bada
bathing cap ['beiðiŋkæp] n
badmössa c
bathing suit ['beiðiŋsu:t] n
baddräkt c; badbyxor pl
bathrobe ['ba:θroub] n
badrock c
bathroom ['ba:θru:m] n
badrum nt; toalett c
batter ['bætə] n smet c
battery ['bætəri] n batteri nt
battle ['bætəl] n slag nt; kamp
c, strid c; v kämpa
bay [bei] n vik c; v skälla
*be [bi:] v *vara
beach [bi:tʃ] n strand c;
nudist ~ nudistbadstrand c
bead [bi:d] n pärla c; **beads**
pl pärlhalsband nt; radband
nt
beak [bi:k] n näbb c
beam [bi:m] n stråle c; bjälke
c
bean [bi:n] n böna c
bear [bɛə] n björn c
*bear [bɛə] v *bära; tåla;
*utstå
beard [biəd] n skägg nt
beast [bi:st] n djur nt; **~ of
prey** rovdjur nt
*beat [bi:t] v *slå; besegra
beautiful ['bju:tifəl] adj
vacker
beauty ['bju:ti] n skönhet c;
parlour skönhetssalong c; **~
salon** skönhetssalong c; **~
treatment** skönhetsvård c
beaver ['bi:və] n bäver c
because [bi'kɔz] conj därför

att; eftersom; **~ of** på grund
av
*become [bi'kʌm] v *bli; klä
bed [bed] n säng c; **~ and
board** helpension c, mat och
logi; **~ and breakfast** rum
med frukost
bedding ['bediŋ] n
sängkläder pl
bedroom ['bedru:m] n
sovrum nt
bee [bi:] n bi nt
beech [bi:tʃ] n bok c
beef [bi:f] n oxkött nt
beefburger ['bi:fbə:gə] n
biffburgare c
beehive ['bi:haiv] n bikupa c
been [bi:n] v (pp be)
beer [biə] n öl nt
beet [bi:t] n beta c
beetle ['bi:təl] n skalbagge c
beetroot ['bi:tru:t] n rödbeta
c
before [bi'fɔ:] prep före;
framför; conj innan; adv
förut; innan
beg [beg] v tigga; *bönfalla;
*be
beggar ['begə] n tiggare c
*begin [bi'gin] v begynna,
börja
beginner [bi'ginə] n
nybörjare c
beginning [bi'giniŋ] n
begynnelse c; början c
on behalf of [bi'ha:f] på ...
vägnar
behave [bi'heiv] v uppföra
sig
behaviour [bi'heivjə] n

uppförande *nt*

behind [bi'haind] *prep*
bakom; *adv* bakom

beige [beiʒ] *adj* beige

being [bi:iŋ] *n* varelse *c*

Belgian [beldʒən] *adj*
belgisk; *n* belgare *c*

Belgium [beldʒəm] Belgien

belief [bi'li:f] *n* tro *c*

believe [bi'li:v] *v* tro

bell [bel] *n* klocka *c*;
ringklocka *c*

bellboy [belbɔi] *n*
hotellpojke *c*

belly [beli] *n* buk *c*

belong [bi'lɔŋ] *v* tillhöra

belongings [bi'lɔŋiŋz] *pl*
tillhörigheter *pl*

beloved [bi'lʌvd] *adj* älskad

below [bi'lou] *prep* nedanför;
under; *adv* nedan

belt [belt] *n* bälte *nt*; garter ~
Am strumpebandshållare *c*

bench [bentʃ] *n* bänk *c*

bend [bend] *n* kurva *c*,
böjning *c*; krök *c*

*bend [bend] *v* böja; ~ **down**
böja sig

beneath [bi'ni:θ] *prep* under;
adv nedanför

benefit [benifit] *n* vinst *c*,
nytta *c*; förmån *c*; *v* **dra
nytta

bent [bent] *adj* (pp bend)
böjd

berry [beri] *n* bär *c*

beside [bi'said] *prep* bredvid

besides [bi'saidz] *adv*
dessutom; förresten; *prep*
utom

best [best] *adj* bäst

bet [bet] *n* vad *nt*; insats *c*

*bet [bet] *v* *slå vad

betray [bi'trei] *v* förråda

better [betə] *adj* bättre

between [bi'twi:n] *prep*
mellan

beverage [bevəridʒ] *n* dryck
c

beware [bi'wɛə] *v* akta sig

beyond [bi'jɔnd] *prep*
bortom; på andra sidan om;
utöver; *adv* bortom

bible [baibəl] *n* bibel *c*

bicycle [baisikəl] *n* cykel *c*

bid [bid] *n* bud *nt*

big [big] *adj* stor; omfångsrik;
tjock; viktig

bike [baik] *n* colloquial cykel
c

bile [bail] *n* galla *c*

bilingual [bai'liŋgwəl] *adj*
tvåspråkig

bill [bil] *n* räkning *c*; nota *c*; *v*
fakturera

billiards [biljədz] *pl* biljard *c*

billion [biljən] *n* miljard *c*

*bind [baind] *v* *binda

binding [baindiŋ] *n* band *nt*;
bård *c*

binoculars [bi'nɔkjələz] *pl*
kikare *c*

biodegradable
[,baioudi'greidəbəl] *adj*
biologiskt nedbrytbar

biology [bai'ɔlədʒi] *n* biologi
c

bipolar [,bai'poulə] *adj*
bipolär

birch [bə:tʃ] *n* björk *c*

bird [bə:d] *n* fågel *c*

birth [bə:θ] *n* födelse *c*

birthday ['bə:θdei] *n*
födelsedag *c*

biscuit ['biskit] *n* kex *nt*

bishop ['biʃəp] *n* biskop *c*

bit [bit] *n* bit *c*; smula *c*

bitch [bitʃ] *n* tik *c*

bite [bait] *n* munsbit *c*; bett *nt*

*bite [bait] *v* *bita

bitter ['bitə] *adj* bitter

black [blæk] *adj* svart; ~
market svarta börsen

blackberry ['blækbəri] *n*
björnbär *c*

Blackberry® ['blækbəri] *n*
Blackberry *c*

blackbird ['blækbə:d] *n*
koltrast *c*

blackboard ['blækbɔ:d] *n*
svarta tavlan

blackcurrant [,blæk'kʌrənt]
n svarta vinbär *c*

blackmail ['blækmeil] *n*
utpressning *c*; *v* utpressa
pengar

blacksmith ['blæksmiθ] *n*
smed *c*

bladder ['blædə] *n* urinblåsa
c

blade [bleid] *n* knivblad *nt*; ~
of grass grässtrå *n*

blame [bleim] *n* klander *nt*; *v*
förebrå, klandra

blank [blæŋk] *adj* blank

blanket ['blæŋkit] *n* filt *c*

blast [blɑ:st] *n* explosion *c*

blazer ['bleizə] *n* blazer *c*

bleach [bli:tʃ] *v* bleka

bleak [bli:k] *adj* karg, kal

*bleed [bli:d] *v* blöda

bless [bles] *v* välsigna

blessing ['blesiŋ] *n*
välsignelse *c*

blind [blaind] *n* persienn *c*,
rullgardin *c*; *adj* blind; *v*
blända

blister ['blistə] *n* blåsa *c*,
vattenblåsa *c*

blizzard ['blizəd] *n* snöstorm
c

block [blɔk] *v* blockera,
spärra; *n* kloss *c*; ~ of flats
hyreshus *nt*

Blog [blɔg] *n* blogg *c*

blond [blɔnd] *adj* blond

blood [blʌd] *n* blod *nt*; ~
pressure blodtryck *nt*

blood poisoning
['blʌd,pɔizəniŋ] *n*
blodförgiftning *c*

blood vessel ['blʌd,vesəl] *n*
blodkärl *c*

bloody ['blʌdi] *adj colloquial*
blodig

blossom ['blɔsəm] *n*
blomma *c*

blot [blɔt] *n* fläck *c*; blotting
paper läskpapper *nt*

blouse [blauz] *n* blus *c*

blow [blou] *n* örfil *c*, slag *nt*;
vindpust *c*

*blow [blou] *v* blåsa

blowout ['blouaut] *n*
punktering *c*

blue [blu:] *adj* blå; nedstämd

blunt [blʌnt] *adj* slö; trubbig

blush [blʌʃ] *v* rodna

board [bɔ:d] *n* bräda *c*; tavla
c; pension *c*; styrelse *c*; ~

and lodging mat och logi, helpension *c*

boarder ['bɔːdə] *n* internatselev *c*, inackordering *c*

boardinghouse ['bɔːdiŋhaus] *n* pensionat *nt*

boarding school ['bɔːdiŋskuːl] *n* internatskola *c*

boast [boust] *v* *skryta

boat [bout] *n* båt *c*, skepp *nt*

body ['bɔdi] *n* kropp *c*

bodyguard ['bɔdigɑːd] *n* livvakt *c*

bog [bɔg] *n* träsk *nt*

boil [bɔil] *v* koka; *n* spikböld *c*

bold [bould] *adj* djärv, fräck

Bolivia [bə'liviə] Bolivia

Bolivian [bə'liviən] *adj* boliviansk; *n* bolivian *c*

bolt [boult] *n* regel *c*; bult *c*

bomb [bɔm] *n* bomb *c*; *v* bombardera

bond [bɔnd] *n* obligation *c*

bone [boun] *n* ben *nt*; fiskben *nt*; *v* urbena

bonnet ['bɔnit] *n* motorhuv *c*

book [buk] *n* bok *c*, reservera; bokföra, *skriva in

booking ['bukiŋ] *n* beställning *c*, reservation *c*

bookmaker ['buk,meikə] *n* vadhållningsagent *c*

bookseller ['buk,selə] *n* bokhandlare *c*

bookstand ['bukstænd] *n* bokstånd *nt*

bookstore ['bukstɔː] *n*

bokhandel *c*, boklåda *c*

boot [buːt] *n* stövel *c*; bagageutrymme *nt*

booth [buːð] *n* bod *c*; hytt *c*

booze [buːz] *n colloquial* sprit

border ['bɔːdə] *n* gräns *c*; kant *c*

bore[1] [bɔː] *v* tråka ut; borra; *n* tråkmåns *c*

bore[2] [bɔː] *v* (p bear)

boring ['bɔːriŋ] *adj* tråkig, långtråkig

born [bɔːn] *adj* född

borrow ['bɔrou] *v* låna

bosom ['buzəm] *n* barm *c*; bröst *nt*

boss [bɔs] *n* chef *c*

botany ['bɔtəni] *n* botanik *c*

both [bouθ] *adj* båda; **both ... and** både ... och

bother ['bɔðə] *v* besvära, störa; *göra sig besvär; *n* besvär *nt*

bottle ['bɔtəl] *n* flaska *c*; ~ **opener** flasköppnare *c*; **hot--water** ~ varmvattensflaska *c*

bottleneck ['bɔtəlnek] *n* flaskhals *c*

bottom ['bɔtəm] *n* botten *c*; bakdel *c*, stjärt *c*; *adj* nedersta

bought [bɔːt] *v* (p, pp buy)

boulder ['bouldə] *n* stenblock *c*

bound [baund] *n* gräns *c*; *be ~ **to** *måste; ~ **for** på väg till

boundary ['baundəri] *n* gränslinje *c*; landgräns *c*

bouquet [bu'kei] *n* bukett *c*

bribery

bourgeois ['buəʒwɑ:] *adj* kälkborgerlig

boutique [bu'ti:k] *n* boutique *c*

bow[1] [bau] *v* bocka

bow[2] [bou] *n* båge *c*; ~ **tie** fluga *c*

bowels [bauəlz] *pl* inälvor *pl*, tarmar *pl*

bowl [boul] *n* skål *c*

bowling ['boulin] *n* kägelspel *nt*, bowling *c*; ~ **alley** bowlingbana *c*

box[1] [bɔks] *v* boxas; **boxing match** boxningsmatch *c*

box[2] [bɔks] *n* ask *c*

box office ['bɔks,ɔfis] *n* biljettlucka *c*, biljettkassa *c*

boy [bɔi] *n* pojke *c*; tjänare *c*; ~ **scout** scout *c*

boyfriend ['bɔifrend] *n* pojkvän *c*

bra [brɑ:] *n* behå *c*

bracelet ['breislit] *n* armband *nt*

braces ['breisiz] *pl* hängslen *pl*

brain [brein] *n* hjärna *c*; förstånd *nt*

brain wave ['breinweiv] *n* snilleblixt *c*

brake [breik] *n* broms *c*; ~ **drum** bromstrumma *c*; ~ **lights** bromsljus *nt*

branch [brɑ:ntʃ] *n* gren *c*; filial *c*

brand [brænd] *n* märke *nt*; brännmärke *nt*

brand-new [,brænd'nju:] *adj* splitter ny

brass [brɑ:s] *n* mässing *c*; ~ **band** mässingsorkester *c*

brave [breiv] *adj* tapper, modig

Brazil [brə'zil] Brasilien

Brazilian [brə'ziljən] *adj* brasiliansk; *n* brasilianare *c*

breach [bri:tʃ] *n* rämna *c*; brott *nt*

bread [bred] *n* bröd *nt*; **wholemeal** ~ fullkornsbröd *nt*

breadth [bredθ] *n* bredd *c*

break [breik] *n* brytning *c*; rast *c*

*break [breik] *v* *bryta; ~ **down** *gå sönder; *bryta samman; analysera

breakdown ['breikdaun] *n* sammanbrott *nt*, motorstopp *nt*

breakfast ['brekfəst] *n* frukost *c*

breast [brest] *n* bröst *nt*

breaststroke ['breststrouk] *n* bröstsim *nt*

breath [breθ] *n* anda *c*

breathe [bri:ð] *v* andas

breathing ['bri:ðin] *n* andning *c*

breed [bri:d] *n* ras *c*; art *c*

*breed [bri:d] *v* uppföda

breeze [bri:z] *n* bris *c*

brew [bru:] *v* brygga

brewery ['bru:əri] *n* bryggeri *nt*

Brexit ['breksit] *n* brexit *c*

bribe [braib] *v* muta

bribery ['braibəri] *n* mutning *c*

brick [brik] *n* tegelsten *c*

bricklayer ['brikleiə] *n* murare *c*

bride [braid] *n* brud *c*

bridegroom ['braidgru:m] *n* brudgum *c*

bridge [bridʒ] *n* bro *c*; bridge *c*

brief [bri:f] *adj* kort; kortfattad

briefcase ['bri:fkeis] *n* portfölj *c*

briefs [bri:fs] *pl* trosor *pl*, kalsonger *pl*

bright [brait] *adj* glänsande; strålande; kvicktänkt, skärpt

brighten ['braitən] *v* göra ljusare

brill [bril] *n* slätvar *c*

brilliant ['briljənt] *adj* briljant; begåvad

brim [brim] *n* brädd *c*

***bring** [briŋ] *v* *ta med, medföra; *ha med sig; ~ back återföra; ~ up uppfostra; *ta upp

brisk [brisk] *adj* pigg

British ['britiʃ] *adj* brittisk

Briton ['britən] *n* britt *c*

broad [brɔ:d] *adj* bred; utsträckt, vidsträckt; allmän

broadband ['brɔ:dæbænd] *n* bredband *c*

broadcast ['brɔ:dka:st] *n* utsändning *c*

***broadcast** ['brɔ:dka:st] *v* utsända

brochure ['brouʃuə] *n* broschyr *c*

broke¹ [brouk] *v* (p break)

broke² [brouk] *adj* pank

broken ['broukən] *adj* (pp break) sönder; trasig

broker ['broukə] *n* mäklare *c*

bronchitis [brɔŋ'kaitis] *n* luftrörskatarr *c*

bronze [brɔnz] *n* brons *c*; *adj* brons-

brooch [broutʃ] *n* brosch *c*

brook [bruk] *n* bäck *c*

broom [bru:m] *n* kvast *c*

brothel ['brɔθəl] *n* bordell *c*

brother ['brʌðə] *n* bror *c*; broder *c*

brother-in-law ['brʌðərinlɔ:] *n* (pl brothers-) svåger *c*

brought [brɔ:t] *v* (p, pp bring)

brown [braun] *adj* brun

bruise [bru:z] *n* blodutgjutning *c*, blåmärke *nt*; *v* *slå gul och blå

brunette [bru:'net] *n* brunett *c*

brush [brʌʃ] *n* borste *c*; pensel *c*; *v* borsta

brutal ['bru:təl] *adj* brutal

bubble ['bʌbəl] *n* bubbla *c*

buck [bʌk] *n colloquial* bock *c*

bucket ['bʌkit] *n* hink *c*

buckle ['bʌkəl] *n* spänne *nt*

bud [bʌd] *n* knopp *c*

buddy ['bʌdi] *n colloquial* kompis *c*

budget ['bʌdʒit] *n* budget *c*

buffet ['bufei] *n* gående bord *c*

bug [bʌg] *n* vägglus *c*; skalbagge *c*; *nAm* insekt *c* *build [bild] v bygga

building ['bildin] n byggnad c

bulb [bʌlb] n blomlök c; light
~ glödlampa c

Bulgaria [bʌl'gɛəriə] n
Bulgarien

Bulgarian [bʌl'gɛəriən] adj
bulgarisk; n bulgar c

bulk [bʌlk] n volym c; massa
c; största delen

bulky ['bʌlki] adj omfångsrik,
skrymmande

bull [bul] n tjur c

bullet ['bulit] n kula c

bulletin ['bulitin] n anslag nt;
~ board n anslag stavla c

bullfight ['bulfait] n
tjurfäktning c

bullring ['bulrin] n
tjurfäktningsarena c

bump [bʌmp] v stöta;
sammanstöta; dunka; n
duns c, slag nt, stöt c

bumper ['bʌmpə] n
kofångare c

bumpy ['bʌmpi] adj gropig

bun [bʌn] n bulle c

bunch [bʌntʃ] n bukett c;
hop c

bundle ['bʌndəl] n bunt c; v
bunta ihop

bunk [bʌŋk] n koj c

buoy [bɔi] n boj c

burden ['bəːdən] n börda c

bureau ['bjuərou] n (pl ~x,
~s) skrivbord nt; nAm byrå c

bureaucracy [bjuə'rɔkrəsi] n
byråkrati c

burglar ['bəːglə] n
inbrottstjuv c

burgle ['bəːgəl] v *göra
inbrott

burial ['beriəl] n begravning
c, gravsättning c

burn [bəːn] n brännsår nt

*burn [bəːn] v *brinna;
bränna; vidbränna

*burst [bəːst] v *spricka;
*brista

bury ['beri] v begrava

bus [bʌs] n buss c

bush [buʃ] n buske c

business ['biznəs] n affärer
pl, handel c; affär c,
affärsverksamhet c;
sysselsättning c; ~ hours
kontorstid c, affärstid c; ~
trip affärsresa c; on ~ i
affärer

business-like ['biznislaik]
adj affärsmässig

businessman ['biznəsmən]
n (pl -men) affärsman c

businesswoman
['biznəswumən] n
affärskvinna c

bust [bʌst] n byst c

bustle ['bʌsəl] n jäkt nt

busy ['bizi] adj upptagen;
livlig

but [bʌt] conj men; dock;
prep utom

butcher ['butʃə] n slaktare c

butter ['bʌtə] n smör nt

butterfly ['bʌtəflai] n fjäril c;
~ stroke fjärilsim nt

buttock ['bʌtək] n skinka c

button ['bʌtən] n knapp c; v
knäppa

buttonhole ['bʌtənhoul] n

buy 230

knapphål *nt*
*buy [bai] *v* köpa; anskaffa
buyer ['baiə] *n* köpare *c*
buzz [bʌz] *n* surr *nt*
by [bai] *prep* av; med; vid

bye-bye [bai'bai] *colloquial* hej då
by-pass ['baipɑːs] *n* omfartsled *c*; *v* *fara förbi; *undvika

C

cab [kæb] *n* taxi *c*
cabaret ['kæbərei] *n* kabaré *c*; nattklubb *c*
cabbage ['kæbidʒ] *n* kål *c*
cab driver ['kæb,draivə] *n* taxichaufför *c*
cabin ['kæbin] *n* kabin *c*; hydda *c*; hytt *c*; kajuta *c*
cabinet ['kæbinət] *n* skåp *nt*; regering *c*
cable ['keibəl] *n* kabel *c*; telegram *nt*; *v* telegrafera
cadre ['kɑːdə] *n* stamanställd *c*; stamtrupp *c*
café ['kæfei] *n* kafé *nt*
cafeteria [,kæfə'tiəriə] *n* kafeteria *c*
caffeine ['kæfiːn] *n* koffein *nt*
cage [keidʒ] *n* bur *c*
cake [keik] *n* kaka *c*; bakverk *nt*, tårta *c*
calamity [kə'læməti] *n* katastrof *c*, olycka *c*
calcium ['kælsiəm] *n* kalcium *nt*
calculate ['kælkjuleit] *v* räkna ut, beräkna
calculation [,kælkju'leifən] *n* beräkning *c*
calculator ['kælkjuleitə] *n* miniräknare *c*

calendar ['kæləndə] *n* kalender *c*
calf [kɑːf] *n* (pl calves) kalv *c*; vad *c*; ~ **skin** kalvskinn *nt*
call [kɔːl] *v* ropa; kalla; ringa; *n* rop *nt*; besök *nt*; påringning *c*; ***be called** heta; ~ **names** skymfa; ~ **on** besöka; ~ **up** *Am* ringa upp
call waiting ['kɔːl̩'weitiŋ] *n* samtal väntar *nt*
caller ID ['kɔːlər̩ai'diː] *n* nummerpresentatör *c*
calm [kɑːm] *adj* stilla, lugn; ~ **down** lugna
calorie ['kæləri] *n* kalori *c*
Calvinism ['kælvinizəm] *n* kalvinism *c*
came [keim] *v* (p come)
camel ['kæməl] *n* kamel *c*
camera ['kæmərə] *n* kamera *c*; filmkamera *c*; ~ **shop** fotoaffär *c*
camp [kæmp] *n* läger *nt*; *v* kampa
campaign [kæm'pein] *n* kampanj *c*
camp bed [,kæmp'bed] *n* tältsäng *c*, fältsäng *c*
camper ['kæmpə] *n* kampare *c*

carefree

camping ['kæmpiŋ] *n*
kamping *c*; ~ **site**
kampingplats *c*

can [kæn] *n* konservburk *c*; ~
opener konservöppnare *c*

***can** [kæn] *v* *kunna

Canada ['kænədə] Kanada

Canadian [kə'neidiən] *adj*
kanadensisk; *n* kanadensare *c*

canal [kə'næl] *n* kanal *c*

canary [kə'neəri] *n*
kanariefågel *c*

cancel ['kænsəl] *v* annullera;
avbeställa

cancellation [,kænsə'leiʃən]
n annullering *c*

cancer ['kænsə] *n* cancer *c*

candidate ['kændidət] *n*
kandidat *c*

candle ['kændəl] *n*
stearinljus *nt*

candy ['kændi] *n*Am
karamell *c*; snask *nt*, godis
nt; ~ **store** Am gottaffär *c*

cane [kein] *n* rör *nt*; käpp *c*

canister ['kænistə] *n*
bleckburk *c*

canoe [kə'nu:] *n* kanot *c*

canteen [kæn'ti:n] *n* kantin *c*

canvas ['kænvəs] *n* smärting
c

cap [kæp] *n* skärmmössa *c*,
mössa *c*

capable ['keipəbəl] *adj*
kapabel, duglig

capacity [kə'pæsəti] *n*
kapacitet *c*; förmåga *c*

cape [keip] *n* cape *c*; udde *c*

capital ['kæpitəl] *n*
huvudstad *c*; kapital *nt*; *adj*
huvudsaklig, huvud-; ~
letter stor bokstav

capitalism ['kæpitəlizəm] *n*
kapitalism *c*

capitulation [kə,pitju'leiʃən]
n kapitulation *c*

capsule ['kæpsju:l] *n* kapsyl *c*

captain ['kæptin] *n* kapten *c*

capture ['kæptʃə] *v*
*tillfångata; *inta; *n*
tillfångatagande *nt*; erövring
c

car [kɑ:] *n* bil *c*; ~ **hire**
biluthyrning *c*; ~ **park**
parkeringsplats *c*; ~ **rental**
Am biluthyrning *c*

caramel ['kærəməl] *n*
karamell *c*

carat ['kærət] *n* karat *c*

caravan ['kærəvæn] *n*
husvagn *c*

carburettor [,kɑ:bju'retə] *n*
förgasare *c*

card [kɑ:d] *n* kort *nt*;
brevkort *nt*

cardboard ['kɑ:dbɔ:d] *n*
papp *c*; *adj* papp-

cardigan ['kɑ:digən] *n* kofta *c*

cardinal ['kɑ:dinəl] *n*
kardinal *c*; *adj* huvudsaklig,
huvud-

care [keə] *n* vård *c*;
bekymmer *nt*; ~ **about** bry
sig om; ~ **for** *vilja ha; tycka
om; *take ~ **of** sköta om, *ta
hand om

career [kə'riə] *n* karriär *c*

carefree ['keəfri:] *adj* sorglös

careful ['kɛəfəl] *adj* försiktig; omsorgsfull

careless ['kɛələs] *adj* vårdslös, slarvig

caretaker ['kɛə,teikə] *n* vaktmästare *c*

cargo ['kɑ:gou] *n* (pl ~es) last *c*, laddning *c*

carjacking ['kɑ:,dʒækiŋ] *n* bilkapning *c*

carnival ['kɑ:nivəl] *n* karneval *c*

carp [kɑ:p] *n* (pl ~) karp *c*

carpenter ['kɑ:pintə] *n* snickare *c*

carpet ['kɑ:pit] *n* matta *c*

carpool ['kɑ:,pu:l] *n* samåkning *c*; *v* samåka

carriage ['kæridʒ] *n* järnvägsvagn *c*; vagn *c*, ekipage *nt*

carriageway ['kæridʒwei] *n* körbana *c*

carrot ['kærət] *n* morot *c*

carry ['kæri] *v* *bära; föra; ~ on *fortsätta; ~ out genomföra

carrycot ['kærikɔt] *n* babykorg *c*

cart [kɑ:t] *n* kärra *c*

cartilage ['kɑ:tilidʒ] *n* brosk *nt*

carton ['kɑ:tən] *n* kartong *c*; cigarrettlimpa *c*

cartoon [kɑ:'tu:n] *n* tecknad film

cartridge ['kɑ:tridʒ] *n* patron *c*

carve [kɑ:v] *v* *skära; *utskära, snida

carving ['kɑ:viŋ] *n* snideri *nt*

case [keis] *n* fall *nt*; resväska *c*; etui *nt*; attaché ~ dokumentportfölj *c*; in ~ ifall; in ~ of i händelse av

cash [kæʃ] *n* kontanter *pl*; *v* lösa in, inkassera; ~ dispenser bankomat *c*

cashier [kæ'ʃiə] *n* kassör *c*; kassörska *c*

cash machine ['kæʃmə'ʃi:n] *n* bankomat *c*; uttagsautomat *c*

cashmere ['kæʃmiə] *n* kaschmir *c*

casino [kə'si:nou] *n* (pl ~s) kasino *nt*

cask [kɑ:sk] *n* tunna *c*

cassette [kə'set] *n* kassett *c*

cast [kɑ:st] *n* kast *nt*

***cast** [kɑ:st] *v* kasta

castle ['kɑ:səl] *n* slott *nt*, borg *c*

casual ['kæʒuəl] *adj* informell; flyktig, oförmodad, tillfällig

casualty ['kæʒuəlti] *n* offer *nt*; olycksfall *nt*

cat [kæt] *n* katt *c*

catacomb ['kætəkoum] *n* katakomb *c*

catalogue ['kætəlɔg] *n* katalog *c*

catarrh [kə'tɑ:] *n* katarr *c*

catastrophe [kə'tæstrəfi] *n* katastrof *c*

***catch** [kætʃ] *v* *fånga; *gripa; överrumpla; *hinna

catchword ['kætʃwə:d] *n* slagord *nt*

category ['kætigəri] n
  kategori c

cathedral [kə'θi:drəl] n
  domkyrka c, katedral c

catholic ['kæθəlik] adj
  katolsk

cattle ['kætəl] pl boskap c

caught [kɔ:t] v (p, pp catch)

cauliflower ['kɔliflauə] n
  blomkål c

cause [kɔ:z] v orsaka; vålla; n
  orsak c; grund c, anledning
  c; sak c; ~ to förmå att

caution ['kɔ:ʃən] n
  försiktighet c; v varna

cautious ['kɔ:ʃəs] adj
  försiktig

cave [keiv] n grotta c

cavern ['kævən] n håla c

caviar ['kævia] n kaviar c

cavity ['kævəti] n hålighet c

CD(-ROM) [si:'di:] n
  CD-(ROM) c

CD player ['si:'di:‿ˌpleiə] n
  CD-spelare c

cease [si:s] v upphöra

ceasefire ['si:sfaiə] n eld
  upphör nt

ceiling ['si:liŋ] n innertak nt

celebrate ['selibreit] v fira

celebration [ˌseli'breiʃən] n
  firande nt

celebrity [si'lebrəti] n
  berömdhet c

celery ['seləri] n selleri c

cell [sel] n cell c; mobil c

cellar ['selə] n källare c

cellphone ['selfoun] n
  mobil(telefon) c

cement [si'ment] n cement nt

cemetery ['semitri] n kyrkogård c, begravningsplats c

censorship ['sensəʃip] n
  censur c

center ['sentə] nAm center nt

centimetre ['sentimi:tə] n
  centimeter c

central ['sentrəl] adj central;
  ~ heating centralvärme c; ~
  station centralstation c

centralize ['sentrəlaiz] v
  centralisera

centre ['sentə] n centrum nt;
  medelpunkt c

century ['sentʃəri] n
  århundrade nt

ceramics [si'ræmiks] pl
  keramik c, lergods nt

ceremony ['serəməni] n
  ceremoni c

certain ['sə:tən] adj säker;
  viss

certainly ['sə:tənli] adv
  säkert

certificate [sə'tifikət] n
  certifikat nt; intyg nt,
  handling c, diplom nt, attest
  c

chain [tʃein] n kedja c

chair [tʃeə] n stol c

chairman ['tʃeəmən] n (pl
  -men) ordförande c

chairwoman ['tʃeəwumən] n
  ordförande (kvinnlig) c

chalet ['ʃælei] n alpstuga c

chalk [tʃɔ:k] n krita c

challenge ['tʃæləndʒ] v
  utmana; n utmaning c

chamber ['tʃeimbə] n
  kammare c

champagne [ʃæm'peɪn] *n*
champagne *c*

champion ['tʃæmpjən] *n*
mästare *c*; förkämpe *c*

chance [tʃɑːns] *n* slump *c*;
chans *c*, tillfällighet *c*; risk *c*;
by ~ av en slump

change [tʃeɪndʒ] *v* förändra,
ändra, växla; klä om sig;
byta; *n* förändring *c*;
småpengar *pl*; for a ~ som
omväxling

channel ['tʃænəl] *n* kanal *c*;
English Channel Engelska
kanalen

chaos ['keɪɔs] *n* kaos *nt*

chaotic [kei'ɔtik] *adj* kaotisk

chap [tʃæp] *n* karl *c*

chapel ['tʃæpəl] *n* kapell *nt*

chaplain ['tʃæplin] *n* kaplan
c

character ['kærəktə] *n*
karaktär *c*

characteristic
[,kærəktə'ristik] *adj*
betecknande, karakteristisk;
n kännetecken *nt*;
karaktärsdrag *nt*

characterize ['kærəktəraiz]
v karakterisera

charcoal ['tʃɑːkoul] *n* träkol *nt*

charge [tʃɑːdʒ] *v* *ta betalt;
*ålägga; anklaga; lasta; *n*
avgift *c*; laddning *c*, börda *c*,
belastning *c*; anklagelse *c*;
free of ~ kostnadsfri; in ~ of
ansvarig för; *take ~ of *ta
hand om

charger [tʃɑːdʒə] *n* laddare *c*

charity ['tʃærəti] *n*
välgörenhet *c*

charm [tʃɑːm] *n* tjusning *c*,
charm *c*; amulett *c*

charming ['tʃɑːmiŋ] *adj*
charmerande

chart [tʃɑːt] *n* tabell *c*;
diagram *nt*; sjökort *nt*;
conversion ~
omräkningstabell *c*

chase [tʃeis] *v* förfölja;
*fördriva, jaga bort; *n* jakt *c*

chasm ['kæzəm] *n* klyfta *c*

chassis ['ʃæsi] *n* (pl ~) chassi
nt

chaste [tʃeist] *adj* kysk

chat [tʃæt] *v* prata, småprata;
n pratstund *c*, prat *nt*,
småprat *nt*

chatterbox ['tʃætəbɔks] *n*
pratmakare *c*

chauffeur ['ʃoufə] *n* chaufför
c

cheap [tʃiːp] *adj* billig;
förmånlig

cheat [tʃiːt] *v* lura, fuska;
*bedra

check [tʃek] *v* kolla,
kontrollera; *n* rutigt
mönster; nota *c*; *nAm* check
c; check! schack!; ~ in
checka in, *skriva in sig; ~
out lämna

checkbook ['tʃekbuk] *nAm*
checkhäfte *nt*

checkerboard ['tʃekəbɔːd]
nAm schackbräde *nt*

checkers ['tʃekəz] *plAm*
damspel *nt*

checkroom ['tʃekruːm] *nAm*

garderob c

checkup ['tʃekʌp] n undersökning c

cheek [tʃi:k] n kind c

cheekbone ['tʃi:kboun] n kindben c

cheeky ['tʃi:ki] adj colloquial fräck

cheer [tʃiə] v heja, hälsa med jubel; ~ **up** muntra upp

cheerful ['tʃiəfəl] adj munter, glad

cheese [tʃi:z] n ost c

chef [ʃef] n kökschef c

chemical ['kemikəl] adj kemisk

chemist ['kemist] n apotekare c; **chemist's** apotek nt; kemikalieaffär c

chemistry ['kemistri] n kemi c

cheque [tʃek] n check c

chequebook ['tʃekbuk] n checkhäfte nt

cherry ['tʃeri] n körsbär nt

chess [tʃes] n schack nt

chest [tʃest] n bröst nt; bröstkorg c; kista c; ~ **of drawers** byrå c

chestnut ['tʃesnʌt] n kastanj c

chew [tʃu:] v tugga

chewing gum ['tʃu:iŋgʌm] n tuggummi nt

chicken ['tʃikin] n kyckling c

chickenpox ['tʃikinpɔks] n vattkoppor pl

chief [tʃi:f] n chef c; adj huvud-, över-

chieftain ['tʃi:ftən] n

hövding c

child [tʃaild] n (pl children) barn nt

childbirth ['tʃaildbə:θ] n förlossning c

childhood ['tʃaildhud] n barndom c

Chile ['tʃili] Chile

Chilean ['tʃiliən] adj chilensk; n chilenare c

chill [tʃil] n rysning nt

chilly ['tʃili] adj kylig

chimes [tʃaimz] pl klockspel nt

chimney ['tʃimni] n skorsten c

chin [tʃin] n haka c

China ['tʃainə] Kina

china ['tʃainə] n porslin nt

Chinese [tʃai'ni:z] adj kinesisk; n kines c

chip [tʃip] n flisa c; spelmark c; v kantstöta, tälja; **chips** pommes frites

chisel ['tʃizəl] n mejsel c

chives [tʃaivz] pl gräslök c

chlorine ['klɔ:ri:n] n klor c

chock-full [tʃɔk'ful] adj fullpackad, proppfull

chocolate ['tʃɔklət] n choklad c; chokladpralin c

choice [tʃɔis] n val nt; urval nt

choir [kwaiə] n kör c

choke [tʃouk] v kvävas; *strypa, kväva; n choke c

***choose** [tʃu:z] v *välja

chop [tʃɔp] n kotlett c; v hacka

Christ [kraist] Kristus

christen ['krisǝn] v döpa

christening ['krisǝniŋ] n dop nt

Christian ['kristʃǝn] adj kristen; ~ name förnamn nt

Christmas ['krismǝs] jul c

chronic ['krɔnik] adj kronisk

chronological [,krɔnǝ'lɔdʒikǝl] adj kronologisk

chuckle ['tʃʌkǝl] v småskratta

chunk [tʃʌŋk] n stycke nt

church [tʃǝ:tʃ] n kyrka c

churchyard ['tʃǝ:tʃjɑ:d] n kyrkogård c

cigar [si'gɑ:] n cigarr c; ~ shop cigarraffär c

cigarette [,sigǝ'ret] n cigarett c

cigarette case [,sigǝ'retkeis] n cigarrettetui nt

cigarette holder [,sigǝ'ret,houldǝ] n cigarrettmunstycke nt

cigarette lighter [,sigǝ'ret,laitǝ] n cigarrettändare c

cinema ['sinǝmǝ] n biograf c

cinnamon ['sinǝmǝn] n kanel c

circle ['sǝ:kǝl] n cirkel c; krets c; balkong c; v *omge, *omsluta

circulation [,sǝ:kju'leiʃǝn] n cirkulation c; blodcirkulation c; omlopp nt

circumstance ['sǝ:kǝmstæns] n

omständighet c

circus ['sǝ:kǝs] n cirkus c

citizen ['sitizǝn] n stadsbo c

citizenship ['sitizǝnʃip] n medborgarskap nt

city ['siti] n stad c

civic ['sivik] adj medborgar-

civil ['sivǝl] adj medborgerlig; hövlig; ~ law civilrätt c; ~ servant statstjänsteman c

civilian [si'viljǝn] adj civil; n civilist c

civilization [,sivǝlai'zeiʃǝn] n civilisation c

civilized ['sivǝlaizd] adj civiliserad

claim [kleim] v kräva, fordra; *påstå; n anspråk nt, fordran c

clamp [klæmp] n klämma c; krampa c

clap [klæp] v applådera

clarify ['klærifai] v *klargöra

class [klɑ:s] n klass c

classical ['klæsikǝl] adj klassisk

classify ['klæsifai] v indela

classmate ['klɑ:smeit] n klasskamrat c

classroom ['klɑ:sru:m] n klassrum nt

clause [klɔ:z] n klausul c

claw [klɔ:] n klo c

clay [klei] n lera c

clean [kli:n] adj ren; v städa, *rengöra

cleaning ['kli:niŋ] n rengöring c; ~ fluid rengöringsmedel nt clear [kliə] adj klar; tydlig; v röja

clearing ['kliəriŋ] n uthuggning c

cleft [kleft] n skreva c

clergyman ['klə:dʒimən] n (pl -men) präst c

clerk [klɑ:k] n kontorist c; bokhållare c; sekreterare c

clever ['klevə] adj intelligent; skicklig, klok

click [klik] v klicka; ~ into place klicka på plats

client ['klaiənt] n kund c; klient c

cliff [klif] n klippa c

climate ['klaimit] n klimat nt

climb [klaim] v klättra; n klättring c

cling [kliŋ] v klänga sig; ~ to klänga sig fast

clinic ['klinik] n klinik c

cloak [klouk] n cape c

cloakroom ['kloukru:m] n kapprum nt

clock [klɔk] n ur nt; at ... o'clock klockan ...

cloister ['klɔistə] n kloster nt

clone [kloun] v klona; n klon c

close¹ [klouz] v stänga, *sluta; closed adj stängd, sluten

close² [klous] adj nära

closet ['klɔzit] n skåp nt; garderob c

cloth [klɔθ] n tyg nt; trasa c

clothes [klouðz] pl kläder pl

clothing ['klouðiŋ] n beklädnad c

cloud [klaud] n moln nt

cloudy ['klaudi] adj mulen, molnig

clover ['klouvə] n klöver c

clown [klaun] n clown c

club [klʌb] n klubb c, förening c; påk c, klubba c

clumsy ['klʌmzi] adj klumpig

clutch [klʌtʃ] n koppling c; grepp nt

coach [koutʃ] n buss c; vagn c; kaross c; tränare c

coal [koul] n kol nt

coarse [kɔ:s] adj grov

coast [koust] n kust c

coat [kout] n överrock c, kappa c

coat hanger ['kout,hæŋə] n galge c

cocaine [kou'kein] n kokain nt

cock [kɔk] n tupp c

cocktail ['kɔkteil] n cocktail c

coconut ['koukənʌt] n kokosnöt c

cod [kɔd] n (pl ~) torsk c

code [koud] n kod c

coffee ['kɔfi] n kaffe nt

cognac ['kɔnjæk] n konjak c

coherence [kou'hiərəns] n sammanhang nt

coin [kɔin] n mynt nt; slant c

coincide [,kouin'said] v *sammanfalla

cold [kould] adj kall; n kyla c; förkylning c; *catch a ~ *bli förkyld

collaborate [kə'læbəreit] v samarbeta

collapse 238

collapse [kə'læps] v
kollapsa, *bryta samman
collar ['kɔlə] n halsband nt;
krage c; ~ stud kragknapp c
collarbone ['kɔləboun] n
nyckelben nt
colleague ['kɔli:g] n kollega
c
collect [kə'lekt] v samla;
hämta; samla in
collection [kə'lekʃən] n
samling c; brevlådstömning
c; kollekt c, insamling c
collective [kə'lektiv] adj
kollektiv
collector [kə'lektə] n
samlare c; insamlare c
college ['kɔlidʒ] n högre
läroanstalt; högskola c
collide [kə'laid] v kollidera
collision [kə'liʒən] n
sammanstötning c, kollision
c; ombordläggning c
Colombia [kə'lɔmbiə]
Colombia
Colombian [kə'lɔmbiən] adj
colombiansk; n colombian c
colonel ['kə:nəl] n överste c
colony ['kɔləni] n koloni c
colour ['kʌlə] n färg c; v
färga; ~ film färgfilm c
colour-blind ['kʌləblaind]
adj färgblind
coloured ['kʌləd] adj färgad
colourful ['kʌləfəl] adj
färgrik, färgstark
column ['kɔləm] n pelare c;
kolumn c; rubrik c
coma ['koumə] n koma c
comb [koum] v kamma; n

kam c
combat ['kɔmbæt] n kamp c,
strid c; v bekämpa, kämpa
combination
[,kɔmbi'neiʃən] n
kombination c
combine [kəm'bain] v
kombinera
*come [kʌm] v *komma; ~
across råka träffa, stöta på;
*få tag i
comedian [kə'mi:diən] n
skådespelare c; komiker c
comedy ['kɔmədi] n lustspel
nt, komedi c; musical ~
musikalisk komedi
comfort ['kʌmfət] n komfort
c, bekvämlighet c; tröst c; v
trösta
comfortable ['kʌmfətəbl]
adj bekväm, komfortabel
comic ['kɔmik] adj komisk
comics ['kɔmiks] pl tecknad
serie
coming ['kʌmiŋ] n ankomst c
comma ['kɔmə] n
kommatecken nt
command [kə'mɑ:nd] v
befalla; n befallning c
commander [kə'mɑ:ndə] n
befälhavare c
commemoration
[kə,memə'reiʃən] n
minnesfest c
commence [kə'mens] v
börja
comment ['kɔment] n
kommentar c; v
kommentera
commerce ['kɔmə:s] n

handel c

commercial [kəˈmɔːʃəl] *adj*
kommersiell, handels-; *n*
reklamsändning c; **~ law**
handelsrätt c

commission [kəˈmiʃən] *n*
kommission c

commit [kəˈmit] *v* anförtro,
överlämna; *begå, föröva

committee [kəˈmiti] *n*
kommitté c, utskott nt

common [ˈkɔmən] *adj*
gemensam; allmän, vanlig;
simpel

commune [ˈkɔmjuːn] *n*
kommun c

communicate
[kəˈmjuːnikeit] *v* meddela

communication
[kə,mjuːniˈkeiʃən] *n*
kommunikation c;
meddelande nt

communism [ˈkɔmjunizəm]
n kommunism c

communist [ˈkɔmjunist] *n*
kommunist c

community [kəˈmjuːnəti] *n*
gemenskap c, samhälle nt

commuter [kəˈmjuːtə] *n*
pendlare c

compact [ˈkɔmpækt] *adj*
kompakt

compact disc [ˈkɔmpækt
disk] *n* CD-skiva c; **~ player**
CD-spelare c

companion [kəmˈpænjən] *n*
följeslagare c

company [ˈkʌmpəni] *n*
sällskap nt; bolag nt; företag
nt, firma c

comparative [kəmˈpærətiv]
adj relativ

compare [kəmˈpɛə] *v*
jämföra

comparison [kəmˈpærisən] *n*
jämförelse c

compartment
[kəmˈpɑːtmənt] *n* kupé c;
fack nt

compass [ˈkʌmpəs] *n*
kompass c

compel [kəmˈpel] *v* tvinga

compensate [ˈkɔmpənseit] *v*
kompensera

compensation
[,kɔmpənˈseiʃən] *n*
kompensation c;
skadeersättning c

compete [kəmˈpiːt] *v* tävla

competition [,kɔmpəˈtiʃən]
n tävlan c; tävling c

competitor [kəmˈpetitər] *n*
medtävlare c

compile [kəmˈpail] *v*
sammanställa, samla ihop

complain [kəmˈplein] *v* klaga

complaint [kəmˈpleint] *n*
reklamation c, klagomål nt;
complaints book
reklamationsbok c

complete [kəmˈpliːt] *adj*
fullkomlig, komplett; *v*
avsluta

completely [kəmˈpliːtli] *adv*
fullkomligt, totalt,
fullständigt

complex [ˈkɔmpleks] *n*
komplex nt; *adj* invecklad

complexion [kəmˈplekʃən] *n*
hy c

complicated

240

complicated ['kɔmplikeitid]
adj komplicerad, invecklad
compliment ['kɔmplimənt] *n*
komplimang *c*; *v*
komplimentera, gratulera
compose [kəm'pouz] *v*
sammanställa
composer [kəm'pouzə] *n*
kompositör *c*
composition [,kɔmpə'ziʃən]
n komposition *c*;
sammansättning *c*
comprehensive
[,kɔmpri'hensiv] *adj*
omfattande, innehållsrik
comprise [kəm'praiz] *v*
*inbegripa, omfatta
compromise ['kɔmprəmaiz]
n kompromiss *c*
compulsory [kəm'pʌlsəri]
adj obligatorisk
computer [kəm'pjutə] *n*
dator *c*
conceal [kən'si:l] *v* *dölja
conceited [kən'si:tid] *adj*
egenkär
conceive [kən'si:v] *v* avla;
tänka ut; fatta
concentrate ['kɔnsəntreit] *v*
koncentrera
concentration
[,kɔnsən'treiʃən] *n*
koncentration *c*
conception [kən'sepʃən] *n*
uppfattning *c*; befruktning *c*
concern [kən'sɔ:n] *v*
beträffa, *angå; *n* oro *c*;
angelägenhet *c*; koncern *c*
concerned [kən'sɔ:nd] *adj*
bekymrad; inblandad

concerning [kən'sə:niŋ]
prep angående, beträffande
concert ['kɔnsət] *n* konsert *c*;
~ **hall** konsertsal *c*
concession [kən'seʃən] *n*
koncession *c*; beviljande *nt*
concise [kən'sais] *adj*
kortfattad, koncis
conclusion [kəŋ'klu:ʒən] *n*
slut *nt*, slutsats *c*
concrete ['kɔŋkri:t] *adj*
konkret; *n* betong *c*
concurrence [kəŋ'kʌrəns] *n*
sammanträffande *nt*
concussion [kəŋ'kʌʃən] *n*
hjärnskakning *c*
condition [kən'diʃən] *n*
villkor *nt*; tillstånd *nt*,
kondition *c*
conditional [kən'diʃənəl] *adj*
villkorlig
conditioner [kən'diʃənə] *n*
sköljmedel
condom ['kɔndəm] *n*
kondom *c*
conduct[1] ['kɔndʌkt] *n*
uppförande *nt*
conduct[2] [kən'dʌkt] *v*
ledsaga; dirigera
conductor [kən'dʌktə] *n*
förare *c*; dirigent *c*
confectioner [kən'fekʃənə]
n konditor *c*
conference ['kɔnfərəns] *n*
konferens *c*
confess [kən'fes] *v* erkänna;
bikta sig; bekänna
confession [kən'feʃən] *n*
bekännelse *c*; bikt *c*
confidence ['kɔnfidəns] *n*

förtroende nt
confident ['kɔnfidənt] adj
tillitsfull
confidential [ˌkɔnfi'denʃəl]
adj konfidentiell
confirm [kən'fəːm] v
bekräfta
confirmation
[ˌkɔnfə'meiʃən] n
bekräftelse c
confiscate ['kɔnfiskeit] v
konfiskera
conflict ['kɔnflikt] n konflikt
c
confuse [kən'fjuːz] v
förvirra
confusion [kən'fjuːʒən] n
förvirring c
congratulate
[kən'grætʃuleit] v
lyckönska, gratulera
congratulation
[kənˌgrætʃu'leiʃən] n
lyckönskning c, gratulation
c
congregation
[ˌkɔŋgri'geiʃən] n
församling c; kongregation c
congress ['kɔŋgres] n
kongress c
connect [kə'nekt] v
*förbinda, koppla; koppla
till; *anknyta; *ansluta
connection [kə'nekʃən] n
förbindelse c; sammanhang
nt, anknytning c
connoisseur [ˌkɔnə'səː] n
kännare c
connotation [ˌkɔnə'teiʃən] n
bibetydelse c

conquer ['kɔŋkə] v erövra;
besegra
conqueror ['kɔŋkərə] n
erövrare c
conquest ['kɔŋkwest] n
erövring c
conscience ['kɔnʃəns] n
samvete nt
conscious ['kɔnʃəs] adj
medveten
consciousness ['kɔnʃəsnəs]
n medvetande nt
conscript ['kɔnskript] n
värnpliktig c
consent [kən'sent] v
samtycka; n samtycke nt,
bifall nt
consequence ['kɔnsikwəns]
n verkan c, följd c
consequently
['kɔnsikwəntli] adv
följaktligen
conservative [kən'səːvətiv]
adj samhällsbevarande,
konservativ
consider [kən'sidə] v
betrakta; överväga; *anse
considerable
[kən'sidərəbəl] adj betydlig;
avsevärd, betydande
considerate [kən'sidərət]
adj hänsynsfull
consideration
[kənˌsidə'reiʃən] n
övervägande nt; hänsyn c,
hänsynsfullhet c
considering [kən'sidəriŋ]
prep med hänsyn till
consignment
[kən'sainmənt] n

försändelse c
consist of [kən'sist] *v *bestå
av
conspire [kən'spaiə] *v*
*sammansvärja sig
constant ['kɔnstənt] *adj*
ständig
constipation
[,kɔnsti'peiʃən] *n*
förstoppning c
constituency
[kən'stitʃuənsi] *n* valkrets c
constitution
[,kɔnsti'tju:ʃən] *n* grundlag
c; sammansättning c
construct [kən'strʌkt] *v*
konstruera; bygga, uppföra
construction [kən'strʌkʃən]
n konstruktion c;
uppförande *nt*; bygge *nt*,
byggnad c
consul ['kɔnsəl] *n* konsul c
consulate ['kɔnsjulət] *n*
konsulat *nt*
consult [kən'sʌlt] *v* rådfråga
consultation [,kɔnsəl'teiʃən]
n konsultation c; ~ **hours**
mottagningstid c
consume [kən'sju:m] *v*
konsumera
consumer [kən'sju:mə] *n*
konsument c
contact ['kɔntækt] *n* kontakt
c, beröring c; *v* kontakta; ~
lenses kontaktlinser *pl*
contagious [kən'teidʒəs] *adj*
smittosam, smittande
contain [kən'tein] *v*
*innehålla; rymma
container [kən'teinə] *n*

behållare c; container c
contemporary
[kən'tempərəri] *adj*
samtida; nutida; *n* samtida
person
contempt [kən'tempt] *n*
förakt *nt*, ringaktning c
content [kən'tent] *adj* nöjd
contents ['kɔntents] *pl*
innehåll *nt*
contest ['kɔntest] *n* strid c;
tävling c
continent ['kɔntinənt] *n*
kontinent c, världsdel c
continental [,kɔnti'nentəl]
adj kontinental
continual [kən'tinjuəl] *adj*
ständig; **continually** *adv*
oupphörligen
continue [kən'tinju:] *v*
*fortsätta, *fortgå
continuous [kən'tinjuəs] *adj*
oavbruten, kontinuerlig
contour ['kɔntuə] *n* kontur c
contraceptive
[,kɔntrə'septiv] *n*
preventivmedel c
contract[1] ['kɔntrækt] *n*
kontrakt *nt*
contract[2] [kən'trækt] *v*
*ådraga sig
contractor [kən'træktə] *n*
entreprenör c
contradict [,kɔntrə'dikt] *v*
*motsäga
contradictory
[,kɔntrə'diktəri] *adj*
motsägande
contrary ['kɔntrəri] *n*
motsats c; *adj* motsatt; **on**

the ~ däremot
contrast ['kɒntrɑːst] *n*
kontrast *c*
contribution
[ˌkɒntri'bjuːʃən] *n* bidrag *nt*
control [kən'troul] *n* kontroll
c; *v* kontrollera
controversial
[ˌkɒntrə'vəːʃəl] *adj*
omtvistad, omstridd
convenience [kən'viːnjəns]
n bekvämlighet *c*
convenient [kən'viːnjənt]
adj bekväm; lämplig,
passande
convent ['kɒnvənt] *n* kloster
nt
conversation
[ˌkɒnvə'seiʃən] *n*
konversation *c*, samtal *nt*
convert [kən'vəːt] *v*
omvända; omräkna
convict[1] [kən'vikt] *v* förklara
skyldig
convict[2] ['kɒnvikt] *n*
brottsling *c*
conviction [kən'vikʃən] *n*
övertygelse *c*; fällande dom
convince [kən'vins] *v*
övertyga
convulsion [kən'vʌlʃən] *n*
kramp *c*
cook [kuk] *n* kock *c*; *v* laga
mat; tillaga
cookbook ['kukbuk] *nAm*
kokbok *c*
cooker ['kukə] *n* spis *c*; gas ~
gasspis *c*
cookery book ['kukəribuk] *n*
kokbok *c*

cookie ['kuki] *nAm* kex *nt*
cool [kuːl] *adj* kylig
cooperation
[kou,ɔpə'reiʃən] *n*
samarbete *nt*; samverkan *c*
co-operative [kou'ɔpərətiv]
adj kooperativ;
samarbetsvillig; *n*
kooperation *c*
coordinate [kou'ɔːdineit] *v*
samordna
coordination
[kou,ɔːdi'neiʃən] *n*
samordning *c*
cope [koup] *v* klara det
copper ['kɒpə] *n* koppar *c*
copy ['kɒpi] *n* kopia *c*;
avskrift *c*; exemplar *nt*; *v*
kopiera; härma; carbon ~
karbonkopia *c*
coral ['kɒrəl] *n* korall *c*
cord [kɔːd] *n* rep *nt*; lina *c*
cordial ['kɔːdiəl] *adj* hjärtlig
corduroy ['kɔːdərɔi] *n*
manchester *c*
core [kɔː] *n* kärna *c*; kärnhus
nt
cork [kɔːk] *n* kork *c*
corkscrew ['kɔːkskruː] *n*
korkskruv *c*
corn [kɔːn] *n* korn *nt*;
spannmål *c*, säd *c*; liktorn *c*;
~ on the cob majskolv *c*
corner ['kɔːnə] *n* hörn *nt*
cornfield ['kɔːnfiːld] *n*
sädesfält *nt*
corpse [kɔːps] *n* lik *nt*
corpulent ['kɔːpjulənt] *adj*
korpulent; tjock
correct [kə'rekt] *adj* riktig,

korrekt, rätt; v rätta, rätta
till
correction [kəˈrekʃən] n
rättelse c
correctness [kəˈrektnəs] n
riktighet c
correspond [ˌkɔriˈspɔnd] v
korrespondera;
överensstämma, motsvara
correspondence
[ˌkɔriˈspɔndəns] n
överensstämmelse c,
brevväxling c
correspondent
[ˌkɔriˈspɔndənt] n
korrespondent c
corridor [ˈkɔridɔː] n korridor
c
corrupt [kəˈrʌpt] adj
korrumperad; v korrumpera
corruption [kəˈrʌpʃən] n
korruption c
corset [ˈkɔːsit] n korsett c
cosmetics [kɔzˈmetiks] pl
skönhetsmedel pl,
kosmetika pl
cost [kɔst] n kostnad c; pris
c
***cost** [kɔst] v kosta
cosy [ˈkouzi] adj mysig,
hemtrevlig
cot [kɔt] nAm turistsäng c
cottage [ˈkɔtidʒ] n stuga c
cotton [ˈkɔtən] n bomull c
cotton wool [ˈkɔtənwul] n
bomull c
couch [kautʃ] n soffa c
cough [kɔf] n hosta c; v hosta
could [kud] v (p can)
council [ˈkaunsəl] n

rådsförsamling c
councillor [ˈkaunsələ] n
rådsmedlem c
counsel [ˈkaunsəl] n
överläggning c, råd nt
counsellor [ˈkaunsələ] n
rådgivare c
count [kaunt] v räkna; räkna
ihop; medräkna; *anse; n
greve c
counter [ˈkauntə] n disk c
counterfeit [ˈkauntəfiːt] v
förfalska
counterfoil [ˈkauntəfɔil] n
talong c
countess [ˈkauntis] n
grevinna c
country [ˈkʌntri] n land nt;
landsbygd c; ~ **house**
lantställe nt
countryman [ˈkʌntrimən] n
(pl -men) landsman c
countryside [ˈkʌntrisaid] n
landsbygd c
county [ˈkaunti] n grevskap
nt
couple [ˈkʌpəl] n par nt
coupon [ˈkuːpɔn] n kupong
c, biljett c
courage [ˈkʌridʒ] n
tapperhet c, mod nt
courageous [kəˈreidʒəs] adj
modig, tapper
course [kɔːs] n kurs c; rätt c;
lopp nt; **intensive ~**
snabbkurs c; **of ~** givetvis,
naturligtvis
court [kɔːt] n domstol c; hov
nt
courteous [ˈkəːtiəs] adj artig

cousin ['kʌzən] n kusin c

cover ['kʌvə] v täcka; n skydd nt; lock nt; pärm c; ~ charge kuvertavgift c

cow [kau] n ko c

coward ['kauəd] n ynkrygg c

cowardly ['kauədli] adj feg

crab [kræb] n krabba c

crack [kræk] n smäll c; spricka c; v smälla; *spricka, spräcka

cracker ['krækə] nAm kex nt

cradle ['kreidəl] n vagga c

cramp [kræmp] n kramp c

crane [krein] n lyftkran c

crankshaft ['kræŋkʃɑːft] n vevaxel c

crap [kræp] n V skit c

crash [kræʃ] n kollision c; v kollidera; störta; ~ barrier vägräcke nt

crate [kreit] n spjällåda c

crater ['kreitə] n krater c

crawl [krɔːl] v *krypa; n crawlsim nt

craze [kreiz] n mani c

crazy ['kreizi] adj galen; vansinnig, tokig

creak [kriːk] v gnissla

cream [kriːm] n kräm c; grädde c; adj gräddfärgad

creamy ['kriːmi] adj grädd-

crease [kriːs] v skrynkla; n veck nt; skrynkla c

create [kriˈeit] v skapa

creative [kriˈeitiv] adj kreativ

creature ['kriːtʃə] n varelse c

credible ['kredibəl] adj trovärdig

credit ['kredit] n kredit c; v kreditera; ~ card kreditkort nt

creditor ['kreditə] n fordringsägare c

credulous ['kredjuləs] adj godtrogen

creek [kriːk] n vik c

*creep [kriːp] v *krypa

creepy ['kriːpi] adj kuslig

cremate [kriˈmeit] v kremera

crew [kruː] n besättning c

cricket ['krikit] n kricket c; syrsa c

crime [kraim] n brott nt

criminal ['kriminəl] n förbrytare c, brottsling c; adj kriminell, brottslig; ~ law strafflag c

criminality [ˌkrimiˈnæləti] n brottslighet c

crimson ['krimzən] adj karmosinröd

crippled ['kripəld] adj invalidiserad

crisis ['kraisis] n (pl crises) kris c

crisp [krisp] adj knaprig, frasig

critic ['kritik] n kritiker c

critical ['kritikəl] adj kritisk, farlig

criticism ['kritisizəm] n kritik c

criticize ['kritisaiz] v kritisera

crochet ['krouʃei] v virka

crockery ['krɔkəri] n lergods nt, porslin nt

crocodile ['krɔkədail] n

krokodil c

crooked ['krukid] *adj* krokig, vriden; oärlig

crop [krɔp] *n* skörd c

cross [krɔs] *v* *gå över; *adj* vresig, arg; *n* kors *nt*

cross-eyed ['krɔsaid] *adj* skelögd

crossing ['krɔsiŋ] *n* överfart c; korsning c; övergångsställe *nt*

crossroads ['krɔsroudz] *n* gatukorsning c

crosswalk ['krɔswɔ:k] *nAm* övergångsställe *nt*

crow [krou] *n* kråka c

crowbar ['krouba:] *n* bräckjärn *nt*

crowd [kraud] *n* folkmassa c, hop c

crowded ['kraudid] *adj* fullpackad; överfull

crown [kraun] *n* krona c; *v* kröna

crucifix ['kru:sifiks] *n* krucifix *nt*

crucifixion [,kru:si'fikʃən] *n* korsfästelse c

crucify ['kru:sifai] *v* korsfästa

cruel [kruəl] *adj* grym

cruise [kru:z] *n* kryssning c

crumb [krʌm] *n* smula c

crusade [kru:'seid] *n* korståg *nt*

crust [krʌst] *n* skorpa c

crutch [krʌtʃ] *n* krycka c

cry [krai] *v* *gråta; *skrika; ropa; *n* skrik *nt*; rop *nt*

crystal ['kristəl] *n* kristall c; *adj* kristall-

Cuba ['kju:bə] Kuba

Cuban ['kju:bən] *adj* kubansk; *n* kuban c

cube [kju:b] *n* kub c; tärning c

cuckoo ['kuku:] *n* gök c

cucumber ['kju:kəmbə] *n* gurka c

cuddle ['kʌdəl] *v* krama, kela med

cuff [kʌf] *n* manschett c

cuff links ['kʌfliŋks] *pl* manschettknappar *pl*

cul-de-sac ['kʌldəsæk] *n* återvändsgränd c

cultivate ['kʌltiveit] *v* odla

culture ['kʌltʃə] *n* kultur c

cultured ['kʌltʃəd] *adj* kultiverad

cunning ['kʌniŋ] *adj* listig

cup [kʌp] *n* kopp c; pokal c

cupboard ['kʌbəd] *n* skåp c

curb [kə:b] *n* trottoarkant c; *v* tygla, kuva

cure [kjuə] *v* bota; *n* kur c; tillfrisknande *nt*

curiosity [,kjuəri'ɔsəti] *n* nyfikenhet c

curious ['kjuəriəs] *adj* vetgirig, nyfiken; märkvärdig

curl [kə:l] *v* locka; krusa; *n* lock c

curler ['kə:lə] *n* papiljott c

curly ['kə:li] *adj* lockig

currant ['kʌrənt] *n* korint c; vinbär *nt*

currency ['kʌrənsi] *n* valuta c; **foreign ~** utländsk valuta

darn

current ['kʌrənt] n ström c; adj nuvarande, gällande; alternating ~ växelström c; direct ~ likström c

curry ['kʌri] n curry c

curse [kə:s] v *svära; förbanna; n svordom c

curtain ['kə:tən] n gardin c; ridå c

curve [kə:v] n kurva c; krökning c

curved [kə:vd] adj böjd

cushion ['kuʃən] n kudde c

custody ['kʌstədi] n häkte nt; förvaring c; förmynderskap nt

custom ['kʌstəm] n vana c; bruk nt

customary ['kʌstəməri] adj vanlig, sedvanlig, bruklig

customer ['kʌstəmə] n kund c; klient c

Customs ['kʌstəmz] pl tull c; ~ duty tull c; ~ officer tulltjänsteman c

cut [kʌt] n snitt nt; skärsår nt

*cut [kʌt] v *skära; klippa; *skära ned; ~ off *skära av; klippa av; stänga av

cutlery ['kʌtləri] n bestick nt

cutlet ['kʌtlət] n kotlett c

cycle ['saikəl] n cykel c; kretslopp nt

cyclist ['saiklist] n cyklist c

cylinder ['silində] n cylinder c; ~ head topplock nt

Czech Republic [ˌtʃek riˈpʌblik] Tjeckiska republiken

D

dad [dæd] n pappa c

daddy ['dædi] n pappa c

daffodil ['dæfədil] n påsklilja c

daily ['deili] adj daglig; n dagstidning c

dairy ['dɛəri] n mejeri nt

dam [dæm] n damm c; jordvall c

damage ['dæmidʒ] n skada c; v förstöra

damn [dæm] v förbanna

damp [dæmp] adj fuktig; n fukt c; v fukta

dance [dɑ:ns] v dansa; n dans c

dandelion ['dændilaiən] n maskros c

dandruff ['dændrəf] n mjäll nt

Dane [dein] n dansk c

danger ['deindʒə] n fara c

dangerous ['deindʒərəs] adj farlig

Danish ['deiniʃ] adj dansk

dare [dɛə] v våga; utmana

daring ['dɛəriŋ] adj djärv, oförskräckt

dark [dɑ:k] adj mörk; n mörker c

darling ['dɑ:liŋ] n älskling c

darn [dɑ:n] v stoppa

dash 248

dash [dæʃ] *v* rusa; *n*
tankstreck *nt*
dashboard ['dæʃbɔːd] *n*
instrumentbräda *c*
data ['deitə] *pl* data *pl*
date[1] [deit] *n* datum *nt*; träff
c; *v* datera; **out of ~**
omodern
date[2] [deit] *n* dadel *c*
daughter ['dɔːtə] *n* dotter *c*
daughter-in-law
['dɔːtərinlɔː] *n* svärdotter *c*
dawn [dɔːn] *n* gryning *c*;
dagning *c*
day [dei] *n* dag *c*; **by ~** om
dagen; **~ trip** dagsutflykt *c*;
per ~ per dag; **the ~ before
yesterday** i förrgår
day spa ['dei͵spɑː] *n* day spa
c
daybreak ['deibreik] *n*
dagbräckning *c*
daylight ['deilait] *n* dagsljus
nt
dead [ded] *adj* död
deaf [def] *adj* döv
deal [diːl] *n* affärsuppgörelse
c, affärstransaktion *c*
***deal** [diːl] *v* dela ut; **~ with**
befatta sig med; *göra
affärer med
dealer ['diːlə] *n* agent *c*,
-handlare
dear [diə] *adj* kär; dyr; dyrbar
death [deθ] *n* död *c*; **~
penalty** dödsstraff *nt*
debate [di'beit] *n* debatt *c*
debit ['debit] *n* debet *c*
debit card ['debit͵kɑːd] *n*
kontokort *nt*

debt [det] *n* skuld *c*
decaf(feinated)
[diːˈkæfineitid] *adj*
koffeinfri
decaffeinated
[diːˈkæfineitid] *adj*
koffeinfri
deceit [di'siːt] *n* bedrägeri *nt*
deceive [di'siːv] *v* *bedra
December [di'sembə]
december
decency ['diːsənsi] *n*
anständighet *c*
decent ['diːsənt] *adj*
anständig
decide [di'said] *v* *besluta,
bestämma, *avgöra
decision [di'siʒən] *n*
avgörande *c*, beslut *nt*
deck [dek] *n* däck *nt*; **~ cabin**
däckshytt *c*; **~ chair** vilstol *c*
declaration [͵deklə'reiʃən] *n*
förklaring *c*; deklaration *c*
declare [di'kleə] *v* förklara;
*uppge; förtulla
decorate ['dekəreit] *v*
dekorera
decoration [͵dekə'reiʃən] *n*
dekoration *c*
decrease [diː'kriːs] *v* *skära
ned, minska; *avta; *n*
minskning *c*
dedicate ['dedikeit] *v* ägna
deduce [di'djuːs] *v* härleda
deduct [di'dʌkt] *v* *dra av
deed [diːd] *n* handling *c*,
gärning *c*
deep [diːp] *adj* djup
deep-freeze [͵diːp'friːz] *n*
frys *c*

deer [diə] *n* (pl ~) hjort *c*
defeat [di'fiːt] *v* besegra; *n* nederlag *nt*
defective [di'fektiv] *adj* bristfällig
defence [di'fens] *n* försvar *nt*
defend [di'fend] *v* försvara
deficiency [di'fiʃənsi] *n* brist *c*
deficit ['defisit] *n* underskott *nt*
define [di'fain] *v* definiera, bestämma
definite ['definit] *adj* bestämd
definition [ˌdefi'niʃən] *n* definition *c*
degree [di'griː] *n* grad *c*
delay [di'lei] *v* försena, *uppskjuta; *n* försening *c*; uppskov *nt*
delegate ['deligət] *n* delegat *c*
delegation [ˌdeli'geiʃən] *n* deputation *c*, delegation *c*
deliberate[1] [di'libəreit] *v* *överlägga, överväga
deliberate[2] [di'libərət] *adj* överlagd
deliberation [diˌlibə'reiʃən] *n* överläggning *c*
delicacy ['delikəsi] *n* delikatess *c*
delicate ['delikət] *adj* fin; ömtålig; känslig
delicatessen [ˌdelikə'tesən] *n* delikatessaffär *c*
delicious [di'liʃəs] *adj* utsökt, läcker
delight [di'lait] *n* förtjusning

c, njutning *c*; *v* *glädja;
delighted förtjust
delightful [di'laitfəl] *adj* härlig, förtjusande
deliver [di'livə] *v* leverera, avlämna; frälsa
delivery [di'livəri] *n* leverans *c*; förlossning *c*; frälsning *c*; ~ van varubil *c*
demand [di'maːnd] *v* fordra, kräva; *n* begäran *c*; efterfrågan *c*
democracy [di'mɔkrəsi] *n* demokrati *c*
democratic [ˌdemə'krætik] *adj* demokratisk
demolish [di'mɔliʃ] *v* *riva
demolition [ˌdemə'liʃən] *n* rivning *c*
demonstrate ['demənstreit] *v* bevisa; demonstrera
demonstration [ˌdemən'streiʃən] *n* demonstration *c*
den [den] *n* lya *c*
Denmark ['denmaːk] Danmark
denomination [diˌnɔmi'neiʃən] *n* benämning *c*
dense [dens] *adj* tät
dent [dent] *n* buckla *c*
dental ['dentl] *adj* dental; **dental floss** *n* tandtråd *c*
dentist ['dentist] *n* tandläkare *c*
denture ['dentʃə] *n* tandprotes *c*
deny [di'nai] *v* förneka; neka, *bestrida, vägra

deodorant [diː'oudərənt] n
deodorant c

depart [di'pɑːt] v avresa,
avlägsna sig; *avlida

department [di'pɑːtmənt] n
avdelning c, departement
nt; ~ **store** varuhus nt

departure [di'pɑːtʃə] n
avgång c, avresa c

dependant [di'pendənt] adj
beroende

depend on [di'pend] bero på;
*vara beroende av; **that
depends on** det beror på

deposit [di'pɔzit] n
inbetalning c; handpenning
c, pant c; avlagring c,
sediment nt; v deponera

depot ['depou] n depå c;
nAm station c

depressed [di'prest] adj
deprimerad

depressing [di'presiŋ] adj
nedslående

depression [di'preʃən] n
depression c; lågtryck nt

deprive of [di'praiv] beröva

depth [depθ] n djup nt

deputy ['depjuti] n
deputerad c;
ställföreträdare c

descend [di'send] v *stiga
ned

descendant [di'sendənt] n
ättling c

descent [di'sent] n
nedstigning c

describe [di'skraib] v
*beskriva

description [di'skripʃən] n
beskrivning c; signalement
nt

desert[1] ['dezət] n öken c; adj
öde

desert[2] [di'zəːt] v desertera;
*överge

deserve [di'zəːv] v förtjäna

design [di'zain] v *planlägga;
n utkast c; mönster nt

designate ['dezigneit] v
bestämma

desirable [di'zaiərəbəl] adj
önskvärd, åtråvärd

desire [di'zaiə] n önskan c;
lust c, begär nt; v önska,
längta

desk [desk] n skrivbord nt;
talarstol c; skolbänk c

despair [di'spɛə] n förtvivlan
c; v förtvivla

despatch [di'spætʃ] v
avsända

desperate ['despərət] adj
desperat

despise [di'spaiz] v förakta

despite [di'spait] prep trots

dessert [di'zəːt] n dessert c

destination [,desti'neiʃən] n
bestämmelseort c

destine ['destin] v *avse,
bestämma

destiny ['destini] n öde nt

destroy [di'strɔi] v förstöra

destruction [di'strakʃən] n
förstörelse c; undergång c

detach [di'tætʃ] v avskilja

detail ['diːteil] n detalj c

detailed ['diːteild] adj
detaljerad, utförlig

detect [di'tekt] v upptäcka

detective [di'tektiv] n
detektiv c; ~ story
detektivroman c

detergent [di'tə:dʒənt] n
rengöringsmedel nt

determine [di'tə:min] v
bestämma, fastställa

determined [di'tə:mind] adj
beslutsam

detest [di'test] v avsky

detour ['di:tuə] n omväg c

devaluation
[,di:vælju'eiʃən] n
devalvering c

devalue [,di:'vælju:] v
devalvera

develop [di'veləp] v
utveckla; framkalla

development [di'veləpmənt]
n utveckling c; framkallning
c

deviate ['di:vieit] v *avvika

devil ['devəl] n djävul c

devise [di'vaiz] v uttänka

devote [di'vout] v ägna, offra

dew [dju:] n dagg c

diabetes [,daiə'bi:ti:z] n
sockersjuka c, diabetes c

diabetic [,daiə'betik] n
diabetiker c, sockersjuk c

diagnose [,daiəg'nouz] v
ställa in diagnos

diagnosis [,daiəg'nousis] n
(pl -ses) diagnos c

diagonal [dai'ægənəl] n
diagonal c; adj diagonal

diagram ['daiəgræm] n
diagram nt; grafisk
framställning c

dial ['daiəl] n urtavla

dialect ['daiəlekt] n dialekt c

diamond ['daiəmənd] n
diamant c

diaper ['daiəpə] nAm blöja c

diaphragm ['daiəfræm] n
diafragma c; bländare c

diarrhoea [daiə'riə] n diarré
c

diary ['daiəri] n
fickalmanacka c; dagbok c

dictaphone ['diktəfoun] n
diktafon c

dictate [dik'teit] v diktera

dictator [dik'teitə] n diktator
c

dictionary ['dikʃənəri] n
ordbok c

did [did] v (p do)

die [dai] v *dö

diesel ['di:zəl] n diesel c

diet ['daiət] n diet c

differ ['difə] v *vara olik

difference ['difərəns] n
skillnad c

different ['difərənt] adj olik;
annan

difficult ['difikəlt] adj svår;
kinkig

difficulty ['difikəlti] n
svårighet c

*dig [dig] v gräva

digest [di'dʒest] v smälta
maten

digestible [di'dʒestəbəl] adj
lättsmält

digestion [di'dʒestʃən] n
matsmältning c

digit ['didʒit] n siffra c

digital ['didʒitəl] adj digital

digital camera ['didʒi-

digital photo
təl_'kæmərə] *n*
digitalkamera *c*

digital photo
['didʒitəl_'foutou] *n*
digitalfoto *nt*

digital projector
['didʒitəl_prə'jektə] *n*
digital projektor *nt*

dignified ['dignifaid] *adj*
värdig

dignity ['digniti] *n* värdighet
c

dike [daik] *n* fördämning *c*

dilapidated [di'læpideitid]
adj förfallen

diligence ['dilidʒəns] *n* nit *c*,
flit *c*

diligent ['dilidʒənt] *adj*
ihärdig, flitig, arbetsam

dilute [dai'lju:t] *v* förtunna,
utspäda

dim [dim] *adj* matt, dunkel;
vag, oklar

dine [dain] *v* *äta middag

dinghy ['diŋgi] *n* jolle *c*

dining car ['dainiŋka:] *n*
restaurangvagn *c*

dining room ['dainiŋru:m] *n*
matsal *c*

dinner ['dinə] *n* middag *c*,
lunch *c*

dinner jacket ['dinə,dʒækit]
n smoking *c*

dinner service ['dinə,sə:vis]
n matservis *c*

diphtheria [dif'θiəriə] *n*
difteri *c*

diploma [di'ploumə] *n*
diplom *nt*

diplomat ['dipləmæt] *n*

diplomat *c*

direct [di'rekt] *adj* direkt; *v*
rikta; vägleda; leda;
regissera

direction [di'rekʃən] *n*
riktning *c*; instruktion *c*;
regi *c*; styrelse *c*, direktion *c*;
directions for use
bruksanvisning *c*

directive [di'rektiv] *n*
direktiv *nt*

director [di'rektə] *n* direktör
c; regissör *c*

directory [di'rektəri] *n*
adress-förteckning *c*

dirt [də:t] *n* smuts *c*

dirty ['də:ti] *adj* smutsig

disabled [di'seibəld] *adj*
invalidiserad, handikappad

disadvantage
[,disəd'va:ntidʒ] *n* nackdel
c

disagree [,disə'gri:] *v* *vara
oenig, *vara oense

disagreeable [,disə'gri:əbəl]
adj obehaglig

disappear [,disə'piə] *v*
*försvinna

disappoint [,disə'pɔint] *v*
*göra besviken; **be
disappointing** *vara en
besvikelse

disappointment
[,disə'pɔintmənt] *n*
besvikelse *c*

disapprove [,disə'pru:v] *v*
ogilla

disaster [di'za:stə] *n*
katastrof *c*, olycka *c*

disastrous [di'za:strəs] *adj*

katastrofal

disc [disk] *n* kota *c*, skiva *c*; grammofonskiva *c*; **slipped**
~ diskbråck *nt*

discard [di'ska:d] *v* kassera

discharge [dis'tʃa:dʒ] *v*
lossa; urladda; ~ **of** *frita
från

discipline ['disiplin] *n*
disciplin *c*

discolour [dis'kʌlə] *v*
urbleka, avfärga;
discoloured missfärgad

disconnect [,diskə'nekt] *v*
åtskilja; stänga av; *ta loss

discontented
[,diskən'tentid] *adj*
missbelåten

discontinue [,diskən'tinju:]
v sluta, *avbryta

discourage [dis'kʌridʒ] *v*
göra modfälld

discount ['diskaunt] *n* rabatt
c, avdrag *c*

discover [di'skʌvə] *v*
upptäcka

discovery [di'skʌvəri] *n*
upptäckt *c*

discuss [di'skʌs] *v*
diskutera; debattera

discussion [di'skʌʃən] *n*
diskussion *c*; överläggning *c*,
debatt *c*, samtal *c*

disease [di'zi:z] *n* sjukdom *c*

disembark [,disim'ba:k] *v*
*landstiga, *gå i land

disgrace [dis'greis] *n* skam *c*

disguise [dis'gaiz] *v* förklä
sig; *n* förklädnad *c*

disgust [dis'gʌst] *n* avsky *c*

disgusting [dis'gʌstiŋ] *adj*
äcklig, vidrig

dish [diʃ] *n* tallrik *c*;
serveringsfat *nt*, fat *nt*;
maträtt *c*

dishonest [di'sɔnist] *adj*
oärlig

dishwasher ['diʃwɔʃə] *n*
tvättmaskin *c*

disinfect [,disin'fekt] *v*
desinfektera

disinfectant [,disin'fektənt]
n desinfektionsmedel *nt*

disk drive ['disk‚draiv] *n*
skivenhet *c*

dislike [di'slaik] *v* inte tycka
om, tycka illa om; *n* antipati
c, motvilja *c*

dislocated ['disləkeitid] *adj*
ur led

dismiss [dis'mis] *v* skicka
bort; avskeda

disorder [di'sɔ:də] *n* oreda *c*

dispatch [di'spætʃ] *v*
avsända

display [di'splei] *v* utställa;
visa; *n* utställning *c*

displease [di'spli:z] *v*
misshaga, förarga

disposable [di'spouzəbəl]
adj engångs-

disposal [di'spouzəl] *n*
förfogande *nt*

dispose of (di'spouz) *göra
sig av med

dispute [di'spju:t] *n* dispyt *c*;
gräl *nt*, tvist *c*; *v* tvista,
*bestrida

dissatisfied [di'sætisfaid]
adj missnöjd

dissolve 254

dissolve [di'zɔlv] v upplösa

dissuade from [di'sweid] avråda

distance ['distəns] n avstånd nt; ~ **in kilometres** kilometeravstånd nt

distant ['distənt] adj avlägsen

distinct [di'stiŋkt] adj tydlig; olik

distinction [di'stiŋkʃən] n skillnad c

distinguish [di'stiŋgwiʃ] v urskilja, *göra skillnad

distinguished [di'stiŋgwiʃt] adj framstående

distress [di'stres] n nöd c; ~ **signal** nödsignal c

distribute [di'stribjuːt] v utdela

distributor [di'stribjutə] n distributör c; strömfördelare c

district ['distrikt] n distrikt nt; område nt; stadsdel c

disturb [di'stəːb] v störa

disturbance [di'stəːbəns] n störning c; oro c

ditch [ditʃ] n dike nt

dive [daiv] v *dyka

diversion [dai'vəːʃən] n trafikomläggning c; förströelse c

divide [di'vaid] v dela; indela; åtskilja

divine [di'vain] adj gudomlig

division [di'viʒən] n delning c; avdelning c

divorce [di'vɔːs] n skilsmässa c; v skiljas, skilja sig

dizziness ['dizinəs] n yrsel c

dizzy ['dizi] adj yr

***do** [duː] v *göra; *vara nog

dock [dɔk] n docka c; kaj c; v docka

docker ['dɔkə] n hamnarbetare c

doctor ['dɔktə] n doktor c, läkare c

document ['dɔkjumənt] n handling c, intyg nt

dog [dɔg] n hund c

doll [dɔl] n docka c

dollar ['dɔlə] n dollar c

dolphin ['dɔlfin] n delfin c

dome [doum] n kupol c

domestic [də'mestik] adj inrikes; n tjänare c

domicile ['dɔmisail] n hemort c

domination [ˌdɔmi'neiʃən] n herravälde nt

dominion [də'minjən] n. makt c

donate [dou'neit] v donera

donation [dou'neiʃən] n donation c

done [dʌn] v (pp do)

donkey ['dɔŋki] n åsna c

donor ['dounə] n donator c

door [dɔː] n dörr c; **revolving** ~ svängdörr c; **sliding** ~ skjutdörr c

doorbell ['dɔːbel] n dörrklocka c

doorkeeper ['dɔːˌkiːpə] n dörrvaktmästare c

doorman ['dɔːmən] n (pl -men) dörrvaktmästare c

dormitory ['dɔːmitri] n

sovsal c

dose [dous] n dos c

dot [dɔt] n punkt c

double ['dʌbəl] adj dubbel

doubt [daut] v tvivla,
betvivla; n tvivel nt; **without**
~ utan tvivel

doubtful ['dautfəl] adj
tvivelaktig; oviss

dough [dou] n deg c

down¹ [daun] adv ned;
omkull, ner, nedåt; adj
nedstående; prep nedåt,
nedför; ~ **payment**
handpenning c

down² [daun] n dun nt

download ['daun,loud] n
nerladdning c

downpour ['daunpɔ:] n
störtregn c

downstairs [,daun'steəz]
adv där nere, ner

downstream [,daun'stri:m]
adv medströms

down-to-earth [,dauntu'ə:θ]
adj omdömesgill

downwards ['daunwədz]
adv nedåt

dozen ['dʌzən] n (pl ~, ~s)
dussin nt

draft [drɑ:ft] n växel c

drag [dræg] v släpa

dragon ['drægən] n drake c

drain [drein] v dränera,
*torrlägga; n avlopp nt

drama ['drɑ:mə] n drama nt;
skådespel nt

dramatic [drə'mætik] adj
dramatisk

drank [dræŋk] v (p drink)

draught [drɑ:ft] n drag nt;
draughts damspel nt; ~
beer fatöl

draw [drɔ:] n dragplåster nt,
oavgjord match; dragning c

*draw [drɔ:] v rita; *dra; *ta
ut; ~ up avfatta, redigera

drawbridge ['drɔ:bridʒ] n
vindbrygga c

drawer ['drɔ:ə] n låda c,
byrålåda c; **drawers**
kalsonger pl

drawing ['drɔ:iŋ] n teckning
c

drawing pin ['drɔ:iŋpin] n
häftstift nt

drawing room ['drɔ:iŋru:m]
n salong c

dread [dred] v frukta; n
fruktan c

dreadful ['dredfəl] adj
förskräcklig, förfärlig

dream [dri:m] n dröm c

*dream [dri:m] v drömma

dress [dres] v klä på, klä sig;
*förbinda; n klänning c

dressing gown ['dresiŋ-
gaun] n morgonrock c

dressing room ['dresiŋru:m]
n påklädningsrum c

dressing table
['dresiŋ,teibəl] n
toalettbord nt

dressmaker ['dres,meikə] n
sömmerska c

drill [dril] v borra; träna; n
borr c

drink [driŋk] n drink c, dryck
c

*drink [driŋk] v *dricka

drinking water ['driŋkiŋ,wɔːtə] *n* dricksvatten *c*

drip-dry [,drip'drai] *adj* strykfri

drive [draiv] *n* väg *c*; biltur *c*

*drive [draiv] *v* köra

driver ['draivə] *n* förare *c*

drive-thru ['draiv,θru:] *v* drive-in

driver's licence, driving licence körkort *nt*

drizzle ['drizəl] *n* duggregn *nt*

drop [drɔp] *v* tappa; *n* droppe *c*

drought [draut] *n* torka *c*

drown [draun] *v* dränka; ***be drowned** drunkna

drug [drʌg] *n* drog *c*; medicin *c*

drugstore ['drʌgstɔ:] *nAm* apotek *nt*, kemikalieaffär *c*; varuhus *nt*

drum [drʌm] *n* trumma *c*

drunk [drʌŋk] *adj* (pp drink) berusad, full

dry [drai] *adj* torr; *v* torka

dry-clean [,drai'kli:n] *v* kemtvätta

dry cleaner's [,drai'kli:nəz] *n* kemtvätt *c*

dryer ['draiə] *n* torktumlare *c*

duchess [dʌtʃis] *n* hertiginna *c*

duck [dʌk] *n* anka *c*

due [dju:] *adj* väntad; ***bör** betalas; betalbar

dues [dju:z] *pl* avgifter

dug [dʌg] *v* (p, pp dig)

duke [dju:k] *n* hertig *c*

dull [dʌl] *adj* tråkig, långtråkig; matt, dov; slö

dumb [dʌm] *adj* stum; dum

dune [dju:n] *n* dyn *c*

dung [dʌŋ] *n* dynga *c*

duration [dju'reiʃən] *n* varaktighet *c*

during ['djuəriŋ] *prep* under

dusk [dʌsk] *n* skymning *c*

dust [dʌst] *n* damm *nt*

dustbin ['dʌstbin] *n* soptunna *c*

dusty ['dʌsti] *adj* dammig

Dutch [dʌtʃ] *adj* holländsk, nederländsk

Dutchman ['dʌtʃmən] *n* (pl -men) holländare *c*, nederländare *c*

duty ['dju:ti] *n* plikt *c*; tullavgift *c*; **Customs ~** tullavgift *c*

duty-free [,dju:ti'fri:] *adj* tullfri

DVD ['di:vi:'di:] *n* DVD *c*

DVD-ROM ['di:vi:di:'rɔm] *n* DVD-ROM *c*

dwarf [dwɔ:f] *n* dvärg *c*

dye [dai] *v* färga; *n* färg *c*

dynamo ['dainəmou] *n* (pl ~s) dynamo *c*

E

each [i:tʃ] *adj* varje, var; ~ **other** varandra

eager ['i:gə] *adj* ivrig, otålig

eagle ['i:gəl] *n* örn *c*

ear [iə] *n* öra *nt*

earache ['iəreik] *n* örsprång *nt*

eardrum ['iədrʌm] *n* trumhinna *c*

earl [ə:l] *n* greve *c*

early ['ə:li] *adj* tidig

earn [ə:n] *v* tjäna, förtjäna

earnest ['ə:nist] *n* allvar *nt*

earnings ['ə:niŋz] *pl* inkomster, intäkter *pl*

earring ['iəriŋ] *n* örhänge *nt*

earth [ə:θ] *n* jord *c*; mark *c*

earthquake ['ə:θkweik] *n* jordbävning *c*

ease [i:z] *n* lätthet *c*; välbefinnande *nt*

east [i:st] *n* öster *c*, öst

Easter ['i:stə] påsk *c*

eastern ['i:stən] *adj* ostlig, östra

easy ['i:zi] *adj* lätt; bekväm; ~ **chair** fåtölj *c*

easy-going ['i:zi,gouiŋ] *adj* avspänd, sorglös

***eat** [i:t] *v* *äta

eavesdrop ['i:vzdrɔp] *v* tjuvlyssna

ebony ['ebəni] *n* ebenholts *c*

eccentric [ik'sentrik] *adj* excentrisk

echo ['ekou] *n* (pl ~es)

genljud *nt*, eko *nt*

eclipse [i'klips] *n* förmörkelse *c*

economic [,i:kə'nɔmik] *adj* ekonomisk

economical [,i:kə'nɔmikəl] *adj* sparsam, ekonomisk

economist [i'kɔnəmist] *n* ekonom *c*

economize [i'kɔnəmaiz] *v* spara

economy [i'kɔnəmi] *n* ekonomi *c*

eco-tourist ['i:kou,tu:rist] *n* ekoturist *c*

ecstasy ['ekstəzi] *n* extas *c*

Ecuador ['ekwədɔ:] Ecuador

Ecuadorian [,ekwə'dɔ:riən] *n* ecuadorian *c*

eczema ['eksimə] *n* eksem *nt*

edge [edʒ] *n* kant *c*

edible ['edibəl] *adj* ätbar

edit ['edit] *v* redigera

edition [i'diʃən] *n* upplaga *c*; **morning** ~ morgonupplaga *c*

editor ['editə] *n* redaktör *c*

educate ['edʒukeit] *v* uppfostra, utbilda

education [,edʒu'keiʃən] *n* uppfostran *c*; utbildning *c*

eel [i:l] *n* ål *c*

effect [i'fekt] *n* verkan *c*; *v* *åstadkomma; **in** ~ faktiskt

effective [i'fektiv] *adj* verksam, effektiv

efficient [i'fiʃənt] *adj*
effektiv, duglig, verksam

effort ['efət] *n* ansträngning *c*

egg [eg] *n* ägg *nt*

eggplant ['egplɑ:nt] *n*
äggplanta *c*

egg yolk ['egjouk] *n* äggula *c*

Egypt ['i:dʒipt] Egypten

Egyptian [i'dʒipʃən] *adj*
egyptisk; *n* egypter *c*

eiderdown ['aidədaun] *n*
duntäcke *nt*

eight [eit] *num* åtta

eighteen [,ei'ti:n] *num* arton

eighteenth [,ei'ti:nθ] *num*
artonde

eighth [eitθ] *num* åttonde

eighty ['eiti] *num* åttio

either ['aiðə] *pron* endera;
either ... or antingen ...
eller

elaborate [i'læbəreit] *v*
utarbeta

elastic [i'læstik] *adj* elastisk;
tänjbar; **~ band** resårband *c*

elasticity [,elæ'stisəti] *n*
elasticitet *c*

elbow ['elbou] *n* armbåge *c*

elder ['eldə] *adj* äldre

elderly ['eldəli] *adj* äldre

eldest ['eldist] *adj* äldst

elect [i'lekt] *v* *välja

election [i'lekʃən] *n* val *nt*

electric [i'lektrik] *adj*
elektrisk; **~ cord** sladd *c*; **~
razor** rakapparat *c*

electrician [,ilek'triʃən] *n*
elektriker *c*

electricity [,ilek'trisəti] *n*
elektricitet *c*

electronic [ilek'trɔnik] *adj*
elektronisk

elegance ['eligəns] *n* elegans
c

elegant ['eligənt] *adj* elegant

element ['elimənt] *n* element
nt, beståndsdel *c*

elephant ['elifənt] *n* elefant *c*

elevator ['eliveitə] *nAm* hiss
c

eleven [i'levən] *num* elva

eleventh [i'levənθ] *num* elfte

elf [elf] *n* (pl elves) älva *c*, alf *c*

eliminate [i'limineit] *v*
eliminera

elm [elm] *n* alm *c*

else [els] *adv* annars

elsewhere [,el'swɛə] *adv*
någon annanstans

elucidate [i'lu:sideit] *v*
belysa, förklara

e-mail [i:meil] *n* e-post *c*; **~
address** *n* e-postadress *c*

emancipation
[i,mænsi'peiʃən] *n*
frigörelse *c*

embankment
[im'bæŋkmənt] *n* vägbank *c*

embargo [em'bɑ:gou] *n* (pl
~es) embargo *nt*

embark [im'bɑ:k] *v* *gå
ombord

embarkation
[,embɑ:'keiʃən] *n*
embarkering *c*

embarrass [im'bærəs] *v*
genera, *göra förlägen;
hindra; **embarrassed**
förlägen; **embarrassing**
pinsam; **embarrassment** *n*

förlägenhet c
embassy ['embəsi] n
    ambassad c
emblem ['embləm] n emblem
    nt
embrace [im'breis] v krama,
    omfamna; n omfamning c
embroider [im'broidə] v
    brodera
embroidery [im'broidəri] n
    broderi nt
emerald ['emərəld] n
    smaragd c
emergency [i'mə:dʒənsi] n
    nödsituation c; nödläge nt; ~
    exit nödutgång c
emigrant ['emigrənt] n
    utvandrare c
emigrate ['emigreit] v
    utvandra
emigration [,emi'greiʃən] n
    utvandring c
emotion [i'mouʃən] n
    sinnesrörelse c, känsla c
emperor ['empərə] n kejsare c
emphasize ['emfəsaiz] v
    betona
empire ['empaiə] n imperium
    nt, kejsardöme nt
employ [im'ploi] v
    *sysselsätta, anställa;
    använda
employee [,emploi'i:] n
    anställd c, löntagare c
employer [im'ploiə] n
    arbetsgivare c
employment [im'ploimənt] n
    anställning c, arbete nt; ~
    exchange arbetsförmedling
    c

empress ['empris] n
    kejsarinna c
empty ['empti] adj tom; v
    tömma
enable [i'neibəl] v
    *möjliggöra
enamel [i'næməl] n emalj c
enamelled [i'næməld] adj
    emaljerad
enchanting [in'tʃɑ:ntiŋ] adj
    förtrollande, bedårande
encircle [in'sə:kəl] v inringa,
    omringa; *innesluta
enclose [iŋ'klouz] v bifoga
enclosure [iŋ'klouʒə] n
    bilaga c
encounter [iŋ'kauntə] v
    möta, träffa; n
    sammanträffande nt
encourage [iŋ'kʌridʒ] v
    uppmuntra
encyclopaedia
    [en,saiklə'pi:diə] n
    uppslagsbok c
end [end] n ände c, slut nt; v
    sluta
ending ['endiŋ] n slut nt
endless ['endləs] adj oändlig
endorse [in'dɔ:s] v endossera
endure [in'djuə] v *stå ut
    med
enemy ['enəmi] n fiende c
energetic [,enə'dʒetik] adj
    energisk
energy ['enədʒi] n energi c;
    kraft c
engage [iŋ'geidʒ] v anställa;
    förplikta sig; **engaged**
    förlovad; upptagen
engagement [iŋ'geidʒmənt]

n förlovning *c*; förpliktelse
c; avtalat möte; ~ **ring**
förlovningsring *c*

engine ['endʒin] *n* maskin *c*,
motor *c*; lokomotiv *nt*

engineer [ˌendʒi'niə] *n*
ingenjör *c*

England ['ɪŋɡlənd] England

English ['ɪŋɡliʃ] *adj* engelsk

Englishman ['ɪŋɡliʃmən] *n*
(pl -men) engelsman *c*

engrave [iŋ'ɡreiv] *v* gravera

engraver [iŋ'ɡreivə] *n* gravör
c

engraving [iŋ'ɡreiviŋ] *n*
gravyr *c*

enigma [i'nigmə] *n* gåta *c*

enjoy [in'dʒɔi] *v* *njuta,
*njuta av

enjoyable [in'dʒɔiəbəl] *adj*
rolig, trevlig

enjoyment [in'dʒɔimənt] *n*
nöje *nt*

enlarge [in'lɑːdʒ] *v* förstora;
utvidga

enlargement [in'lɑːdʒmənt]
n förstoring *c*

enormous [i'nɔːməs] *adj*
väldig, enorm

enough [i'nʌf] *adv* nog; *adj*
tillräcklig

enquire [iŋ'kwaiə] *v*
underrätta sig, förhöra sig;
undersöka

enquiry [iŋ'kwaiəri] *n*
undersökning *c*; förfrågan *c*

enter ['entə] *v* *gå in, inträda;
*skriva in

enterprise ['entəpraiz] *n*
företag *c*

entertain [ˌentə'tein] *v*
*underhålla, roa; *mottaga
som gäst

entertainer [ˌentə'teinə] *n*
underhållare *c*

entertaining [ˌentə'teiniŋ]
adj underhållande, roande

entertainment
[ˌentə'teinmənt] *n*
underhållning *c*

enthusiasm [in'θjuːziæzəm]
n entusiasm *c*

enthusiastic
[inˌθjuːzi'æstik] *adj*
entusiastisk

entire [in'taiə] *adj* hel

entirely [in'taiəli] *adv* helt

entrance ['entrəns] *n* ingång
c; tillträde *nt*; inträde *nt*

entrance fee ['entrənsfiː] *n*
inträdesavgift *c*

entry ['entri] *n* ingång *c*;
tillträde *nt*; anteckning *c*; **no**
~ tillträde förbjudet

envelop [in'veləp] *v* svepa in

envelope ['envəloup] *n*
kuvert *nt*

envious ['enviəs] *adj*
avundsjuk, avundsam

environment
[in'vaiərənmənt] *n* miljö *c*;
omgivning *c*

envoy ['envɔi] *n* envoyé *c*

envy ['envi] *n* avundsjuka *c*; *v*
avundas

epic ['epik] *n* epos *nt*; *adj*
episk

epidemic [ˌepi'demik] *n*
epidemi *c*

epilepsy ['epilepsi] *n* epilepsi

c

epilogue ['epilɔg] n epilog c

episode ['episoud] n episod c

equal ['i:kwəl] adj lika; v
*vara likvärdig

equality [i'kwɔləti] n
jämlikhet c

equalize ['i:kwəlaiz] v
utjämna

equally ['i:kwəli] adv lika

equator [i'kweitə] n
ekvatorn

equip [i'kwip] v utrusta,
ekipera

equipment [i'kwipmənt] n
utrustning c

equivalent [i'kwivələnt] adj
motsvarande, likvärdig

eraser [i'reizə] n radergummi
nt

erect [i'rekt] v uppbygga,
upprätta; adj
upprättstående, upprätt

err [ə:] v *ta fel, *missta; irra

errand ['erənd] n ärende c

error ['erə] n misstag nt, fel nt

escalator ['eskəleitə] n
rulltrappa c

escape [i'skeip] v
*undslippa; *undgå, fly; n
flykt c

escort¹ ['eskɔ:t] n eskort c

escort² [i'skɔ:t] v eskortera

especially [i'speʃəli] adv
särskilt, i synnerhet

esplanade [,esplə'neid] n
esplanad c

essay ['esei] n essä c; uppsats
c

essence ['esəns] n essens c;

väsen nt, kärna c

essential [i'senʃəl] adj
oumbärlig; väsentlig

essentially [i'senʃəli] adv
väsentligen

establish [i'stæbliʃ] v
etablera; fastställa

estate [i'steit] n
lantegendom c

esteem [i'sti:m] n aktning c,
respekt c; v uppskatta

estimate¹ ['estimeit] v
värdera

estimate² ['estimət] n
beräkning c

estuary ['estʃuəri] n
flodmynning c

etcetera [et'setərə] och så
vidare

etching ['etʃiŋ] n etsning c

eternal [i'tə:nəl] adj evig

eternity [i'tə:nəti] n evighet c

Ethiopia [iθi'oupiə] Etiopien

Ethiopian [iθi'oupiən] adj
etiopisk; n etiopier c

e-ticket ['i:,tikət] n e-biljett c

EU ['i:'ju] EU

Euro ['ju:rou] n euro c

Europe ['juərəp] Europa

European [,juərə'pi:ən] adj
europeisk; n europé c; ~
Union Europeiska
Unionen

evacuate [i'vækjueit] v
evakuera

evaluate [i'væljueit] v
värdera

evaporate [i'væpəreit] v
avdunsta

even ['i:vən] adj jämn, plan,
lika; adv till och med

evening ['i:vniŋ] *n* kväll *c*; ~
dress aftonklädsel *c*
event [i'vent] *n* händelse *c*
eventual [i'ventʃuəl] *adj*
slutlig
eventually [i'ventʃuəli] *adv*
så småningom
ever ['evə] *adv* någonsin;
alltid
every ['evri] *adj* varje
everybody ['evri,bɔdi] *pron*
var och en
everyday ['evridei] *adj* daglig
everyone ['evriwʌn] *pron*
envar, var och en
everything ['evriθiŋ] *pron*
allting
everywhere ['evriweə] *adv*
överallt
evidence ['evidəns] *n* bevis
nt
evident ['evidənt] *adj* tydlig
evil ['i:vəl] *n* ondska *c*; *adj*
ond, elak
evolution [,i:və'lu:ʃən] *n*
utveckling *c*
exact [ig'zækt] *adj* exakt
exactly [ig'zæktli] *adv* exakt
exaggerate [ig'zædʒəreit] *v*
*överdriva
exam [ig'zæm] *n colloquial*
examen *c*
examination
[ig,zæmi'neiʃən]
undersökning *c*
examine [ig'zæmin] *v*
undersöka
example [ig'zɑ:mpəl] *n*
exempel *nt*; **for** ~ till
exempel

excavation [,ekskə'veiʃən] *n*
utgrävning *c*
exceed [ik'si:d] *v*
*överskrida; överträffa
excel [ik'sel] *v* utmärka sig
excellent ['eksələnt] *adj*
förträfflig
except [ik'sept] *prep* med
undantag av, utom
exception [ik'sepʃən] *n*
undantag *nt*
exceptional [ik'sepʃənəl] *adj*
enastående, ovanlig
excerpt ['eksə:pt] *n* utdrag *nt*
excess [ik'ses] *n* överdrift *c*
excessive [ik'sesiv] *adj*
överdriven
exchange [iks'tʃeindʒ] *v*
växla, utbyta, byta ut; *n* byte
nt; börs *c*; ~ **office**
växelkontor *nt*; ~ **rate**
växelkurs *c*
excite [ik'sait] *v* upphetsa
excited [ik'saitəd] *adj*
upphetsad
excitement [ik'saitmənt] *n*
uppståndelse *c*, spänning *c*
exciting [ik'saitiŋ] *adj*
spännande
exclaim [ik'skleim] *v* utropa
exclamation
[,eksklə'meiʃən] *n* utrop *nt*
exclude [ik'sklu:d] *v*
*utesluta
exclusive [ik'sklu:siv] *adj*
exklusiv
exclusively [ik'sklu:sivli]
adv enbart, uteslutande
excursion [ik'skə:ʃən] *n*
utflykt *c*

excuse[1] [ik'skju:s] n orsäkt c

excuse[2] [ik'skju:z] v ursäkta

execute ['eksikju:t] v utföra

execution [,eksi'kju:ʃən] n avrättning c; utförande nt

executioner [,eksi'kju:ʃənə] n bödel c

executive [ig'zekjutiv] adj verkställande; n verkställande myndighet; direktör c

executive assistant [ig'zekjətiv,ə'sistənt] n chefssekreterare c

exempt [ig'zempt] v *frita, frikalla, befria; adj befriad

exemption [ig'zempʃən] n befrielse c

exercise ['eksəsaiz] n övning c; skriftligt prov; v öva; utöva

exhale [eks'heil] v utandas

exhaust [ig'zɔ:st] n avgas c; v utmatta; ~ **gases** avgaser pl

exhibit [ig'zibit] v ställa ut; förevisa, uppvisa

exhibition [,eksi'biʃən] n utställning c

exile ['eksail] n landsflykt c; landsflykting c

exist [ig'zist] v existera

existence [ig'zistəns] n existens c

exit ['eksit] n utgång c; utfart c

exotic [ig'zɔtik] adj exotisk

expand [ik'spænd] v utvidga; utbreda

expansion [ik'spænʃən] n expansion c

expect [ik'spekt] v vänta sig

expectation [,ekspek'teiʃən] n förväntan c

expedition [,ekspə'diʃən] n expedition c; snabbhet c

expel [ik'spel] v utvisa

expenditure [ik'spenditʃə] n utgifter, pl

expense [ik'spens] n utgift c; **expenses** pl omkostnader pl

expensive [ik'spensiv] adj dyrbar, dyr; kostsam

experience [ik'spiəriəns] n erfarenhet c; v *erfara, uppleva; **experienced** erfaren

experiment [ik'sperimənt] n experiment nt, försök nt; v experimentera

expert ['ekspə:t] n fackman c, expert c; adj sakkunnig

expire [ik'spaiə] v utlöpa, *förfalla; utandas; **expired** ogiltig

explain [ik'splein] v förklara

explanation [,eksplə'neiʃən] n förklaring c

explicit [ik'splisit] adj tydlig, uttrycklig

explode [ik'sploud] v explodera

exploit [ik'splɔit] v *utsuga, utnyttja

explore [ik'splɔ:] v utforska

explosion [ik'splouʒən] n explosion c

explosive [ik'splousiv] adj explosiv; n sprängämne nt

export[1] [ik'spɔ:t] v exportera

export² ['ekspɔ:t] *n* export *c*

expose [ik'spous] *v* utsätta

exposition [,ekspə'ziʃən] *n* utställning *c*

exposure [ik'spouʒə] *n* utsättande *nt*; exponering *c*; ~ **meter** exponeringsmätare *c*

express [ik'spres] *v* uttrycka; *ge uttryck åt; adj snabbgående; uttrycklig; ~ **train** expresståg *nt*

expression [ik'spreʃən] *n* uttryck *nt*; yttrande *nt*

exquisite [ik'skwizit] *adj* utsökt

extend [ik'stend] *v* förlänga; utvidga; bevilja

extension [ik'stenʃən] *n* förlängning *c*; utvidgande *nt*; anknytningslinje *c*; ~ **cord** förlängningssladd *c*

extensive [ik'stensiv] *adj* omfångsrik; vidsträckt, omfattande

extent [ik'stent] *n* utsträckning *c*, omfång *nt*

exterior [ek'stiəriə] *adj* yttre; *n* yttre *nt*

external [ek'stə:nəl] *adj* utvändig

extinguish [ik'stiŋgwiʃ] *v* släcka

extort [ik'stɔ:t] *v* utpressa

extortion [ik'stɔ:ʃən] *n* utpressning *c*

extra ['ekstrə] *adj* extra

extract¹ [ik'strækt] *v* *utdra

extract² ['ekstrækt] *n* utdrag *nt*

extradite ['ekstrədait] *v* utlämna

extraordinary [ik'strɔ:dənri] *adj* utomordentlig

extravagant [ik'strævəgənt] *adj* överdriven, extravagant, slösaktig

extreme [ik'stri:m] *adj* extrem; ytterlig, yttersta; *n* ytterlighet *c*

exuberant [ig'zju:bərənt] *adj* översvallande

eye [ai] *n* öga *nt*

eyebrow ['aibrau] *n* ögonbryn *nt*

eyelash ['ailæʃ] *n* ögonfrans *c*

eyelid ['ailid] *n* ögonlock *nt*

eyebrow pencil ['ai,pensəl] *n* ögonbrynspenna *c*

eye shadow ['ai,ʃædou] *n* ögonskugga *c*

eyewitness ['ai,witnəs] *n* ögonvittne *nt*

F

fable ['feibəl] n fabel c

fabric ['fæbrik] n tyg nt; struktur c

façade [fə'sɑ:d] n fasad c

face [feis] n ansikte nt; v konfrontera, *vara vänd mot; ~ massage ansiktsmassage c; **facing** mittemot

face cream ['feiskri:m] n ansiktskräm c

face pack ['feispæk] n ansiktsmask c

face-powder ['feis,paudə] n ansiktspuder nt

facilities [fə'silətis] pl möjligheter pl; **cooking** ~ pl kokmöjligheter pl

fact [fækt] n faktum nt; **in** ~ i själva verket

factor ['fæktə] n faktor c

factory ['fæktəri] n fabrik c

factual ['fæktʃuəl] adj faktisk

faculty ['fækəlti] n förmåga c; fallenhet c, talang c; fakultet c

fade [feid] v blekna

fail [feil] v misslyckas; fattas; försumma; kuggas; **without** ~ helt säkert

failure ['feiljə] n misslyckande nt

faint [feint] v svimma; adj vag, svag

fair [fɛə] n marknad c; varumässa c; adj just,

rättvis; ljushårig, blond; fager

fairly ['fɛəli] adv tämligen, ganska

fairy ['fɛəri] n fe c

fairytale ['fɛəriteil] n saga c

faith [feiθ] n tro c; tillit c

faithful ['feiθful] adj trogen

fake [feik] n förfalskning c

fall [fɔ:l] n fall nt; nAm höst c

*fall [fɔ:l] v *falla

false [fɔ:ls] adj falsk; fel, oäkta; ~ **teeth** löständer pl

falter ['fɔ:ltə] v vackla; stamma

fame [feim] n ryktbarhet c, berömmelse c; rykte nt

familiar [fə'miljə] adj välkänd; familjär

family ['fæməli] n familj c; släkt c; ~ **name** efternamn nt

famous ['feiməs] adj berömd

fan [fæn] n fläkt c; solfjäder c; beundrare c; ~ **belt** fläktrem c

fanatical [fə'nætikəl] adj fanatisk

fancy ['fænsi] v *ha lust att, tycka om; tänka sig, föreställa sig; n nyck c; fantasi c

fantastic [fæn'tæstik] adj fantastisk

fantasy ['fæntəzi] n fantasi c

far [fɑ:] adj avlägset; **by** ~

fare 266

betydligt; **so ~** hittills; **~
away** långt bort
fare [feə] *n* biljettpris *nt*; mat
c, kost *c*
farm [fɑ:m] *n* lantbruk *nt*
farmer ['fɑ:mə] *n* lantbrukare
c; **farmer's wife**
lantbrukarhustru *c*
farmhouse ['fɑ:mhaus] *n*
lantgård *c*
far-off ['fɑ:rɔf] *adj* avlägsen
farther ['fɑ:ðə] *adj* mera
fascinate ['fæsineit] *v*
fascinera
fascism ['fæʃizəm] *n* fascism
c
fascist ['fæʃist] *adj* fascistisk;
n fascist *c*
fashion ['fæʃən] *n* mode *nt*;
sätt *nt*
fashionable ['fæʃənəbəl] *adj*
modern
fast [fɑ:st] *adj* snabb, hastig
fasten ['fɑ:sən] *v* fästa,
spänna fast; stänga
fastener ['fɑ:sənə] *n* spänne
nt
fat [fæt] *adj* tjock, fet; *n* fett
nt
fat free ['fæt,'fri:] *adj* fettfri
fatal ['feitəl] *adj* ödesdiger,
fatal, dödlig
fate [feit] *n* öde *nt*
father ['fɑ:ðə] *n* far *c*; pater *c*
father-in-law ['fɑ:ðərinlɔ:] *n*
(pl fathers-) svärfar *c*
fatty ['fæti] *adj* fet
faucet ['fɔ:sit] *nAm*
vattenkran *c*
fault [fɔ:lt] *n* fel *nt*; defekt *c*

faultless ['fɔ:ltləs] *adj* felfri;
oklanderlig
faulty ['fɔ:lti] *adj* bristfällig
favour ['feivə] *n* välvilja *c*,
tjänst *c*; *v* favorisera, gynna
favourable ['feivərəbəl] *adj*
gynnsam
favourite ['feivərit] *n* favorit
c, gunstling *c*; *adj* älsklings-
fawn [fɔ:n] *adj* gulbrun; *n*
rådjurskalv *c*, hjortkalv *c*
fax [fæks] *n* (tele)fax *nt*; **send
a ~** skicka ett fax, faxa
fear [fiə] *n* rädsla *c*, oro *c*; *v*
frukta
feasible ['fi:zəbəl] *adj*
utförbar
feast [fi:st] *n* fest *c*
feat [fi:t] *n* bragd *c*,
prestation *c*
feather ['feðə] *n* fjäder *c*
feature ['fi:tʃə] *n*
kännemärke *nt*; ansiktsdrag
nt
February ['februəri] februari
federal ['fedərəl] *adj*
förbunds-
federation [,fedə'reiʃən] *n*
federation *c*; förbundsstat *c*
fee [fi:] *n* arvode *c*
feeble ['fi:bəl] *adj* svag
***feed** [fi:d] *v* mata; **fed up
with** utled på
***feel** [fi:l] *v* känna; känna på;
~ like *ha lust att
feeling ['fi:liŋ] *n* känsla *c*;
känsel *c*
feet [fi:t] *pl* fötter *pl*
fell [fel] *v* (p fall)
fellow ['felou] *n* karl *c*

felt¹ [felt] *n* filt *c*

felt² [felt] *v* (p, pp feel)

female ['fi:meil] *adj* hon- *pref*

feminine ['feminin] *adj*
feminin

fence [fens] *n* stängsel *nt*;
staket *nt*; *v* fäkta

ferment [fə:'ment] *v* jäsa

ferry-boat ['feribout] *n* färja
c

fertile ['fə:tail] *adj* fruktbar

festival ['festival] *n* festival *c*

festive ['festiv] *adj* festlig

fetch [fetʃ] *v* hämta

feudal ['fju:dəl] *adj* feodal

fever ['fi:və] *n* feber *c*

feverish ['fi:vəriʃ] *adj* febrig

few [fju:] *adj* få

fiancé [fi'ɑ:sei] *n* fästman *c*

fiancée [fi'ɑ:sei] *n* fästmö *c*

fibre ['faibə] *n* fiber *c*

fiction ['fikʃən] *n*
skönlitteratur *c*, fiktion *c*

field [fi:ld] *n* fält *nt*, åker *c*; ~
glasses fältkikare *c*

fierce [fiəs] *adj* vild, häftig

fifteen [,fif'ti:n] *num* femton

fifteenth [,fif'ti:nθ] *num*
femtonde

fifth [fifθ] *num* femte

fifty ['fifti] *num* femtio

fig [fig] *n* fikon *c*

fight [fait] *n* slagsmål *nt*;
kamp *c*, strid *c*

***fight** [fait] *v* *strida, *slåss,
kämpa

figure ['figə] *n* figur *c*; siffra *c*

file [fail] *n* fil *c*; brevpärm *c*,
dossié *c*; rad *c*

fill [fil] *v* fylla; ~ **in** fylla i;

filling station bensinstation
c; ~ **out** *Am* fylla i; ~ **up**
tanka

filling ['filiŋ] *n* plomb *c*;
fyllning *c*

film [film] *n* film *c*; *v* filma

filter ['filtə] *n* filter *nt*

filthy ['filθi] *adj* lortig,
smutsig

final ['fainəl] *adj* slutlig

finally ['fainəli] *adv* slutligen

finance [fai'næns] *v*
finansiera

finances [fai'nænsiz] *pl*
finanser *pl*

financial [fai'nænʃəl] *adj*
finansiell

finch [fintʃ] *n* bofink *c*

***find** [faind] *v* hitta, *finna

fine [fain] *n* böter *pl*; *adj* fin;
skön; härlig, utmärkt; ~ **arts**
de sköna konsterna

finger ['fiŋgə] *n* finger *nt*;
little ~ lillfinger *nt*

fingerprint ['fiŋgəprint] *n*
fingeravtryck *nt*

finish ['finiʃ] *n* avsluta, sluta;
fullborda; *n* slut *nt*; mållinje
c; **finished** färdig

Finland ['finlənd] Finland

Finn [fin] *n* finländare *c*

Finnish ['finiʃ] *adj* finsk

fire [faiə] *n* eld *c*; eldsvåda *c*;
v *skjuta; avskeda

fire alarm ['faiərə,lɑ:m] *n*
brandalarm *c*

fire brigade ['faiəbri,geid] *n*
brandkår *c*

fire escape ['faiəri,skeip] *n*
brandstege *c*

fire extinguisher
['faiərik‚stiŋgwiʃə] *n*
brandsläckare *c*

firefighter ['faiə‚faitə] *n*
brandman c

fireplace ['faiəpleis] *n* öppen
spis

fireproof ['faiəpruːf] *adj*
brandsäker; eldfast

firewall ['faiə‚wɔːl] *n*
brandvägg *c*

firm [fəːm] *adj* fast; solid; *n*
firma *c*

first [fəːst] *num* första; **at ~**
först; i början; **~ name**
förnamn *nt*

first aid [‚fəːst'eid] *n* första
hjälpen; **~ kit** förbandslåda
c; **~ post** hjälpstation *c*

first-class [‚fəːst'klɑːs] *adj*
förstklassig

first-rate [‚fəːst'reit] *adj*
förstklassig

fir tree ['fəːtriː] *n* gran *c*,
barrträd *nt*

fish¹ [fiʃ] *n* (pl ~, ~es) fisk *c*; **~
shop** fiskaffär *c*

fish² [fiʃ] *v* fiska; meta;
fishing gear fiskredskap *nt*;
fishing hook metkrok *c*;
fishing industry
fiskerinäring *c*; **fishing
licence** fiskekort *nt*; **fishing
line** metrev *c*; **fishing net**
fisknät *nt*; **fishing rod**
metspö *nt*; **fishing tackle**
fiskedon *nt*

fishbone ['fiʃboun] *n* fiskben
nt

fisherman ['fiʃəmən] *n* (pl

-men) fiskare *c*

fist [fist] *n* knytnäve *c*

fit [fit] *adj* lämplig; *n* anfall *nt*;
v passa; **fitting room**
provrum *nt*

five [faiv] *num* fem

fix [fiks] *v* laga

fixed [fikst] *adj* fästad,
orörlig

fizz [fiz] *n* brus *nt*

flag [flæg] *n* flagga *c*

flame [fleim] *n* låga *c*

flamingo [flə'miŋgou] *n* (pl
~s, ~es) flamingo *c*

flannel ['flænəl] *n* flanell *c*

flash [flæʃ] *n* blixt *c*, glimt *c*

flash bulb ['flæʃbʌlb] *n*
blixtlampa *c*

flashlight ['flæʃlait] *n*
ficklampa *c*

flask [flɑːsk] *n* plunta *c*;
thermos ~ termos *c*

flat [flæt] *adj* flat, platt; *n*
lägenhet *c*; **~ tyre**
punktering *c*

flavour ['fleivə] *n* smak *c*; *v*
smaksätta, krydda

flee [fliː] *v* fly

fleet [fliːt] *n* flotta *c*

flesh [fleʃ] *n* kött *nt*

flew [fluː] *v* (p fly)

flex [fleks] *n* sladd *c*

flexible ['fleksibəl] *adj* böjlig;
smidig

flight [flait] *n* flygresa *c*;
charter ~ charterflyg *nt*

flint [flint] *n* flintsten *c*

float [flout] *v* *flyta; *n* flöte
nt, flottör *c*

flock [flɔk] *n* hjord *c*

flood [flʌd] *n* översvämning
c; flod *c*

floor [flɔ:] *n* golv *nt*; våning *c*

florist ['flɔrist] *n*
blomsterhandlare *c*

flour [flauə] *n* mjöl *nt*,
vetemjöl *nt*

flow [flou] *v* *flyta, strömma

flower [flauə] *n* blomma *c*

flowerbed ['flauəbed] *n*
rabatt *c*

flower shop ['flauəʃɔp] *n*
blomsterhandel *c*

flown [floun] *v* (pp fly)

flu [flu:] *n* influensa *c*

fluent ['flu:ənt] *adj* flytande

fluid ['flu:id] *adj* flytande; *n*
vätska *c*

flute [flu:t] *n* flöjt *c*

fly [flai] *n* fluga *c*; gylf *c*

***fly** [flai] *v* *flyga

foam [foum] *n* skum *nt*; *v*
skumma

foam rubber ['foum,rʌbə] *n*
skumgummi *nt*

focus ['foukəs] *n* brännpunkt
c

fog [fɔg] *n* dimma *c*

foggy ['fɔgi] *adj* dimmig

foglamp ['fɔglæmp] *n*
dimlykta *c*

fold [fould] *v* *vika; *n* veck *nt*

folk [fouk] *n* folk *nt*; ~ **song**
folkvisa *c*

folk dance ['foukdɑ:ns] *n*
folkdans *c*

folklore ['fouklɔ:] *n* folklore
c

follow ['fɔlou] *v* följa efter;
following *adj* nästa,

följande

***be fond of** [bi: fɔnd ɔv]
tycka om

food [fu:d] *n* mat *c*; föda *c*; ~
poisoning matförgiftning *c*

foodstuffs ['fu:dstʌfs] *pl*
matvaror *pl*

fool [fu:l] *n* dumbom *c*, dåre
c; *v* skoja, lura

foolish ['fu:liʃ] *adj* löjlig,
dåraktig; dum

foot [fut] *n* (pl feet) fot *c*; ~
powder fotpuder *nt*; **on** ~
till fots

football ['futbɔ:l] *n* fotboll *c*;
~ **match** fotbollsmatch *c*

foot brake ['futbreik] *n*
fotbroms *c*

footpath ['futpɑ:θ] *n*
gångstig *c*

footwear ['futweə] *n* skodon
nt

for [fɔ:, fə] *prep* till; i, av, på
grund av, för; *conj* för

forbid [fə'bid] *v* *förbjuda

force [fɔ:s] *v* tvinga, forcera;
n makt *c*, kraft *c*; våld *nt*; **by**
~ med tvång; **driving** ~
drivkraft *c*

forecast ['fɔ:kɑ:st] *n*
förutsägelse *c*; *v* *förutsäga

foreground ['fɔ:graund] *n*
förgrund *c*

forehead ['fɔred] *n* panna *c*

foreign ['fɔrin] *adj* utländsk;
främmande

foreigner ['fɔrinə] *n*
utlänning *c*

foreman ['fɔ:mən] *n* (pl
-men) förman *c*

foremost ['fɔ:moust] *adj* förnämst

forest ['fɔrist] *n* skog *c*

forester ['fɔristə] *n* skogsvaktare *c*

forever, for ever [fə'revə] *adv* för alltid

forge [fɔ:dʒ] *v* förfalska

*forget [fə'get] *v* glömma

forgetful [fə'getfəl] *adj* glömsk

*forgive [fə'giv] *v* *förlåta

fork [fɔ:k] *n* gaffel *c*; vägskäl *nt*; *v* förgrenas, dela sig

form [fɔ:m] *n* form *c*; formulär *nt*; klass *c*; *v* forma

formal ['fɔ:məl] *adj* formell

formality [fɔ:'mæləti] *n* formalitet *c*

former ['fɔ:mə] *adj* förutvarande; före detta; formerly förr, förut

formula ['fɔ:mjulə] *n* (pl ~e, ~s) formel *c*

fortnight ['fɔ:tnait] *n* fjorton dagar

fortress ['fɔ:tris] *n* fästning *c*

fortunate ['fɔ:tʃənət] *adj* lycklig

fortunately *adv* lyckligtvis

fortune ['fɔ:tʃu:n] *n* förmögenhet *c*; öde *nt*, lycka *c*

forty ['fɔ:ti] *num* fyrtio

forward ['fɔ:wəd] *adv* fram, framåt; *v* eftersända

foster parents ['fɔstə,peərənts] *pl* fosterföräldrar *pl*

fought [fɔ:t] *v* (p, pp fight)

foul [faul] *adj* osnygg; gemen

found¹ [faund] *v* (p, pp find)

found² [faund] *v* grunda, stifta

foundation [faun'deiʃən] *n* stiftelse *c*; ~ cream underlagskräm *c*

fountain ['fauntin] *n* fontän *c*; källa *c*

fountain pen ['fauntinpen] *n* reservoarpenna *c*

four [fɔ:] *num* fyra

fourteen [,fɔ:'ti:n] *num* fjorton

fourteenth [,fɔ:'ti:nθ] *num* fjortonde

fourth [fɔ:θ] *num* fjärde

fowl [faul] *n* (pl ~s, ~) fjäderfä *nt*

fox [fɔks] *n* räv *c*

foyer ['fɔiei] *n* foajé *c*

fraction ['frækʃən] *n* bråkdel *c*

fracture ['fræktʃə] *v* *bryta; *n* brott *nt*

fragile ['frædʒail] *adj* skör; bräcklig

fragment ['frægmənt] *n* brottstycke *nt*

frame [freim] *n* ram *c*; montering *c*

France [frɑ:ns] Frankrike

franchise ['fræntʃaiz] *n* koncession *c*, rösträtt *c*

fraternity [frə'tə:nəti] *n* broderlighet *c*

fraud [frɔ:d] *n* bedrägeri *nt*

fray [frei] *v* fransa sig

free [fri:] *adj* fri; gratis; ~ of charge kostnadsfri; ~ ticket fribiljett *c*

freedom ['fri:dəm] *n* frihet *c*

*freeze [fri:z] *v* **frysa

freezer ['fri:zə] *n* frys *c*

freezing ['fri:ziŋ] *adj* iskall

freezing point ['fri:ziŋpɔint]
n fryspunkt *c*

freight [freit] *n* frakt *c*, last *c*

freight train ['freittrein]
nAm godståg *nt*

French [frentʃ] *adj* fransk;
the ~ *pl* fransmännen *pl*;
~ fries *pl* pommes frites *pl*

Frenchman ['frentʃmən] *n*
(pl -men) fransman *c*

frequency ['fri:kwənsi] *n*
frekvens *c*; förekomst *c*

frequent ['fri:kwənt] *adj* ofta
förekommande, vanlig;
frequently ofta

fresh [freʃ] *adj* färsk; ny;
uppfriskande; **~ water**
sötvatten *nt*

friction ['frikʃən] *n* friktion *c*

Friday ['fraidi] fredag *c*

fridge [fridʒ] *n* kylskåp *nt*

friend [frend] *n* vän *c*;
väninna *c*

friendly ['frendli] *adj* vänlig,
vänskaplig

friendship ['frendʃip] *n*
vänskap *c*

fright [frait] *n* fruktan *c*,
skräck *c*

frighten ['fraitən] *v* skrämma

frightened ['fraitənd] *adj*
skrämd; ***be ~** *bli
förskräckt

frightful ['fraitfəl] *adj*
förskräcklig, förfärlig

fringe [frindʒ] *n* frans *c*

frog [frɔg] *n* groda *c*

from [frɔm] *prep* från; av;
från och med

front [frʌnt] *n* framsida *c*;
in ~ of framför

frontier ['frʌntiə] *n* gräns *c*

frost [frɔst] *n* frost *c*

frozen ['frouzən] *adj* frusen;
~ food djupfryst mat

fructose ['frʌktouz] *n*
fruktos *c*; **fructose-free** *adj*
fruktosfri

fruit [fru:t] *n* frukt *c*

fry [frai] *v* steka

frying pan ['fraiiŋpæn] *n*
stekpanna *c*

fuck [fʌk] *v* V knulla

fuel ['fju:əl] *n* bränsle *nt*;
bensin *c*; **~ pump** *Am*
bensinpump *c*

full [ful] *adj* full; **~ board**
helpension *c*; **~ stop** punkt
c; **~ up** fullsatt

fun [fʌn] *n* nöje *nt*; skoj *nt*

function ['fʌŋkʃən] *n*
funktion *c*

fund [fʌnd] *n* fond *c*

fundamental
[ˌfʌndə'mentəl] *adj*
grundläggande

funeral ['fju:nərəl] *n*
begravning *c*

funnel ['fʌnəl] *n* tratt *c*

funny ['fʌni] *adj* rolig, lustig;
konstig

fur [fə:] *n* päls *c*

furious ['fjuəriəs] *adj*
ursinnig, rasande

furnace ['fə:nis] *n* ugn *c*

furnish ['fə:niʃ] *v* leverera,

*förse; möblera; ~ with
*förse med
furniture ['fɜ:nitʃə] n möbler
pl
furrier ['fʌriə] n körsnär c
further ['fɜ:ðə] adj
avlägsnare; ytterligare
furthermore ['fɜ:ðəmɔ:] adv

dessutom
furthest ['fɜ:ðist] adj längst
bort
fuse [fju:z] n propp c;
stubintråd c
fuss [fʌs] n bråk nt, väsen nt
future ['fju:tʃə] n framtid c;
adj framtida

G

gable ['geibəl] n gavel c
gadget ['gædʒit] n grej c
gain [gein] v *vinna; n
förvärv nt, förtjänst c
gale [geil] n storm c
gall [gɔ:l] n galla c; ~ **bladder**
gallblåsa c
gallery ['gæləri] n galleri nt;
konstgalleri nt
gallon ['gælən] n (Brit 4,55 l;
Am 3,79 l) gallon c
gallop ['gæləp] n galopp c
gallows ['gæləuz] pl galge c
gallstone ['gɔ:lstoun] n
gallsten c
game [geim] n spel nt;
villebråd nt; ~ **reserve**
djurreservat c
gang [gæŋ] n gäng nt; skift nt
gangway ['gæŋwei] n
landgång c
gap [gæp] n öppning c
garage ['gærɑ:ʒ] n garage nt;
v ställa in i garaget
garbage ['gɑ:bidʒ] n avfall
nt, sopor pl
garden ['gɑ:dən] n trädgård
c; **public** ~ offentlig park;

zoological gardens
djurpark c
gardener ['gɑ:dənə] n
trädgårdsmästare c
gargle ['gɑ:gəl] v gurgla
garlic ['gɑ:lik] n vitlök c
gas [gæs] n gas c; nAm
bensin c; ~ **cooker** gaskök
nt; ~ **pump** Am bensinpump
c; ~ **station** bensinstation c;
~ **stove** gasspis c
gasoline ['gæsəli:n] nAm
bensin c
gastric ['gæstrik] adj mag-; ~
ulcer magsår nt
gasworks ['gæswə:ks] n
gasverk nt
gate [geit] n port c; grind c
gather ['gæðə] v samla;
samlas; skörda
gauge [geidʒ] n mätare c
gave [geiv] v (p give)
gay [gei] adj munter; brokig
gaze [geiz] v stirra
gazetteer [ˌgæzə'tiə] n
geografiskt lexikon
gear [giə] n växel c;
utrustning c; **change** ~

växla; ~ lever växelspak c

gearbox ['giəbɔks] n växellåda c

geese [gi:s] pl gäss pl

gem [dʒem] n juvel c, ädelsten c; klenod c

gender ['dʒendə] n genus nt

general ['dʒenərəl] adj allmän; n general c; ~ practitioner allmänpraktiserande läkare; in ~ i allmänhet

generate ['dʒenəreit] v alstra

generation [,dʒenə'reiʃən] n generation c

generator ['dʒenəreitə] n generator c

generosity [,dʒenə'rɔsəti] n givmildhet c

generous ['dʒenərəs] adj generös, givmild

genital ['dʒenitəl] adj köns-

genius ['dʒi:niəs] n geni nt

gentle ['dʒentəl] adj mild; blid; varsam

gentleman ['dʒentəlmən] n (pl -men) herre c

genuine ['dʒenjuin] adj äkta

geography [dʒi'ɔgrəfi] n geografi c

geology [dʒi'ɔlədʒi] n geologi c

geometry [dʒi'ɔmətri] n geometri c

germ [dʒə:m] n bacill c; grodd c

German ['dʒə:mən] adj tysk; n tysk c

Germany ['dʒə:məni] Tyskland

gesticulate [dʒi'stikjuleit] v gestikulera

***get** [get] v *få; hämta; *bli; ~ **back** *gå tillbaka, *komma tillbaka; ~ **off** *stiga av; ~ **on** *stiga på; *göra framsteg; ~ **up** resa sig, *stiga upp

ghost [goust] n spöke nt; ande c

giant ['dʒaiənt] n jätte c

giddiness ['gidinəs] n yrsel c

giddy ['gidi] adj yr

gift [gift] n gåva c; talang c

gift card ['gift‿ka:d] n presentkort nt

gifted ['giftid] adj begåvad

gigantic [dʒai'gæntik] adj väldig

giggle ['gigəl] v fnittra

gill [gil] n gäl c

gilt [gilt] adj förgylld

ginger ['dʒindʒə] n ingefära c

gipsy ['dʒipsi] n zigenare c

girdle ['gə:dəl] n gördel c

girl [gə:l] n flicka c;

girlfriend ['gə:lfrend] n flickvän c

***give** [giv] v *ge; överräcka; ~ **away** förråda; ~ **in** *ge efter; ~ **up** *ge upp

glacier ['glæsiə] n glaciär c

glad [glæd] adj glad; **gladly** gärna, med glädje

gladness ['glædnəs] n glädje c

glamorous ['glæmərəs] adj charmerande, förtrollande

glance [glɑ:ns] n blick c; v kasta en blick

gland [glænd] n körtel c

glare [gleə] n skarpt sken; sken nt

glaring ['gleəriŋ] adj bländande; påfallande; gräll

glass [glɑːs] n glas nt; glas-; **glasses** glasögon pl; **magnifying ~** förstoringsglas nt

glaze [gleiz] v glasa; glasera

glide [glaid] v *glida

glider ['glaidə] n segelflygplan nt

glimpse [glimps] n skymt c; glimt c; v skymta

global ['gloubəl] adj världsomfattande; **global positioning system** n GPS c; **global warming** n global uppvärmning c

globalization [ˌgloubəlai'zeiʃən] n globalisering c

globalize ['gloubə,laiz] v globalisera

globe [gloub] n jordklot nt, glob c

gloom [gluːm] n dunkelhet c

gloomy ['gluːmi] adj dyster

glorious ['glɔːriəs] adj praktfull

glory ['glɔːri] n berömmelse c, ära c, lovord nt

gloss [glɔs] n glans c

glossy ['glɔsi] adj blank

glove [glʌv] n handske c

glow [glou] v glöda; n glöd c

glue [gluː] n lim nt

gluten ['gluːtən] n gluten nt; **gluten-free** adj glutenfri

***go** [gou] v *gå; *bli; **~ ahead**

~fortsätta; ~ away *fara; **~ back** *gå tillbaka; **~ home** *gå hem; **~ in** *gå in; **~ on** *fortsätta; **~ out** *gå ut; **~ through** *genomgå

goal [goul] n mål nt

goalkeeper ['goul,kiːpə] n målvakt c

goat [gout] n get c

god [gɔd] n gud c

goddess ['gɔdis] n gudinna c

godfather ['gɔd,fɑːðə] n gudfar c

godmother ['gɔd,mʌðə] n gudmor c

goggles ['gɔgəlz] pl skyddsglasögon pl

gold [gould] n guld nt; **~ leaf** bladguld c

golden ['gouldən] adj gyllene

goldsmith ['gouldsmiθ] n guldsmed c

golf [gɔlf] n golf c

golfclub ['gɔlfklʌb] n golfklubb c

golf course ['gɔlfkɔːs] n golfbana c

gondola ['gɔndələ] n gondol c

gone [gɔn] adv (pp go) borta

good [gud] adj bra, god; snäll

goodbye! [ˌgud'bai] adjö!

good-humoured [ˌgud'hjuːməd] adj gladlynt

good-looking [ˌgud'lukiŋ] adj snygg

good-natured [ˌgud'neitʃəd] adj godmodig

goods [gudz] pl varor pl; **~ train** godståg nt

good-tempered
[ˌgud'tempəd] adj godlynt

goodwill [ˌgud'wil] n välvilja c

goose [guːs] n (pl geese) gås c

gooseberry ['guzbəri] n krusbär nt

goose flesh ['guːsfleʃ] n gåshud c

gorge [gɔːdʒ] n bergsklyfta c

gorgeous ['gɔːdʒəs] adj praktfull

gospel ['gɔspəl] n evangelium c

gossip ['gɔsip] n skvaller nt; v skvallra

got [gɔt] v (p, pp get)

gourmet ['guəmei] n gastronom c

gout [gaut] n gikt c

govern ['gʌvən] v regera

governess ['gʌvənis] n guvernant c

government ['gʌvənmənt] n regering c, styrelse c

governor ['gʌvənə] n guvernör c

gown [gaun] n klänning c

GPS ['dʒiːpiː'es] n GPS c

grace [greis] n grace c; nåd c

graceful ['greisfəl] adj graciös; intagande; behaglig

grade [greid] n grad c; v klassificera

gradient ['greidiənt] n stigning c

gradual ['grædʒuəl] adj gradvis

graduate ['grædʒueit] v *ta

examen

grain [grein] n korn nt, sädeskorn c

gram [græm] n gram nt

grammar ['græmə] n grammatik c

grammatical [grə'mætikəl] adj grammatisk

gramophone ['græməfoun] n grammofon c

grand [grænd] adj storslagen

grandchild ['græn,tʃaild] n barnbarn c

granddaughter ['græn,dɔːtə] n sondotter c, dotterdotter c

grandfather ['græn,faːðə] n farfar c, morfar c

grandmother ['græn,mʌðə] n farmor c; mormor c

grandparents ['græn,peərənts] pl morföräldrar pl, farföräldrar pl

grandson ['grænsʌn] n sonson c, dotterson c

granite ['grænit] n granit c

grant [graːnt] v bevilja, *medge; n bidrag nt, stipendium nt

grapefruit ['greipfruːt] n grapefrukt c

grapes [greips] pl vindruvor pl

graph [græf] n diagram nt

graphic ['græfik] adj grafisk

grasp [graːsp] v *gripa; n grepp nt

grass [graːs] n gräs nt

grasshopper ['graːs,hɔpə] n

gräshoppa c
grate [greit] n spisgaller c; v
 *riva
grateful ['greitfəl] adj
 tacksam
grater ['greitə] n rivjärn nt
gratis [grætis] adj gratis
gratitude ['grætitju:d] n
 tacksamhet c
gratuity [grə'tju:əti] n
 gratifikation c
grave [greiv] n grav c; adj
 allvarlig
gravel ['grævəl] n grus nt
gravestone ['greivstoun] n
 gravsten c
graveyard ['greivja:d] n
 begravningsplats c
gravity ['grævəti] n
 tyngdkraft c; allvar nt
gravy ['greivi] n sky c
graze [greiz] v beta; n
 skrubbsår nt
grease [gri:s] n fett nt; v
 *smörja
greasy ['gri:si] adj flottig,
 oljig
great [greit] adj stor; **Great
 Britain** Storbritannien
Greece [gri:s] Grekland
greed [gri:d] n habegär nt
greedy ['gri:di] adj hagalen;
 glupsk
Greek [gri:k] adj grekisk; n
 grek c
green [gri:n] adj grön; ~ **card**
 grönt kort
greengrocer ['gri:n,grousə]
 n grönsakshandlare c
greenhouse ['gri:nhaus] n

drivhus nt, växthus nt
greens [gri:nz] pl grönsaker
 pl
greet [gri:t] v hälsa
greeting ['gri:tiŋ] n hälsning
 c
grey [grei] adj grå
greyhound ['greihaund] n
 vinthund c
grief [gri:f] n sorg c,
 bedrövelse c
grieve [gri:v] v sörja
grill [gril] n grill c; v grilla
grillroom ['grilru:m] n
 grillrestaurang c
grim [grim] adj barsk
grin [grin] v flina; n flin nt
 *grind** [graind] v mala;
 finmala
grip [grip] v *gripa; n grepp
 nt; nAm kappsäck c
grit [grit] n grus nt
groan [groun] v stöna
grocer ['grousə] n
 specerihandlare c; **grocer's**;
 grocery speceriaffär c
groceries ['grousəriz] pl
 specerier pl
groin [grɔin] n ljumske c
groom [gru:m] n brudgum c
groove [gru:v] n skåra c, fåra
 c
gross[1] [grous] n (pl ~) gross
 nt
gross[2] [grous] adj grov;
 brutto-
grotto ['grɔtou] n (pl ~es, ~s)
 grotta c
ground[1] [graund] n grund c,
 mark c; ~ **floor** bottenvåning

c; **grounds** mark c

ground² [graund] v (p, pp grind)

group [gru:p] n grupp c

grouse [graus] n (pl ∼) vildhönsfågel c, ripa c

grove [grouv] n skogsdunge c

*__grow__ [grou] v växa; odla; *bli

growl [graul] v morra

grown-up [grounʌp] adj vuxen; n vuxen c

growth [grouθ] n växt c; svulst c

grudge [grʌdʒ] v missunna

grumble [ˈgrʌmbəl] v knorra

guarantee [ˌgærənˈti:] n garanti c; säkerhet c; v garantera

guard [gɑːd] n vakt c; v bevaka

guardian [ˈgɑːdiən] n förmyndare c

guess [ges] v gissa; förmoda; n förmodan c

guest [gest] n gäst c

guesthouse [ˈgesthaus] n pensionat nt

guest room [ˈgestruːm] n gästrum nt

guide [gaid] n reseledare c; guide c; v vägleda; guida

guide dog [ˈgaiddɔg] n

ledarhund c

guidebook [ˈgaidbuk] n resehandbok c

guideline [ˈgaidlain] n riktlinje c

guilt [gilt] n skuld c

guilty [ˈgilti] adj skyldig

guinea pig [ˈginipig] n marsvin nt

guitar [giˈtɑː] n gitarr c

gulf [gʌlf] n bukt c

gull [gʌl] n mås c

gum [gʌm] n tandkött nt; gummi nt; klister nt

gun [gʌn] n gevär nt; kanon c

gunpowder [ˈgʌn,paudə] n krut nt

gust [gʌst] n kastby c

gusty [ˈgʌsti] adj stormig

gut [gʌt] n tarm c; **guts** mod nt

gutter [ˈgʌtə] n rännsten c

guy [gai] n karl c

gymnasium [dʒimˈneiziəm] n (pl ∼s, -sia) gymnastiksal c

gymnast [ˈdʒimnæst] n gymnast c

gymnastics [dʒimˈnæstiks] pl gymnastik c

gynaecologist [ˌgainəˈkɔlədʒist] n gynekolog c

H

habit ['hæbit] *n* vana *c*
habitable ['hæbitəbəl] *adj* beboelig
habitual [hə'bitʃuəl] *adj* invand
had [hæd] *v* (p, pp have)
haddock ['hædək] *n* (pl ~) kolja *c*
haemorrhage ['heməridʒ] *n* blödning *c*
haemorrhoids ['hemərɔidz] *pl* hemorrojder *pl*
hail [heil] *n* hagel *nt*
hair [heə] *n* hår *nt*; ~ cream hårkräm *c*; ~ gel hårgelé *nt*; ~ piece löshår *nt*; ~ rollers hårrullar *pl*
hairbrush ['heəbrʌʃ] *n* hårborste *c*
haircut ['heəkʌt] *n* hårklippning *c*
hairdo ['heəduː] *n* frisyr *c*
hairdresser ['heə,dresə] *n* damfrisör *c*
hairdrier, hairdryer ['heə,draiə] *n* hårtork *c*
hairgrip ['heəgrip] *n* hårspänne *c*
hair net ['heənet] *n* hårnät *c*
hair oil ['heərɔil] *n* hårolja *c*
hairpin ['heəpin] *n* hårnål *c*
hair spray ['heəsprei] *n* hårspray *c*
hairy ['heəri] *adj* hårig
half[1] [hɑːf] *adj* halv; *adv* till hälften

half[2] [hɑːf] *n* (pl halves) hälft *c*
half time [,hɑːf'taim] *n* halvlek *c*
halfway [,hɑːf'wei] *adv* halvvägs
halibut ['hælibət] *n* (pl ~) helgeflundra *c*
hall [hɔːl] *n* hall *c*; sal *c*
halt [hɔːlt] *v* stanna
halve [hɑːv] *v* halvera
ham [hæm] *n* skinka *c*
hamlet ['hæmlət] *n* liten by
hammer ['hæmə] *n* hammare *c*
hammock ['hæmək] *n* hängmatta *c*
hamper ['hæmpə] *n* matkorg *c*
hand [hænd] *n* hand *c*; *v* överlämna; ~ cream handkräm *c*
handbag ['hændbæg] *n* handväska *c*
handbook ['hændbuk] *n* handbok *c*
handbrake ['hændbreik] *n* handbroms *c*
handcuffs ['hændkʌfs] *pl* handbojor *pl*
handful ['hændful] *n* handfull *c*
handheld ['hand,held] *adj* handhållen
handicap ['hændikæp] *n* handikapp *nt*

handicapped ['hændikæpt]
adj handikappad

handicraft ['hændikrɑːft] *n*
hantverk *nt;* konsthantverk
nt

handkerchief ['hæŋkətʃif] *n*
näsduk *c*

handle ['hændəl] *n* skaft *nt,*
handtag *nt; v* hantera;
behandla

hand-made [,hænd'meid] *adj*
handgjord

handshake ['hændʃeik] *n*
handslag *c*

handsome ['hænsəm] *adj*
snygg

handwork ['hændwɔːk] *n*
hantverk *nt*

handwriting ['hænd,raitiŋ] *n*
handstil *c*

***hang** [hæŋ] *v* hänga

hanger ['hæŋə] *n*
klädhängare *c*

hangover ['hæŋ,ouvə] *n*
baksmälla *c*

happen ['hæpən] *v* hända,
ske

happening ['hæpəniŋ] *n*
händelse *c*

happiness ['hæpinəs] *n*
lycka *c*

happy ['hæpi] *adj* belåten,
lycklig

harbour ['hɑːbə] *n* hamn *c*

hard [hɑːd] *adj* hård; **hardly**
knappast

hardware ['hɑːdwɛə] *n*
järnvaror *pl;* ~ **store**
järnhandel *c*

hare [hɛə] *n* hare *c*

harm [hɑːm] *n* skada *c;* ont
nt; v skada, *göra illa

harmful ['hɑːmfəl] *adj*
skadlig

harmless ['hɑːmləs] *adj*
oförarglig

harmony ['hɑːməni] *n*
harmoni *c*

harp [hɑːp] *n* harpa *c*

harpsichord ['hɑːpsikɔːd] *n*
cembalo *c*

harsh [hɑːʃ] *adj* sträv; sträng;
grym

harvest ['hɑːvist] *n* skörd *c*

has [hæz] *v* (pr have)

haste [heist] *n* brådska *c,* hast
c

hasten ['heisən] *v* skynda sig

hasty ['heisti] *adj* hastig

hat [hæt] *n* hatt *c;* ~ **rack**
hatthylla *c*

hatch [hætʃ] *n* lucka *c*

hate [heit] *v* hata; *n* hat *nt*

hatred ['heitrid] *n* hat *nt*

haughty ['hɔːti] *adj*
högdragen

haul [hɔːl] *v* släpa

***have** [hæv] *v* *ha; *få; ~ **to**
*måste

hawk [hɔːk] *n* hök *c;* falk *c*

hay [hei] *n* hö *nt;* ~ **fever**
hösnuva *c*

hazard ['hæzəd] *n* risk *c*

haze [heiz] *n* dis *nt*

hazelnut ['heizəlnʌt] *n*
hasselnöt *c*

hazy ['heizi] *adj* disig

he [hiː] *pron* han

head [hed] *n* huvud *nt; v* leda;
~ **of state** statsöverhuvud *nt;*

~ **teacher** överlärare c

headache ['hedeik] n
huvudvärk c

heading ['hediŋ] n överskrift
c

headlamp ['hedlæmp] n
strålkastare c

headlight ['hedlait] n
strålkastare c

headline ['hedlain] n rubrik c

headmaster [,hed'mɑːstə] n
rektor c

headquarters
[,hed'kwɔːtəz] pl
högkvarter n

head-strong ['hedstrɔŋ] adj
envis

head waiter [,hed'weitə] n
hovmästare c

heal [hiːl] v läka

health [helθ] n hälsa c; ~
centre hälsovårdscentral c;
~ **certificate** friskintyg nt

healthy ['helθi] adj frisk

heap [hiːp] n hög c

*****hear** [hiə] v höra

hearing ['hiəriŋ] n hörsel c

heart [hɑːt] n hjärta nt;
innersta nt; **by ~** utantill; ~
attack hjärtattack c

heartburn ['hɑːtbəːn] n
halsbränna c

hearth [hɑːθ] n eldstad c

heartless ['hɑːtləs] adj
hjärtlös

hearty ['hɑːti] adj hjärtlig

heat [hiːt] n hetta c, värme c;
v uppvärma; **heating pad**
värmedyna c

heater ['hiːtə] n kamin c;

immersion ~ doppvärmare
c

heath [hiːθ] n hed c

heathen ['hiːðən] n hedning
c; adj hednisk

heather ['heðə] n ljung c

heating ['hiːtiŋ] n
uppvärmning c

heaven ['hevən] n himmel c

heavy ['hevi] adj tung

Hebrew ['hiːbruː] n
hebreiska c

hedge [hedʒ] n häck c

hedgehog ['hedʒhɔg] n
igelkott c

heel [hiːl] n häl c; klack c

height [hait] n höjd c;
höjdpunkt c

heir [eə] n arvinge c

heiress ['eərəs] n
arvtagerska c

helicopter ['helikɔptə] n
helikopter c

hell [hel] n helvete nt

hello! [he'lou] hej!; **say hello
to** säg hej till

helm [helm] n rorkult c

helmet ['helmit] n hjälm c

helmsman ['helmzmən] n
rorsman c

help [help] v hjälpa; n hjälp c

helper ['helpə] n hjälp c

helpful ['helpfəl] adj
hjälpsam

helping ['helpiŋ] n portion c

hem [hem] n fåll c

hemp [hemp] n hampa c

hen [hen] n höna c

her [həː] pron henne; adj
hennes

herb [hə:b] *n* ört *c*

herd [hə:d] *n* hjord *c*

here [hiə] *adv* här; ~ **you are** var så god

hereditary [hi'reditəri] *adj* ärftlig

hernia ['hə:niə] *n* brock *nt*

hero ['hiərou] *n* (pl ~es) hjälte *c*

heron ['herən] *n* häger *c*

herring ['heriŋ] *n* (pl ~, ~s) sill *c*

herself [hə:'self] *pron* sig; själv

hesitate ['heziteit] *v* tveka

heterosexual [,hetərə'sekʃuəl] *adj* heterosexuell

hiccup ['hikʌp] *n* hicka *c*

hide [haid] *n* djurhud *c*, skinn *nt*

***hide** [haid] *v* gömma; *dölja

hideous ['hidiəs] *adj* avskyvärd

hierarchy ['haiəra:ki] *n* hierarki *c*

high [hai] *adj* hög

highway ['haiwei] *n* landsväg *c*; *nAm* motorväg *c*

hijack ['haidʒæk] *v* kapa

hijacker ['haidʒækə] *n* kapare *c*

hike [haik] *v* vandra

hill [hil] *n* kulle *c*; backe *c*

hillside ['hilsaid] *n* sluttning *c*

hilltop ['hiltɔp] *n* backkrön *nt*

hilly ['hili] *adj* backig, kuperad

him [him] *pron* honom

himself [him'self] *pron* sig; själv

hinder ['hində] *v* hindra

hinge [hindʒ] *n* gångjärn *nt*

hint [hint] *n* vink *c*

hip [hip] *n* höft *c*

hip-hop ['hip,hɔp] *n* hip-hop *c*

hire [haiə] *v* hyra; **for** ~ till uthyrning

hire purchase[,haiə'pə:tʃəs] *n*, **installment plan** *nAm* avbetalningsköp *nt*

his [hiz] *adj* hans

historian [hi'stɔ:riən] *n* historiker *c*

historic [hi'stɔrik] *adj* historisk

historical [hi'stɔrikəl] *adj* historisk

history ['histəri] *n* historia *c*

hit [hit] *n* schlager *c*

***hit** [hit] *v* *slå; träffa

hitchhike ['hitʃhaik] *v* lifta

hitchhiker ['hitʃ,haikə] *n* liftare *c*

hoarse [hɔ:s] *adj* skrovlig, hes

hobby ['hɔbi] *n* hobby *c*

hobbyhorse ['hɔbihɔ:s] *n* käpphäst *c*

hockey ['hɔki] *n* hockey *c*

hoist [hɔist] *v* hissa

hold [hould] *n* lastrum *nt*

***hold** [hould] *v* *hålla fast, *hålla; *bibehålla; ~ **on** *hålla sig fast; ~ **up** stötta, *hålla uppe

hold-up ['houldʌp] *n* väpnat rån

hole [houl] *n* hål *nt*

holiday ['hɔlədi] *n* semester *c*; helgdag *c*; ~ **camp** ferieläger *nt*; ~ **resort** semesterort *c*; **on** ~ på semester

Holland ['hɔlənd] Holland

hollow ['hɔlou] *adj* ihålig

holy ['houli] *adj* helig

homage ['hɔmidʒ] *n* hyllning *c*

home [houm] *n* hem *nt*; hus *nt*, vårdhem *nt*; *adv* hemma, hem; **at** ~ hemma

home-made [,houm'meid] *adj* hemgjord

homesickness ['houm,siknəs] *n* hemlängtan *c*

homework ['houm,wə:k] *n* läxa *c*

homosexual [,houmə'sekʃuəl] *adj* homosexuell

honest ['ɔnist] *adj* ärlig; uppriktig

honesty ['ɔnisti] *n* ärlighet *c*

honey ['hʌni] *n* honung *c*

honeymoon ['hʌnimu:n] *n* smekmånad *c*, bröllopsresa *c*

honk [hʌŋk] *vAm* tuta

honour ['ɔnə] *n* heder *c*; *v* hedra, ära

honourable ['ɔnərəbəl] *adj* ärofull; rättskaffens

hood [hud] *n* kapuschong *c*; *nAm* motorhuv *c*

hoof [hu:f] *n* hov *c*

hook [huk] *n* krok *c*

hoot [hu:t] *v* tuta

hooter ['hu:tə] *n* signalhorn *nt*

hoover ['hu:və] *v* *dammsuga

hop¹ [hɔp] *v* hoppa; *n* hopp *nt*

hop² [hɔp] *n* humle *nt*

hope [houp] *n* hopp *nt*; *v* hoppas

hopeful ['houpfəl] *adj* hoppfull

hopeless ['houpləs] *adj* hopplös

horizon [hə'raizən] *n* horisont *c*

horizontal [,hɔri'zɔntəl] *adj* horisontal

horn [hɔ:n] *n* horn *nt*; blåsinstrument *nt*; signalhorn *nt*

horrible ['hɔribəl] *adj* förskräcklig; ryslig, avskyvärd, gräslig

horror ['hɔrə] *n* skräck *c*, fasa *c*

hors d'œuvre [ɔ:'də:vr] *n* förrätt *c*

horse [hɔ:s] *n* häst *c*

horseman ['hɔ:smən] *n* (pl -men) ryttare *c*

horsepower ['hɔ:s,pauə] *n* hästkraft *c*

horserace ['hɔ:sreis] *n* hästkapplöpning *c*

horseradish ['hɔ:s,rædiʃ] *n* pepparrot *c*

horseshoe ['hɔ:sʃu:] *n* hästsko *c*

horticulture ['hɔ:tikʌltʃə] *n* trädgårdsodling *c*

hosiery ['houʒəri] n
trikåvaror pl

hospitable ['həspitəbəl] adj
gästfri

hospital ['həspitəl] n sjukhus
nt, lasarett nt

hospitality [,həspi'tæləti] n
gästfrihet c

host [houst] n värd c

hostage ['həstidʒ] n gisslan c

hostel ['həstəl] n härbärge nt

hostess ['houstis] n värdinna
c

hostile ['həstail] adj fientlig

hot [hət] adj varm, het

hotel [hou'tel] n hotell nt

hotspot ['hət,spət] n
inneställe c

hot-tempered [,hət'tempəd]
adj hetlevrad

hour [auə] n timme c

hourly ['auəli] adj varje
timme

house [haus] n hus nt; bostad
c; ~ agent fastighetsmäklare
c; ~ block Am husblock nt;
public ~ restaurang c

houseboat ['hausbout] n
husbåt c

household ['haushould] n
hushåll nt

housekeeper ['haus,ki:pə] n
hushållerska c

housekeeping ['haus,ki:piŋ]
n hushållning c,
hushållssysslor pl

housemaid ['hausmeid] n
hembiträde nt

housewife ['hauswaif] n
hemmafru c

housework ['hauswə:k] n
hushållsarbete nt

how [hau] adv hur; så; ~
many hur många; ~ much
hur mycket

however [hau'evə] conj
likväl, emellertid

hug [hʌg] v omfamna; n kram
c

huge [hju:dʒ] adj kolossal,
jättestor, väldig

hum [hʌm] v nynna

human ['hju:mən] adj
mänsklig; ~ being människa
c

humanity [hju'mænəti] n
mänsklighet c

humble ['hʌmbəl] adj
ödmjuk

humid ['hju:mid] adj fuktig

humidity [hju'midəti] n
fuktighet c

humorous ['hju:mərəs] adj
skämtsam, humoristisk,
lustig

humour ['hju:mə] n humor c

hundred ['hʌndrəd] n hundra

Hungarian [hʌŋ'geəriən] adj
ungersk; n ungrare c

Hungary ['hʌŋgəri] Ungern

hunger ['hʌŋgə] n hunger c

hungry ['hʌŋgri] adj hungrig

hunt [hʌnt] v jaga; n jakt c

hunter ['hʌntə] n jägare c

hurricane ['hʌrikən] n orkan
c; ~ lamp stormlykta c

hurry ['hʌri] v skynda sig; n
brådska c; in a ~ fort

*hurt [hə:t] v värka, skada;
såra

hurtful ['hə:tfəl] adj skadlig

husband ['hʌzbənd] n äkta man, make c

hut [hʌt] n hydda c

hydrogen ['haidrədʒən] n väte n

hygiene ['haidʒi:n] n hygien c

hygienic [hai'dʒi:nik] adj hygienisk

hymn [him] n hymn c, psalm c

hyphen ['haifən] n bindestreck nt

hypocrisy [hi'pɔkrəsi] n hyckleri nt

hypocrite ['hipəkrit] n hycklare c

hypocritical [,hipə'kritikəl] adj hycklande, skenhelig

hysterical [hi'sterikəl] adj hysterisk

I

I [ai] pron jag

ice [ais] n is c

ice bag ['aisbæg] n isblåsa c

ice cream ['aiskri:m] n glass c

Iceland ['aislənd] Island

Icelander ['aisləndə] n islänning c

Icelandic [ais'lændik] adj isländsk

icon ['aikɔn] n ikon c

idea [ai'diə] n idé c; tanke c, infall nt; begrepp nt, föreställning c

ideal [ai'diəl] adj idealisk; n ideal nt

identical [ai'dentikəl] adj identisk

identification [ai,dentifi'keiʃən] n identifiering c; legitimation c

identify [ai'dentifai] v identifiera

identity [ai'dentəti] n identitet c; ~ card

identitetskort nt

idiom ['idiəm] n idiom nt

idiomatic [,idiə'mætik] adj idiomatisk

idiot ['idiət] n idiot c

idiotic [,idi'ɔtik] adj idiotisk

idle ['aidəl] adj overksam; lat; gagnlös, tom

idol ['aidəl] n avgud c; idol c

if [if] conj om; ifall

ignition [ig'niʃən] n tändning c; ~ coil tändspole c

ignorant ['ignərənt] adj okunnig

ignore [ig'nɔ:] v ignorera

ill [il] adj sjuk; dålig; elak

illegal [i'li:gəl] adj olaglig, illegal

illegible [i'ledʒəbəl] adj oläslig

illiterate [i'litərət] n analfabet c

illness ['ilnəs] n sjukdom c

illuminate [i'lu:mineit] v lysa upp

illumination [i,lu:mi'neiʃən]

285 **impossible**

n belysning *c*

illusion [i'lu:ʒən] *n* illusion *c*;
villfarelse *c*

illustrate ['iləstreit] *v*
illustrera

illustration [,ilə'streiʃən] *n*
illustration *c*

image ['imidʒ] *n* bild *c*

imaginary [i'mædʒinəri] *adj*
inbillad

imagination
[i,mædʒi'neiʃən] *n* fantasi *c*,
inbillning *c*

imagine [i'mædʒin] *v*
föreställa sig; inbilla sig;
tänka sig

imitate ['imiteit] *v* imitera,
efterlikna

imitation [,imi'teiʃən] *n*
imitation *c*

immediate [i'mi:djət] *adj*
omedelbar

immediately [i'mi:djətli] *adv*
genast, omedelbart

immense [i'mens] *adj*
enorm, oerhörd, oändlig

immigrant ['imigrənt] *n*
invandrare *c*

immigrate ['imigreit] *v*
immigrera

immigration [,imi'greiʃən] *n*
invandring *c*

immodest [i'mɔdist] *adj*
oblyg

immunity [i'mju:nəti] *n*
immunitet *c*

immunize ['imjunaiz] *v*
immunisera

impartial [im'pɑ:ʃəl] *adj*
opartisk

impassable [im'pɑ:səbəl]
adj oframkomlig

impatient [im'peiʃənt] *adj*
otålig

impede [im'pi:d] *v* hindra

impediment [im'pedimənt] *n*
hinder *nt*

imperfect [im'pə:fikt] *adj*
ofullkomlig

imperial [im'piəriəl] *adj*
kejserlig; imperial-

impersonal [im'pə:sənəl] *adj*
opersonlig

impertinence [im'pə:tinəns]
n näsvishet *c*

impertinent [im'pə:tinənt]
adj oförskämd, fräck, näsvis

implement¹ ['implimənt] *n*
redskap *nt*, verktyg *nt*

implement² ['impliment] *v*
utföra, *fullgöra

imply [im'plai] *v* antyda;
*innebära

impolite [,impə'lait] *adj*
ohövlig

import¹ [im'pɔ:t] *v* införa,
importera

import² ['impɔ:t] *n* import *c*,
införsel *c*, importvara *c*; ~
duty importtull *c*

importance [im'pɔ:təns] *n*
betydelse *c*

important [im'pɔ:tənt] *adj*
viktig, betydelsefull

importer [im'pɔ:tə] *n*
importör *c*

imposing [im'pouziŋ] *adj*
imponerande

impossible [im'pɔsəbəl] *adj*
omöjlig

impotence ['impətəns] n
impotens c

impotent ['impətənt] adj
impotent

impress [im'pres] v *göra
intryck på, imponera

impression [im'prefən] n
intryck nt

impressive [im'presiv] adj
imponerande

imprison [im'prizən] v
fängsla

imprisonment
[im'prizənmənt] n
fångenskap c

improbable [im'prɔbəbəl]
adj otrolig

improper [im'prɔpə] adj
opassande, felaktig

improve [im'pruːv] v
förbättra

improvement
[im'pruːvmənt] n
förbättring c

improvise ['imprəvaiz] v
improvisera

impudent ['impjudənt] adj
oförskämd

impulse ['impʌls] n impuls c;
stimulans c

impulsive [im'pʌlsiv] adj
impulsiv

in [in] prep i; om, på; adv in

inaccessible [i,næk'sesəbəl]
adj otillgänglig

inaccurate [i'nækjurət] adj
oriktig

inadequate [i'nædikwət] adj
otillräcklig

incapable [iŋ'keipəbəl] adj

oduglig

incense ['insens] n rökelse c

inch [intʃ] n (2,54 cm) tum c

incident ['insidənt] n
händelse c

incidental [,insi'dentəl] adj
tillfällig

incite [in'sait] v sporra

inclination [,iŋkli'neifən] n
benägenhet c

incline [iŋ'klain] n sluttning c

inclined [iŋ'klaind] adj
benägen; lutande; *be ~ to
*vara benägen att

include [iŋ'kluːd] v innefatta,
omfatta; **included**
inberäknad

inclusive [iŋ'kluːsiv] adj
inklusive

income ['iŋkəm] n inkomst c

income tax ['iŋkəmtæks] n
inkomstskatt c

incompetent [iŋ'kɔmpətənt]
adj inkompetent

incomplete [,iŋkəm'pliːt] adj
ofullständig

inconceivable
[,iŋkən'siːvəbəl] adj
ofattbar

inconspicuous
[,iŋkən'spikjuəs] adj
oansenlig, försynt

inconvenience
[,iŋkən'viːnjəns] n
olägenhet c, besvär nt

inconvenient
[,iŋkən'viːnjənt] adj
olämplig; besvärlig

incorrect [,iŋkə'rekt] adj
felaktig, oriktig

increase¹ [iŋ'kriːs] v öka;
*tillta

increase² ['iŋkriːs] n ökning
c

incredible [iŋ'kredəbəl] adj
otrolig

incurable [iŋ'kjuərəbəl] adj
obotlig

indecent [in'diːsənt] adj
opassande

indeed [in'diːd] adv
verkligen

indefinite [in'definit] adj
obestämd

indemnity [in'demnəti] n
skadeersättning c,
gottgörelse c

independence
[,indi'pendəns] n
självständighet c

independent [,indi'pendənt]
adj självständig; oberoende

index ['indeks] n register nt,
förteckning c; ~ finger
pekfinger nt

India ['indiə] Indien

Indian ['indiən] adj indisk;
indiansk; n indier c; indian c

indicate ['indikeit] v påpeka,
antyda, visa

indication [,indi'keiʃən] n
tecken nt, antydan c

indicator ['indikeitə] n
indikator c, blinker c

indifferent [in'difərənt] adj
likgiltig

indigestion [,indi'dʒestʃən]
n matsmältningsbesvär nt

indignation [,indig'neiʃən] n
harm c, upprördhet c

indirect [,indi'rekt] adj
indirekt

individual [,indi'vidʒuəl] adj
enskild, individuell; n
individ c, enskild person

Indonesia [,ində'niːziə]
Indonesien

Indonesian [,ində'niːziən]
adj indonesisk; n indones c

indoor ['indɔː] adj inomhus-

indoors [,in'dɔːz] adv
inomhus

indulge [in'dʌldʒ] v *ge efter

industrial [in'dʌstriəl] adj
industriell; ~ area
industriområde nt

industrious [in'dʌstriəs] adj
flitig

industry ['indəstri] n industri
c

inedible [i'nedibəl] adj
oätbar

inefficient [,ini'fiʃənt] adj
ineffektiv; oduglig

inevitable [i'nevitəbəl] adj
oundviklig

inexpensive [,inik'spensiv]
adj billig

inexperienced
[,inik'spiəriənst] adj
oerfaren

infant ['infənt] n spädbarn nt

infantry ['infəntri] n infanteri
nt

infect [in'fekt] v infektera,
smitta

infection [in'fekʃən] n
infektion c

infectious [in'fekʃəs] adj
smittsam

infer [in'fəː] *v* *innebära, *dra en slutsats

inferior [in'fiəriə] *adj* underlägsen, sämre; mindervärdig; nedre

infinite ['infinət] *adj* oändlig

infinitive [in'finitiv] *n* infinitiv *c*

inflammable [in'flæməbəl] *adj* eldfarlig

inflammation [,inflə'meiʃən] *n* inflammation *c*

inflatable [in'fleitəbəl] *adj* uppblåsbar

inflate [in'fleit] *v* blåsa upp

inflation [in'fleiʃən] *n* inflation *c*

inflict [in'flikt] *v* tillfoga

influence ['influəns] *n* påverkan *c*; *v* påverka

influential [,influ'enʃəl] *adj* inflytelserik

influenza [,influ'enzə] *n* influensa *c*

inform [in'fɔːm] *v* informera; meddela, underrätta

informal [in'fɔːməl] *adj* informell

information [,infə'meiʃən] *n* uppgift *c*; upplysning *c*, meddelande *nt*; ~ **bureau** upplysningsbyrå *c*

infra-red [,infrə'red] *adj* infraröd

infrequent [in'friːkwənt] *adj* sällsynt

ingredient [iŋ'griːdiənt] *n* ingrediens *c*

inhabit [in'hæbit] *v* bebo

inhabitable [in'hæbitəbəl] *adj* beboelig

inhabitant [in'hæbitənt] *n* invånare *c*

inhale [in'heil] *v* inandas

inherit [in'herit] *v* ärva

inheritance [in'heritəns] *n* arv *nt*

inhibit [in'hibit] *v* hämma

initial [i'niʃəl] *adj* ursprunglig, första; *n* initial *c*; *v* parafera

initiate [i'niʃieit] *v* påbörja

initiative [i'niʃətiv] *n* initiativ *nt*

inject [in'dʒekt] *v* inspruta

injection [in'dʒekʃən] *n* injektion *c*

injure ['indʒə] *v* skada, såra

injury ['indʒəri] *n* skada *c*, oförrätt *c*

injustice [in'dʒʌstis] *n* orättvisa *c*

ink [iŋk] *n* bläck *nt*

inlet ['inlet] *n* sund *nt*, inlopp *nt*

inn [in] *n* värdshus *nt*

inner ['inə] *adj* inre; ~ **tube** innerslang *c*

innocence ['inəsəns] *n* oskuld *c*

innocent ['inəsənt] *adj* oskyldig

inoculate [i'nɔkjuleit] *v* ympa

inoculation [i,nɔkju'leiʃən] *n* ympning *c*

inquire [iŋ'kwaiə] *v* *ta reda på, förhöra sig, förfråga

inquiry [iŋ'kwaiəri] *n* förfrågan *c*; undersökning *c*

~ **office** upplysningsbyrå c
inquisitive [iŋ'kwizətiv] adj
frågvis
insane [in'sein] adj
sinnessjuk
inscription [in'skripʃən] n
inskription c
insect ['insekt] n insekt c; ~
repellent insektsmedel nt
insecticide [in'sektisaid] n
insektsgift nt
insensitive [in'sensətiv] adj
känslolös
insert [in'sə:t] v infoga,
stoppa in
inside [,in'said] n insida c;
adj inre; adv inne; inuti; ~
prep innanför, in, i; ~ **out** in
och in
insight ['insait] n insikt c
insignificant
[,insig'nifikənt] adj
obetydlig; oansenlig,
intetsägande; oviktig
insist [in'sist] v insistera;
*vidhålla
insolence ['insələns] n
oförskämdhet c
insolent ['insələnt] adj
oförskämd, fräck
insomnia [in'sɔmniə] n
sömnlöshet c
inspect [in'spekt] v
inspektera, undersöka,
granska
inspection [in'spekʃən] n
inspektion c; kontroll c
inspector [in'spektə] n
inspektör c, inspektör c
inspire [in'spaiə] v inspirera

install [in'stɔ:l] v installera
installation [,instə'leiʃən] n
installation c
instalment [in'stɔ:lmənt] n
avbetalning c
instance ['instəns] n
exempel nt; fall nt; **for** ~ till
exempel
instant ['instənt] n ögonblick
nt
instant message
['instənt ,mesədʒ] n
direktmeddelande c
instantly ['instəntli] adv
ögonblickligen, omedelbart
instead of [in'sted ɔv] i
stället för
instinct ['instiŋkt] n instinkt
c
institute ['institju:t] n
institut nt; anstalt c; v stifta,
inrätta
institution [,insti'tju:ʃən] n
institution c, grundande nt
instruct [in'strʌkt] v
instruera
instruction [in'strʌkʃən] n
undervisning c
instructive [in'strʌktiv] adj
lärorik
instructor [in'strʌktə] n
lärare c, instruktör c
instrument ['instrumənt] n
instrument nt; **musical** ~
musikinstrument nt
insufficient [,insə'fiʃənt] adj
otillräcklig
insulate ['insjuleit] v isolera
insulation [,insju'leiʃən] n
isolering c

insulator ['insjuleitə] *n*
isolator *c*

insult[1] [in'sʌlt] *v* förolämpa

insult[2] ['insʌlt] *n*
förolämpning *c*

insurance [in'ʃuərəns] *n*
försäkring *c*; ~ **policy**
försäkringsbrev *nt*

insure [in'ʃuə] *v* försäkra

intact [in'tækt] *adj* intakt

integrate ['intəgreit] *v*
integrera

intellect ['intəlekt] *n*
förstånd *nt*, intellekt *nt*

intellectual [,intə'lektʃuəl]
adj intellektuell

intelligence [in'telidʒəns] *n*
intelligens *c*

intelligent [in'telidʒənt] *adj*
intelligent

intend [in'tend] *v* ämna

intense [in'tens] *adj* intensiv;
häftig

intention [in'tenʃən] *n* avsikt
c

intentional [in'tenʃənəl] *adj*
avsiktlig

intercourse ['intəkɔːs] *n*
umgänge *c*

interest ['intrəst] *n* intresse
nt; ränta *c*; *v* intressera

interested ['intristid] *adj*
intresserad

interesting ['intrəstiŋ] *adj*
intressant

interfere [,intə'fiə] *v*
*ingripa; ~ with blanda sig i

interference [,intə'fiərəns] *n*
inblandning *c*

interim ['intərim] *n* mellantid
c

interior [in'tiəriə] *n* insida *c*;
interiör *c*; inrikesärenden

interlude ['intəluːd] *n*
mellanspel *nt*

intermediary [,intə'miːdjəri]
n förmedlare *c*

intermission [,intə'miʃən] *n*
paus *c*

internal [in'təːnəl] *adj* inre;
invärtes; inhemsk, invändig

international [,intə'næʃənəl]
adj internationell

Internet ['intənet] *n* Internet
nt

interpret [in'təːprit] *v* tolka

interpreter [in'təːpritə] *n*
tolk *c*

interrogate [in'terəgeit] *v*
förhöra

interrogation
[in,terə'geiʃən] *n* förhör *nt*

interrogative [,intə'rɔgətiv]
adj interrogativ

interrupt [,intə'rʌpt] *v*
*avbryta

interruption [,intə'rʌpʃən] *n*
avbrott *c*

intersection [,intə'sekʃən] *n*
skärning *c*, vägkorsning *c*

interval ['intəvəl] *n* paus *c*;
intervall *c*

intervene [,intə'viːn] *v*
*ingripa

interview ['intəvjuː] *n*
intervju *c*

intestine [in'testin] *n* tarm *c*

intimate ['intimət] *adj*
förtrolig

into ['intu] *prep* in i

291   **issue**

intolerable [in'tɔlərəbəl] *adj*
   outhärdlig
intoxicated [in'tɔksikeitid]
   adj berusad
intrigue [in'tri:g] *n* intrig *c*
introduce [,intrə'dju:s] *v*
   presentera, introducera;
   införa
introduction [,intrə'dʌkʃən]
   n presentation *c*; inledning *c*
invade [in'veid] *v* invadera
invalid¹ ['invəli:d] *n* invalid
   c; *adj* invalidiserad
invalid² [in'vælid] *adj* ogiltig
invasion [in'veiʒən] *n*
   invasion *c*
invent [in'vent] *v* *uppfinna;
   uppdikta
invention [in'venʃən] *n*
   uppfinning *c*
inventive [in'ventiv] *adj*
   uppfinningsrik
inventor [in'ventə] *n*
   uppfinnare *c*
inventory ['inventri] *n*
   inventering *c*
invert [in'və:t] *v* kasta om,
   vända upp och ner
invest [in'vest] *v* investera;
   placera pengar
investigate [in'vestigeit] *v*
   efterforska, utreda
investigation
   [in,vesti'geiʃən] *n*
   utredning *c*
investment [in'vestmənt] *n*
   investering *c*,
   kapitalplacering *c*
investor [in'vestə] *n*
   aktieägare *c*, investerare *c*

invisible [in'vizəbəl] *adj*
   osynlig
invitation [,invi'teiʃən] *n*
   inbjudan *c*
invite [in'vait] *v* *inbjuda
invoice ['invɔis] *n* faktura *c*
involve [in'vɔlv] *v* inblanda
inwards ['inwədz] *adv* inåt
iodine ['aiədi:n] *n* jod *c*
Iran [i'rɑ:n] Iran
Iranian [i'reiniən] *adj* iransk;
   n iranier *c*
Iraq [i'rɑ:k] Irak
Iraqi [i'rɑ:ki] *adj* irakisk; *n*
   irakier *c*
Ireland ['aiələnd] Irland
Irish ['aiəriʃ] *adj* irländsk
iron ['aiən] *n* järn *nt*;
   strykjärn *nt*; järn-; *v* *stryka
ironical [ai'rɔnikəl] *adj*
   ironisk
irony ['aiərəni] *n* ironi *c*
irregular [i'regjulə] *adj*
   oregelbunden
irreparable [i'repərəbəl] *adj*
   oreparerbar
irrevocable [i'revəkəbəl] *adj*
   oåterkallelig
irritable ['iritəbəl] *adj*
   lättretad
irritate ['iriteit] *v* irritera, reta
is [iz] *v* (pr be)
island ['ailənd] *n* ö *c*
isolate ['aisəleit] *v* isolera
isolation [,aisə'leiʃən] *n*
   isolering *c*
Israel ['izreil] Israel
Israeli [iz'reili] *adj* israelisk; *n*
   israelier *c*
issue ['iʃu:] *v* *utge; *n*

utgivning c, upplaga c; fråga c, tvisteämne nt; resultat nt, utgång c, följd c, konsekvens c

it [it] pron den, det

Italian [i'tæljən] adj italiensk; n italienare c

Italy ['itəli] Italien

itch [itʃ] n klåda c; v klia

item ['aitəm] n post c; punkt c

itinerary [ai'tinərəri] n resrutt c, resplan c

its pron dess

itself [it'self] sig; by ~ automatiskt

ivory ['aivəri] n elfenben nt

ivy ['aivi] n murgröna c

J

jack [dʒæk] n domkraft c

jacket ['dʒækit] n kavaj c, jacka c; bokomslag nt

jade [dʒeid] n jade c

jail [dʒeil] n fängelse c

jam [dʒæm] n sylt c; trafikstockning c

janitor ['dʒænitə] n portvakt c

January ['dʒænjuəri] januari

Japan [dʒə'pæn] Japan

Japanese [,dʒæpə'niːz] adj japansk; n japan c

jar [dʒɑː] n kruka c; skakning c

jaundice ['dʒɔːndis] n gulsot c

jaw [dʒɔː] n käke c

jealous ['dʒeləs] adj svartsjuk

jealousy ['dʒeləsi] n svartsjuka c

jeans [dʒiːnz] pl jeans pl

jelly ['dʒeli] n gelé c

jellyfish ['dʒelifiʃ] n manet c

jersey ['dʒəːzi] n jerseytyg nt; ylletröja c

jet [dʒet] n stråle c; jetplan nt

jet lag ['jet‿læg] n jet lag c

jetty ['dʒeti] n hamnpir c

Jew [dʒuː] n jude c

jewel ['dʒuːəl] n smycke c

jeweller ['dʒuːələ] n juvelerare c; guldsmedsaffär c

jewellery ['dʒuːəlri] n smycken; juveler

Jewish ['dʒuːiʃ] adj judisk

job [dʒɔb] n jobb nt; plats c, arbete nt

jobless ['dʒɔbles] adj arbetslös

jockey ['dʒɔki] n jockey c

join [dʒɔin] v *förbinda; *ansluta sig till; förena, sammanfoga

joint [dʒɔint] n led c; sammanfogning c; adj gemensam, förenad

jointly ['dʒɔintli] adv gemensamt

joke [dʒouk] n vits c, skämt nt

jolly ['dʒɔli] adj lustig; glad; trevlig; livad

293   kill

Jordan ['dʒɔːdən] Jordanien
Jordanian [dʒɔːˈdeiniən] *adj*
  jordansk; *n* jordanier *c*
journal ['dʒəːnəl] *n* journal *c*,
  tidskrift *c*
journalism ['dʒəːnəlizəm] *n*
  journalism *c*
journalist ['dʒəːnəlist] *n*
  journalist *c*
journey ['dʒəːni] *n* resa *c*
joy [dʒɔi] *n* fröjd *c*, glädje *c*
joyful ['dʒɔiful] *adj* förtjust,
  glad; glädjande
jubilee ['dʒuːbiliː] *n* jubileum
  nt
judge [dʒʌdʒ] *n* domare; *v*
  döma; bedöma
judgment ['dʒʌdʒmənt] *n*
  dom *c*
jug [dʒʌg] *n* tillbringare *c*
juice [dʒuːs] *n* saft *c*, juice *c*
juicy ['dʒuːsi] *adj* saftig

July [dʒuˈlai] juli
jump [dʒʌmp] *v* hoppa; *n*
  språng *nt*, hopp *nt*
jumper ['dʒʌmpə] *n* jumper *c*
junction ['dʒʌŋkʃən] *n*
  vägkorsning *c*; knutpunkt *c*
June [dʒuːn] juni
jungle ['dʒʌŋgəl] *n* djungel *c*,
  urskog *c*
junior ['dʒuːnjə] *adj* junior
junk [dʒʌŋk] *n* skräp *nt*;
  djonk *c*
jury ['dʒuəri] *n* jury *c*
just [dʒʌst] *adj* rättvis,
  berättigad; riktig; *adv* just;
  precis
justice ['dʒʌstis] *n* rätt *c*;
  rättvisa *c*
justify ['dʒʌstifai] *v* försvara

K

kangaroo [ˌkæŋgəˈruː] *n*
  känguru *c*
keel [kiːl] *n* köl *c*
keen [kiːn] *adj* livlig,
  angelägen; skarp
*keep [kiːp] *v* *hålla; bevara;
  *fortsätta; ~ **away from**
  hålla sig på avstånd från; ~
  off *låta vara; ~ **on**
  *fortsätta; ~ **quiet** *tiga; ~
  up *hålla ut; ~ **up with**
  hänga med
kennel ['kenəl] *n* hundkoja *c*;
  kennel *c*

Kenya ['kenjə] Kenya
kerosene ['kerəsiːn] *n*
  fotogen *c*
kettle ['ketəl] *n* kittel *c*
key [kiː] *n* nyckel *c*
keyhole ['kiːhoul] *n*
  nyckelhål *nt*
khaki ['kɑːki] *n* kaki *c*
kick [kik] *v* sparka; *n* spark *c*
kickoff [ˌkiˈkɔf] *n* avspark *c*
kid [kid] *n* barn *nt*, unge *c*;
  getskinn *nt*; *v* *driva med
kidney ['kidni] *n* njure *c*
kill [kil] *v* *slå ihjäl, döda

kilogram ['kiləgræm] n kilo nt

kilometre ['kilə,mi:tə] n kilometer c

kind [kaind] adj snäll, vänlig; god; n sort c

kindergarten ['kində,ga:tən] n lekskola c

king [kiŋ] n kung c

kingdom ['kiŋdəm] n kungarike nt; rike nt

kiosk ['ki:ɔsk] n kiosk c

kiss [kis] n kyss c, puss c; v kyssa

kit [kit] n utrustning c

kitchen ['kitʃin] n kök nt; ~ garden köksträdgård c; ~ towel kökshandduk c

knapsack ['næpsæk] n ryggsäck c

knee [ni:] n knä nt

kneecap ['ni:kæp] n knäskål c

*kneel [ni:l] v knäböja

knew [nju:] v (p know)

knife [naif] n (pl knives) kniv c

knight [nait] n riddare c

*knit [nit] v sticka

knob [nɔb] n handtag c

knock [nɔk] v knacka; n knackning c; ~ against stöta emot; ~ down *slå omkull

*know [nou] v *veta, känna

knowledge ['nɔlidʒ] n kunskap c

knuckle ['nʌkəl] n knoge c

L

label ['leibəl] n etikett c; v etikettera

laboratory [lə'bɔrətəri] n laboratorium nt

labour ['leibə] n arbete nt; förlossningsarbete nt; v anstränga sig; **labor permit** Am arbetstillstånd nt

labourer ['leibərə] n arbetare c

labour-saving ['leibə,seiviŋ] adj arbetsbesparande

labyrinth ['læbərinθ] n labyrint c

lace [leis] n spets c; skosnöre nt

lack [læk] n saknad c, brist c; v sakna

lactose ['læktous] n laktos c; **lactose-free** adj laktosfri

lactose intolerant ['læktous ,in'tɔlərənt] adj laktosintolerant

lacquer ['lækə] n lack nt

lad [læd] n pojke c, gosse c

ladder ['lædə] n stege c

lady ['leidi] n dam c; **ladies' room** damtoalett c

lagoon [lə'gu:n] n lagun c

lake [leik] n sjö c

lamb [læm] n lamm nt; lammkött nt

lame [leim] adj ofärdig, halt, förlamad

lamentable ['læməntəbəl]
  adj bedrövlig
lamp [læmp] n lampa c
lampshade ['læmpʃeid] n
  lampskärm c
land [lænd] n land nt; v landa;
  *gå i land
landlady ['lænd,leidi] n
  hyresvärdinna c
landlord ['lændlɔ:d] n
  hyresvärd c
landmark ['lændmɑ:k] n
  landmärke nt
landscape ['lændskeip] n
  landskap nt
lane [lein] n gränd c, smal
  gata; körfil c
language ['læŋgwidʒ] n
  språk nt; ~ laboratory
  språklaboratorium nt
lantern ['læntən] n lykta c
lapel [lə'pel] n rockslag nt
lap [læp] n knä nt
laptop ['læp,tɔp] n bärbar
  dator c
large [lɑ:dʒ] adj stor; rymlig
lark [lɑ:k] n lärka c
laryngitis [,lærin'dʒaitis] n
  strupkatarr c
last [lɑ:st] adj sist; förra; v
  vara; at ~ till sist; till slut
lasting ['lɑ:stiŋ] adj varaktig
latchkey ['lætʃki:] n
  portnyckel c
late [leit] adj sen; för sent
lately ['leitli] adv på sista
  tiden, nyligen
lather ['lɑ:ðə] n lödder nt
Latin America ['lætin
  ə'merikə] Latinamerika

Latin-American
  [,lætinə'merikən] adj
  latinamerikansk
latitude ['lætitju:d] n
  breddgrad c
laugh [lɑ:f] v skratta; n skratt
  nt
laughter ['lɑ:ftə] n skratt nt
launch [lɔ:ntʃ] v lansera;
  *sjösätta; *avskjuta; n slup c
launching ['lɔ:ntʃiŋ] n
  sjösättning c
launderette [,lɔ:ndə'ret] n
  tvättomat c
laundry ['lɔ:ndri] n
  tvättinrättning c; tvätt c
lavatory ['lævətəri] n toalett c
lavish ['læviʃ] adj slösaktig
law [lɔ:] n lag c; juridik c; ~
  court domstol c
lawful ['lɔ:fəl] adj laglig
lawn [lɔ:n] n gräsmatta c
lawsuit ['lɔ:su:t] n rättegång
  c, process c
lawyer ['lɔ:jə] n advokat c;
  jurist c
laxative ['læksətiv] n
  avföringsmedel nt
*lay [lei] v placera, *lägga,
  *sätta; ~ bricks mura
layer [leiə] n lager nt
layman ['leimən] n lekman c
lazy ['leizi] adj lat
*lead [li:d] v leda
lead¹ [li:d] n försprång nt;
  ledning c; koppel nt
lead² [led] n bly nt
leader ['li:də] n ledare c
leadership ['li:dəʃip] n

ledarskap *nt*
leading ['liːdiŋ] *adj* förnämst, ledande
leaf [liːf] *n* (pl leaves) löv *nt*, blad *nt*
league [liːg] *n* förbund *nt*
leak [liːk] *v* läcka; *n* läcka *c*
leaky ['liːki] *adj* otät
lean [liːn] *adj* mager
*lean [liːn] *v* luta sig
leap [liːp] *n* hopp *nt*
*leap [liːp] *v* skutta, hoppa
leap year ['liːpjiə] *n* skottår *nt*
*learn [ləːn] *v* lära sig
learner ['ləːnə] *n* nybörjare *c*
lease [liːs] *n* hyreskontrakt *nt*; arrende *nt*; *v* hyra, arrendera ut; arrendera
leash [liːʃ] *n* koppel *nt*
least [liːst] *adj* minst; **at ~** åtminstone
leather ['leðə] *n* läder *nt*; läder-, skinn-
leave [liːv] *n* ledighet *c*
*leave [liːv] *v* lämna, *ge sig av, resa bort, *låta; **~ behind** efterlämna; **~ out** utelämna
Lebanese [,lebə'niːz] *adj* libanesisk; *n* libanes *c*
Lebanon ['lebənən] Libanon
lecture ['lektʃə] *n* föreläsning *c*, föredrag *nt*
left[1] [left] *adj* vänster
left[2] [left] *v* (p, pp leave)
left-hand ['lefthænd] *adj* vänster
left-handed [,left'hændid] *adj* vänsterhänt
leg [leg] *n* ben *nt*

legacy ['legəsi] *n* legat *nt*
legal ['liːgəl] *adj* legal, laglig; juridisk
legalization [,liːgəlai'zeiʃən] *n* legalisering *c*
legation [li'geiʃən] *n* legation *c*
legible ['ledʒibəl] *adj* läslig
legitimate [li'dʒitimət] *adj* rättmätig, legitim
leisure ['leʒə] *n* ledighet *c*
lemon ['lemən] *n* citron *c*
lemonade [,lemə'neid] *n* läskedryck *c*
*lend [lend] *v* låna ut
length [leŋθ] *n* längd *c*
lengthen ['leŋθən] *v* förlänga
lengthways ['leŋθweiz] *adv* på längden
lens [lenz] *n* lins *c*; **telephoto ~** teleobjektiv *nt*; **zoom ~** zoomlins *c*
leprosy ['leprəsi] *n* spetälska *c*
less [les] *adv* mindre
lessen ['lesən] *v* förminska
lesson ['lesən] *n* läxa *c*, lektion *c*
*let [let] *v* *låta; hyra ut; **~ down** *svika
letter ['letə] *n* brev *nt*; bokstav *c*; **~ of credit** kreditiv *nt*; **~ of recommendation** rekommendationsbrev *nt*
letterbox ['letəbɔks] *n* brevlåda *c*
lettuce ['letis] *n* grönsallad *c*
level ['levəl] *adj* slät; plan, jämn; *n* plan *nt*, nivå *c*;

vattenpass *nt*; *v* jämna, utjämna; **~ crossing** järnvägsövergång *c*

lever ['li:və] *n* hävstång *c*, spak *c*

liability [,laiə'biləti] *n* skyldighet *c*

liable ['laiəbəl] *adj* ansvarig, benägen; **~ to** utsatt för

liar ['laiə] *n* lögnare *c*

liberal ['libərəl] *adj* liberal; frikostig, rundhänt, givmild

liberation [,libə'reiʃən] *n* frigörelse *c*, befrielse *c*; frigivande *nt*

Liberia [lai'biəriə] Liberia

Liberian [lai'biəriən] *adj* liberiansk; *n* liberian *c*

liberty ['libəti] *n* frihet *c*

library ['laibrəri] *n* bibliotek *nt*

licence ['laisəns] *n* licens *c*; tillståndsbevis *nt*; **driving ~** körkort *nt*; **~ number** *nAm* registreringsnummer *nt*; **~ plate** *nAm* registreringsskylt *c*

license ['laisəns] *v* *ge rättighet, auktorisera

lick [lik] *v* slicka; övertrumfa

lid [lid] *n* lock *nt*

lie [lai] *v* *ljuga; *n* lögn *c*

***lie** [lai] *v* *ligga; **~ down** *lägga sig

life [laif] *n* (pl lives) liv *nt*; **~ insurance** livförsäkring *c*; **~ jacket** flytväst *c*

life support ['laif_sə,pɔ:t] *n* livsuppehållande (maskin) *c*

lifebelt ['laifbelt] *n* livbälte *nt*

lifetime ['laiftaim] *n* livstid *c*

lift [lift] *v* lyfta, höja; *n* hiss *c*; skjuts *c*

light [lait] *n* ljus *nt*; *adj* lätt; ljus; **~ bulb** glödlampa *c*

***light** [lait] *v* tända

lighter ['laitə] *n* tändare *c*

lighthouse ['laithaus] *n* fyr *c*

lighting ['laitiŋ] *n* belysning *c*

lightning ['laitniŋ] *n* blixt *c*

like [laik] *v* tycka om; *adj* lik; *conj* såsom; *prep* liksom

likely ['laikli] *adj* sannolik

like-minded [,laik'maindid] *adj* likasinnad

likewise ['laikwaiz] *adv* likaså, likaledes

lily ['lili] *n* lilja *c*

limb [lim] *n* lem *c*

lime [laim] *n* kalk *c*; lind *c*; grön citron

limetree ['laimtri:] *n* lind *c*

limit ['limit] *n* gräns *c*; *v* begränsa

limp [limp] *v* halta; *adj* slapp

line [lain] *n* rad *c*; streck *nt*; lina *c*; linje *c*; **stand in ~** *Am* köa

linen ['linin] *n* linne *nt*

liner ['lainə] *n* linjefartyg *nt*

lingerie ['lɔ̃ʒəri:] *n* damunderkläder *pl*

lining ['lainiŋ] *n* foder *nt*

link [liŋk] *v* *sammanbinda; *n* länk *c*

link [liŋk] *n* (computer) länk *c*

lion ['laiən] *n* lejon *nt*

lip [lip] *n* läpp *c*

liposuction ['lipou,sʌkʃən] *n* fettsugning *c*

lipstick ['lipstik] n läppstift nt

liqueur [li'kjuə] n likör c

liquid ['likwid] adj flytande; n vätska c

liquor ['likə] n sprit c

liquorice ['likəris] n lakrits c

list [list] n lista c; v *inskriva

listen ['lisən] v lyssna

listener ['lisnə] n lyssnare c

literary ['litrəri] adj litterär, litteratur-

literature ['litrətʃə] n litteratur c

litre ['li:tə] n liter c

litter ['litə] n avfall nt; kull c

little ['litəl] adj liten; föga

live¹ [liv] v leva; bo

live² [laiv] adj levande

livelihood ['laivlihud] n uppehälle nt

lively ['laivli] adj livfull

liver ['livə] n lever c

living ['liviŋ] n levnadssätt nt; ~ room vardagsrum nt

lizard ['lizəd] n ödla c

load [loud] n last c; börda c; v lasta

loaf [louf] n (pl loaves) limpa c

loan [loun] n lån nt

lobby ['lɔbi] n vestibul c; foajé c

lobster ['lɔbstə] n hummer c

local ['loukəl] adj lokal-, lokal; ~ call lokalsamtal nt; ~ train lokaltåg nt

locality [lou'kæləti] n samhälle nt

locate [lou'keit] v lokalisera

location [lou'keiʃən] n läge nt

lock [lɔk] v låsa; n lås nt; sluss c; ~ up låsa in

locker ['lɔkə] n förvaringsbox c

locomotive [,loukə'moutiv] n lok nt

lodge [lɔdʒ] v inkvartera; n jaktstuga c

lodger ['lɔdʒə] n inackordering c

lodgings ['lɔdʒiŋz] pl inkvartering c

log [lɔg] n stock c; ~ in v logga in; ~ off v logga ut

logic ['lɔdʒik] n logik c

logical ['lɔdʒikəl] adj logisk

lonely ['lounli] adj ensam

long [lɔŋ] adj lång; långvarig; ~ for längta efter; no longer inte längre

longing ['lɔŋiŋ] n längtan c

longitude ['lɔndʒitju:d] n längdgrad c

look [luk] v titta; tyckas, *se ut; n blick c; utseende nt; ~ after sköta, passa, *ta hand om; ~ at *se på, titta på; ~ for leta efter; ~ out *se upp; ~ up *slå upp

looking-glass ['lukiŋglɑ:s] n spegel c

loop [lu:p] n ögla c

loose [lu:s] adj lös

loosen ['lu:sən] v lossa

lord [lɔ:d] n lord c

lorry ['lɔri] n lastbil c

***lose** [lu:z] v mista, förlora

loser ['lu:sə] n förlorare c

loss [lɔs] n förlust c

lost [lɔst] adj vilsegången; försvunnen; ~ **and found** hittegods nt; ~ **property office** hittegodsmagasin nt

lot [lɔt] n lott c; mängd c, hög c

lottery ['lɔtəri] n lotteri nt

loud [laud] adj högljudd, gäll

loudspeaker [,laud'spi:kə] n högtalare c

lounge [laundʒ] n sällskapsrum nt

louse [laus] n (pl lice) lus c

love [lʌv] v älska, *hålla av; n kärlek c; **in** ~ förälskad

lovely ['lʌvli] adj söt, förtjusande, ljuvlig

lover ['lʌvə] n älskare c

love story ['lʌv,stɔ:ri] n kärlekshistoria c

low [lou] adj låg; djup; nedstämd; ~ **tide** ebb c

lower ['louə] v sänka; minska; adj lägre, undre

lowlands ['louləndz] pl lågland nt

loyal ['lɔiəl] adj lojal

lubricate ['lu:brikeit] v *smörja, olja

lubrication [,lu:bri'keiʃən] n smörjning c; ~ **oil** smörjolja c; ~ **system** smörjsystem nt

luck [lʌk] n tur c; **bad** ~ otur c; **good** ~! lycka till!

lucky ['lʌki] adj lyckosam, tursam; ~ **charm** amulett c

ludicrous ['lu:dikrəs] adj löjeväckande, löjlig

luggage ['lʌgidʒ] n bagage nt; **hand** ~ handbagage nt; **left** ~ **office** bagageinlämning c; ~ **rack** bagagehylla c; ~ **van** resgodsfinka c

lukewarm ['lu:kwɔ:m] adj ljum

lumbago [lʌm'beigou] n ryggskott nt

luminous ['lu:minəs] adj lysande

lump [lʌmp] n klump c, bit c; bula c; ~ **of sugar** sockerbit c; ~ **sum** klumpsumma c

lumpy ['lʌmpi] adj klimpig

lunacy ['lu:nəsi] n vansinne nt

lunatic ['lu:nətik] adj vansinnig; n sinnessjuk c

lunch [lʌntʃ] n lunch c

luncheon ['lʌntʃən] n lunch c

lung [lʌŋ] n lunga c

lust [lʌst] n åtrå c

luxurious [lʌg'ʒuəriəs] adj luxuös

luxury ['lʌkʃəri] n lyx c

M

machine [mə'ʃiːn] *n* maskin
c, apparat *c*

machinery [mə'ʃiːnəri] *n*
maskineri *nt*

mackerel ['mækrəl] *n* (pl ~)
makrill *c*

mackintosh ['mækintɔʃ] *n*
regnrock *c*

mad [mæd] *adj*
sinnesförvirrad, vanvettig,
tokig; rasande

madness ['mædnəs] *n*
vansinne *nt*

magazine [,mægə'ziːn] *n*
tidskrift *c*; magasin *nt*

magic ['mædʒik] *n* magi *c*,
trollkonst *c*; *adj* magisk

magician [mə'dʒiʃən] *n*
trollkarl *c*

magistrate ['mædʒistreit] *n*
rådman *c*

magnetic [mæg'netik] *adj*
magnetisk

magneto [mæg'niːtou] *n* (pl
~s) magnetapparat *c*

magnificent [mæg'nifisənt]
adj ståtlig; magnifik,
praktfull

magnify ['mægnifai] *v*
förstora

maid [meid] *n* hembiträde *nt*

maiden name ['meidən
neim] flicknamn *nt*

mail [meil] *n* post *c*; *v* posta; ~
order *Am* postanvisning *c*

mailbox ['meilbɔks] *nAm*

brevlåda *c*

main [mein] *adj* huvud-;
störst; ~ **deck** överdäck *nt*; ~
line huvudlinje *c*; ~ **road**
huvudväg *c*; ~ **street**
huvudgata *c*

mainland ['meinlənd] *n*
fastland *nt*

mainly ['meinli] *adv*
huvudsakligen

mains [meinz] *pl*
huvudledning *c*

maintain [mein'tein] *v*
*upprätthålla

maintenance ['meintənəns]
n underhåll *nt*

maize [meiz] *n* majs *c*

major ['meidʒə] *adj* större;
störst; *n* major *c*

majority [mə'dʒɔrəti] *n*
majoritet *c*

*make [meik] *v* *göra; tjäna;
*hinna med; ~ **do with** klara
sig med; ~ **good** *gottgöra; ~
up *sätta upp, *göra upp

make-up ['meikʌp] *n* smink *c*

malaria [mə'leəriə] *n* malaria
c

Malay [mə'lei] *n* malajier *c*

Malaysia [mə'leiziə]
Malaysia

Malaysian [mə'leiziən] *adj*
malaysisk

male [meil] *adj* han-, mans-,
manlig

malicious [mə'liʃəs] *adj*

marry

illvillig
malignant [mə'lignənt] *adj*
elakartad
mall [mɔ:l] *nAm* köpcenter *nt*
mallet ['mælit] *n* klubba *c*
malnutrition
[ˌmælnjuˈtriʃən] *n*
undernäring *c*
mammal ['mæməl] *n*
däggdjur *nt*
man [mæn] *n* (pl men) man *c*;
människa *c*; **men's room**
herrtoalett *c*
manage ['mænidʒ] *v* styra;
lyckas
manageable ['mænidʒəbəl]
adj hanterlig
management
['mænidʒmənt] *n* styrelse *c*;
direktion *c*
manager ['mænidʒə] *n*
direktör *c*, chef *c*
mandarin ['mændərin] *n*
mandarin *c*
mandate ['mændeit] *n*
mandat *nt*
manger ['meindʒə] *n*
foderbehållare *c*
manicure ['mænikjuə] *n*
manikyr *c*; *v* manikyrera
mankind [mæn'kaind] *n*
mänsklighet *c*
mannequin ['mænəkin] *n*
skyltdocka *c*
manner ['mænə] *n* sätt *nt*, vis
nt; **manners** *pl* uppförande
nt
man-of-war [ˌmænəv'wɔ:] *n*
örlogsfartyg *nt*
manor house ['mænəhaus] *n*

herrgård *c*
mansion ['mænʃən] *n*
patricierhus *nt*
manual ['mænjuəl] *adj* hand-
manufacture
[ˌmænjuˈfæktʃə] *v* tillverka
manufacturer
[ˌmænjuˈfæktʃərə] *n*
fabrikant *c*
manure [mə'njuə] *n* gödsel *c*
manuscript ['mænjuskript]
n manuskript *nt*
many ['meni] *adj* många
map [mæp] *n* karta *c*; plan *c*
maple ['meipəl] *n* lönn *c*
marble ['mɑ:bəl] *n* marmor *c*;
spelkula *c*
March [mɑ:tʃ] mars
march [mɑ:tʃ] *v* marschera; *n*
marsch *c*
mare [meə] *n* sto *nt*
margarine [ˌmɑ:dʒə'ri:n] *n*
margarin *c*
margin ['mɑ:dʒin] *n* marginal *c*
maritime ['mæritaim] *adj*
maritim
mark [mɑ:k] *v* märka;
markera; utmärka; *n* märke
nt; betyg *nt*; skottavla *c*
market ['mɑ:kit] *n* marknad
c, saluhall *c*
marketplace ['mɑ:kitpleis] *n*
torg *nt*; marknadsplats *c*
marmalade ['mɑ:məleid] *n*
marmelad *c*
marriage ['mæridʒ] *n*
äktenskap *nt*
marrow ['mærou] *n* märg *c*
marry ['mæri] *v* gifta sig

marsh [mɑːʃ] n sumpmark c

martyr ['mɑːtə] n martyr c

marvel ['mɑːvəl] n under nt;
v förundra sig

marvellous ['mɑːvələs] adj
underbar

mascara [mæ'skɑːrə] n
maskara c

masculine ['mæskjulin] adj
manlig

mash [mæʃ] v mosa; **mashed
potatoes** pl potatismos nt

mask [mɑːsk] n mask c

Mass [mæs] n mässa c

mass [mæs] n mängd c,
massa c; klump c; ~
production
massproduktion c

massage ['mæsɑːʒ] n
massage c; v massera

masseur [mæ'səː] n massör c

massive ['mæsiv] adj massiv

mast [mɑːst] n mast c

master ['mɑːstə] n mästare c;
arbetsgivare c; lektor c,
lärare c; v bemästra

masterpiece ['mɑːstəpiːs] n
mästerverk nt

mat [mæt] n matta c; adj matt

match [mætʃ] n tändsticka c;
jämlike c, match c, parti nt;
v passa ihop

matchbox ['mætʃbɔks] n
tändsticksask c

material [mə'tiəriəl] n
material nt; tyg nt; adj
materiell

mathematical
[,mæθə'mætikəl] adj
matematisk

mathematics
[,mæθə'mætiks] n
matematik c

matrimony ['mætriməni] n
äktenskap nt

matter ['mætə] n materia c,
ämne nt; angelägenhet c,
fråga c; v *vara viktigt; **as a
~ of fact** faktiskt, i själva
verket

matter-of-fact
[,mætərəv'fækt] adj torr
och saklig

mattress ['mætrəs] n
madrass c

mature [mə'tjuə] adj mogen

maturity [mə'tjuərəti] n
mogen ålder, mognad c

mausoleum [,mɔːsə'liːəm] n
mausoleum nt

mauve [mouv] adj rödlila

May [mei] maj

***may** [mei] v *kunna; *få

maybe ['meibi] adv kanske

mayor [meə] n borgmästare c

maze [meiz] n labyrint c;
virrvarr nt

me [miː] pron mig

meadow ['medou] n äng c

meal [miːl] n måltid c, mål nt

mean [miːn] adj gemen;
medel-; n genomsnitt nt

***mean** [miːn] v betyda; mena

meaning ['miːniŋ] n mening
c

meaningless ['miːniŋləs] adj
meningslös

means [miːnz] n medel nt; by
no ~ inte alls

in the meantime [in ðə

'miːntaim] under tiden

meanwhile ['miːnwail] adv under tiden

measles ['miːzəlz] n mässling c

measure ['meʒə] v mäta; n mått nt; åtgärd c

meat [miːt] n kött nt

mechanic [mi'kænik] n mekaniker c, montör c

mechanical [mi'kænikəl] adj mekanisk

mechanism ['mekənizəm] n mekanism c

medal ['medəl] n medalj c

media ['miːdiə] pl media pl

mediaeval [,medi'iːvəl] adj medeltida

mediate ['miːdieit] v medla

mediator ['miːdieitə] n medlare c

medical ['medikəl] adj medicinsk

medicine ['medsin] n medicin c; läkarvetenskap c

meditate ['mediteit] v meditera

Mediterranean [,meditə'reiniən] Medelhavet

medium ['miːdiəm] adj genomsnittlig, medel-, medelmåttig

***meet** [miːt] v träffa, möta

meeting ['miːtiŋ] n sammanträde nt; möte nt

meeting place ['miːtiŋpleis] n mötesplats c

melancholy ['melənkəli] n vemod nt

mellow ['melou] adj mjuk, fyllig

melodrama ['melə,drɑːmə] n melodrama nt

melody ['melədi] n melodi c

melon ['melən] n melon c

melt [melt] v smälta

member ['membə] n medlem c; **Member of Parliament** riksdagsman c

membership ['membəʃip] n medlemskap nt

memo ['memou] n (pl ~s) memorandum nt

memorable ['memərəbəl] adj minnesvärd

memorial [mə'mɔːriəl] n minnesmärke nt

memorize ['meməraiz] v lära sig utantill

memory ['meməri] n minne nt

mend [mend] v laga, reparera

menstruation [,menstru'eiʃən] n menstruation c

mental ['mentəl] adj mental

mention ['menʃən] v nämna, omnämna; n omnämnande nt

menu ['menjuː] n matsedel c, meny c

merchandise ['məːtʃəndaiz] n handelsvaror c

merchant ['məːtʃənt] n köpman c

merciful ['məːsifəl] adj barmhärtig

mercury ['məːkjuri] n kvicksilver nt

mercy ['mɔːsi] *n*
barmhärtighet *c*

mere [miə] *adj* blott och bar

merely ['miəli] *adv* endast

merge [mɔːdʒ] *v* slå ihop

merger ['mɔːdʒə] *n*
sammanslagning *c*

merit ['merit] *v* förtjäna; *n*
förtjänst *c*

merry ['meri] *adj* munter

merry-go-round
['merigou,raund] *n* karusell
c

mesh [meʃ] *n* maska *c*

mess [mes] *n* oordning *c*,
oreda *c*; ~ **up** spoliera

message ['mesidʒ] *n*
meddelande *c*

message board
['mesədʒ,bɔːd] *n*
meddelandeforum *c*

messenger ['mesindʒə] *n*
bud *c*

metal ['metəl] *n* metall *c*;
metall-

meter ['miːtə] *n* mätare *c*

method ['meθəd] *n* metod *c*,
förfaringssätt *nt*; ordning *c*

methodical [mə'θɔdikəl] *adj*
metodisk

metre ['miːtə] *n* meter *c*

metric ['metrik] *adj* metrisk

Mexican ['meksikən] *adj*
mexikansk; *n* mexikanare *c*

Mexico ['meksikou] Mexiko

mice [mais] *pl* möss *pl*

microphone ['maikrəfoun] *n*
mikrofon *c*

midday ['middei] *n* mitt på
dagen

middle ['midəl] *n* mitt *c*; *adj*
mellersta; **Middle Ages**
Medeltiden; ~ **class**
medelklass *c*; **middle-class**
adj borgerlig

midnight ['midnait] *n*
midnatt *c*

midst [midst] *n* mitt *c*

midsummer ['mid,sʌmə] *n*
midsommar *c*

midwife ['midwaif] *n* (pl
-wives) barnmorska *c*

might [mait] *n* makt *c*

*****might** [mait] *v* *kunna

mighty ['maiti] *adj* mäktig

migraine ['miːgrein] *n* migrän
c

mild [maild] *adj* mild

mildew ['mildjuː] *n* mögel *nt*

milestone ['mailstoun] *n*
milstolpe *c*

milieu ['miːljɔː] *n* miljö *c*

military ['militəri] *adj*
militär-; ~ **force** krigsmakt *c*

milk [milk] *n* mjölk *c*

milkman ['milkmən] *n* (pl
-men) mjölkbud *nt*

milkshake ['milkʃeik] *n*
milkshake *c*

milky ['milki] *adj* mjölkig

mill [mil] *n* kvarn *c*; fabrik *c*

miller ['milə] *n* mjölnare *c*

million ['miljən] *n* miljon *c*

millionaire [,miljə'neə] *n*
miljonär *c*

mince [mins] *v* finhacka

mind [maind] *n* begåvning *c*;
v *ha något emot; bry sig
om, akta, akta sig för

mine [main] *n* gruva *c*

miner ['mainə] n
gruvarbetare c

mineral ['minərəl] n mineral
nt; ~ water mineralvatten nt

mingle ['mingl] v mingla

miniature ['minjətʃə] n
miniatyr c

minimum ['miniməm] n
minimum nt

mining ['mainiŋ] n gruvdrift
c

minister ['ministə] n minister
c; präst c; Prime Minister
statsminister c

ministry ['ministri] n
departement nt

mink [miŋk] n mink c

minor ['mainə] adj liten,
mindre; underordnad; n
minderårig c

minority [mai'nɔrəti] n
minoritet c

mint [mint] n mynta c

minus ['mainəs] prep minus

minute¹ ['minit] n minut c;
minutes protokoll nt

minute² [mai'nju:t] adj
ytterst liten

miracle ['mirəkəl] n mirakel
nt

miraculous [mi'rækjuləs]
adj otrolig

mirror ['mirə] n spegel c

misbehave [,misbi'heiv] v
uppföra sig illa

miscarriage [mis'kærid3] n
missfall nt

miscellaneous
[,misə'leiniəs] adj blandad

mischief ['mistʃif] n ofog nt;

skada c, förtret c, åverkan c

mischievous ['mistʃivəs] adj
odygdig, skadlig

miserable ['mizərəbəl] adj
olycklig, eländig

misery ['mizəri] n elände nt;
nöd c

misfortune [mis'fɔ:tʃən] n
otur c, olycka c

mishap ['mishæp] n missöde
nt

*mislay [mis'lei] v *förlägga

misplaced [mis'pleist] adj
malplacerad

mispronounce
[,misprə'nauns] v uttala fel

miss¹ [mis] fröken c

miss² [mis] v missa

missing ['misiŋ] adj
försvunnen; ~ person
försvunnen person

mist [mist] n dimma c

mistake [mi'steik] n fel nt,
misstag nt

*mistake [mi'steik] v
förväxla, *missförstå

mistaken [mi'steikən] adj
felaktig; *be ~ *missta sig

mister ['mistə] herr

mistress ['mistrəs] n husmor
c; föreståndarinna c;
älskarinna c

mistrust [mis'trʌst] v misstro

misty ['misti] adj disig

*misunderstand
[,misʌndə'stænd] v
*missförstå

misunderstanding
[,misʌndə'stændiŋ] n
missförstånd nt

misuse [mis'ju:s] n missbruk
nt

mittens ['mitənz] pl
tumvantar pl

mix [miks] v blanda; ~ **with**
*umgås med

mixed [mikst] adj blandad

mixer ['miksə] n mixer c

mixture ['mikstʃə] n
blandning c

moan [moun] v jämra sig

moat [mout] n vallgrav c

mobile ['moubail] n mobil c;
adj mobil; ~ **phone**
mobil(telefon) c

mock [mɔk] v håna

mockery ['mɔkəri] n hån nt

model ['mɔdəl] n modell c;
mannekäng c; v modellera,
forma

modem ['moudem] n modem
nt

moderate ['mɔdərət] adj
måttlig, moderat;
medelmåttig

modern ['mɔdən] adj modern

modest ['mɔdist] adj
blygsam, anspråkslös

modesty ['mɔdisti] n
blygsamhet c

modify ['mɔdifai] v ändra

moist [mɔist] adj fuktig

moisten ['mɔisən] v fukta

moisture ['mɔistʃə] n
fuktighet c; **moisturizing
cream** fuktighetsbevarande
kräm

molar ['moulə] n kindtand c

moment ['moumənt] n
ögonblick nt

momentary ['mouməntəri]
adj tillfällig

monarch ['mɔnək] n monark
c

monarchy ['mɔnəki] n
monarki c

monastery ['mɔnəstri] n
kloster nt

Monday ['mʌndi] måndag c

monetary ['mʌnitəri] adj
monetär; ~ **unit** myntenhet c

money ['mʌni] n pengar pl; ~
exchange växelkontor nt; ~
order postanvisning c

monk [mʌŋk] n munk c

monkey ['mʌŋki] n apa c

monologue ['mɔnəlɔg] n
monolog c

monopoly [mə'nɔpəli] n
monopol nt

monotonous [mə'nɔtənəs]
adj monoton

month [mʌnθ] n månad c

monthly ['mʌnθli] adj
månatlig; ~ **magazine**
månadstidning c

monument ['mɔnjumənt] n
monument nt, minnesmärke
nt

mood [mu:d] n humör nt

moon [mu:n] n måne c

moonlight ['mu:nlait] n
månsken nt

moose [mu:s] n (pl ~, ~s) älg
c

moped ['mouped] n moped c

moral ['mɔrəl] n moral c; adj
sedlig, moralisk

morality [mə'ræləti] n
morallära c

mouth

more [mɔː] *adj* fler; **once ~** en gång till

moreover [mɔːˈrouvə] *adv* dessutom, för övrigt

morning [ˈmɔːniŋ] *n* morgon *c*, förmiddag *c*; **~ paper** morgontidning *c*; **this ~** i morse

Moroccan [məˈrɔkən] *adj* marockansk; *n* marockan *c*

Morocco [məˈrɔkou] Marocko

morphine [ˈmɔːfiːn] *n* morfin *nt*

morsel [ˈmɔːsəl] *n* bit *c*

mortal [ˈmɔːtəl] *adj* dödlig

mortgage [ˈmɔːgidʒ] *n* hypotek *nt*, inteckning *c*

mosaic [məˈzeiik] *n* mosaik *c*

mosque [mɔsk] *n* moské *c*

mosquito [məˈskiːtou] *n* (pl ~es) mygga *c*; moskit *c*

mosquito net [məˈskiːtounet] *n* myggnät *nt*

moss [mɔs] *n* mossa *c*

most [moust] *adj* (de) flesta); **at ~** på sin höjd; **~ of all** mest av allt

mostly [ˈmoustli] *adv* för det mesta

motel [mouˈtel] *n* motell *nt*

moth [mɔθ] *n* mal *c*

mother [ˈmʌðə] *n* mor *c*; **~ tongue** modersmål *nt*

mother-in-law [ˈmʌðərinlɔː] *n* (pl mothers-) svärmor *c*

mother of pearl [ˌmʌðərəvˈpəːl] *c*

motion [ˈmouʃən] *n* rörelse *c*; motion *c*

motivate [ˈmoutiveit] *v* motivera

motive [ˈmoutiv] *n* motiv *nt*

motor [ˈmoutə] *n* motor *c*; *v* bila; **~ body** *Am* karosseri *nt*; **starter ~** startmotor *c*

motorbike [ˈmoutəbaik] *nAm* moped *c*

motorboat [ˈmoutəbout] *n* motorbåt *c*

motorcar [ˈmoutəkaː] *n* bil *c*

motorcycle [ˈmoutəˌsaikəl] *n* motorcykel *c*

motorist [ˈmoutərist] *n* bilist *c*

motorway [ˈmoutəwei] *n* motorväg *c*

motto [ˈmɔtou] *n* (pl ~es, ~s) motto *nt*

mouldy [ˈmouldi] *adj* möglig

mound [maund] *n* kulle *c*

mount [maunt] *v* *bestiga; montera; *n* berg *nt*; montering *c*

mountain [ˈmauntin] *n* berg *nt*; **~ pass** bergspass *nt*; **~ range** bergskedja *c*

mountaineering [ˌmauntiˈniəriŋ] *n* bergsbestigning *c*

mountainous [ˈmauntinəs] *adj* bergig

mourning [ˈmɔːniŋ] *n* sorg *c*

mouse [maus] *n* (pl mice) mus *c*

moustache [məˈstaːʃ] *n* mustasch *c*

mouth [mauθ] *n* mun *c*; gap

nt, käft *c*; mynning *c*

mouthwash ['mauθwɔʃ] *n* munvatten *nt*

movable ['mu:vəbəl] *adj* flyttbar

move [mu:v] *v* *sätta i rörelse; flytta; röra sig; röra; *n* drag *nt*, steg *nt*; flyttning *c*

movement ['mu:vmənt] *n* rörelse *c*

movie ['mu:vi] *n* film *c*; **movies** *Am* bio *c*; ~ **theater** bio *c*

much [mʌtʃ] *adj* många; *adv* mycket; **as** ~ lika mycket; likaså

mud [mʌd] *n* gyttja *c*

muddle ['mʌdəl] *n* oreda *c*, röra *c*, virrvarr *nt*; *v* förvirra

muddy ['mʌdi] *adj* lerig

muffler ['mʌflə] *nAm* ljuddämpare *c*

mug [mʌg] *n* mugg *c*

mule [mju:l] *n* mulåsna *c*

multicultural [,mʌlti'kʌltʃərəl] *adj* multikulturell

multiplex ['mʌlti,pleks] *n* multiplex *c*

multiplication [,mʌltipli'keiʃən] *n* multiplikation *c*

multiply ['mʌltiplai] *v* multiplicera

mumps [mʌmps] *n* påssjuka *c*

municipal [mju:'nisipəl] *adj* kommunal-

municipality [mju:,nisi'pæləti] *n*

kommun *c*

murder ['mə:də] *n* mord *nt*; *v* mörda

murderer ['mə:dərə] *n* mördare *c*

muscle ['mʌsəl] *n* muskel *c*

muscular ['mʌskjulə] *adj* muskulös

museum [mju:'zi:əm] *n* museum *nt*

mushroom ['mʌʃru:m] *n* svamp *c*

music ['mju:zik] *n* musik *c*; ~ **academy** konservatorium *nt*

musical ['mju:zikəl] *adj* musikalisk; *n* musikal *c*

music hall ['mju:zikhɔ:l] *n* revyteater *c*

musician [mju:'ziʃən] *n* musiker *c*

muslin ['mʌzlin] *n* muslin *nt*

mussel ['mʌsəl] *n* blåmussla *c*

*must [mʌst] *v* *måste

mustard ['mʌstəd] *n* senap *c*

mute [mju:t] *adj* stum

mutiny ['mju:tini] *n* myteri *nt*

mutton ['mʌtən] *n* fårkött *nt*

mutual ['mju:tʃuəl] *adj* inbördes, ömsesidig

my [mai] *adj* min

myself [mai'self] *pron* mig; själv

mysterious [mi'stiəriəs] *adj* gåtfull, mystisk

mystery ['mistəri] *n* mysterium *nt*

myth [miθ] *n* myt *c*

N

nag [næg] v tjata

nail [neil] n nagel c; spik c

nail file ['neilfail] n nagelfil c

nail polish ['neil,pɔliʃ] n nagellack nt

nail scissors ['neil,sizəz] pl nagelsax c

naïve [naːˈiːv] adj naiv

naked ['neikid] adj naken; kal

name [neim] n namn nt; v uppkalla; **in the ~ of** i ... namn

namely ['neimli] adv nämligen

nap [næp] n tupplur c

napkin ['næpkin] n servett c

nappy ['næpi] n blöja c

narcosis [naːˈkousis] n (pl -ses) narkos c

narcotic [naːˈkɔtik] n narkotika c; narkoman c

narrow ['nærou] adj trång, snäv, smal

narrow-minded [,nærouˈmaindid] adj inskränkt

nasty ['naːsti] adj smutsig, obehaglig; otäck

nation ['neiʃən] n nation c; folk nt

national ['næʃənəl] adj nationell; folk-; stats-; **~ anthem** nationalsång c; **~ dress** nationaldräkt c; **~ park** nationalpark c

nationality [,næʃəˈnælɪti] n nationalitet c

nationalize ['næʃənəlaiz] v nationalisera

native ['neitiv] n inföding c; adj infödd, inhemsk; **~ country** fosterland nt, hemland nt; **~ language** modersmål nt

natural ['nætʃərəl] adj naturlig; medfödd

naturally ['nætʃərəli] adv naturligtvis

nature ['neitʃə] n natur c

naughty ['nɔːti] adj odygdig, stygg

nausea ['nɔːsiə] n illamående nt

naval ['neivəl] adj flott-

navel ['neivəl] n navel c

navigable ['nævigəbəl] adj segelbar

navigate ['nævigeit] v navigera; segla

navigation [,næviˈgeiʃən] n navigation c; sjöfart c

navy ['neivi] n flotta c

near [niə] adj nära, närbelägen

nearby ['niəbai] adj närliggande

nearly ['niəli] adv närapå, nästan

neat [niːt] adj prydlig; oblandad; ren; klar, koncis

necessary ['nesəsəri] adj

nödvändig
necessity [nə'sesəti] n
nödvändighet c
neck [nek] n hals c; **nape of
the ~** nacke c
necklace ['nekləs] n
halsband nt
necktie ['nektai] n slips c
need [ni:d] v behöva, *måste;
n behov nt; nödvändighet c;
~ to *måste
needle ['ni:dəl] n nål c
needlework ['ni:dəlwə:k] n
handarbete nt
negative ['negətiv] adj
nekande, negativ; n negativ
nt
neglect [ni'glekt] v
försumma; n slarv nt
neglectful [ni'glektfəl] adj
försumlig
negligee ['negliʒei] n negligé
c
negotiate [ni'gouʃieit] v
förhandla
negotiation [ni,gouʃi'eiʃən]
n förhandling c
neighbour ['neibə] n granne
c
neighbourhood ['neibəhud]
n grannskap nt
neighbouring ['neibəriŋ] adj
angränsande
neither ['naiðə] pron
ingendera; **neither ... nor**
varken ... eller
nephew ['nefju:] n systerson
c, brorson c
nerve [nə:v] n nerv c;
fräckhet c

nervous ['nə:vəs] adj nervös
nest [nest] n bo nt
net [net] n nät nt; adj netto-
the Netherlands
['neðələndz] Nederländerna
network ['netwə:k] n nätverk
nt
networking ['net,wə:kiŋ] n
nätverksarbete c
neuralgia [njuə'rældʒə] n
neuralgi c
neurosis [njuə'rousis] n
neuros c
neuter ['nju:tə] adj neutrum
neutral ['nju:trəl] adj neutral
never ['nevə] adv aldrig
nevertheless [,nevəðə'les]
adv inte desto mindre
new [nju:] adj ny; **New Year**
nyår nt
news [nju:z] n nyhet c,
dagsnyheter pl
newsagent ['nju:,zeidʒənt]
n tidningsförsäljare c
newspaper ['nju:z,peipə] n
dagstidning c
newsreel ['nju:zri:l] n
journalfilm c
newsstand ['nju:zstænd] n
tidningskiosk c
New Zealand [nju: 'zi:lənd]
Nya Zeeland
next [nekst] adj nästa,
följande; **~ to** bredvid
next-door [,nekst'dɔ:] adv
näst intill
nice [nais] adj snäll, söt,
trevlig; god; sympatisk
nickel ['nikəl] n nickel c
nickname ['nikneim] n

note

smeknamn *nt*
nicotine ['nikəti:n] *n* nikotin *nt*
niece [ni:s] *n* systerdotter *c*, brorsdotter *c*
Nigeria [nai'dʒiəriə] Nigeria
Nigerian [nai'dʒiəriən] *adj* nigeriansk; *n* nigerian *c*
night [nait] *n* natt *c*; kväll *c*; **by ~** om natten; **~ flight** nattflyg *nt*; **~ rate** nattaxa *c*; **~ train** nattåg *nt*
nightclub ['naitklʌb] *n* nattklubb *c*
night cream ['naitkri:m] *n* nattkräm *c*
nightingale ['naitiŋgeil] *n* näktergal *c*
nightly ['naitli] *adj* nattlig
nightmare ['naitmeə] *n* mardröm *c*
nil [nil] ingenting, noll
nine [nain] *num* nio
nineteen [,nain'ti:n] *num* nitton
nineteenth [,nain'ti:nθ] *num* nittonde
ninety ['nainti] *num* nittio
ninth [nainθ] *num* nionde
nitrogen ['naitrədʒən] *n* kväve *nt*
no [nou] nej; *adj* ingen; **~ one** ingen
nobility [nou'biləti] *n* adel *c*
noble ['noubəl] *adj* adlig; ädel
nobody ['noubədi] *pron* ingen
nod [nɔd] *n* nick *c*; *v* nicka
noise [nɔiz] *n* ljud *nt*; oväsen

nt, buller *nt*
noisy ['nɔizi] *adj* bullrig; högljudd
nominal ['nɔminəl] *adj* nominell, obetydlig
nominate ['nɔmineit] *v* nominera, utnämna
nomination [,nɔmi'neiʃən] *n* nominering *c*; utnämning *c*
none [nʌn] *pron* ingen
nonsense ['nɔnsəns] *n* dumheter *pl*
non-smoker [,nɔn'smoukə] *n* icke-rökare *c*
noon [nu:n] *n* klockan tolv
nor [nɔ:]; inte heller
normal ['nɔ:məl] *adj* vanlig, normal
north [nɔ:θ] *n* nord *c*; *adj* nordlig; **North Pole** Nordpolen
north-east [,nɔ:θ'i:st] *n* nordost *c*
northern ['nɔ:ðən] *adj* norra
north-west [,nɔ:θ'west] *n* nordväst *c*
Norway ['nɔ:wei] Norge
Norwegian [nɔ:'wi:dʒən] *adj* norsk; *n* norrman *c*
nose [nouz] *n* näsa *c*
nosebleed ['nouzbli:d] *n* näsblod *nt*
nostril ['nɔstril] *n* näsborre *c*
nosy ['nouzi] *adj* colloquial nyfiken
not [nɔt] *adv* inte
notary ['noutəri] *n* juridiskt ombud
note [nout] *n* anteckning *c*; fotnot *c*; ton *c*; *v* anteckna;

observera, notera
notebook ['noutbuk] *n* anteckningsbok *c*
noted ['noutid] *adj* välkänd
notepaper ['nout,peipə] *n* brevpapper *nt*
nothing ['nʌθiŋ] *n* ingenting, intet *nt*
notice ['noutis] *v* *lägga märke till, uppmärksamma, märka; *se; *n* meddelande *nt*, uppsägning *c*; uppmärksamhet *c*
noticeable ['noutisəbəl] *adj* märkbar; anmärkningsvärd
notify ['noutifai] *v* meddela; underrätta
notion ['noufən] *n* aning *c*, begrepp *nt*
notorious [nou'tɔːriəs] *adj* beryktad
nought [nɔːt] *n* nolla *c*
noun [naun] *n* substantiv *nt*
nourishing ['nʌriʃiŋ] *adj* närande
novel ['nɔvəl] *n* roman *c*
novelist ['nɔvəlist] *n* romanförfattare *c*
November [nou'vembə] november
now [nau] *adv* nu; ~ **and then** då och då
nowadays ['nauədeiz] *adv* nuförtiden
nowhere ['nouwɛə] *adv* ingenstans

nozzle ['nɔzəl] *n* munstycke *nt*
nuance [nju:'ɑːs] *n* nyans *c*
nuclear ['nju:kliə] *adj* kärn-; ~ **energy** kärnkraft *c*
nucleus ['nju:kliəs] *n* kärna *c*
nude [nju:d] *adj* naken; *n* akt *c*
nuisance ['nju:səns] *n* besvär *nt*
numb [nʌm] *adj* utan känsel; domnad, förlamad
number ['nʌmbə] *n* nummer *nt*; tal *nt*, antal *nt*
numeral ['nju:mərəl] *n* räkneord *nt*
numerous ['nju:mərəs] *adj* talrik
nun [nʌn] *n* nunna *c*
nurse [nəːs] *n* sjuksköterska *c*; barnsköterska *c*; *v* vårda; amma
nursery ['nəːsəri] *n* barnkammare *c*; daghem *nt*; plantskola *c*
nut [nʌt] *n* nöt *c*; mutter *c*
nutcrackers ['nʌt,krækəz] *pl* nötknäppare *c*
nutmeg ['nʌtmeg] *n* muskotnöt *c*
nutritious [nju:'triʃəs] *adj* närande
nutshell ['nʌtʃel] *n* nötskal *nt*
nylon ['nailɔn] *n* nylon *nt*

O

oak [ouk] *n* ek *c*

oar [ɔː] *n* åra *c*

oasis [ou'eisis] *n* (pl oases) oas *c*

oath [ouθ] *n* ed *c*

oats [outs] *pl* havre *c*

obedience [ə'biːdiəns] *n* lydnad *c*

obedient [ə'biːdiənt] *adj* lydig

obey [ə'bei] *v* lyda

object¹ ['ɔbdʒikt] *n* objekt *nt*; föremål *nt*; syfte *nt*

object² [əb'dʒekt] *v* invända, protestera

objection [əb'dʒekʃən] *n* invändning *c*

objective [əb'dʒektiv] *adj* objektiv; *n* mål *nt*

obligatory [ə'bligətəri] *adj* obligatorisk

oblige [ə'blaidʒ] *v* förplikta; *be obliged to* *vara tvungen att; *måste

obliging [ə'blaidʒiŋ] *adj* tillmötesgående

oblong ['ɔblɔŋ] *adj* avlång, rektangulär; *n* rektangel *c*

obscene [əb'siːn] *adj* oanständig

obscure [əb'skjuə] *adj* dunkel, skum, oklar, mörk

observation [,ɔbzə'veiʃən] *n* iakttagelse *c*, observation *c*

observatory [əb'zəːvətri] *n* observatorium *nt*

observe [əb'zəːv] *v* observera, *iaktta

obsession [əb'seʃən] *n* besatthet *c*

obstacle ['ɔbstəkəl] *n* hinder *nt*

obstinate ['ɔbstinət] *adj* envis; hårdnackad

obtain [əb'tein] *v* *erhålla, skaffa sig

obtainable [əb'teinəbəl] *adj* anskaffbar

obvious ['ɔbviəs] *adj* tydlig

occasion [ə'keiʒən] *n* tillfälle *nt*; anledning *c*

occasionally [ə'keiʒənəli] *adv* då och då

occupant ['ɔkjupənt] *n* innehavare *c*

occupation [,ɔkju'peiʃən] *n* sysselsättning *c*; ockupation *c*

occupy ['ɔkjupai] *v* ockupera, *uppta, *besätta; **occupied** *adj* ockuperad, upptagen

occur [ə'kəː] *v* ske, hända, *förekomma

occurrence [ə'kʌrəns] *n* händelse *c*

ocean ['ouʃən] *n* världshav *nt*

October [ɔk'toubə] oktober

octopus ['ɔktəpəs] *n* bläckfisk *c*

oculist ['ɔkjulist] *n* ögonläkare *c*

odd [ɔd] *adj* underlig, konstig; udda

odour ['oudə] *n* lukt *c*

of [ɔv, əv] *prep* av

off [ɔf] *adv* av; iväg; *prep* från

offence [ə'fens] *n* förseelse *c*; kränkning *c*, anstöt *c*

offend [ə'fend] *v* såra, kränka; *förgå sig

offensive [ə'fensiv] *adj* offensiv; anstötlig, kränkande; *n* offensiv *c*

offer ['ɔfə] *v* *erbjuda; *bjuda; *n* erbjudande *nt*

office ['ɔfis] *n* kontor *nt*; ämbete *nt*; ~ **hours** kontorstid *c*

officer ['ɔfisə] *n* officer *c*

official [ə'fiʃəl] *adj* officiell

off-licence ['ɔf,laisəns] *n*, **liquor store** *nAm* systembolag *nt*

often ['ɔfən] *adv* ofta

oil [ɔil] *n* olja *c*; **fuel ~** brännolja *c*; ~ **filter** oljefilter *nt*; ~ **pressure** oljetryck *nt*

oil painting [,ɔil'peintiŋ] *n* oljemålning *c*

oil refinery ['ɔilri,fainəri] *n* oljeraffinaderi *nt*

oil well ['ɔilwel] *n* oljekälla *c*, oljefyndighet *c*

oily ['ɔili] *adj* oljig

ointment ['ɔintmənt] *n* salva *c*

okay! [,ou'kei] *int* fint!

old [ould] *adj* gammal; ~ **age** ålderdom *c*

old-fashioned [,ould'fæʃənd] *adj*

gammaldags, gammalmodig

olive ['ɔliv] *n* oliv *c*; ~ **oil** olivolja *c*

omelette ['ɔmlət] *n* omelett *c*

ominous ['ɔminəs] *adj* olycksbådande

omit [ə'mit] *v* utelämna

omnipotent [ɔm'nipətənt] *adj* allsmäktig

on [ɔn] *prep* på; vid

once [wʌns] *adv* en gång; **at ~** på en gång; **for ~** för en gångs skull; ~ **more** en gång till

oncoming ['ɔn,kʌmiŋ] *adj* förestående, mötande

one [wʌn] *num* en; *pron* man

oneself [wʌn'self] *pron* själv

onion ['ʌnjən] *n* lök *c*

only ['ounli] *adj* enda; *adv* endast, bara, blott; *conj* men

onwards ['ɔnwədz] *adv* framåt, vidare

onyx ['ɔniks] *n* onyx *c*

opal ['oupəl] *n* opal *c*

open ['oupən] *v* öppna; *adj* öppen

opener ['oupnə] *n* öppnare *c*

opening ['oupəniŋ] *n* öppning *c*

opera ['ɔpərə] *n* opera *c*; ~ **house** operahus *c*

operate ['ɔpəreit] *v* fungera; operera

operation [,ɔpə'reiʃən] *n* funktion *c*; operation *c*

operator ['ɔpəreitə] *n* telefonist *c*

opinion [ə'pinjən] *n* uppfattning *c*, åsikt *c*

opponent [ə'pounənt] n
motståndare c

opportunity [,ɔpə'tju:nəti] n
tillfälle nt

oppose [ə'pouz] v opponera
sig

opposite ['ɔpəzit] prep
mittemot; adj motstående,
motsatt

opposition [,ɔpə'ziʃən] n
opposition c

oppress [ə'pres] v förtrycka,
tynga

optician [ɔp'tiʃən] n optiker
c

optimism ['ɔptimizəm] n
optimism c

optimist ['ɔptimist] n
optimist c

optimistic [,ɔpti'mistik] adj
optimistisk

optional ['ɔpʃənəl] adj valfri

or [ɔ:] conj eller

oral ['ɔ:rəl] adj muntlig

orange ['ɔrindʒ] n apelsin c;
adj brandgul

orbit ['ɔ:bit] n omlopp nt

orchard ['ɔ:tʃəd] n
fruktträdgård c

orchestra ['ɔ:kistrə] n
orkester c; ~ seat Am
parkett c

order ['ɔ:də] v befalla;
beställa; n ordningsföljd c,
ordning c; befallning c,
order c; beställning c; in ~ i
ordning; in ~ to för att;
made to ~ gjord på
beställning; out of ~
funktionsoduglig; postal ~

postanvisning c

order form ['ɔ:dəfɔ:m] n
orderblankett c

ordinary ['ɔ:dənri] adj vanlig,
alldaglig

ore [ɔ:] n malm c

organ ['ɔ:gən] n organ nt;
orgel c

organic [ɔ:'gænik] adj
organisk

organization
[,ɔ:gənai'zeiʃən] n
organisation c

organize ['ɔ:gənaiz] v
organisera

Orient ['ɔ:riənt] n Orienten c

oriental [,ɔ:ri'entəl] adj
orientalisk

orientate ['ɔ:riənteit] v
orientera sig

origin ['ɔridʒin] n ursprung
nt; härstamning c, härkomst
c

original [ə'ridʒinəl] adj
ursprunglig, originell

originally [ə'ridʒinəli] adv
ursprungligen

ornament ['ɔ:nəmənt] n
utsmyckning c

ornamental [,ɔ:nə'mentəl]
adj prydnads-, dekorativ

orphan ['ɔ:fən] n föräldralöst
barn

orthodox ['ɔ:θədɔks] adj
ortodox

ostrich ['ɔstritʃ] n struts c

other ['ʌðə] adj annan

otherwise ['ʌðəwaiz] conj
annars; adv annorlunda

ought [ɔ:t] v bör

*ought to [ɔːt] **böra

ounce ['auns] n uns nt

our [auə] adj vår

ours ['auəz] pron vår

ourselves [auə'selvz] pron
oss; själva

out [aut] adv ute, ut; ~ **of**
utanför, från

outbreak ['autbreik] n
utbrott nt

outcome ['autkʌm] n följd c,
resultat nt

*outdo [,aut'duː] v överträffa

outdoors [,aut'dɔːz] adv
utomhus

outfit ['autfit] n utrustning c

outing ['autiŋ] n utflykt c

outline ['autlain] n ytterlinje
c; v teckna konturerna av,
skissera

outlook ['autluk] n utsikt c;
syn c

output ['autput] n
produktion c

outrage ['autreidʒ] n
illgärning c, våldsdåd nt

outside [,aut'said] adv
utomhus; prep utanför; n
utsida c

outsize ['autsaiz] n
extrastorlek c

outskirts ['autskəːts] pl
utkant c

outsource ['aut,sɔːs] v lägga
ut på entreprenad

outstanding [,aut'stændiŋ]
adj framstående,
framträdande, utestående

outward ['autwəd] adj yttre

outwards ['autwədz] adv

utåt

oval ['ouvəl] adj oval

oven ['ʌvən] n ugn c;
microwave ~ mikrovågsugn
c

over ['ouvə] prep över,
ovanför; adv över; adj över;
~ **there** där borta

overall ['ouvərɔːl] adj
sammanlagd

overalls ['ouvərɔːlz] pl
overall c

overcast ['ouvəkɑːst] adj
mulen

overcoat ['ouvəkout] n
överrock c

*overcome [,ouvə'kʌm] v
*övervinna

overdo [,ouvə'duː] v
överdriva

overdraft ['ouvədrɑːft] n
övertrassering c

overdraw [,ouvə'drɔː] v
övertrassera

overdue [,ouvə'djuː] adj
försenad; förfallen till
betalning

overgrown [,ouvə'groun] adj
igenvuxen

overhaul [,ouvə'hɔːl] v
undersöka, *genomgå;
*hinna ifatt

overhead [,ouvə'hed] adv
ovan

overlook [,ouvə'luk] v
*förbise

overnight [,ouvə'nait] adv
över natten

overseas [,ouvə'siːz] adj
över haven

pair

oversight ['ouvəsait] n
förbiseende nt; uppsikt c

*oversleep [,ouvə'sli:p] v
*försova sig

overstrung [,ouvə'strʌŋ] adj
överspänd

*overtake [,ouvə'teik] v köra
om; no overtaking
omkörning förbjuden

over-tired [,ouvə'taiəd] adj
uttröttad

overture ['ouvətʃə] n
ouvertyr c

overweight ['ouvəweit] n
övervikt c

overwhelm [,ouvə'welm] v
överväldiga

overwork [,ouvə'wə:k] v
överanstränga sig

owe [ou] v *vara skyldig; *ha
att tacka för; owing to med
anledning av

owl [aul] n uggla c

own [oun] v äga; adj egen

owner ['ounə] n ägare c,
innehavare c

ox [ɔks] n (pl oxen) oxe c

oxygen ['ɔksidʒən] n syre nt

oyster ['ɔistə] n ostron nt

ozone ['ouzoun] n ozon nt

P

pace [peis] n sätt att *gå; steg
nt; tempo nt

Pacific Ocean [pə'sifik
'ouʃən] Stilla havet

pacifism ['pæsifizəm] n
pacifism c

pacifist ['pæsifist] n pacifist
c; pacifistisk

pack [pæk] v packa; ~ up
packa in

package ['pækidʒ] n paket nt

packet ['pækit] n paket nt

packing ['pækiŋ] n packning
c, förpackning c

pact [pækt] n pakt c

pad [pæd] n dyna c;
anteckningsblock nt

paddle ['pædəl] n paddel c

padlock ['pædlɔk] n hänglås
nt

pagan ['peigən] adj hednisk;

n hedning c

page [peidʒ] n sida c

pail [peil] n ämbar nt

pain [pein] n smärta c; pains
möda c

painful ['peinfəl] adj
smärtsam

painkiller ['peinkilə] n
smärtstillande medel nt

painless ['peinləs] adj
smärtfri

paint [peint] n målarfärg c; v
måla

paintbox ['peintbɔks] n
färglåda c

paintbrush ['peintbrʌʃ] n
pensel c

painter ['peintə] n målare c

painting ['peintiŋ] n målning
c

pair [pɛə] n par nt

Pakistan [ˌpɑːkiˈstɑːn]
Pakistan
Pakistani [ˌpɑːkiˈstɑːni] adj
pakistansk; n pakistanier c
palace [ˈpæləs] n palats nt
pale [peil] adj blek; ljus-
palm [pɑːm] n palm c;
handflata c
palpable [ˈpælpəbəl] adj
kännbar, påtaglig
palpitation [ˌpælpiˈteiʃən] n
hjärtklappning c
pan [pæn] n panna c
pane [pein] n ruta c
panel [ˈpænəl] n panel c
panelling [ˈpænəliŋ] n panel
c
panic [ˈpænik] n panik c
pant [pænt] v flämta
panties [ˈpæntiz] pl trosor pl
pants [pænts] pl underbyxor
pl; plAm byxor pl
pant suit [ˈpæntsuːt] n
byxdräkt c
panty hose [ˈpæntihouz] n
strumpbyxor pl
paper [ˈpeipə] n papper nt;
tidning c; pappers-; carbon
~ karbonpapper nt; ~ bag
papperspåse c; ~ napkin
pappersservett c; typing ~
skrivmaskinspapper nt;
wrapping ~ omslagspapper
nt
paperback [ˈpeipəbæk] n
pocketbok c
paper knife [ˈpeipənaif] n
papperskniv c
parade [pəˈreid] n parad c
paradise [ˈpærədais] n

paradis nt
paraffin [ˈpærəfin] n fotogen
c
paragraph [ˈpærəɡrɑːf] n
paragraf c
parakeet [ˈpærəkiːt] n
papegoja c
paralise [ˈpærəlaiz] v
paralysera
parallel [ˈpærəlel] adj
jämlöpande, parallell; n
parallell c
paralyse [ˈpærəlaiz] v
paralysera
parcel [ˈpɑːsəl] n paket nt
pardon [ˈpɑːdən] n förlåtelse
c; benådning c
parent [ˈpɛərənt] n förälder c
parents [ˈpɛərənts] pl
föräldrar pl
parents-in-law
[ˈpɛərəntsinlɔː] pl
svärföräldrar pl
parish [ˈpæriʃ] n församling c
park [pɑːk] n park c; v
parkera
parking [ˈpɑːkiŋ] n parkering
c; no ~ parkering förbjuden;
~ fee parkeringsavgift c; ~
light parkeringsljus nt; ~ lot
Am parkeringsplats c; ~
meter parkeringsmätare c; ~
zone parkeringszon c
parliament [ˈpɑːləmənt] n
riksdag c, parlament nt
parliamentary
[ˌpɑːləˈmentəri] adj
parlamentarisk
parrot [ˈpærət] n papegoja c
parsley [ˈpɑːsli] n persilja c

319

pawn

parson ['pɑ:sən] n präst c
parsonage ['pɑ:sənidʒ] n
prästgård c
part [pɑ:t] n del c; stycke nt; v
skilja; spare ~ reservdel c
partial ['pɑ:ʃəl] adj
ofullständig; partisk
participant [pɑ:'tisipənt] n
deltagare c
participate [pɑ:'tisipeit] v
*delta
particular [pə'tikjulə] adj
särskild; noga; in ~ särskilt
partition [pɑ:'tiʃən] n
skiljevägg c; delning c, del c
partly ['pɑ:tli] adv delvis
partner ['pɑ:tnə] n partner c;
kompanjon c
partridge ['pɑ:tridʒ] n
rapphöna c
party ['pɑ:ti] n parti nt; kalas
nt, fest c; sällskap nt
pass [pɑ:s] v *förflyta,
passera; *ge; *bli godkänd;
vAm köra om; n bergspass
nt; pass nt; no passing Am
omkörning förbjuden; ~ by
*gå förbi; ~ through *gå
igenom
passage ['pæsidʒ] n passage
c; överfart c; avsnitt nt;
genomresa c
passenger ['pæsəndʒə] n
passagerare c; ~ car Am
järnvägsvagn c
passer-by [,pɑ:sə'bai] n
förbipasserande c
passion ['pæʃən] n lidelse c,
passion c; raseri nt
passionate ['pæʃənət] adj

lidelsefull
passive ['pæsiv] adj passiv
passport ['pɑ:spɔ:t] n pass
nt; ~ control passkontroll c;
~ photograph passfoto nt
password ['pɑ:swə:d] n
lösenord nt
past [pɑ:st] n det förflutna;
adj förfluten, förra; prep
förbi
paste [peist] n pasta c; v
klistra
pastime ['pɑ:staim] n
tidsfördriv nt
pastry ['peistri] n bakelser
pl; ~ shop konditori nt
pasture ['pɑ:stʃə] n
betesmark c
pasty ['peisti] n pirog c
patch [pætʃ] v lappa
patent ['peitənt] n patent nt,
patentbrev nt
path [pɑ:θ] n stig c
patience ['peiʃəns] n
tålamod nt
patient ['peiʃənt] adj
tålmodig; n patient c
patriot ['peitriət] n patriot c
patrol [pə'troul] n patrull c; v
patrullera; övervaka
pattern ['pætən] n mönster c
pause [pɔ:z] n paus c; v
pausa
pave [peiv] v *stenlägga
pavement ['peivmənt] n
trottoar c; gatubeläggning c
pavilion [pə'viljən] n
paviljong c
paw [pɔ:] n tass c
pawn [pɔ:n] v *pantsätta; n

schackbonde
pawnbroker ['pɔːn,brəukə] n
pantlånare c
pay [pei] n avlöning c, lön c
pay [pei] v betala; löna sig; ~
attention to
uppmärksamma; **paying**
lönande; ~ **off** slutbetala; ~
on account avbetala
pay desk ['peidesk] n kassa c
payee [pei'iː] n
betalningsmottagare c
payment ['peimənt] n
betalning c
pea [piː] n ärta c
peace [piːs] n fred c
peaceful ['piːsfəl] adj fridfull
peach [piːtʃ] n persika c
peacock ['piːkɔk] n påfågel c
peak [piːk] n topp c;
höjdpunkt c; ~ **hour**
rusningstid c; ~ **season**
högsäsong c
peanut ['piːnʌt] n jordnöt c
pear [pɛə] n päron nt
pearl [pəːl] n pärla c
peasant ['pezənt] n bonde c
pebble ['pebəl] n strandsten c
peculiar [pi'kjuːljə] adj
egendomlig, säregen
peculiarity [pi,kjuːli'ærəti] n
egendomlighet c
pedal ['pedəl] n pedal c
pedestrian [pi'destriən] n
fotgängare c; **no
pedestrians** förbjudet för
fotgängare; ~ **crossing**
övergångsställe för
fotgängare
peel [piːl] v skala; n skal nt

peep [piːp] v kika
peg [peg] n pinne c, hängare
c, sprint c
pelican ['pelikən] n pelikan c
pelvis ['pelvis] n bäcken nt
pen [pen] n penna c
penalty ['penəlti] n böter pl;
straff nt; ~ **kick** straffspark c
pencil ['pensəl] n
blyertspenna c
pencil sharpener
['pensəl,ʃɑːpnə] n
pennvässare c
pendant ['pendənt] n
hängsmycke nt
penetrate ['penitreit] v
genomtränga
penguin ['peŋgwin] n
pingvin c
penicillin [,peni'silin] n
penicillin nt
peninsula [pə'ninsjulə] n
halvö c
penknife ['pennaif] n (pl
-knives) pennkniv c
penny ['peni] n penny c
pension[1] ['pɑːsiɔ̃ː] n
pensionat nt
pension[2] ['penʃən] n
pension c
Pentecost ['pentikəst] n
pingst c
people ['piːpəl] pl folk pl; n
folk nt
pepper ['pepə] n peppar c
peppermint ['pepəmint] n
pepparmint nt
per [pəː] prep per; ~ **cent**
procent c
perceive [pə'siːv] v

*förnimma

percentage [pə'sentidʒ] *n*
procent *c*

perceptible [pə'septibəl] *adj*
märkbar

perception [pə'sepʃən] *n*
förnimmelse *c*

perch [pɜ:tʃ] (pl ~) abborre *c*

percolator ['pɜ:kəleitə] *n*
kaffebryggare *c*

perfect ['pɜ:fikt] *adj* perfekt,
fullkomlig

perfection [pə'fekʃən] *n*
fullkomlighet *c*

perform [pə'fɔ:m] *v* utföra

performance [pə'fɔ:məns] *n*
föreställning *c*

perfume ['pɜ:fju:m] *n*
parfym *c*

perhaps [pə'hæps] *adv*
kanske; kanhända

peril ['peril] *n* fara *c*

perilous ['periləs] *adj*
livsfarlig

period ['piəriəd] *n* period *c*;
punkt *c*

periodical [,piəri'ɔdikəl] *n*
tidskrift *c*; *adj* periodisk

perish ['periʃ] *v* *omkomma

perishable ['periʃəbəl] *adj*
ömtålig

perjury ['pɜ:dʒəri] *n* mened *c*

permanent ['pɜ:mənənt] *adj*
varaktig, beständig, ständig;
fast, stadigvarande; ~ **wave**
permanent *c*

permission [pə'miʃən] *n*
tillåtelse *c*, tillstånd *nt*; lov
nt, tillståndsbevis *c*

permit[1] [pə'mit] *v* *tillåta

permit[2] ['pɜ:mit] *n*
tillståndsbevis *nt*, tillstånd *nt*

peroxide [pə'rɔksaid] *n*
vätesuperoxid *c*

perpendicular
[,pɜ:pən'dikjulə] *adj* lodrät

Persia ['pɜ:ʃə] Persien

Persian ['pɜ:ʃən] *adj* persisk;
n perser *c*

person ['pɜ:sən] *n* person *c*;
per ~ per person

personal ['pɜ:sənəl] *adj*
personlig; **personal
identification number** *n*
PIN *c*

personality [,pɜ:sə'næləti] *n*
personlighet *c*

personnel [,pɜ:sə'nel] *n*
personal *c*

perspective [pə'spektiv] *n*
perspektiv *nt*

perspiration [,pɜ:spə'reiʃən]
n transpiration *c*, svettning
c, svett *c*

perspire [pə'spaiə] *v*
transpirera, svettas

persuade [pə'sweid] *v*
övertala; övertyga

persuasion [pə'sweiʒən] *n*
övertygelse *c*

pessimism ['pesimizəm] *n*
pessimism *c*

pessimist ['pesimist] *n*
pessimist *c*

pessimistic [,pesi'mistik]
adj pessimistisk

pet [pet] *n* sällskapsdjur *nt*;
kelgris *c*; älsklings-

petal ['petəl] *n* kronblad *nt*

petition [pi'tiʃən] *n* petition *c*

petrol ['petrəl] *n* bensin *c*; ~ pump bensinpump *c*; ~ station bensinmack *c*; ~ tank bensintank *c*; unleaded ~ blyfri bensin *c*

petroleum [pi'trouliəm] *n* råolja *c*

petty ['peti] *adj* oväsentlig, obetydlig, liten; ~ cash kontorskassa *c*

pewter ['pju:tə] *n* tennlegering *c*

phantom ['fæntəm] *n* fantom *c*

pharmacist ['fɑ:məsist] *n* apotekare *c*

pharmacology [,fɑ:mə'kɔlədʒi] *n* farmakologi *c*

pharmacy ['fɑ:məsi] *n* apotek *nt*

phase [feiz] *n* fas *c*

pheasant ['fezənt] *n* fasan *c*

Philippine ['filipain] *adj* filippinsk

Philippines ['filipi:nz] *pl* Filippinerna

philosopher [fi'lɔsəfə] *n* filosof *c*

philosophy [fi'lɔsəfi] *n* filosofi *c*

phone [foun] *n* telefon *c*; *v* telefonera, ringa upp

phone card ['foun,kɑ:d] *n* telefonkort *nt*

phonetic [fə'netik] *adj* fonetisk

photo ['foutou] *n* (pl ~s) foto *nt*

photocopy ['fəutəukɔpi] *n*

fotokopia *c*; *v* fotokopiera

photograph ['foutəgrɑ:f] *n* fotografi *nt*; *v* fotografera

photographer [fə'tɔgrəfə] *n* fotograf *c*

photography [fə'tɔgrəfi] *n* fotografering *c*

photo message ['foutou,mesədʒ] *n* fotomeddelande *c*

phrase [freiz] *n* fras *c*

phrase book ['freizbuk] *n* parlör *c*

physical ['fizikəl] *adj* fysisk

physician [fi'ziʃən] *n* läkare *c*

physicist ['fizisist] *n* fysiker *c*

physics ['fiziks] *n* fysik *c*, naturvetenskap *c*

physiology [,fizi'ɔlədʒi] *n* fysiologi *c*

pianist ['pi:ənist] *n* pianist *c*

piano [pi'ænou] *n* piano *nt*; grand ~ flygel *c*

pick [pik] *v* plocka; *välja; n* val *nt*; ~ up plocka upp; hämta; pick-up van skåpvagn *c*

pickles ['pikəlz] *pl* pickels *pl*

picnic ['piknik] *n* picknick *c*; *v* picknicka

picture ['piktʃə] *n* tavla *c*; film *c*, illustration *c*; bild *c*; ~ postcard vykort *nt*; pictures bio *c*

picturesque [,piktʃə'resk] *adj* pittoresk

piece [pi:s] *n* bit *c*, stycke *c*

pier [piə] *n* pir *c*

pierce [piəs] v *göra hål, genomborra

pig [pig] n gris c

pigeon ['pidʒən] n duva c

piggy bank ['pigibæŋk] n spargris c

pig-headed [,pig'hedid] adj tjurskallig

piglet ['piglət] n spädgris c

pigskin ['pigskin] n svinläder nt

pike [paik] (pl ~) gädda c

pile [pail] n hög c; v stapla; **piles** pl hemorrojder pl

pilgrim ['pilgrim] n pilgrim c

pilgrimage ['pilgrimidʒ] n pilgrimsfärd c

pill [pil] n piller nt

pillar ['pilə] n pelare c, stolpe c

pillarbox ['piləbɔks] n brevlåda c

pillow ['pilou] n huvudkudde c, kudde c

pillowcase ['piloukeis] n örngott nt

pilot ['pailət] n pilot c; lots c

pimple ['pimpəl] n finne c

pin [pin] n knappnål c; v fästa med nål; **bobby** ~ Am hårklämma c

PIN [pin] n PIN c

pincers ['pinsəz] pl kniptång c

pinch [pintʃ] v *nypa

pine [pain] n tall c; furu c

pineapple ['pai,næpəl] n ananas c

ping-pong ['piŋpɔŋ] n bordtennis c

pink [piŋk] adj skär

pioneer [,paiə'niə] n pionjär c

pious ['paiəs] adj from

pip [pip] n kärna c

pipe [paip] n pipa c; rör nt; ~ **cleaner** piprensare c; ~ **tobacco** piptobak c

pirate ['paiərət] n sjörövare c

pistol ['pistəl] n pistol c

piston ['pistən] n kolv c; ~ **ring** kolvring c

pit [pit] n grop c; gruva c

pitcher ['pitʃə] n krus nt

pity ['piti] n medlidande nt; v *ha medlidande med, beklaga; **what a pity!** så synd!

placard ['plækɑːd] n plakat nt

place [pleis] n ställe nt; v placera, *sätta; ~ **of birth** födelseort c; ***take** ~ äga rum

plague [pleig] n plåga c

plaice [pleis] (pl ~) rödspätta c

plain [plein] adj tydlig; enkel, vanlig; n slätt c

plan [plæn] n plan c; v planera

plane [plein] adj plan; n flygplan nt; ~ **crash** flygolycka c

planet ['plænit] n planet c

planetarium [,plæni'teəriəm] n planetarium c

plank [plæŋk] n planka c

plant [plɑːnt] n planta c; fabrik c; v plantera

plantation [plæn'teiʃən] n
plantage c

plaster ['plɑːstə] n rappning
c, gips c; plåster nt

plastic ['plæstik] adj plast-; n
plast c

plate [pleit] n tallrik c; platta
c

plateau ['plætou] n (pl ~x, ~s)
platå c

platform ['plætfɔːm] n
plattform c; ~ **ticket**
perrongbiljett c

platinum ['plætinəm] n
platina c

play [plei] v leka; spela; n lek
c; pjäs c; **one-act** ~ enaktare
c; ~ **truant** skolka

player [pleiə] n spelare c

playground ['pleigraund] n
lekplats c

playing card ['pleiiŋkɑːd] n
spelkort c

playwright ['pleirait] n
skådespelsförfattare c

plea [pliː] n svaromål nt;
anhållan c; ursäkt c

plead [pliːd] v plädera

pleasant ['plezənt] adj
angenäm, trevlig

please [pliːz] var god; v
*glädja; **pleased** nöjd;
pleasing angenäm

pleasure ['pleʒə] n nöje nt,
glädje c

plentiful ['plentifəl] adj riklig

plenty ['plenti] n riklighet c;
överflöd nt

pliers [plaiəz] pl tång c

plimsolls ['plimsəlz] pl
gymnastikskor pl

plot [plɔt] n komplott c,
sammansvärjning c;
handling c; jordlott c

plough [plau] n plog c; v
plöja

plucky ['plʌki] adj käck

plug [plʌg] n plugg c,
stickkontakt c; ~ **in** *sticka
in, *ansluta

plum [plʌm] n plommon nt

plumber ['plʌmə] n
rörmokare c

plump [plʌmp] adj knubbig

plural ['pluərəl] n plural c

plus [plʌs] prep plus

pneumatic [njuː'mætik] adj
luft-

pneumonia [njuː'mouniə] n
lunginflammation c

poach [poutʃ] v *tjuvskjuta

pocket ['pɔkit] n ficka c

pocketbook ['pɔkitbuk] n
plånbok c; anteckningsbok
c

pocketknife ['pɔkitnaif] n (pl
-knives) fickkniv c

poem ['pouim] n dikt c

poet ['pouit] n skald c

poetry ['pouitri] n poesi c

point [pɔint] n punkt c; spets
c; v peka; ~ **of view**
synpunkt c; ~ **out** visa,
utpeka

pointed ['pɔintid] adj spetsig

poison ['pɔizən] n gift nt; v
förgifta

poisonous ['pɔizənəs] adj
giftig

Poland ['poulənd] Polen

pole [poul] *n* påle *c*; pol *c*

police [pə'li:s] *pl* polis *c*

policeman [pə'li:smən] *n* (pl -men) poliskonstapel *c*, polis *c*

police station [pə'li:s,steiʃən] *n* polisstation *c*

policy ['polisi] *n* politik *c*; försäkringsbrev *nt*

polio ['pouliou] *n* polio *c*, barnförlamning *c*

Polish ['pouliʃ] *adj* polsk

polish ['poliʃ] *v* polera

polite [pə'lait] *adj* artig

political [pə'litikəl] *adj* politisk

politician [,poli'tiʃən] *n* politiker *c*

politics ['politiks] *n* politik *c*

poll [poul] *n* röstning *c*; **go to the polls** gå till val

pollute [pə'lu:t] *v* förorena

pollution [pə'lu:ʃən] *n* förorening *c*

pond [pond] *n* damm *c*

pony ['pouni] *n* ponny *c*

pool [pu:l] *n* bassäng *c*; ~ **attendant** badvakt *c*

poor [puə] *adj* fattig; usel

pope [poup] *n* påve *c*

pop music [pop 'mju:zik] popmusik *c*

poppy ['popi] *n* vallmo *c*

popular ['popjulə] *adj* populär; folk-

population [,popju'leiʃən] *n* befolkning *c*

populous ['popjuləs] *adj* folkrik

porcelain ['po:səlin] *n* porslin *nt*

porcupine ['po:kjupain] *n* piggsvin *nt*

pork [po:k] *n* griskött *nt*

port [po:t] *n* hamn *c*; babord

portable ['po:təbəl] *adj* bärbar

porter ['po:tə] *n* bärare *c*; dörrvaktmästare *c*

porthole ['po:thoul] *n* hyttventil *c*

portion ['po:ʃən] *n* portion *c*

portrait ['po:trit] *n* porträtt *nt*

Portugal ['po:tjugəl] Portugal

Portuguese [,po:tju'gi:z] *adj* portugisisk; *n* portugis *c*

posh [poʃ] *adj* colloquial stilig

position [pə'ziʃən] *n* position *c*; läge *nt*; inställning *c*; ställning *c*

positive ['pozətiv] *adj* positiv

possess [pə'zes] *v* äga; **possessed** *adj* besatt

possession [pə'zeʃən] *n* ägo, innehav *nt*; **possessions** ägodelar *pl*

possibility [,posə'biləti] *n* möjlighet *c*

possible ['posəbəl] *adj* möjlig; eventuell

post [poust] *n* stolpe *c*; tjänst *c*; post *c*; *v* posta; **post-office** postkontor *nt*

postage ['poustidʒ] *n* porto *nt*; ~ **paid** portofri; ~ **stamp** frimärke *c*

postcard ['poustkɑ:d] *n*

brevkort *nt*; vykort *nt*

poster ['pousta] *n* affisch *c*

poste restante [poust
re'stɑ:t] poste restante

postman ['poustmən] *n* (pl
-men) brevbärare *c*

post-paid [,poust'peid] *adj*
franko

postpone [pə'spoun] *v*
*uppskjuta

pot [pɔt] *n* gryta *c*

potato [pə'teitou] *n* (pl ~es)
potatis *c*

pottery ['pɔtəri] *n* keramik *c*;
lergods *nt*

pouch [pautʃ] *n* pung *c*

poulterer ['poultərə] *n*
vilthandlare *c*

poultry ['poultri] *n* fjäderfä
nt

pound [paund] *n* pund *nt*

pour [pɔ:] *v* hälla

poverty ['pɔvəti] *n* fattigdom
c

powder ['paudə] *n* puder *nt*;
~ **compact** puderdosa *c*; **talc**
~ talk *c*

powder room ['paudəru:m]
n damtoalett *c*

power [pauə] *n* styrka *c*, kraft
c; energi *c*; makt *c*

powerful ['pauəfəl] *adj*
mäktig; stark

powerless ['pauələs] *adj*
maktlös

power station
['pauə,steiʃən] *n* kraftverk
nt

practical ['præktikəl] *adj*
praktisk

practically ['præktikli] *adv*
nästan

practice ['præktis] *n*
utövande *nt*, praktik *c*

practise ['præktis] *v*
praktisera; öva sig

praise [preiz] *v* berömma; *n*
beröm *nt*

pram [præm] *n* barnvagn *c*

prawn [prɔ:n] *n* räka *c*

pray [prei] *v* *bedja

prayer [prɛə] *n* bön *c*

preach [pri:tʃ] *v* predika

precarious [pri'kɛəriəs] *adj*
vansklig

precaution [pri'kɔ:ʃən] *n*
försiktighet *c*;
försiktighetsåtgärd *c*

precede [pri'si:d] *v* *föregå

preceding [pri'si:diŋ] *adj*
föregående

precious ['preʃəs] *adj* dyrbar

precipice ['presipis] *n* stup *nt*

precipitation [pri,sipi'teiʃən]
n nederbörd *c*

precise [pri'sais] *adj* precis,
noga; noggrann

predecessor ['pri:disesə] *n*
föregångare *c*

predict [pri'dikt] *v* förutspå

prefer [pri'fə:] *v* *föredra

preferable ['prefərəbəl] *adj*
att föredra

preference ['prefərəns] *n*
förkärlek *c*

prefix ['pri:fiks] *n* förstavelse
c

pregnant ['pregnənt] *adj*
havande, gravid

prejudice ['predʒədis] *n*

fördom c

preliminary [pri'liminəri] adj
inledande; preliminär

premature ['premətʃuə] adj
förhastad, förtidig

premier ['premjə] n
premiärminister c

premises ['premisiz] pl
fastighet c

premium ['pri:miəm] n
försäkringspremie c;
belöning c

prepaid [,pri:'peid] adj
betald i förskott

preparation [,prepə'reiʃən] n
förberedelse c

prepare [pri'pεə] v
förbereda; *göra i ordning

prepared [pri'pεəd] adj
beredd

preposition [,prepə'ziʃən] n
preposition c

prescribe [pri'skraib] v
ordinera

prescription [pri'skripʃən] n
recept nt

presence ['prezəns] n
närvaro c

present[1] ['prezənt] n gåva c,
present c; nutid c; adj
nuvarande; närvarande

present[2] [pri'zent] v
presentera; *framlägga

presently ['prezəntli] adv
snart, strax

preservation [,prezə'veiʃən]
n bevarande nt,
konservering c

preserve [pri'zə:v] v bevara;
konservera

president ['prezidənt] n
president c; ordförande c

press [pres] n trängsel c,
press c; v trycka; pressa; ~
conference presskonferens
c

pressing ['presiŋ] adj
brådskande, trängande

pressure ['preʃə] n tryck nt;
påtryckning c; **atmospheric**
~ lufttryck nt

pressure cooker
['preʃə,kukə] n tryckkokare
c

prestige [pre'sti:ʒ] n prestige
c

presumable [pri'zju:məbəl]
adj trolig

presumptuous
[pri'zʌmpʃəs] adj
övermodig; anspråksfull

pretence [pri'tens] n
förevändning c

pretend [pri'tend] v låtsa,
simulera

pretext ['pri:tekst] n
svepskäl c

pretty ['priti] adj söt, vacker;
adv ganska, tämligen

prevent [pri'vent] v
förhindra; förebygga

preventive [pri'ventiv] adj
förebyggande

preview ['pri:vju:] n
förhandsvisning c

previous ['pri:viəs] adj
föregående, tidigare

price [prais] n pris nt; v
*prissätta

priceless ['praisləs] adj

price list   328

ovärderlig
price list ['prais,list] *n*
prislista *c*
prick [prik] *v* *sticka
pride [praid] *n* stolthet *c*
priest [pri:st] *n* katolsk präst
primary ['praiməri] *adj*
primär; huvudsaklig;
elementär
prince [prins] *n* prins *c*
princess [prin'ses] *n*
prinsessa *c*
principal ['prinsəpəl] *adj*
huvud-; *n* rektor *c*
principle ['prinsəpəl] *n*
princip *c*, grundsats *c*
print [print] *v* trycka; *n*
avtryck *nt*; tryck *nt*; **printed
matter** trycksak *c*
prior [praiə] *adj* föregående
priority [prai'ɔrəti] *n*
företräde *nt*, prioritet *c*
prison ['prizən] *n* fängelse *nt*
prisoner ['prizənə] *n* intern *c*,
fånge *c*; ~ **of war** krigsfånge
c
privacy ['praivəsi] *n*
avskildhet *c*, privatliv *nt*
private ['praivit] *adj* privat;
personlig
privilege ['privilidʒ] *n*
privilegium *c*
prize [praiz] *n* pris *nt*;
belöning *c*
probable ['prɔbəbəl] *adj*
sannolik, trolig
probably ['prɔbəbli] *adv*
sannolikt
problem ['prɔbləm] *n*
problem *nt*; spörsmål *nt*

pro-choice ['prou'tʃɔis] *adj*
pro-choice
procedure [prə'si:dʒə] *n*
procedur *c*
proceed [prə'si:d] *v*
*fortsätta; *gå tillväga
process ['prouses] *n* process
c, förlopp *c*
procession [prə'seʃən] *n*
procession *c*
proclaim [prə'kleim] *v*
*kungöra, utropa
produce[1] [prə'dju:s] *v*
framställa
produce[2] ['prɔdju:s] *n*
produkt *c*
producer [prə'dju:sə] *n*
producent *c*
product ['prɔdʌkt] *n* produkt
c
production [prə'dʌkʃən] *n*
produktion *c*
profession [prə'feʃən] *n*
yrke *nt*
professional [prə'feʃənəl]
adj yrkes-, yrkesskicklig
professor [prə'fesə] *n*
professor *c*
profit ['prɔfit] *n* vinst *c*,
behållning *c*; nytta *c*; *v* *ha
nytta; *dra fördel
profitable ['prɔfitəbəl] *adj*
vinstbringande
profound [prə'faund] *adj*
djup, djupsinnig
programme ['prougræm] *n*
program *nt*
progress[1] ['prougres] *n*
framsteg *nt*
progress[2] [prə'gres] *v* *göra

framsteg
progressive [prə'gresiv] *adj*
framstegsvänlig, progressiv;
tilltagande
prohibit [prə'hibit] *v*
*förbjuda
prohibition [,proui'biʃən] *n*
förbud *nt*
prohibitive [prə'hibitiv] *adj*
oöverkomlig
project ['prɔdʒekt] *n* projekt
nt, plan *c*
pro-life ['prou‿'laif] *adj* pro-
-life
promenade [,prɔmə'nɑ:d] *n*
promenad *c*
promise ['prɔmis] *n* löfte *nt*;
v lova
promote [prə'mout] *v*
befordra, främja
promotion [prə'mouʃən] *n*
befordran *c*
prompt [prɔmpt] *adj*
omgående
pronoun ['prounaun] *n*
pronomen *nt*
pronounce [prə'nauns] *v*
uttala
pronunciation
[,prənʌnsi'eiʃən] *n* uttal *nt*
proof [pru:f] *n* bevis *nt*;
provtryck *nt*
propaganda [,prɔpə'gændə]
n propaganda *c*
propel [prə'pel] *v* *driva
framåt
propeller [prə'pelə] *n*
propeller *c*
proper ['prɔpə] *adj* passande;
riktig, lämplig, anständig,

tillbörlig
property ['prɔpəti] *n*
egendom *c*, ägodelar *pl*;
egenskap *c*
prophet ['prɔfit] *n* profet *c*
proportion [prə'pɔ:ʃən] *n*
proportion *c*
proportional [prə'pɔ:ʃənəl]
adj proportionell
proposal [prə'pouzəl] *n*
förslag *nt*
propose [prə'pouz] *v*
*föreslå
proposition [,prɔpə'ziʃən] *n*
förslag *nt*
proprietor [prə'praiətə] *n*
ägare *c*
prospect ['prɔspekt] *n* utsikt
c
prospectus [prə'spektəs] *n*
prospekt *nt*
prosperity [prə'sperəti] *n*
framgång *c*, välstånd *nt*;
välgång *c*
prosperous ['prɔspərəs] *adj*
blomstrande, framgångsrik
prostitute ['prɔstitju:t] *n*
prostituerad *c*
protect [prə'tekt] *v* skydda
protection [prə'tekʃən] *n*
skydd *nt*
protein ['prouti:n] *n* protein
nt
protest[1] ['proutest] *n* protest
c
protest[2] [prə'test] *v*
protestera
Protestant ['prɔtistənt] *adj*
protestantisk
proud [praud] *adj* stolt;

högmodig
prove [pruːv] *v* bevisa; visa sig vara
proverb ['prɔvəːb] *n* ordspråk *nt*
provide [prə'vaid] *v* *förse, skaffa; **provided that** förutsatt att
province ['prɔvins] *n* län *nt*; landskap *nt*
provincial [prə'vinʃəl] *adj* provinsiell
provisional [prə'viʒənəl] *adj* provisorisk
provisions [prə'viʒənz] *pl* proviant *c*
prune [pruːn] *n* katrinplommon *nt*
psychiatrist [sai'kaiətrist] *n* psykiater *c*
psychic ['saikik] *adj* psykisk
psychoanalyst [ˌsaikou'ænəlist] *n* psykoanalytiker *c*
psychological [ˌsaikɔ'lɔdʒikəl] *adj* psykologisk
psychologist [sai'kɔlədʒist] *n* psykolog *c*
psychology [sai'kɔlədʒi] *n* psykologi *c*
public ['pʌblik] *adj* offentlig; allmän; *n* publik *c*; ~ **garden** offentlig park; ~ **house** pub *c*
publication [ˌpʌbli'keiʃən] *n* offentliggörande *nt*; publikation *c*
publicity [pʌ'blisəti] *n* publicitet *c*

publish ['pʌbliʃ] *v* *offentliggöra, *ge ut, publicera
publisher ['pʌbliʃə] *n* förläggare *c*
puddle ['pʌdəl] *n* pöl *c*
pull [pul] *v* *dra; ~ **out** *ta fram, *dra upp, *avgå; ~ **up** stanna
pulley ['puli] *n* (pl ~s) block *nt*
Pullman ['pulmən] *n* sovvagn *c*
pullover ['puˌlouvə] *n* pullover *c*
pulpit ['pulpit] *n* predikstol *c*, talarstol *c*
pulse [pʌls] *n* puls *c*
pump [pʌmp] *n* pump *c*; *v* pumpa
pun [pʌn] *n* ordlek *c*
punch [pʌntʃ] *v* *slå; *n* knytnävsslag *nt*
punctual ['pʌŋktʃuəl] *adj* punktlig
puncture ['pʌŋktʃə] *n* punktering *c*
punctured ['pʌŋktʃəd] *adj* punkterad
punish ['pʌniʃ] *v* straffa
punishment ['pʌniʃmənt] *n* straff *nt*
pupil ['pjuːpəl] *n* elev *c*
puppet-show ['pʌpitʃou] *n* dockteater *c*
purchase ['pəːtʃəs] *v* köpa; *n* köp *nt*, uppköp *nt*; ~ **price** köpesumma *c*
purchaser ['pəːtʃəsə] *n* köpare *c*

pure [pjuə] *adj* ren
purple ['pə:pəl] *adj* purpur
purpose ['pə:pəs] *n* ändamål
nt, avsikt *c*, syfte *nt*; on ~
med vilja
purse [pə:s] *n* portmonnä *c*,
kassa *c*
pursue [pə'sju:] *v* förfölja;
eftersträva
pus [pʌs] *n* var *nt*
push [puʃ] *n* knuff *c*; *v*
*skjuta; knuffa, *driva på
push button ['puʃ,bʌtən] *n*

knapp *c*, strömbrytare *c*
*put [put] *v* *lägga, ställa,
placera; stoppa; ~ away
ställa på plats; ~ off
*uppskjuta; ~ on klä på sig;
~ out släcka
puzzle ['pʌzəl] *n* pussel *nt*;
huvudbry *nt*; *v* förbrylla;
jigsaw ~ pussel *nt*
puzzling ['pʌzliŋ] *adj*
förbryllande
pyjamas [pə'dʒɑ:məz] *pl*
pyjamas *c*

Q

quack [kwæk] *n* charlatan *c*,
kvacksalvare *c*
quail [kweil] *n* (pl ~, ~s)
vaktel *c*
quaint [kweint] *adj*
egendomlig; gammaldags
qualification
[,kwɔlifi'keiʃən] *n*
kvalifikation *c*;
inskränkning *c*, förbehåll *nt*
qualified ['kwɔlifaid] *adj*
kvalificerad; kompetent
qualify ['kwɔlifai] *v*
kvalificera sig
quality ['kwɔləti] *n* kvalitet *c*;
egenskap *c*
quantity ['kwɔntəti] *n*
kvantitet *c*; antal *nt*
quarantine ['kwɔrənti:n] *n*
karantän *c*
quarrel ['kwɔrəl] *v* kivas,
gräla; *n* gräl *nt*, kiv *nt*
quarry ['kwɔri] *n* stenbrott *nt*

quarter ['kwɔ:tə] *n* kvart *c*;
kvartal *nt*; kvarter *nt*; ~ of
an hour kvart *c*
quarterly ['kwɔ:təli] *adj*
kvartals-
quay [ki:] *n* kaj *c*
queen [kwi:n] *n* drottning *c*
queer [kwiə] *adj* underlig,
konstig; besynnerlig
query ['kwiəri] *n* förfrågan *c*;
v betvivla
question ['kwestʃən] *n* fråga
c; problem *nt*, spörsmål *nt*; *v*
fråga ut; ifrågasätta; ~ mark
frågetecken *nt*
queue [kju:] *n* kö *c*; *v* köa
quick [kwik] *adj* kvick
quick-tempered
[,kwik'tempəd] *adj* lättretlig
quiet ['kwaiət] *adj* stillsam,
stilla, lugn; *n* ro *c*, stillhet *c*
quilt [kwilt] *n* täcke *nt*
quit [kwit] *v* upphöra, *ge

upp
quite [kwait] *adv* fullkomligt, helt; någorlunda, ganska, alldeles
quiz [kwiz] *n* (pl ~zes) frågesport *c*

quota ['kwoutə] *n* kvot *c*
quotation [kwou'teiʃən] *n* citat *nt*; ~ **marks** citationstecken *pl*
quote [kwout] *v* citera

R

rabbit ['ræbit] *n* kanin *c*
rabies ['reibiz] *n* rabies *c*
race [reis] *n* kapplöpning *c*, lopp *nt*; ras *c*
racecourse ['reiskɔːs] *n* hästkapplöpningsbana *c*
racehorse ['reishɔːs] *n* kapplöpningshäst *c*
racetrack ['reistræk] *n* tävlingsbana *c*
racial ['reiʃəl] *adj* ras-
racket ['rækit] *n* oväsen *nt*; *n* (*tennis*) racket *c*
radiator ['reidieitə] *n* värmeelement *nt*
radical ['rædikəl] *adj* radikal
radio ['reidiou] *n* radio *c*
radish ['rædiʃ] *n* rädisa *c*
radius ['reidiəs] *n* (pl radii) radie *c*
raft [rɑːft] *n* flotte *c*
rag [ræg] *n* trasa *c*
rage [reidʒ] *n* ursinne *nt*, raseri *nt*; *v* rasa, *vara rasande
raid [reid] *n* räd *c*
rail [reil] *n* ledstång *c*, räcke *nt*
railing ['reiliŋ] *n* räcke *nt*
railroad ['reilroud] *nAm* järnväg *c*

railway ['reilwei] *n* järnväg *c*
rain [rein] *n* regn *nt*; *v* regna
rainbow ['reinbou] *n* regnbåge *c*
raincoat ['reinkout] *n* regnrock *c*
rainy ['reini] *adj* regnig
raise [reiz] *v* höja; öka; uppfostra, uppföda, odla; *pålägga; *nAm* löneförhöjning *c*
raisin ['reizən] *n* russin *nt*
rake [reik] *n* kratta *c*
rally ['ræli] *n* massmöte *nt*
ramp [ræmp] *n* ramp *c*
ramshackle ['ræm,ʃækəl] *adj* fallfärdig
rancid ['rænsid] *adj* härsken
rang [ræŋ] *v* (p ring)
range [reindʒ] *n* räckvidd *c*
range finder ['reindʒ,faində] *n* avståndsmätare *c*
rank [ræŋk] *n* rang *c*; rad *c*
ransom ['rænsəm] *n* lösen *c*
rap [ræp] *n* rapp *c*
rape [reip] *v* *våldta
rapid ['ræpid] *adj* snabb, hastig
rapids ['ræpidz] *pl* fors *c*
rare [rɛə] *adj* sällsynt

rarely ['reəli] *adv* sällan

rascal ['rɑːskəl] *n* lymmel *c*, skälm *c*

rash [ræʃ] *n* hudutslag *nt*; *adj* obetänksam, förhastad

raspberry ['rɑːzbəri] *n* hallon *nt*

rat [ræt] *n* råtta *c*

rate [reit] *n* taxa *c*, pris *nt*; fart *c*; at any ~ i varje fall; ~ of exchange valutakurs *c*

rather ['rɑːðə] *adv* ganska, någorlunda, rätt; hellre, snarare

ration ['ræʃən] *n* ranson *c*

rattan [ræ'tæn] *n* rotting *c*

raven ['reivən] *n* korp *c*

raw [rɔː] *adj* rå; ~ material råmaterial *nt*

ray [rei] *n* stråle *c*

rayon ['reiən] *n* konstsiden *c*

razor ['reizə] *n* rakkniv *c*

razor blade ['reizəbleid] *n* rakblad *nt*

reach [riːtʃ] *v* nå; *n* räckhåll *nt*

react [ri'ækt] *v* reagera

reaction [ri'ækʃən] *n* reaktion *c*

*read [riːd] *v* läsa

reading ['riːdiŋ] *n* läsning *c*

reading lamp ['riːdiŋlæmp] *n* läslampa *c*

reading room ['riːdiŋruːm] *n* läsesal *c*

ready ['redi] *adj* klar, färdig

ready-made [ˌredi'meid] *adj* konfektionssydd

real [riəl] *adj* verklig

reality [ri'æləti] *n* verklighet *c*

realizable ['riəlaizəbəl] *adj* utförbar

realize ['riəlaiz] *v* *inse*; realisera, förverkliga

really ['riəli] *adv* verkligen, faktiskt; egentligen

rear [riə] *n* baksida *c*; *v* uppfostra, uppföda

rear light [riə'lait] *n* baklykta *c*

reason ['riːzən] *n* orsak *c*, skäl *nt*; förnuft *nt*, förstånd *nt*; *v* resonera

reasonable ['riːzənəbəl] *adj* förnuftig; rimlig

reassure [ˌriːə'ʃuə] *v* lugna

rebate ['riːbeit] *n* rabatt *c*

rebellion [ri'beljən] *n* uppror *nt*

recall [ri'kɔːl] *v* erinra sig; återkalla; upphäva

receipt [ri'siːt] *n* kvitto *nt*, mottagningsbevis *nt*; mottagande *nt*

receive [ri'siːv] *v* *motta*

receiver [ri'siːvə] *n* telefonlur *c*; hälare *c*

recent ['riːsənt] *adj* ny, färsk

recently ['riːsəntli] *adv* häromdagen, nyligen

reception [ri'sepʃən] *n* mottagande *nt*; mottagning *c*; ~ office reception *c*

receptionist [ri'sepʃənist] *n* receptionist *c*

recession [ri'seʃən] *n* tillbakagång *c*

recipe ['resipi] *n* recept *nt*

recital [ri'saitəl] *n* solistframträdande *nt*

reckon ['rekən] v räkna; *anse; förmoda

recognition [,rekəg'niʃən] n erkännande nt

recognize ['rekəgnaiz] v känna igen; erkänna

recollect [,rekə'lekt] v minnas

recommence [,ri:kə'mens] v börja om

recommend [,rekə'mend] v rekommendera, förorda; tillråda

recommendation [,rekəmen'deiʃən] n rekommendation c

reconciliation [,rekənsili'eiʃən] n försoning c

reconstructive surgery [,ri:kən'strʌktiv_'sə:dʒəri] n rekonstruktiv kirurgi c

record¹ ['rekɔ:d] n grammofonskiva c; rekord nt; protokoll nt; **long- -playing ~** LP-skiva c

record² [ri'kɔ:d] v anteckna, inregistrera; inspela

recorder [ri'kɔ:də] n bandspelare c

recording [ri'kɔ:diŋ] n inspelning c

record player ['rekɔ:d,pleiə] n skivspelare c, grammofon c

recover [ri'kʌvə] v *återfå; tillfriskna

recovery [ri'kʌvəri] n tillfrisknande nt

recreation [,rekri'eiʃən] n förströelse c, avkoppling c; ~ **centre** fritidscenter nt; ~ **ground** bollplan c

recruit [ri'kru:t] n rekryt c

rectangle ['rektæŋgəl] n rektangel c

rectangular [rek'tæŋgjulə] adj rektangulär

rectum ['rektəm] n ändtarm c

recyclable [,ri:'sʌikləbl] adj återvinningsbar

recycle [,ri:'sʌikl] v återvinna

red [red] adj röd

redeem [ri'di:m] v frälsa, återköpa,

reduce [ri'dju:s] v reducera, minska, förvandla, *skära ned

reduction [ri'dʌkʃən] n prisnedsättning c, reduktion c

redundant [ri'dʌndənt] adj överflödig

reed [ri:d] n vass c

reef [ri:f] n rev nt

referee [,refə'ri:] n skiljedomare c

reference ['refrəns] n hänvisning c, referens c; sammanhang nt; **with ~ to** beträffande

refer to [ri'fə:] hänvisa till

refill ['ri:fil] n påfyllningsförpackning c

refinery [ri'fainəri] n raffinaderi nt

reflect [ri'flekt] v reflektera

reflection [ri'flekʃən] n

reflex *c*; spegelbild *c*
reflector [ri'flektə] *n*
    reflektor *c*
reformation [,refə'meiʃən] *n*
    Reformationen *c*
refresh [ri'freʃ] *v* fräscha
    upp, svalka
refreshment [ri'freʃmənt] *n*
    förfriskning *c*
refrigerator [ri'fridʒəreitə] *n*
    kylskåp *nt*
refugee [,refju'dʒi:] *n*
    flykting *c*
refund¹ [ri'fʌnd] *v* återbetala
refund² [ri:'fʌnd] *n*
    återbetalning *c*
refusal [ri'fju:zəl] *n* vägran *c*
refuse¹ [ri'fju:z] *v* vägra
refuse² ['refju:s] *n* avfall *nt*
regard [ri'gɑ:d] *v* *anse;
    betrakta; *n* hänsyn *c*; **as**
    regards med hänsyn till,
    angående
regarding [ri'gɑ:diŋ] *prep*
    angående, beträffande;
    rörande
regatta [ri'gætə] *n*
    kappsegling *c*
régime [rei'ʒi:m] *n* regim *c*
region ['ri:dʒən] *n* region *c*;
    område *nt*
regional ['ri:dʒənəl] *adj*
    regional
register ['redʒistə] *v*
    *inskriva sig;
    rekommendera; **registered**
    letter rekommenderat brev
registration [,redʒi'streiʃən]
    n registrering *c*; **~ form**
    inskrivningsblankett *c*; **~**

number
    registreringsnummer *nt*; **~**
    plate nummerplåt *c*
regret [ri'gret] *v* beklaga;
    ångra; *n* beklagande *nt*
regular ['regjulə] *adj*
    regelbunden, regelmässig;
    normal, reguljär
regulate ['regjuleit] *v* reglera
regulation [,regju'leiʃən] *n*
    regel *c*, reglemente *nt*;
    reglering *c*
rehabilitation
    [,ri:hə,bili'teiʃən] *n*
    rehabilitering *c*
rehearsal [ri'hə:səl] *n*
    repetition *c*
rehearse [ri'hə:s] *v* repetera
reign [rein] *n* regeringstid *c*; *v*
    regera
reimburse [,ri:im'bə:s] *v*
    återbetala
reindeer ['reindiə] *n* (pl ~)
    ren *c*
reject [ri'dʒekt] *v* *avslå,
    avvisa; förkasta
relate [ri'leit] *v* berätta
related [ri'leitid] *adj*
    besläktad
relation [ri'leiʃən] *n*
    förhållande *nt*, relation *c*;
    släkting *c*
relative ['relətiv] *n* släkting *c*;
    adj relativ
relax [ri'læks] *v* koppla av,
    slappna av
relaxation [,rilæk'seiʃən] *n*
    avkoppling *c*
reliable [ri'laiəbəl] *adj*
    pålitlig

relic ['relik] *n* relik *c*

relief [ri'li:f] *n* lättnad *c*; hjälp *c*; relief *c*

relieve [ri'li:v] *v* lätta, lindra, avlösa

religion [ri'lidʒən] *n* religion *c*

religious [ri'lidʒəs] *adj* religiös

rely on [ri'lai] lita på

remain [ri'mein] *v* *förbli; *återstå

remainder [ri'meində] *n* rest *c*, återstod *c*

remaining [ri'meiniŋ] *adj* övrig, resterande

remark [ri'mɑ:k] *n* anmärkning *c*; *v* påpeka, anmärka

remarkable [ri'mɑ:kəbəl] *adj* anmärkningsvärd

remedy ['remədi] *n* läkemedel *nt*; botemedel *nt*

remember [ri'membə] *v* *komma ihåg; minnas

remembrance [ri'membrəns] *n* hågkomst *c*, minne *nt*

remind [ri'maind] *v* påminna

remit [ri'mit] *v* översända

remittance [ri'mitəns] *n* penningförsändelse *c*

remnant ['remnənt] *n* rest *c*, kvarleva *c*

remote [ri'mout] *adj* avsides, avlägsen

remote control [ri'mout ˌkən'troul] *n* fjärrkontroll *c*

removal [ri'mu:vəl] *n*

undanröjning *c*

remove [ri'mu:v] *v* avlägsna

remunerate [ri'mju:nəreit] *v* belöna; *ersätta

remuneration [riˌmju:nə'reiʃən] *n* belöning *c*

renew [ri'nju:] *v* förnya; förlänga

renewable [ri'nju:əbəl] *adj* förnybar

rent [rent] *v* hyra; *n* hyra *c*

repair [ri'pɛə] *v* reparera; *n* reparation *c*

reparation [ˌrepə'reiʃən] *n* reparation *c*

*repay [ri'pei] *v* återbetala

repayment [ri'peimənt] *n* återbetalning *c*

repeat [ri'pi:t] *v* upprepa

repellent [ri'pelənt] *adj* frånstötande, motbjudande

repentance [ri'pentəns] *n* ånger *c*

repertory ['repətəri] *n* repertoar *c*

repetition [ˌrepə'tiʃən] *n* upprepning *c*

replace [ri'pleis] *v* *ersätta

reply [ri'plai] *v* svara; *n* svar *nt*; in ~ som svar

report [ri'pɔ:t] *v* rapportera; meddela; anmäla sig; *n* redogörelse *c*, rapport *c*

reporter [ri'pɔ:tə] *n* reporter *c*

represent [ˌrepri'zent] *v* representera; föreställa

representation [ˌreprizen'teiʃən] *n*

representation c;
framställning c
representative [ˌrepriˈzentətiv] adj
representativ
reprimand [ˈreprimɑːnd] v
tillrättavisa
reproach [riˈprəutʃ] n
förebråelse c; v förebrå
reproduce [ˌriːprəˈdjuːs] v
*återge
reproduction
[ˌriːprəˈdʌkʃən] n
återgivning c, reproduktion
c; fortplantning c
reptile [ˈreptail] n kräldjur nt
republic [riˈpʌblik] n
republik c
republican [riˈpʌblikən] adj
republikansk
repulsive [riˈpʌlsiv] adj
frånstötande
reputation [ˌrepjuˈteiʃən] n
renommé nt; anseende nt
request [riˈkwest] n begäran
c; förfrågan c; v begära
require [riˈkwaiə] v kräva
requirement [riˈkwaiəmənt]
n krav nt
requisite [ˈrekwizit] adj
erforderlig
rescue [ˈreskjuː] v rädda; n
räddning c
research [riˈsəːtʃ] n
forskning c
resemblance [riˈzembləns] n
likhet c
resemble [riˈzembəl] v likna
resent [riˈzent] v *ta illa upp
reservation [ˌrezəˈveiʃən] n

reservation c
reserve [riˈzəːv] v reservera;
beställa; n reserv c
reserved [riˈzəːvd] adj
reserverad
reservoir [ˈrezəvwɑː] n
reservoar c
reside [riˈzaid] v bo
residence [ˈrezidəns] n
bostad c; ～ **permit**
uppehållstillstånd nt
resident [ˈrezidənt] n
invånare c; adj bofast;
inneboende
resign [riˈzain] v *avgå
resignation [ˌrezigˈneiʃən] n
avsked nt, avskedsansökan c
resist [riˈzist] v *göra
motstånd mot
resistance [riˈzistəns] n
motstånd nt
resolute [ˈrezəluːt] adj
resolut, beslutsam
respect [riˈspekt] n respekt c;
aktning c, vördnad c; v
respektera
respectable [riˈspektəbəl]
adj respektabel,
aktningsvärd
respectful [riˈspektfəl] adj
respektfull
respective [riˈspektiv] adj
respektive
respiration [ˌrespəˈreiʃən] n
andning c
respite [ˈrespait] n uppskov
nt
responsibility
[riˌspɒnsəˈbiləti] n ansvar nt
responsible [riˈspɒnsəbəl]

adj ansvarig

rest [rest] *n* vila *c*; rest *c*; *v* vila

rest room ['restru:m] *nAm* toalett *c*

rest home ['resthoum] *n* vilohem *nt*

restaurant ['restərɔ̃:] *n* restaurang *c*

restful ['restfəl] *adj* lugn

restless ['restləs] *adj* rastlös

restrain [ri'strein] *v* *hålla tillbaka, tygla

restriction [ri'strikʃən] *n* inskränkning *c*, begränsning *c*

result [ri'zʌlt] *n* resultat *nt*; följd *c*; utgång *c*; *v* resultera

resume [ri'zju:m] *v* *återuppta

résumé ['rezjumei] *n* sammanfattning *c*

retail ['ri:teil] *v* *sälja i detalj

retailer ['ri:teilə] *n* detaljist *c*

retina ['retinə] *n* näthinna *c*

retire [ri'taiə] *v* dra sig tillbaka

retired [ri'taiəd] *adj* pensionerad

retirement [ri'taiəmənt] *n* pensionering *c*

return [ri'tə:n] *v* återvända, *komma tillbaka; *n* återkomst *c*; ~ **flight** returflyg *nt*; ~ **journey** återresa *c*

reunite [,ri:ju:'nait] *v* återförena

reveal [ri'vi:l] *v* uppenbara, avslöja

revelation [,revə'leiʃən] *n* avslöjande *nt*; uppenbarelse *c*

revenge [ri'vendʒ] *n* hämnd *c*

revenue ['revənju:] *n* inkomst *c*

reverse [ri'və:s] *n* motsats *c*; avigsida *c*; backväxel *c*; motgång *c*; *adj* omvänd; *v* backa

review [ri'vju:] *n* recension *c*; tidskrift *c*

revise [ri'vaiz] *v* revidera

revision [ri'viʒən] *n* revision *c*

revival [ri'vaivəl] *n* återupplivande *nt*; förnyelse *c*

revolt [ri'voult] *v* *göra uppror; *n* revolt *c*

revolting [ri'voultiŋ] *adj* motbjudande, upprörande, äcklig

revolution [,revə'lu:ʃən] *n* revolution *c*; varv *nt*

revolutionary [,revə'lu:ʃənəri] *adj* revolutionär

revolver [ri'vɔlvə] *n* revolver *c*

revue [ri'vju:] *n* revy *c*

reward [ri'wɔ:d] *n* belöning *c*; *v* belöna

rheumatism ['ru:mətizəm] *n* reumatism *c*

rhinoceros [rai'nɔsərəs] *n* (pl ~, ~es) noshörning *c*

rhubarb ['ru:ba:b] *n* rabarber *c*

rhyme [raim] *n* rim *nt*

rhythm ['riðəm] n rytm c

rib [rib] n revben nt

ribbon ['ribən] n band nt

rice [rais] n ris nt

rich [ritʃ] adj rik

riches ['ritʃiz] pl rikedom c

rid [rid] v befria;

get ~ of göra sig av med

riddle ['ridəl] n gåta c

ride [raid] n körning c

***ride** [raid] v åka; *rida

rider ['raidə] n ryttare c

ridge [ridʒ] n rygg c,
upphöjning c, kam c

ridicule ['ridikju:l] v
förlöjliga

ridiculous [ri'dikjuləs] adj
löjlig

riding ['raidiŋ] n ridning c

riding school ['raidiŋsku:l] n
ridskola c

rifle ['raifəl] v gevär nt

right [rait] n rättighet c; adj
riktig, rätt; höger; rättvis; **all
right!** bra!; ***be ~** *ha rätt; ~
of way förkörsrätt c

righteous ['raitʃəs] adj
rättfärdig

right-hand ['rait'hænd] adj
höger

rightly ['raitli] adv med rätta

rim [rim] n fälg c; kant c

ring [riŋ] n ring c; cirkusarena
c

***ring** [riŋ] v ringa; ~ **up** ringa
upp

rinse [rins] v skölja; n
sköljning c

riot ['raiət] n upplopp nt

rip [rip] v *riva sönder

ripe [raip] adj mogen

rise [raiz] n löneförhöjning c;
upphöjning c; stigning c;
uppsving nt

***rise** [raiz] v *stiga upp; *gå
upp; *stiga

rising ['raiziŋ] n uppror nt

risk [risk] n risk c; fara c; v
riskera

risky ['riski] adj vågad,
riskfylld

rival ['raivəl] n rival c;
konkurrent c; v rivalisera,
konkurrera

rivalry ['raivəlri] n rivalitet c;
konkurrens c

river ['rivə] n å c, flod c; ~
bank flodstrand c

riverside ['rivəsaid] n
flodstrand c

roach [routʃ] n (pl ~) mört c

road [roud] n gata c, väg c; ~
fork vägskäl nt; ~ **map**
vägkarta c; ~ **system** vägnät
nt; ~ **up** vägarbete nt

roadhouse ['roudhaus] n
värdshus nt

roadrage ['roud,reidʒ] n
aggressivt beteende hos
bilförare c

roadside ['roudsaid] n
vägkant c; ~ **restaurant**
värdshus nt

roadway ['roudwei] nAm
körbana c

roam [roum] v ströva

roar [rɔ:] v *tjuta, *ryta; n
vrål nt, dån nt

roast [roust] v grilla, halstra

rob [rɔb] v råna

robber ['rɔbə] n rånare c

robbery ['rɔbəri] n rån nt, stöld c

robe [roub] n klänning c; ämbetsdräkt c

robin ['rɔbin] n rödhake c

robust [rou'bʌst] adj robust

rock [rɔk] n klippa c; v gunga

rocket ['rɔkit] n raket c

rocky ['rɔki] adj klippig

rod [rɔd] n stång c

roe [rou] n rom c

roll [roul] v rulla; n rulle c; kuvertbröd nt

Rollerblade ['roulə,bleid] n Rollerblade® c

roller-skating ['roulə,skeitiŋ] n rullskridskoåkning c

Roman Catholic ['roumən 'kæθəlik] romersk katolsk

romance [rə'mæns] n romans c

romantic [rə'mæntik] adj romantisk

roof [ru:f] n tak nt; **thatched** ~ halmtak nt

room [ru:m] n rum nt; utrymme nt, plats c; ~ **and board** mat och logi; ~ **service** rumsbetjäning c; ~ **temperature** rumstemperatur c

roomy ['ru:mi] adj rymlig

root [ru:t] n rot c

rope [roup] n rep nt

rosary ['rouzəri] n radband nt

rose [rouz] n ros c; adj rosa

rotten ['rɔtən] adj rutten

rouge [ru:ʒ] n rouge c

rough [rʌf] adj ojämn, hård

roulette [ru:'let] n rulett c

round [raund] adj rund; prep runt om, omkring; n rond c; ~ **trip** Am tur och retur

roundabout ['raundəbaut] n rondell c

rounded ['raundid] adj rundad

route [ru:t] n rutt c

routine [ru:'ti:n] n rutin c

row[1] [rou] n rad c; v ro

row[2] [rau] n bråk nt

rowdy ['raudi] adj busig

rowing boat ['rouiŋbout] n roddbåt c

royal ['rɔiəl] adj kunglig

rub [rʌb] v *gnida

rubber ['rʌbə] n gummi nt; suddgummi nt; ~ **band** gummiband nt

rubbish ['rʌbiʃ] n skräp nt; trams nt, strunt nt; **talk** ~ prata strunt

rubbish bin ['rʌbiʃbin] n sophink c

ruby ['ru:bi] n rubin c

rucksack ['rʌksæk] n ryggsäck c

rudder ['rʌdə] n roder nt

rude [ru:d] adj ohövlig

rug [rʌg] n liten matta; pläd c

ruin ['ru:in] v *ödelägga, ruinera; n undergång c; **ruins** ruin c

rule [ru:l] n regel c; makt c, regering c, styrelsesätt nt; v regera, styra; **as a** ~ vanligen, som regel

ruler ['ru:lə] *n* härskare *c*, regent *c*; linjal *c*

Rumania [ru:'meiniə] Rumänien

Rumanian [ru:'meiniən] *adj* rumänsk; *n* rumän *c*

rumour ['ru:mə] *n* rykte *nt*

***run** [rʌn] *v* *springa; ~ **into** råka träffa

runaway ['rʌnəwei] *n* rymling *c*

rung [rʌn] *v* (pp ring)

runner ['rʌnə] *n* löpare *c*

runway ['rʌnwei] *n* start-, landningsbana

rural ['ruərəl] *adj* lantlig

ruse [ru:z] *n* list *c*

rush [rʌʃ] *v* rusa; *n* säv *c*

rush hour ['rʌʃauə] *n* rusningstid *c*

Russia ['rʌʃə] Ryssland

Russian ['rʌʃən] *adj* rysk; *n* ryss *c*

rust [rʌst] *n* rost *c*

rustic ['rʌstik] *adj* rustik

rusty ['rʌsti] *adj* rostig

S

sack [sæk] *n* säck *c*

sacred ['seikrid] *adj* helig

sacrifice ['sækrifais] *n* offer *nt*; *v* offra

sacrilege ['sækrilidʒ] *n* helgerån *nt*

sad [sæd] *adj* sorgsen; vemodig, bedrövad

saddle ['sædəl] *n* sadel *c*

sadness ['sædnəs] *n* sorgsenhet *c*

safe [seif] *adj* säker; *n* kassaskåp *nt*

safety ['seifti] *n* säkerhet *c*

safety belt ['seiftibelt] *n* säkerhetsbälte *nt*

safety pin ['seiftipin] *n* säkerhetsnål *c*

safety razor ['seifti,reizə] *n* rakhyvel *c*

sail [seil] *v* segla; *n* segel *nt*

sailing boat ['seiliŋbout] *n* segelbåt *c*

sailor ['seilə] *n* sjöman *c*

saint [seint] *n* helgon *nt*

salad ['sæləd] *n* sallad *c*

salad-oil ['sælədɔil] *n* salladsolja *c*

salary ['sæləri] *n* avlöning *c*, lön *c*

sale [seil] *n* försäljning *c*; **clearance ~** realisation *c*; **for ~** till salu; **sales** realisation *c*

saleable ['seiləbəl] *adj* säljbar

salesgirl ['seilzgə:l] *n* försäljerska *c*

salesman ['seilzmən] *n* (pl -men) försäljare *c*; expidit *c*

salmon ['sæmən] *n* (pl ~) lax *c*

salon ['sælɔ̃:] *n* salong *c*

saloon [sə'lu:n] *n* bar *c*

salt [sɔ:lt] *n* salt *nt*

salt cellar ['sɔ:lt,selə] *n*, salt

salty

shaker *nAm* saltkar *nt*

salty ['sɔ:lti] *adj* salt

salute [sə'lu:t] *v* hälsa

same [seim] *adj* samma

sample ['sɑ:mpəl] *n* varuprov *nt*

sand [sænd] *n* sand *c*

sandal ['sændəl] *n* sandal *c*

sandpaper ['sænd,peipə] *n* sandpapper *nt*

sandwich ['sænwidʒ] *n* smörgås *c*

sandy ['sændi] *adj* sandig

sanitary ['sænitəri] *adj* sanitär; ~ **towel** dambinda *c*

sapphire ['sæfaiə] *n* safir *c*

sardine [sɑ:'di:n] *n* sardin *c*

satchel ['sætʃəl] *n* skolväska *c*

satellite ['sætəlait] *n* satellit *c*

satellite dish ['sætəlait‿ˌdiʃ] *n* parabol *c*

satellite radio ['sætəlait‿ˌreidiou] *n* satellitradio *c*

satin ['sætin] *n* satäng *c*

satisfaction [ˌsætis'fækʃən] *n* tillfredsställelse *c*, belåtenhet *c*

satisfactory [ˌsætis'fæktəri] *adj* tillfredsställande

satisfy ['sætisfai] *v* tillfredsställa; **satisfied** tillfredsställd, belåten

sat nav ['sætnæv] *n* navigationssystem *nt*, GPS *c*

Saturday ['sætədi] *n* lördag *c*

sauce [sɔ:s] *n* sås *c*

saucepan ['sɔ:spən] *n* kastrull *c*

saucer ['sɔ:sə] *n* tefat *nt*

Saudi Arabia [ˌsaudiə'reibiə] Saudiarabien

Saudi Arabian [ˌsaudiə'reibiən] *adj* saudiarabisk

sauna ['sɔ:nə] *n* bastu *c*

sausage ['sɔsidʒ] *n* korv *c*

savage ['sævidʒ] *adj* vild

save [seiv] *v* rädda; spara

savings ['seivinz] *pl* besparingar *pl*; ~ **bank** sparbank *c*

saviour ['seivjə] *n* frälsare *c*

savoury ['seivəri] *adj* välsmakande

saw¹ [sɔ:] *v* (p see)

saw² [sɔ:] *n* såg *c*

sawdust ['sɔ:dʌst] *n* sågspån *c*

sawmill ['sɔ:mil] *n* sågverk *nt*

*say [sei] *v* *säga

scaffolding ['skæfəldiŋ] *n* byggnadsställning *c*

scale [skeil] *n* skala *c*; tonskala *c*; fiskfjäll *nt*; vågskål *c*; **scales** *pl* våg *c*

scan [skæn] *v* skanna; skanning *c*

scandal ['skændəl] *n* skandal *c*

Scandinavia [ˌskændi'neiviə] Skandinavien

Scandinavian [ˌskændi'neiviən] *adj* skandinavisk; *n* skandinav *c*

scanner ['skænə] *n* skanner *c*

scapegoat ['skeipgout] *n* syndabock *c*

seabird

scar [skɑ:] n ärr nt
scarce [skeəs] adj knapp
scarcely ['skeəsli] adv knappast
scarcity ['skeəsəti] n knapphet c
scare [skeə] v skrämma; n skräck c
scarf [skɑ:f] n (pl ~s, scarves) halsduk c
scarlet ['skɑ:lət] adj scharlakansröd
scary ['skeəri] adj oroväckande, skrämmande
scatter ['skætə] v strö, *sprida, skingra
scene [si:n] n scen c
scenery ['si:nəri] n landskap nt
scenic ['si:nik] adj naturskön
scent [sent] n doft c
schedule ['ʃedju:l] n tidtabell c, tidsschema nt
scheme [ski:m] n schema nt; plan c
scholar ['skɔlə] n lärd c; stipendiat c
scholarship ['skɔləʃip] n stipendium nt
school [sku:l] n skola c
schoolboy ['sku:lbɔi] n skolpojke c
schoolgirl ['sku:lgə:l] n skolflicka c
schoolmaster ['sku:l,mɑ:stə] n skollärare c, lärare c
schoolteacher ['sku:l,ti:tʃə] n lärare c
science ['saiəns] n vetenskap

c
scientific [,saiən'tifik] adj vetenskaplig
scientist ['saiəntist] n vetenskapsman c
scissors ['sizəz] pl sax c
scold [skould] v skälla, gräla på; skälla ut
scooter ['sku:tə] n vespa c; sparkcykel c
score [skɔ:] n poängsumma c; v *få poäng
scorn [skɔ:n] n hån nt, förakt nt; v förakta
Scotland ['skɔtlənd] n Skottland
Scottish ['skɔtiʃ] adj skotsk
scout [skaut] n boyscout c
scrap [skræp] n bit c
scrapbook ['skræpbuk] n klippbok c
scrape [skreip] v skrapa
scratch [skrætʃ] v rispa, skrapa; n repa c, skråma c
scream [skri:m] v *tjuta, *skrika; n skrik nt, skri nt
screen [skri:n] n skärm c; bildskärm c, filmduk c
screw [skru:] n skruv c; v skruva
screwdriver ['skru:,draivə] n skruvmejsel c
scrub [skrʌb] v skura; n snårmark c
sculptor ['skʌlptə] n skulptör c
sculpture ['skʌlptʃə] n skulptur c
sea [si:] n hav nt
seabird ['si:bə:d] n sjöfågel c

seashore 344

seashore ['si:kɔust] n kust c

seagull ['si:gʌl] n fiskmås c

seal [si:l] n sigill nt; säl c

seam [si:m] n söm c

seaman ['si:mən] n (pl -men) matros c

seamless ['si:mləs] adj utan söm

seaport ['si:pɔ:t] n hamnstad c

search [sə:tʃ] v söka; genomsöka, visitera; n visitering nt

searchlight ['sə:tʃlait] n strålkastare c

seascape ['si:skeip] n marinmålning c

seashell ['si:ʃel] n snäcka c

seashore ['si:ʃɔ:] n havsstrand c

seasick ['si:sik] adj sjösjuk

seasickness ['si:,siknəs] n sjösjuka c

seaside ['si:said] n kust c; ~ resort badort c

season ['si:zən] n årstid c, säsong c; high ~ högsäsong c; low ~ lågsäsong c; off ~ lågsäsong c

season ticket ['si:zən,tikit] n abonnemangskort nt

seat [si:t] n säte c; plats c, sittplats c

seat belt ['si:tbelt] n säkerhetsbälte nt

sea urchin ['si:,ə:tʃin] n sjöborre c

sea water ['si:,wɔ:tə] n havsvatten nt

second ['sekənd] num andra;

n sekund c; ögonblick nt

secondary ['sekəndəri] adj sekundär; ~ school läroverk nt

second-hand [,sekənd'hænd] adj begagnad

secret ['si:krət] n hemlighet c; adj hemlig

secretary ['sekrətri] n sekreterare c

section ['sekʃən] n sektion c; avdelning c

secure [si'kjuə] adj säker; v *göra säker; *binda fast; trygga

security [si'kjuərəti] n säkerhet c; borgen c

sedative ['sedətiv] n lugnande medel

seduce [si'dju:s] v förföra

*see [si:] v *se; *inse, *förstå; ~ to sörja för

seed [si:d] n frö nt

*seek [si:k] v söka

seem [si:m] v synas, verka

seen [si:n] v (pp see)

seesaw ['si:sɔ:] n gungbräda c

seize [si:z] v *gripa

seldom ['seldəm] adv sällan

select [si'lekt] v utplocka, *utvälja; adj utvald

selection [si'lekʃən] n urval nt

self [self] n jag nt

self-centred [,self'sentəd] adj självupptagen

self-evident [,sel'fevidənt] adj självklar

self-government
[ˌself'gʌvəmənt] *n*
självstyre *nt*
selfie ['selfi] *n* selfie *c*
selfish ['selfiʃ] *adj* självisk
selfishness ['selfiʃnəs] *n*
egoism *c*
self-service [ˌself'səːvis] *n*
självbetjäning *c*; ~
restaurant självservering *c*
*sell [sel] *v* *sälja
semblance ['sembləns] *n*
utseende *nt*
semi- ['semi] halv-
semicircle [ˌsemi,səːkəl] *n*
halvcirkel *c*
semicolon [ˌsemi'koulən] *n*
semikolon *nt*
senate ['senət] *n* senat *c*
senator ['senətə] *n* senator *c*
*send [send] *v* skicka, sända;
~ **back** skicka tillbaka,
returnera; ~ **for** skicka efter;
~ **off** skicka iväg
sender ['sendə] *n* avsändare
c
senile ['siːnail] *adj* senil
sensation [sen'seiʃən] *n*
sensation *c*; känsla *c*,
förnimmelse *c*
sensational [sen'seiʃənəl]
adj sensationell,
uppseendeväckande
sense [sens] *n* sinne *nt*;
förnuft *nt*; betydelse *c*,
mening *c*; *v* *förnimma,
märka; ~ **of honour**
hederskänsla *c*
senseless ['sensləs] *adj*
vanvettig, orimlig

sensible ['sensəbəl] *adj*
förnuftig
sensitive ['sensitiv] *adj*
känslig
sentence ['sentəns] *n*
mening *c*; dom *c*; *v* döma
sentimental [ˌsenti'mentəl]
adj sentimental
separate¹ ['sepəreit] *v* skilja
separate² ['sepərət] *adj*
åtskild, särskild
separately ['sepərətli] *adv*
separat
September [sep'tembə]
september
septic ['septik] *adj* septisk;
*become ~ *bli
inflammerad
sequel ['siːkwəl] *n* följd *c*
sequence ['siːkwəns] *n*
ordningsföljd *c*
serene [sə'riːn] *adj* fridfull;
klar
serial ['siəriəl] *n* följetong *c*
series ['siəriːz] *n* (pl ~) serie *c*
serious ['siəriəs] *adj*
allvarlig, seriös
seriousness ['siəriəsnəs] *n*
allvar *nt*
sermon ['səːmən] *n* predikan
c
servant ['səːvənt] *n* betjänt *c*
serve [səːv] *v* servera
service ['səːvis] *n* tjänst *c*;
betjäning *c*; ~ **charge**
betjäningsavgift *c*; ~ **station**
bensinstation *c*
serviette [ˌsəːvi'et] *n* servett
c
session ['seʃən] *n* session *c*

set [set] *n* grupp *c*,
uppsättning *c*
*****set** [set] *v* **sätta; ~ menu**
fast meny; **~ out** *ge sig av
setting ['setiŋ] *n* infattning *c*,
omgivning *c*; **~ lotion**
läggningsvätska *c*
settle ['setəl] *v* ordna, *göra
upp; **~ down** *slå sig ned,
lugna sig
settlement ['setəlmənt] *n*
förlikning *c*, uppgörelse *c*,
överenskommelse *c*
seven ['sevən] *num* sju
seventeen [ˌsevən'tiːn] *num*
sjutton
seventeenth [ˌsevən'tiːnθ]
num sjuttonde
seventh ['sevənθ] *num*
sjunde
seventy ['sevənti] *num*
sjuttio
several ['sevərəl] *adj* flera,
åtskilliga
severe [si'viə] *adj* sträng,
häftig
*****sew** [sou] *v* sy; **~ up** sy ihop
sewer ['suːə] *n* kloak *c*
sewing machine
['souiŋməˌʃiːn] *n* symaskin *c*
sex [seks] *n* kön *nt*
sexual ['sekʃuəl] *adj* sexuell
sexuality [ˌsekʃu'æləti] *n*
sexualitet *c*
shade [ʃeid] *n* skugga *c*;
nyans *c*
shadow ['ʃædou] *n* skugga *c*
shady ['ʃeidi] *adj* skuggig
*****shake** [ʃeik] *v* skaka
shaky ['ʃeiki] *adj* ostadig,

skakig
*****shall** [ʃæl] *v* *ska
shallow ['ʃælou] *adj* grund
shame [ʃeim] *n* skam *c*;
shame! fy!
shampoo [ʃæm'puː] *n*
schampo *nt*
shape [ʃeip] *n* form *c*; *v*
forma
share [ʃeə] *v* dela; *n* del *c*;
aktie *c*
shark [ʃɑːk] *n* haj *c*
sharp [ʃɑːp] *adj* vass
sharpen ['ʃɑːpən] *v* vässa,
slipa
shave [ʃeiv] *v* raka sig
shaver ['ʃeivə] *n* rakapparat
c
shaving brush ['ʃeiviŋbrʌʃ]
n rakborste *c*
shaving cream
['ʃeiviŋkriːm] *n* rakkräm *c*
shaving soap ['ʃeiviŋsoup]
n raktvål *c*
shawl [ʃɔːl] *n* schal *c*
she [ʃiː] *pron* hon
shed [ʃed] *n* skjul *nt*
*****shed** [ʃed] *v* *utgjuta;
*sprida
sheep [ʃiːp] *n* (pl **~**) får *nt*
sheer [ʃiə] *adj* pur, ren;
genomskinlig, skir, brant
sheet [ʃiːt] *n* lakan *nt*; ark *nt*;
plåt *c*
shelf [ʃelf] *n* (pl shelves) hylla
c
shell [ʃel] *n* snäckskal *nt*; skal
nt
shellfish ['ʃelfiʃ] *n* skaldjur
nt

shrinkproof

shelter ['ʃeltə] n skydd nt; v
skydda

shepherd ['ʃepəd] n herde c

shift [ʃift] n ombyte nt, skift
nt, förändring c

***shine** [ʃain] v *skina; glänsa;
blänka

ship [ʃip] n fartyg nt; v
skeppa; **shipping line**
linjerederi cn

shipowner ['ʃi,pounə] n
skeppsredare c

shipyard ['ʃipjɑːd] n
skeppsvarv nt

shirt [ʃəːt] n skjorta c

shiver ['ʃivə] v huttra, skälva;
n rysning c

shock [ʃɔk] n chock c; v
chockera; **~ absorber**
stötdämpare c

shocking ['ʃɔkiŋ] adj
chockerande

shoe [ʃuː] n sko c; **~ polish**
skokräm c

shoelace ['ʃuːleis] n
skosnöre c

shoemaker ['ʃuː,meikə] n
skomakare c

shoe shop ['ʃuːʃɔp] n
skoaffär c

shook [ʃuk] v (p shake)

***shoot** [ʃuːt] v *skjuta

shop [ʃɔp] n butik c; v
handla; **~ assistant** affärsbiträde nt

shopkeeper ['ʃɔp,kiːpə] n
affärsinnehavare c

shopping bag kasse c;
shopping centre
affärscentrum nt; **shopping**

trolley kundvagn c

shopwindow [,ʃɔp'windou]
n skyltfönster nt

shore [ʃɔː] n strand c

short [ʃɔːt] adj kort; liten; **~
circuit** kortslutning c

shortage ['ʃɔːtidʒ] n brist c

shorten ['ʃɔːtən] v förkorta

shortly ['ʃɔːtli] adv snart,
inom kort

shorts [ʃɔːts] pl shorts pl;
plAm kalsonger pl

short-sighted [,ʃɔːt'saitid]
adj närsynt

shot [ʃɔt] n skott nt; spruta c;
bild c

***should** [ʃud] v borde

shoulder ['ʃouldə] n axel c

shout [ʃaut] v *skrika; n
skrik nt

shovel ['ʃʌvəl] n skovel c

show [ʃou] n uppförande nt,
föreställning c; utställning c

***show** [ʃou] v visa; utställa,
framvisa; bevisa

showcase ['ʃoukeis] n
monter c

shower ['ʃauə] n dusch c;
regnskur c, störtskur c; **~ gel**
n duschgelé c or nt

showroom ['ʃouruːm] n
utställningslokal c

shriek [ʃriːk] v *skrika; n
illtjut nt

shrimp [ʃrimp] n räka c

shrine [ʃrain] n reliksskrin nt,
helgedom c

***shrink** [ʃriŋk] v krympa

shrinkproof ['ʃriŋkpruːf] adj
krympfri

shrub [ʃrʌb] *n* buske *c*

shudder ['ʃʌdə] *n* rysning *c*

shuffle ['ʃʌfəl] *v* blanda

*****shut** [ʃʌt] *v* stänga; ~ **in** stänga in

shutter ['ʃʌtə] *n* fönsterlucka *c*, persienn *c*

shy [ʃai] *adj* skygg, blyg

shyness ['ʃainəs] *n* blyghet *c*

Siamese [,saiə'mi:z] *adj* siamesisk; *n* siames *c*

sick [sik] *adj* sjuk; illamående

sickness ['siknəs] *n* sjukdom *c*; illamående *nt*

side [said] *n* sida *c*; parti *nt*; **onesided** *adj* ensidig

sideburns ['saidbə:nz] *pl* polisonger *pl*

sidelight ['saidlait] *n* sidoljus *nt*

side street ['saidstri:t] *n* sidogata *c*

sidewalk ['saidwɔ:k] *nAm* gångbana *c*, trottoar *c*

sideways ['saidweiz] *adv* åt sidan

siege [si:dʒ] *n* belägring *c*

sieve [siv] *n* sil *c*; *v* sila

sift [sift] *v* sikta

sight [sait] *n* synhåll *c*; syn *c*, åsyn *c*; sevärdhet *c*

sign [sain] *n* tecken *nt*; gest *c*; *v* underteckna

signal ['signəl] *n* signal *c*; tecken *nt*; *v* signalera

signature ['signətʃə] *n* signatur *c*

significant [sig'nifikənt] *adj* betydelsefull

signpost ['sainpoust] *n* vägvisare *c*

silence ['sailəns] *n* tystnad *c*; *v* tysta

silencer ['sailənsə] *n* ljuddämpare *c*

silent ['sailənt] *adj* tyst; *****be ~** *****tiga

silk [silk] *n* siden *nt*

silly ['sili] *adj* dum

silver ['silvə] *n* silver *nt*; silver-

silversmith ['silvəsmiθ] *n* silversmed *c*

silverware ['silvəweə] *n* silver *nt*

similar ['similə] *adj* liknande, dylik

similarity [,simi'lærəti] *n* likhet *c*

simple ['simpəl] *adj* enkel, okonstlad; vanlig

simply ['simpli] *adv* enkelt, helt enkelt

simulate ['simjuleit] *v* låtsa

simultaneous [,siməl'teiniəs] *adj* samtidig; **simultaneously** *adv* samtidigt

sin [sin] *n* synd *c*

since [sins] *prep* sedan; *adv* sedan dess; *conj* sedan; eftersom

sincere [sin'siə] *adj* uppriktig

sincerely [sin'siəli] *adv* uppriktigt

sinew ['sinju:] *n* sena *c*

*****sing** [siŋ] *v* *****sjunga

singer ['siŋə] *n* sångare *c*; sångerska *c*

single ['siŋgəl] adj en enda;
ofift; ~ **room** enkelrum nt

singular ['siŋgjulə] n
singularis nt; adj säregen

sinister ['sinistə] adj
olycksbådande

sink [siŋk] n vask c

*****sink** [siŋk] v *sjunka

sip [sip] n liten klunk

sir [sə:] min herre

siren ['saiərən] n siren c

sister ['sistə] n syster c

sister-in-law ['sistərinlɔ:] n
(pl sisters-) svägerska c

*****sit** [sit] v *sitta; ~ **down**
*sätta sig

site [sait] n tomt c; läge nt

sitting room ['sitiŋru:m] n
vardagsrum nt

situated ['sitʃueitid] adj
belägen

situation [,sitʃu'eiʃən] n
situation c; läge nt,
anställning c

six [siks] num sex

sixteen [,siks'ti:n] num
sexton

sixteenth [,siks'ti:nθ] num
sextonde

sixth [siksθ] num sjätte

sixty ['siksti] num sextio

size [saiz] n storlek c,
dimension c; format nt

skate [skeit] v åka skridskor;
n skridsko c

skating ['skeitiŋ] n
skridskoåkning c

skating rink ['skeitiŋriŋk] n
skridskobana c

skeleton ['skelitən] n skelett

nt

sketch [sketʃ] n skiss c,
teckning c; v teckna,
skissera

ski[1] [ski:] v åka skidor

ski[2] [ski:] n (pl ~, ~s) skida c;
~ **boots** pjäxor pl; ~ **pants**
skidbyxor pl; ~ **poles** Am
skidstavar pl; ~ **sticks**
skidstavar pl

skid [skid] v slira, sladda

skier ['ski:ə] n skidåkare c

skiing ['ski:iŋ] n skidåkning c

ski jump ['ski:dʒʌmp] n
backhoppning c

skilful ['skilfəl] adj händig,
duktig, skicklig

ski lift ['ski:lift] n skidlift c

skill [skil] n skicklighet c

skilled [skild] adj skicklig;
yrkesutbildad

skin [skin] n hud c, djurskinn
nt; skal nt; ~ **cream**
hudkräm c

skip [skip] v skutta; hoppa
över

skirt [skə:t] n kjol c

skull [skʌl] n skalle c

sky [skai] n himmel c; luft c

skyscraper ['skai,skreipə] n
skyskrapa c

slack [slæk] adj slak

slacks [slæks] pl långbyxor
pl

slam [slæm] v *slå igen

slander ['slɑ:ndə] n förtal nt

slang [slæŋ] n slang c

slant [slɑ:nt] v slutta

slanting ['slɑ:ntiŋ] adj
lutande, sned, sluttande

slap

slap [slæp] v *slå; n örfil c

slate [sleit] n skiffer nt

slave [sleiv] n slav c

sledge [sledʒ] n släde c, kälke c

sleep [sli:p] n sömn c

*sleep [sli:p] v *sova

sleeping bag ['sli:piŋbæg] n sovsäck c

sleeping car ['sli:piŋka:] n sovvagn c

sleeping pill ['sli:piŋpil] n sömntablett c

sleepless ['sli:pləs] adj sömnlös

sleepy ['sli:pi] adj sömnig

sleeve [sli:v] n ärm c; skivfodral nt

sleigh [slei] n släde c, kälke c

slender ['slendə] adj slank

slice [slais] n skiva c

slide [slaid] n glidning c; rutschbana c; diapositiv nt

*slide [slaid] v *glida

slight [slait] adj lätt; svag

slim [slim] adj slank; v magra

slip [slip] v halka, slira; n felsteg nt; underklänning c

slipper ['slipə] n toffel c

slippery ['slipəri] adj slipprig, hal

slogan ['slougən] n slogan c, partiparoll c

slope [sloup] n sluttning c; v slutta

sloping ['sloupiŋ] adj sluttande

sloppy ['slɔpi] adj oordentlig

slot [slɔt] n myntöppning c

slot machine ['slɔt,məʃi:n] n

350

spelautomat c

slow [slou] adj trögtänkt, långsam; ~ **down** fördröja, sakta ned

slum [slʌm] n fattigkvarter nt

slump [slʌmp] n prisfall nt

slush [slʌʃ] n snöslask nt

sly [slai] adj slug

smack [smæk] v *ge en örfil; n klatsch c

small [smɔ:l] adj liten

smallpox ['smɔ:lpɔks] n smittkoppor pl

smart [sma:t] adj chic; klipsk, duktig

smartphone ['sma:tfoun] n smartmobil c, smarttelefon c

smash [smæʃ] n slag nt; v krossa

smell [smel] n lukt c

*smell [smel] v lukta; lukta illa

smelly ['smeli] adj illaluktande

smile [smail] v *le; n leende nt

smith [smiθ] n smed c

smoke [smouk] v röka; n rök c; **no smoking** rökning förbjuden

smoker ['smoukə] n rökare c; rökkupé c

smoke-free ['smouk'fri:] adj rökfritt

smoking compartment ['smoukiŋkəm,pa:tmənt] n rökkupé c

smooth [smu:ð] adj slät, jämn; mjuk

smuggle ['smʌgəl] v

smuggla

snack [snæk] n mellanmål nt

snack bar [ˈsnækbɑː] n snackbar c

snail [sneil] n snigel c

snake [sneik] n orm c

snapshot [ˈsnæpʃɔt] n ögonblicksbild c, kort nt

sneakers [ˈsniːkəz] plAm gymnastikskor pl

sneeze [sniːz] v *nysa

sniper [ˈsnaipə] n prickskytt c

snooty [ˈsnuːti] adj mallig, överlägsen

snore [snɔː] v snarka

snorkel [ˈsnɔːkəl] n snorkel c

snout [snaut] n nos c

snow [snou] n snö c; v snöa

snowstorm [ˈsnoustɔːm] n snöstorm c

snowy [ˈsnoui] adj snöig

so [sou] conj så; adv så, till den grad; **and ~ on** och så vidare; **~ far** hittills; **~ that** så att, så

soak [souk] v blöta

soap [soup] n tvål c; **~ powder** tvättvättmedel nt

sober [ˈsoubə] adj nykter; sansad

so-called [ˌsouˈkɔːld] adj så kallad

soccer [ˈsɔkə] n fotboll c; **~ team** fotbollslag nt

social [ˈsouʃəl] adj social, samhälls-

socialism [ˈsouʃəlizəm] n socialism c

socialist [ˈsouʃəlist] adj

socialistisk; n socialist c

society [səˈsaiəti] n samfund nt; sammanslutning c, sällskap nt; förening c

sock [sɔk] n socka c

socket [ˈsɔkit] n glödlampshållare c; urtag nt

soda [ˈsoudə] nAm läsk c **~ water** sodavatten nt

sofa [ˈsoufə] n soffa c

soft [sɔft] adj mjuk; **~ drink** alkoholfri dryck

soften [ˈsɔfən] v mjuka upp

software [ˈsɔftweə] n programvara c

soil [sɔil] n jord c; jordmån c

soiled [sɔild] adj nedsmutsad

solar [ˈsoulə] adj sol- **~ system** n solsystem nt

sold [sould] v (p, pp sell); **~ out** utsåld

soldier [ˈsouldʒə] n soldat c

sole[1] [soul] adj ensam

sole[2] [soul] n sula c; sjötunga c

solely [ˈsoulli] adv uteslutande

solemn [ˈsɔləm] adj högtidlig

solicitor [səˈlisitə] n advokat c, jurist c

solid [ˈsɔlid] adj gedigen, massiv; n fast kropp

soluble [ˈsɔljubəl] adj löslig

solution [səˈluːʃən] n lösning c

solve [sɔlv] v lösa

sombre [ˈsɔmbə] adj dyster

some [sʌm] adj några; pron somliga; något; **~ day** någon gång; **~ more** lite mer; **~**

time en gång, någon gång
somebody ['sʌmbədi] *pron*
någon
somehow ['sʌmhau] *adv* på
något sätt
someone ['sʌmwʌn] *pron*
någon
something ['sʌmθiŋ] *pron*
något
sometimes ['sʌmtaimz] *adv*
ibland
somewhat ['sʌmwɔt] *adv*
tämligen
somewhere ['sʌmwɛə] *adv*
någonstans
son [sʌn] *n* son *c*
song [sɔŋ] *n* sång *c*
son-in-law ['sʌninlɔ:] *n* (pl
sons-) svärson *c*
soon [su:n] *adv* inom kort,
fort, snart; **as ~ as** så snart
som
sooner ['su:nə] *adv* hellre
sore [sɔ:] *adj* öm; *n* ömt
ställe; sår *nt*; **~ throat**
halsont *nt*
sorrow ['sɔrou] *n* sorg *c*,
bedrövelse *c*
sorry ['sɔri] *adj* ledsen;
sorry! ursäkta!, förlåt!
sort [sɔ:t] *v* ordna, sortera; *n*
sort *c*, slag *nt*; **all sorts of** all
slags
soul [soul] *n* själ *c*
sound [saund] *n* ljud *nt*; *v*
*låta; adj pålitlig
soundproof ['saundpru:f]
adj ljudisolerad
soup [su:p] *n* soppa *c*
soup plate ['su:ppleit] *n*

sopptallrik *c*
soup spoon ['su:pspu:n] *n*
soppsked *c*
sour [sauə] *adj* sur
source [sɔ:s] *n* källa *c*
south [sauθ] *n* söder *c*; **South
Pole** Sydpolen
South Africa [sauθ 'æfrikə]
Sydafrika
southeast [,sauθ'i:st] *n*
sydost *c*
southerly ['sʌðəli] *adj* sydlig
southern ['sʌðən] *adj* södra
southwest [,sauθ'west] *n*
sydväst *c*
souvenir ['su:vəniə] *n*
souvenir *c*; **~ shop**
souvenirbutik *c*
sovereign ['sɔvrin] *n*
härskare *c*
Soviet ['souviət] *adj* sovjetisk
*sow [sou] *v* så
spa [spɑ:] *n* kurort *c*
space [speis] *n* rymd *c*; **~
shuttle** rymdraket *c*
spacious ['speiʃəs] *adj*
rymlig
spade [speid] *n* spade *c*
Spain [spein] Spanien
Spaniard ['spænjəd] *n*
spanjor *c*
Spanish ['spæniʃ] *adj* spansk
spanking ['spæŋkiŋ] *n* smäll
c
spare [spɛə] *adj* reserv-,
extra; *v *vara utan; **~ part**
reservdel *c*; **~ room** gästrum
nt; **~ time** fritid *c*; **~ tyre**
reservdäck *nt*; **~ wheel**
reservhjul *nt*

spark [spɑːk] n gnista c
sparking plug ['spɑːkiŋplʌg]
 n tändstift nt
sparkling ['spɑːkliŋ] adj
 gnistrande; mousserande
sparrow ['spærou] n sparv c
*speak [spiːk] v tala
speaker phone
 ['spiːkə‿ˌfoun] n
 högtalartelefon c
spear [spiə] n spjut nt
special ['speʃəl] adj speciell,
 särskild; ~ delivery
 expressutdelning c
specialist ['speʃəlist] n
 specialist c
speciality [ˌspeʃi'æləti] n
 specialitet c
specialize ['speʃəlaiz] v
 specialisera sig
specially ['speʃəli] adv i
 synnerhet
species ['spiːʃiːz] n (pl ~) art
 c
specific [spə'sifik] adj
 specifik
specimen ['spesimən] n
 exemplar nt, specimen nt
speck [spek] n fläck c
spectacle ['spektəkəl] n
 skådespel nt; spectacles
 glasögon pl
spectator [spek'teitə] n
 åskådare c
speculate ['spekjuleit] v
 spekulera
speech [spiːtʃ] n talförmåga
 c; anförande nt, tal nt; språk
 nt
speechless ['spiːtʃləs] adj

mållös
speed [spiːd] n hastighet c;
 fart c; cruising ~ marschfart
 c; ~ limit fartbegränsning c,
 hastighetsbegränsning c
*speed [spiːd] v köra (för)
 fort
speed dial(ing)
 ['spiːd‿ˌdail(iŋ)] n
 snabbuppringning c
speeding ['spiːdiŋ] n
 fortkörning c
speedometer [spiː'dɔmitə] n
 hastighetsmätare c
spell [spel] n förtrollning c
*spell [spel] v stava
spelling ['speliŋ] n stavning c
*spend [spend] v förbruka,
 spendera; tillbringa
sphere [sfiə] n klot nt; sfär c
spice [spais] n krydda c
spiced [spaist] adj kryddad
spicy ['spaisi] adj kryddstark
spider ['spaidə] n spindel c;
 spider's web spindelnät nt
*spill [spil] v spilla
*spin [spin] v *spinna; snurra
spinach ['spinidʒ] n spenat c
spine [spain] n ryggrad c
spire [spaiə] n spira c
spirit ['spirit] n ande c; spöke
 nt; spirits spritdrycker pl;
 sinnesstämning c; ~ stove
 spritkök nt
spiritual ['spiritʃuəl] adj
 andlig
spit [spit] n spott nt, saliv c;
 spett nt
*spit [spit] v spotta
spite [spait] n ondska c; in ~

spiteful   354

of trots
spiteful ['spaitfəl] *adj*
ondskefull
splash [splæʃ] *v* stänka
splendid ['splendid] *adj*
strålande, praktfull
splendour ['splendə] *n* prakt
c
splint [splint] *n* spjäla *c*
splinter ['splintə] *n* splitter *nt*
***split** [split] *v* *klyva
***spoil** [spɔil] *v* fördärva;
skämma bort
spoke[1] [spouk] *v* (p speak)
spoke[2] [spouk] *n* eker *c*
sponge [spʌndʒ] *n*
tvättsvamp *c*
spool [spu:l] *n* spole *c*
spoon [spu:n] *n* sked *c*
spoonful ['spu:nful] *n* sked *c*
sport [spɔːt] *n* sport *c*; ~
utility vehicle SUV *c*
sports car ['spɔːtskaː] *n*
sportbil *c*
sports jacket
['spɔːts,dʒækit] *n*
sportjacka *c*
sportsman ['spɔːtsmən] *n*
(pl -men) idrottsman *c*
sportswear ['spɔːtsweə] *n*
sportkläder *pl*
sportswoman
['spɔːtswumən] *n* (pl
-women) idrottskvinna *c*
spot [spɔt] *n* fläck *c*; ställe *nt*,
plats *c*
spotless ['spɔtləs] *adj*
fläckfri
spotlight ['spɔtlait] *n*
strålkastare *c*

spotted ['spɔtid] *adj* fläckig
spout [spaut] *n* stråle *c*; pip *c*,
ränna *c*
spray [sprei] *n* spray *c*
spread [spred] *v* *sprida
spring [spriŋ] *n* vår *c*; fjäder
c; källa *c*
springtime ['spriŋtaim] *n* vår
c
sprouts [sprauts] *pl*
brysselkål *c*
spy [spai] *n* spion *c*
squadron ['skwɔdrən] *n*
skvadron *c*
square [skweə] *adj*
kvadratisk; *n* kvadrat *c*;
öppen plats, torg *nt*
squash [skwɔʃ] *n* fruktsaft *c*;
squash *c*
squeeze [skwiːz] *v* klämma
squirrel ['skwirəl] *n* ekorre *c*
squirt [skwɔːt] *n* stråle *c*
stable ['steibəl] *adj* stabil; *n*
stall *nt*
stack [stæk] *n* stack *c*, stapel
c
stadium ['steidiəm] *n*
stadion *nt*
staff [staːf] *n* personal *c*
stage [steidʒ] *n* scen *c*;
stadium *nt*, fas *c*; etapp *c*
stain [stein] *v* fläcka ned; *n*
fläck *c*; **stained glass** färgat
glas; ~ **remover**
fläckborttagningsmedel *nt*
stainless ['steinləs] *adj*
fläckfri; ~ **steel** rostfritt stål
staircase ['steəkeis] *n* trappa

c

stairs [steəz] *pl* trappa *c*

stale [steil] *adj* gammal

stall [stɔːl] *n* stånd *nt*; parkett
c

stamp [stæmp] *n* frimärke *nt*;
stämpel *c*; *v* frankera;
stampa; ~ **machine**
frimärksautomat *c*

stand [stænd] *n* ställ *nt*, stånd
nt; läktare *c*

*****stand** [stænd] *v* *stå

standard [stændəd] *n* norm
c; standard-; ~ **of living**
levnadsstandard *c*

stanza [stænzə] *n* strof *c*

staple [steipəl] *n*
häftklammer *c*; stapelvara *c*

star [stɑː] *n* stjärna *c*

starboard [stɑːbəd] *n*
styrbord

stare [steə] *v* stirra

starling [stɑːliŋ] *n* stare *c*

start [stɑːt] *v* börja; *n* början
c

starting point [stɑːtiŋpɔint]
n utgångspunkt *c*

starve [stɑːrv] *v* *svälta

state [steit] *n* stat *c*; tillstånd
nt; *v* fastställa

the States [ðə steits] Förenta
Staterna

statement [steitmənt] *n*
uppgift *c*, redogörelse *c*

statesman [steitsmən] *n* (pl
-men) statsman *c*

station [steiʃən] *n*
järnvägsstation *c*; position *c*

stationary [steiʃənəri] *adj*
stillastående

stationer's [steiʃənəz] *n*
pappershandel *c*

stationery [steiʃənəri] *n*
kontorsartiklar *c*

statistics [stətistiks] *pl*
statistik *c*

statue [stætʃuː] *n* staty *c*

stay [stei] *v* *förbli, stanna
kvar; vistas, *uppehålla sig;
n vistelse *c*

steadfast [stedfɑːst] *adj*
orubblig

steady [stedi] *adj* stadig

steak [steik] *n* biff *c*

*****steal** [stiːl] *v* *stjäla

steam [stiːm] *n* ånga *c*

steamer [stiːmə] *n* ångare *c*

steel [stiːl] *n* stål *nt*

steep [stiːp] *adj* brant

steeple [stiːpəl] *n* tornspira
c

steer [stiə] *v* styra

steering column
[stiəriŋ,kɔləm] *n* rattstång *c*

steering wheel [stiəriŋwiːl]
n ratt *c*

steersman [stiəzmən] *n* (pl
-men) rorsman *c*

stem [stem] *n* stjälk *c*

stem cell [stem ,sel] *n*
stamcell *c*

step [step] *n* steg *nt*; *v* trampa

stepchild [steptʃaild] *n* (pl
-children) styvbarn *nt*

stepfather [step,fɑːðə] *n*
styvfar *c*

stepmother [step,mʌðə] *n*
styvmor *c*

sterile [sterail] *adj* steril

sterilize [sterilaiz] *v*

stereo 356

sterilisera
stereo [steriou] *n* stereo *c*
steward ['stju:əd] *n* steward *c*
stewardess ['stju:ədes] *n* flygvärdinna *c*
stick [stik] *n* pinne *c*, käpp *c*
***stick** [stik] *v* fästa, klistra
sticker ['stikə] *n* klistermärke *nt*
sticky ['stiki] *adj* klibbig
stiff [stif] *adj* stel
still [stil] *adv* ännu; likväl; *adj* stilla
stimulant ['stimjulənt] *n* stimulans *c*; stimulantia *pl*
stimulate ['stimjuleit] *v* stimulera
sting [stiŋ] *n* sting *nt*, stick *nt*
***sting** [stiŋ] *v* *sticka
stingy ['stindʒi] *adj* småaktig
***stink** [stiŋk] *v* *stinka
stipulate ['stipjuleit] *v* stipulera, bestämma
stipulation [,stipju'leiʃən] *n* bestämmelse *c*
stir [stə:] *v* röra sig; röra om
stitch [stitʃ] *n* stygn *nt*, håll *nt*
stock [stɔk] *n* lager *nt*; *v* lagra; ~ **exchange** fondbörs *c*; ~ **market** fondmarknad *c*; **stocks and shares** värdepapper *pl*
stocking ['stɔkiŋ] *n* strumpa *c*
stole¹ [stoul] *v* (p steal)
stole² [stoul] *n* stola *c*
stomach ['stʌmək] *n* mage *c*
stomach ache ['stʌməkeik] *n* magont *nt*

stone [stoun] *n* sten *c*; ädelsten *c*; kärna *c*; sten-; **pumice** ~ pimpsten *c*
stood [stud] *v* (p, pp stand)
stop [stɔp] *v* stoppa, upphöra; *halla upp med; *n* hållplats *c*; **stop!** stopp!
stopper ['stɔpə] *n* propp *c*
storage ['stɔ:ridʒ] *n* lagring *c*
store [stɔ:] *n* lager *nt*; affär *c*; *v* lagra
store house ['stɔ:haus] *n* magasin *nt*
storey ['stɔ:ri] *n* våning *c*
stork [stɔ:k] *n* stork *c*
storm [stɔ:m] *n* storm *c*
stormy ['stɔ:mi] *adj* stormig
story ['stɔ:ri] *n* historia *c*
stout [staut] *adj* korpulent, tjock; kraftig
stove [stouv] *n* ugn *c*; köksspis *c*
straight [streit] *adj* rak; hederlig; *adv* rakt; ~ **ahead** rakt fram; ~ **away** omedelbart, genast; ~ **on** rakt fram
strain [strein] *n* ansträngning *c*; påfrestning *c*; *v* överanstränga; sila
strainer ['streinə] *n* durkslag *nt*
strange [streindʒ] *adj* främmande; besynnerlig
stranger ['streindʒə] *n* främling *c*; okänd person *c*
strangle ['stræŋgəl] *v* *strypa
strap [stræp] *n* rem *c*
straw [strɔ:] *n* strå *nt*, halm *c*;

357   substantial

sugrör *nt*
strawberry ['strɔːbəri] *n*
  jordgubbe *c*; **wild ~**
  smultron *nt*
stream [striːm] *n* bäck *c*;
  ström *c*; *v* strömma
street [striːt] *n* gata *c*
streetcar ['striːtkaː] *nAm*
  spårvagn *c*
strength [streŋθ] *n* kraft *c*,
  styrka *c*
stress [stres] *n* stress *c*;
  betoning *c*; *v* betona
stretch [stretʃ] *v* tänja; *n*
  sträcka *c*
stretcher ['stretʃə] *n* bår *c*
strict [strikt] *adj* sträng;
  strikt
strike [straik] *n* strejk *c*
***strike** [straik] *v* *slå; *slå till;
  strejka
striking ['straikiŋ] *adj*
  slående, markant,
  påfallande
string [striŋ] *n* snöre *nt*;
  sträng *c*
strip [strip] *n* remsa *c*
stripe [straip] *n* rand *c*
striped [straipt] *adj* randig
stroke [strouk] *n* slaganfall *c*
stroll [stroul] *v* flanera; *n*
  promenad *c*
strong [strɔŋ] *adj* stark;
  kraftig
stronghold ['strɔŋhould] *n*
  fästning *c*
structure ['strʌktʃə] *n*
  struktur *c*; byggnadsverk *nt*
struggle ['strʌgəl] *n* strid *c*,
  kamp *c*; *v* slåss, kämpa

stub [stʌb] *n* talong *c*
stubborn ['stʌbən] *adj* envis
student ['stjuːdənt] *n*
  student *c*; studentska *c*;
  studerande *c*
studies ['stʌdiz] *pl* studier *pl*
study ['stʌdi] *v* studera; *n*
  studium *nt*; arbetsrum *nt*
stuff [stʌf] *n* material *nt*;
  grejor *pl*
stuffed [stʌft] *adj* fylld
stuffing ['stʌfiŋ] *n* fyllning *c*
stuffy ['stʌfi] *adj* kvav
stumble ['stʌmbəl] *v* snubbla
stung [stʌŋ] *v* (p, pp sting)
stupid ['stjuːpid] *adj* dum
style [stail] *n* stil *c*
subject¹ ['sʌbdʒikt] *n*
  subjekt *nt*; undersåte *c*; **~ to**
  utsatt för
subject² [səb'dʒekt] *v*
  underkuva
submarine ['sʌbməriːn] *n*
  u-båt *c*
submit [səb'mit] *v*
  underkasta sig
subordinate [sə'bɔːdinət]
  adj underordnad
subscriber [səb'skraibə] *n*
  prenumerant *c*
subscription [səb'skripʃən]
  n prenumeration *c*,
  abonnemang *nt*; insamling *c*
subsequent ['sʌbsikwənt]
  adj följande
subsidy ['sʌbsidi] *n*
  understöd *nt*
substance ['sʌbstəns] *n*
  substans *c*
substantial [səb'stænʃəl] *adj*

verklig; ansenlig

substitute ['sʌbstitjuːt] *v*
*ersätta; *n* surrogat *nt*;
ställföreträdare *c*

subtitle ['sʌb‚taitəl] *n*
undertitel *c*

subtle ['sʌtəl] *adj* subtil

subtract [səb'trækt] *v*
minska, *dra ifrån

suburb ['sʌbəːb] *n* förstad *c*,
förort *c*

suburban [sə'bəːbən] *adj*
förstads-

subway ['sʌbwei] *nAm*
tunnelbana *c*

succeed [sək'siːd] *v* lyckas;
efterträda

success [sək'ses] *n* succé *c*

successful [sək'sesfəl] *adj*
framgångsrik

succumb [sə'kʌm] *v* duka
under

such [sʌtʃ] *adj* sådan,
liknande; *adv* så; ~ **as** sådan
som

suck [sʌk] *v* *suga

sudden ['sʌdən] *adj* plötslig

suddenly ['sʌdənli] *adv*
plötsligt

suede [sweid] *n* mockaskinn
nt

suffer ['sʌfə] *v* *lida; tåla

suffering ['sʌfəriŋ] *n* lidande
nt

suffice [sə'fais] *v* räcka

sufficient [sə'fiʃənt] *adj*
tillräcklig

suffrage ['sʌfridʒ] *n* rösträtt
c

sugar ['ʃugə] *n* socker *nt*

suggest [sə'dʒest] *v* *föreslå

suggestion [sə'dʒestʃən] *n*
förslag *nt*

suicide ['suːisaid] *n*
självmord *nt*

suicide attack
['sjuːəsaid‚ə‚tæk] *n*
självmordsattack *c*

suicide bomber
['sjuːəsaid‚‚bɔmə] *n*
självmordsbombare *c*

suit [suːt] *v* passa; avpassa; *n*
dräkt *c*, kostym *c*

suitable ['suːtəbəl] *adj*
passande

suitcase ['suːtkeis] *n*
resväska *c*

suite [swiːt] *n* svit *c*

sum [sʌm] *n* summa *c*

summary ['sʌməri] *n*
sammandrag *nt*, översikt *c*

summer ['sʌmə] *n* sommar *c*;
~ **time** sommartid *c*

summit ['sʌmit] *n* topp *c*

sun [sʌn] *n* sol *c*

sunbathe ['sʌnbeið] *v*
solbada

Sunday ['sʌndi] söndag *c*

sunglasses ['sʌn‚glɑːsiz] *pl*
solglasögon *pl*

sunlight ['sʌnlait] *n* solljus *nt*

sunny ['sʌni] *adj* solig

sunrise ['sʌnraiz] *n*
soluppgång *c*

sunset ['sʌnset] *n*
solnedgång *c*

sunshade ['sʌnʃeid] *n*
solparasoll *nt*

sunshine ['sʌnʃain] *n*
solsken *nt*

sunstroke ['sʌnstrouk] *n*
solsting *nt*

suntan oil ['sʌntænɔil]
sololja *c*

super ['sju:pə] *adj colloquial*
super

superb [su'pə:b] *adj*
storartad, utsökt

superficial [,su:pə'fiʃəl] *adj*
ytlig

superfluous [su'pə:fluəs]
adj överflödig

superior [su'piəriə] *adj*
större, bättre, överlägsen

superlative [su'pə:lətiv] *adj*
superlativ; *n* superlativ *c*

supermarket ['su:pə,ma:kit]
n snabbköp *nt*

superstition [,su:pə'stiʃən]
n vidskepelse *c*

supervise ['su:pəvaiz] *v*
övervaka

supervision [,su:pə'viʒən] *n*
kontroll *c*, uppsikt *c*

supervisor ['su:pəvaizə] *n*
arbetsledare *c*,
uppsyningsman *c*

supper ['sʌpə] *n* kvällsmat *c*

supple ['sʌpəl] *adj* böjlig,
mjuk, smidig

supplement ['sʌplimənt] *n*
tidningsbilaga *c*

supply [sə'plai] *n* leverans *c*;
förråd *nt*; utbud *nt*; *v* *förse

support [sə'pɔ:t] *v* *hålla
uppe, stödja, understödja; *n*
stöd *nt*; ~ hose
stödstrumpor *pl*

supporter [sə'pɔ:tə] *n*
anhängare *c*

suppose [sə'pouz] *v*
förmoda, *anta; supposing
that *anta att

suppository [sə'pɔzitəri] *n*
stolpiller *c*

suppress [sə'pres] *v*
undertrycka

surcharge ['sə:tʃɑ:dʒ] *n*
tillägg *nt*; överbelastning *c*

sure [ʃuə] *adj* säker

surely ['ʃuəli] *adv* säkerligen

surf (the Net) [sə:f] *v* surfa
(på Nätet)

surface ['sə:fis] *n* yta *c*

surfboard ['sə:fbɔ:d] *n*
surfingbräda *c*

surgeon ['sə:dʒən] *n* kirurg
c; veterinary ~ veterinär *c*

surgery ['sə:dʒəri] *n* kirurgi
c; läkarmottagning *c*

surname ['sə:neim] *n*
efternamn *nt*

surplus ['sə:pləs] *n* överskott
nt

surprise [sə'praiz] *n*
överraskning *c*; *v* överraska;
förvåna

surrender [sə'rendə] *v* *ge
sig; *n* kapitulation *c*

surround [sə'raund] *v*
omringa, *omge

surrounding [sə'raundiŋ]
adj kringliggande

surroundings [sə'raundiŋz]
pl omgivning

survey ['sə:vei] *n* översikt *c*

survival [sə'vaivəl] *n*
överlevnad *c*

survive [sə'vaiv] *v* överleva

suspect[1] [sə'spekt] *v*

misstänka; *anta
suspect² ['sʌspekt] n
misstänkt c
suspend [sə'spend] v
suspendera
suspenders [sə'spendəz]
plAm hängslen pl; ~ **bridge**
hängbro c
suspension [sə'spenʃən] n
upphängningsanordning nt,
fjädring c
suspicion [sə'spiʃən] n
misstanke c;
misstänksamhet c, misstro c
suspicious [sə'spiʃəs] adj
misstänkt; misstrogen,
misstänksam
sustain [sə'stein] v *utstå
SUV ['esyu:'vi:] n SUV c
Swahili [swə'hi:li] n swahili
swallow ['swɔlou] v sluka,
*svälja; n svala c
swam [swæm] n (p swim)
swamp [swɔmp] n träsk nt
swan [swɔn] n svan c
swap [swɔp] v byta
***swear** [swɛə] v *svära
sweat [swet] n svett c; v
svettas
sweater ['swetə] n tröja c
Swede [swi:d] n svensk c
Sweden ['swi:dən] Sverige
Swedish ['swi:diʃ] adj
svensk
***sweep** [swi:p] v sopa
sweet [swi:t] adj söt; snäll; n
karamell c; dessert c;
sweets sötsaker pl
sweeten ['swi:tən] v söta
sweetheart ['swi:thɑ:t] n

älskling c, raring c
sweetshop ['swi:tʃɔp] n
gottaffär c
swell [swel] adj tjusig
***swell** [swel] v svälla; svullna;
öka
swelling ['sweliŋ] n svullnad
c
swift [swift] adj rask
***swim** [swim] v simma
swimmer ['swimə] n
simmare c
swimming ['swimiŋ] n
simning c; ~ **pool**
simbassäng c
swimmingtrunks
['swimiŋtrʌŋks] pl
badbyxor pl
swimsuit ['swimsu:t]n,
swimming suit nAm
baddräkt c
swindle ['swindəl] v svindla;
n svindel c
swindler ['swindlə] n
svindlare c
swing [swiŋ] n gunga c
***swing** [swiŋ] v svänga;
gunga
Swiss [swis] adj schweizisk;
n schweizare c
switch [switʃ] n växel c;
strömbrytare c, spö nt; v
växla; ~ **off** koppla av,
stänga av; ~ **on** koppla på
switchboard ['switʃbɔ:d] n
kopplingsbord nt
Switzerland ['switsələnd]
Schweiz
sword [sɔ:d] n svärd nt
swum [swʌm] v (pp swim)

syllable ['siləbəl] *n* stavelse *c*

symbol ['simbəl] *n* symbol *c*

sympathetic [,simpə'θetik] *adj* deltagande

sympathy ['simpəθi] *n* sympati *c*; medkänsla *c*

symphony ['simfəni] *n* symfoni *c*

symptom ['simtəm] *n* symptom *nt*

synagogue ['sinəgɔg] *n* synagoga *c*

synonym ['sinənim] *n* synonym *c*

synthetic [sin'θetik] *adj* syntetisk

Syria ['siriə] Syrien

Syrian ['siriən] *adj* syrisk; *n* syrier *c*

syringe [si'rindʒ] *n* injektionsspruta *c*

syrup ['sirəp] *n* sockerlag *c*, saft *c*

system ['sistəm] *n* system *nt*; **decimal** ~ decimalsystem *nt*

systematic [,sistə'mætik] *adj* systematisk

T

table ['teibəl] *n* bord *nt*; tabell *c*; ~ **of contents** innehållsförteckning *c*; ~ **tennis** bordtennis *c*

tablecloth ['teibəlklɔθ] *n* bordduk *c*

tablespoon ['teibəlspu:n] *n* matsked *c*

tablet ['tæblit] *n* tablett *c*; pekdator *c*; surfplatta *c*

taboo [tə'bu:] *n* tabu *nt*

tactics ['tæktiks] *pl* taktik *c*

tag [tæg] *n* prislapp *c*, adresslapp *c*

tail [teil] *n* svans *c*

taillight ['teillait] *n* baklykta *c*

tailor ['teilə] *n* skräddare *c*

tailor-made ['teiləmeid] *adj* skräddarsydd

***take** [teik] *v* *ta; *gripa; *begripa, *förstå, fatta; ~

away *ta bort; ~ **off** *ta av; ~ **up** *uppta

take-off ['teikɔf] *n* start *c*

tale [teil] *n* berättelse *c*, saga *c*

talent ['tælənt] *n* begåvning *c*

talented ['tæləntid] *adj* begåvad

talk [tɔ:k] *v* tala, prata; *n* samtal *nt*

talkative ['tɔ:kətiv] *adj* pratsam

tall [tɔ:l] *adj* hög; lång

tame [teim] *adj* tam; *v* tämja

tampon ['tæmpən] *n* tampong *c*

tangerine [,tændʒə'ri:n] *n* mandarin *c*

tangible ['tændʒibəl] *adj* gripbar

tank [tæŋk] n tank c

tanker ['tæŋkə] n tankfartyg nt

tanned [tænd] adj solbränd

tap [tæp] n kran c; slag nt; v knacka

tape [teip] n ljudband nt; snöre nt; adhesive ~ klisterremsa c, tejp c

tape measure ['teip,meʒə] n måttband nt

tap water ['tæpwɔːtə] n kranvatten nt

tar [taː] n tjära c

target ['taːgit] n måltavla c

tariff ['tærif] n tariff c

task [taːsk] n uppgift c

taste [teist] n smak c; v smaka

tasteless ['teistləs] adj smaklös

tasty ['teisti] adj välsmakande

taught [tɔːt] v (p, pp teach)

tavern ['tævən] n taverna c

tax [tæks] n skatt c; v beskatta

taxation [tæk'seiʃən] n beskattning c

tax-free ['tæksfriː] adj skattefri

taxi ['tæksi] n taxi c; ~ rank taxistation c; ~ stand Am taxistation c

taxi driver ['tæksi,draivə] n taxichaufför c

taximeter ['tæksi,miːtə] n taxameter c

tea [tiː] n te nt; eftermiddagste nt

*teach [tiːtʃ] v undervisa, lära

teacher ['tiːtʃə] n lärare c; lärarinna c

teachings ['tiːtʃiŋz] pl lära c

tea cloth ['tiːklɔθ] n kökshandduk c

teacup ['tiːkʌp] n tekopp c

team [tiːm] n lag nt

teapot ['tiːpɔt] n tekanna c

*tear [tɛə] v *riva

tear¹ [tiə] n tår c

tear² [tɛə] n reva c

tease [tiːz] v reta

tea set ['tiːset] n teservis c

tea-shop ['tiːʃɔp] n tesalong c

teaspoon ['tiːspuːn] n tesked c

teaspoonful ['tiːspuːn,ful] n tesked c

technical ['teknikəl] adj teknisk

technical support ['teknikəl sə'pɔːt] n teknisk support c

technician [tek'niʃən] n tekniker c

technique [tek'niːk] n teknik c

technological [,teknə'lɔdʒikəl] adj teknologisk

technology [tek'nɔlədʒi] n teknologi c

teenager ['tiː,neidʒə] n tonåring c

telecommunications [,telikəmjuːni'keiʃənz] n telekommunikation c

Thai

telegram ['teligræm] n
telegram nt
telegraph ['teligra:f] v
telegrafera
telepathy [ti'lepəθi] n
telepati c
telephone ['telifoun] n
telefon c; ~ **book** Am
telefonkatalog c; ~ **booth**
telefonhytt c; ~ **call**
telefonsamtal nt; ~
directory telefonkatalog c;
~ **operator** telefonist c
television ['teliviʒən] n
television c; **cable** ~ kabel-
-TV c; **satellite** ~ satellit-TV
c; ~ **set** televisionsapparat c
telex ['teleks] n telex nt
*tell [tel] v tala om; berätta,
*säga
telly ['teli] n colloquial tv c
temper ['tempə] n humör nt
temperature ['temprətʃə] n
temperatur c
tempest ['tempist] n oväder
nt
temple ['tempəl] n tempel nt;
tinning c
temporary ['tempərəri] adj
tillfällig, provisorisk
tempt [tempt] v fresta
temptation [temp'teiʃən] n
frestelse c
ten [ten] num tio
tenant ['tenənt] n hyresgäst c
tend [tend] v tendera; vårda;
~ to tendera åt
tendency ['tendənsi] n
benägenhet c, tendens c
tender ['tendə] adj öm; mör

tendon ['tendən] n sena c
tennis ['tenis] n tennis c; ~
shoes tennisskor pl
tennis court ['teniskɔ:t] n
tennisplan c, tennisbana c
tense [tens] adj spänd
tension ['tenʃən] n spänning
c
tent [tent] n tält nt
tenth [tenθ] num tionde
tepid ['tepid] adj ljum
term [tə:m] n term c; period
c, termin c; villkor nt
terminal ['tə:minəl] n
ändstation c
terrace ['terəs] n terrass c
terrain [te'rein] n terräng c
terrible ['teribəl] adj
förskräcklig, hemsk,
förfärlig
terrific [tə'rifik] adj
storartad
terrify ['terifai] v förskräcka;
terrifying skrämmande
territory ['teritəri] n område
nt, territorium nt
terror ['terə] n skräck c
terrorism ['terərizəm] n
terrorism c, terror c
terrorist ['terərist] n terrorist
c
test [test] n prov nt, prövning
c; v pröva, testa
testify ['testifai] v vittna
text [tekst] n text c
textbook ['teksbuk] n
lärobok c
texture ['tekstʃə] n struktur c
Thai [tai] adj thailändsk; n
thailändare c

Thailand ['tailænd] Thailand

than [ðæn] *conj* än

thank [θæŋk] *v* tacka; ~ **you** tack *nt*

thankful ['θæŋkfəl] *adj* tacksam

that [ðæt] *adj* den, den där; *pron* den där; som; *conj* att

thaw [θɔ:] *v* smälta, töa; *n* töväder *nt*

the [ðə,ði] *art* -en *suf*; **the ...** **the ...** ju ... desto

theatre ['θiətə] *n* teater *c*

theft [θeft] *n* stöld *c*

their [ðeə] *adj* deras

them [ðem] *pron* dem

theme [θi:m] *n* tema *nt*, ämne *nt*

themselves [ðəm'selvz] *pron* sig; själva

then [ðen] *adv* då; sedan, därefter

theology [θi'ɔlədʒi] *n* teologi *c*

theoretical [θiə'retikəl] *adj* teoretisk

theory ['θiəri] *n* teori *c*

therapy ['θerəpi] *n* terapi *c*

there [ðeə] *adv* där; dit

therefore ['ðeəfɔ:] *conj* därför

thermometer [θə'mɔmitə] *n* termometer *c*

thermostat ['θə:məstæt] *n* termostat *c*

these [ði:z] *adj* de här

thesis ['θi:sis] *n* (pl theses) tes *c*

they [ðei] *pron* de

thick [θik] *adj* tät; tjock

thicken ['θikən] *v* tjockna, *göra tjock

thickness ['θiknəs] *n* tjocklek *c*

thief [θi:f] *n* (pl thieves) tjuv *c*

thigh [θai] *n* lår *nt*

thimble ['θimbəl] *n* fingerborg *c*

thin [θin] *adj* tunn; mager

thing [θiŋ] *n* sak *c*

think [θiŋk] *v* tycka; tänka; ~ **of** tänka på; ~ **over** fundera på

thinker ['θiŋkə] *n* tänkare *c*

third [θə:d] *num* tredje

thirst [θə:st] *n* törst *c*

thirsty ['θə:sti] *adj* törstig

thirteen [,θə:'ti:n] *num* tretton

thirteenth [,θə:'ti:nθ] *num* trettonde

thirty ['θə:ti] *num* trettio

this [ðis] *adj* den här; *pron* denna

thistle ['θisəl] *n* tistel *c*

thorn [θɔ:n] *n* tagg *c*

thorough ['θʌrə] *adj* grundlig, ordentlig

thoroughfare ['θʌrəfeə] *n* huvudväg *c*, huvudgata *c*

those [ðouz] *pron* de, de där; dessa

though [ðou] *conj* även om, fastän, ehuru; *adv* emellertid

thought¹ [θɔ:t] *v* (p, pp think)

thought² [θɔ:t] *n* tanke *c*

thoughtful ['θɔ:tfəl] *adj* tankfull; omtänksam

tin opener

thousand ['θauzənd] *num*
tusen

thread [θred] *n* tråd *c*; *v* trä
upp

threadbare ['θredbɛə] *adj*
trådsliten

threat [θret] *n* hot *nt*

threaten ['θretən] *v* hota

three [θri:] *num* tre

three-quarter [,θri:'kwɔ:tə]
adj trefjärdedels-

threshold ['θreʃould] *n*
tröskel *c*

threw [θru:] *v* (p throw)

thrifty ['θrifti] *adj*
ekonomisk

throat [θrout] *n* strupe *c*; hals
c

throne [θroun] *n* tron *c*

through [θru:] *prep* genom

throughout [θru:'aut] *adv*
överallt

throw [θrou] *n* kast *nt*

*throw [θrou] *v* slänga, kasta

thrush [θrʌʃ] *n* trast *c*

thumb [θʌm] *n* tumme *c*

thumbtack ['θʌmtæk] *nAm*
häftstift *nt*

thump [θʌmp] *v* dunka

thunder ['θʌndə] *n* åska *c*; *v*
åska

thunderstorm ['θʌndəstɔ:m]
n åskväder *nt*

thundery ['θʌndəri] *adj* åsk-

Thursday ['θə:zdi] torsdag *c*

thus [ðʌs] *adv* således

thyme [taim] *n* timjan *c*

tick [tik] *n* bock *c*; ~ off pricka
av

ticket ['tikit] *n* biljett *c*; böter

pl; ~ **collector** konduktör *c*;
~ **machine** biljettautomat *c*

tickle ['tikəl] *v* kittla

tide [taid] *n* tidvatten *nt*; **high**
~ högvatten *nt*; **low** ~
lågvatten *nt*

tidy ['taidi] *adj* städad; ~ **up**
städa

tie [tai] *v* *binda, *knyta; *n*
slips *c*

tiger ['taigə] *n* tiger *c*

tight [tait] *adj* stram; trång;
adv fast

tighten ['taitən] *v* *dra till,
*dra åt; åtstrama

tights [taits] *pl* trikåer *pl*,
strumpbyxor *pl*

tile [tail] *n* kakel *nt*;
tegelpanna *c*

till [til] *prep* tills, till; *conj* till
dess att, ända till

timber ['timbə] *n* timmer *nt*

time [taim] *n* tid *c*; gång *c*;
all the ~ hela tiden; **in** ~ i
tid; ~ **of arrival** ankomsttid
c; ~ **of departure**
avgångstid *c*

time-saving ['taim,seiviŋ]
adj tidsbesparande

timetable ['taim,teibəl] *n*
tidtabell *c*

timid ['timid] *adj* blyg

timidity [ti'midəti] *n* blyghet
c

tin [tin] *n* tenn *nt*;
konservburk *c*, burk *c*;
tinned food konserver *pl*

tinfoil ['tinfɔil] *n* folie *c*

tin opener ['ti,noupənə] *n*
konservöppnare *c*

tiny ['taini] *adj* pytteliten

tip [tip] *n* spets *c*; dricks *c*

tire¹ [taiə] *n* däck *nt*

tire² [taiə] *v* trötta

tired [taiəd] *adj* trött

tiring [taiəriŋ] *adj* tröttsam

tissue ['tiʃuː] *n* vävnad *c*; ansiktsservett *c*, pappersnäsduk *c*

title ['taitəl] *n* titel *c*

to [tuː] *prep* till, i; åt; för att

toad [toud] *n* padda *c*

toadstool ['toudstuːl] *n* svamp *c*

toast [toust] *n* rostat bröd; skål *c*

tobacco [tə'bækou] *n* (pl ~s) tobak *c*; ~ pouch tobakspung *c*

tobacconist [tə'bækənist] *n* tobakshandlare *c*; tobacconist's tobaksaffär *c*

today [tə'dei] *adv* idag

toddler ['tɔdlə] *n* litet barn

toe [tou] *n* tå *c*

toffee ['tɔfi] *n* kola *c*

together [tə'geðə] *adv* tillsammans

toilet ['tɔilət] *n* toalett *c*; ~ case necessär *c*

toilet paper ['tɔilət,peipə] *n* toalettpapper *nt*

toiletry ['tɔilətri] *n* toalettartiklar *pl*

token ['toukən] *n* tecken *nt*; bevis *nt*; pollett *c*

told [tould] *v* (p, pp tell)

tolerable ['tɔlərəbəl] *adj* uthärdlig

toll [toul] *n* vägavgift *c*

tomato [tə'mɑːtou] *n* (pl ~es) tomat *c*

tomb [tuːm] *n* grav *c*

tombstone ['tuːmstoun] *n* gravsten *c*

tomorrow [tə'mɔrou] *adv* i morgon

ton [tʌn] *n* ton *nt*

tone [toun] *n* ton *c*; klang *c*

tongs [tɔŋz] *pl* tång *c*

tongue [tʌŋ] *n* tunga *c*

tonic ['tɔnik] *n* stärkande medel

tonight [tə'nait] *adv* i natt, i kväll

tonsilitis [,tɔnsə'laitis] *n* halsfluss *c*

tonsils ['tɔnsəlz] *pl* halsmandlar *pl*

too [tuː] *adv* alltför; också

took [tuk] *v* (p take)

tool [tuːl] *n* redskap *nt*, verktyg *nt*; ~ kit vertygssats *c*

toot [tuːt] *vAm* tuta

tooth [tuːθ] *n* (pl teeth) tand *c*

toothache ['tuːθeik] *n* tandvärk *c*

toothbrush ['tuːθbrʌʃ] *n* tandborste *c*

toothpaste ['tuːθpeist] *n* tandkräm *c*

toothpick ['tuːθpik] *n* tandpetare *c*

toothpowder ['tuːθ,paudə] *n* tandpulver *nt*

top [tɔp] *n* topp *c*; översida *c*; lock *nt*; övre; on ~ of ovanpå; ~ side översida *c*

topic ['tɔpik] *n* samtalsämne *nt*

topical ['tɔpikəl] adj aktuell

torch [tɔːtʃ] n fackla c; ficklampa c

torment¹ [tɔːˈment] v plåga

torment² [tɔːˈment] n pina c

torture [ˈtɔːtʃə] n tortyr c; v tortera

toss [tɔs] v kasta

tot [tɔt] n litet barn

total [ˈtoutəl] adj total, fullständig; n summa c

totalitarian [ˌtoutæliˈteəriən] adj totalitär

touch [tʌtʃ] v vidröra, röra; beröra; n beröring c; känsel c

touching [ˈtʌtʃiŋ] adj rörande

tough [tʌf] adj seg

tour [tuə] n rundresa c

tourism [ˈtuərizəm] n turism c

tourist [ˈtuərist] n turist c; ~ class turistklass c; ~ office turistbyrå c

tournament [ˈtuənəmənt] n turnering c

tow [tou] v *ta på släp, bogsera

towards [təˈwɔːdz] prep mot; gentemot; åt

towel [tauəl] n handduk c

towelling [ˈtauəliŋ] n handduktyg nt

tower [tauə] n torn nt

town [taun] n stad c; ~ centre stadscentrum nt; ~ hall stadshus nt

townspeople [ˈtaunzˌpiːpəl] pl stadsbor pl

toxic [ˈtɔksik] adj giftig

toy [tɔi] n leksak c

toyshop [ˈtɔiʃɔp] n leksaksaffär c

trace [treis] n spår nt; v spåra

track [træk] n järnvägsspår nt; bana c

tractor [ˈtræktə] n traktor c

trade [treid] n handel c; yrke nt; v *driva handel

trade union [ˌtreidˈjuːnjən] n fackförening c

trademark [ˈtreidmaːk] n varumärke nt

trader [ˈtreidə] n affärsman c

tradesman [ˈtreidzmən] n (pl -men) handelsman c

tradeswoman [ˈtreidzwumən] n handelsidkare (kvinnlig) c

tradition [trəˈdiʃən] n tradition c

traditional [trəˈdiʃənəl] adj traditionell

traffic [ˈtræfik] n trafik c; ~ jam trafikstockning c; ~ light trafikljus nt

trafficator [ˈtræfikeitə] n körriktningsvisare c

tragedy [ˈtrædʒədi] n tragedi c

tragic [ˈtrædʒik] adj tragisk

trail [treil] n spår nt, stig c

trailer [ˈtreilə] n släpvagn c; nAm husvagn c

train [trein] n tåg nt; v träna, dressera; stopping ~ persontåg nt; through ~ snälltåg nt; ~ ferry tågfärja c

trainee [trei'ni:] *n* praktikant
c

trainer ['treinə] *n* tränare *c*

training ['treiniŋ] *n* träning *c*

trait [treit] *n* drag *nt*

traitor ['treitə] *n* förrädare *c*

tram [træm] *n* spårvagn *c*

tramp [træmp] *n* luffare *c*; *v*
vandra

tranquil ['træŋkwil] *adj* lugn

tranquillizer ['træŋkwilaizə]
n lugnande medel

transaction [træn'zækʃən] *n*
transaktion *c*

transatlantic
[ˌtrænzət'læntik] *adj*
transatlantisk

transfer [træns'fə:] *v*
överföra

transform [træns'fɔ:m] *v*
förvandla, omvandla

transformer [træns'fɔ:mə] *n*
transformator *c*

transition [træn'siʃən] *n*
övergång *c*

translate [træns'leit] *v*
*översätta

translation [træns'leiʃən] *n*
översättning *c*

translator [træns'leitə] *n*
översättare *c*

transmission [trænz'miʃən]
n sändning *c*

transmit [trænz'mit] *v*
sända

transmitter [trænz'mitə] *n*
sändare *c*

transparent [træn'speərənt]
adj genomskinlig

transport[1] ['trænspɔ:t] *n*

transport *c*

transport[2] [træn'spɔ:t] *v*
transportera

transportation
[ˌtrænspɔ:'teiʃən] *n*
transport *c*

trap [træp] *n* fälla *c*

trash [træʃ] *n* smörja *c*; ~ **can**
Am soptunna *c*

travel ['trævəl] *v* resa; ~
agency resebyrå *c*; ~
insurance reseförsäkring *c*;
travelling expenses
resekostnader *pl*

traveller ['trævələ] *n* resenär
c; **traveller's cheque**
resecheck *c*

tray [trei] *n* bricka *c*

treason ['tri:zən] *n* förräderi
nt

treasure ['treʒə] *n* skatt *c*

treasurer ['treʒərə] *n*
skattmästare *c*

treasury ['treʒəri] *n*
föreningskassa *c*,
skattkammare *c*

treat [tri:t] *v* behandla

treatment ['tri:tmənt] *n*
behandling *c*

treaty ['tri:ti] *n* traktat *c*

tree [tri:] *n* träd *nt*

tremble ['trembəl] *v* skälva,
darra

tremendous [tri'mendəs] *adj*
oerhörd

trendy ['trendi] *adj colloquial*
trendig

trespass ['trespəs] *v*
inkräkta

trespasser ['trespəsə] *n*

369

Turkey

inkräktare *c*
trial [traiəl] *n* rättegång *c*;
prov *nt*
triangle ['traiæŋgəl] *n*
triangel *c*
triangular [trai'æŋgjulə] *adj*
trekantig
tribe [traib] *n* stam *c*
tributary ['tribjutəri] *n* biflod
c
tribute ['tribju:t] *n* hyllning *c*
trick [trik] *n* spratt *nt*;
konststycke *nt*, trick *nt*
trigger ['trigə] *n* avtryckare
c
trim [trim] *v* trimma
trip [trip] *n* tripp *c*, resa *c*,
utflykt *c*
triumph ['traiəmf] *n* triumf *c*;
v triumfera
triumphant [trai'ʌmfənt] *adj*
segerrik
troops [tru:ps] *pl* trupper *pl*
tropical ['trɔpikəl] *adj*
tropisk
tropics ['trɔpiks] *pl*
tropikerna *pl*
trouble ['trʌbəl] *n* möda *c*,
besvär *nt*, bekymmer *nt*; *v*
besvära
troublesome ['trʌbəlsəm]
adj besvärlig
trousers ['trauzəz] *pl*
långbyxor *pl*
trout [traut] *n* (pl ~) forell *c*
truck [trʌk] *nAm* lastbil *c*
true [tru:] *adj* sann; äkta,
verklig; trofast, trogen
trumpet ['trʌmpit] *n* trumpet
c

trunk [trʌŋk] *n* koffert *c*; stam
c; *nAm* bagageutrymme *nt*;
trunks gymnastikbyxor *pl*
long-distance call
['lɔŋkkɔ:l] *n* rikssamtal *nt*
trust [trʌst] *v* lita på; *n*
förtroende *nt*
trustworthy ['trʌst,wə:ði]
adj pålitlig
truth [tru:θ] *n* sanning *c*
truthful ['tru:θful] *adj*
sannfärdig
try [trai] *v* försöka, bemöda
sig; *n* försök *nt*; ~ **on** prova
tube [tju:b] *n* rör *nt*; tub *c*
tuberculosis
[tju:,bə:kju'lousis] *n*
tuberkulos *c*
Tuesday ['tju:zdi] tisdag *c*
tug [tʌg] *n* bogsera; *n*
bogserbåt *c*; ryck *nt*
tuition [tju:'iʃən] *n*
undervisning *c*
tulip ['tju:lip] *n* tulpan *c*
tumour ['tju:mə] *n* tumör *c*
tuna ['tju:nə] *n* (pl ~, ~s)
tonfisk *c*
tune [tju:n] *n* melodi *c*, visa *c*;
~ **in** ställa in
tuneful ['tju:nfəl] *adj*
melodisk
tunic ['tju:nik] *n* tunika *c*
Tunisia [tju:'niziə] Tunisien
Tunisian [tju:'niziən] *adj*
tunisisk; *n* tunisier *c*
tunnel ['tʌnəl] *n* tunnel *c*
turbine ['tə:bain] *n* turbin *c*
turbojet [,tə:bou'dʒet] *n*
turbojet *c*
Turkey ['tə:ki] Turkiet

turkey ['tə:ki] *n* kalkon *c*

Turkish ['tə:kiʃ] *adj* turkisk; ~ **bath** turkiskt bad

turn [tə:n] *v* vända, svänga, *vrida om; *n* varv *nt*, vändning *c*; tur *c*; ~ **back** vända tillbaka; ~ **down** förkasta; ~ **into** förvandlas till; ~ **off** stänga av; ~ **on** *sätta på, tända, skruva på; ~ **over** vända upp och ner; ~ **round** vända på; vända sig om

turning ['tə:niŋ] *n* kurva *c*

turning point ['tə:niŋpɔint] *n* vändpunkt *c*

turnover ['tə:,nouvə] *n* omsättning *c*; ~ **tax** omsättningsskatt *c*

turnpike ['tə:npaik] *nAm* motorväg *c*

turpentine ['tə:pəntain] *n* terpentin *nt*

turtle ['tə:təl] *n* sköldpadda *c*

tutor ['tju:tə] *n* informator *c*; förmyndare *c*

tuxedo [tʌk'si:dou] *nAm* (pl ~s, ~es) smoking *c*

TV [,ti:'vi:] *n colloquial* TV *c*; **on** ~ på TV

tweed [twi:d] *n* tweed *c*

tweezers ['twi:zəz] *pl* pincett

c

twelfth [twelfθ] *num* tolfte

twelve [twelv] *num* tolv

twentieth ['twentiəθ] *num* tjugonde

twenty ['twenti] *num* tjugo

twice [twais] *adv* två gånger

twig [twig] *n* kvist *c*

twilight ['twailait] *n* skymning *c*

twine [twain] *n* snodd *c*

twins [twinz] *pl* tvillingar *pl*; **twin beds** dubbelsängar *pl*

twist [twist] *v* *vrida; *n* vridning *c*

two [tu:] *num* två

two-piece [,tu:'pi:s] *adj* tvådelad

type [taip] *v* *skriva maskin; *n* typ *c*

typewriter ['taipraitə] *n* skrivmaskin *c*

typhoid ['taifɔid] *n* tyfus *c*

typical ['tipikəl] *adj* karakteristisk, typisk

typist ['taipist] *n* maskinskriverska *c*

tyrant ['taiərənt] *n* tyrann *c*

tyre [taiə] *n* däck *nt*; ~ **pressure** slangtryck *nt*

U

ugly ['ʌgli] *adj* ful

ulcer ['ʌlsə] *n* sår *nt*

ultimate ['ʌltimət] *adj* sista

ultraviolet [,ʌltrə'vaiələt] *adj*

ultraviolett

umbrella [ʌm'brelə] *n* paraply *nt*

umpire ['ʌmpaiə] *n* domare *c*

unable [ʌ'neibəl] *adj*
oförmögen

unacceptable
[ˌʌnək'septəbəl] *adj*
oantagbar

unaccountable
[ˌʌnə'kauntəbəl] *adj*
oförklarlig

unaccustomed
[ˌʌnə'kʌstəmd] *adj* ovan

unanimous [ju:'næniməs]
adj enstämmig

unanswered [ˌʌ'nɑːnsəd] *adj*
obesvarad

unauthorized
[ˌʌ'nɔːθəraizd]
adj oberättigad

unavoidable [ˌʌnə'vɔidəbəl]
adj oundviklig

unaware [ˌʌnə'wɛə] *adj*
omedveten

unbearable [ʌn'bɛərəbəl] *adj*
outhärdlig

unbreakable [ˌʌn'breikəbəl]
adj okrossbar

unbroken [ʌn'broukən] *adj*
intakt

unbutton [ˌʌn'bʌtən] *v*
knäppa upp

uncertain [ʌn'səːtən] *adj*
oviss, osäker

uncle ['ʌŋkəl] *n* farbror *c*,
morbror *c*

unclean [ˌʌn'kliːn] *adj* oren

uncomfortable
[ʌn'kʌmfətəbəl] *adj*
obekväm

uncommon [ʌn'kɔmən] *adj*
sällsynt, ovanlig

unconditional
[ˌʌnkən'diʃənəl] *adj*
ovillkorlig

unconscious [ʌn'kɔnʃəs]
adj medvetslös

uncork [ˌʌn'kɔːk] *v* korka
upp

uncover [ʌn'kʌvə] *v* avtäcka

uncultivated
[ˌʌn'kʌltiveitid] *adj*
ouppodlad, okultiverad

under ['ʌndə] *prep* under,
nedanför

undercurrent ['ʌndəˌkʌrənt]
n underström *c*

underestimate
[ˌʌndə'restimeit] *v*
underskatta

underground ['ʌndəgraund]
adj underjordisk; *n*
tunnelbana *c*

underline [ˌʌndə'lain] *v*
*stryka under

underneath [ˌʌndə'niːθ] *adv*
under

underpants ['ʌndəpænts]
plAm kalsonger *pl*

undershirt ['ʌndəʃəːt] *n*
undertröja *c*

***understand** [ˌʌndə'stænd] *v*
*förstå

understanding
[ˌʌndə'stændiŋ] *n* förstårelse
c

understatement
[ˌʌndə'steitmənt] *n*
underdrift *c*

***undertake** [ˌʌndə'teik] *v*
*företa

undertaking [ˌʌndə'teikiŋ] *n*
företag *nt*

underwater ['ʌndəˌwɔːtə]

adj undervattens-
underwear ['ʌndəwɛə] *n*
underkläder *pl*
undesirable
[ˌʌndi'zaiərəbəl] *adj*
ovälkommen; ej önskvärd
***undo** [ˌʌn'du:] *v* lösa upp
undoubtedly [ʌn'dautidli]
adv otvivelaktigt
undress [ˌʌn'dres] *v* klä av
sig
unearned [ˌʌ'nə:nd] *adj*
oförtjänt
uneasy [ʌ'ni:zi] *adj* olustig
uneducated [ˌʌ'nedjukeitid]
adj obildad
unemployed [ˌʌnim'plɔid]
adj arbetslös
unemployment
[ˌʌnim'plɔimənt] *n*
arbetslöshet *c*
unequal [ˌʌ'ni:kwəl] *adj*
olika
uneven [ˌʌ'ni:vən] *adj* ojämn
unexpected [ˌʌnik'spektid]
adj oanad, oväntad
unfair [ˌʌn'fɛə] *adj* ojust,
orättvis
unfaithful [ˌʌn'feiθfəl] *adj*
otrogen
unfamiliar [ˌʌnfə'miljə] *adj*
obekant
unfasten [ˌʌn'fɑ:sən] *v* lossa
unfavourable
[ˌʌn'feivərəbəl] *adj*
ogynnsam
unfit [ˌʌn'fit] *adj* olämplig
unfold [ʌn'fould] *v* veckla ut
unfortunate [ʌn'fɔ:tʃənət]
adj olycklig

unfortunately
[ʌn'fɔ:tʃənətli] *adv* tyvärr,
dessvärre
unfriendly [ˌʌn'frendli] *adj*
ovänlig
ungrateful [ʌn'greitfəl] *adj*
otacksam
unhappy [ʌn'hæpi] *adj*
olycklig
unhealthy [ʌn'helθi] *adj*
ohälsosam
unhurt [ˌʌn'hə:t] *adj* oskadad
uniform ['ju:nifɔ:m] *n*
uniform *c*; *adj* likformig,
konstant
unimportant [ˌʌnim'pɔ:tənt]
adj oviktig
uninhabitable
[ˌʌnin'hæbitəbəl] *adj*
obeboelig
uninhabited [ˌʌnin'hæbitid]
adj obebodd
unintentional
[ˌʌnin'tenʃənəl] *adj*
oavsiktlig
union ['ju:njən] *n*
fackförening *c*; förening *c*;
union *c*
unique [ju:'ni:k] *adj* unik
unit ['ju:nit] *n* enhet *c*
unite [ju:'nait] *v* förena
united [ju'naitid] *adj*
förenad
United States [ju:'naitid
steits] Förenta Staterna
unity ['ju:nəti] *n* enhet *c*
universal [ˌju:ni'və:səl] *adj*
universell, allmän
universe ['ju:nivə:s] *n*
universum *nt*

university [ˌjuːniˈvəːsəti] *n*
universitet *nt*

unjust [ˌʌnˈdʒʌst] *adj*
orättvis

unkind [ʌnˈkaind] *adj* ovänlig

unknown [ˌʌnˈnoun] *adj*
okänd

unlawful [ˌʌnˈlɔːfəl] *adj*
olaglig

unlearn [ˌʌnˈləːn] *v* lära sig av
med

unless [ənˈles] *conj* såvida
inte

unlike [ˌʌnˈlaik] *adj* olik

unlikely [ʌnˈlaikli] *adj*
osannolik

unlimited [ʌnˈlimitid] *adj*
obegränsad

unload [ˌʌnˈloud] *v* lasta av

unlock [ˌʌnˈlɔk] *v* låsa upp

unlucky [ʌnˈlʌki] *adj* oturlig,
olycklig

unnecessary [ʌnˈnesəsəri]
adj onödig

unoccupied [ˌʌˈnɔkjupaid]
adj ledig

unofficial [ˌʌnəˈfiʃəl] *adj*
inofficiell

unpack [ˌʌnˈpæk] *v* packa
upp

unpleasant [ʌnˈplezənt] *adj*
otrevlig, obehaglig,
oangenäm

unpopular [ʌnˈpɔpjulə] *adj*
illa omtyckt, impopulär

unprotected [ˌʌnprəˈtektid]
adj oskyddad

unqualified [ˌʌnˈkwɔlifaid]
adj okvalificerad

unreal [ˌʌnˈriəl] *adj* overklig

unreasonable
[ʌnˈriːzənəbəl] *adj* orimlig,
oresonlig

unreliable [ˌʌnriˈlaiəbəl] *adj*
opålitlig

unrest [ˌʌnˈrest] *n* oro *c*;
rastlöshet *c*

unsafe [ʌnˈseif] *adj* riskabel

unsatisfactory
[ˌʌnsætisˈfæktəri] *adj*
otillfredsställande

unscrew [ˌʌnˈskruː] *v* skruva
av

unselfish [ʌnˈselfiʃ] *adj*
osjälvisk

unsound [ʌnˈsaund] *adj*
osund

unstable [ʌnˈsteibəl] *adj*
instabil

unsteady [ˌʌnˈstedi] *adj*
ostadig, vacklande; villrådig

unsuccessful
[ˌʌnsəkˈsesfəl] *adj*
misslyckad

unsuitable [ˌʌnˈsuːtəbəl] *adj*
opassande

unsurpassed [ˌʌnsəˈpɑːst]
adj oöverträffad

untidy [ʌnˈtaidi] *adj*
oordentlig

untie [ˌʌnˈtai] *v* *knyta upp

until [ənˈtil] *prep* tills, till

untrue [ˌʌnˈtruː] *adj* osann

untrustworthy
[ˌʌnˈtrʌstˌwəːði] *adj*
opålitlig

unusual [ʌnˈjuːʒuəl] *adj*
ovanlig

unwell [ˌʌnˈwel] *adj* krasslig

unwilling [ˌʌnˈwiliŋ] *adj*

ovillig

unwise [ˌʌn'waiz] *adj* oförståndig

unwrap [ˌʌn'ræp] *v* veckla upp, öppna

up [ʌp] *adv* upp, uppåt

upholster [ʌp'houlstə] *v* stoppa möbler; inreda

upkeep ['ʌpkiːp] *n* underhåll *nt*

uplands ['ʌpləndz] *pl* högland *nt*

upload ['ʌpˌloud] *v* ladda upp

upon [ə'pɔn] *prep* på

upper ['ʌpə] *adj* över-, övre

upright ['ʌprait] *adj* upprätt; *adv* upprätt

upscale ['ʌpˌskeil] *adj* exklusiv

upset [ˌʌp'set] *adj* upprörd

*upset [ˌʌp'set] *v* kullkasta; förvirra, såra

upside down [ˌʌpsaid'daun] *adv* upp och ner

upstairs [ˌʌp'steəz] *adv* upp; uppför trappan; en trappa upp

upstream [ˌʌp'striːm] *adv* uppför strömmen

upwards ['ʌpwədz] *adv* upp, uppåt

urban ['əːbən] *adj* stads-

urge [əːdʒ] *v* uppmana; *n* starkt behov

urgency ['əːdʒənsi] *n* nödtvång *nt*

urgent ['əːdʒənt] *adj*

brådskande

urine ['juərin] *n* urin *nt*

Uruguay ['juərəgwai] Uruguay

Uruguayan [ˌjuərə'gwaiən] *adj* uruguaysk; *n* uruguayare *c*

us [ʌs] *pron* oss

usable ['juːzəbəl] *adj* användbar

usage ['juːzidʒ] *n* sedvänja *c*

use¹ [juːz] *v* använda; ***be used to** *vara van vid; **~ up** förbruka

use² [juːs] *n* användning *c*; ***be of ~** *vara till nytta

useful ['juːsfəl] *adj* användbar, nyttig

useless ['juːsləs] *adj* lönlös, oanvändbar, oduglig

user ['juːzə] *n* förbrukare *c*

usher ['ʌʃə] *n* platsanvisare *c*

usherette [ˌʌʃə'ret] *n* platsanviserska *c*

usual ['juːʒuəl] *adj* vanlig

usually ['juːʒuəli] *adv* vanligtvis

utensil [juː'tensəl] *n* redskap *nt*, verktyg *nt*; köksredskap *nt*

utility [juː'tiləti] *n* nyttighet *c*

utilize ['juːtilaiz] *v* utnyttja, använda

utmost ['ʌtmoust] *adj* yttersta

utter ['ʌtə] *adj* fullständig, total; *v* yttra

V

vacancy ['veikənsi] n vakans c

vacant ['veikənt] adj ledig

vacate [və'keit] v utrymma

vacation [və'keiʃən] n lov nt

vaccinate ['væksineit] v vaccinera

vaccination [,væksi'neiʃən] n vaccination c

vacuum ['vækjuəm] n vakuum nt; vAm *dammsuga; ~ cleaner dammsugare c; ~ flask termosflaska c

vague [veig] adj vag

vain [vein] adj fåfänglig; tom, fruktlös; in ~ förgäves

valet ['vælit] n betjänt c; v passa upp

valid ['vælid] adj giltig

valley ['væli] n dal c, dalsänka c

valuable ['væljubəl] adj värdefull, dyrbar; **valuables** pl värdesaker pl

value ['vælju:] n värde nt; v värdera

valve [vælv] n ventil c

van [væn] n transportbil c

vanilla [və'nilə] n vanilj c

vanish ['væniʃ] v *försvinna

vapour ['veipə] n ånga c

variable ['veəriəbəl] adj växlande

variation [,veəri'eiʃən] n förändring c

varied ['veərid] adj varierad

variety [və'raiəti] n art c, omväxling c

various ['veəriəs] adj åtskilliga, olika

varnish ['vɑ:niʃ] n lack nt, fernissa c; v fernissa, lacka

vary ['veəri] v variera; ändra; *vara olik

vase [vɑ:z] n vas c

vast [vɑ:st] adj vidsträckt, ofantlig

vault [vɔ:lt] n valv nt; kassavalv nt

veal [vi:l] n kalvkött nt

vegan ['vi:gən] n vegan c; adj vegansk

vegetable ['vedʒətəbəl] n grönsak c; ~ merchant grönsakshandlare c

vegetarian [,vedʒi'teəriən] n vegetarian c

vegetation [,vedʒi'teiʃən] n vegetation c

vehicle ['vi:əkəl] n fordon nt

veil [veil] n slöja c

vein [vein] n åder c; varicose ~ åderbrock nt

velvet ['velvit] n sammet c

velveteen [,velvi'ti:n] n bomullssammet c

venerable ['venərəbəl] adj vördnadsvärd

venereal disease [vi'niəriəl di'zi:z] könssjukdom c

Venezuela [,veni'zweilə]
Venezuela

Venezuelan [,veni'zweilən]
adj venezuelansk; *n*
venezuelan *c*

ventilate ['ventileit] *v*
ventilera, lufta, vädra

ventilation [,venti'leiʃən] *n*
ventilation *c*

ventilator ['ventileitə] *n*
ventilator *c*

venture ['ventʃə] *n* våga

veranda [və'rændə] *n*
veranda *c*

verb [və:b] *n* verb *nt*

verbal ['və:bəl] *adj* muntlig

verdict ['və:dikt] *n* dom *c*,
domslut *nt*

verge [və:dʒ] *n* kant *c*; gräns
c

verify ['verifai] *v* verifiera,
kontrollera; bekräfta

verse [və:s] *n* vers *c*

version ['və:ʃən] *n* version *c*;
översättning *c*

versus ['və:səs] *prep* kontra

vertical ['və:tikəl] *adj* lodrät

very ['veri] *adv* mycket; *adj*
verklig, sann; absolut

vessel ['vesəl] *n* fartyg *nt*;
kärl *nt*

vest [vest] *n* undertröja *c*;
nAm väst *c*

veterinary surgeon
['vetrinəri 'sə:dʒən]
veterinär *c*

via [vaiə] *prep* via

viaduct ['vaiədʌkt] *n* viadukt
c

vibrate [vai'breit] *v* vibrera

vibration [vai'breiʃən] *n*
vibration *c*

vicinity [vi'sinəti] *n* närhet *c*,
omgivningar

vicious ['viʃəs] *adj*
ondskefull

victim ['viktim] *n* offer *nt*

victory ['viktəri] *n* seger *c*

video ['vidiou] *n* video; ~
camera videokamera *c*; ~
cassette videokassett *c*; ~
game videospel *nt*; ~
recorder videospelare *c*; ~
recording videoinspelning *c*

view [vju:] *n* utsikt *c*; åsikt *c*,
uppfattning *c*; *v* betrakta

viewfinder ['vju:,faində] *n*
sökare *c*

vigilant ['vidʒilənt] *adj*
vaksam

villa ['vilə] *n* villa *c*

village ['vilidʒ] *n* by *c*

villain ['vilən] *n* skurk *c*

vine [vain] *n* vinranka *c*

vinegar ['vinigə] *n* vinäger *c*

vineyard ['vinjəd] *n* vingård
c

vintage ['vintidʒ] *n* vinskörd
c

violation [vaiə'leiʃən] *n*
kränkning *c*

violence ['vaiələns] *n* våld *nt*

violent ['vaiələnt] *adj*
våldsam, häftig

violet ['vaiələt] *n* viol *c*; *adj*
violett

violin [vaiə'lin] *n* fiol *c*

VIP [,vi: ai'pi:] *n* VIP *c*

virgin ['və:dʒin] *n* jungfru *c*

virtue ['və:tʃu:] *n* dygd *c*

virus ['vairəs] n virus c
visa ['vi:zə] n visum nt
visibility [,vizə'biləti] n sikt c
visible ['vizəbəl] adj synlig
vision ['viʒən] n vision c
visit ['vizit] v besöka; n besök nt, visit c; **visiting hours** besökstid c
visitor ['vizitə] n besökare c
vital ['vaitəl] adj livsviktig
vitamin ['vitəmin] n vitamin nt
vivid ['vivid] adj livlig
vocabulary [və'kæbjuləri] n ordförråd nt; ordlista c
vocal ['voukəl] adj vokal-
vocalist ['voukəlist] n vokalist c
voice [vɔis] n röst c
voice mail ['vois.,meil] n röstbrevlåda c
void [vɔid] adj ogiltig
volcano [vɔl'keinou] n (pl ~es, ~s) vulkan c

volt [voult] n volt c
voltage ['voultidʒ] n spänning c
volume ['vɔljum] n volym c; bokband nt
voluntary ['vɔləntəri] adj frivillig
volunteer [,vɔlən'tiə] n frivillig c
vomit ['vɔmit] v kräkas, spy
vote [vout] v rösta; n röst c; röstning c
voter ['voutə] n väljare c
voucher ['vautʃə] n kupong c, bong c
vow [vau] n löfte nt, ed c; v *svära
vowel [vauəl] n vokal c
voyage ['vɔiidʒ] n resa c
vulgar ['vʌlgə] adj vulgär, vanlig
vulnerable ['vʌlnərəbəl] adj sårbar
vulture ['vʌltʃə] n gam c

W

wade [weid] v vada
wafer ['weifə] n rån nt
waffle ['wɔfəl] n våffla c
wages ['weidʒiz] pl lön c
waggon ['wægən] n vagn c
waist [weist] n midja c
waistcoat ['weiskout] n väst c
wait [weit] v vänta; ~ **on** uppassa
waiter ['weitə] n kypare c,

vaktmästare c
waiting ['weitiŋ] n väntan c
waiting list ['weitiŋlist] n väntelista c
waiting room ['weitiŋru:m] n väntrum c
waitress ['weitris] n servitris c
***wake** [weik] v väcka; ~ **up** vakna
walk [wɔ:k] v *gå;

walker   378

promenera; *n* promenad *c*;
sätt att gå; **walking** till fots
walker ['wɔːkə] *n* vandrare *c*
walking stick ['wɔːkiŋstik] *n*
promenadkäpp *c*
wall [wɔːl] *n* mur *c*; vägg *c*
wallet ['wɔlit] *n* plånbok *c*
wallpaper ['wɔːl,peipə] *n*
tapet *c*
walnut ['wɔːlnʌt] *n* valnöt *c*
waltz [wɔːls] *n* vals *c*
wander ['wɔndə] *v* ströva
omkring, vandra
want [wɔnt] *v* *vilja; önska; *n*
behov *nt*; brist *c*
war [wɔː] *n* krig *nt*
warden ['wɔːdən] *n*
intendent *c*, föreståndare *c*
wardrobe ['wɔːdroub] *n*
garderob *c*, klädskåp *nt*
warehouse ['weəhaus] *n*
förrådsbyggnad *c*, magasin
nt
wares [weəz] *pl* varor *pl*
warm [wɔːm] *adj* varm; *v*
värma
warmth [wɔːmθ] *n* värme *c*
warn [wɔːn] *v* varna
warning ['wɔːniŋ] *n* varning
c
wary ['weəri] *adj* varsam
was [wɔz] *v* (p be)
wash [wɔʃ] *v* tvätta; **~ and
wear** strykfri; **~ up** diska
washable ['wɔʃəbəl] *adj*
tvättbar
washbasin ['wɔʃ,beisən] *n*
handfat *c*
washing ['wɔʃiŋ] *n* tvätt *c*
washing machine

['wɔʃiŋmə,ʃiːn] *n*
tvättmaskin *c*
washing powder
['wɔʃiŋ,paudə] *n* tvättmedel
nt
washroom ['wɔʃruːm] *nAm*
toalett *c*
wasp [wɔsp] *n* geting *c*
waste [weist] *v* slösa bort; *n*
slöseri *nt*; *adj* öde
wasteful ['weistfəl] *adj*
slösaktig
wastepaper basket
[weist'peipə,baːskit] *n*
papperskorg *c*
watch [wɔtʃ] *v* *iaktta,
betrakta; övervaka; *n* klocka
c; **~ for** *hålla utkik; **~ out**
*se upp
watchmaker ['wɔtʃ,meikə] *n*
urmakare *c*
watchstrap ['wɔtʃstræp] *n*
klockarmband *nt*
water ['wɔːtə] *n* vatten *nt*;
iced ~ isvatten *nt*; **running ~**
rinnande vatten; **~ pump**
vattenpump *c*; **~ ski**
vattenskida *c*
watercolo(u)r ['wɔːtə,kʌlə] *n*
vattenfärg *c*; akvarell *c*
watercress ['wɔːtəkres] *n*
vattenkrasse *c*
waterfall ['wɔːtəfɔːl] *n*
vattenfall *nt*
watermelon ['wɔːtə,melən]
n vattenmelon *c*
waterproof ['wɔːtəpruːf] *adj*
vattentät
water softener
[,wɔːtə,sɔfnə] *n*

avkalkningsmedel *nt*
waterway ['wɔːtəwei] *n*
  farled *c*
watt [wɔt] *n* watt *c*
wave [weiv] *n* våg *c*; *v* vinka
wavelength ['weivleŋθ] *n*
  våglängd *c*
wavy ['weivi] *adj* vågig
wax [wæks] *n* vax *nt*
waxworks ['wækswɔːks] *pl*
  vaxkabinett *nt*
way [wei] *n* vis *nt*, sätt *nt*; väg
  c; håll *nt*, riktning *c*; avstånd
  nt; **any ~** hur som helst; **by
  the ~** förresten; **one-way
  traffic** enkelriktad trafik;
  out of the ~ avsides; **the
  other ~ round** tvärtom; **~
  back** tillbakaväg *c*; **~ in**
  ingång *c*; **~ out** utgång *c*
wayside ['weisaid] *n* vägkant
  c
we [wiː] *pron* vi
weak [wiːk] *adj* svag; tunn
weakness ['wiːknəs] *n*
  svaghet *c*
wealth [welθ] *n* rikedom *c*
wealthy ['welθi] *adj*
  förmögen
weapon ['wepən] *n* vapen *nt*;
  **weapons of mass
  destruction** *n*
  massförstörelsevapen *c*
*wear [weə] *v* *vara klädd i,
  *bära; **~ out** *slita ut
weary ['wiəri] *adj* trött,
  modlös; tröttsam
weather ['weðə] *n* väder *nt*;
  ~ forecast
  väderleksrapport *c*

*weave [wiːv] *v* väva
weaver ['wiːvə] *n* vävare *c*
website ['web,sait] *n*
  webbplats *c*
wedding ['wediŋ] *n* bröllop
  nt
wedding ring ['wediŋriŋ] *n*
  vigselring *c*
wedge [wedʒ] *n* klyfta *c*, kil *c*
Wednesday ['wenzdi]
  onsdag *c*
weed [wiːd] *n* ogräs *nt*
week [wiːk] *n* vecka *c*
weekday ['wiːkdei] *n* vardag
  c
weekly ['wiːkli] *adj* vecko-
*weep [wiːp] *v* *gråta
weigh [wei] *v* väga
weighing machine
  ['weiiŋmə,ʃiːn] *n* våg *c*
weight [weit] *n* vikt *c*
welcome ['welkəm] *adj*
  välkommen; *n* välkomnande
  nt; *v* välkomna
weld [weld] *v* svetsa
welfare ['welfeə] *n*
  välbefinnande *nt*;
  socialhjälp *c*
well[1] [wel] *adv* bra; *adj* frisk;
  as ~ likaså; **as ~ as** såväl
  som; **well!** ja ja!
well[2] [wel] *n* brunn *c*
well-founded [,wel'faundid]
  adj välgrundad
well-known [wel'noun] *adj*
  välkänd
well-to-do [,weltə'duː] *adj*
  välbärgad
went [went] *v* (p go)
were [wəː] *v* (p be)

west [west] *n* väst *c*, väster *c*

westerly ['westəli] *adj* västlig

western ['westən] *adj* västlig

wet [wet] *adj* våt

whale [weil] *n* val *c*

wharf [wɔːf] *n* (pl ~s, wharves) lastkaj *c*

what [wɔt] *pron* vad; **~ for** varför

whatever [wɔ'tevə] *pron* vad som än

wheat [wiːt] *n* vete *nt*

wheel [wiːl] *n* hjul *nt*

wheelbarrow ['wiːl,bærou] *n* skottkärra *c*

wheelchair ['wiːltʃeə] *n* rullstol *c*

when [wen] *adv* när; *conj* då, när

whenever [we'nevə] *conj* närhelst

where [weə] *adv* var; *conj* var

wherever [weə'revə] *conj* varhelst

whether ['weðə] *conj* om; **whether ... or** vare sig ... eller

which [witʃ] *pron* vilken; som

whichever [wi'tʃevə] *adj* vilken ... än

while [wail] *conj* medan; *n* stund *c*

whilst [wailst] *conj* medan

whim [wim] *n* nyck *c*, infall *nt*

whip [wip] *n* piska *c*; *v* vispa, piska

whiskers ['wiskəz] *pl* polisonger *pl*

whisper ['wispə] *v* viska; *n* viskning *c*

whistle ['wisəl] *v* vissla; *n* visselpipa *c*

white [wait] *adj* vit

whiting ['waitiŋ] *n* (pl ~) vitling *c*

who [huː] *pron* vem; som

whoever [huː'evə] *pron* vem som än

whole [houl] *adj* fullständig, hel; oskadad; *n* helhet *c*

wholesale ['houlseil] *n* grosshandel *c*; **~ dealer** grossist *c*

wholesome ['houlsəm] *adj* hälsosam

wholly ['houlli] *adv* helt och hållet

whom [huːm] *pron* till vem

whore [hɔː] *n* hora *c*

whose [huːz] *pron* vars; vems

why [wai] *adv* varför

wicked ['wikid] *adj* ond

wide [waid] *adj* vid, bred

widen ['waidən] *v* vidga

widow ['widou] *n* änka *c*

widower ['widouə] *n* änkling *c*

width [widθ] *n* bredd *c*

wife [waif] *n* (pl wives) maka *c*, hustru *c*

wi-fi, WiFi® ['waifai] *n* Wi-Fi (*nt*), WLAN *nt*; **wi-fi hotspot** *n* Wi-Fi hotspot *c*

wig [wig] *n* peruk *c*

wild [waild] *adj* vild

woodland

will [wil] *n* vilja *c*; testamente *nt*

***will** [wil] *v* *vilja; *ska

willing ['wiliŋ] *adj* villig

willpower ['wilpauə] *n* viljekraft *c*

***win** [win] *v* *vinna

wind [wind] *n* vind *c*

***wind** [waind] *v* slingra sig; *vrida, linda, *dra upp

winding ['waindiŋ] *adj* slingrande

windmill ['windmil] *n* väderkvarn *c*

window ['windou] *n* fönster *nt*

windowsill ['windousil] *n* fönsterbräde *nt*

windscreen ['windskri:n] *n* vindruta *c*; ~ **wiper** vindrutetorkare *c*

windshield ['windʃi:ld] *nAm* vindruta *c*; ~ **wiper** *nAm* vindrutetorkare *c*

windy ['windi] *adj* blåsig

wine [wain] *n* vin *nt*

wine cellar ['wain,selə] *n* vinkällare *c*

wine list ['wainlist] *n* vinlista *c*

wine merchant ['wain,mə:tʃənt] *n* vinhandlare *c*

wing [wiŋ] *n* vinge *c*

winkle ['wiŋkəl] *n* strandsnäcka *c*

winner ['winə] *n* segrare *c*

winning ['winiŋ] *adj* vinnande; **winnings** *pl* vinst *c*

winter ['wintə] *n* vinter *c*; ~ **sports** vintersport *c*

wipe [waip] *v* torka av, torka bort

wire [waiə] *n* tråd *c*; ståltråd *c*

wireless ['waiələs] *adj* trådlös

wisdom ['wizdəm] *n* visdom *c*

wise [waiz] *adj* vis

wish [wiʃ] *v* önska, *vilja ha; *n* längtan *c*, önskan *c*

wit ['wit] *n* vett *nt*

witch [witʃ] *n* häxa *c*

with [wið] *prep* med; av

***withdraw** [wið'dro:] *v* *dra tillbaka

within [wi'ðin] *prep* inom; *adv* inuti

without [wi'ðaut] *prep* utan

witness ['witnəs] *n* vittne *nt*

wits [wits] *pl* förstånd *nt*

witty ['witi] *adj* spirituell

wolf [wulf] *n* (pl wolves) varg *c*

woman ['wumən] *n* (pl women) kvinna *c*

womb [wu:m] *n* livmoder *c*

won [wʌn] *v* (p, pp win)

wonder ['wʌndə] *n* under *nt*; förundran *c*; *v* undra

wonderful ['wʌndəfəl] *adj* härlig, underbar

wood [wud] *n* trä *nt*; skog *c*

wood carving ['wud,ka:viŋ] *n* snideriarbete *nt*

wooded ['wudid] *adj* skogig

wooden ['wudən] *adj* trä-; ~ **shoe** träsko *c*

woodland ['wudlənd] *n*

wool   382

skogstrakt *c*

wool [wul] *n* ull *c*; **darning ~**
stoppgarn *nt*

woollen ['wulən] *adj* ylle-

word [wə:d] *n* ord *nt*

wore [wɔ:] *v* (p wear)

work [wə:k] *n* arbete *nt*;
syssla *c*; *v* arbeta; fungera;
working day arbetsdag *c*; **~
of art** konstverk *nt*; **~ permit**
arbetstillstånd *nt*

workaholic [,wə:kə'hɔlik] *n*
arbetsnarkoman *c*

worker ['wə:kə] *n* arbetare *c*

working ['wə:kiŋ] *n* funktion
c

working day ['wə:kiŋ] *n*
arbetsdag *c*

workman ['wə:kmən] *n* (pl
-men) arbetare *c*

works [wə:ks] *pl* fabrik *c*

workshop ['wə:kʃɔp] *n*
verkstad *c*

world [wə:ld] *n* värld *c*; **~ war**
världskrig *nt*

world-famous
[,wə:ld'feiməs] *adj*
världsberömd

world-wide ['wə:ldwaid] *adj*
världsomspännande

worm [wə:m] *n* mask *c*

worn [wɔ:n] *adj* (pp wear)
sliten

worn-out [,wɔ:n'aut] *adj*
utsliten

worried ['wʌrid] *adj* ängslig

worry ['wʌri] *v* oroa sig; *n* oro
c, bekymmer *nt*

worse [wə:s] *adj* värre; *adv*
värre

worship ['wə:ʃip] *v* dyrka; *n*
andakt *c*, gudstjänst *c*

worst [wə:st] *adj* värst; *adv*
värst

worth [wə:θ] *n* värde *nt*; ***be ~
*vara värd; **be worth-while**
*vara lönande

worthless ['wə:θləs] *adj*
värdelös

worthy of ['wə:ði əv]
värdig

would [wud] *v* (p will)

wound[1] [wu:nd] *n* sår *nt*; *v*
såra

wound[2] [waund] *v* (p, pp
wind)

wrap [ræp] *v* slå in

wreck [rek] *n* vrak *nt*; *v*
*ödelägga

wrench [rentʃ] *n* skiftnyckel
c; ryck *nt*; *v* *vrida

wrinkle ['riŋkəl] *n* rynka *c*

wrist [rist] *n* handled *c*

wristwatch ['ristwɔtʃ] *n*
armbandsur *nt*

***write** [rait] *v* *skriva; **in
writing** skriftligen; **~ down**
*skriva ner

writer ['raitə] *n* författare *c*

writing pad ['raitiŋpæd] *n*
skrivblock *nt*,
anteckningsblock *nt*

writing paper ['raitiŋ,peipə]
n brevpapper *nt*

written ['ritən] *adj* (pp write)
skriftlig

wrong [rɔŋ] *adj* orätt, fel; *n*
orätt *c*; *v* *göra orätt; **be ~**
*ha fel

wrote [rout] *v* (p write)

X

Xmas ['krisməs] n jul c

X-ray ['eksrei] n röntgenbild c; v röntga

Y

yacht [jɔt] n lustjakt c
yacht club ['jɔtklʌb] n segelsällskap nt
yachting ['jɔtiŋ] n segelsport c
yard [jɑːd] n gård c
yarn [jɑːn] n garn nt
yawn [jɔːn] v gäspa
year [jiə] n år nt
yearly ['jiəli] adj årlig
yeast [jiːst] n jäst c
yell [jel] v *tjuta; n tjut nt
yellow ['jelou] adj gul
yes [jes] ja
yesterday ['jestədi] adv igår
yet [jet] adv ännu; conj dock, likväl

yield [jiːld] v *ge avkastning; *ge efter
yoghurt ['jɔgət] n yoghurt c
yoke [jouk] n ok nt
yolk [jouk] n äggula c
you [juː] pron du; dig; ni; er
young [jʌŋ] adj ung
your [jɔː] adj din; er
yours [jɔːz] pron din; er
yourself [jɔːˈself] pron dig; själv
yourselves [jɔːˈselvz] pron er; själva
youth [juːθ] n ungdom c; ~ hostel ungdomshärbärge nt
yuppie ['jʌpi] n yuppie c

Z

zap [zæp] v knäppa
zeal [ziːl] n iver c
zealous ['zeləs] adj ivrig
zebra ['ziːbrə] n sebra c
zebra crossing ['ziːbrə krɔsiŋ] n, **crosswalk** nAm övergångsställe nt
zenith ['zeniθ] n zenit;

höjdpunkt c
zero ['ziərou] n (pl ~s) nolla c
zest [zest] n lust c
zinc [ziŋk] n zink c
zip [zip] n blixtlås nt; ~ **code** nAm postnummer nt
zipper ['zipə] n blixtlås nt

zodiac ['zoudiæk] *n*
djurkretsen

zone [zoun] *n* zon *c*; område
nt

zoo [zu:] *n* (pl ~s) zoo *nt*

zoology [zou'ɔlədʒi] *n*
zoologi *c*

Some Basic Phrases

Några vanliga uttryck

Please.	Var så god.
Thank you very much.	Tack så mycket.
Don't mention it.	Ingen orsak.
Good morning.	God morgon.
Good afternoon.	Hej. / God dag.
Good evening.	God kväll.
Good night.	God natt.
Good-bye.	Hejdå.
See you later.	Vi ses.
Where is/Where are…?	Var är…?
What do you call this?	Vad heter det här?
What does that mean?	Vad betyder det?
Do you speak English?	Talar du engelska?
Do you speak German?	Talar du tyska?
Do you speak French?	Talar du franska?
Do you speak Spanish?	Talar du spanska?
Do you speak Italian?	Talar du italienska?
Could you speak more slowly, please?	Kan du vara snäll och tala lite långsammare?
I don't understand.	Jag förstår inte.
Can I have…?	Kan jag få…?
Can you show me…?	Kan du visa mig…?
Can you tell me…?	Kan du säga mig…?
Can you help me, please?	Kan du hjälpa mig?
I'd like…	Jag skulle vilja ha…
We'd like…	Vi skulle vilja ha…
Please give me…	Var snäll och ge mig…
Please bring me…	Var snäll och hämta…
I'm hungry.	Jag är hungrig.
I'm thirsty.	Jag är törstig.
I'm lost.	Jag har gått vilse.
Hurry up!	Skynda på!
There is/There are…	Det finns…
There isn't/There aren't…	Det finns inte…

Arrival

Your passport, please.
Do you have anything to
declare?
No, nothing at all.
Can you help me with my
luggage, please?
Where's the bus to the centre
of town, please?
This way, please.
Where can I get a taxi?
What's the fare to…?
Take me to this address,
please.
I'm in a hurry.

Hotel

My name is…
Do you have a reservation?
I'd like an ensuite room.

What's the price per night?

May I see the room?
What's my room number,
please?
There's no hot water.
May I see the manager,
please?
Did anyone call?
Is there any mail for me?
May I have my bill (check),
please?

Eating out

Do you have a fixed-price
menu?
May I see the menu?

Ankomst

Passet, tack.
Har du någonting att förtulla?

Nej, ingenting alls.
Kan du vara snäll och hjälpa
mig med mitt bagage?
Var står bussen till centrum?

Den här vägen.
Var kan jag få tag på en taxi?
Vad kostar det till…?
Var snäll och kör mig till den
här adressen, tack.
Jag har bråttom.

Hotell

Mitt namn är…
Har du reserverat?
Jag skulle vilja ha ett rum
med badrum eller dusch.
Hur mycket kostar det per
natt?
Kan jag få se på rummet?
Vilket rumsnummer har jag?

Det finns inget varmvatten.
Kan jag få tala med
hotelldirektören, tack?
Har någon ringt mig?
Finns det någon post till mig?
Kan jag få räkningen, tack?

Äta ute

Har ni någon fast meny?

Kan jag få se på menyn?

May we have an ashtray, please?	Kan vi få en askkopp, tack?
Where's the toilet, please?	Var är toaletten?
I'd like a starter.	Jag skulle vilja ha en förrätt.
Do you have any soup?	Har ni någon soppa?
I'd like some fish.	Jag skulle vilja ha fisk.
What kind of fish do you have?	Vad har ni för fisk?
I'd like a steak.	Jag skulle vilja ha biff.
What vegetables have you got?	Vad finns det för grönsaker?
Nothing more, thanks.	Ingenting mer, tack.
What would you like to drink?	Vad vill du ha att dricka?
I'll have a beer, please.	Jag tar en öl, tack.
I'd like a bottle of wine.	Jag skulle vilja ha en flaska vin.
May I have the bill (check), please?	Får jag be om notan, tack?
Is service included?	Ingår dricks?
Thank you, that was very good.	Tack, det var mycket gott.

Travelling

På resa

Where's the railway station, please?	Var ligger järnvägsstationen?
Where's the ticket office, please?	Var är biljettluckan?
I'd like a ticket to…	Jag skulle vilja ha en biljett till…
First or second class?	Första eller andra klass?
First class, please.	Första klass, tack.
Single or return (one way or roundtrip)?	Enkel eller tur och retur?
Do I have to change trains?	Måste jag byta tåg?
What platform does the train for… leave from?	Från vilken perrong avgår tåget till…?
Where's the nearest underground (subway) station?	Var ligger närmaste tunnelbanestation?

Where's the bus station, please?
Var ligger busstationen?

When's the first bus to…?
När går första bussen till…?

Please let me off at the next stop.
Kan du släppa av mig vid nästa hållplats?

Nöjen

Relaxing

Vad går det på bio?
What's on at the cinema (movies)?

När börjar filmen?
What time does the film (movie) begin?

Finns det några biljetter till i kväll?
Are there any tickets for tonight?

Var kan vi gå och dansa?
Where can we go dancing?

Träffa folk

Meeting people

Hej.
(*formal*) How do you do?

Hur står det till?
How are you?

Tack bra. Och själv?
Very well, thank you. And you?

Får jag presentera…?
May I introduce…?

Jag heter…
My name is…

Roligt att träffas.
I'm very pleased to meet you.

Hur länge har du varit här?
How long have you been here?

Det var trevligt att träffas.
It was nice meeting you.

Har du något emot att jag röker?
Do you mind if I smoke?

Förlåt, har du eld?
Do you have a light, please?

Vill du ha något att dricka?
May I get you a drink?

Får jag bjuda dig på middag i kväll?
May I invite you for dinner tonight?

Var ska vi träffas?
Where shall we meet?

Handel och service

Var ligger närmaste bank?

Var kan jag lösa in
resecheckar?
Kan jag få lite växel, tack?

Var finns närmaste apotek?

Hur kommer jag dit?
Kan man gå dit?
Kan du hjälpa mig?
Hur mycket kostar den här?
Och den där?
Det är inte riktigt vad jag vill
ha.
Den här tycker jag om.
Kan du rekommendera
någonting mot solsveda?
Jag skulle vilja klippa mig.
Jag skulle vilja ha manikyr.

Fråga om vägen

Kan du visa mig på kartan var
jag är?
Du är på fel väg.
Kör/Gå rakt fram.
Det är till vänster/till höger.

Nödsituationer

Ring genast efter en läkare.
Ring efter en ambulans.
Var snäll och ring polisen.

Shops, stores and services

Where's the nearest bank,
please?
Where can I cash some
travellers' cheques?
Can you give me some small
change, please?
Where's the nearest chemist's
(pharmacy)?
How do I get there?
Is it within walking distance?
Can you help me, please?
How much is this? And that?

It's not quite what I want.

I like it.
Can you recommend
something for sunburn?
I'd like a haircut, please.
I'd like a manicure, please.

Street directions

Can you show me on the map
where I am?
You are on the wrong road.
Go/Walk straight ahead.
It's on the left/on the right.

Emergencies

Call a doctor quickly.
Call an ambulance.
Please call the police.

Swedish Abbreviations

AB	*aktiebolag*	Ltd., Inc.
adr.	*adress*	address
ang.	*angående*	regarding
ank.	*ankomst, ankommande*	arrival, arriving
anm.	*anmärkning*	remark
avd.	*avdelning*	department
avg.	*avgång, avgående*	departure, departing
avs.	*avseende; avsändare*	respect; sender
bet.	*betydelse; betalt*	meaning; paid
bil.	*bilaga*	enclosure, enclosed
bl.a.	*bland annat*	among other things
ca	*cirka*	approximately
doc.	*docent*	senior lecturer, associate professor
dvs.	*det vill säga*	i. e.
eftr.	*efterträdare*	successor (firm)
e.Kr.	*efter Kristus*	A.D.
el.	*eller; elektrisk*	or; electrical
em.	*eftermiddag*	(in the) afternoon
f.d.	*före detta*	former, ex-
f.Kr.	*före Kristus*	B.C.
fm.	*förmiddag*	(in the) morning
f.n.	*för närvarande*	at present
FN	*Förenta Nationerna*	UN
forts.	*fortsättning*	continued
fr.o.m.	*från och med*	as of
f.v.b.	*för vidare befordran*	please forward
ggr	*gånger*	times
HKH	*Hans/Hennes Kunglig Höghet*	His/Her Royal Highness
ind.omr.	*industriområde*	industrial area
inv.	*invånare*	inhabitants, population
JK	*justitiekansler*	Attorney General
JO	*justitieombudsman*	Ombudsman for the Judiciary and Civil Administration
kl.	*klockan; klass*	o'clock; class
kr.	*krona (kronor)*	crown(s) (currency)

LO	*Landsorganisationen*	Association of Swedish Trade Unions
moms	*mervärdeskatt*	VAT, value added tax
n.b.	*nedre botten; nota bene (märk väl)*	ground floor (exit); nota bene
ngn	*någon*	any(one), some(one)
ngt	*något*	any(thing), some(thing)
obs.	*observera*	note
o.s.a.	*om svar anhålles*	please reply
osv.	*och så vidare*	etc.
p.g.a.	*på grund av*	because of
RÅ	*riksåklagare*	Director of Public Prosecutions
s.	*sidan*	page
sa/s:a	*summa*	the sum, total
sek.	*sekund*	second (clock)
SJ	*Statens Järnvägar*	Swedish National Railways
skr.	*svenska kronor*	Swedish crowns
SR	*Sveriges Radio*	Swedish Broadcasting Corporation
st.	*styck*	piece
STF	*Svenska Turistföreningen*	Swedish Tourist Association
t.h.	*till höger*	to the right
tim.	*timme*	hour
t.o.m.	*till och med*	up to (and including)
tr.	*trappa (trappor)*	stairs; floor
t.v.	*till vänster; tills vidare*	to the left; until further notice
UD	*Utrikesdepartementet*	Swedish Foreign Office
vard.	*vardagar*	working days
VD	*verkställande direktör*	managing director
v.g.	*var god*	please
v.g.v.	*var god vänd*	P.T.O., please turn over
ö.g.	*över gården*	across/in the courtyard
ö.h.	*över havet*	above sea level

Engelska förkortningar

AA	*Automobile Association*	brittisk motororganisation
AAA	*American Automobile Association*	amerikansk motororganisation
ABC	*American Broadcasting Company*	privat amerikanskt radio- och TV-bolag
A.D.	*anno Domini*	e.Kr.
Am.	*America; American*	Amerika; amerikansk
a.m.	*ante meridiem (before noon)*	för tid mellan kl. 00.00 och 12.00
Amtrak	*American railroad corporation*	sammanslutning av privata amerikanska järnvägar
AT & T	*American Telephone and Telegraph Company*	privat amerikanskt telefonbolag
Ave.	*avenue*	aveny
BBC	*British Broadcasting Corporation*	statligt brittiskt radio- och TV-bolag
B.C.	*before Christ*	f.Kr.
bldg.	*building*	byggnad, hus
Blvd.	*boulevard*	boulevard
Brit.	*Britain; British*	Storbritannien; brittisk
Bros.	*brothers*	bröder (i firmanamn)
¢	*cent*	1/100 dollar
Can.	*Canada; Canadian*	Kanada; kanadensisk
CBS	*Columbia Broadcasting System*	privat amerikanskt radio- och TV-bolag
CID	*Criminal Investigation Department*	kriminalpolisen (Scotland Yard)
c/o	*(in) care of*	under adress
Co.	*company*	bolag
Corp.	*corporation*	korporation, bolag
D.C.	*District of Columbia*	Columbiadistriktet (Washington, D.C.)
DDS	*Doctor of Dental Science/Surgery*	tandläkare
dept.	*department*	departement, avdelning
EU	*European Union*	Europeiska Unionen

e.g.	*for instance*	t.ex.
Eng.	*England; English*	England; engelsk
excl.	*excluding; exclusive*	ej inräknad, exklusive
ft.	*foot/feet*	fot (mått)
GB	*Great Britain*	Storbritannien
H.E.	*His/Her Excellency; His Eminence*	Hans/Hennes Excellens; Hans Höghet
H.H.	*His Holiness*	Hans Helighet (påven)
H.M.	*His/Her Majesty*	Hans/Hennes Majestät
H.M.S.	*Her Majesty's ship*	Hennes Majestäts fartyg (brittiskt örlogsfartyg)
hp	*horsepower*	hästkrafter
Hwy	*highway*	huvudväg, allmän landsväg
i.e.	*that is to say*	dvs.
in.	*inch*	tum
Inc.	*incorporated*	AB, aktiebolag
incl.	*including, inclusive*	inräknad, inklusive
£	*pound sterling*	brittiskt pund
L.A.	*Los Angeles*	Los Angeles
Ltd.	*limited*	AB, aktiebolag
M.D.	*Doctor of Medicine*	leg. läk.
M.P.	*Member of Parliament*	ledamot av parlamentet
mph	*miles per hour*	miles per timma
Mr.	*Mister*	titel före namn för en man, motsvaras närmast av 'herr' i svenskan
Mrs.	*polite or formal title used in front of the name of a woman who is married*	titel före namn för en gift kvinna, motsvaras närmast av 'fru' i svenskan
Ms.	*polite or formal title used in front of the name of a woman's surname when you do not know whether she is married or not*	titel före namn för en kvinna med okänt civilstånd, motsvaras närmast av 'fru' i svenskan
nat.	*national*	nationell
NBC	*National Broadcasting Company*	privat amerikanskt radio- och TV-bolag

394

No.	number	nummer
N.Y.C.	New York City	New York (staden)
O.B.E.	Officer (of the Order) of the British Empire	Riddare av brittiska imperieorden
p.	page; penny/pence	sida; 1/100 pund
p.a.	per annum	per år
Ph.D.	Doctor of Philosophy	fil. dr.
p.m.	post meridiem (after noon)	för tid mellan kl. 12.00 och 24.00
PO	Post Office	postkontor
POO	post office order	postanvisning
pop.	population	folkmängd, befolkning
P.T.O.	please turn over	var god vänd
RAC	Royal Automobile Club	Kungliga Brittiska Automobilklubben
RCMP	Royal Canadian Mounted Police	Kanadas ridande polis
Rd.	road	väg
ref.	reference	referens, hänvisning
Rev.	reverend	pastor
RFD	rural free delivery	utbärning av post på landsbygden
RR	railroad	järnväg
RSVP	please reply	o.s. a., om svar anhålles
$	dollar	dollar
Soc.	society	förening
St.	saint; street	sankt(a); gata
UN	United Nations	FN
UPS	United Parcel Service	privat företag som levererar paket
US	United States	Förenta staterna
VAT	value added tax	moms, mervärdeskatt
VIP	very important person	vip, betydelsefull person
Xmas	Christmas	jul
yd.	yard	yard (mått)
YMCA	Young Men's Christian Association	KFUM
YWCA	Young Women's Christian Association	KFUK
ZIP	ZIP code	postnummer

Mini Grammar

Articles

All Swedish nouns are either common or neuter in gender.

1. Indefinite article (a/an)

common:	**en** man	a man
neuter:	**ett** barn	a child

2. Definite article (the)

Whereas in English we say "the house", the Swedes say the equivalent of "house-the", i. e. they tag the definite article onto the end of the noun. Common nouns take an -(e)n ending, neuter nouns an -(e)t ending.

common:	**mannen**	*the man*
neuter:	**barnet**	*the child*

Nouns

1. As already noted, nouns are either common or neuter. There are no easy rules for determining gender. Learn each new word with its accompanying article.

2. The plural is formed according to one of five declensions.

		singular		indefinite plurals	
Declension	1	**flicka**	girl	**flickor**	girls
	2	**bil**	car	**bilar**	cars
	3	**dam**	lady	**damer**	ladies
		sko	shoe	**skor**	shoes
	4	**äpple**	apple	**äpplen**	apples
	5	**hus**	house	**hus**	houses

	definite plurals
flickorna	the girls
äpplena	the apples
husen	the houses

There are also various irregular plurals.

3. Possession is shown by adding **-s** (singular and plural).

Note: There is no apostrophe.

Görans **bror**	George's brother
hotellets **ägare**	the owner of the hotel
veckans **första dag**	the first day of the week
den resandes **väska**	the traveller's suitcase
barnens **rum**	the children's room

Adjectives

1. Adjectives agree with the noun in gender and number. For the indefinite form, the neuter is formed by adding **-t**; the plural by adding **-a**.

(en) stor hund	(a) big dog	**stora hundar**	big dogs
(ett) stort hus	(a) big house	**stora hus**	big houses

2. For the definite declension of the adjective, add the ending **-a** (common, neuter and plural). This form is used when the adjective is preceded by **den, det, de** (the definite article used with adjectives) or by a demonstrative or a possessive adjective.

den stora hunden	the big dog
de stora hundarna	the big dogs
det stora huset	the big house
de stora husen	the big houses

3. Demonstrative adjectives

	common	neuter	plural
this/these	**den här/ denna**	**det här/ detta**	**de här/ dessa**
that/those	**den där/ den**	**det där/ det**	**de där/ de**

4. Possessive adjectives agree in number and gender with the
   noun they modify, i. e. with the thing possessed and not the
   possessor.

	common	neuter	plural
my	**min**	**mitt**	**mina**
your	**din**	**ditt**	**dina**
his			
her }	**sin**	**sitt**	**sina**
its			
our	**vår**	**vårt**	**våra**
your	**er**	**ert**	**era**
their	**sin**	**sitt**	**sina**

In modern Swedish the forms **er, ert, era** correspond to the personal pronoun **ni** and refer to several possessors.

The forms **sin, sitt, sina** always refer back to the subject:

Han har sin bok.	He has his (own) book.
De har sina böcker.	They have their (own) books.

The genitive forms of the personal pronouns (see p. 398) are
also used to show possession. However, the meaning changes:

Han har hans bok.	He has his (another person's) book.

5. Comparative and superlative

The comparative and superlative are normally formed by adding the endings **-(a)re** and **-(a)st**, respectively, to the adjective
(and an umlaut where necessary, see stor/större/störst below),
or by putting **mer** and **mest** (more, most) before the adjective.

Hans arbete är lätt.	His work is easy.
Hans arbete är lättare.	His work is easier.
Hans arbete är lättast.	His work is easiest.
Er bil är stor.	Your car is big.
Er bil är större.	Your car is bigger.
Er bil är störst.	Your car is the biggest.
Det är imponerande.	It's impressive.
Det är mer imponerande.	It's more impressive.
Det är mest imponerande.	It's most impressive.

Adverbs

Adverbs are generally formed by adding **-t** to the corresponding adjective.

Hon går snabb*t*.   She walks quickly.

Personal pronouns

	subject	object	genitive
I	**jag**	**mig**	–
you	**du**	**dig**	–
he	**han**	**honom**	**hans**
she	**hon**	**henne**	**hennes**
it	**den/det**	**den/det**	**dess**
we	**vi**	**oss**	–
you	**ni**	**er**	–
they	**de**	**dem**	**deras**

Like many other languages, Swedish has two forms for "you". The formal word **ni**, traditionally the correct form of address between all but close friends and children, has now been replaced by the informal **du**.

Verbs

Here we are concerned only with the infinitive, imperative, and present tense. The present tense is simple, because it has the same form throughout. The infinitive of most Swedish verbs ends in **-a** (a few verbs of one syllable end in other vowels). Here are three useful auxiliary verbs:

	to be	to have	to be able to
Infinitive	**(att) vara**	**(att) ha**	**(att) kunna**
Present tense (same form throughout)	**är**	**har**	**kan**
Imperative	**var**	**ha**	–

The present tense of Swedish verbs ends in **-r**:

	to ask	to buy	to believe	to do/make
Infinitive	(att) fråga	(att) köpa	(att) tro	(att) göra
Present tense (same form throughout)	frågar	köper	tror	gör
Imperative	fråga	köp	tro	gör

There is no equivalent of the English present continuous tense. Thus:

Jag reser.   I travel/I am travelling.

Negatives

Negation is expressed by using the adverb **inte** (not). It is usually placed immediately after the verb in a main clause. In compound tenses **inte** comes between the auxiliary and the main verb.

Jag talar svenska.   I speak Swedish.
Jag talar inte svenska.   I do not speak Swedish.
Hon har inte skrivit.   She has not written.

Questions

Questions are formed by reversing the order of the subject and the verb:

Bussen stannar här.   The bus stops here.
Stannar bussen här?   Does the bus stop here?

Jag kommer i kväll.   I am coming tonight.
Kommer du i kväll?   Are you coming tonight?

400

Irregular Verbs

The following list contains the most common irregular Swedish verbs. Only one form of the verb is shown below as the form is conjugated the same throughout within a given tense. There is a large number of prefixes in Swedish, like *an-*, *av-*, *be-*, *efter-*, *fram-*, *från-*, *för-*, *in-*, *med-*, *ned-*, *ner-*, *om-*, *und-*, *under-*, *upp-*, *ut-*, *vid-*, *åter-*, *över-*, etc. A prefixed verb is conjugated in the same way as the stem verb. The supine form is a special form of the past participle; the past participle itself is only used as an adjective. The perfect tense is formed by using the auxiliary *att ha* (to have) together with the supine.

Infinitive	Present	Imperfect	Supine	
be(dja)	ber	bad	bett	ask, pray
binda	binder	band	bundit	bind, tie
bita	biter	bet	bitit	bite
bjuda	bjuder	bjöd	bjudit	offer; invite; bid
bli(va)	blir	blev	blivit	become; remain
brinna	brinner	brann	brunnit	burn
brista	brister	brast	brustit	burst
bryta	bryter	bröt	brutit	break
bära	bär	bar	burit	carry
böra	bör	borde	bort	ought to
dra(ga)	drar	drog	dragit	pull
dricka	dricker	drack	druckit	drink
driva	driver	drev	drivit	propel, drive
dyka	dyker	dök/dykte	dykt	dive
dö	dör	dog	dött	die
dölja	döljer	dolde	dolt	conceal
falla	faller	föll	fallit	fall
fara	far	for	farit	go away, leave
finna	finner	fann	funnit	find
flyga	flyger	flög	flugit	fly
flyta	flyter	flöt	flutit	float, flow
frysa	fryser	frös	frusit	be cold; freeze
få	får	fick	fått	get, may
förnimma	förnimmer	förnam	förnummit	perceive
försvinna	försvinner	försvann	försvunnit	disappear

ge (giva)	ger	gav	gett/givit	*give*
gjuta	gjuter	göt	gjutit	*cast (iron)*
glida	glider	gled	glidit	*glide, slide*
glädja	gläder	gladde	glatt	*delight, please*
gnida	gnider	gned	gnidit	*rub*
gripa	griper	grep	gripit	*seize, grasp*
gråta	gråter	grät	gråtit	*weep, cry*
gå	går	gick	gått	*go, walk*
göra	gör	gjorde	gjort	*do, make*
ha	har	hade	haft	*have*
hinna	hinner	hann	hunnit	*have time, catch*
hugga	hugger	högg	huggit	*hew, cut*
hålla	håller	höll	hållit	*hold, keep*
kliva	kliver	klev	klivit	*stride, climb*
klyva	klyver	klöv	kluvit	*split*
knipa	kniper	knep	knipit	*pinch*
knyta	knyter	knöt	knutit	*tie*
komma	kommer	kom	kommit	*come*
krypa	kryper	kröp	krupit	*crawl, creep*
kunna	kan	kunde	kunnat	*can*
le	ler	log	lett	*smile*
lida	lider	led	lidit	*suffer*
ligga	ligger	låg	legat	*lie*
ljuda	ljuder	ljöd	ljudit	*sound*
ljuga	ljuger	ljög	ljugit	*tell a lie*
låta	låter	lät	låtit	*let; sound*
lägga	lägger	lade	lagt	*lay, put*
måste*	måste	–	–	*must*
niga	niger	neg	nigit	*curtsy*
njuta	njuter	njöt	njutit	*enjoy*
nypa	nyper	nöp	nupit	*pinch someone*
nysa	nyser	nös/nyste	nyst/nysit	*sneeze*
pipa	piper	pep	pipit	*chirp*
rida	rider	red	ridit	*ride*
rinna	rinner	rann	runnit	*run, flow*
riva	river	rev	rivit	*tear; demolish*
ryta	ryter	röt	rutit	*roar*
se	ser	såg	sett	*see*

---

* present tense

402

sitta	sitter	satt	suttit	*sit*
sjuda	sjuder	sjöd	sjudit	*seethe*
sjunga	sjunger	sjöng	sjungit	*sing*
sjunka	sjunker	sjönk	sjunkit	*sink*
ska*	ska	skulle	–	*shall*
skina	skiner	sken	skinit	*shine*
skjuta	skjuter	sköt	skjutit	*shoot; push*
skrida	skrider	skred	skridit	*stride, stalk*
skrika	skriker	skrek	skrikit	*shout*
skriva	skriver	skrev	skrivit	*write*
skryta	skryter	skröt	skrutit	*boast*
skära	skär	skar	skurit	*cut*
slippa	slipper	slapp	sluppit	*not need to*
slita	sliter	slet	slitit	*wear out; tear*
sluta	sluter	slöt	slutit	*close*
slå	slår	slog	slagit	*beat; strike*
smita	smiter	smet	smitit	*slip away*
smyga	smyger	smög	smugit	*sneak, snuggle*
smörja	smörjer	smorde	smort	*grease*
snyta (sig)	snyter	snöt	snutit	*blow one's nose*
sova	sover	sov	sovit	*sleep*
spinna	spinner	spann	spunnit	*spin; purr*
spricka	spricker	sprack	spruckit	*burst, crack*
sprida	sprider	spred	spritt	*spread*
springa	springer	sprang	sprungit	*run*
sticka	sticker	stack	stuckit	*sting*
stiga	stiger	steg	stigit	*rise*
stinka	stinker	stank	–	*stink*
stjäla	stjäl	stal	stulit	*steal*
strida	strider	stred	stridit	*fight*
stryka	stryker	strök	strukit	*iron*
strypa	stryper	ströp/strypte	strypt	*strangle*
stå	står	stod	stått	*stand*
suga	suger	sög	sugit	*suck*
supa	super	söp	supit	*booze*
svida	svider	sved	svidit	*smart*
svika	sviker	svek	svikit	*betray, let down*
svälja	sväljer	svalde	svalt	*swallow*
svär(j)a	svär	svor	svurit	*swear; curse*

---

* present tense

säga	säger	sa(de)	sagt	*say*
sälja	säljer	sålde	sålt	*sell*
sätta	sätter	satte	satt	*place, set*
ta(ga)	tar	tog	tagit	*take*
tiga	tiger	teg	tigit	*be silent*
tjuta	tjuter	tjöt	tjutit	*yell*
tvinga	tvingar	tvingade/	tvingat/	*force*
		tvang	tvungit	
umgås	umgås	umgicks	umgåtts	*associate with*
vara	är	var	varit	*be*
veta	vet	visste	vetat	*know*
vika	viker	vek	vikit/vikt	*fold*
vilja	vill	ville	velat	*want, will*
vina	viner	ven	vinit	*howl, whine (storm)*
vinna	vinner	vann	vunnit	*win*
vrida	vrider	vred	vridit	*twist, wrench*
välja	väljer	valde	valt	*choose; elect*
vänja	vänjer	vande	vant	*accustom, get used to*
äta	äter	åt	ätit	*eat*

Minigrammatik

Artiklar

Den **bestämda artikeln** har samma form i sing. och plur.: **the**

the room, the rooms   rummet, rummen

Den **obestämda artikeln** har två former: **a** som används framför ord som börjar på konsonant och **an** som används framför vokal eller stumt h.

a coat	en kappa
an umbrella	ett paraply
an hour	en timme
a small village	en liten by
an old town	en gammal stad

Some anger obestämd mängd eller obestämt antal. Det används framför substantiv i både sing. och plur. och motsvarar på svenska någon, något, lite, några.

I'd like some tea, please.	Jag skulle vilja ha lite te.
Give me some stamps, please.	Var snäll och ge mig några frimärken.

Any betyder någon eller vilken som helst och används mest i nekande och frågande satser.

There isn't any soap.	Det finns inte någon tvål.
Do you have any stamps?	Har ni (du) några frimärken?
Is there any mail for me?	Finns det någon post till mig?

Substantiv

Pluralis bildas som regel genom att lägga -(e)s till singularformen.

cup – cups	kopp – koppar
dress – dresses	klänning – klänningar

Obs! Om ett substantiv slutar på **-y** i sing. ändras stavningen i
plur. till **-ies** om **y** föregås av en konsonant. Om det föregås av
en vokal används den normala pluraländelsen **-s**.

lady – ladies	dam – damer
day – days	dag – dagar

Men ingen regel utan undantag ...

man – men	man – män
woman – women	kvinna – kvinnor
child – children	barn – barn
foot – feet	fot – fötter

Genitiv

1. Då ägaren är en person och då substantivet inte slutar på **-s**
   lägger man till **'s**.

the boy's room	pojkens rum
the children's clothes	barnens kläder

Om substantivet slutar på **-s** lägger man endast till apostrofen (').

the boys' room	pojkarnas rum

2. Då ägaren inte är en person används prepositionen of.

the end of the journey	resans slut (slutet på resan)

Adjektiv

Adjektivet förblir oförändrat både framför substantivet och
när det står ensamt.

a large brown suitcase	en stor brun resväska

Det finns två sätt att bilda **komparativ** och **superlativ**.

1. Adjektiv med en stavelse och de flesta med två stavelser
   får ändelsen -(e)r och -(e)st.

small – smaller – smallest	liten – mindre – minst
pretty – prettier – prettiest	söt – sötare – sötast

Obs! **-y** efter konsonant ändras till **i** framför **-er** och **-est**.

2. Adjektiv med fler än två stavelser och vissa adjektiv med två stavelser (t.ex. de som slutar på **-ful** eller **-less**) bildar komparativ och superlativ med hjälp av **more** och **most**.

expensive (dyr) – **more expensive** – **most expensive**
careful (försiktig) – **more careful** – **most careful**

Följande adjektiv är oregelbundna:

good (bra) – **better** – **best**
bad (dålig) – **worse** – **worst**
little (lite) – **less** – **least**
much (mycket) }
many (många) } – **more** – **most**

Pronomen

	personliga		possessiva	
	subjekts-form	objekts-form	förenade	själv-ständiga
jag	**I**	**me**	**my**	**mine**
du	**you**	**you**	**your**	**yours**
han	**he**	**him**	**his**	**his**
hon	**she**	**her**	**her**	**hers**
den/det	**it**	**it**	**its**	–
vi	**we**	**us**	**our**	**ours**
ni	**you**	**you**	**your**	**yours**
de	**they**	**them**	**their**	**theirs**

Exempel på förenat possessivt pronomen:

Where's my key? Var är min nyckel?

Exempel på självständigt possessivt pronomen:

It's not mine.   Det är inte min.
It's yours.   Det är er (din).

Obs! Engelskan har inte skilda former för "du" och "ni".
Båda heter **you.**

Oregelbundna verb

Nedanstående lista innehåller de vanligaste engelska oregelbundna verben. Sammansatta verb och de verb som har en förstavelse (prefix) böjs som de enkla verben: t.ex. *withdraw* böjs
som *draw* och *mistake* som *take*.

Infinitiv	Imperfektum	Perfekt particip	
arise	arose	arisen	*uppstå*
awake	awoke	awoken/ awaked	*vakna*
be	was	been	*vara*
bear	bore	borne	*bära*
beat	beat	beaten	*slå*
become	became	become	*bli*
begin	began	begun	*börja*
bend	bent	bent	*böja*
bet	bet	bet	*slå vad*
bid	bade/bid	bidden/bid	*bjuda*
bind	bound	bound	*binda*
bite	bit	bitten	*bita*
bleed	bled	bled	*blöda*
blow	blew	blown	*blåsa*
break	broke	broken	*bryta*
breed	bred	bred	*uppföda*
bring	brought	brought	*medföra*
build	built	built	*bygga*
burn	burnt/burned	burnt/burned	*bränna, brinna*
burst	burst	burst	*brista*
buy	bought	bought	*köpa*
can*	could	–	*kunna*
cast	cast	cast	*kasta; gjuta*
catch	caught	caught	*fånga*
choose	chose	chosen	*välja*
cling	clung	clung	*klänga sig fast*
clothe	clothed/clad	clothed/clad	*klä*
come	came	come	*komma*
cost	cost	cost	*kosta*

* presens indikativ

creep	crept	crept	*krypa*
cut	cut	cut	*skära*
deal	dealt	dealt	*handla med; dela ut*
dig	dug	dug	*gräva*
do (he does*)	did	done	*göra*
draw	drew	drawn	*rita; dra*
dream	dreamt/ dreamed	dreamt/ dreamed	*drömma*
drink	drank	drunk	*dricka*
drive	drove	driven	*köra*
dwell	dwelt	dwelt	*vistas*
eat	ate	eaten	*äta*
fall	fell	fallen	*falla*
feed	fed	fed	*(ut)fodra, mata*
feel	felt	felt	*känna (sig)*
fight	fought	fought	*slåss*
find	found	found	*finna*
flee	fled	fled	*fly*
fling	flung	flung	*kasta*
fly	flew	flown	*flyga*
forsake	forsook	forsaken	*överge*
freeze	froze	frozen	*frysa*
get	got	got	*få*
give	gave	given	*ge*
go (he goes*)	went	gone	*resa*
grind	ground	ground	*mala*
grow	grew	grown	*växa*
hang	hung	hung	*hänga*
have (he has*)	had	had	*ha*
hear	heard	heard	*höra*
hew	hewed	hewed/hewn	*hugga*
hide	hid	hidden	*gömma*
hit	hit	hit	*slå*
hold	held	held	*hålla*
hurt	hurt	hurt	*såra; värka*
keep	kept	kept	*behålla*
kneel	knelt	knelt	*knäböja*

---

* presens indikativ

knit	knitted/knit	knitted/knit	*sticka*
know	knew	known	*veta; kunna*
lay	laid	laid	*lägga*
lead	led	led	*leda*
lean	leant/leaned	leant/leaned	*luta (sig)*
leap	leapt/leaped	leapt/leaped	*hoppa*
learn	learnt/learned	learnt/learned	*lära sig*
leave	left	left	*lämna*
lend	lent	lent	*låna (ut)*
let	let	let	*låta, tillåta*
lie	lay	lain	*ligga*
light	lit/lighted	lit/lighted	*tända*
lose	lost	lost	*förlora*
make	made	made	*göra*
may*	might	–	*få, kunna (kanske)*
mean	meant	meant	*mena*
meet	met	met	*möta*
mow*	mowed	mowed/mown	*meja*
must*	must	–	*vara tvungen*
ought* (to)	ought	–	*böra*
pay	paid	paid	*betala*
put	put	put	*sätta*
read	read	read	*läsa*
rid	rid	rid	*befria*
ride	rode	ridden	*rida*
ring	rang	rung	*ringa*
rise	rose	risen	*stiga upp*
run	ran	run	*springa*
saw	sawed	sawn	*såga*
say	said	said	*säga*
see	saw	seen	*se*
seek	sought	sought	*söka*
sell	sold	sold	*sälja*
send	sent	sent	*sända*
set	set	set	*sätta*
sew	sewed	sewed/sewn	*sy*
shake	shook	shaken	*skaka*

---

* presens indikativ

410

shall*	should	–	skola
shed	shed	shed	fälla
shine	shone	shone	skina
shoot	shot	shot	skjuta
show	showed	shown	visa
shrink	shrank	shrunk	krympa
shut	shut	shut	stänga
sing	sang	sung	sjunga
sink	sank	sunk	sjunka
sit	sat	sat	sitta
sleep	slept	slept	sova
slide	slid	slid	glida
sling	slung	slung	slunga
slink	slunk	slunk	smita
slit	slit	slit	sprätta upp
smell	smelled/smelt	smelled/smelt	lukta
sow	sowed	sown/sowed	så
speak	spoke	spoken	tala
speed	sped/speeded	sped/speeded	hasta
spell	spelt/spelled	spelt/spelled	stava
spend	spent	spent	tillbringa; ge ut
spill	spilt/spilled	spilt/spilled	spilla
spin	spun	spun	spinna
spit	spat	spat	spotta
split	split	split	klyva
spoil	spoilt/spoiled	spoilt/spoiled	skämma (bort); förstöra
spread	spread	spread	sprida
spring	sprang	sprung	rusa upp
stand	stood	stood	stå
steal	stole	stolen	stjäla
stick	stuck	stuck	fästa
sting	stung	stung	sticka, stinga
stink	stank/stunk	stunk	stinka
strew	strewed	strewed/strewn	strö
stride	strode	stridden	kliva
strike	struck	struck/stricken	slå (till)
string	strung	strung	trä (upp)

---

* presens indikativ

strive	strove	striven	*sträva*
swear	swore	sworn	*svär(j)a*
sweep	swept	swept	*sopa*
swell	swelled	swollen/ swelled	*svälla*
swim	swam	swum	*simma*
swing	swung	swung	*svänga, gunga*
take	took	taken	*ta*
teach	taught	taught	*lära (ut)*
tear	tore	torn	*slita sönder*
tell	told	told	*berätta*
think	thought	thought	*tänka*
throw	threw	thrown	*kasta*
thrust	thrust	thrust	*stöta*
tread	trod	trodden	*trampa*
wake	woke/waked	woken/waked	*vakna; väcka*
wear	wore	worn	*ha på sig*
weave	wove	woven	*väva*
weep	wept	wept	*gråta*
will*	would	–	*vilja*
win	won	won	*vinna*
wind	wound	wound	*veva (upp)*
wring	wrung	wrung	*vrida (ur)*
write	wrote	written	*skriva*

---

* presens indikativ

Numerals

Cardinal numbers

0	noll
1	en/ett
2	två
3	tre
4	fyra
5	fem
6	sex
7	sju
8	åtta
9	nio
10	tio
11	elva
12	tolv
13	tretton
14	fjorton
15	femton
16	sexton
17	sjutton
18	arton
19	nitton
20	tjugo
21	tjugoen/tjugoett
30	trettio
31	trettioen/trettioett
40	fyrtio
41	fyrtioen/fyrtioett
50	femtio
51	femtioen/femtioett
60	sextio
61	sextioen/sextioett
70	sjuttio
80	åttio
90	nittio
100	ett hundra
101	hundraen/hundraett
200	två hundra
1 000	ett tusen
2 000	två tusen
1 000 000	en miljon
2 000 000	två miljoner

Ordinal numbers

1:a	första
2:a	andra
3:e	tredje
4:e	fjärde
5:e	femte
6:e	sjätte
7:e	sjunde
8:e	åttonde
9:e	nionde
10:e	tionde
11:e	elfte
12:e	tolfte
13:e	trettonde
14:e	fjortonde
15:e	femtonde
16:e	sextonde
17:e	sjuttonde
18:e	artonde
19:e	nittonde
20:e	tjugonde
21:a	tjugoförsta
22:a	tjugoandra
23:e	tjugotredje
24:e	tjugofjärde
25:e	tjugofemte
26:e	tjugosjätte
27:e	tjugosjunde
28:e	tjugoåttonde
29:e	tjugonionde
30:e	trettionde
31:a	trettioförsta
40:e	fyrtionde
50:e	femtionde
60:e	sextionde
70:e	sjuttionde
80:e	åttionde
90:e	nittionde
100:e	hundrade
1 000:e	tusende
10 000:e	tiotusende

Räkneord

Grundtal

0	zero
1	one
2	two
3	three
4	four
5	five
6	six
7	seven
8	eight
9	nine
10	ten
11	eleven
12	twelve
13	thirteen
14	fourteen
15	fifteen
16	sixteen
17	seventeen
18	eighteen
19	nineteen
20	twenty
21	twenty-one
22	twenty-two
23	twenty-three
24	twenty-four
25	twenty-five
30	thirty
40	forty
50	fifty
60	sixty
70	seventy
80	eighty
90	ninety
100	a/one hundred
230	two hundred and thirty
1,000	a/one thousand
10,000	ten thousand
100,000	a/one hundred thousand
1,000,000	a/one million

Ordningstal

1st	first
2nd	second
3rd	third
4th	fourth
5th	fifth
6th	sixth
7th	seventh
8th	eighth
9th	ninth
10th	tenth
11th	eleventh
12th	twelfth
13th	thirteenth
14th	fourteenth
15th	fifteenth
16th	sixteenth
17th	seventeenth
18th	eighteenth
19th	nineteenth
20th	twentieth
21st	twenty-first
22nd	twenty-second
23rd	twenty-third
24th	twenty-fourth
25th	twenty-fifth
26th	twenty-sixth
27th	twenty-seventh
28th	twenty-eighth
29th	twenty-ninth
30th	thirtieth
40th	fortieth
50th	fiftieth
60th	sixtieth
70th	seventieth
80th	eightieth
90th	ninetieth
100th	hundredth
230th	two hundred and thirtieth
1,000th	thousandth

Time

Although official time in Sweden is based on the 24-hour clock, the 12-hour system is used in conversation.

If you have to indicate that it is a.m. or p.m., add *på morgonen*, *på förmiddagen*, *på eftermiddagen*, *på kvällen*, *på natten*.

Thus:

klockan sju på morgonen	7 a.m.
klockan elva på förmiddagen	11 a.m.
klockan två på eftermiddagen	2 p.m.
klockan sju på kvällen	7 p.m.
klockan två på natten	2 a.m.

Days of the week

söndag	Sunday	*torsdag*	Thursday
måndag	Monday	*fredag*	Friday
tisdag	Tuesday	*lördag*	Saturday
onsdag	Wednesday		

Klockan

Engelsmännen och amerikanerna använder 12-timmarssyste-
met vid tidsangivelser. För att ange vilken tid på dygnet det är,
lägger man till *a.m.* för tiden mellan midnatt och kl. 12 och
p.m. för tiden mellan kl. 12 och midnatt. I Storbritannien börjar man mer och mer att använda 24-timmarssystemet vid offi-
ciella tidsangivelser.

I'll come at seven a.m.	Jag kommer kl. 7 på morgonen.
I'll come at three p.m.	Jag kommer kl. 3 på eftermiddagen.
I'll come at eight p.m.	Jag kommer kl. 8 på kvällen.

Veckodagar

Sunday	söndag	*Thursday*	torsdag
Monday	måndag	*Friday*	fredag
Tuesday	tisdag	*Saturday*	lördag
Wednesday	onsdag		

Conversion Tables/Omvandlingstabeller

Metres and feet

The figure in the middle stands for both metres and feet, e.g.
1 metre = 3.281 ft. and 1 foot = 0.30 m.

Meter och fot

Siffran i mitten gäller för både meter och fot,
dvs. 1 meter = 3,281 fot och 1 fot = 0,30 meter.

C°	F°	Metres/Meter		Feet/Fot
100	212	0.30	1	3.281
		0.61	2	6.563
		0.91	3	9.843
40	105	1.22	4	13.124
36,9	98,6	1.52	5	16.403
35		1.83	6	19.686
	90	2.13	7	22.967
30		2.44	8	26.248
	80	2.74	9	29.529
25		3.05	10	32.810
20	70	3.66	12	39.372
		4.27	14	45.934
15	60	6.10	20	65.620
		7.62	25	82.023
10	50	15.24	50	164.046
		22.86	75	246.069
5	40	30.48	100	328.092
0	32			
-5	30			
	20			
-10	10			
-15				
-20	0			

Temperature

To convert Centigrade to Fahrenheit, multiply by 1.8 and add 32.
To convert Fahrenheit to Centigrade, subtract 32 from Fahrenheit and divide by 1.8.

Temperatur

För att räkna om Celsius till Fahrenheit multiplicerar man med 1,8 och lägger till 32.
För att räkna om Fahrenheit till Celsius, drar man ifrån 32 och dividerar med 1,8.